ENGLISH DRAMATIC FORM

ENGLISH DRAMATIC FORM

A HISTORY
OF ITS DEVELOPMENT

By

M. C. BRADBROOK

LITT.D.

*Reader in English, Cambridge University,
and Fellow of Girton College*

1965
CHATTO & WINDUS
LONDON

Published by
Chatto & Windus Ltd.
42 William IV Street
London W.C.2

*

Clarke, Irwin & Co. Ltd
Toronto

0701105585

To
THE SHAKESPEARE SOCIETY
OF JAPAN

Preface

D RAMA today is full of experiment, springing from the actors' and audiences' part in total theatre. The author starts off an activity; he does not control it. This idea has spread from the French theatre, incomparably the most lively of the day, to others. Plays are conceived in terms of action and response.

My theory of the drama as a species of game implies none the less that the claim of the playwright must be maintained, against the modern counterclaims of the director, if no longer in quite the old terms. "The poetry behind the text" derives from the text.

I do not know of any recent psychological theory of drama, and therefore in writing Part One I have relied solely on the work of psychiatrists and psychologists. I am very conscious of my temerity, and I have been extremely grateful to Dr D. H. Heard of the Tavistock Clinic for sparing time to read Chapter 2 and giving me advice upon it.

In Part Two, I have tried to show how the great imaginative drama of Marlowe and Shakespeare rested upon two medieval traditions; processional civic pageants and courtly games which received poetic form from Chaucer. In relating Chaucer and Shakespeare I have considered the imaginative effect upon their audiences of characters projected as an interacting group.

In Part Three, from the time when imaginative theatre revived to the present day, I have been more concerned with the development of the theatre as a whole than in Part Two, which depends on selected plays of Marlowe, Shakespeare, Webster and Dryden. But in Part Three I have also specially considered two poets, Yeats and Eliot, whose influence rests on a transfusion of imaginative life, not confined to their own achievements as dramatists nor to drama in verse. The modern form of imaginative drama is more often prose.

Each part, representing an approach to a different kind of material, has necessarily been written in a somewhat different way, but the case is none the less a single one, and I hope the connexions between the different parts will be apparent.

While this book was in proof, the Aldwych plays of 1964 showed how earnestly preaching has begun on some of the matters handled in Chapters 2 and 10. Seventy years ago Strindberg recognised the imaginative basis upon which, in *The Murder of Marat*, his disciple Weiss has built a play—and filled it with statement and doctrine in the manner of Brecht. As the epilogue puts it:

> Everything that we see and hear
> Can add to or increase us in some way,
> And so it might be with this play.
> Some seeds have drifted from our stage. A few
> May even have entered and taken root in you.
> But what these seeds are—even though
> In your darkest places they feed and grow,
> Whatever these seeds are—you will never know.

M. C. BRADBROOK

Cambridge, October 1964

Contents

ix

PART ONE

A Psychological Theory of Drama

Chapter One

INTRODUCTION

I THE ICON AND THE DREAM

THE dramatist, it has been said, by the intensity of imaginative experience, enters ideally into the minds of all his characters and speaks from within them. His own reading of life cannot be extracted from the drama in which it is embodied; but so fully has he entered the world of his play that what he reveals within its framework seems to be only a part of what he knows about his characters, as what a man reveals within any one action is only a part of what he is. The dramatist "knowing in each the image of a living creature, and knowing it far beyond the purposes for which he uses it on the surface of the play", (1) seeks response through a technique of evocation rather than of statement. The unfocused aspects of character work within the minds of those who encounter them, like yeast in bread.

No literary form can be thought of as if it could sustain the kind of definition given to physical objects, least of all drama, the most collaborative and therefore the most volatile of the arts. Yet, if used with discretion, descriptive terms may employ such words, and the drama may be seen as embodied on the stage. The Shakespearean form may be termed the drama of human relationships, since he has in the highest degree the capacity to enter into all his characters; but this evolved historically from two other forms, which I have termed Theatre of the Icon and Theatre of the Dream; these identifications cover the play in being as well as the dramatist's idea of it. They include the response of the audience, as part of the play. For the history of the drama is the history of interaction between the author's imagination, the actor's skill and the spectators' expectation. The conjunction of all these issues from and evokes an inner drama that is played by each of the actors and each member of the audience.

Medieval pageantry—the plays of the craft guilds being its most developed kind—employed speaking as only one of the properties (as it is today in the "total theatre" of Barrault). The personages were identified by traditional garments, postures and emblems—St Catharine's wheel, St Barbara's tower; they were heroic but familiar. Such icons represent the ideals or fears of a community; the Manger, the Pietà, St George and his dragon are still familiar today. In drama, the icons lead to plays of heroic monolithic design; the central character, though humiliated by the vulnerability of human flesh, wears a heroic mask. Marlowe created his theatre largely within this tradition, and Tamburlaine the Great is a figure at once traditional and new; traditional in conception, new in poetic power and action.

The medieval ritual of the dream began in courtly games and ceremonies, which raised life towards the level of poetry. Chaucer read his poems to an audience who were themselves the subjects of his verse, but who saw themselves reflected in an idealized form. John of Gaunt acted his silent rôle as the elegy for his wife was recited to him in the midst of their household. The audience of courtly poetry provided both spectators and dumb actors for the poet-presenter, who, in his dream-visions presented an interior drama, a drama of sentiment and feeling rather than of history. Free from the limits of mundane possibility, it constituted a special kind of fantastic "game".

The icon inhabits an eternal present, but the ritual of the dream follows a story. The icon may be attached to a simple story or myth, which does not need to be enacted in full, but can be presented by a tableau; in the dream, the rôles are conventional—for instance, the knight, the lady, the monster —but the adventures are endless.

The Icon offers a tragic form, the Dream vision more fre-

14

quently is comic. Marlowe, the great dramatist of the Icon, Chaucer and Lyly, poet and dramatist of the Dream vision, the courtly game, each assumed full participation. Alleyn as Tamburlaine dominated his audience, compelled attention by his presence and voice—though the style did not persist, and Hamlet compares it to the town crier's proclamation (2). The audience of Chaucer and Lyly saw themselves reflected in the "shadows" of the poem, which projected actual relationships; the Dreamer himself was only the means of entering a world in which he might not play a central part. The interplay of characters within a developing narrative (though not a logical one), and the contrast between the world of the play and the world outside it, when transferred to the later drama, produced the mirror effect of the play within the play, which in *The Taming of the Shrew*, for instance, is combined with the idea of the play as dream.

Shakespeare brought the drama to full life, while the wilder hyperbole of medieval romance persisted in a popular form, subjected to the ironic critical parody of a society which by now played the old games in new ways (3).

The Bardic audience which had listened to sung or recited romance, sought traditional ideals, realized in habit; the courtly audience had always enjoyed debate. Poetry was an enlargement of the daily world, an imaginative vision either communal, or subtle and more individual. It was also not an experience, but a performance.

The delicate balance which Shakespeare established did not long survive his day; in the plays of Webster and Jonson i is beginning to tilt towards the icon in a new form. In the heroic plays of Dryden, the wheel has come full circle, while Restoration comedy briefly revived something of a courtly game. By the latter part of the seventeenth century, dramatic form had congealed. *Tamburlaine* (1587) and *Aurengzebe* (1675) may be held to define the limits of the first great age of English dramatic form.

The theatre survived and flourished as a social institution, and so continued for about two hundred years. In the eighteenth century and the greater part of the nineteenth century, the English theatre was devoid of literary originality; it lived on scenic tradition and shrivelled reproductions of Shakespearean forms.

2 MODERN DRAMA

When, at the end of the nineteenth century, the art of imaginative playwriting was revived, it was necessary to re-create traditions for actors and audience. By now, theatre was an international art. The genuine national traditions of earlier times, including the English tradition, became absorbed; Italian comedy alone retained some independence. In the nineteenth century, Paris supplied a common centre of theatrical life, but the dramatists themselves came from lands on the fringe and periphery of Europe—from Russia, Scandinavia, Ireland, Sicily. They were nourished by the experimental stage and the critical traditions of Paris.

The two greatest dramatists of the nineteenth century, Ibsen and Chekhov, worked for the picture stages of the time. The audience, in their silent and darkened auditorium, watched a peepshow in the little lighted box before them, but were drawn into Ibsen's plays by the problems he raised; they were intellectually disturbed, even outraged. Ibsen made his reputation as a bold iconoclast, and as a "thinker"; the imaginative and poetic qualities of his plays, which have ensured their survival, were hardly noticed by Shaw and other *avant garde* writers of the 'nineties who introduced them to the English stage. The theme of tragic sacrifice in *The Wild Duck* and *Rosmersholm*, that "hunger of the imagination that preys upon life" and the demonic presence of the dead within living minds found symbolic form in offstage scenes—the ocean depths of the dusty attic where the Wild Duck splashed its

16

broken wing, the haunted white waters of the mill-race grinding the corn and receiving upon the thunder of its spray the imprint of galloping white horses who were the returning dead.

It is these poetic images of life and death which have maintained Ibsen; and in the form they took they were translatable. It was his great good fortune to return from verse to prose and to move all the poetic statement of his plays into these imagined forms, or into the form of stage objects—Rebecca's white shawl (bridal veil and shroud), or the pistols of Hedda Gabler.

Chekhov relied upon the acting of the Moscow Arts Theatre to present his delicate and subtle prose poems, where problems have vanished and only questions remain. The pathos of the inarticulate, of the unstated, shown in the speech of characters who do not communicate with each other, requires prose. Yet the achievements of Ibsen and Chekhov, though their greatness was recognized, did not lead to the recognition that, in the modern imaginative theatre, full drama could be achieved without verse.

Consequently, attempts to re-establish the theatre in England as an imaginative form were led by lyric poets. The two great English poets of modern times, Yeats and Eliot, who have striven to restore poetic life to the theatre, succeeded in creating a situation where drama of the imagination became possible. Their criticism and their practical interest in the stage supplied an incentive and an example to others; they were propagandists for the imaginative drama as well as practitioners, and perhaps their greatest service has been in what they made it possible for others to do. They held the vital clue that drama should work by evocation, not by statement; they came to learn that action is centred within the spectators, each one responding as an individual. Eliot in particular insisted on the audience's right to its own interpretation, as being of equal validity with the poet's.

B 17

Long after the subjective principle had been recognized pragmatically in the work of Strindberg, and Pirandello, it received full formulation in the work of Existentialists. Interior drama, by transforming the rôle of the spectator from a passive to an active one, has also transformed the relation of actor, dramatist and audience.

Within the last dozen years, theatre has evolved an analogous form to the medieval "game"; for the play is now a game played between actors and audience with material provided by the dramatist. The rules of the game, like the rules of civilized conversation, are flexible.

This new theatre is once again centred in Paris, as the product of an international group. Beckett was born in Dublin, Ionesco in Roumania, Adamov in Kislovodsk, Arrabal in Spain, Schéhadé in the Lebanon, Tardieu and Pinget in Switzerland, Ghelderode in Belgium (4).

In Weiss, Genet, Gelber, the audience are reminded of theatrical illusion by some sort of play within the play. They are involved in an action which is itself fantastic, irrational ritual, and within this, they are shown a play. Beckett makes use of stage clowns, Genet uses masks.

The play produces its effect, not as witnessed story, but as direct Act. Although completely different in intention, the great influence of Brecht has also been exerted to disturb and probe, to set before the audience the needs for decision and action. His technique of alienation alerts them; and equally with the French anti-theatre (which also likes to label itself anti-Brecht) he would reject the psychological study of characters in favour of a drama of situation.

Because the theatre now calls directly upon the more primitive forms of communication, upon contact and rapport, upon gesture and direct appeal to preconscious levels of engagement, the words of the play give only a part of the writer's original statement. Artaud's collected manifestoes, which Barrault termed the most important writings on the modern theatre, recall the primitive level of the action as the most serious. All is summed up in the opening sentence of the First Manifesto:

We cannot go on prostituting the idea of the theatre, whose only value is in its excruciating, magical relation to reality and danger.

Instead of continuing to rely upon texts considered definitive and sacred, it is essential to put an end to the subjugation of the theatre to the text and to recover the notion of a kind of unique language, half way between gesture and thought.

The Theatre and its Double, tr. Richards (1958), p. 89.

He cites, as an example of pure theatre, the Balinese, with its devil masks and ritual movement: his "theatre of cruelty" sought to project the "actual poetry" behind the "poetry of the texts" as the Aldwych plays do now.

In Barrault's "total theatre" the text has not been displaced to this extent—the great productions of Claudel's plays alone would prove the contrary. But the audience is involved by shock and by calling out what is below the civilized, trained level of response in the plays of such very different writers as Genet, Ionesco, Beckett, Pinter, Gelber and Albee.

For reasons which the next chapter will indicate, I cannot accept this subjugation of language to more primitive forms of communication, though I think the recognition that they exist and their integration with speech is the great achievement of the modern theatre.

When Jan Kott can praise *Titus Andronicus* as great Shakespearean theatre—"il savait déjà modeler de grandes figures, mais il était encore incapable de donner toute leur voix à ces géants . . . c'est déjà le théâtre shakespearien, ce n'est pas encore le texte shakespearien" (5), it may be seen how far the theories of Artaud could influence the reading of a great dramatist. Kott goes on to suggest that the cinema gives a more authentic form to Shakespeare than the stage, and that Olivier's films are more true than any theatre could be to the particular Shakespeare of our time, "Un Shakespeare cruel et vrai".

The Royal Shakespeare Theatre's performances have largely spread these views—a *King Lear* in which Edmund is allowed no repentance, a *Henry VI* which is true to the old seventeenth-century traditions of "Shakespeare Improved". The period in which the script dominated in the theatre has been remarkably brief; perhaps a hundred years.

It is undeniable that Shakespeare is somehow important to the most extraordinary range of people—that his plays are adapted by West Indian negroes and Russians of the steppes, who can have slight access either to the language or the social assumptions behind the plays. The Russian Academician Samarin made the point at Stratford that a Russian Shakespeare is as legitimate as an English Chekhov (6).

The degree of divergence in individual interpretation that is compatible with taking part in a public performance is difficult fully to grasp; in the case of Shakespeare such variety of interpretation extends not only between person and person, but between different periods and different countries. Tolerance and acceptance of different versions must be dependent on whether the new interpretation shows some initial respect and attention to the author's intentions, as transmitted in his words—the kind of respect and attention that in human relations would provide the basis of mutual understanding. The poet provides a permanent substratum, upon which infinite variations are possible, but "the poetry behind the texts" is accessible only through the texts.

NOTES TO CHAPTER ONE

(1) Una Ellis Fermor, *Shakespeare the Dramatist* (1961), p. 58. This passage is generally indebted to the late Miss Ellis Fermor's perceptive study.

(2) For a study of Alleyn's style, based on Hamlet's speech to the player, see A. Gurr, "Who Strutted and Bellowed?" (*Shakespeare Survey*, 16 (1963)). For another discussion of this speech which has bearings on the acting, and which is discussed below, Chapter III, p. 57, see Harry Levin, *The Question of Hamlet* (Oxford 1959).

(3) See below, Chapter IV, p. 70, for a discussion of *The Knight of the Burning Pestle*, and the Jacobean court masque. For games as art, cf. Ninian Smart and Ruth Saw, *British Journal of Aesthetics*, III, 4 (October, 1963).

(4) R. N. Coe, *Ionesco* (1961), p. 40.

(5) Jan Kott, *Shakespeare notre Contemporain* (René Julliard, Paris, 1962), pp. 260 ff. The theories of M. Kott have some likeness to the plays of Adamov, especially such early works as *La Grande et la Petite Manoeuvre*.

(6) See R. M. Samarin in *Shakespeare Survey*, 16 (1963).

Chapter Two

THE INNER AND THE
OUTER DRAMA

I THE "INTERNAL SOCIETY"

Spectators of a play, who participate in its collective action, together with the actors, go through a curve of experience traced for them by the author. At the end they reach

> A condition at once exuberant and reposed: the sense of having passed through a great experience, one which testifies to the superb wealth and range of life, and to the splendid rather than the disastrous powers of man. . . .
> Such a work is not a statement or insight or special kind of information—not these things essentially, though it may be all of them incidentally—but is momentous and energising *experience* . . . before it is a source of insight, great imaginative literature is a source of *power* . . . inviting and demanding an intense and varied emotion, a general heightening of all the powers of apprehension, and a great access of life-giving energy.
> John Holloway, *The Story of the Night*, pp. 17–19.

To become absorbed in such an experience collectively is a natural strengthening of personal security; it affirms their *existenz* to each of the participants, at the same time that it offers them a common cohesion. This is the life-bearing aspect of ritual—which at its primary level is shared by the theatre with tribal dancing, popular games and primitive religious ceremonies.

At the finer levels of organization which are recognized as art, however, powerful collective responses do not submerge the identity of the participants. Each within himself acts his intrapersonal drama, which may indeed make a strong sensi-

22

tive impress on those about him; the quality of attentiveness is certainly felt by the actors, as the "feel" of the "house" comes over.

For certain societies, where "people live from their affects" and "the ego has almost no autonomy" (1), group life is held together by emotion, and participation in any such ritual is likely to be expressed by gestures, cries and a loss of the distinction between actors and spectators. Collective experience will submerge personal response.

For those societies where individuated structure has developed strongly, a complex group of dramatic characters in action will evoke variant patterns of action within each member of the audience.

First projected by the writer's inner vision, then interpreted by the actors, the characters are reformed within each spectator, and move there dynamically, in accordance with the drama of his own "Internal Society".

For within each individual there plays a private drama, following established habits but responding also to external stimulus. These inward images that shape and dominate the deeper levels of thought and feeling in everyone have been implanted in childhood; and though differently charged with love or hate, and differently grouped, are basically the same in all. The formation of a coherent personality depends upon the satisfactory integration of this "Inner Society" round a core, which is the centre of being; in other words, upon confidence and ontological security, originally given to the child by its relation with its mother.

Speaking descriptively, the ego is a boundary phenomenon between an internal world (an internal society it might be called, since the unconscious seems to be almost exclusively preoccupied with personal relationships) and an external world revealed through the sense organs. . . . These internalized objects may be pictured as having an arrangement in depth; the most primitive are the most deeply buried,

23

but with each "layer" (representing a phase of development) influencing the deposition of, and the freedom of movement in the more superficial layers above it (2); furthermore and more difficult to conceive, in each layer the same objects (the parents, siblings and other relations or their surrogates are always the central figures) reoccur again and again. . . . Achievements, however sublime or base, are not made alone for their effect on contemporary society or posterity, but also to adjust the relations of the "internal society".

> John Rickman, *Selected Contributions to Psycho-Analysis*, ed. Scott, 1957, p. 159.

Parts of the internal society may form the basis of relations with other people; others may form the basis for general social activities, e.g. in the case of one who "takes after" a parent in occupation or interest. There are also the satellite selves, dark stars which never come to light; these deeply buried or subsidiary or rejected forms may yet exert a powerful gravitational pull which will affect conscious life. Not all these dark forms, certainly, are hostile to the conscious light of day, but some are; these enjoy play in fantasy only, without access to the level of overt decision or willed action, or verbal formulation; they will appear in symbolic forms, in dreams or in the primitive language of gesture or "pantomime".

2 FANTASY AND IMAGINATION

All action and experience involves a certain amount of imagination and of fantasy, that is of both conscious and unconscious experiences which take the form of plastic images (representing the Internal Society) and dramatic representations. Fantasy is not merely what is popularly known as "wish-fulfilment", it is a means of conjoining the buried selves to any and every action. Fantasy therefore exerts a continuous influence both with adjusted and maladjusted persons,

24

the difference lying in the specific characters of the dominant fantasies, the desire or anxiety associated with them, and their interplay with each other and with external reality (3). In normal characters, fantasies are neither perceived by themselves or by others, but operate like breathing, heartbeat, digestion and other unconscious vital processes; only when they erupt through the consciousness of a disordered personality do they become a source of discomfort and perhaps of danger. In general, fantasy is like a lubricant for the bolts and hinges of life. A mature relationship is not one devoid of fantasy, but one in which fantasy is regulated and allowed to soften the difficulties without destroying the firmness of the main structure. The normal amount of fantasy in any one life may vary at different times and places, and will depend on temperament. It is joined to imagination (the conscious aspect of this process) in more intimate relationships. Lovers may play at children's games together, or play at being children; in Genet's *The Balcony* and the brothel sequence of *Ulysses*, gross fantasies are indulged in as sexual games.

When two individuals meet whose fantasies complement each other, they will be able to enjoy at least that form of happiness which is "the perpetual possession of being well deceived". The person who needs to be thought important and the person who needs someone to look up to may succeed in satisfying each other, whatever the world may think of both, and notwithstanding the possibility that the "hero" may be extremely inefficient or dependent in other ways upon the hero-worshipper. Fantasy will reinforce, underlie and sustain a planned course of activity.

At a slightly higher level, dreaming or day-dreaming may help to solve problems of living by bringing the primitive parts of the mind to bear upon a problem; dreams may point towards a real solution, and need not represent merely the sort of gratification that a hungry baby may obtain for a short

25

time by sucking its thumb (4). Eccentricities of dress, or of personal equipment (such as cars and pets) may, as Bacon said of poetry, "give some show of satisfaction to the mind, wherein the nature of things doth seem to deny it".

3 THE INNER CONFLICT

The levels of conflict within the ordinary person include those caused by outward events, "the nature of things"; by the imaginative or fantasy systems of others impinging on himself in his relationships; the acknowledged conflicts of his own contradictory impulses, divided wishes and fears, duty and pleasure; the conflicts between the light and the dark, the conscious and unconscious parts of his being; conflicts totally inaccessible.

Transformation at lower levels will bring new adjustment at higher levels—this is the purpose of psychotherapy, which aims at altering behaviour. Transformation of the conscious rôles will regroup, strengthen or diminish the "satellite selves". Flexibility of engagement or withdrawal, of commitment and playfulness, of perseverence and adaptation, belong only to stable personalities. Where the foundations are insecure, there must be a compensatory rigidity in the superstructure. "But the tragic paradox is that the more the self is defended in this way, the more it is destroyed" (5).

The unhappy being who experiences the torments of a deeply divided self will have to protect his vulnerable core, his inner self by playing an act or assuming a false self in ordinary life; he splits into two halves, the secret inner self, and the outer manipulated rôles with which he faces the world. The separate parts of his Internal Society are liable to break off and appear as eccentric aspects of his public self, which distort and finally disrupt any appearance of conformity. In a schizophrenic these various selves may appear to hold dialogues with each other, so that apparently discon-

26

nected ravings can be interpreted as a dialogue. As examples of sanity and of creative art, such poems as Andrew Marvell's *Dialogue between Soul and Body* or Yeats's *Dialogue between Self and Soul* may be compared with the following family "dialogue" between a mother and two daughters in the mind of the younger daughter, a chronic schizophrenic.

In listening to Julie, it was often as though one were doing group psychotherapy with one patient . . . it seemed one was in the presence of various fragments, or incomplete elements or different personalities in operation at the same time . . . Julie seemed to speak of herself in the first, second or third person. . . . One of the simplest instances . . . is seen when she issued herself an order and proceeded to obey it. Thus "she" would say "Sit down, stand up", and "she" would sit down and stand up . . . or "she" would say something which "she" would greet with derisive laughter, System A would say to me "She's a Royal Queen" while System B laughs derisively.

There was the peremptory bully who was always ordering her about; the same peremptory voice would make endless complaints to me about "this child": "this is a wicked child. This child is wasted time. This child is just a cheap tart. You'll never do anything with this child" . . . it was evident that this bullying figure within her was for much of the time "the boss". . . . She was basically an internal female persecutor who contained in concentrated form all the bad that Julie ascribed to her mother.

Two other partial systems could be readily identified. One fulfilled the rôle of an advocate on her behalf to me, and a protector or buffer against persecution. "She" frequently referred to Julie as her little sister. . . . The third partial system that I shall introduce was an entirely good, compliant, propitiating little girl . . . a derivative very similar to the false self [of earlier stages]. When this system spoke, "she" said "I'm a good girl, I go to the lavatory regularly."

There were derivatives also of what seemed to have been an "inner" self; finally . . . there were periods of precarious sanity when she spoke in a pathetically scared, barely audible tone, but seemed to be more nearly speaking "in her own person" than at any other time.

"I was born under a black sun. I wasn't born, I was crushed out. It's not one of those things you get over like that. I wasn't mothered, I was smothered. She wasn't a mother. I'm choosey who I have for a mother. Stop it. Stop it. She's killing me. She's cutting out my tongue. I'm rotten, base, I'm wicked. I'm wasted time."

The first six sentences are spoken sanely. Suddenly she appears to be subjected to some terrifying attack, presumably from the bad mother. She breaks off—"Stop it, stop it." Addressing me, "She's killing me." Then . . . her bad mother's condemnation of her. . . .

R. D. Laing, The Divided Self, pp. 214–20.

Intrapersonal conflict may be expressed in certain forms of psychotherapy; the use of socio-dramatic techniques for group therapy by J. L. Moreno utilize "the inescapable emotional tie uniting actors and audience" (see J. L. Moreno, *Who Shall Survive?* New York, 1953). The school for maladjusted children at Fleury, near Paris, used masks, which were made and assumed by the children to dramatize their troubles. External conflicts may also be assisted by being symbolized or debated in group therapy; a simple case, two strangers with marital difficulties succeeded in discussing things together which they were unable to face with their partners (S. H. Foukes and E. J. Antony, *Group Psycho-Therapy*, 1957, p. 231). In some forms of therapy, the analyst and an assistant may engage in dramas with the patient (for it is a curious fact, especially curious in view of three being the standard number of actors of Greek drama, that three is the basic number of figures required in the therapeutic situation, although one may be present only in fantasy) (6).

4 THE PUBLIC PLAY

Anything which can be expressed in verbal terms is on the way to integration; the earliest and the terminal stages of schizophrenia are speechless. In ordinary persons the darker and more primitive, the remote and outlying aspects of the self can be expressed only in more primitive forms, in pantomimic gesture or wordless cries. Language is a delicate and complicated tool, and anything which can be handled by this tool must be relatively accessible to reshaping. Hence the importance in any curative process of the patient's ability to recognize a situation by putting it into words (especially the release of emotion from a pre-verbal era of life).

Laing says of one psychotic young man that the only situation in which he could let himself go was in listening to jazz (op. cit., p. 52). Primitive dances, beating of drums with cries and gesticulation, may be powerful collective integrators.

The engagement or participation of spectator and actor in drama includes these primitive elements, which belong especially to the Chorus of early plays, but unites them with the power of speech, of narrative, of a series of events that approximates more elaborately than in any other form of art to "reality"; that is closest to an imitation of life. Hence its peculiar potency in reconciling primitive and advanced modes of expression.

The difference of effect between drama which is merely entertainment and drama which is art lies in the complexity and degree of tolerated conflict involved by the spectators' participation in the action.

> Everyone who has observed the gallery during [a melodrama] is aware that its inmates are living on the stage, and always of course, in the part of the hero or heroine. The illusion of reality which attaches to the play allows the daydreaming to be conducted much more efficiently than in the case of the novel. . . .

If we rise higher in the scale of art . . . the reader no longer identifies himself merely with the hero, but rather with all the characters at once. He finds portrayed the complexes or partial tendencies that exist in his own mind —and in the action of the novel he reads the conflicts and struggles which he experiences in his own life. . . . The reason that such productions appeal only to a limited class is that they presuppose in their audience the possession of mental processes sufficiently complicated to enable this identification to occur.

Bernard Hart, The Psychology of Insanity
(5th ed., 1957), p. 116.

Owing to their participation as part of an audience, it appears possible for people to gain from drama what they could not gain from other forms of art, for their level of appreciation is raised (not necessarily consciously) by the actors' interpretation and by the transmitted response of the other spectators. Among its other advantages, therefore, drama enlarges the territory of the individual sensibility.

Drama may evoke both superficial and deeply buried "satellite selves", so that internal conflicts may be worked out to a more harmonious adjustment, a regrouping of impulses, a harmonizing of partial systems.

In this way, participation may correspond to the therapeutic function of a dream (7), and the final result will not by any means be just a fantasy gratification. The play dynamically frees and flexes relatively fixed and rigid images of the inner society. Therefore, if several rôles attract identification, the plot becomes an exercise in the dynamics of adjustment, uniquely assisted by the fact that participation in drama is itself a social act. Conflicts can be projected more directly and more intensively.

It cannot be expected that a given play will precisely correspond with the needs of any individual or at least, the odds are against it. Nevertheless, the result will not be fantasy gratification alone; it will be a return, through the release afforded by the exercise of fantasy in a context suggesting reality, to full reality. As the maladjusted are encouraged to express their fantasies in direct analysis, or as personal difficulties may be directly handled in group therapy (8), so response to a play can strengthen inner freedom and balance among the participants. In particular, the multiplicity of layers in a good performance, the degree with which various aspects of the plot and characters are realized and the degree to which they are only suggested or mimed or "floated in" as part of the spectacle, will greatly widen the area of communication and the possibility of individual selection by each member of the audience.

The degree of flexibility and adjustment which the play itself provides will depend partly on mounting and production. It will depend even more on the basis supplied by the author —although a great actor can transform a mediocre script, particularly if it has obvious connexions with the emotional preoccupations of the audience.

The language of a great poet will include latent and half-focused imagery, a wide power of suggestion and a controlling rhythm. In addition, his characters and actions will be set in some kind of natural perspective, some being more prominent and many-sided, others toned down, or faded out; so that the scope for reinterpretation is extended, even for the simpler members of the audience. Moreover, the dramatist can make use of silence, of irony, so that "what he reveals within the framework of the play seems to be only a part of what he knows" (9).

A play which draws largely on traditional materials, which contains heroic figures, which assumes or maintains relatively inflexible codes of behaviour will embody fantasies associated with conscience; while an inconsequent, improvised dream-play will more probably embody primitive gratifications. The theatre of the idol and the theatre of the dream show the constituent bias which underlies them. Between them lies the great theatre of men and women, where fantasy has great freedom and where imaginative and realistic elements are more elaborately varied; where the two deviant forms are united.

The Hero and Chorus of *Oedipus Tyrannus* have been compared by two analysts with the leader and group in ordinary communities, and with the leader and the group in group-therapy. The Chorus is relatively helpless, but the Hero, who both embodies its forbidden wishes and also takes decisions which resolve the conflict, enables the Chorus finally to regain the power of action (10). These observations were more entertainingly recognized by A. E. Housman in his *Fragment of Greek Tragedy*:

CHORUS
STROPHE: In speculation
I would not willingly acquire a name
For ill-digested thought:
But after pondering much
To this conclusion I at last have come,
Life is uncertain.
This truth I have written deep
In my reflective midriff,
On tablets not of wax,
Nor with a pen did I inscribe it there.

Its native ingenuity sufficed
My well-taught diaphragm.
ERIPHYLA (within):
O, I am smitten with a hatchet's jaw,
And that in deed and not in word alone.
CHORUS: I thought I heard a sound within the house,
Unlike the sound of one that jumps for joy.
ERIPHYLA: He splits my skull, not in a friendly way,
Once more; he purposes to strike me dead.
CHORUS: I would not be reported rash; but yet
I doubt if all be well within the house.

ERIPHYLA: O, O, another stroke, that makes the third.
He stabs me to the heart against my wish.
CHORUS: If that be so, thy state of health is poor,
But thine arithmetic is quite correct.

At appropriate moments, some equally blinding glimpse of the obvious may strike a spectator, because it chimes with his inner needs. It is not often that the direct action of the plot will have this effect; a change of heart or a change of opinion is not the purpose of art. G. B. Shaw boasted that the lives of spectators had been changed by witnessing his plays; there had been some sort of conversion—and they had been moved to join a good cause, sign a cheque, leave or reassume the path of virtue (11). Such decisions may be precipitated by a play, but they are not its highest way of working. It is this exceptional process that Hamlet proposes to employ against his uncle:

> *I have heard*
> *That guilty creature sitting at a play*
> *Have by the very cunning of the scene*
> *Been so struck to the soul, that presently*
> *They have proclaimed their malefactions. . . .*

Such sharp and direct results are at the opposite end of the scale from the subtle and largely unperceived flexing and re-grouping of impulse on many different levels, which those who are moderately integrated can enjoy from "the great access of life-giving energy, testifying to the superb wealth and range of life, and to the splendid rather than the disastrous powers of man".

5 THE AUTHOR AND THE ACTORS

For the author, composition may well prove a difficult and painful process; his creative act may involve the recovery of deeply-buried material, the overcoming of inner resistance. T. S. Eliot has said:

C
33

What you start from is nothing so definite as an emotion in the ordinary sense; it is still more certainly not an idea; it is . . .

> *a bodiless childful of life in the gloom*
> *Crying with frog voice, 'what shall I be?'*

. . . he (the writer) is oppressed by a burden which he must bring to birth in order to obtain relief . . . and when the words are finally arranged in the right way . . . he may experience a moment of exhaustion, of appeasement, of absolution, and of something which is very near annihilation, which is in itself indescribable. . . . It is likely of course, that it is in the beginning the pressure of some rude unknown *psychic material* that directs the poet to tell that particular story, to develop that particular situation. And, on the other hand, the frame once chosen . . . may itself evoke other psychic material. . . . All that matters is that the voices in the end should be heard in harmony; and I have said, I doubt whether in any real poem only one voice is audible.

"The Three Voices of Poetry" (*On Poetry and Poets*, 1957, pp. 98–101).

This account would not apply to poets of easy and ready habits in composition, more of whose organizing has been done at a preconscious level. Such was probably the case with Shakespeare (12). But Milton's "Bardic voice", the lofty and remote accents of *Paradise Lost* and *Samson Agonistes*—which have the effect of evoking an invisible audience—enable him perhaps to bring together, as otherwise he could not have done, themes of the largest public significance with some very intimate personal experience. The lovers in Eden, Samson and Delilah, Satan cast down, have obvious personal implications, but they are enlarged to heroic scale, they are distanced, by a ritualized form of speech (13).

The process of composition, as it is experienced by any artist, is difficult to describe without sounding banal, but

34

there appears generally a large element of the "given" as well as the kind of struggle described by Eliot (14).

Among the main types of actor and theories of acting, there is the type defined by Diderot in *Paradoxe sur le Comédien*, who does not in any way identify himself with his part, and the one who, like the First Actor in *Hamlet* (and reputedly, Richard Burbage), sheds real tears. Both types, however, are dependent upon response from the audience. Ideally, it may be hazarded, neither the personality of the author nor of the actor should obtrude in the final total experience; they should be fused in the great collective experience, the activity of the play-in-being.

Although the ideas and observations of psychology and psychiatry may throw light on the dramatic process of play-going and playwriting it is obviously impossible to apply them to plays. Various systems of psychiatry, which may be used to give a reductive account of maladjusted individuals, with the object of bringing about an adjustment in their behaviour, are not applicable to works of art, which are not susceptible of the kind of scrutiny and dynamic tests that a living being responds to. Nor can the author be directly interrogated by a study of his work, which may reflect quite a different aspect of himself from that realized in behaviour or formulated in beliefs. In a play, a much greater degree of paradox can be tolerated than would be acceptable as an intellectual belief.

More especially the attempt directly to apply psychiatric theories is too often a method of gratifying some particular interest (15). A tentative approach to some well-marked historic phases of the drama has been offered here, in the hope that it will enable the reader more clearly to distinguish the nature and effect of the plays; not to give an explanation of their origins.

Although among the more persistent forms of art, the theatre is notably liable to brief periods of great activity and splendour that seldom last more than half a century, interspersed with long periods of static activity, decline or even eclipse. At any given time, the theatre may function as an open or a relatively closed institution, the plays may be traditional and few in number, frequently repeated; or they may succeed each other in great profusion. Therefore, in considering primarily two periods of great fertility—the High Renaissance and Baroque, roughly 1580–1680, and the modern theatre of the last hundred years—I have chosen a few selected examples from these periods, more in the hope that my hypothesis will throw light on the examples, than that the examples will establish my hypothesis.

By the dramatists' own self-effacement in their action, by the opportunities given for collaboration of actors and spectators, drama is the most "open" of the arts. This openness is shown in the characteristic speech of drama, which is not that of exposition, but of implication. Dramatic speech must of its nature be highly condensed and richly evocative, so that a single line may reverberate and link with the whole poetic movement, in the speech of other characters. The flash of revelation—the "Qu'il mourût!" of *Horace*, the "Consummatum est!" of *Faustus*—or the loaded richness of "Absent thee from felicity awhile", "His delights were dolphin-like", open out upon a whole play. This quality of poetic drama, which ensures the strongest possible local effect with the strongest possible degree of unity and integration in the work as a whole, brings about full harmony of performance, the "power to move men, to touch the depth of their imaginations, to free them and to set at work the powers of life" (16).

For if language is a delicate and complicated tool, compared with gesture, display or costume, the language of the poetic dramatist is to that of ordinary speech, as ordinary speech to the disconnected first words of the infant.

36

NOTES TO CHAPTER TWO

(1) C. G. Jung, *Memories, Dreams, Reflections*, 1963, p. 228 (speaking of N. Africa).

(2) One way of picturing the layers is the autocosmic (or autistic), when external objects are not separate from the body: the microcosmic, when objects can be magically transformed at will: and the macrocosmic, in which the independence and stability of the external world is recognized. A story which illustrates how the Internal Society forms tells of a small boy who came to his father's room at an early hour and was sent back to his own bed. Hearing murmurs, the father got up and went to the child's room. He was lying down, but stuck a leg out of bed, and then addressed it severely, "Don't dare to get up till half past seven!" He then drew back the offending limb, and repeated this game.

(3) Susan Isaacs, "The Nature and Function of Phantasy" in *Developments in Psycho-Analysis*, ed. J. Rivière, 1952.

(4) See J. A. Hadfield, *Dreams and Nightmares*, 1954, Part II.

(5) R. D. Laing, *The Divided Self*, 1960, p. 81. See, in this work, Chapters V, VI, XI (the last is quoted below).

(6) Rickman, op. cit., p. 152; R. D. Laing, *The Self and Others*, 1961, p. 140.

(7) See J. A. Hadfield, *Dreams and Nightmares*, 1954, Part II.

(8) See S. H. Foulkes and E. J. Antony, *Group Psychotherapy*, 1957, Chapter 8, on communication at twelve levels.

(9) Una Ellis Fermor, *Shakespeare the Dramatist*, 1961, p. 16. Her whole discussion of the implications of character are relevant here. cf. also John Bayley, *The Characters of Love*, 1960, Chapter I, pp. 7–8 particularly.

(10) J. Friedman and S. Gassel, *Psycho Analytical Quarterly*, vol. XIX, No. 2, New York, 1950. "The chorus in Sophocles' *Oedipus Tyrannus*."

(11) Another form of irrelevant direct response is that of the schoolgirl or schoolboy who develops a passion for a particular actor; who proceeds to imitate the appearance, cherish the photograph, or write "fan mail".

37

(12) See D. W. Harding, "The Hinterland of Thought" in *Experience into Words* (1963).

(13) Incidentally the Chorus of *Samson Agonistes* provides a notable example of how this passive element can take on new life at the end of the drama. The final speech of the Chorus is pure triumph.

(14) See Rosamond Harding, *The Anatomy of Inspiration* (1940), pp. 13–16.

(15) See Kenneth Muir, "Some Freudian Interpretations of Shakespeare" in *Proceedings of the Leeds Philosophical Society*, vol. VII, Part I, July 1952, pp. 43–52 for a discussion of some psychiatrists' deductions.

(16) Una Ellis Fermor, op. cit., p. 4.

PART TWO

The Evolution of Poetic Drama

Chapter Three

THE INHERITANCE OF
CHRISTOPHER MARLOWE

I PAGEANTRY AND THE SACRED IMAGE

FULL poetic drama did not emerge in England till the time of Marlowe and Shakespeare. Before this, there were pageants, with or without recited speech; there were poetic courtly games, and bardic sessions with the minstrels for the populace; there were moral dialogues and debates for the churchmen.

The basic conditions for full drama did not exist. Drama is metropolitan; it is the poetry of the City. This I take to be simply a historic fact; the theatre reached its greatest heights in fifth-century Athens, in Elizabethan London, in the Paris of Louis XIV; Ibsen, the one dramatist of the modern world who can be mentioned in the company of Sophocles, Shakespeare and Racine, attained full stature only when he left the north for Italy and Germany, the "new countries" of the nineteenth century. Ireland has produced great dramatists but until Dublin became a metropolis she produced no great drama; Sheridan and Goldsmith, Wilde and Shaw wrote for the London stage. Irish poetry sprang not from the great City, not even from the village, but from the shebeen in the hills. The harper and his song, ballad and romance flourish in such a land, as they also flourished in medieval England; the theatre was born in London.

City pageants, which London saw from Chaucer's day onwards, were triumphant ceremonies involving some human icon or idol. For a Royal Entry, the crowd waited in the narrow city streets, pressed round some conduit head or gatehouse upon which a gorgeous figure stood eminent; as the even more gorgeous procession approached, the pageant image would move forward, like a clock wound up to strike, deliver a single speech and relapse into statuary once more. The figure might be human or wax; and in either case the speech might come from a Presenter with silver tipped verge or wand, who pointed out the "speakers" in turn and delivered their lines for them.

In religious feasts, the shaky but majestic pageant, trundling through the streets halted at set intervals and the figures of its dumb show "played"; their speech was proclamatory or narrative rather than fully dramatic. These animated figures reproduced those to be found in great churches: to walk round King's College Chapel at Cambridge or to look at the roof bosses in the transept of Norwich Cathedral is to progress through the pageant stations of a medieval play (1). This theatre lives yet in the processions of Holy Week at Seville, when the church images are carried from their shrines on gilded and flowerdecked pageants; each pageant, weighing about four tons and borne on the shoulders of forty men, advances haltingly through the narrow streets towards the Cathedral. As they converge in the winding Street of the Serpent, gypsies in the crowd break into their high song of greeting; it is a rite of participation, sustained for twelve hours a day throughout the seven days of the week, to the slow roll of drums. The chief part, however, is silent.

Each church sends out two pageants, baroque cars bearing waxen images. Christ's passion is presented in realistic sequence, one pageant from each church; alternating with these, in single glory, graciously bending forward under her royal canopy, banks of candles blazing before her, glides the youthful, waxen Queen of Heaven—image after image, blazing with jewels, the tears on her cheeks real pearls, her crown towering high, her rich embroidered mantle sweeping low. The Son is Human, agonized; the Mother is Divine, her grief transmuted into supernatural glory; while His crown of thorns stabs like the darts in the neck of the bull.

42

The slow movement, the menacing drum rolls, the regal glory aloft and the patient marching of the invisible human beasts of burden below build up in the packed crowd a single response, ponderous and utterly alien to modern susceptibilities. Many there have attended from infancy; layers of memory accumulate with each year. They settle down to wait for hours, creating their own social unity as they eat nuts and spit the shells about, or chat to their neighbours among the hooded fraternities who, bearing lighted candles or carrying crosses, are escorting the images. Sudden concentration tightens as an image approaches; the crowds rise and cross themselves, the gypsies' wailing song begins. All this tide of feeling beating on the image and rolling back in reflected power, animates the community in veneration; and the communal veneration of the image generates a dynamic akin to drama. It is possible only because the image is familiar, and because animated life is transferred to it by the occasion.

The most beloved of all the many Madonnas bears a scar on her left cheek, where in a frenzy of excitement a drunkard once hurled his glass at La Macarena as she passed by. For the next eight years he expiated this by walking in chains behind the image.

2 THE IMAGE OF THE "ETAYN"

Besides sacred images, the streets and castle halls of Chaucer's day knew Gog and Magog, Jack o' Lent with his crown of straw, and the wild green men or snorting dragons who burst into Christmas feasts. The city dragon is still to be seen in Norwich Castle. "Etayns" or monstrous giants still walk in Carnival time.

In the most splendid of all English romances, *Sir Gawain and the Grene Knight*, written by some north country poet of Chaucer's day, a gorgeous and terrifying figure rides into King Arthur's Christmas feast, after the King had given the usual cue for the pageant-entry; he would not eat till he had seen a marvel. The head and trunk of the green and gold clad challenger were huge, his lower limbs were shapely and suited for horsemanship; his flowing hair and beard fell round him, like a cape, to elbow length. Was he really "half-etayn" or half a man and half a wicker frame? The crowd are uncertain, as he issues his Challenge to take and return a blow; for the playful decapitation of such a monster, as in a St George's play, would be quite feasible. After Gawain's blow has severed the head, and the crowd of revellers have kicked it round the hall like a football, an eerie menace is revealed. The headless knight picks up his own head, issues a fresh challenge, and gallops out. But the King and Gawain, putting on an appearance of nonchalance, "grin" at the sport which has trapped them, and Arthur reassures the Queen that if not an interlude, it was very much the same:

Wel bycommes such craft vpon cristmasse,
Layking of enterludez, to laȝe and to syng.

The mystery is not solved till at the very end the Green Knight confesses to Gawain that he was sent by Morgan le Fay in this magic shape; her conjuring at once reduces the fearfulness of the opening scene, and the end of the tale dissolves the enchantment of the beginning. It restores to the scene in Arthur's hall something of the comic transformation act that a reveller at Kenilworth performed before Queen Elizabeth, when he tore off Arion's head and proclaimed himself to be honest Harry Goldingham come to bid her majesty welcome. The severed head that plays such a large part in Shakespearean drama from *King Henry VI* to *Macbeth* belongs to the tradition of *Sir Gawain and the Grene Knight*.

Several characteristics of the Green Knight remain with the monstrous ominous strangers, Turks or Moors, who appear on the English stages of the sixteenth and seventeenth

44

century—such as his power of insulting jest, his gigantic, splendid and alarming appearance, his strange galvanic energy, his use of his womenfolk as decoys. The only Christmas disguisings for the Hall which actually survive are those of John Lydgate, where the unhappy, pious child-king Henry VI was saluted by angels descending with the fleur-de-lis, and a dove brought Clovis' golden ampoule for his anointing at Rheims. This was the boy for whom Shakespeare's Henry V had hoped such glory when he wooed Katherine of France:

> Shall not thou and I, between St Denis and St George, compound a boy, half French, half English, that shall go to Constantinople and take the Turk by the beard? shall we not? what sayest thou, my fair flower de luce?

But Henry VI was no Gawain. Indeed he was much more like the hen-pecked husbands who presented their petitions to him in the Christmas Mumming at Hertford.

Giants and dwarfs marched together in street pageants; early in the sixteenth century, the grotesque figure of the "drouchis" or dwarf makes a sudden eruption, set down by a whirlwind at the Market Cross of Edinburgh, proclaiming himself Turk, giant and goblin all in one:

> *Harry, harry, hobbillschowe!*
> *Se quha is cummyn nowe,*
> *Bot I wait nevir howe,*   *wait: wot.*
>   *With the quhorle wynd?*   *quhorle: whirl*
> *A Soldan out of Seriand land,*
> *A gyand strang for to stand*
> *That with the strength of my hand*
>   *Beres may bynd.*
> *Yit I trowe that I vary,*
> *I am the nakit Blind Harry,*   *Blind Harry: a goblin*
> *That lang has bene in the fary,*
>   *Farleis to find.*   *farleis: wonders*

45

After blowing himself out by proclaiming his giant ancestry, and by his shouted claims and monstrous jests drawing a crowd, the "drouchis" reveals himself a poor player, who has come to cry his play. He introduces three fellow-players, demands from among the crowd first a wife and then a drink; those who have enjoyed his "lude" may "skynk first to me the can".

The poor tatterdemalion jester shows plainly through the ranting, roaring lines: William Dunbar, who wrote *The Manere of Crying of ane Playe*, played his own part at the court of James IV of Scots with the same galvanic, demonic energy and bawdy frankness as the great Elizabethan clowns.

Far removed from this boisterous bawdry is the stately civic procession which Dunbar described at the welcome of James IV's Queen, the English Margaret, to the royal burgh of Aberdeen. Burgesses in their caps of gold and velvet gowns presented her with four pageants—the Salutation of the Virgin, the Three Kings, Adam and Eve, followed by secular ancestors, Robert the Bruce and a line of Stuarts. Finally, out tripped four and twenty maidens, playing and singing; they were dressed in green, with hats of white embroidered in gold—the Aberdeen Girls' Choir!

On another May morning, Dunbar brings in a pageant ship, under "saill als quhite as blossom upon spray", and another troupe of lovely ladies in green kirtles, their hair bound with gold thread, who shoot at the Golden Targe of Reason, and take the poet prisoner (2).

Games of this kind produced their own images; these returned to the pageants. More figures acquired emblematic shapes; Fortune or Love might appear as monsters with "two faces in a hood", and a favourite form for the Moral play appears to have been the game of Chess or Cards (3). Among the "four knaves of the pack" the Knave of Clubs was chief, and he took the Vice's part when

46

Iniquity came in like Hokus Pokus, in a juggler's jerkin,
with false skirts, like the Knave of Clubs.
    Ben Jonson, *The Staple of News*, Act II, *ad fin.*

Thomas Nashe once played the Varlet of Clubs in a college
play. This old tradition is behind the most startling theatrical success of the Elizabethan and Jacobean theatre, Thomas
Middleton's *Game at Chess*, which as late as 1624 revived an
obsolete model to make a highly contemporary protest
against the Spanish marriage proposed for Charles Prince of
Wales. Black and white chess men represent Spain and England; at the height of his temptation the White Knight
(Charles) is shown, "an altar, and statues, with a song", during which the statues move round the altar in a dance—"all
move portentously, the right hand way".

"Checkmate by discovery" follows, consigning all the
Black party to perdition; a gaping Hell-mouth receives them
as, scrabbling and fighting, they are thrust in "the Bag".

> *There behold the Bag's mouth, like Hell opens*
> *To take her due, and the lost sons appear*
> *Greedily gaping for increase of fellowship.*

3 MARLOWE'S TAMBURLAINE

The Reformation involved a general destruction of sacred
images in England. The simple mechanisms that jerked the
eyes or flexed the joints of wonderworking forms were triumphantly torn out. The Rood of Bromholm was battered to
pieces at Paul's Cross, before the great covered pulpit where
spectacles of the faith were played. Unfortunate heretics did
penance here, bearing a faggot as sign of the doom overhanging them, while in the intervals of a denunciatory sermon,
the preacher would come down and lash the offender, who
himself must throw his books into the flames.

The first great poetic drama of the English stage is a

47

pageant of iconoclasm, and of iconclastic ruthlessness. It is a challenge to orthodoxy, culminating in the burning of sacred books. Yet Marlowe's *Tragical Discourses of Tamburlaine the Great* (1587) derives its energies from the tradition it abjures.

A mounted King of the Moors, dressed in red satin and silver paper, led the way in many street processions of the sixteenth century. He rode under a canopy of state, followed by a train of slaves and concubines; he or his followers acted as "whifflers" and cleared the way with their swords.

> Marlowe owes the form of *Tamburlaine* to processional pageants, as the stage directions constantly remind us . . . it is the transmutation of spectacle into words . . . The language of Tamburlaine reaches beyond the resources of pageant inventory—the silver paper, dummy lances and fireworks; reaches towards glorification of earthly sovereignty.
>
> J. P. Brockbank, *Dr Faustus*, pp. 23–4.

He may at times recall the gigantic exploits of Magog, as recounted by Dunbar's "drouchis":

> *He wald apone his tais stand,*
> *And tak the sternis downe with his hand,*
> *And set them in a gold garland*
> *Abone his wifis haire.*

When he puts on armour and takes a curtle axe, the force of this shepherd appears simpler and more archaic than that of common humanity; his elemental form releases the same energy as the Green Knight, shown in a like sardonic wit and calling out a like response, which includes fear and admiration, horror and attraction.

"Threatening the world with high astounding terms", this Challenger storms his way to a throne in a story derived from Pedro Mexia the Sevillian, student of Salamanca, mathematician and cosmographer. These were the new arts by which man was challenging the traditions of his own past. The gigantic imaginative form of Tamburlaine seems of cosmic proportions, like that of Shakespeare's Antony, whose "reared arm crested the world".

> *Of stature tall and straightly fashioned,*
> *Like his desires, lift upwards and divine . . .*
> *Pale of complexion, wrought in him with passion,*
> *Thirsting with sovereignty and love of arms.*
> *His lofty brows, in folds do figure death,*
> *And in their smoothness, amity and life.*
> *About them hangs a knot of amber hairs,*
> *Wrapped in curls, as fierce Achilles' was,*
> *On which the breath of heaven delights to play,*
> *Making it dance with wanton majesty. . . .*   2.1.461–80

Intervening lines, which seem to describe the head of some extraordinary jewelled image rather than a man, term his eyes "the piercing instruments of sight" whose rolling is the rolling of the heavens. To his enemies, Tamburlaine is a Titan, to be buried under a volcano—a monstrous slave who "ne'er was sprung of human race"; they cannot tell if he be God or Fiend, Spirit or transformed Monster. To his friends, he seems a Jove thrusting down old Saturn. "To wear a crown enchased with pearl and gold" is to be "more glorious than a god"; power resides in the gorgeous and costly metals and stones, and power at once material and symbolic. Marlowe's doctrine of power, like that of his age, was largely a doctrine of sovereignty. In every parish church of the land, a copy of Foxe's *Book of Martyrs* displayed the Pope riding in triumph, with kings at his stirrup; then Henry VIII enthroned, and spurning the crown from the head of the Pope, now his abject footstool.

The hard metallic ruthlessness of Tamburlaine as Lord of Death is contrasted with tremulous images of air and fire, which belong to his aspiring mind as Lord of Life. As such, he appears to his love, Zenocrate:

Ah, life and soul, still hover in his breast,
And leave my body senseless as the earth,
Or else unite you to his life and soul,
That I may live and die with Tamburlaine. . . .
As looks the sun through Nilus' flowing stream,
Or when the morning holds him in her arms,
So looks my lordly love, fair Tamburlaine. 3.2.1006–34

A lambent light plays upon him, with the dangerous beauty of that surrounding Faustus' Helena, who is "fairer than the evening air, clad in the beauty of a thousand stars". A delicacy of translucence is reflected from the shadowing wing of the Prince of the Powers of the Air. When the two queens, holding the crowns of their monarchs, bandy words during the combat of Tamburlaine with Bajazeth, they have only the dead, flat brilliance of playing cards; Bajazeth encaged and used as a footstool is but obeying a kind of gravitational destiny, by which Tamburlaine soars as he sinks; he represents the submission of mere flesh and blood, rags of greatness, to the now visionary Sun King in the widening, dazzling luminosity of his ascent. Mere humanity finally expires with Arabia, Zenocrate's earthly betrothed lover.

Then his two followers join with Tamburlaine in the final tableau to crown Zenocrate as Queen of an earthly Heaven. This Coronation of the Virgin by a trinity of love and power has a blasphemous force, which only the old familiar images of the coronation of another Virgin will bring home; but the visual pattern is unmistakable once it has been seen. In a later scene, the reckless burning of Mahomet's scriptures reveals the dark aspects of one who worships

> *a God full of revenging wrath,*
> *From whom the lightening and the thunder breaks,*
> *Whose scourge I am. . . .* Part II, 5.1

Alternations of the dark and bright aspects of Tamburlaine do not provide a fully dramatic figure, only a virtuoso display for the magnificent voice and presence of Edward Alleyn. His first cry of pain at self-confrontation, the bewildered suffering of an inner conflict, brings him fully to life as a man. He sees the effect of the murder of the Virgins of Damascus upon Zenocrate, after they had vainly come forward with their simple laurel offerings to his black tent. He suffers; but does not melt.

> *What is beauty, saith my sufferings, then?* 5.2.1941

To suffer, yet to surmount feelings which have subdued the gods themselves to shepherds' level, proves that this shepherd is fit to be a king.

The inner conflict of Tamburlaine, roused by the tears of Zenocrate, prefigures that of Faustus:

> *Angels in their crystal armours fight*
> *A doubtful battle with my tempted thoughts.*

Only this once, as the Challenger recalls his shepherd's life for the last time, does he speak in personal accents of wit, tenderness and pain. His relation to Zenocrate reaches its climax in dumb show when "he goes to her and takes her away lovingly by the hand, looking wrathfully on Agydas, and says nothing".

The tableaux of this play, the heraldry of Tamburlaine's white, red and black pavilions, the clash of swords and the sparkle of jewels are incorporated in the poetry, which is still that of proclamation and display. His succession of victories suggest the tournament as much as the theatre.

4 DR FAUSTUS, AND THE JEW OF MALTA

In the prologue to *Tamburlaine*, Marlowe rejected clowning; in *Dr Faustus* he succumbed to it, splendidly. This full drama of guilt and responsibility includes a much wider range of tradition, though not till the final scene does the realization of his action come to the doomed magician when, like Everyman, but with such different anticipation, he is called to his reckoning. The jests of the clowns, which reflect ironically upon Faustus' powers, are not altogether separate from the tragic story; images of hell-fire and of the torn flesh of victims may emerge from their patter with unexpected menace:

WAGNER: . . . the villain's out of service, and so hungry that I know he would give his soul to the devil for a shoulder of mutton, though it were blood-raw.
CLOWN: Not so, neither, I had need to have it well roasted, and good sauce to it, if I pay so dear, I can tell you.

1.4.8–12

Faustus' own tricks vary from those of the common conjuror to those of the eldritch shape-changer; his transformations, though lacking the dramatic depths that glow in the scenes of choice, combine the comic and the horrific, being designed to raise at once a shudder and a guffaw. Benvolio and the knights who cut off Faustus' head, only to find that "Zounds, the devil's alive again" are deceived by the same trick that the Green Knight played on Gawain. On the other hand, the early jests about false legs and false limbs which Faustus sheds so lightly gain a terrible retrospective irony when in the last scenes his scholars find his mangled remains—and it may be that the stage properties were identical.

> *Oh help us, heaven! see, here are Faustus' limbs*
> *All torn asunder by the hand of death.*　5.3.7–8

In his conjuring, Faustus has acted as puppet master, turning the Pope into a kind of property doll, calling up the shadows of Alexander and Helen; now the puppet limbs of the conjuror strew the stage as the devil jerks the strings.

Lucifer's pageant of the Seven Deadly Sins is a popular

medieval show; it had been treated in a poem of William Dunbar with the same eldritch mirth. His "seir bumbard belly hudrouns" skip through fire and jag each other with knives; they are meant to make us laugh, but, as C. S. Lewis observed, we are meant to be laughing at torture. The menaces of the Devil are extended with unnerving jollity in many medieval poems; even Mephistophilis cannot sustain his grand melancholy except with Faustus. The grotesque hobgoblin pranks by which he transforms the clowns to a dog and an ape might come from popular jestbooks, which were filled with a mixture of the horrific and the obscene (4).

The play of *Faustus* offers such a bold intellectual challenge that it demands this compensatory or protective relief—any situation of unusual danger will often call out the impulse to ridicule or laughter. In spite of the orthodox conclusion, the words of Faustus are a defiance to divinity, which once said, cannot be unsaid. The play broke very strong taboos, and the audience went in fear that the devil might materialize upon the stage—stories were current of performances in which one more actor appeared. The audience are involved in the event in a new complex way, and at different levels of response.

His soliloquies, above all the final one, bring Faustus to life through an interior conflict. Good and Bad Angels have disappeared, as he disintegrates into competing and contradictory voices, and his freedom of choice, even of movement, slips away. Caught between the grinding wheels of Nature's clock and the gaping mouth of Hell, the agony of Faustus' self-consciousness in the hour of his dissolution creates a new kind of dramatic poetry. Where the imaginative form of Tamburlaine had expanded to fill the whole universe, Faustus, after searching the heavens, and seeking with the giants who warred on Jove to be buried under hills and mountains finds himself faced with a Nature coldly external to himself, impervious to his vulnerable shrinking. The trap closes; his body becomes a prison from which he longs to escape into some lower form of life:

> *Ah, Pythagoras' metempsychosis, were that true,*
> *This soul should fly from me, and I be changed*
> *Unto some brutish beast. . . .*

Who is the "me" that is neither body nor soul—that in his last words appeals to them both to dissolve? The new, tormented self that can speak these words is "Faustus, and a man".

When Faustus sold his soul, he obliterated his ability to possess a past, since every action that fell behind him into the past pushed him nearer to his final end; nor could he look at the future, but only at the present. His magic annihilated Space, but his bondage contracted Time; the last hour, as it closes in, shows him only where he is, and where in effect he had been living for four and twenty years. Such a realization was perhaps only possible in the world of the new cosmology, in Galileo's world. The groundlings who paid their penny to see the devil's fireworks got more than their pennyworth.

The Jew of Malta derives from a medieval tradition best seen in *The Croxton Play of the Sacrament*, where five Jews purchase the Host and conduct upon it a series of experimental tortures. Jonathas, their leader, prays devoutly to "Mahomet" for the great wealth he enjoys—amethysts, beryls, sapphires, rich spices and fruits which he enumerates in a speech that is very close to Barabas' opening. The marvels which result from his experimental stabbing, boiling and baking of the Host (to find why the Christians "believe in a cake") cause his own hand to stick fast to the Host and then to drop off, like Faustus' limbs. The hand and the Host are thrown into a cauldron like that which finally receives Barabas, and which boils with blood; finally, the oven to which it

54

is consigned bursts asunder and an Image of Christ appears, Who speaks to the Jews, while His wounds trickle blood. After the conversion and baptism of the Jews, the Image is changed into bread again and borne to church.

In the prologue to Marlowe's play, Machiavelli—in Elizabethan eyes a kind of anti-Christ—comes to question more radically than Jonathas's religious verbal magic, "the word spoken with power". It is a heroic speech of defiance.

> *Let them know that I am Machiaval,*
> *And weigh not men and therefore not men's words....*

But Barabas himself, in his defiance of the Christians, sinks from a neutral and sceptical philosophic attitude to one of emotional fury and general hatred. His relationship to the world is entirely through "things"—his wealth; when this is disrupted, he reveals the lack of any affective tie to men. Superb in his energy, he lives in a world of puppets, himself the only image which has come to life.

The old story of the Sacrament is also behind the Shakespearean *Merchant of Venice* (in another version) (5), but Shakespeare's flexibility is much greater even than Marlowe's. Richard III, most Marlovian of his heroes, combines the scepticism of Machiavel with the diabolic sadism of Barabas, and something of Kyd's Revenger. His is the first part in which Shakespeare displayed his special power of synthesis, of uniting very different traditions into a single powerful form. It remains the oldest "live" part to be acted on the stage; but as I have written about it at some length elsewhere, I shall not elaborate upon it further (6).

5 SHAKESPEARE AND THE IMAGE

Richard III is Shakespeare's first and clearest icon—a diabolic one. In his early plays, he often employs at an emotional climax some icon which presents a woeful or gracious pageant to the spectators, although his flexible style led him rather to other modes.

Richard II, who played so many parts, from the king's to the beggar's, suddenly sees himself transformed to the mechanical figure of a timepiece, as he sits in his last prison hammering out his thoughts. Richard, a character of particularly strong interior life, is the very antithesis of a Marlovian Challenger.

> *I wasted time and now doth time waste me,*
> *For now hath time made me his numbering clock:*
> *My thoughts are minutes: and with sighs they jar*
> *Their watches on unto mine eyes, the outward watch,*
> *Whereto my finger, like a dial's point,*
> *Is pointed still in cleansing them from tears.*
> *Now, sir, the hour that tells what hour it is*
> *Are clamourous groans, that strike upon my heart,*
> *Which is the bell; so sighs and tears and groans*
> *Show minutes, times and hours; but my time*
> *Runs posting on, in Bolingbroke's proud joy,*
> *While I stand fooling here, his Jack o' the clock.*
>
> 5.1.50–60

This could not have been written without Faustus; but the actor has become so different from an image, that the state can now be recalled within the poetry as an tragic symbol. As King, Richard had shown a strange mechanical lifelessness, whether in throwing down his warder in the lists at Coventry and giving the signal for a hundred years' bloodshed to begin; or descending in his sunbright armour from the battlements of Flint Castle to the base court. Only after, at his deposition, he has shattered his own image in the glass, can he see himself for what he is, in this strange vision of the clock. And to *see* this image is to transcend it. Ionesco has based a complete play upon these last scenes of Richard II's life—*Exit the King*.

Boy players were often called upon to give the effect of an image; it suited their limited range. In *Titus Andronicus*, the mutilated Lavinia is described in a series of images taken from street pageants—the tree of flourishing and withered leaves, and the conduit with "three issuing spouts" are gruesomely revived emblems from City festivities used to suggest the immobility of this pageanty of woe.

Portia waits the choice of caskets like a figure taken from an old tapestry. Ancient imagery is more violently used in the Player's Speech of *Hamlet*. The terrifying figure of Pyrrhus, all in black, horridly smeared with blood, like some mechanical figure of destruction, or like the red-and-black suited Tamburlaine, stands transfixed over Priam with his sword arrested in mid air. There is in the Fall of Troy, as Harry Levin has finely said "a glaring nightmare of smoke and screams and ruins", but it may owe more than a little to Marlowe's *Tragedy of Dido*, a play in which all the characters move like puppets at the bidding of the gods. This, Marlowe's only play for children, may have been recalled in both the magniloquence of the older style, and its stagey inflexibility, as Hamlet contrasts the actor's emotion with his own.

In the later plays of Shakespeare, images of death are miraculously converted into flesh and blood. In *Pericles* Thaisa, taken from her coffin, "begins to blow into life's flower again"; while within the Chapel where the image of Hermione has been kept "holy, apart", at the end of *The Winter's Tale*, Paulina presents Leontes with a "lively mockery" of life. He shrinks at first, feeling "more stone than it", but Perdita, in the authentic spirit of veneration, recovers herself to say:

Give me leave,
And do not say 'tis superstition, that
I kneel to implore her blessing. 5.3.42–3

57

So, to heavenly music, the mother and queen descends; she is stone no more (7).

Such ceremony found its later form in the discoveries of the Jacobean masque. As the divinity of kings became more doctrinal, the sudden revelation of a genuine royal figure by the opening of a rock or descent from a cloud enhanced this divinity symbolically.

Oberon the Fairy Prince played by Henry Prince of Wales, represented *himself*; it was an imaginative way of sweeping the small courtly audience into his kingdom-to-be. The slight elegant figures of Charles I and his Queen danced in an Arcadian world where Cupid ruled; their masquing was to culminate in the last and most tragic spectacle of the Whitehall stage, Charles's supreme rôle, when

> *the Royal Actor borne*
> *The tragic scaffold might adorn*
> *Whilst round the armed bands*
> *Did clap their bloody hands.*

The great open scene on which Charles perished re-assembled a tragic scaffold that had by then passed away. The enclosed theatre of the Hall had long been the setting for drama. Marlowe's plays belong essentially to those early stages which were based on still earlier "game places", or open circles beyond the city walls, whose traditions perhaps went back to the arena. It is to be found today, surviving in the Spanish bullring, where the "lords' room" and "minstrels' gallery" are still to be seen with their pillared roof and shawl-draped balcony placed above the tiers of seats. The theatre of Marlowe shows an archaic simplicity, even compared with the early Shakespeare, reflecting more primitive conditions of acting, which was still close to the street performances of the first part of Elizabeth's reign. The public theatre had been established in London for a little over a decade when Marlowe's Tamburlaine first appeared on the boards; and it was upon this public theatre that Shakespeare's first plays were also seen. Unlike Marlowe, however, he was able to draw upon another tradition, with finer poetic possibilities; this was the courtly tradition, springing from the ceremonies and "games" of a great household.

NOTES TO CHAPTER THREE

(1) See M. D. Anderson, *Drama and Imagery in English Medieval Churches* (1963), for an account of the Norwich roof bosses. I have given a more iconographical account of Marlowe in *Theology*, vol. *LXVII* (July, August 1964).

(2) Such scenes are connected with the courtly games dealt with in the next chapter. The ship pageant was common in courtly entertainments; see Glynne Wickham, *Early English Stages*, Vol. I (1959).

(3) See T. W. Craik, *The Tudor Interlude* (1958), pp. 63–4. Two faces in a hood were characteristic of the medieval demon (he might also have a face at the belly, or the anus). I have collected about a dozen instances of the playing card figures. The latest appearance of the "four knaves of the pack" is in Jonson's *Fortunate Isles*, 1626.

(4) I have dealt more fully with this aspect of Dr Faustus in "Faustus and the Eldritch Tradition" in *Essays on Shakespeare and Elizabethan Drama, in honor of Hardin Craig*, ed. R. Hosley (1962).

(5) See M. D. Anderson, op. cit., p. 202. Two Judges, sent by the Emperor Constantine to search for the True Cross, find a Christian merchant in Antonio's plight and release him by the quibble that Portia uses. To escape the heavy penalty he has incurred, the Jew reveals to Constantine's mother, St Helena, the burial place of the True Cross. The story comes from the *Cursor Mundi*.

(6) See my *Shakespeare and Elizabethan Poetry*, Chapter VIII; also *The Rise of the Common Player*, Chapter V. Compare Bernard Spivack, *Shakespeare and the Allegory of Evil* (1958), and A. P. Rossitter, *Angel with Horns* (1961).

(7) I do not think it has been noted that there is a similar statue scene in *The Trial of Chivalry* (an anonymous play of Derby's men, *c.* 1605). The "statue" of Ferdinand on his tomb comes to life when his lady places a ring on his hand, and declares herself his wife.

Chapter Four

THE DREAM VISION FROM CHAUCER TO SHAKESPEARE

I SHAKESPEARE'S COURTLY COMEDY

SHAKESPEARE's dramatic career began in the popular theatres. The envy of Robert Greene, who attacked "this upstart crow beautified with our feathers", shows that in Marlowe's lifetime he had already made his mark; in comparing him with one of the dumb actors in animal masks, who appeared in shows of detraction and scorn, Greene strove to thrust him down among the lowest kind of entertainer (1). Shakespeare's reply was to publish a gorgeous courtly poem, *Venus and Adonis*, dedicated to a courtly patron, the Earl of Southampton. Perhaps at this time he was actually living in Southampton's house, for plague had closed the theatres and the acting troupes were broken, scattered or fled. He could well have taken to the kind of life that has been depicted for us in the recently discovered autobiography of Whythorne the musician. If so, this might explain how in the plays written round 1592–94, he suddenly develops a new and intimate understanding of the courtly life, with its long tradition of ceremonious games. This gave shape to two comedies, *Love's Labour's Lost* and *A Midsummer Night's Dream*, which were evidently written in the first place for a noble household. One indication of this may be found in the exceptionally large number of boys' parts—six in *Love's Labour's Lost* and about a dozen in *A Midsummer Night's Dream*. No acting company could have filled them; Shakespeare was evidently free to draw upon the pages or choristers of a great household.

Still more noticable, however, is the enclosed privacy of

61

the royal park, the atmosphere of intimate jest in *Love's Labour's Lost*. The messenger of death who closes the play bears a sharp reminder of what might have been happening beyond the gates of some rural seat in Hampshire, in 1593 or 1594; at the end, Berowne goes out to jest in a hospital as penance for his vow against love.

Such an ending would have been comprehensible to Chaucer, and the shaping spirit of these two plays—so different from the pallid courtship of an earlier work, *Two Gentlemen of Verona*—derived from Chaucer's tradition. The outward form had changed, but the audience and their relation to the poetry was not so different. Chaucer used the dream vision to separate the "performance" of poetry from ordinary living; in drama the play within the play gives a similar perspective, and releases the audience, as participants, from the limitations of everyday existence.

2 CHAUCER'S DREAM POETRY

In Richard II's time, the court settled down in the neighbourhood of London; Chaucer, who was a Londoner by birth, derived his intimate rapport with the court as its Master of Ceremonies from having spent his youth in royal service. His verses were spoken on behalf of his audience, and projected an ideal version of the life they led; each was assigned a part in the "play". Crowded together in the hall and solar, courtiers needed such a protective ritual, if personal relations were to develop in utter absence of privacy. The convention of the dream vision lent psychic distance; in poetry "dreams" provide a way of introducing "games"—of playing with reality. A variety of interpretations would always be permitted; and while the lord or lady to whom the poet made his offering would hold the subtlest clues, all could participate, for an "example" of love behaviour was always an "example" of some general truth, and not a code message.

Poetry, as already remarked, was not only experience but performance.

In *The House of Fame* Chaucer explicitly discusses the nature of dreams as if they represented for him the whole problem of consciousness. The complexity of his material and the variety of his terms make most modern discussions look rather crude. But the controlled involvement of his "dream" or "game" may be shown from his first vision, *The Book of the Duchess*.

Chaucer and his wife were both entered in the household of Blanche, Duchess of Lancaster; this elegy was offered to her husband, John of Gaunt, when she died at the age of twenty-nine. The form is unexpected. Instead of prolonged tragic lament, or heavy didactic complaint, Chaucer celebrates lost happiness in a delicate May morning vision, where, as in a reliquary, the memory of a ten years' marriage is enshrined with all the lightness of gold and jewelled filigree.

The poem opens with someone sleepless with grief. He summons a servant to read—as John of Gaunt might have done; the tale is one of bereavement in marriage, of constancy and sorrow.

> *Farewel, swete, my worldes blisse*
> *I pray God your sorwe lisse:*
> *To litel while our blisse lasteth.*

Sleep and dreams come at last. The Dreamer thinks he wakes in a splendid chamber painted with scenes from the *Romaunt of the Rose*—that vision of the Earthly Paradise of lovers, the happy garden from which half of human existence was excluded—the old, the sorrowful, the poor were all banished outside the walls.

Such was to be the enclosed garden or park of *Love's Labour's Lost*, where at the end the dark figure of mourning was to penetrate—Marcadé, messenger of death.

63

Chaucer's dreamer, entering the park, meets much earlier the figure of Sorrow, in the person of the Black Knight. His first words tell the whole secret, as the Dreamer overhears them:

> *my lady brighte*
> *which I have loved with all my might*
> *Is fro me deed and is agoon.*

Yet the unfolding of the story begins at a high level of reticence and artifice—this information is for the audience only. To the Dreamer the Black Knight will only say that at a game of Chess against Fortune, the mummer with the monster's head, he has lost his Queen. To explain why he is so stifled with melancholy that "I am sorwe and sorwe ys I", the Black Knight recounts the whole story of his service of love.

This leads into a long description of the White Lady—no mere catalogue of her features, as in the French original, but an evocation of her gaiety, sparkle, tenderness. He describes her in a simile which Shakespeare was to put into the mouth of Romeo.

> *She was lyk to torch bryght,*
> *That every man may take of lyght*
> *Ynogh and it hath never the less* (2).

In the delightful interplay of a comedy of love, the Knight's feelings evoke a sceptical protest. "I believe you," says the Dreamer, "you thought her the most beautiful lady in the world, and so would anyone who looked with your eyes." "With mine?" cries the Knight. "Why, everyone thought so; even if they had not, I would have loved her, for I was constrained to it—no, no, what nonsense, I wanted to do it, but I had no choice because of her great virtues, which equalled those of Penelope or Lucrece." When at last he won her, their perfect happiness made each day a bridal:

64

Our joye was ever yliche ynewe:
Our hertes were so even a payre
That nevere was there noon contrayre
To that other for no woo.

In a blankness which his own love-mazedness may explain
(3), the Dreamer puts the blundering intolerable question:

Sir, quod I, where is she now?

The Black Knight cries out sharply "Now?", relapses into his
former stony immobility, and finally achieves his curt revelation:

She ys ded.—Nay—Yis, be my trouthe.—
Is that youre los? By God, hyt ys routhe.

With this awestruck, helpless exclamation the game stops,
the Knight turns towards his castle, the clock strikes twelve
and the Dreamer wakes.

The paradox of consoling grief by an aery love vision would
be striking to the first audience as wearing white at a funeral,
or playing love songs for a requiem. Its fantasy and apparent
inconsequence were well designed to dissolve the stony
rigidity of grief.

Each of Chaucer's later love visions has its own quality;
The Parlement of Foules moves from a grand opening—Scipio's
vision of the universe—to the Earthly Paradise, to the contrasted courts of Venus and Nature; and finally to the mating
of the birds on St Valentine's Day, whose delicate piping song
closes the long *decrescendo*. Yet here, again, is a paradox; the
chief lovers, like Shakespeare's, do not pair. Given a free
choice (which royalty might hope for only in a dream) the
Princess hesitates, clinging to Nature even if it means a scolding or a beating, and asks for a year to make up her mind.
This girlish recoil, in subtly satisfying anticlimax, acknow-
ledges the feminine point of view; it does not need a comparison of the closing rondel and the owl and cuckoo songs to

E   65

reveal that the author of *Love's Labour's Lost* had read *The Parlement of Foules*.

The kingdom of the birds is exactly parallel to human society, with its soldiers, kings, counsellors, robbers and peasants. The noisy court proceedings—controlled by Nature's peremptory "Hold your tongues there!"—introduce a great variety of lovers, each defined by his speech, from the modest eloquence of the royal eagle, the bluff soldierly oaths of his first rival and the clerkly legal distinctions of the second, down to the rowdy cries of the proletarian ducks and cuckoos.

Chaucer supplied his royal patrons with a form of ceremonious game in which he himself might play a part. After the prologue to *The Legend of Good Women*, where he is condemned for heresy against love, and enjoined the penance of writing only of good women and of faithless men, he contrives to end a particularly tragic tale with

Trusteth, as in love, no man but me.

The bookish and needy writers who succeeded him betray their insecurity by straining after pomp or instruction or by exploiting the jester's privilege of bawdy familiarity. Lydgate is stately and stiff; Dunbar reduced the dream vision to allegorical compliment or pageantry, while also writing burlesque tournaments of the tailors and shoemakers—a battle of the slop-pails.

Tales of adventure and chivalry, such as the story of Chaucer's young Squire in *The Canterbury Tales*, offer instead of the ordered dream vision an unfettered day-dream and these were a popular form of entertainment up to the seventeenth century. Launcefal or Gawain is rewarded with an enchanted princess and a fairy kingdom. Or else he undergoes strange ordeals, overcoming giants, Saracens, and etayns, the range of conquest being quite unchecked by any ironic queries. Often the hero begins as an unknown, simple countryman, who turns out in the end to be of royal birth.

To judge from the titles of lost early plays, this kind of story, made into a play of adventures, was popular with everyone. Throughout the sixteenth century, games, shows and academic morals that all somehow contrived to involve the audience, were preparing the way for the great drama to come; they ranged from courtly games of the Flower and the Leaf and the Holly and the Ivy to the village "skimmity ride". Compliment to the Chief Spectator, or else a glancing shaft of malice at some general enemy, was expected. To "shadow" contemporary events was so much to be expected that "Shadow" was used later as the surname for an actor. Even in Shakespeare's days, there was constant need to re-assure the audience that particular persons were not being "touched".

The possibilities were uncertain, and the situation confused, because the language of these dramas is clumsy. To evolve a proper dramatic relation, the poet had to be clear what he was doing—as Chaucer had been. I have indicated some of the stages of this development in a previous book, *The Rise of the Common Player*, and shall not return to it now. When Shakespeare looked back historically across the troubles of the fifteenth century to the formal and elegant beauty of the court of Richard II, he indicated the nature of his own poetic inheritance. The fair garden, with Richard as "that sweet lovely rose", the high point of late medieval art in England, was separated from Shakespeare by a dreary waste; in which, here and there, some sturdy tale of Arthur or Gawain, with its simple appeal to the championship of a national cause, suggested what the theme of national unity might become in more skilful hands.

3 GEORGE PEELE

A Londoner, son of a pageant writer, George Peele united the broken shards of many traditions into simple dramatic forms. He belonged to a generation earlier than Marlowe or Shakespeare, for he was at Oxford when they were in petty school. His versatility ranged from *The Arraignement of Paris*, a dramatic courtly game, to a dream vision of the House of Fame for a Garter feast. City pageants were his speciality.

The crude violence of his worst plays reflect the debased tradition of popular romance; yet in one play Peele reached true imaginative form, weaving together fairy tales and sequences derived from the players' repertoire. The device of the play within a play gave him finally the dramatic equivalent of the Dream Vision's psychic depth. The Induction to *The Old Wives' Tale* shows three servants of a noble lord, whose names proclaim them to be players, seeking the creature comforts of fire, food and sleep in the woodland cottage of Clunch and Madge. Antic goes to bed and to dream off stage, while Frolic and Fantastic sit up with old Madge that they may be "ready . . . extempore" in the morning. Her tale "of the Gyant and the King's daughter and I know not what" comes to life in the telling, and soon old Madge is dreaming out the rest.

The play had been written for the Queen's own players, but survives in a form that it took when, in the time of the plague, they had fallen on evil days and turned country strollers (4). In its mangled state it has the strangely satisfying incompleteness that is found also in *Faustus*; here, once again, is true oral poetry; its lack of formal structure invites the spectators to fill in the gaps. The characters of the main play had all been seen many times before. They need no set action or plot sequence, but have only to display themselves for what they are—the princess "white as snow and red as blood", the enchanter who holds her captive; her two brothers, who wander in search of her; Erestus, the enchanted knight, who, like William of Palerne in the old romance, has been changed into the form of a white bear, and lives at the cross roads in the wood. When the Two Brothers meet him,

68

he does not need to be told their story, but can ask at once: "Is she fair?"

Some of the incidents belong to other plays of the same company (5), so if any particular character pleased the audience it would be natural for them to demand a little more, and for the actor to fit in another "turn". Juan y Bango, the Spanish braggart, might be summoned back with the cry "Let him roar again"—as a minstrel, after due encouragement, would give another "fitte" of his tale. The play, with no less than twenty-four named parts, some of which are wordless, seems to be built for expansion or contraction in the manner of the Italian commedia dell'arte, where the performers built up a play by selections from their repertoire of jokes and love-scenes. Five miniature sets, which must have been packed away in the property carts of the strollers, were set out in a semicircle, in emblematic representation of the "places". The pageant cars had shrunk, drawn up and stationed themselves upon the scaffold as stylized objects. The old wife's cottage, the magician's cell, the enchanted wood and the enchanted ground with its hillock where characters could be blasted with flames of fire, the well of life from which rose an enchanted head—all allowed the characters to be lightly transported from place to place with the feeling of floating freely that is one of the conditions of a dream. For this medley is held together within the dream-framework till Madge's last words give a rustic awakening:

> When this was done, I took a piece of bread and cheese and came my way, and so shall you have too, before you go, to your breakfast.

The midsummer woodland of Shakespeare's dream play, no less than the improvised properties of his workmen's "tragedy", represent a courtly version of this simple form; the likeness is as plain as the difference. There is no element of parody in Peele. The dream-like flatness of his dialogue is filled out by the rich sensuous beauty of songs, whose clustered images spread summer pleasure, and carry only by implication the beautiful wantonness of a woman's body.

> *When as the rye reach to the chin,*
> *And chopcherry, chopcherry ripe within,*
> *Strawberries swimming in the cream,*
> *And schoolboys playing in the stream:*
> > *Then O, then O, then O, my true love said,*
> > *Till that time come again*
> > *She could not live a maid.*

It was only some fourteen years or so later that such romance-plays were being looked back upon as too unsophisticated for the stage. In another play-within-the-play, the citizen's wife of Beaumont's *Knight of the Burning Pestle* (1608) emulates the simplicity of old Madge; she knows old wives' tales that go back to the days of Gawain and the Green Knight:

> they say the King of Portugal cannot sit at his meat, but the giants and the etayns will come and snatch it from him.

The citizen party have never been to a theatre before, though well acquainted with the Lord Mayor's Show and the May Lords with scarfs and rings. The manners of these citizens are those of a street audience; they chat freely to all around, are constantly interrupting to admonish or advise; call for the actors as readily as they call for beer, and proudly pay to bring in the Waits of Southwark. The climax of adventure for the bold 'prentice, turned Grocer-Errant, is to return and lead the city musters at Mile End. In this play the citizens cannot distinguish play from reality; they break up the comedy which the actors are trying to stage and impose their own; the Grocer and his wife, though deeply involved in the actors' story, cannot have enough of their own

70

'prentice. Their impatience when he leaves the stage is vehement, for he is *their* performer in their "game"; his dying speech leaves him still very much alive, but his mistress has the last word in the comedy.

4 JOHN LYLY

Such was the popular tradition, as seen through the amused parody of a "little theatre" group in the early years of King James. The original "little theatre" group was a courtly one, and in the plays of John Lyly the Chaucerian tradition of courtly games was given dramatic form. Lyly, whose plays were shown in the 1580s, was given to describing them as "shadows" or "dreams" of the royal court whose dalliance they reflected.

The Queen was invited to imagine herself "in a deep dream" before witnessing *Sapho and Phao*, the play where she appeared in transparent disguise as the beauty who disarmed Cupid; "all is but a poet's dream" would excuse the more dangerous satire of *The Woman in the Moon*. The prologue to *Endimon* begs that "none will apply pastimes because they are fancies"; but even pastime had lost its innocence, since courtship had become a trade. Lyly, like the nobles for whom he designed his offerings, was in search of reward.

Pointed, dexterous and precise in their symmetry of plot and characters, Lyly's plays remain poetry of the surface; their delicate fantasy and airy malice, as played by the diminutive choristers of St Paul's or the Chapel, depended on the immediate occasion. The audience was invited to a collaboration simpler than that which Peele demanded, even if the style of the plays is so much more elaborate; for the tinkling musical box of courtly compliment, though it chimed so sweetly, could play only one tune. Participation did not invite intimacy; it only underlined a certain exclusiveness. The plays deployed in witty manoeuvre for the benefit of

71

Oxford or Leicester; the sharpness of the wit combats betray underlying tensions that could be felt in the dulcet praise of Elizabeth. Courtly comedy lent itself to competitive display in the direct interest of social climbers; reward was uncertain, and competition ruthless. While the queen was invited to dream of gods and goddesses, the poet was dreaming of the Mastership of the Revels; his tribute, unlike Chaucer's, was not "fre" and the clearest note in his plays is one of controlled frustration (6).

The plays were unified round courtly debates on set themes; the characters were flat and simplified; Cupid, not Venus was the presiding deity—Desire only, not Love herself. Liable at any moment to change their nature, their shape or even their sex, characters do not speak with individual voices; "the mind dances on the tautness of the dialogue . . . theirs is a world in which idleness never bores, flirtation never palls, in which wealth does not oppress, and power exists without responsibility; it is, in short, a world of wish-fulfilment" (7).

Lyly's aim was "to move inward delight, not outward lightness . . . soft smiling, not loud laughing"; he appealed to manners and not to feelings. His plays, which leave open the possibility of various "applications", made an immediate impression of great sharpness, they were perfectly adapted for a particular moment, but that moment was brief. They have the ephemeral quality of the true "games" or "dream"; long before Elizabeth's reign was over, Lyly's particular style had fallen out of fashion and was cast aside while he himself was piteously excusing his "tediousness" and begging the reward which had never come his way.

5 SHAKESPEARE AND *A MIDSUMMER NIGHT'S DREAM*

Shakespeare's mastery of his art in *A Midsummer Night's Dream* is complete and assured. Written in all probability for a noble wedding festivity, it takes up Lyly's theme of

transformation, and his contrasted groups of characters—
monarchs, fairies, lovers and rustics. Puck stages his own
"fond pageant" of the lovers' metamorphosis with all the
airy malice and elegant symmetry that had been Lyly's a
decade before; once all have entered the enchanted wood for
a "rite of May", the speed of their changes is such that when at
last they wake, the actors seem remote "as far off mountains
turned into clouds". In the romance of *Huon of Bordeaux*,
Oberon ruled a magic wood to the east of the world, and so
the spiced Indian air is familiar to Titania; but this wood is
filled with English spirits and beasts, small creatures of the
wild that the fairies hunt. By day it is the palace wood, part
of Theseus' hunting desmesne, and the rustics meet "at the
duke's oak". To Shakespeare, it is a Warwickshire woodland
by moonlight, its dusk warm with the scent of musk rose and
eglantine—a kingdom where spells and charms are laws,
where changelings, mermaids and monsters may be met, and
where the discords of the mortal world are finally resolved.
At first Puck the shapechanger, auditor and actor in the
tradesmens' play, scatters and hunts the tragedians, who
tumble out of their theatre in panic, to find themselves, as in
some Bankside scramble, rifled by the underworld.

> *senseless things begin to do them wrong,*
> *For briars and thorns at their apparel snatch,*
> *Some sleeves, some hats, from yielders all things snatch.* (8)

Like Chaucer's Dreamer, Shakespeare here found his way
to an enchanted wood where he was to return again and
again, satisfying at once the impulse to retreat and the impulse to explore. This fantastic shelter of dappled boughs,
whether called the Forest of Arden, Windsor Forest or a
Wood near Milford Haven, became his kingdom of Dream.
Here, like Chaucer, he found his own depths, from which
new depths were transferred to his own writing. For if it be
enquired where is the dialogue in depth that enlivens this

73

play it is plain that one character and one alone is unmistakably gifted with the full range of human voice and human personality—Bottom the Weaver. His magic encounter with the Queen of the Enchanted Wood, when like Sir Launcefal or Thomas of Ercildoune, he finds himself wooed by a fairy bride, wakes the whole woodland to a full natural life. Once he has donned the ass's head of the mome, he enters the kingdom of the cowslip-pensioners; the blossoms rise, move, nod and curtsey to him; the moths hover, the cobwebs twinkle; a silvery voice whispers:

Out of the wood do not desire to go.

The delicate woodland life of flowers and spirits encroaches upon the bewildered lovers, who dwindle into properties for Puck's pageant. "You puppet, you!" cries Helena, and Hermia retorts "Painted maypole!" while Bottom presents Love's Pageant with its Monster. Nothing could be more ridiculous than the triple incongruity of the ass's head, the tradesman's sturdy insensibility and the fairy's dotage.

But who, it may be asked, is Bottom? A stage-struck artisan, who loves to rant and knows how to "kill a calf" in high style (9); who later finds himself playing before a King and Queen (heaven knows how insufficiently), his play miraculously chosen out of a whole collection of devices (some by very learned men and satirical), which the Master of the Revels holds in readiness for the royal entertainment.

Bottom's dialogue in depth is held with the whole collective spirit of the woodland, though he sleeps in the arms of Titania. It is by contrast with the delicate life of the woodland that Moon and Wall, in their laborious explanations, become doubly absurd (10); behind the harmless roars of the Lion lurks the dangerous form of the shapechanger Puck, "a hog, a headless bear, sometimes a fire", who slips in to speak the epilogue. Contrast between shadow and substance is

74

further complicated by glimpses of an outer world, where Queen Elizabeth walks in the moonlight beside the western seas, or the chambers of a great household are blessed for a bridal. To the dialogue between Bottom and the Woodland, since a third voice has always been needed for a full exchange, may be added that of Theseus, personification of kindly reason, who rejects belief in "these antic fables and these fairy toys" yet welcomes the poor players:

Our sport shall be to take what they mistake:
And what poor duty cannot do, noble respect
Takes it in might, not merit. . . .
The best in this kind are but shadows; and the worst no worse, if
   imagination amend them.

"It must be your imagination then, and not theirs," tartly responds the lady on the dais, in accents by no means unfamiliar to an Elizabethan.

The play must have had its special moment of presentation, but courtly tale—partly and more obviously derived from Lyly, but more deeply from Chaucer (11)—released in Shakespeare his "shaping spirit of imagination" and led him through forms of things unknown into work filled with shapes of common humanity.

As imagination bodies forth
The forms of things unknown, the poet's pen
Turns them to shapes and gives to airy nothing
A local habitation and a name.
Such tricks hath strong imagination
That if it would but apprehend some joy,
It comprehends some bringer of that joy. . . .

The difference between imagination and insensibility is hilariously developed in the "tedious brief scene" of the tradesmen's play, with the players determined to represent everything in a solid form, as if this were a City pageant. The courtiers vouchsafe interested speculation (always

75

courteously gratified by Bottom) and increasingly vehement encouragement:

Well roared, Lion.
Well run, Thisbe.
Well shone, Moon. Truly, the Moon shines with a good grace.

Against this early naturalism, Puck makes his apology:

If we shadows have offended
Think but this and all is mended
That you have but slumbered here
While these visions did appear.
And this weak and idle theme
No more yielding but a dream,
Gentles, do not reprehend.
If you pardon, we will mend.

The life of dreams is the life of the imagination; and the direct apprehension of that life, not in conceptual terms but with full realization of its power, takes form when it can be presented dynamically, as Shakespeare does in this play. It is a witness to his own freedom and to his understanding of it. Within a single action, players, poet and spectators are involved; this action reaches from a simple gesture of homage to something imperishable.

The flexibility with which the imagination moves from dream to waking and on to the illusion of the play-within-the-play and then back to the fairy world (as the woodland invades the hall to bless the bridal) is proof of a mastery which could not have grown, though it was richly developed, within the small world of the court. Shakespeare's sojourn within that world may perhaps have lasted from 1592 till 1594, when the theatres reopened after the intermission of the plague time (12). He returned to the world of the public stage and to the great company which then assembled under the leadership of James and Richard Burbage—the Lord Chamberlain's Men. From the rarified, delicate plays in

76

which his poetry had been perfected and his strong sense of symmetry in action had become welded to the imaginative forms of things unknown, he brought back to the common stages a freedom, a natural sympathy, and a flexibility of style which were essential to the development of his full dramatic form.

(1) See my article "Beasts and Gods", *Shakespeare Survey*, 16 (1962), for a discussion of the social implications of Greene's attack on Shakespeare and the riposte.

(2) Compare Romeo's "Oh, she doth teach the torches to burn bright!" The description of Blanche is of course indebted to Machaut, but Chaucer has completely transformed the borrowing from a simple descriptive catalogue of beauties to a lively image.

(3) There are a number of explanations for this; G. L. Kittredge suggested that the Dreamer is "drawing out" the Knight to cure his melancholy—as Chaucer might have done with John of Gaunt. Or it may be that any remarks merely overheard do not form part of the exchange but are recorded by convention, as it were.

(4) *The Old Wives' Tale* was not published till 1595, after the probable date of Shakespeare's *Midsummer Night's Dream*. It was written for the Queen's Men, the leading troupe of the previous decade.

(5) I have dealt with this and other aspects in "*The Old Wives' Tale;* a play of Enchantment", *English Studies*, October 1962. For the emblematic mode of staging, see Glynne Wickham, *Early English Stages* (1963), II (I), pp. 314–19.

(6) See G. H. Hunter, *John Lyly, the Humanist as Courtier*, 1962, pp. 31–5.

(7) Hunter, op. cit., p. 254.

(8) The panic sounds like a transmuted recollection of some theatre scene with the audience like birds "rising and cawing at the gun's report"—the image of the birds recalls the fleeing crowd as seen from the stage.

(9) "My mistress with a Monster is in Love" (2.2.6). The ass's head was a regular mumming disguise. "To kill a calf" was to make a ranting speech—compare Hamlet on Polonius' acting "it was a brute part in him to kill so capital a calf there". Aubrey, hearing this phrase applied to Shakespeare in his youth, took it literally and assumed his father must have been a butcher.

(10) They are not much more absurd than some of the personifications of City pageants—Thames with his Fishes, the Sun. Glynne Wickham describes the "wall" as it was actually used; it was a painted canvas on a stretched frame, and was collapsible ("thus Wall away doth go")—see Wickham, op. cit., p. 212.

(11) The quarrelling lovers and Duke Theseus come from *The Knight's Tale*; the fairy queen and king intervene in human affairs in *The Merchant's Tale*; Pyramus and Thisbe are in *The Legend of Good Women*; the dreamer and the magic wood have several parallels.

(12) Professor Harbage has recently suggested a much earlier date for *Love's Labour's Lost* (*Philological Quarterly*, October 1962) but I cannot agree; nor do I think the sentiments appropriate for a children's troupe. Their limit is better suggested by Marlowe's *Dido*.

Chapter Five

MEN AND WOMEN:
SHAKESPEARE AND TRADITION

I TRADITION AND EXPERIMENT

THE public audience who came to Shakespeare's plays were attentive; they "rejoiced much to be at plays" and might soon grow excitable and violent; they had traditional expectations, but were also prepared to be tickled by novelty. We may hear voices from the crowd from time to time in the plays themselves—Francis Feeble the tailor, with "the only man-sized voice in Gloucestershire" or the clown's confidential apology for a defeated amateur actor: "He is a marvellous good neighbour i'faith and a very good bowler—but for Alisaunder, alas, you see how 'tis; a little o'er parted."

The plays incorporated familiar and traditional stories or characters, as they also incorporated proverbs and the phrases of common life, but combined them in unexpected contrast with a fashionable, or literary appeal to the more sophisticated. For each kind of writing, sometimes for single characters, there was an appropriate language, a particular set of metaphors. The themes and images which modern critics have distinguished in Shakespeare's plays should not be opposed to character or plot, for they are its direct symbolic expression.

The medium of drama is "not words but people moving about on a stage using words" and certain rôles attracted poetic words and phrases. The imagery of Revenge tragedy is as easily identified as the typical Revenger's part. It carries the emotional charge, the affect, which is attached to this kind of play; so directing the audience how to respond. Images of hell and night, blood and furies are the medium in which the play is built up. The binding effect of these images works

80

indirectly and need not be perceived by the audience; though trained rhetoricians would probably notice them.

In this chapter, four examples of Shakespeare's dramatic form will be considered, to show the literary and dramatic traditions which he used, and what he made of them, more especially in the relationships of men and women. In *The Taming of the Shrew*, a popular dramatic tradition is taken up and considerably modified; it is joined to an elegant Italian subplot, and it is sustained by the usual imagery for this kind of play—that of animal taming.

Romeo and Juliet transfers lyric material to dramatic form, but with characteristic Shakespearean power of presenting the mesh or web of human relationships. The depth both of personal and of social interplay depends on the variety of poetry and prose, in which Shakespeare embodies them. *Troilus and Cressida*, written for a small private audience, ironically refashions heroic material, and in particular the great poem of personal love and social enmities, Chaucer's *Troilus and Criseyde*. *Cymbeline* is a "magical history", with some features of the old romances, and some very fine and intricate detail; it is the first play written for the new theatre at Blackfriars, which offered Shakespeare a different dramatic medium from that of the great open stages.

The first two plays, which imply a strong sympathetic collaboration between actors and audience, have pleased many and pleased long. Only within the present century has the third gained general popularity on the stage. The fourth still remains something of a connoisseur's piece. Originally each of these was rooted in a strong tradition, upon which it provided a variation; such a mixture of tradition and experiment, which both stimulates and reassures an audience, was the basis of Shakespeare's popular appeal, in his own day.

2 THE TAMING OF THE SHREW

England was proverbially known as "hell of horses, purgatory of servants, paradise of women". The highest of all the inferiors to man enjoyed exceptional advantages. In medieval drama, the shrew was often permitted to triumph; this was the oldest and indeed the only native comic rôle for a woman —one exceptionally suitable to be played by a man.

Unlike earlier shrews, Katharine is young and at first unmarried, but the great novelty of her story is the nature of Petruchio, her tamer, and the very special means he employs. High theological argument or a taste of the stick (1) were the usual remedies for the shrew; neither is used here.

Chaucer's Wyf of Bath, first and greatest of the Shrews Triumphant, overcame both these hazards. She claimed to have been the whip and purgatory of five husbands: "welcome the sixte, when that ever he shalle!" The tradesman's widow enjoyed a unique opportunity for independence, riches and social freedom; so that by literary tradition the shrew becomes placed among tradesmen and artisans: the Wyf is a wealthy trader in cloth. Yet after her tremendous manifesto in praise of the sovereignty of women, she tells a charming fairy story in which, once she has been allowed her will, the fairy bride becomes obedient to her knightly husband. The Wyf of Bath is brilliantly inconsistent and inconsequential; this is part of her invulnerable self-assurance.

Simpler paradoxes underly Dunbar's *Twa Mariit Weman and the Wedow*, which opens in a courtly vision of three lovely ladies, seated in an arbour on Midsummer Eve; they turn out to be two dissatisfied wives, and a hypocritical widow, who piously recounts the "legend" of her own life. The courtly vision dissolves, and a series of artful tricks are satirically set out. The basic attitude is a throughly conventional anti-feminism. This mock vision might be called the first anti-play!

Mrs Noah, the leading shrew of the mystery plays, evolves from simple boozing and brawling to a notable housewife; in some plays, she is the centre of a gossips' league. Lydgate's *Mumming at Hertford* shows six termagents, whose spouses appeal to Henry VI for a "new statute" enfranchizing husbands. The women in turn appeal to the "old testament" and to the powerful precedent of the Wyf of Bath; the King gives judgment in their favour. (He himself was to come under this statute when he married the masterful Margaret of Anjou.)

Two short plays from the early Tudor stage, *Johan Johan* (*c.* 1533) and *Tom Tyler and his Wife* (*c.* 1560), also show rebellious husbands; Johan, a cuckold, denounces his wife and proclaims his intention of beating her horribly, which directs the audience's attention firmly to his abject but boastful state. Tom Tyler is another meek-hearted man who has married Strife. With her gossips, Sturdy and Tipple, she forms a drinking party, but chases Tom back to work when he ventures to seek a pot of beer. His brave friend Tom Taylor puts on Tyler's coat and attempts to correct her; but Tom Tyler foolishly confesses the trick and gets a final drubbing from Strife, who throughout has exploited him as drudge and provider:

> *What a husband have I, as light as a fly?*
> *I leap and I skip, I carry the whip . . .*
> *I will teach him to know the way to Dunmow,*
> *At board and at bed, I will crack the knave's head.*

This very popular farce is close to ballads and jigs, in which the wife is often beaten into submission. In *The Wife Wrapped in a Wether's Skin*, Robin beats his high-born wife, after he has "disguised" her in a wether's skin; in a more savage version she is beaten insensible and wrapped in the skin of Morell, an old horse. Tom Tyler and Tom Taylor, at the height of their triumph, rejoice in a song which puts a wife among the higher domestic animals:

83

Blame not Thomas if Tom be sick,
His mare doth prance, his mare doth kick,
She snorts and holds her head so high,
Go tie the Mare, Tomboy, tie the Mare, tie.

In Petruchio's central soliloquy to the audience, where he explains his method of wife-taming, this popular imagery is revived. By starving Kate and keeping her awake, Petruchio is applying the classical method of taming a falcon (or kite). Kate is not to be wrapt in a wether's skin, a more subtle form of the animal tamer's art is called for; but it is animal-taming none the less.

My falcon now is sharp and passing empty,
And till she stoop she must not be full gorged. . . .
. . . to watch her as we watch these kites
That beat and beat and will not be obedient.

It allows him to maintain the pretence that "all is done in reverend care of her"; and he ends with direct and triumphant appeal to the spectators:

He that knows better how to tame a shrew,
Now let him speak; 'tis charity to shew.

Petruchio owes his victory to his eloquence and his natural vigour; the challenge exhilarates him. His provocative display of wit and bawdry furnish his courting plumage. At the beginning, both characters are shown at their least attractive; Kate's speech is vulgar, thick sown with proverbs; she threatens to comb her suitor's noddle with a three legged stool; and is defined as a "devil", "this fiend of hell". The basis of Petruchio's wooing is bluntness, "russet yeas and honest kersey noes". He meets Kate with a teasing shower of contradictory epithets "plain . . . bonny . . . sometimes curst . . . prettiest Kate in Christendom" but ends according to a plan of lofty diplomacy and imagination already confided to the audience:

84

SHAKESPEARE AND TRADITION

Hearing thy mildness praised in every town,
Myself am come to woo thee for my wife.

At the marriage he appears as a madman, having assumed the part to which shrews were supposed to reduce their husbands (2). The broken-down horse, the mad attire and wild behaviour, suggest that if she is a devil, he is "a devil, a devil, a very fiend . . . tut, she's a lamb, a dove, a fool to him". Yet all the time he assumes a virtue for her if she has it not; maintains her sweetness, obedience, ignores her threats and tears—or, for those members of the audience who were prepared to look below the farce, he is appealing to the desire to be mastered and cherished which Kate's angry, thwarted, provocative abuse unconsciously betrays. This mastery he asserts immediately after the wedding with a mimic marriage by capture, and an assertion of his legal rights.

I will be master of what is my own,
She is my goods, my chattels, she is my house,
My household stuff, my field, my barn,
My horse, my ox, my ass, my anything.

All the usual desires of the shrew for feasts, clothes, company are withheld till Kate capitulates and enters Petruchio's private universe, in which "it shall be what o'clock I say it is", in which he decides whether the sun or the moon is shining in the sky.

Petruchio's last demand is a mere flouting of decorum. He wants a kiss in the public street; he gets it. The shrew's rôle is transformed, and the charming young woman whom Petruchio imagined, he has now, like Pygmalion, obtained in the flesh.

Her final oration to the other wives recalls the man's part as breadwinner, protector and temporal lord. The audience has been given a lovers' battle, a war of wits between the two; Katharine is the first shrew to be shown as youthful bride. Her sister, Bianca, who had begun by sweet obedience,

85

now takes over the shrew's part; while the third bride in the play, being a widow, uses an easy tone of practised insolence.

The Italian subplot in which Bianca's lovers are entangled in a series of mistaken identities, sets off by its flat characters and complicated disguises the depth and simplicity of the main plot. A third level of artifice is given by the Induction, for the whole story is presented as a play within a play. Old Sly's son of Burton Heath, who is caught up into a dream of food, drink and obsequious service through the prank of a young lord, is even presented with a modest obedient "wife"—a page in disguise. After he has been entertained by a troupe of actors, he wakes declaring that he has now learned how to tame his own shrew (3). The question of identity has been worked out at three levels.

The moral of the play would appear to be the old proverb, "Better marry a shrew than a sheep"; all the wryness, sting and satire is taken out of Katharine's rôle. It is well within the compass of a boy player; "she" is on the stage for a remarkably short time, most of which is taken up with listening to Petruchio. This play has always done better on the boards than in the study. Fletcher wrote a sequel to it, *The Woman's Prize or the Tamer Tamed* (1604–10), where Petruchio in old age comes to London for a second wife; the lady, under the leadership of "Colonel Bianca", barricades herself on the wedding night and starts a campaign against husbands. By a series of tricks which include pretending that her husband has caught the plague, shutting him up and depriving him of his goods, and finally, when he shams dead, preaching a sermon on his unmanliness to the "corpse", Maria sufficiently shews the mettle of her pasture. At one point she recalls the animal taming of the earlier play and praises the wild bird, the haggard:

> (*Which is that woman that hath wing and knows it,*
> *Spirit and plume), will make a hundred checks,*
> *To shew her freedom, sail in every air. . . .*

The tanner's wife who leads a regiment of country wives to the battle, invokes the older play, swearing that Maria shall march off with terms of victory:

> *She shall, Tom Tyler's,*
> *And brave ones too.*

The gossips' league is also revived; yet Maria submits in the end, having won her victory. There is a feeling here that the audience are being asked to play old parts and strike old attitudes; the romp is a little too self-conscious; there is too much burlesque in the farce.

In *The Silent Woman* Ben Jonson, himself married to "a shrew but honest", sketches a variety of women in rebellion. There is the low comedy of a shop-keeping termagent, Mistress Otter; the lofty pretensions of the Ladies Collegiate, women of fashion "that live from their husbands; and give entertainment to all the wits and braveries of the time"; and Epicoene herself, the Silent Woman, transformed from modesty to scolding and at last shown up as a boy in disguise. Truewit, the connoisseur of women, delivers a tremendous Character of an Ill Wife; the audience are invited to identify themselves with the Wits, whose view is detached, ironic and merciless. The whole plot turns on Dauphine's stratagem of "marrying" his uncle Morose to a boy; but life and vivacity is stronger in the parts of the cheated, than in that of the cool young cavalier who plays so dexterously with his victim. Morose, the hero-victim, serves as dark antithesis to his nephew; a wit himself, in spite of his defeat he impresses by a massiveness that the young men can not show. Although the conscious identification is with Youth, and against Crabbed Age, yet it is in Dauphine's saturnine foe that the deeper, more Shakespearean complexity of character is to be found.

87

3 ROMEO AND JULIET

In *The Taming of the Shrew*, a traditionally comic rôle was made part of a relationship in depth; this in turn was linked to an ingenious farce whose complexities belonged to the professional traditions of the Italian stage. *Romeo and Juliet* presents what Edwin Muir termed a "universe of two"—the full transcript of "true love acted". This explores something new in feminine psychology—the imaginative realization of the woman's rôle as a positive one. Juliet moves rapidly from bold speech to bold action, while among Petrarchan poets, the woman had remained an object to be wooed, adored, scolded, renounced. For them, masculine fluctuation of mood predominated; the lady remained a remote and glittering Image. So Romeo describes Rosaline, his first love; and his first approach to Juliet is that of a pilgrim to a shrine, but her replies are so gaily turned, in their demure promptness, that Romeo has kissed her twice before they have had time to speak a sonnet between them, when Chaucer's Black Knight took years to win his Blanche.

The family feud deprives Juliet of this conventional reluctance. Their names are enough to tell the pair that all their world is opposed to their love.

> *be but sworn my love,*
> *and I'll no longer be a Capulet.*

The secret marriage that makes her a Montague is both a natural mating and a sacramental union, but it lacks the third essential for a full marriage; it is not a socially acknowleged bond. The lovers' sad presages prove true; society destroys them, and Juliet's grave is proved her marriage bed.

The feud is as instinctive and passionate as their love. "I hate hell, all Montagues, and thee" is Tybalt's comprehensive declaration. From the beginning the lovers are alienated from everyone except the Friar. Even in the orchard, death may break in, with Capulet retainers. Set apart from the brawling daytime streets, love belongs to the night, where every meeting, except the marriage, takes place; the "universe of two" takes into itself all the beauty of a sleeping Garden of the Rose. The mask of Night protects Juliet, while under the brilliant summer sky with the moon silvering her Eden of apple trees, she seems to Romeo

> *as glorious to the night, being o'er my head*
> *As is a winged messenger of heaven.*

In her epithalamium, she summons Romeo as "a day in night"; at the dawn parting, as the severing clouds part like curtains round the marriage bed, she cries:

> *Then window, let day in, and let life out.*

Nature is with the lovers, though society parts them, until the shadow of the plague and the grave brings into opposition the two fundamental categories of Shakespeare's imagination —love and death (4).

The prologue speak of "star crossed lovers" in "the fearful passage of their death-marked love", evoking images of the plague cross and the plague marks. Behind the lyric beauty, as memory and experience, Shakespeare drew on the audience's recent plague terrors, in the great epidemic of 1592 to 1594. The tragedy is connected to a real disaster in the most natural and most powerful way. In the event, it is not the feud, but the plague that stays the messenger, which actually brings the lovers to death; but before this the physical horrors of the charnel have been vividly realized in the description of Tybalt, yet "green in earth" and "festering in his bloody shroud".

The powerful images of sun and stars work to opposite effect, and enlarge the confines of narrow meeting places— the little orchard of a great town house, the curtained bed chamber, the lowering vault, transformed by Juliet to "a feasting presence full of light". Yet marriage and burial are also united in metaphor throughout the story. The friar will not have Romeo lay one love in a grave and take out another —a grim picture of plague time. Lady Capulet cries petulently, "I would the fool were married to her grave" and her husband later mourns:

> *Oh, son, the night before thy wedding day*
> *Hath death lain with thy wife.*

The image of death as the rival lover haunts Romeo's sick fancy as he opens the tomb. The dead bridegroom, whom Juliet wakes to find, returns to his bride in many a ballad, from *Clerk Saunders* to Housman's *The True Lover*.

Though the lovers' laments can grow fantastical, when they are together their language reaches a clear ballad-like simplicity; "my husband", "my wife" are their terms of consolation. The strength of their love lies in its consistency and constancy. "Well, Juliet, I will lie with thee tonight", the grim jest with which Romeo announces his resolution to die, takes the form of a promise to his bride.

Between the two there is a continuum of feeling on every level from that of idealized fancy to "the modesty of true love acted". In the world about them it is otherwise. The elegant wooing of Paris and the bluntness of old Capulet's household are far apart. "Green sickness carrion . . . baggage . . . tallow-face" represents the abuse the old man heaps on his child, while the Nurse can anxiously work out what seems to her a reasonable solution—"I think it *best* you married with the County" she says, pondering the interests of her nurseling with due care. Mercutio's vision of Queen Mab and his last ironic jest at his death's wound show how great a range may be achieved within a single short part.

The variety of language in this play, and the variety within individual parts, imply a new dramatic assurance. It could not have been predicted that the author of *Romeo and*

Juliet would develop into the author of *Hamlet*, yet his dramatic imagination, in its characteristically Shakespearean form, is already present in the earlier play.

This variety can be parallelled only in Chaucer. The likelihood that the creator of Angelica the Nurse had learnt from the creator of the Wyf of Bath is not to be measured by the number of traceable parallel passages. Characterization through the voice and accent, characterization in depth, ironic and yet sympathetic, is best realized, before Shakespeare, in *The Canterbury Tales* and not in stage dialogue.

4 TROILUS AND CRESSIDA

Written perhaps half a dozen years later, *Troilus and Cressida* was designed to be read as literature, and not only for the boards of the theatre. It was to serve as "commentary" to human "actions", and it "was never clapperclawed with the palms of the vulgar". The formal debates in camp and citadel show conscious labour and effort; the tone of the play, disturbing and ambiguous, controls and directs the response. Shakespeare may have set out to write a bitter comedy for the Inns of Court; but no play of his can be pigeonholed.

The sack of Troy was in the sixteenth century the highest secular symbol of Disaster, the Great Crash; it was what 1914 was to writers of the 'twenties and 'thirties. Shakespeare had to quarry out the story of the siege from a number of rambling narratives (5); he selected, recombined and rearranged the material with the utmost freedom. For the love story which presents the miniature human version of disaster he went to Chaucer; here his treatment is at once consistent and paradoxical. The high and heroic romance of *Troilus and Criseyde* is in every way deflated: a poetic ideal, Chaucer's own "universe of two", is ironically distorted and defaced (6). Compression and inversion direct Shakespeare's use of Chaucer. Each of Chaucer's five books is represented by one or two scenes in Shakespeare, the division between Chaucer's books corresponding roughly to the division between Shakespeare's acts. Chaucer's story is leisurely and protracted: as Shakespeare tells it

> *Injurious Time, now with a robber's haste,*
> *Crams his rich thievery up, he knows not how.* 4.4.44–5

Pandarus and Cressid distort Chaucer's two subtlest creations—it was precisely to the most original parts of Chaucer that Shakespeare turned for his bitterest refashioning. For Chaucer's delicate and subtle fencing between these two, when Pandarus comes to plead ("I shal felen what he meneth, ywis"), there is substituted a brutal and frank exchange, culminating in the open taunt, "You are a Bawd". Cressid's soliloquy in Act I proclaims her simple creed, the art of the coquette raised to a rule of life, while Chaucer's Creseyde will not admit, even to herself, the natural flattery which she feels at the prospect of a royal lover; she is a young widow, sensitive, loath to make any emotional commitment. Though (on Pandarus' word) still a virgin, Shakespeare's Cressid is both wily and raw, and, warm from her first meeting with Troilus, generalizes glibly:

> *Prithee tarry, you men will never tarry,*
> *O foolish Cressid, I might have still held off,*
> *And then you would have tarried.* 4.2.15–17

As Ulysses was to observe, she is a natural "daughter of the game".

Shakespeare's destruction of Pandarus is as thorough as is that of Creseyde. In Shakespeare he gloats with obscene insistence, while in Chaucer he drily mocks the lovers; his jests with his niece on the morning after her surrender to Troilus contrast very neatly the high rhetoric of courtesy in Chaucer, and the low rhetoric of the stews, in Shakespeare.

At corresponding points in the story, both authors address the spectators. Chaucer, at his ending, speaks first to his book "litel my tragedie", then to his audience, the "yonge fresshe folkes, he or she", then his fellow poets, and finally he appeals to the Trinity in words which he took from Dante's *Paradiso*. The human tragedy, while subsumed into something greater, remains beautiful in itself.

> *Thinketh al nis but a faire,*
> *This world, that passeth soone as floures faire.*

Chaucer's lines might serve for the epitaph of Juliet, "flower that she was, deflowered" by Death. But now Shakespeare chooses to end with a reference to the celebrated brothels of the Bankside owned by the Bishop of Winchester. Pandarus prays those of his Livery in the audience to condole with him:

> *As many as be here of* Pandars *hall,*
> *Your eyes half out, weep out at Pandars fall . . .*
> *Brethren and sisters of the hold-door trade. . . .*   5.10.48–52

It completes his lacerative destruction of Chaucer's vision.

Chaucer's lovers, after their parting in Troy, never meet again; the prisoner Creseyde, caught in the war machine, is battered into submission. She ends so broken that her final pitiful letter shows her incapable even of the consistent lie.

Shakespeare uses the extreme form of shock, of dramatic reversal, where Chaucer dwelt on the pangs of suspense and of ebbing hope. In Shakespeare's tent scene, by a blinding demonstration, the hero is shown the quicksands of the heroine's faith. The irony is pointed by Cressid's resumption of her old arts, in words that echo the earlier scenes; and, in reply to her new lover's "Will you then?", perhaps the savagest line of the play:

> *In faith, I will lo, never trust me else.*   5.2.59

After her maudlin tears over the pledge Troilus had given her, in which she rises to verse at the thought of Troilus' "memorial dainty kisses" to her glove, she veers:

93

Well, well, 'tis done, 'tis past; and yet it is not.
I will not keep my word. 5.2.97–98

Ulysses, who has read her at a glance, watches half incredulously the despair of Troilus; the gloating of Pandarus is replaced by the savagery of Thersites; three different readings of events are supplied by three different watchers.

Shakespeare's Troilus, like Chaucer's, had had fears; but the suddenness and completeness of this metamorphosis destroys more than his image of Cressid; it destroys his whole world. Chaos is come again; the principle of contradiction no longer works—a thing may be itself and also something other.

If there be rule in unity itself,
This was not she. 5.2.141–2

If the outward and inward ever correspond—if beauty have a soul—this was not she. The varying points of view represented by the three watchers of his betrayal are not further apart than the incompatible fighting images within Troilus.

Within my soul there doth conduce a fight
Of this strange nature, that a thing inseparate
Divides more wider than the sky and earth.

The inward strife that breaks up a whole imagined world was to form the basis of greater tragedies to come; for the strength of this play lies in the vision not of the grandeur but of the pettiness of evil; the squalor and meanness and triviality of betrayal, which here enjoy their hour. It is not surprising that *Troilus and Cressida* should enjoy a modern vogue and that Jan Kott should find it most congenial of all Shakespeare's plays. (7)

5 CYMBELINE

Troilus had cried:

Let it not be believed for womanhood!
Think, we had mothers

94

and when Posthumus is convinced that his constant wife has played him false, his whole world darkens, his own birth taking on the aspect of a betrayal:

> *Is there no way for men to be, but women*
> *Must be half workers? We are all bastards,*
> *And that most venerable man which I*
> *Did call my father was I know not where*
> *When I was stamp'd. Some coiner with his tools*
> *Made me a counterfeit. . . .*   2.5

Posthumus, like Troilus, lives largely in an imaginative relation; the horrors of his too lively fantasy are abruptly stopped when he receives the bloody napkin that is supposed to be a token of Imogen's death; "the idea of her life" (8) returns to him and is reinstated in his mind. He imposes on himself a voluntary penance, and finds himself in prison more fettered by conscience than by the locks upon his limbs:

> *Must I repent,*
> *I cannot do it better than in gyves*
> *Desir'd more than constrained.*   5.4

He offers to the gods his own life, in exchange for the one he took; for it is they to whom it belongs, and who now give it authentic value.

> *For Imogen's dear life take mine; and though*
> *'Tis not so dear, yet 'tis a life; you coin'd it.*

So in fantasy, at least, he regains her; he is reconciled within himself.

> *O Imogen,*
> *I'll speak to thee in silence.*

As he sleeps, a whole visionary company surrounds him; and Jove himself descends with an oracular message. Only as a prisoner does Posthumus regain his inner freedom. This paradox was to become a central theme of tragedy on the Jacobean and Caroline stage.

The married lovers live separated, with dreams, imaginations, tokens and letters for consolation. Imogen, vulnerable yet resolved in the midst of open trials and secret betrayals, shows a fineness of breeding, a sensitive dignity that relates her to Chaucer's great ladies rather than to the heroines of the Elizabethan stage. The same qualities are found in Hermione and Queen Katherine. This delicacy, like the vivid impulsive imagination of Posthumus, keeps their relationship highly strung.

Yet this relationship is presented as part of an old-fashioned romance, a "magical history" (9) of long-lost children, wicked stepmothers, and sleeping potions. Imogen takes the same kind of drug that Juliet had taken, and wakes to find a dead man beside her; but her tragic dream dissolves in the end. The magical history blends elements of such old wives' tales as might have been gathered by a winter's fire with the sophisticated baroque fashions of the new tragicomedy. As a play, *Cymbeline* is powerful in some places and weak in others; it represents in all probability Shakespeare's first attempt at meeting the conditions of the new indoor theatre at Blackfriars. It alternates vivid passions of rage, grief, jealousy, mourning, with dream-like transitions, as it alternates small closed spaces—bedchamber, cave or prison —with the wide mountainsides of Wales; ancient legendary Britain with modern Italy and classical Rome. Shakespeare, who had an acute sense of history, must have known what he was doing when he made a Machiavellian, "bold Iachimo, Sienna's brother", lead the troops of Augustus Caesar. He was returning to the old form of the medley, refashioned after twenty years' experience.

For the majority of Shakespeare's contemporaries, jealousy was a comic emotion, and the jealous man an object of scorn. The rage of Posthumus or of Leontes is shown as an invasion of their natural peace and stability; the outer consequences are averted only by the actions of others. "My life stands in the level of your dreams," Hermione says. The part which imagination plays in the closest relationships is the controlling principle of the romances.

The first two of our plays put life into familiar models by creating for each a spouse with whom a deep relationship becomes established—for the shrew, as for the Petrarchan lover, a true reciprocity brings into activity new aspects of the traditional figure.

The last two plays show the danger to any such relationship when its imaginative aspect predominates. Though Petruchio's imagination creates the new image for Kate, he had read the situation correctly. Troilus and Posthumus, in very different circumstances, each recovers at heavy cost, from his own error of projecting an imaginative form. Coleridge described "Constancy to an Ideal Object":

> *She is not Thou and only Thou art She . . .*
> *And art thou nothing? Such thou art, as when*
> *The woodsman, winding westward up the glen*
> *At wintry dawn, where o'er the sheep track's maze*
> *The viewless snow mist weaves a glittering haze,*
> *Sees full before him, gliding without tread,*
> *An image with a glory round its head:*
> *The enamour'd rustic worships its fair hues,*
> *Nor knows he makes the shadow he pursues.*

Shakespeare seems to have believed in love at first sight. The prompt and complete projection of an ideal image which this involves would come naturally to an easy, fluent, spontaneous artist. The dangers of the process are obvious; Romeo is shown as justified, Troilus as deceived. Posthumus, at the end, finds that his dream is truth; he is embraced by "a piece of tender air"—as Imogen is described by the oracle—that is also flesh and blood.

This is a potentially tragic theme, to which *Troilus and*

Cressida, generally placed immediately before *Hamlet,* served as introduction. At the end of the great tragedies comes *Cymbeline.* Between them stretch Elsinore, Dunsinane, the wild heaths of ancient Britain and the rocky citadel of Cytheria, where Desdemona died.

At Elsinore, the greatest fortress-palace of Northern Europe looks out over the waters of the Sound. Its military strength and Renaissance splendour were well known to English tragedians, who had been welcomed there by a king. Shakespeare must have heard of the great Hall, equally designed for drama or duels—perhaps of the cellerage too, for the triple series of underground defences which surround the fortress were the most modern and formidable military fortifications of the day, capable of holding three thousand troops during the Thirty Years' War.

To set a play in Kronborg Castle was to choose a setting that was at once palace and a prison. The palace and the prison were to provide the scene for many tragedies of the coming age.

NOTES TO CHAPTER FIVE

(1) Theology winds up the inferior version *The Taming of A Shrew*, which I take to be a later and debased form. (I have dealt at greater length with these plays in an article in *Shakespeare Jahrbuch*, Band 94, 1958, pp. 132–50.)

(2) As the Abbess explains to Adriana, the shrewish wife of *The Comedy of Errors*, 5.1. 68–86.

(3) This ending is kept only in *The Taming of A Shrew*. Note that the players have been acting a version of the Wife of Bath's Tale, and that Petruchio also knows this story of the woman's victory (1.2.69).

(4) According to Edward A. Armstrong, *Shakespeare's Imagination* (1963), pp. 100–11.

(5) See Robert K. Presson, *Shakespeare's Troilus and Cressida and the Legends of Troy* (Wisconsin, 1953). What follows is condensed from my article, "What Shakespeare did to Chaucer's *Troilus and Criseyde*", *Shakespeare Quarterly*, IX, 3; Summer, 1958.

(6) In the sixteenth century, Henryson's *Testament of Cresseid* was printed as a sequel to Chaucer's poem. The imagery of disease, so violently used in it, may have influenced Shakespeare. To have encountered so harsh, jarring an ending to the delicacy and complexity of Chaucer's story must have been very bewildering to a sensitive reader unaware of the historic explanation of its presence.

(7) Jan Kott, *Shakespeare notre Contemporain* (1962, Paris)— "Troilus et Cressida surprisants et modernes".

(8) *Much Ado about Nothing*, 4.1. Posthumus finds that the dead Imogen re-instates herself in his imagination; the Friar in *Much Ado* knew likewise that if Hero were thought dead, Claudio would repent even "though he thought his accusation true".

(9) See J. P. Brockbank, "History and Histrionics in *Cymbeline*", *Shakespeare Survey*, II (1958).

Chapter Six

PRISONERS AND POLITICS: THE SOCIAL IMAGE FROM SHAKESPEARE TO DRYDEN

I HAMLET

THE summit of the English dramatic tradition is *Hamlet*. But of such a work, in a survey such as this, there is comparatively little that may be said. It is traditional—the refashioning of an older play. It is original—in the depth, complexity and acuteness of the inner conflict. It has received more criticism than any other play in the language, and the range of interpretations that may be thought valid is very great; for direct identification with Hamlet himself can satisfy a multitude of needs, and he has consequently been seen as all things by all men, from angel to devil.

But there is also great variety of mood and temper in the exceptionally large number of developed minor characters. *Hamlet* contains a whole society of individuals, not a row of nobles or servants, and evolves the hero in relation to them, as well as in the isolation and scepticism of his self-communing. From:

> *So, gentlemen,*
> *With all my love I do commend me to you*

to the epitaph on a spy:

> *Thou wretched, rash, intruding fool, farewell!*

Hamlet flashes, consistently inconsistent.

Among other things, the play can be entered upon as a masked duel, a struggle for power, a long fencing match between Hamlet and Claudius, mercurial and saturnine princes. Claudius' first act is to restrain Hamlet to "open confinement" at his court; Hamlet retaliates by becoming a sort of changeling—he is no longer there, but hidden behind the antic disposition, which is something more than a rôle; how much more, remains his secret. This is the *Hamlet* Kott saw in Cracow in 1956, "le drame du crime politique"; Hamlet is the prisoner of a police system.

In the rage, despair and self-probing of his soliloquies, Hamlet plays many other parts; none, perhaps, is final. The liberating processes set out in Chapter Two are therefore particularly well established in this play; each individual member of the audience is drawn in by the great variety of rôle and mood offered, till with Yeats's Brahmin, he may feel:

> *I have been a king,*
> *I have been a slave,*
> *Nor is there anything,*
> *Fool, rascal, knave,*
> *That I have not been.*

From the mysterious glimpses of the moon upon the ghostly armour of the dead, rising from his prison house, to the mirrored mazes of the players' scene, with Hamlet talking theatre gossip of the hour; from the lyrical reflections of Ophelia's songs and the story of her death, to the final duel, Shakespeare pulls out all the stops. The orchestration is magisterial: an interior drama of great complexity is presented in Hamlet himself; an interior drama of even greater complexity is evoked in the audience.

In some dozen or fourteen years the tragic play had evolved from *Tamburlaine* to *Hamlet*: the primitive drama, now lost, upon which Shakespeare's play is based must have supplied a steady plinth for the experimental form erected upon it. Kyd's *Spanish Tragedy*, the earliest of the English Revenge plays to survive, may give some hint of what this could have been. The Revenge play offered the only native tragic performance or poetic "shape"; many poets, as they engaged themselves in it, bettered their best. *The Revenger's Tragedy*, Webster's *White Devil* and *Duchess of Malfi* not only share some features of plotting and some rôles, but also a common tone of lively but ironic questioning, a dark scepticism, that finds its outward embodiment in images of prison, treacherous revels by torchlight, secret murder, cries of bewilderment and of dereliction—"Must I believe it?" "O, I am lost", or

> *In what a shadow or deep pit of darkness*
> *Doth womanish and fearful mankind live.*

In the original *Spanish Tragedy* as in Shakespearean plays like *Richard III* and *Titus Andronicus*, though the weight of guilt petrifies, an ethical basis of crime and punishment is felt to be secure. Power derives from the gods. Hieronymo the judge, outraged by the actions of a tyrant, turns to revenge, "a kind of wild justice", as Titus, too, turns to seek "Revenge's cave". The chthonic gods, if cruel, are unambiguous; and if the price of an accomplished Revenge is high, it is stoically paid. Justice and kingly sway may be inverted; they are not totally dissolved and abolished. In the later Revenge plays, from Shakespeare's *Hamlet* onwards, this fixed ethical framework has disappeared; promptings of ghosts and spirits replace the harsh Senecan edicts, and the struggle for power is a struggle for worldly rule. The "Malcontent", a deprived and intelligent criminal, may assume heroic stature.

Guilt and responsibility also become more diffused. The courage of an isolated, self-questioning hero leads him into strange and dangerous countries of the mind. Madness or imbalance is an integral part of tragic experience in all these plays. In Hamlet as in Lear, a certain depth of insight can be reached only when the surface view of things is broken up and ruined.

Webster's plays, coming some dozen years after *Hamlet*, mark the end of the Revenge tradition. Macabre superstition, omens and curses build up an atmosphere of doom in which the inner solitude of victims who torment each other creates a suspended, timeless void. Their restlessness of activity has no significance. *L'enfer, c'est les autres*.

2 WEBSTER'S DUCHESS OF MALFI

The questioning, sceptical temper of *Troilus and Cressida* and of *Hamlet* is carried on in the writings of Jacobean dramatists generally, and particularly in those of Webster. Fate and Chance—fixed determinism and random accident—seem to alternate in his plots. The White Devil gains the height of her ambition, marriage with Brachiano, only to lose him, poisoned at his wedding celebration. Ferdinand sends the masque of madmen to reduce his sister to despair; she dies unbroken, and it is he who grows demented.

The internal prison that darkens *Hamlet*—"Oh, God, I could be bounded in a nutshell and count myself a king of infinite space were it not that I have bad dreams"—has in *The Duchess of Malfi* become a true prison. The image of the prisoner is charged with particular poignancy for this age; the "absurd", incongruous conjunction of adverse circumstances in Webster could be paralleled in Sartre or Camus. The Revenge action of Webster's play uncoils in a double spiral; the long revenge of the Arragonian princes upon their sister, then Bosola the Malcontent's counter revenge for her murder—which he himself had carried out at the brothers' bidding.

The Duchess and Ferdinand are twins, but her feminine part of the aristocratic recklessness they share ensures only that she and her sober husband become the sort of people that things are done to. The power of society is against her, although the Duchess' marriage is a pitiably small and personal demand for freedom of choice.

A detached curiosity appears in torturer and victim as the ceremony of the Duchess' destruction advances. Like

Richard II in his prison cell, she sees herself as an image or Icon.

What do I look like now?

she asks her maid, who replies:

> *Like to your picture in the gallery:*
> *A deal of life in shew, but none in practice.*

Before capturing her children, Bosola enquires curiously "Can they prattle?" and the Duchess bandies jest for jest about her own grave: "Tell me, of what fashion wilt though make it?" Each minute detail measures tension, by the incongruous power of its effect. When the trap jaws are concealed, the perils and dangers of the world cease to be avoidable, and security hangs on trifles. The Duchess, who gave herself to Antonio under the name of his blind Fortune, says in prison that Fortune has regained her eyesight "to behold my Tragedy". Utter privation confers its own kind of clarity. It is true that in her dungeon, the Duchess curses the "stars", the whole material frame of things

> *and those three smiling seasons of the year*
> *Into a Russian winter; nay, the world*
> *To its first Chaos*

but Bosola, her jailor, the instrument of Fate, imposes an implacable calm:

> *Look you, the stars shine still.*

The Duchess's reply, another bitter jest, implies the contagious nature of a curse: "Oh, but you must remember my curse hath a great way to go". Such curses, the last weapon left to the helpless, invoke the aid of gods against other gods. Indeed, a curse, irrespective of the guilt or the innocence of the individual, may lie in the "royal blood of Arragon and Castile" to which the Duchess and her brothers belong— the physical tie which twinned her with Ferdinand, and which is the only cause of her tragedy.

Damn her, that body of hers,
While that my blood ran pure in't, was more worth
Than that which thou wouldst comfort (call'd a soul)

he cries to Bosola, but this blood, which she has contaminated
by a low marriage, carried, as all would know, the curse of
the madness which overtook Ferdinand. In her death hour
she completely masters her own instinctive revulsions and
pardons her brothers:

I have so much obedience in my blood,
I wish it in their veins, to do them good.

A more than natural strength develops:

I am acquainted with sad misery,
As the tanned galley slave is with his oar.

Her misery is *sad* because it is settled and established, because
it is adult and mature, and because it is massive and heavy as
the physical burden of the oar: but

Necessity makes me suffer constantly,
And custom makes it easy.

She has reached this stage of ultimate calm through torments which take strange and unearthly form—the madmen's charivari, the waxen figures of her husband and children, looking as if they were murdered; the dead man's hand,
or Hand of Glory (among the most powerful charms of
witches). These the Duchess sums up by recalling the great
curse of Deuteronomy, the ominous weight of which makes the
weight of the galley oar by comparison light:

The heaven o'er my head seems made of molten brass,
The earth of flaming sulphur, yet I am not mad. 4.2.25–8 (1)

For her guilty brother, the Cardinal, only the shadow of the
devil appears as a reflection in the fish ponds as he walks in
his garden—"a thing arm'd with a rake, that seems to strike
at me".

Omens and witchcraft surround the Duchess in her prison; but her executioner Bosola is a hardened soldier of fortune, who has chosen loyalty to the spy's payroll, crushing down his weak impulses of pity and sympathy. He himself compares the Duchess's imprisonment to animal taming—the chained mastiffs, caged birds, a fly in a trap. It is questionable whether the Duchess or Bosola provide the tragic centre of the play; for in Webster's plays the spectator is offered, in modern manner, alternative points of view. (2) In performance, the part of Bosola can certainly dominate the play. He is bought by the devil's agent as Faustus was, and makes a clear-eyed bargain; but when he is paid with a pardon for having carried out his orders, this unexpected example of principles with which he is perfectly familiar converts him: only, it is too late.

The sardonic, the pitiful and the melodramatic are better mingled in performance of this play than they can be in the reading; for the disjointed brilliance of Webster's style needs to be filled out with stage action. On the other hand, *The Revenger's Tragedy*, which has a much more tight and organized structure, does not succeed in the theatre, because the characters remain too didactic. Only the great central speech of the Revenger, Vindice, carries sufficient depth to evoke a full dramatic response. Somewhat against my will, I have come to accept the evidence that would make this play an early work of Thomas Middleton (3). Its close ironic structure and the control of the parts by the whole cannot be matched on the Elizabethan stage, outside Middleton's and Jonson's plays; the extreme bitterness, the Swiftian disillusion, and the narrow intensity of this darkest of all Elizabethan revenge plays might well represent his early, youthful extemity of horror and disgust; its naïvety that accompanies an intense purity of response might also fit the future author of *The Changeling*.

3 SHAKESPEARE

By any Jacobeans, the tragic hero is liable to be presented within a traditional frame of reference but not from the traditional point of view. Shakespeare's Othello, as a negro, would be expected by the groundlings to show all the villainous characteristics of the stage blackamoor, as developed in the Marlovian plays of Turks and Moors (4); Iago as Machiavel, would be his fellow in crime. The shock of meeting a "Noble Moor" must in itself greatly have stimulated the original audience; there is contemporary evidence how deeply they were fascinated by this play, and it was much imitated by later writers. Led by his too powerful imagination to a strange and appalling ritual act of murder, Othello at the end, like the Duchess of Malfi, reaches a calm beyond suffering; he anticipates and carries out upon himself the judgment of the court. His last act is not a suicide but an execution of that "Turkish" aspect of himself which he identifies with the enemy. It is a deed at once of justice and of expiation.

The inward gaze upon "black and grained spots that will not leave their tinct", which Hamlet taught to Gertrude, comes to Lady Macbeth only in sleep. Then she sees her hands as Macbeth had seen his before the blood had dried. In this tragedy, even innocence must wear an ambiguous face: the hard possibility of political treachery that Malcolm and Macduff explore together (5) is contrasted with the insubstantial witches, who can melt as breath into the wind; with the terror of dreams and of the walking dead with sightless eyes. Life itself becomes "a walking shadow, a poor player". This petitionary term—as in "Your Majesty's Poor Players", the usual form of address—brings for the actor who speaks it and the audience who accept it a strange sense of vertigo, that makes the practised and familiar appeal itself most horrible.

Life's but a walking shadow, a poor player
That struts and frets his hour upon the stage,
And then is heard no more; it is a tale
Told by an idiot, full of sound and fury,
Signifying nothing.

The immediate dramatic reversal of these lines as spoken on a stage is extraordinary.

The primitive sacrificial levels of *King Lear*, the archaic simplicity of its world, have often proved overwhelming to those who, like Dr Johnson, maintain a difficult control over their own troubled imagination (Dr Johnson could not bear to read the end). In the present age, *King Lear* seems to speak more clearly to our condition than any other of Shakespeare's plays; it is a play that presents suffering of such magnitude as to turn a prison cell into a refuge; last century's strictures upon its theatrical power now sound very remote. The three aspects of inner storm represented by Lear, Poor Tom and the Fool achieve their own harmony and balance in the heath and the night; the lacerative pity of the straw-crowned monarch wandering among the flowers, the grotesque exorcism of the fiend at Dover Cliff are fully comprehensible to a theatre that knows Strindberg, Claudel and Brecht. *King Lear* can now be staged in a bare style where its characteristic form does not appear unusual; it has grown far more accessible than it could naturally have been to the eighteenth or the nineteenth centuries.

King Lear forms an exception to the sceptical, questing, self-critical plays of Jacobean times. There are no contrasting points of view; the effect is massive, unqualified; "a condition of complete simplicity, costing not less than everything". It presents the struggle for power in terms of natural authority; of inheritance; and of criminal treachery. But the power that Lear surrenders is never really conceived of in political terms; what is shown are the *effects* of power—all that Macbeth summed up as being lost to him:

PRISONERS AND POLITICS

that which should accompany old age
As honour, love, obedience, troops of friends,

which for Lear are never entirely alienated: he loses the
hundred knights, his two daughters, but not all.

4 POLITICAL TRAGEDY AND SOCIAL COMEDY

With *Coriolanus*, Shakespeare returned to the solid world
of Rome, which was his usual method in approaching a
dilemma. He returns also to a hero singularly lacking in insight. The political manoeuvres to which Coriolanus submits
and which trap him in the end, contradict in an obscure way
what he is by nature, for good as well as evil. They contradict his ingenuousness as well as his pride. He suffers, from
the beginning, an initial imprisonment within a narrow pat-
rician code, that imposes, above all, the taboo on tenderness.
Eliot has caught this in his verses on the Triumph:

the eyes watchful, waiting, perceiving, indifferent.
O hidden under the dove's wing, hidden in the turtle's breast,
Under the palmtree at noon, under the running water
At the still point of the turning world. O hidden.

Virgilia, his "gracious silence" with her dove's eyes "that
can make gods foresworn" is the only one who knows this
Coriolanus. The wonderful archaic simile with which he
goes to banishment—

I go alone
Like to a lonely dragon, that his fen
Makes feared and talked of more than seen—

represents what Coriolanus fears at the centre of his being—a
very large, very dangerous, magical, ancient, and imprisoned
beast. It is the self which cannot get out. Meanwhile he is
trapped, "with cautelous baits and practices".

But, unlike Tamburlaine who does not surrender his

109

revenge to the pleas of Zenocrate, Coriolanus melts before the pleas of his wife and mother; he who had seemed in his wrath "a god made by some other deity than Nature" proves his humanity when it is challenged, and thereby surrenders his last claim to worldly power.

Chapman's two Byron plays belong to the same year as *Coriolanus* (1607–8), but handle with great boldness an almost contemporary story. The primal energy of the great soldier lifts him above the shame of his treachery, although his intransigence brings him to deserved execution. The King's hard decision that the death sentence must stand is statesmanlike. Yet Byron remains a man to whom mere events are, in a sense, unimportant. His great defiance of his Fate—

> *Give me a spirit that on this life's rough sea*
> *Loves t'have his sails fill'd with a lusty wind . . .*

is justified by the pride of his last speech on the scaffold.

Chapman, like Jonson in *Sejanus*, is concerned with the flaw within the moral order, though he focuses the problem in one man, while Jonson deals with a group (6). The political cut and thrust of the rival factions in *Sejanus* distributed crime among all the seekers after power; it is perhaps the most "Machiavellian" of all Jacobean political plays, because the corrupting effects of power are shown in group action, with all the complex risks and subtle shifts of interest traced out. It evokes a questing, uncertain attitude in the spectators, and a criticial approach to *all* the rôles; the social framework is what matters, and not the individuals.

In the seventeenth century, with its growing political incertitudes, tragic drama often reflected a struggle for power; in writers other than Jonson, the hero is isolated, as the one against the many. Political or cameristic plotting was better suited to the small indoor theatres than it had been to the great open stages of early Jacobean times. Glynne Wickham sees an indoor theatre with naturalistic scenery replacing the open stage with its formal emblematic objects; this coincided with a move away from poetry and towards prose drama. It fitted naturally with a more artificial and limited view of society.

The change was slow, but from about 1608, when the King's Men took over the closed theatre of the Blackfriars, it was inevitable. Red Bull melodrama still flourished, and shares at the Globe Theatre were worth quarrelling about, but gradually the King's Men, who were the most closely dependent on the court of all the companies, concentrated the talent of the time; they were the only company effectively to survive the great closing of the theatres for plague at the end of James's reign. Their later traditions foreshadow those of the Restoration stage; the plays are aimed at small court audiences, the issues grow limited and personal. The social order is no longer questioned; it provides a frame of reference within which action is bounded. The early 1620s are a real dividing line between late Elizabethan and Cavalier plays.

In Middleton, Massinger and Ford, the social assumptions underlying their tragedies are those of a class-structured society. In such a society, individual passions may become incongruous, dislocative, even "Absurd" without being ethically condemned. Social presumptions shield the ignorance of Beatrice Joanna in Middleton's *The Changeling*, as she repulses De Flores:

> *Think but upon the difference that creation*
> *Set 'twixt thy blood and mine and keep thee there—*

as social pressure explains, later, the corruption of Bianca in *Women Beware Women*, followed by that of Leantio. In these plays, human relationships are thwarted by rigid social patterns. In Ford's *The Broken Heart*, the presumption of Ithocles' passion, in daring to love a Princess, is a postulate of the play, and depends on a cult of royalty; any merely

III

"human" feeling must appear misplaced. The Princess is isolated in the same way as the Spanish Infanta of Corneille's *Le Cid*.

On the other hand, Ford's *Perkin Warbeck* is a play of self deception, a private tragedy of the Pretender; there are none of the hierarchical implications that such a story would have carried in Shakespeare's day. The centre of interest is the riddle of what Perkin believes about himself; it is left a mystery. The "Absurd" passions of Bassanes' jealousy, or Giovanni and Annabella's helpless infatuation with each other, belong to beings ruled by the powers of the "blood"— a state of psychological determinism.

The reverse of this determinism is the utter irresponsibility of social comedy; Fletcher's gay young Wittipols and Mirabels, who spend their lives in pursuit of a fortune, offer a stylish model of blithe and easy living. Even the satire of city comedy at this time bears very little relation to actual social problems of the day: its tricks and its morality grow increasingly artificial.

The personal image has sharpened and drawn apart from the dynamic of the plot—Ben Jonson's "humourous" characters, with their neat definitions, may have speeded up this process. Inner direction of a solitary passion-driven character collides against the random effects of chance. The gods have departed from the plays of Middleton and Ford, Massinger and Shirley, while the human strata have petrified: relations between the characters of the play contract within specific social limits.

The whole process might be compared to the formation of a planetary system. The luminous burning cloud of Marlowe's dramatic poetry condenses and shrinks, particular rôles grow more distinct, then detach themselves, held together only by mutual tension and attraction across a void; shaken down into beads of moisture, then into smaller, denser spheres, they revolve upon themselves. As character becomes more personal, society imposes position but no longer supplies a function. By the time the theatres closed for the long interregnum of the Civil War, little of the early Jacobean vitality remained to be destroyed.

5 THE RESTORATION: HEROIC PLAYS

When the theatres re-opened at the Restoration of Charles II, they could draw in equal measure upon the remains of the English tradition, and on the courtiers' experience of France. The French theatre of the seventeenth century, beginning somewhat in the rear of English and Spanish drama, had developed suddenly with the coming of Corneille. *Le Cid* (1637), first of the great plays, set a model of heroic love which Dryden found congenial; *Cinna* (1640-1), the most mature political play of the age, was beyond the range of imitators. Auguste, the hero of this play, who recognizes that the price of sovereignty is not only vigilance, magnanimity and isolation but, if necessary, a choice of evils that will leave the conscience burdened, has to pass beyond despair before he can make his choice to pardon the conspirators. Corneille writes tragedy for a civilized people for whom disorder and political chaos are the ultimate worst thing. Though the *language* was far more mature, politically speaking the audience was no more unified than the English audience: John Lough's book would suggest rather less so. Corneille's heroes are always masters of their fate. The choice can be made and imposed on the self absolutely. "Rentre en toi-même" Auguste admonishes himself in the great scene of decision; and to his enemy:

Apprendes à te connaître et descends en toi-même 5.1

but when the Emperor descends, the vision of an eternal succession of wrongs, in which he has played his part, shuts him into an interior prison.

Mais quoi! toujours du sang, et toujours des supplices! . . .
Meurs, puisqu c'est un mal que tu ne peux guérir:
Meurs enfin, puisqu'il faut ou tout perdre, ou mourir.
La vie est peu de chose. . . . 4.2

The mood is echoed by Dryden from Aurengzebe's dungeon:

> *When I consider life, 'tis all a cheat;*
> *Yet, fooled with hope, men foster the deceit;*
> *Trust on, and think tomorrow will repay:*
> *Tomorrow's falser than the former day* . . .
> *I'm tired of waiting for this chemic gold*
> *Which fools us young and beggars us when old.* 4.1

Upon the "sure foundations of despair" Corneille built his heroic plays with all the assurance of a Cartesian intellectualism (7). Yet the exploits of *Le Cid* depend upon the extreme, the fantastic "point of honour" being maintained; honour is essentially competitive, and "la gloire" demands the impossible as a matter of course; though later

Albe vous a nommé, je ne vous connais plus

brings from Horace's opponent the unanswerable:

Je vous connais encore. 2.3

This extreme simplicity at the centre of the tragic conflict is the best proof of Corneille's mastery. His artifice is justified because it leads to such moments as these. His is drama of situation, not of individual characters; Emilie, for instance, seems almost an embodiment of the violent, feminine, irrational aspects of the conspiracy; she is less a person than an emanation. (She would not be satisfied with a vengeance that was not due to her act.) The extraordinary contest of honour in which Cinna and Emilie compete before Auguste for the primacy in the plot to assassinate him is at once mastered and transformed by his own final intervention; he doubles the stakes and deflates the artifice of honour at one stroke.

Soyons amis, Cinna. . . .

While Emilie assumes that because she has changed her mind about Auguste, Heaven must do so too.

It was Machiavelli's opinion that the victim of an intended conspiracy might either issue a general pardon or order a general destruction of his enemies; he must not take half measures. Auguste, who has played the subtle game of sounding his counsellors, who waits upon intuition to precipitate the solution where reason cannot choose, dominates by cunning and by flair, as well as magnanimity. He is a figure of heroically accepted guilt.

The solution is no less beautiful for being expected. In attempting to translate Corneille's passionate chess-play of motive, Dryden left several essentials lacking. Nevertheless, his heroic plays establish their own precarious validity, at least in *The Conquest of Granada*; this play unites the Icon and the Dream.

A post-war society of disillusioned Cavaliers, who found that Restoration of the monarch gave them back little of what had been lost in his father's cause, felt a need to believe in the heroic together with an incapacity to do so. They suffered from what Keats described as "the feel of not to feel it"—the absence of what is most passionately desired, yet not believed any longer to exist. In the cynical and venal court which such men of experience as Andrew Marvell contemplated almost with despair (8), only an inflated image could be offered. Almanzor is protected against the possibility of parody, for his language contains within itself the grotesque and self-corrective elements that would anticipate all effects of such a parody. An invincible Champion and Challenger, whose single defection changes the course of battle, Almanzor is at the mercy of his thirst for glory and his heroic love

115

for Almahide. She in turn is imprisoned within a highly artificial set of rules, or points of honour, which effectually keep
the lovers apart throughout ten acts. Towards the end of this
protracted wooing Almanzor lurks outside his mistress's
chamber:

ALMAHIDE: My light will sure discover those who talk—
Who dares to interrupt my private walk?
ALMANZOR: He who dares love, and for that love must
die,
And knowing this, yet dares love on, am I.

The lines were famous and they were mocked; but Almanzor
himself, after a short bout of dialectic, declares:

My love's too full of zeal to think of sense.
Be you alike; dull reason hence remove . . .
Love eagerly.

Almahide intrepidly wheels into an ascending spiral of heroic
asceticism:

. . . And would you all that secret joy of mind
Which great souls only in great actions find,
All that, for one tumultuous minute lose?

which Almanzor counters:

Love's the best return for flesh and blood.

This can be repulsed only by the lady's final argument—
the threat to yield and then to kill herself. Everyone in this
play has "great celerity in dying" or indeed in renunciation
of any kind.

"All that delirium of the brave" was over for the playwright and his audience, but it could be recovered as a
mirage, in this form of extreme artifice. Everything about
the play is theatrical, is an acknowledged "game" culminating in the hyperbolical flattery of the epilogue, at the expense
of the Jacobean poets:

116

If love and honour now are higher raised,
'Tis not the poet but the age is praised.
Wit's now arrived to a more high degree:
Our native language more refined and free.
Our ladies and our men now speak more wit
In conversation, than those poets writ.

Tragedy was usually punctured by the epilogue, if it had
not already been punctured by a satiric subplot. The sudden revival of "martyred" Nell Gwynn at the end of *Tyrannic
Love*, repulsing a stage attendant who came to bear her off—

Hold, are you mad, you damned confounded dog?
I am to rise and speak the epilogue!—

is only the most celebrated deflation of violence and grandeur.
To disbelieve and yet to crave the heroic produced a strange,
transitory form which could exist only by denying what it
offered.

Feign then what's by a decent tact believed:
And act that state is only so conceived:
And build an edifice of form
For house where phantoms may keep warm. (9)

The alternative to heroic tragedy was the melting pathos of
All for Love or *Venice Preserved*, plays in which it is assumed that
private virtue and domestic joys are the sole consolation for
man in a rapacious and treacherous society. This surrender
to sentiment has as its counterpart a crude delight in atrocity.

Complete independence of any social obligation had been
the boast of Almanzor; even more finally than Chapman's
heroes he owned no obedience beyond himself:

Know that I alone am king of me.
I am as free as Nature first made man
Ere the base laws of servitude began,
When wild in woods the noble savage ran.

If his erratic freedom were not joined with such stringent rules of conduct as makes him resign Almahide, he might indeed be considered a noble savage; but his vengeful swoops are constantly being arrested by some inner power that he does not comprehend and which forces him to follow the highly artificial code of honour that is so fittingly presented in his artificial speeches.

Dryden "improved" Shakespeare into good Restoration theatre by applying "the mechanick beauties". Corneillean symmetry was provided in *Troilus and Cressida*, or *Truth Found too Late*, with its blameless heroine, noble heroes and final tableau:

All the Trojans die upon the place, Troilus last.

Spectacle became an increasing necessity, as language grew more inflated and yet more unequal to tragic statement.

However, in Restoration comedy, the audience could play a verbal game with the lighter fashions and conventions that governed their own behaviour. These plays, addressed to the few who could claim to be Wits, offered an "in-game" at the expense of outsiders. Here, there is once more a clear line of development from the comedy of Jacobean and Caroline times; the repartee is neater, the fop has become a hero, gallantry is sharpened by the presence of actresses, but the patterns of character and action are often taken over and "improved".

In Congreve, the pretty and delicate game of talk itself constitutes the action. Wit here implies both precision and restraint; judgment is displayed in what is *not* said. To toy with feelings, to banter the earnest, to mock the dotard, requires the deliberate withholding of some kinds of response. If "the feel of not to feel it" projected the vast heroic Images of Dryden, it fortified also the elegant assurance of those charming fantasies which were spun out in the last imaginative form of the seventeenth century.

NOTES TO CHAPTER SIX

(1) The Book of Deuteronomy, xxviii, 23, 34. See my article, "Two Notes upon Webster", *Modern Language Review*, xlii, 3; July 1947.

(2) Gunnar Boklund has developed the subject in *The Duchess of Malfi* (Harvard, 1962); and also in his previous book on *The White Devil* (1957).

(3) See George R. Price, "The Authorship and Bibliography of *The Revenger's Tragedy*", *The Library*, third series, vol. xv, 1960, pp. 262–77.

(4) See above, Chapter III. There are about twenty plays based on villainous Moors and Turks, listed in Bang's *Materialien*, before *Mulleasses the Turk*.

(5) See my article "The Sources of *Macbeth*", *Shakespeare Survey*, 4 (1951).

(6) I am indebted here to K. M. Burton, "The Political Tragedies of Chapman and Ben Jonson," *Essays in Criticism*, II, 4: October 1952.

(7) Jacques Maritain's description of Cartesianism as "the sin of angelism" would seem to me to apply to Corneille. But cf. P. J. Yarrow, *Corneille* (1963) Chapter II.

(8) See *Andrew Marvell* (by myself and M. G. Lloyd Thomas), Chapters IV and V.

(9) W. Empson, "This Last Pain", *Poems* (1935) p. 29.

PART THREE
Contemporary Theatre of the Imagination

Chapter Seven

YEATS AND THE REVIVAL

Aᴼᴛᴇʀ an interval of two hundred years, the last years of the nineteenth century saw the theatre re-established as an imaginative activity, by the revival of poetic drama upon the boards. Paradoxically, it was to show that, in the theatre, verse is no longer a necessary form for the dramatic imagination. Two lyric poets, Yeats and Eliot, have successively lent their efforts to the revival, which took forms they could not have foreseen. Unlike those earlier poets of the nineteenth century who occasionally took to drama—Byron, Tennyson, Browning—Yeats and Eliot recognized that the language of poetry is but a part of any theatrical communication; at first both began by stressing ritual—stylized movement, non-realistic décor, speaking to drumbeats, the use of dance and song. Neither poet had much affinity with the exuberance and spontaneity of the live theatre, but they believed that this was the one form by which poetry could regain a proper social function, and they turned to the theatre in the service of their art rather than from natural inclination. At first their plays gained only a limited audience; but besides opening the way for other writers, Yeats and Eliot evolved the first coherent theories of poetic drama to be put forward in England since Dryden's day.

To those who object to older poets, "We know so much more than they did," Eliot once retorted: "Precisely, and they are that which we know."

Yeats, whose experiments covered forty years, discovered in the end a highly individual form, which might be called post-dramatic theatre; a theatre in which the individual recognized the evocative power of the play, and opened himself to imaginative experience, as distinct from the traffic of the stage. Each member of the audience recognizes the interior drama, the releasing of imagination within. This kind of play had already been developed by Strindberg and Andreyev.

If, in the last decade, the work of both Yeats and Eliot has receded into history, a number of features in the new theatre derive from them. Yeats's Icon of the tramp, the old mad beggar, the outcast, is still in the centre of the scene. And the most important aspect of Eliot's theory was the "concealed lighting" or unperceived radiation of poetic rhythm, in dialogue which at first sounds repetitive, stammering, in-articulate—the demotic common speech of the day. Eliot's theory of verse drama indicated the right direction, but not the right technique. He clung to a certain kind of verse, where the imaginative effects of Beckett or Pinter depend upon powerful "poetic" prose rhythms.

2 YEATS AND THE COMMON DREAM, 1892–1907

Yeats said in 1901:

There is only one kind of good poetry, for the poetry of the coteries, which presupposes the written tradition, does not differ in kind from the true poetry of the people, which pre-supposes the unwritten tradition.

It was for this reason that English poetic drama returned to the stage by way of the Irish theatre; the Irish could re-store, after two hundred years of reproductive playwriting, the vital pliancy out of which drama springs. They called up the rhythms of a language in which elemental feelings might still be evoked, in words that were quick with life. They learnt also the interplay between poetry and painting, sculp-ture and the decorative arts which came back to the stage through the French theatre. And they developed a great common theme, the past and future of Ireland, from an inherited tradition of bardic poetry that reached back to late medieval times (1).

Yeats escaped the risks of a propagandist (thought too early hardened into conviction, and visions dwindled to "the pattern in the carpet"). He realized clearly, at the end of his life, what he had always thought: in 1937 he said:

> I have spent my life in clearing out of poetry every phrase written for the eye, and bringing all back to syntax that is for the ear alone. . . . "Write for the ear," I thought, so that you may be instantly understood as when actor or folk singer stands before an audience. I would have poetry turn its back upon all that modish curiosity, psychology.

In returning to the bardic tradition, he developed elements of old Irish stories; then through his lifelong studies of Eastern and Greek and medieval mythologies moved towards personal Icons which finally he made from his own life and those of his friends; for

> a poet writes always of his personal life, in his finest work out of its tragedy; he never speaks directly, as to someone at the breakfast table . . . he has been reborn as an idea, something intended, complete. He is Lear, Romeo, Oedipus . . . he is part of his own phantasmagoria. . . .

This was a slow, lifetime's achievement; it took a lifetime to discover himself, and to discover that the buried self is largely an archaic self.

His earlier psychic explorations, at London with the Golden Dawn, and at Sligo with George Pollexfen and Mary Battle, had prepared Yeats to recognize the underlying levels of communication so essential to the dramatist, and the images which are its vehicles. These images, he learnt, must be reborn for the individual before he can "animate them as experience". From the first, unlike such medievalists as Maeterlinck, Yeats knew the legends in association with the deep levels of interior life, and not merely as book lore; they were linked with visions, and "the drowning of the dykes between man and man".

> I have never said that I condemn all that is not tradition, that there is a subject matter which has descended like that "deposit" the philosophers speak of. . . . I have received [it] from the generations, part of the compact with my fellow men made in my name before I was born. I cannot break from it, without breaking some part of my own nature, and I think it allied to the wisdom or instinct that guides a migrating bird. . . .
>
> When that is no longer possible we are broken off and separate, some sort of dry faggot, and the time has come to read criticism and talk of our point of view.

Yeats's early poetry of dreamy withdrawal provided an immediate defence against the reductive and simplified scientism of the time; in the service of Ireland he found a cause that eventually led him to drama. "In dreams begin responsibilities." It was Synge who, encouraged by Yeats, brought the poetic speech of the countryside into the complex stage language which he evolved, while Yeats was still writing verse "not quite suitable for anybody except mythological kings and queens".

The innocent courage and hopefulness that in the last years of the nineteenth century sustained their little performances in concert rooms and church halls of Dublin united actors and audience. Later, Yeats was to dismiss his first play as "tapestry", his second as "sentimental" and to confess "the nationalism we called up was romantic and poetical", but only radical innocence could have created the whole live theatrical situation as well as the plays. Eliot's summary is just:

> He cared, I think, more for the theatre as an organ for the expression of the consciousness of a people, than as a means

to his own fame and achievement; and I am convinced that it is only if you serve it in this spirit that you can hope to accomplish anything with it.

Yeats rejected the superficial conventions that passed for naturalism, recognizing, before it became a matter of commonplace, that any "scientific" observation is a reductive abstraction from total experience. He had learnt, as Ibsen and Strindberg had also learnt, that interior images will shape and direct the artist's conceptual thought; that the emergence of this process in words is something more than a code transmission (2). Although their developments were in opposite directions, Yeats and Strindberg both began by recognizing that the old stable life of the ego had disintegrated; both turned for some structure of belief to alchemy and Rosicrucian doctrines. But whereas Strindberg began with images of great violence and moved towards the idyllic, replacing his demon women with such angelic figures as Elena or Kirsten, Yeats moved from dreams to violence. His first play, *The Countess Cathleen*, bestows a Christian halo on the heroine, which is, perhaps, only reflected from her lover's eyes. Christian beliefs were but an ornament and Yeats was surprised when he encountered the dogmatic opposition of the Catholic hierarchy.

The very qualities which released him from contemporary convictions prevented Yeats from becoming a full dramatist. He was absorbed in the transition from one state of being to another—from the literal and material to the enlightened; from the temporal to the eternal; and thus was very slightly engaged in the conflict of mind with mind, or the development of an action with many centres. A lonely and solitary mind, Yeats learnt from other poets, and adopted a cause without being able to establish a strong *rapport* with his audience. "Talk to me of originality and I will turn on you with rage. I am a crowd, I am a lonely man, I am nothing."

The writer's inheritance must always remain much greater

than his achievements; by a study of old masters, Yeats was at last enabled to project himself "reborn as idea"—or to use another of his phrases which has become famous, "to turn all to mask and image and so become a phantom in his own eyes". His plays centred upon the hero, but with all rôles including some reflection of the dramatist himself, so that John Bayley says: "Yeats seems to be trying to achieve negative capability by numbers." The level or state of being of each of his characters is of more importance than their relations to one another; conflict lies within the individual and issues in a single act of choice—Cathleen's surrender to the goetic powers, Mary Bruin's beguilement, Seanchan's death for poetry, or Michael Gillane's for Cathleen ni Houlihan; Forgael and Dectora's scorn of life.

Yeats's early work may be termed bardic rather than dramatic; it introduces the heroic character, and invites unqualified assent. Action is faint, though some of the plays are drawn out for several acts; but Yeats never succeeded except in a one-act play.

Synge produced drama of action; it was perhaps the intoxication of this that caused the famous riots. The phrase about a "drift of chosen females standing in their shifts" might not have offended if the drift of chosen females, Pegeen Mike and the rest, had not been actually standing before the audience. Nowadays even the final scrimmage of *The Playboy* is put on in a decent quiet way that would disturb nobody, but this tragic farce originally presented a mask of violence (like *The Shadow of the Glen*), and the violence should be theatrically presented. In Synge's most formal play, *Riders to the Sea*, the repetitive patterns and brilliant colours of ballad poetry lead up to Maurya's lament for her sons, which is also paradoxically a triumph, since "there's nothing more the sea can do to me". Maurya, like Yeats's characters, has crossed a boundary, and entered a new state of being, no less surely than her drowned sons.

The Wise Man, who is the hero of Yeats's *Hour Glass*, a Faustian story, crosses both boundaries almost simultaneously. Two of the leading Icons of Yeats's plays now appear, in the Fool and the Wise Man; at the end they become identified, because as the Fool says, "We know everything, but we will not speak." The death of the Wise Man, the too-credulous materialist whose eyes were opened by the Angel, marks his irreversible transformation or transfiguration: this is the essential subject of all Yeats's early plays. The Fool lives in the white magic of a natural world—his second sight has no connexion with sanctity or morals—but the Wise Man has to choose submission and annihilation before he is borne away by the masked and gilded Angel. Yeats distinguished four levels of life; the natural level, those of black and white magic, and the level of momentary illumination. Black or white magic is expressed in a world of dream—that of the Fairy Child, or the Demons. The dream that enchanted Yeats himself, as he afterwards said, was

> *Character isolated by a deed*
> *To engross the present and dominate memory.*

This "extremity of act" can transform terror into joy, and substitute, as if by metamorphosis, an immortal Icon for mortal flesh. Death's challenge, if heroically met, affirms the identity of the hero. In ancient battle stories, the hero proclaims aloud his name and those of his ancestors as he advances upon his fate (3).

The single deed which isolates characters in Yeats is the act of death: it "shackles accident and bolts up change".

3 FROM MYTH TO ICON, 1913-26

Such metamorphosis renounces the fluid play of events in natural sequence. Yeats himself also came to the end of his natural *rapport* with the Irish audience, when they rejected Synge's *Playboy of the Western World* because he had violated their verbal taboos. The uproar that greeted this play exposed the utter lack of flexibility in their imagination; this seems to have broken Yeats's dramatic impulse, for after 1907 he did not compose any new dramas, but stammeringly reworked over the whole problem of the theatre for ten years, in shaping and reshaping old plays. The many versions of *The Green Helmet*, and the long struggle with *The Player Queen*, witness to this disturbance; so does the violent imagery of his epigram *On those that Hated "The Playboy of the Western World"*:

> *Once when midnight smote the air,*
> *Eunuchs ran through Hell and met*
> *On every crowded street to stare*
> *Upon great Juan riding by:*
> *Even like these to rail and sweat*
> *Staring upon his sinewy thigh.*

From Ezra Pound, with whom he lived in 1913-14, Yeats learned the assumption of a Mask, or many Masks, as the guarantee of honesty. "If we cannot imagine ourselves as different from what we are, we cannot impose a discipline upon ourselves." Such tensions or vacillations as that between the acceptance and the mockery of old Irish legend led to a search for new and stronger images—the stony faces of the Magi, images of dead poets, or dead friends (Mabel Beardsley and Robert Gregory). In the poem "Wisdom" it is ironically proclaimed that true faith is found when "painted panel, statuary" amend the tale of "some peasant gospeller".

Yeats's scepticism deepened after the violence of the Easter Rising in 1916, and all that followed. His refusal to commit himself, either in religion or in politics, was a costly choice; but only in the accepted tensions of his "antinomies" could

130

he impose the secret discipline of his vocation. His continued exploration of the occult is as far removed from credulity as might be imagined; it was a personal affair, not a matter of affiliation.

He first turned away from his early style in *The Green Helmet*, which retells an Irish version of *Sir Gawain and the Grene Knight*. A grotesque comedy, full of loud quarrelsome women, boasting men, cat-headed monsters out of the sea, it presents a stylish disengaged hero, Cuchulain, who was to be the centre of many later plays. In the first version, he offers his own neck to the blow in place of a coward, as a noble sacrifice for Ireland:

RED MAN: If my debt is not paid, no peace shall come to Ireland, and Ireland shall lie weak before her enemies. But if my debt is paid, there shall be peace.

CUCHULAIN: The quarrels of Ireland shall end. What is one man's life? I will pay the debt with my own head. Do not cry out, Emer, for if I were not myself, if I were not Cuchulain, one of those that God has made reckless, the women of Ireland had not loved me, and you had not held your head so high. What do you wait for, old man? Come, raise up your sword.

RED MAN: I will not harm you, Cuchulain. I am the guardian of this land, and age after age I come up out of the sea to try the men of Ireland. I give you the championship because you are without fear, and you shall win many battles with laughing lips, and endure wounding and betrayal without bitterness of heart. . . .

(*The Golden Helmet*, 1908) *

The later version permits no such dignity to the grotesque sea demon and cuts the patriotic appeal. Cuchulain has grown more Byronic; the mockery of his tumbling verses uses something like Synge's "mask of violence" for the defence of Synge's cause:

* The title of the first version of *The Green Helmet*

131

CUCHULAIN: He played and paid with his head, and it's
  right that we pay him back,
And give him more than he gave, for he comes in here as a
  guest.
So I will give him my head (Emer begins to keen). Little
  wife, little wife, be at rest. . . .
Bear children and sweep the house. Wail, but keep from
  the road.
Quick to your work, old Radish, you will fade when the
  cocks have crowed.
RED MAN: I have not come for your head, I'm the Rector of
  this land,
And with my spitting catheads, my frenzied moon-bred
  band,
Age after age, I sift it, and choose for my championship
The man who hits my fancy. And I choose the laughing lip
That shall not turn from laughing, whatever rise or fall:
The heart that grows no bitterer, although betrayed by all:
The hand that loves to scatter; the life like a gambler's
  throw. . . .

(The Green Helmet, 1910)

This is an early example of how Yeats refashioned his Icons.
Gradually the main figures of his imaginative life became
vivid, precise, original, by what Eliot termed "the purging
out of ornament"; the course of improvement is "towards a
greater and greater starkness" and towards an increasing irony
in shaping the internal myth. In the gap of time between his
first and his second group of plays, [which was written between 1916 and 1926] Yeats struggled with his own doubts, as
much as with the theatre. "I wanted a dance, because where
there are no words, there is less to spoil." Yet the unspoken
climax is validated and defined by the speech which builds up
to it, as when Deirdre in the hour of her betrayal sits down to
the chessboard, or when, in *Resurrection*, the silent Figure
crosses the floor of the Upper Room.

From the traditions of the Japanese Noh plays Yeats, by

free selection, established a personal form which would reserve his plays for initiates only (4). In medieval times, ritual
had calmed a turbulent, yeasty mob, or ceremony shaped
into semblance of order the feast and the dance. For Yeats,
ritual and ceremony were a means of keeping apart

> against a pushing world. . . . The arts which interest me,
> while seeming to separate from the world and us a group
> of figures, images, symbols, enable us to pass for a few mo-
> ments into a deep of the mind that had hitherto been too
> subtle for our habitation. As a deep of the mind can only
> be approached through what is most human, most delicate,
> we should distrust bodily distance, mechanism and loud
> noise.
>
> (*On Certain Noble Plays of Japan*)

Yugen, the deep interior harmony that lies beyond ordinary life, is the essence of Noh.

I have no thought—my mind has been swept bare, says the
Wise Man after his illumination; and after his life's glass has
run and the Fool has given the white butterfly which is his
soul to the Angel's keeping, he himself returns to his humbler
insights:

> *I hear the wind ablow*
> *I hear the grass agrow,*
> *And all that I know, I know.*
> *But I will not speak, I will run away.*

The Fool, who meets Angels on the hills every day, the Wise
Man whose thoughts have run

> *Into some cloudy thunderous spring*
> *That is its mountain source*

share the illumination that is incommunicable to the rational
mind in its own terms.

Yeats's plays for dancers, intended for an audience about
fifty in number, assume that the high state of tragedy is gained

by withdrawal and not by sympathy. No longer does he portray the crossing of a boundary between the visible and the invisible world because these now interpenetrate each other. He assumes the constant presence of the supernatural—the Woman of the Sidhe, the voice of Swift, the dead bride and galloping horse of *Purgatory* dominate the stage. The masks or Idols of "the superhuman" must be accepted, and for all plays except the last, this demands a measure of esoteric knowledge as well as natural imagination. In Noh plays, the central act is by tradition a struggle with a ghost or spirit; Yeats's spirits too are no longer "mild, proud shadows" but the predatory hawk, the sea-demon. The great figures of Conchubar the ruler and Cuchulain the hero were radically remade. At the hawk's well, the young Cuchulain first meets the feminine demon; afterwards the menacing Fand comes out of the sea and in his last hour, Cuchulain meets the Morrigu, the woman headed like a crow. The evil supernatural has taken a feminine form again; the lyric of another mythologist might be taken as summing up the mood of the Plays for Dancers:

> *Her strong enchantments failing,*
> *Her towers of fear in wrack,*
> *Her limbecks dried of poison,*
> *And the sword at her neck,*

> *The Queen of Air and Darkness*
> *Begins to shrill and cry,*
> *"O young man, O my slayer,*
> *Tomorrow you shall die."*

> *"O Queen of air and darkness,*
> *I think 'tis true you say,*
> *And I shall die tomorrow,*
> *But you will die today."*

In *Last Poems*, the bronze head of Maud Gonne, who had first formed the image of the Countess Cathleen, then of Cath-

leen ni Houlihan, then Helen of Troy, becomes that of a
Sphinx:

> *supernatural,*
> *As though a sterner eye looked through her eye,*
> *On this foul world in its decline and fall;*
> *On gangling stocks grown great, great stocks run dry,*
> *Heroic reverie mocked by clown and knave,—*
> *And wondered what was left for massacre to save.*

4 THE REVIVAL OF THE ICON, 1935–39

In Yeats's last play, Cuchulain surmounts the ignominy of
death at the hands of a blind beggar man who, when the
chieftain is wounded and bound to a pillar, cuts his throat for a
reward of twelve pennies. From the long perspective of old
age, Yeats looked back at the story of Ireland and himself,
and having learnt the bitterness both of victory and defeat,
no longer dealt in battles or dreams, but a single ritual murder. The death of Cuchulain is ironically contrasted in prologue and epilogue with the squalor of the present time; but,
as in *The Words upon the Window Pane* and *Purgatory*, the fable
of an old age of humiliation is enclosed in a wider story; the
blood, nerve and impulse of helpless and ignorant life en-
closes a Godlike power. In *A Full Moon in March* it is the ritual
murder of the poet that puts song into his dead lips.

In *Purgatory*, a monodrama, the speaker plays back his own
life and that of his parents. Action takes place in his own
mind and that of his dead mother, issuing in the ritual killing
of his son. A great house and family had been destroyed when
his mother married a drunken groom whom the hero himself,
at the age of sixteen, had killed. Now, a "wretched foul old
man" as he watches in the ruins of his burnt-out home the
ghostly re-enactment of his own begetting, he kills again—
"my father and my son on the same jack-knife"—that pollution may not be passed on. For an instant, the dead tree,

symbol of his family, shines out with cold radiance, but the hoof beats of his father's horse return, for his mother's earth-bound soul cannot be released from its dream of the past.

Thus the re-enactment of "the past which is always present" in the compulsive violence of the ancestral dream revolves upon the double impulse of lust and murder. The dead woman who had followed her fancy, the drunkard whose shadow "like a tired beast" leans on the burnt-out window frame of the house he destroyed are both guilty:

> *he killed the house: to kill a house*
> *When great men grew up, married, died,*
> *I here declare a capital offence.*

The old man's murder of his drunken father in the burning house, like the murder of the son he has begot "upon a tinker's daughter in a ditch", are the violent but necessary consequences of preceding acts; as the rape of Leda sealed the doom of Troy.

> *A shudder in the loins engendered there*
> *The broken wall, the burning roof and tower,*
> *And Agamemnon dead.*
>
> Leda and the Swan

. . . . .

> *The window is dimly lit again.*
> *Do not let him touch you! It is not true*
> *That drunken men cannot beget*
> *And if he touch he must beget*
> *And you must bear his murderer.*
>
> Purgatory

Shuttling between the living past and the horror of recognition ("my wits are out"), the old man, at the moment when his mother passes into the bride sleep, destroys the son of his own begetting and assumes the all-protecting rôle that she, who died in giving birth, had never known. He had lived in imagination through her pleasure and remorse, as the two ghosts had lain upon the mattress begetting him; now in grotesque metamorphosis of the generations, he sings to the dead boy a heroic lullaby:

> *Hush a bye, baby, thy father's a knight,*
> *Thy mother a lady, lovely and bright.*

The re-animation of the mother in her son does not save her ghost from its penance:

> *Twice a murderer and all for nothing!*
> *And she must animate that dead night*
> *Not once, but many times.*
> *O God,*
> *Release my mother's soul from its dream!*
> *Mankind can do no more. Appease*
> *The misery of the living and the remorse of the dead.*

The dramatic perspectives of this play depend on the transformation of one generation into another; it is a play of recognition, not of action; the limits of individual suffering have been reached in the separateness and unity of the mad old man with his ghosts.

"It is myself that I remake," Yeats had protested as justification for the reshaping of his poems. Some raw material for this monodrama can be found in the poem published with it, "Why should not old men be mad?" and in the "Private Thoughts". Like some grand musical finale, Yeats's whole dramatic development is summed up here (5), and in the lineaments of the Old Man can be seen the traces of many earlier masks—the Wise Man learning that wisdom comes of beggary, Synge's Joker who killed his "da": Tom the Lunatic from the poems, where the lit-up ruins of Castle Dargan are recalled again and again. Swift, in *The Words upon the Window Pane*, had said "I have that in my blood which no child must inherit", but here the great house represents the total inheritance of Swift's Ireland, for good and ill; and all is squandered.

That so much has been brought to bear on this brief play may explain its force; in *The Death of Cuchulain*, there is more statement, theory, protest. This hero, killed also by a blind beggar, no longer gives the harper matter for heroic song:

> *An old man looking back on life*
> *Imagines it in scorn.*

"Observed facts do not mean much till I can make them parts of my experience" was among Yeats's last "Private Thoughts"; this was the necessary condition for that "remaking of himself" which prompted his daedal art, and in which he finally grew "expert beyond experience". Yet the final concentration which turns gesture and proclamation into vision must come as a gift.

5 THE INHERITANCE BEQUEATHED

These later plays incorporate so much that is alien, harsh and negative as to become paradoxical. Beauty is now inseparable from terror and violence; scepticism must salt and season all belief. Yeats could mock at his own images—as in *The Circus Animals' Desertion*—and he spoke of the "harsh geometry of *A Vision*"—as "incomplete interpretation"; it was meant only for "my schoolmates", those who would not misunderstand the particular grammar of assent. Religious and political concepts are alike dissolved; Yeats imagined

> A Christ not shut off in history but flowing, concrete, phenomenal . . . that Unity of Being Dante compared to a perfectly proportioned human body

while

> State and Nation are the work of intellect, and when you consider what comes before and after they are . . . not worth the blade of grass God gives for the nest of the linnet.

138

Yeats said in the preface to *A Vision* that abstract definition is "incidental and temporary" and that "whatsoever is defined is taken out of experience . . . and that spiritual realities especially can be known only in the animation of experience", and finally in *Wheels and Butterflies* that "mythology . . . draws one onward to the unknown".

His strict dramatic form transmitted material that otherwise might remain inaccessible. In early plays, where the divine was mediated through a woman, and death came like the loosening of long hair, the sensuous appeal of the verse was soft and indefinite, the themes were touching and simple. Later, as the images grew murderous or goetic, the transformations more fantastic, the writing became harder and firmer, more condensed; it anticipates the work of later men. The image of the tramp, the beggar or the blind man has become the most potent Icon of the modern stage—in Beckett and Genet, Pinter and Ionesco, the lineaments traced by Yeats maintain their form. Only by living with them throughout a lifetime did the Fool and Blind Man from *On Baile's Strand* become individualized; still as Yeats said: "I seek an image of the modern mind's discovering itself."

Yeats's contribution to modern drama is therefore not to be reckoned in terms of the number of performances which his plays obtain. In the first period of his play-writing, roughly from 1892 to 1908, his exertions also provided the stage with other poets and drew those who would support it to help him. In his second period, roughly from 1916 to 1926, he provided a poetic approach upon which other writers had advanced, while himself withdrawing from the public stage. This was inevitable, since the interior drama which he projected was without a basis in popular acceptance or understanding. Nowadays every youth who has read his Fromm is "enlightened" on what Yeats "really" meant by the symbol of the hawk's well—by indulging all those projective fantasies of which the poet so painfully divested himself. Yeats's poems

139

of experience, being the hard-won searchings of his "dark" self, will repel those who cannot accept the brutal and archaic levels within their own being, or who expect to find in another's symbolic forms the exact reflexion of their own. As he said:

> The drama has need of cities that it may find men in sufficient numbers. . . . It has one day when the emotions of cities still remember the emotions of sailors and husbandmen; it has another day, now beginning, when thought and scholarship discover their desire.

Yeats appeals to a deep of the mind and not to the level of simple routine; in his very last plays, by means of those Icons he evolved as personal refashioning of traditional images, he speaks not *of* the Dream but *to* the Dream that everyone carries within. Not until their inner Dream has been partially subjected to insight and control, can his statements convey very much to the Dreamer.

Eliot praised the final plays of Yeats because they solved the problem of speech in verse; but Yeats gave much more than a speech rhythm. He achieved the rhythm as a consequence of his separation of the personae of his inward drama, who had been animated from icons to images that were dynamic and "self-begotten". The "conversational" tone of his later poetry—it is really not conversational at all—the return of natural voice to his verse, constitutes proof that he had projected his inner drama, into the common tongue.

For each language, and for each generation, such elements must be formed afresh. Compared with the work of Ibsen or of Strindberg, Yeats's achievement may look limited; but without the Irish dramatic movement, imaginative drama would not have returned to the English stage. And Yeats was at the centre of that recovery of a great area for poetry and for the work of the imagination—this was a great public service to the language, which Yeats himself proffered as his best claim to the Nobel prize for literature, wishing only that Synge and Lady Gregory could have shared it with him.

The first phase of Yeats's dramatic career gave service to the good estate of poetry in the modern world. The second phase, not a matter of the public stages, supplied later writers with themes. "Yeats had nothing and we have had Yeats." The influence of his work is out of all proportion to its scale. The theatre of Samuel Beckett, in particular, is deeply endebted to Yeats's *Purgatory*, without which *Waiting for Godot* and the dramas which followed would hardly have been conceivable.

A parallel with Marlowe is not entirely absurd. Both were poets of soaring imagination whose work is concentrated and yet of great apparent simplicity; who carve out monolithic heroic figures with a powerful mixture of high idealism and mordant ironic disclaimer; who admit a dark streak of violence, from goetic powers. That Marlowe's work was crowded into a few years only and Yeats's spread over a long lifetime does not prevent it being true of the one as of the other, that a great personal achievement was also the foundation for great work to follow. Each of these poets was founder of a drama quite different from his own.

Yet, the likeness breaks down completely if Marlowe and Yeats are seen in terms of the stage. The one achieved dazzling popularity with the common people as well as the poets, and wrote for the great open "game place" or for a small courtly group with equal ease. Yeats had only one or two public successes, and the Old Man who speaks the prologue to *The Death of Cuchulain* wanted an audience of fifty or a hundred. "If there are more than a hundred I won't be able to escape people who are educating themselves out of Book Societies and the like, sciolists all, pickpockets and opinionated bitches."

This is more like the Epistle to *Troilus and Cressida* than like Marlowe.

NOTES TO CHAPTER SEVEN

(1) For example *The Midnight Court*, written in the eighteenth century (and translated by Frank O'Connor), is a medieval dream vision that could have been written by Dunbar.

(2) See the essay, "Authors and Readers", in D. W. Harding, *Experience into Words*, 1963, for a discussion of this subject.

(3) As in *The Battle of Maldon*; in some of Shakespeare's Roman plays also. See Yeats, "Tomorrow's Revolution", *On the Boiler*, "Asiatic conquerors before battle invoked their ancestors, and a few years ago a Japanese admiral thanked his for guiding the torpedoes".

(4) Yeats had always thought that drama should be ritualistic, in order to be "remote, spiritual, ideal." But he had hoped to "bring the country to the town" and the dream of scholars to the city. His disillusionment with the stage, the complex feelings stirred by the Easter Rising and the Civil War left him deeply divided; feeling that only a part of the old Ireland survived, he turned increasingly for his mythology towards the Anglo-Irish civilization of the eighteenth century. The first of the Plays for Dancers, *At the Hawk's Well*, has been five times revived in Tokyo; the power of all these plays has been fully shown in recent productions in Belfast; and in England, by the Wiltshire Players.

(5) The Fool and Beggarman come in *On Baile's Strand*, where Cuchulain kills his son; the Fool and Wise Man in *The Hour Glass*; the ritual sacrifice in *The Green Helmet*. Perhaps this last sacrifice is an ironic reversal also of the Countess Cathleen's immolation for Ireland—Maud Gonne appears in "Why should not old men be mad?" The political echo here (of the destruction of Coole Park) is not of the same kind that Yeats put into *The Dreaming of the Bones* in 1917, it does not belong to the core of the play. T. R. Henn thinks the Old Man stands for the Body and that the overcoming of Cuchulain by a squalid beggar is an acknowledgement of physical death.

Chapter Eight

EUROPEAN DEVELOPMENTS FROM STRINDBERG TO SARTRE

I MODERN FORMS

A<small>N</small> outline of the history of Western drama in the first half of the twentieth century would trace sharp irregular curves, for different theatrical experiments cut across and repeat each other. The one constant feature is the appeal to the spectators' direct response, as individuals. The "little theatre" audience offered no collective endorsement; each member made his response alone. The commercial theatre had dwindled to a social ritual. Although as social history, the story of the public stages is full of interest, it does not belong to the history of imaginative art.

Strindberg's work, covering the end of the nineteenth and the first decade of the twentieth century, initiated a new Theatre of the Dream. From his early dramas to the later plays of vision, he was continually regrouping his images and breaking up old forms. Pirandello, whose reputation suddenly blossomed at the end of the First World War, attempted a more cerebral drama of masks, which, though influential, was in itself too closely bound to the conventions it professed to evade. With Chekhov, these two represented the strongest influences of the time.

The French stage, though hospitable to all sorts of dramatic experiment throughout the nineteenth century, had not seen many native playwrights; but in the 'twenties and 'thirties of the present century a new play of masks evolved, based on Greek myth. It was a drama of crisis, determinist and ironic in mood, which lasted approximately from the mid-'twenties to the Second World War, built up by Cocteau, Giraudoux, and the early work of Anouilh and Montherlant.

The existentialist stage of Camus and Sartre, which predominated from the middle of the war for about a dozen years (roughly 1942–55), met an even sharper crisis with a new philosophy; a drama of situation cracked the rigid framework of the earlier mythological plays. This now has been succeeded by a new theatre of the Dream, often termed Theatre of the Absurd, which is related to the philosophies of Existentialism, but uses them for a quite different kind of play.

Meanwhile, in parallel development, the expressionist drama of the revolutionary writers of Eastern Europe, Andreyev and the German Kaiser and Toller had provided between 1904 and 1930 a theatre of masks for the transmission of propaganda messages. Brecht's doctrine of alienation was a necessary reaction from this simple fervour. In his complex forcing of paradoxes upon the audience, Brecht engages them not in the play itself, but in the conflict which it symbolizes.

2 STRINDBERG

Strindberg's first play, *The Father*, appeared in 1887, his last in 1909. Pirandello's two masterpieces, *Six Characters in Search of an Author* and *Henry IV*, were written within a few weeks of each other in 1920: he died in 1936. Thus the minor curve of Yeats's development, if seen within the major curve of European drama, would be contained within the achievements of these two playwrights, whose work corresponds in time to his first and second phase—Strindberg's with the dream-plays, Pirandello with the Icons.

Strindberg's interior drama was incipient in the great works of Ibsen, especially *Peer Gynt*; it emerged more fully, in Ibsen's very latest plays. In the preface to *Lady Julie* (1888) Strindberg dissolved the unexamined current assumptions about fixed characters—"a man permanently settled and

144

finished"—in favour of the dynamic and the turbulent; what
Yeats was to term "the unfinished man and his pain". Pirandello, who reached maturity in his fifties, elaborated his
position in the preface of *Six Characters*, a document more professional and less profound. Both dramatists explore the
shifting boundary between the inner and the outer world, in
minds whose balance is delicately adjusted and tremulous.
The question of identity—"Who am I?"—is seen not primarily as a matter of an adjustment in society, but as adjustment of conflicting systems of belief and behaviour within the
self. Strindberg penetrated to the waking dream of madness
and recorded his experiences in *Inferno*; Pirandello for nearly
twenty years lived with a wife who suffered from a hysterical
form of insanity, facing a daily struggle to maintain his identity against the twisted version of himself that her pathologi-
cal jealousy imposed.

In his early plays Strindberg recognized, with a clarity that
outraged his contemporaries, the element of hatred and
aggression that is present in all powerful relationships, the
reverse side of love. These dealt a far more drastic blow at the
hypocrisy and prudery of nineteenth-century society than the
revelations of the social realists, for they attacked the individual within his citadel. It is astonishing that when they
were written, Freud was still an unknown practising doctor
in Vienna.

For his dreams of love and hate, fantasy and violence,
Strindberg demanded paradoxically a greater naturalism of
setting. There must be lifelike spontaneity of movement;
natural postures; real furniture, not painted canvas; the cook
with her stove, the last insult of a woman's shawl wrapped
round the Captain in *The Father*. Strindberg uses his stage
as Ibsen might have done, when the Captain hurls a lighted
lamp at his wife as the light of reason goes out in him; for
Laura might be seen as a savager version of Mrs Alving,
drawn from Captain Alving's point of view. She preserves

herself and her child by what could be a largely unconscious plan for destroying her husband, as the heroine of
Ghosts had done. But Laura's mind is never disclosed, her
acts and their consequences imprison the Captain in a world
of objects, and he ends pillowed on the breast of his old Nurse,
strapped in a strait jacket.

In *Lady Julie*, the valet, recalled to duty by the imperious
ringing of his master's bell, changes into his service coat
before he issues to his mistress the whispered order for her
self-destruction. The dramatic force of these two plays is
therefore traditional, as well as experimental, and they have
remained the most actable, the most adaptable of Strindberg's
work.

In the plays of his second period (1897–1909) Strindberg
entered a world of dissolving shapes, where objects take on a
life of their own—the growing castle, the terrifying bottle of
Japanese soy brandished by the demon cook, the flowerpot
with its Easter lily or hyacinth. *To Damascus* (1898–1904)
holds no such stable series of events as the life of Lady Julie
and her parents (which was so fully accounted for, that part
of the explanation had to be crammed into the preface).
Characters now melt into each other, while events continually repeat themselves in a cycle of frustration and horror.
Traumatic incidents from the Stranger's childhood—often
taken from Strindberg's own childhood—may suddenly erupt,
and new figures reveal themselves as belonging to earlier
strata.

In *The Ghost Sonata* (1907) a simple though melodramatic
story is discernible through the powerful fantasies; the sinister plotter is unmasked as "the clock strikes"—which releases
a perfect flood of information about his criminal past. This
in turn does not prevent his receiving the hypocritical tribute
of a pious public funeral. Action remains superficial; the
unmaskings are important only for what they allow to be
affirmed:

They say Jesus Christ descended into hell. It means only his wanderings on this earth—his descent to that madhouse, jail, charnel, the earth. . . . Sleep, my lovely, my heartbroken girl! you've suffered so much, and none of it deserved. Sleep . . . but don't dream . . . and wake to no scorching sun, no dusty room, no tainted friendship, no damaged love. . . . (1)

The Victim who redeems—particularly the young girl— is the central figure of the last plays. Strindberg's tormented and demonic heroes are constantly being faced by accusations, menaced, condemned; or else, they are assaulted by the boredom and pettiness of living, the humiliations of sickness, the tyranny of servants, the smell of cooked cabbage, and a chronic shortage of cash. All these occur not as part of a fixed routine, such as the popular plays of environment might have shown, but as fragmentary, nightmarish intrusions upon the inner world. Like Kafka, Strindberg places the centre within, but this comes to be no longer exclusively the consciousness of the hero. In the later plays there is no longer any central character. There are victims, representatives of innocence and youth, and there are tyrants—though in *Easter* the bogeyman with sinister squeaking goloshes dwindles to a benevolent old man. But there is no longer a conflict of love and hatred. Holiness and wickedness are opposed quite simply. All characters are victims of an unstable universe, which may at any time be convulsed, so that all events reveal themselves as ambiguous. The solution is by transfiguration, or miracle; by a divine descent upon the world.

In two plays, written in 1901, *The Bridal Crown*, and *The Dream Play*, Strindberg draws unexpectedly near to the work that Yeats was writing, about this time. *The Bridal Crown* is a folk tale, set in the lakeland province of Dalecarlia, although the story was a familiar theme under all sorts of guises—the betrayed girl, the murdered child, the cruel penalty. Kirsten, who submits to her fate, is the redeeming Victim of the play;

147

she stands for all that is naturally good, but she is transformed by her sufferings to a state of holiness, such as that of Elena in *Easter*. The daughter of Indra, who descends to earth in the *The Dream Play*, makes the same sacrifice (in Buddhist terms) as the Countess Cathleen in Yeats.

That Strindberg could write these fairy tales, combining the idyllic and the violent, at the same time that he was producing *The Dance of Death*, his most appalling study of marital hatred, serves only as one indication of his range. He is almost the only writer of his time who succeeded both as dramatist and novelist; the fluid, molten quality of his imagination never allowed him to revise—he rewrote. His works run to something like forty volumes, and although some of them were ephemeral, there is a certain kind of power which comes only with professional habit, a technical assurance that in lesser writers may be dangerous, but which, when allied to such a genius as Strindberg's, confers true authority.

"It is myself that I remake"—Yeats's words would apply to his great contemporary with particular force, for the autobiographical element is everywhere distinguishable. It was by self-exploration that Strindberg discovered the murderous yet too-recognizable conflicts that make up his plays and novels. When he began to write, psychiatry was in a very early stage of its modern development—the Nancy school beginning its studies. Strindberg, in non-scientific terms, explored the same regions of the mind.

The Captain's distorted vision controls *The Father*, but the later plays are not directed from any particular point of view. Only the fact that they are designed for some select few to understand prevents them from being transcripts of nightmare or madness; but this narrow distinction indicates the imaginative triumph. Many an unfortunate might endorse Strindberg's plays; none but Strindberg composed them. Ravings do not communicate to others, as these plays do; on on the other hand, like the violent later plays of Yeats, they certainly demand a level of insight which could not have been expected of an audience in Strindberg's day. By now they might be comprehensible to a public trained by Harold Pinter, Ann Jellicoe, and the films of Hitchcock.

3 PIRANDELLO

Many of Pirandello's plays have lost their original force; the notion that truth varies with the eye of the beholder is no longer novel. *Right you are* (*if you think so*) demolishes the notion of "plain unvarnished truth" somewhat laboriously, with the aid of a commentator. Two people each explain that the other suffers from illusions about the identity of a third. The third person appears and says they are both right. This complicated shuttling to and fro of rival versions of truth transforms the traditional Italian stagecraft about mistaken identity into a philosophical puzzle; basically, it is not unlike Goldoni. The real protest is against the cruel prying vulgarity of the crowd of town gossips, given in the anguish of the three principals at the attempt to tear out the facts of their privacy; but the indictment of this brutality is not pursued, and indeed it is often overlooked, in accounts of the play.

A witty burlesque of conventional behaviour—the code for jealous husbands—had been started by Chiarelli with *The Mask and the Face* (1916), and a burlesque of theatrical material can be found in Pirandello, who likes to invert conventional situations. Such mockery loses its force when the object of mockery itself disappears; Pirandello implies a heavy, solid layer of accepted commonplace, to be flouted; of bourgeois respectability, to be dazzled. Both are now much diminished. In *Each in His Own Way* (1924) the drama suddenly turns out to be a play-within-the-play; the curtain having fallen rises at once to show spectators hurrying out to discuss the latest "line of nonsense by Pirandello". The hall of mirrors is extended when some of the "spectators" begin to re-enact the "play" which is about their "real" life; finally the manager declares the whole thing must stop.

In such plays, the pathos and puzzle are united by contrasting acting with life, as a way of contrasting illusion and reality. Some of Pirandello's plays are improvised in the traditional Italian way (2), but his two masterpieces depend on the-play-within-the play, the restless switching of levels and the rather oppressive pathos of a trapped and vulnerable hero.

The six characters in search of an author had haunted Pirandello—"born alive, they wished to live". But he could not find a philosophical significance to justify them, till he realized that this situation in itself supplied the justification.

The three main rôles had in fact appeared in previous plays (3); here their confused story is too well known to them to be communicated clearly, as they drift in from outer space to the stage of a public threatre, begging for incarnation.

> One is born to life in many forms, in many shapes, as tree or as stone, as water, as butterfly, or as woman. So one may also be born a character in a play . . . he who has the luck to be born a character can laugh even at death. He cannot die. . . . We want to live . . . only for a moment . . . in you.

The inarticulate misery of the Mother, the strident passion of the Daughter and the remorse of the Father stand out in high relief from the old-fashioned melodrama which is their "story". The Son refuses to take up his rôle. When the two children are killed, in which world does this occur? The Father cries out to the theatre manager:

> Pretence? Reality, sir, reality!

In *Henry IV* the hero had long lived within a historical masquerade, which to his disordered fancy was reality; he emerges from it to avenge his lost years by a murder, which drives him back to the safety and prison of makebelieve.

The tragic dreamer is imprisoned in his mask and not liberated; Pirandello suffered from the disabling weight of Italian professional theatre—probably the most powerful tradition in Europe of its kind. His cerebral drama gives an exaggerated display of intellectual agility, that does not disguise emotional poverty. The only motive used is marital jealousy or infidelity, sometimes with the cuckold as hero. The claim to be writing mockery only intensifies the meagre brittleness of the lesser plays; within each of them, there is an opera by Leoncavallo demanding to be let out.

The imprisoned author is presented clearly in *When You are Somebody* (1933) where the hero is not permitted to tamper with his own public image, and is made to repudiate uncharacteristic writings.

Between his overwhelming technical inheritance, and his rather limited intellectual puzzles, Pirandello acquired a dangerous fluency and wrote himself out. The contrast with Strindberg shows on the one hand, a questing, untrammelled mind, too powerful to accept any regular form; on the other, an intellectual rebel who was largely a conformist in disguise. Strindberg, by the turn of the century, had already anticipated, for example, much of the work of D. H. Lawrence. Pirandello was content merely to dazzle; he never rejected Mussolini's régime, though he courageously directed that neither Church nor State should offer any professional ministrations at his death.

No flowers on the bed, and no lighted candle. A pauper's cart. Naked. And let no one accompany me, neither relatives nor friends. The cart, the horse, a driver, *è basta*. Burn me. . . .

Pirandello's influence, on the French stage in particular, is of more importance than his achievement. The two great plays apart, he will not stand up to comparison with a great traditionalist such as Lorca, who was also an experimenter.

4 THE ICONS OF CRISIS; DRAMA IN THE 'TWENTIES AND 'THIRTIES

Drama had been used as a political weapon in Russia at the time of the abortive revolution of 1904; in Germany the revolutionary Expressionists, especially Kaiser and Toller, influenced the whole drama of the 'thirties. In America, Eugène O'Neill and Elmer Rice, in Ireland Sean O'Casey, were influenced by expressionism; in England, political drama in the 'thirties climbed rapidly to the protest of the year of Munich, and then fell off abruptly.

From Andreyev's *Play of Man* (1908) onwards, the Icon of Everyman is set in a world dominated by blind forces, and inhabited by puppets. Man addresses his useless prayers and curses to the faceless Grey One, and ends by hurling a speech of defiance into the void. In the evil Cities of Kaiser and Toller, Man is opposed by machines and mechanical villainy. Morality is a matter of black and white; wicked choruses of stockbrokers, armaments men, military leaders are seen as "them", while Man is "us". This Marxist drama snatches at shock techniques—broken sequences, ballet and cinema interludes, songs and tableaux; it records the abolition of Man. There is a reductive treatment of the Enemy, while all the suffering and sensibility is concentrated in one Promethean figure, the victim–hero. These Revolutionary plays are only tolerable in a revolutionary context; they survive as documentaries of the times in which they appeared. The dichotomy is too drastic, the instructive aim too narrow; they are the Morality Plays of the new religion. From them came the blank featureless figures used by the political poets of the 'thirties in England; Auden's Mr and Mrs A in the *The Ascent of F.6* (1936) and the whole structure of *On*

152

the Frontier (1938); Stephen Spender's *Trial of a Judge* (1938), and MacNeice's *Out of the Picture* (1937) (4). As early as 1928, Sean O'Casey had borrowed a scene from Toller, when in *The Silver Tassie* the crucified soldier hears the prayer of the guns.

The marks of extreme violence never found their place in England; in France they appeared in more traditional form. In Germany, Brecht developed his theory of alienation in natural opposition to the earlier doctrinaire style. The passionate fervour of Toller's *Hinkelmann* or *Masses and Men* could not be accepted for very long. Even in such an early play as *The Exception and the Rule*, written for schoolchildren, Brecht could show the ineffectual goodness of the peasants failing against the initiative and ruthless vigour of the capitalist; "The weak man dies, the hardy man survives"—to be acquitted for his crimes in a court of Injustice. It is the hardihood of Azdak and of the peasant heroine that triumph in *The Caucasian Chalk Circle*. Brecht's kind of conviction allows for irony as well as decision; *Mother Courage* unites pity and scorn.

The French use of myth reinforced a more ironic determinism. It allowed the dramatists to blame the gods without necessarily subscribing to their existence; and yet, on the other hand, by sharp deflation of a heroic story, to create a stimulating paradox. The modern instance is superimposed upon the ancient heroics, in the manner of Shakespeare's *Troilus and Cressida*, when in Giraudoux's *Tiger at the Gates*, the Gates of War swing open to show Helen seducing Troilus. Aegisthus is in love with Electra, and Clytemnestra murders her husband because she loathes certain trivial habits (*Electre*, 1937).

These plays of Giraudoux, with Cocteau's *Orphée* (1926) and *La Machine Infernal* (1934), Montherlant's *Pasiphae* (1938) and various adaptations of Greek plays had established the mythological drama before the Second World War; it was in the 'forties, however, that it became re-animated much more powerfully—not then to support determinism but to repudiate it.

In Sartre's heroic Orestes, the pangs of privation, the "feel of not to feel it", become paradoxically the sign of triumph, for where there is pain there is life, and where there is life, the power of free choice.

ORESTES: You are king of the gods, Jupiter, king of stones and of stars, king of the waves of the sea. But not king of men.
JUPITER: I am not your king, presumptuous insect? Who created you?
ORESTES: You did. But there was no need to create me with free will.
JUPITER: I gave you freedom to serve me.
ORESTES: Perhaps you did. But my free will has turned against you now, and neither of us can do anything about it (5).

In these plays of crisis, the authors had "learnt a style from a despair"; violence was necessary for their drama of protest, and they found it in ancient myth. *The Flies* appeared in 1943, Anouilh's *Antigone* in 1944. As Antigone goes to bury her brother with a child's wooden spade, all the defenceless-ness of the unarmed rebel is behind the detail; the pathos is not deflating. "I am not here to understand, I am here to say NO" was a line that meant more to the first audiences than it ever could do again; but unlike the German Expressionist drama, this is not merely a documentary of the Resistance, for the enemy are not reduced to puppets.

Plays of Greek myth ceased after 1945; Camus expressly repudiated them (6). Instead, a sumptuous variety of historic settings stock the new cultural supermarket. Anouilh and Audiberti have taken Joan of Arc as subject, Monther-land Spanish and Italian history (in *The Master of Santiago*, 1948 and *Malatesta*, 1950). Sartre used German settings for *Lucifer and the Lord* (1951) and *Altona* (1959)—though in the last the name of the hero is Franz, a transparent disguise for an indictment that Sartre is making much nearer home than Hamburg. The plague-stricken city of *The Flies* reappears in Camus' *State of Siege* (1948); and has been widely used as a general symbol, because of Artaud's application of it to the theatre in *The Theatre and its Double*. Plays about the theatre and its masks, from Cocteau's *Impromptu de Paris* (1937) and Anouilh's *Eurydice* (1942) to Sartre's *Kean* (1953), Ionesco's *Impromptu de l'Alma* (1956) and Genet's *The Blacks* (1959), have mixed the older influence of Pirandello with more violent contemporary forces.

It seems unlikely that any myth could at the moment establish itself with the authority that Expressionism had for the revolutionary writers of the 'twenties or that classical myth assumed thirty years ago. Icons are needed at times of definite and sharply experienced crisis, but in the troubled, ominous, unstable world of today, the Dream and the "game" of theatrical illusion open a more valid way.

5 EXISTENTIALIST THEATRE; SARTRE AND CAMUS

A tradition which is both denied and believed—believed with the will, but not the intellect—produces plays of paradox and contradiction. The estrangement of the writer from his beliefs is shown by an irony which the affirmations succeed—but only narrowly succeed—in containing. The poignancy of the human condition is strengthened, while its pretensions are sharply deflated. This has already been seen in the plays of Dryden.

The Existentialist paradox, that man is condemned to be free, means that nowhere more exclusively than in the hour of defeat can he assert his identity as an act of will, or choice. Alone of natural beings, man can create his own identity out of what he is given—in Yeats's term, the "body of fate". All men know that their acts may be vain, as many are; yet vulnerable spirits in the grip of hostile forces may sustain themselves by the great Images of the heroic past, to a limited extent. Since, however, the Image represent a security of belief that belongs to the past, it produces a paradox to superimpose this past upon the present. True Icons inhabit an eternal Present, so that time does not enter into their ceremonies, or enters only to be overcome. The ironic flash which joins heroic past to squalid present in such plays as Sartre's (or in Yeats's *Death of Cuchulain*) isolates the hero's act of choice, which serves to join these two incompatibles together. As Sartre has said, the Icon is a means of escaping from the merely psychological conception of events:

> The theatre as conceived of in the period between the wars, and as perhaps it is still thought of in the United States, is a theatre of characters. . . . What is universal to our way of thinking is not nature but the situations in which man finds himself; that is, not the sum total of all the psychological traits, but the limits that enclose him on all sides. . . . He is faced with the necessity of having to work and die, of being hurled into a life which is already complete, which is yet his own enterprise and in which he can never have a second chance; where he must play his cards and take the risks, no matter what the cost. This is why we feel the urge to put on the stage certain situations which throw light on the main aspects of the condition of man, and to have the spectator participate in the free choice which man makes in these situations. . . . For us, psychology is the most abstract of the sciences because it studies our passions without plunging them back into their true human surroundings (7).

It follows that Corneille rather than Racine was the model for these playwrights of crisis, since he "shows will at the core of passion". The Greek myth was for French dramatists an inherited form; it gave some measure of continuity within the native tradition. The mingling of inflation and irony it allowed can again be compared—as the reference to Corneille will suggest—with something of the same mixture in Dryden's post-war theatre.

To accept the paradox of man who "deprived of general truths", is tormented by an absolute aspiration (8), it is assumed that all established creeds and the stability that comes from them must be abandoned; and yet that man is condemned to be no less than man—a rational animal. The anguish of the gap between what man can conceive or imagine, and what circumstances permit him to be, springs from his homeless alienated state. He is estranged from Nature, "heartless, witless Nature", since

> *the crime of being born*
> *Blackens all our lot.*

Yet, whatever their differences, Sartre, Camus and others of the existentialists would claim

> *as by a soldier's right*
> *A charter to commit the crime once more—*

the crime of being born and thereby alienated from the unconscious state of Nature, yet dying with the prospect of total annihilation, rejecting all consolation, whether offered in Christian or Marxist-Expressionist terms.

Altona represents the most acute torments of this position in the hero, Franz, who, after helping a Rabbi to escape a concentration camp, is sent to the Eastern front as an honourable alternative to suicide. Living in torment with his memories of how he tortured Russian partisans, he can support existence only by imagining that Germany is still starving and broken, and therefore he was justified in staving off defeat at any cost. Life on "the other side of despair" need not demand the presence of the torturers, as in the war play, *Men without Shadows*; the will of his haughty family brings

157

Franz to the conflict of power, where the responsibility for criminal acts must be acknowledged, and yet the self must be judged only by itself. The audience may here project themselves and feel the choice to be their own, in its strength and vulnerability. Strong hero or weak chorus are equally themselves.

Thus, though Fate may be fixed, the responsibility for choice is not denied and this entails a direct and full relation of the hero with other characters. The moment of choice creates a man out of his "makings".

The doctrine of the Absurd, as formulated by Camus, postulated a total dissociation between the random chancy events of Nature (the dance of the atoms, the fortuitous groupings of society) and the interior world of man. In spite of the overwhelming pressure of external things upon sentient beings, which could produce situations of extreme horror and incongruity, man must nevertheless attempt by means of *la raison* to adjust and reconcile himself with the envelope or shell of things. The gap between the random and the rational, which is the same as that between the irresponsible and the responsible, between necessity and freedom, is the region of tragic choice. In *Caligula*, the hero who suddenly perceives this gap decides to act out all the random irrational atrocity which the frame of things allows, as a demonstration of the position to his fellow men. He becomes a kind of Black Icon, tragic in the style of Marlowe's Jew of Malta.

In *The Just*, the exact limits of terrorism that are permitted is the subject of debate; the hero rejects the lure of cheap escape or consolation, and the sole prospect that is left of any union in love is the community of death "a dark night . . . on the same rope". The pressure of environment may drive man to an act for which, nevertheless, as conscious and responsible man, he has to pay. This is not so far as might at first appear from the stern and paradoxical doctrines of Claudel. It is much firmer and more committed than the analogous

158

discussions about the limits of crime that are permissable for the cause in Sartre's *Crime Passionel*—a play in which psychology, in spite of good intentions, seems once more to be breaking in.

As early as *The Myth of Sisyphus* (1942), Camus formulated his doctrine of the Absurd—that which does not cohere, which is incongruous. In defining the relation between man and his world as "absurd" in this musico-mathematical sense, Camus emphasized that all easy ways of escaping the conflict, such as suicide, must be ruled out. In "the harrowing and marvellous wager of the absurd" man must vote for life. This attitude Camus calls Revolt, and "L'homme revolté" is he who has recovered the unity of existence.

> The body, compassion, the created world, action, human nobility will then resume their place in this insane world. Man will find again the wine of absurdity and the bread of indifference, which nourished his greatness (9).

The assertion of values is in the last resort a matter of choice. As Camus said in the *Lettre à un ami allemand*: "I have chosen justice . . . so as to keep faith with the earth."

Sisyphus, hero of the Absurd, is tragic because he recognizes his plight.

> Where would his tortures be indeed, if at every step the hope of succeeding upheld him? . . . The lucidity that was to constitute his torture at the same time crowns his victory. There is no fate that cannot be surmounted by scorn.
>
> This universe henceforth without a master seems to him neither sterile nor futile. Each atom of that stone, each mineral flake of that night-filled mountain in itself forms a world. The struggle itself towards the heights is enough to fill a man's heart. One must imagine Sisyphus happy.

Like Dante's Brunetto on the burning sand, he seems as one who has won, although he lost. There is no higher fate than human destiny. Sisyphus is the last and most heroic of the Icons, whose outward act of complete futility is transformed by inward revolt.

NOTES TO CHAPTER EIGHT

(1) *The Ghost Sonata*, scene 3. My own translation.

(2) In 1930 he wrote *Tonight we Improvise*, in which he attacked the all-powerful theatre director. It is amusing to realize that improvising is the latest (1964) fashion on the New York stage.

(3) They had appeared in the play immediately preceding, *All for the Best*, but in reversed positions; this play in turn had inverted a simple anti-romantic comedy of 1916, *Think of it, Giacomino!* All these plays depict the cuckold as hero—a theme which was to be given some fashion by Crommelynik's *Le Cocu Magnifique* (1921).

(4) The figures in these plays repeat each other, e.g. Stagworth, Valerian, Spielmann are basically the same capitalist villain; the Judge's wife, Lady Isobel, Clara de Croot provide feminine counterparts.

(5) Sartre, *The Flies*, III, 2. My own translation.

(6) See John Cruikshank, *Albert Camus* (1959), p. 192.

(7) Sartre, *Forgers of Myths* (1946). Quoted from Toby Cole, *Playwrights on Playwriting* (New York, 1961).

(8) Iris Murdoch, *Sartre* (1953), p. 69. For the comparison with Dryden, see Chapter Six above, p. 115.

(9) Walter Kaufman, *Existentialism, Dostoievsky to Sartre* (New York, 1956), gives the full translation of *The Myth of Sisyphus*, from which these quotations are taken.

Chapter Nine

ELIOT AS DRAMATIST

Eliot's debt to Yeats has been generously acknowledged. Ezra Pound supplied a link between them as dramatists; a close friend of both, he introduced them to the Noh plays of Japan, which in turn they took as a model.

Transformation, or metamorphosis of character became the foundation of Eliot's plays as it had been of Yeats's drama. Superimposing the past upon the present in a more intricate pattern, Eliot used sharp transitions from one to the other as a means of ordering futility in the present. Deep firm lines from a tragic tale of ancient Thebes are scored on the harsh but unheroic ground of a north country squire's family troubles; the shades of Colonus deepen the colour of a beech tree in the Home Counties. Eliot's usual background, however, had not been rural, like that of Yeats; and a modern metropolitan scene is implied in all the later plays. The heroes are public figures, though met only in private life.

Eliot learnt from the French theatre of the 'thirties that irony could be strengthened by setting together ancient heroism and modern triviality; it gives what Yeats termed "an emotion of multitude"—like that of plot and contrasted subplot. The spectator is forced to respond in two different ways simultaneously to the same situation, and so his own personal interpretation is stirred up.

Although he had made his reputation as a poet for the few, Eliot's first notion for the theatre was to revive music hall. *Sweeney Agonistes*, though but a fragment, is perhaps his most modern play. Returning to the London stage by way of pageanty and festival drama, he "aspired to Shaftesbury

162

Avenue" and in at least one play, *The Cocktail Party*, achieved this kind of success. Eliot asked that all his plays should be judged as experiments, and has expressed his dissatisfaction with all; but his influence, example and prestige were vital at a certain period—roughly the twenty years between 1935 and 1955—for the development of English imaginative drama. He has been more influential as a propagandist for drama than as a dramatist; his dramatic ideas, which provided, with those of Yeats, the only attempt since Dryden to construct a theory of the drama in England, have undergone radical changes as a result of his practice.

From the early 'twenties Eliot wrote on the Elizabethan dramatists and on classical drama, but it was not till his religious and social preoccupations of the 'thirties gave him the necessary drive towards public statement that he produced *Murder in the Cathedral* (1935), a play designed for those who go to religious festivals and expect to be patiently bored but who are "prepared to put up with poetry". It may be that Eliot's mastery of the dramatic monologue was a handicap in his search for a full dramatic form; in his first play, as he has admitted, there was only one dramatic character, the hero. (Angus Wilson once remarked that the Puritan mentality tends to see a central character who is very large, surrounded by much smaller characters; in Eliot the doctrinal Anglo-Catholic does not succeed in overlaying completely the temperamental Puritan.)

Murder in the Cathedral gratified Eliot's ten-year-old ambition; it is also a landmark in English dramatic history; for it proved that English verse drama could still succeed, and Eliot's younger contemporaries hastened to follow him. A number of verse plays came out in the later 'thirties, though none of these has maintained itself as *Murder in the Cathedral* has done. His first play may well turn out to be Eliot's most enduring stage success, for though not often professionally performed it can be successfully played by amateurs.

163

The formal simplicity of the character groups, the contrast between the crisp verse of the Hero or his enemies, and the nightmare dreams of the Chorus, or its lyrical hymns, achieve a consistent simplification. It is a classically severe style.

I once saw a performance of a play of Euripides in the Theatre of Herodas Atticus under the Acropolis. The main characters were formal and hieratic, as they stood in their masks; they might have been reciting an old ballad, worn smooth with familiarity. The Chorus of women, supple, responsive in mood, moving in a slow dance of fear or joy, evoked an immediate response, and carried all the emotional significance of the story.

Something like this may be felt in *Murder in the Cathedral*. Thomas à Becket's story is known, to him, to the tempters, to the audience; death and what comes after death is already settled; the fine point of decision is all the finer. This play exists as a moment in time, a moment of choice which brings in something outside time. "The point of the intersection of Time with the Timeless" is the point of Incarnation, and Thomas, after surmounting the temptation of the senses, of power, of private revenge and "the last temptation" of pride makes his decision, on behalf of all. He is the one who sees, who has the responsibility of making the choice. By this decision he crosses an internal boundary line, after which he is "not in danger; only near to death". The actual murder is a ritual performance by the Knights, who then are rapidly transformed into modern demagogues and address the audience rather than the Chorus in their ingenious justifications. By his death, Thomas has released new spiritual forces into the world, as the Chorus see in the end.

The Chorus, those who "do not wish anything to happen", the humble women of Canterbury, acknowledge their share of the guilt. For them, there is still hope and fear, pleading and remorse, new assaults from the powers of darkness whose presence they scent upon the air. In a sense although

164

Thomas is the Hero, the Chorus remains the chief actor. Eliot has said that he wrote the play as a protest against totalitarianism in Europe, and the final speeches of the Knights now bear only too familiar a sound. Thomas is not to be allowed the glory of being a martyr; the verdict is that his death was self-provoked, "suicide while of unsound mind".

The poets of the 'thirties took up such political themes; and within the last few years the story of Beckett has been used by other playwrights. Anouidh's Beckett chooses the honour of God, and thus is bound to ignore the honour of the King. Like Antigone, he says:

I shan't try to convince you. I shall only say no (1).

The severity and simplicity of Eliot's medieval pageant play are at the opposite extreme to the complexity of *The Family Reunion* (1939). There is a close relation between the plot and that of *Sweeney Agonistes*, written in 1926. A "nightmare dream" of a drowned murdered woman, interspersed with ominous songs, and the cheap clichés of the uncomprehending Chorus, build up a comedy of menace. In the one story, the murderer "does a girl in" and keeps her in a bath; in the other, she is lost in the Atlantic Ocean, but the remorse and isolation of the "murderers" are the same.

Sweeney came from Eliot's own personal mythology. The author was perhaps influenced to some extent by Cocteau in choosing the rhythms of the music hall for *Sweeney Agonistes*, but he based the fragment on Pound's Noh, and Yeats's adaptations; expecting the primitive drum-beat to be maintained throughout. He wrote with the idea that the spectators, like the characters, would be graded in degrees of understanding; that only a few would understand the hero. For the rest, since he hoped for a popular audience, he depended on "doing monkey tricks behind the audience's back" (2).

This is a play full of gaps in communication, and Sweeney cannot hope to explain.

I gotta use words when I talk to you.
But if you understand me or if you don't,
That's nothing to me and nothing to you.

The three main phases of Eliot's dramatic writing show him moving from the idea of a rhetorical, "distanced" presentation—that of *Sweeney Agonistes* and the critical writings of the 'twenties—to a theatre that would be socially useful—his view in the early 'thirties. Finally he became preoccupied with the technique of making effects indirectly. Concealed and unobtrusive rhythm replaced the drum beat, and like "concealed lighting" on a picture, made its effect without being noticed. By this means, Eliot hoped to cut across all stratifications of public taste.

One of his chief difficulties has always been the method by which the superhuman may be presented. In *Murder in the Cathedral* he was able to write from Christian presuppositions, but in other plays the problem has produced some very eccentric solutions. An unpublished ending for *Sweeney Agonistes* introduced (to the sound of the Angelus) a figure resembling Father Christmas, who bore a champagne bottle (empty) and an alarm clock; he wore evening dress with a carnation in the buttonhole

THE OLD GENTLEMAN: Good evening. My name is Time. ... I wait for the lost trains that bring in the last souls after midnight. The time by the exchange clock is now 9.46.
SWEENEY: Have you nothing else to say?
OLD GENTLEMAN: Have you nothing to ask me?
SWEENEY: Yes.
OLD GENTLEMAN. Good.
SWEENEY: When will the barnfowl fly before morning?
When will the owl be operated on for cataract?
When will the eagle get out of his barrel-roll?

OLD GENTLEMAN: When the camel is too tired to walk
  further,
Then shall the pigeon pie blossom in the desert
At the wedding breakfast of life and death . . . (3).

It was perhaps as well that Eliot suppressed this ending;
but the wedding breakfast of life and death concludes *The
Family Reunion* (1939), in the bizarre ritual of blowing out
candles on the birthday cake. ("Out, out, brief candle".)
  This drama, which appeared less than six months after
Yeats's *Purgatory*, includes in its houseparty a troupe of family
ghosts; like Yeats's beggar man, Lord Monchensey inhabits
"the past that is always present". The core of Eliot's third
tragic monodrama is played out among dead shadows and
live puppets. Harry Monchensey, who is "rather psychic, as
they say", endures his inner solitude without hope of release
or of understanding. He is one of the Hollow Men. His dead
father's wish to kill his mother produced the fearful waking
dream in which he saw himself as the murderer of his wife; the
misery of the dead threw a shadow of remorse on the living.
Agatha, who exorcises the dead, had loved his father, and
prevented the murder to save the unborn child—himself.
She is therefore his true mother, and he, in accepting a
vicarious suffering and continuing to endure it, becomes mo-
mentarily both her lover and her child.

> *You are the consciousness of your unhappy family,*
> *Its bird sent flying through the purgatorial flame.*

The exchange of "death's dream kingdom" for enlightenment frees him from his invisible chains, and from the rôle
that his original mother would impose; his election takes him
away on an unknown quest, for "liberty is a different kind
of pain from prison". This act of choice kills his mother,
since she has maintained herself by the trivialities of routine
and now "the clock has stopped in the dark".

The most innocent is he who suffers most; Harry's ruth-lessness, which appears as shock or discontinuity, marks his escape from "the war of phantoms". The question of re-sponsibility or "punishment", which has misled some literal-minded critics, has been handled with sure insight by D. W. Harding (4), who sees the play as a study in separation ex-perience, or psychological weaning—the final parting of Harry and his mother. Like Thomas crossing an internal boundary line, Harry enters into a new relation with every-one and passes to a state "on the other side of despair". The Furies become transformed to "the bright angels"; instead of fleeing, he must follow.

For the moment of enlightenment, Eliot took as immediate model Jean Cocteau's *The Infernal Machine* (1934), a play on the story of Oedipus. Agatha, enlightening Harry, like the Sphinx enlightening Oedipus, holds the threads of fate, steps into the place left vacant by the Furies between the windows, assumes the goddess (5). The flashback in time enlarges the scene.

The Sphinx, as Nemesis, says:

I weave, I winnow, I wind, I knit, I plait, I cross, I go over it again and again, I tie and untie again and again, retain-ing the smallest knots.

And Agatha, as Athena:

A curse comes to birth
As a child is formed. . . .
According to the phase
Of the determined moon . . .
The knot shall be unknotted,
And the crooked made straight.

The Infernal Machine, "one of the most perfect ever con-structed by the infernal gods for the destruction of a mortal", is the vehicle of a determinist ethic. It gives a grand and cosmic assertion of a purely negative kind. Cocteau, "the first of his generation, even before Giraudoux, to reinterpret Greek tragedy, because the new era needed a Racine" (6), reinterpreted it in the light of *Phèdre*. This return to tradition, when used as a basis for "Freudian" studies of character, gave grandeur to statements of cosmic unbelief and defiance.

It was natural that Eliot should take this determinist pattern and adapt it to "play tricks behind the audience's back". Much earlier, he had defined the uses of myth, and praised the method of Yeats's Plays for Dancers:

Myth . . . is simply a way of controlling, ordering, of giving shape and significance to the great panorma of futility and anarchy which is contemporary history. . . . Instead of narrative method we may now use mythical method. It is, I believe, a step towards making the modern world possible for art . . . towards form (7).

The form was not clearly established, but I would think that the story is not only one of separation, but of initiation. Harry sets out on a quest, the goal being unknown, while the Chorus, who have "lost their way in the dark", regain their unreal trivial existence; they recoil from the possibility of initiation

as if the earth should open
Right to the centre, as I was about to cross Pall Mall.

There are large and deliberate gaps in knowledge here; there are also mistakes. Eliot acknowledged the injudiciousness of presenting the Furies visually. He has also said that his sympathy is now with the mother, and Harry seems an insufferable prig. This perhaps only proves the completeness with which he has dissociated himself from the limitations of his hero.

Harry's ironic wit, his torments, the nature of his relations with his mother are reminiscent not only of Orestes, but of Hamlet. There is no way in which Harry can communicate

169

the nature of his inner suffering, or even recognize it, and Eliot noted this as a characteristic of *Hamlet*. "Loathing diffused" when he is inside his waking dream, dissociated obsession when he is outside, are represented dramatically for the audience by the gaps or jumps between different dramatic levels; and these in turn are represented by different kinds of verse. Characters engaged in ordinary conversation suddenly enter a trancelike state, in which they utter prophecies, while the Chorus of uncles and aunts occasionally emerge from their satisfied triviality to utter a general confession of fear or discomfort.

> *And the past is about to happen, and the future was long*
> *   since settled.*
> *And the wings of the future darken the past, the beak and*
> *   claws have desecrated . . .*
> *Have torn*
> *The roof from the house, or perhaps it was never there.*

In all three plays, Eliot presents on the dramatic level a contrast between the Hero who bears the burden of guilt and insight, and the Chorus, who can respond, if at all, only by intuition. In *Sweeney Agonistes*, the ominous pounding rhythm, the echoes and repetitions, sustain an atmosphere of menace. In *Murder in the Cathedral*, the crisp astringent dialogue of Thomas with his enemies or his uncomprehending friends alternates with the poetic rhythms of the Chorus and with the prose of Thomas's sermon or the address of the murderers. These are spoken directly to the audience—for this, of course, Eliot had precedent in his medieval model, since *Everyman* concludes with a sermon on pride. The technical problems involved in presenting different dramatic levels of speech, including the most familiar and banal, have been treated by Eliot as the most important aspect of his work. Earlier poets who wrote for the stage were content to produce lines that "could not have been spoken by anyone but a poetry reciter". To maintain a certain level of artifice and yet to avoid the limitations of the consciously "poetic" posed a problem which Eliot succeeded in solving for himself, but which he could not solve for others.

Gradually the ghosts and choruses of the Greek models are dispensed with, until, in his last three plays, Eliot confines himself to the flat speech of everyday. To have taken the superficial talk of the drawing room and exposed what lies beneath is perhaps not an unexpected thing for the author of *Prufrock* and *Portrait of a Lady* to have done. The drawing room at least has the advantage that its range of tone and inflection is restricted. For one of the chief difficulties which Eliot had to meet was the strong individuality of his own poetic accent. When "the author and character are speaking in unison" the lines become powerful and memorable. Ironic wit or the lyric cry are within Eliot's compass; but he cannot present Doris and Dusty, Eggerson or Mrs Piggott except sardonically. "May I pour a drop of oil on these troubled waters?" or "She'll come back to tell us more about the peace and quiet" hit off a type, almost too neatly.

The difficulty of integrating a deep and central vision with alien trivialities has been met by applying a great deal of theory, a great deal of reading and taking a great deal of pains. In this Eliot resembles that Elizabethan dramatist whose achievement he once brilliantly summarized—Ben Jonson. Much of his art, like Jonson's, is an art of caricature; it is judicious, and passionate at the core, but it remains an art for the few. These few, however, include his fellow-writers, who do not imitate him directly but have been stimulated by his work to develop on quite different lines of their own. His drama has worked like yeast, not upon the stage, but upon the writers. He should not be held responsible for Christopher Fry—who would probably have written in any case—but seen rather as an indirect influence behind the very different work of Pinter or Albee.

2 LATER PLAYS; THE ICONS

In Eliot's last three plays, the themes of Initiation, Adoption and the Quest are pursued, with some faint resonance from the Greek myths of Alcestis, Ion and Oedipus at Colonus. By now, the dramatic theory that poetry "should be put on a thin diet" had evolved; the rhythm had become almost imperceptible, for to Eliot his first necessity was to accept the language of ordinary speech, even its deterioration. The poet should be prepared to lay down a tradition which he could not hope to perfect, to submit himself to the language available, in the available dramatic forms.

Eliot therefore took the shabby professional form of drawing room comedy—a much less promising medium than the music hall. It remained stiffly detachable from what he chose to put into it. The sets for *The Cocktail Party* were carefully commonplace, the cigarettes by Abdulla and the stockings by Kayser Bondor. So strict was the purging of ornament that Eliot said: "It is perhaps an open question whether there is any poetry in the play at all."

From time to time, however, the façade of social banality rolls away to reveal some deliberate piece of mystification. Gaps in knowledge remain around the hero and the sacrificial victim. The mysterious sanatorium recalls that

> *The whole world is our hospital*
> *Endowed by the ruined millionaire*
> *(Little Gidding)*

The Libations are vaguely religious, Sir Henry dismisses his patients with the adjuration of Buddha to his disciples and the leading lady is crucified offstage (for which reason, I have been told, the play cannot be staged in France, as no leading lady will forgo her appearance in the last act). Except for Sir Henry's brief assumption of the role of Hercules when he first appears (including a bawdy song), and his

172

quotation of *Prometheus Unbound* at the end, to describe his
psychic vision, there is not much in the way of supernatural
shock for the audience. Flat mystification, seen from the outside, does not extend the boundaries of the play; on the contrary, it merely blocks the spectator's way to inserting his
own cosmic views. The Initiates, who know the way of
illumination, are gradually revealed, but their peculiar
ritual is bound to seem trivial; perhaps if it were in a really
unknown language, like the Sanscrit benediction at the end of
The Waste Land, the effect would be less disturbing. The Unknown Guest, who turns out to be the Unknown God of
modern secular society, the analyst, carries his burden of insight, leads the novices to make their choices, and sends them
on their several quests. One after another, the puppets admit
their private, vulnerable, secret life; in the end, all are saved
and the play is called a Comedy.

Although Eliot's model has not been directly copied, yet
the younger playwrights have worked upon principles which
he was the first to point out. They have used broken, repetitive, almost inarticulate speech, charged with the ominous
power that Eliot sought in his underlying rhythm, the "hidden" drumbeat. In particular, Harold Pinter's earlier comedy
seems to reflect Eliot indirectly. *The Birthday Party,* whose
very title is reminiscent, shows the unlucky hero being ab-
ducted, after a scene of mystification, by two diabolical
Guardians, to be treated at an unknown destination by a
sinister and powerful character, Monty (who may be either
military or sartorial or diabolic). The hero's inability to
communicate is crucial.

Eliot has made the point that a major writer deserves to be
read as a whole, and his last three plays offer a special kind
of interest for the light they throw on each other and on the
themes of his earlier work. The images of the various
characters in these plays have acquired an identity that per-
sists from one play to the next. For example, Gomez and

Mrs Cargill, the man of affairs and the prying chatterbox, seem dark refashionings of Alex and Julia from *The Cocktail Party*. Given the peculiar flatness of character and the brief, abrupt, nature of the action, it is particularly tempting to trace such patterns, derived presumably from Eliot's Internal Society.

The most persistent, I think, is the Imaginary Murder, which can be found also in the lyrics. In *Sweeney Agonistes* and *The Family Reunion*, it is murder of a woman, wife or mistress; in *The Elder Statesman*, of an old man. There are two real murders, which are both martyrdoms, Thomas's and Celia's; two offstage deaths of parents caused by the son's defection. External action culminates in Initiation; to the martyrs by death; to Harry, by the divine Agatha, as Athena; to Colby, by another incarnation of Athena, Mrs Guzzard; to Lord Claverton and his son, by his "ghosts". Ghosts and messengers from another world appear everywhere—Pereira on the telephone, an ominous threatening visitant; Thomas's tempters, from his past life; Harry's Furies; Celia, and by way of parody, Lavinia's aunt; Mrs Guzzard, with the news of Colby's dead father: Gomez and Maisie.

The sacrament of Initiation is penance or confession, which admits to the divine Adoption; with adoption a new identity is acquired and a new kind of suffering, which is purgatorial.

The symmetry of the plot is always so obvious that careful impressions of spontaneity have to be created by parties, reunions, conferences and sessions. Eliot has evolved for himself a sort of personal and idiosyncratic comedy of masks.

The taking up and dropping of rôles is of great importance. In the family patterns sisters are nearly always good, and brothers bad; women can be simply divided into goddesses and tarts, though they may assume disguises. Men take up public rôles and cower behind them; sons reject their parents at great cost, but if parents repudiate children, they are most

174

severely punished. Men in public life are usually better than artists, who tend to be mediocre. Relations with the dead are as important as relations with the living. There is no such things as accident; every act is part of a cosmic design.

The chief embarassment continues to be the supernatural. The cosmic jokes of *The Cocktail Party* and *The Confidential Clerk* are almost as unfortunate as Father Time; the religious games of the Libation and the descent of Mrs Guzzard show traces of misplaced facetiousness. The position is recovered in *The Elder Statesman*, where Mrs Piggott's stagey briskness conveys the insufferable patronage that is one of the humiliations reserved for decrepitude. The diabolic visitants here employ a crisp astringent accent, which seems to record that "the character and the author are speaking in unison". Even the music hall star, since she knows her man, can rise to epigram:

> *Your conscience was clear!*
> *I've very seldom heard people mention their consciences*
> *Except to observe that their conscience was clear. . . .*

The transparent valedictory quality of this play gives it a distinction which is not that of a work for the stage; all the characters are disembodied from the start. Monica, the only one to achieve a complete absolution of solitude, a complete capacity for love, finds that in her the "obstinate silent self" who is the unspeaking director of ordinary persons has been replaced by "a love that's lived in, but not looked at"; and "this love is silent".

Monica is the only character permitted to reach the emotional level of poetry; Mrs Cargill defines Lord Claverton as one of the Hollow Men ("Or did she say 'yellow'? I'm not quite sure.") He, who had become an idol to his daughter, is permitted at last to walk off the stage, after he has confessed himself and stripped off all his public rôles. The "broken-down actor" can then change into his own clothes and

speak as himself; Monica, too, released from the deep pos-
sessiveness that holds her back, can acknowledge her love.
"The dead has poured out a blessing on the living."

The force of this play is concentrated in the last act.
Claverton has to learn to live with his ghosts; "what he has to
pass beyond are not the faults but the savagely unforgiving
judge within him" (8).

Ordinary human love is the subject of initiation in this
play, and no extraordinary vocation or distant quest.

In all the plays, what has been sought is the release from
solitude, and from a sense of guilt that goes with it. For
Harry it is "the solitude in the crowded desert", when the
self is reduced to an eye, watching. For Celia, too, it is an
"awareness of solitude":

> a revelation about my relationship
> With everybody

Colby, who does not seem to need people, needs yet to know
his own identity—what he has it in him to be. Lord Claverton cannot bear company, but neither can he bear to be
alone; he is afraid of "the private self" that may be met in
solitude.

For the characters of the earlier plays, solitude is only to
be overcome at great cost, and in the pursuit of a difficult
quest. Edward and Lavinia come together in humility,
knowing that they do not understand each other, but what
they achieve is limited. They can

> choose, whether to put on proper costumes
> Or huddle quickly into new disguises;
> They have, for the first time, somewhere to start from.

The loneliness of the individual, which had been the theme
of much of Eliot's lyric, is in itself a paradoxical subject for
dramatic communication. The direct appeal to introspec-
tion is strong. Eliot's plays, even more thoroughly than

Yeats's, reveal a solitary man essaying a public art and for his purpose evolving a doctrine of masks. His plays consist of a single action, the distinctive act of choice; as such they offer a deep, incisive judgment with which the spectator may concur. It is as definition and judgment, rather than experience, that they are valid.

Eliot's dramas of responsibility and choice, based upon classical myth, have clearly much in common with the French theatre of Cocteau and Giraudoux, Sartre and Camus. The choice of the hero is an existentialist's choice. The drama is a drama of crisis. If it involves such depths of the self as can hardly be described, only recalled, it also involves the public world. Edward and Lavinia end by giving another Cocktail Party.

This attempt to retain an accepted structure goes with Eliot's experiments in verse, with his determined use of the traditional materials to hand. In the precarious and uncertain period during which he wrote, these explorations were needed. But for the last decade the theatre has been in revolt. Quite suddenly a breakthrough was achieved, and already Eliot's dramatic achievement has become a part of history.

(1) Anouilh's *Beckett or the Honour of God* (1959). Christopher Fry wrote *Curtmantle* in 1961. Osborne's play on Luther may owe something to this tradition. Eliot was the first to see the parallel which early conflicts of church and state might supply to the modern totalitarian conflict.

(2) "A Letter to Ezra Pound", *The Townsman*, I (July, 1938), *The Use of Poetry and the Use of Criticism* (1933), pp. 152–3.

(3) Hallie Flanagan, *Dynamo*, New York, 1943, p. 82. Quoted by Carol H. Smith, *T. S. Eliot's Dramatic Theory and Practice*, Oxford, 1963, pp. 62–3.

(4) D. W. Harding, "Progression of Theme in Eliot's Modern Plays" in *Experience into Words*, 1963.

(5) Her position as head of a woman's college points to her role as Athene, the presiding goddess in the *Oresteia's* final movement, on which story the play is based. Eliot also described Mrs Guzzard of *The Confidential Clerk* as "a cross between Pallas Athene and a suburban housewife".

(6) Jacques Guicharnaud, *Modern French Theatre*, Yale, 1961, p. 50.

(7) This is part of a review of Joyce's *Ulysses*, published in 1923. The comparison with Yeats's plays for dancers occurs in the course of the review.

(8) D. W. Harding, op. cit., p. 160. The connexion between the use of the Icon and the possession of a strong conscience (or superego) is very clear in Eliot's plays.

Chapter Ten

THE THEATRE TODAY

I THEATRE OF THE DREAM

THE drama has now become very openly and generally a "game" between the interior drama of the spectators and the action on the stage; the problem of communication is explicitly present. The very process by which drama works makes such exploration much easier in the theatre than in any other form of literature; for here the demonstration goes on within the statement, "as if a man should read the anatomy lecture upon himself". Theatre today represents an experimental exploration of the interior life, and its relation to the "public" world of objects and events. But it is not a return to the study of character.

Modern drama goes far beyond Hume in rejecting the notion of personal identity; it does not believe in the existence, the being, the integrity of the person. The most brilliant modern dramatists have denied even the approximate coherence of the selves which trade under a single name. They do not believe in dialogue (1).

The audience is no longer led through an imaginative series of events, as in the theatre of Sartre or Eliot. As abstract painting dispenses with representation, so the theatre of the Dream dispenses with events in favour of the interior or fantasy world. There is little possibility of ironic detachment or appeal to judgment in this post-dramatic theatre; its public affiliations are of a more direct and primitive kind. The audience is nearer to the Bardic circle of medieval times, who listened to tales of marvels and ordeals, etayns and dragons.

From the existentialist theatre, this new theatre has inherited extreme violence. Murder in the most lurid form is often at the centre of the play; it is no longer Eliot's imaginary murder or Sartre's political assassinations, the torture of the police barracks, the savagery of war. Instead, senseless crimes of bizarre violence, dismemberment, cannibalism and monstrous perversions or mutilations represent infantile fantasies or acts of insanity. Such a progression becomes inevitable once an orderly sequence of events is abandoned; for nonsense can hold the attention only when it is violent. Since the basis of these plays is the irrational, unless they were monstrously horrific or bizarre, they would not engage the audience.

In the "theatre of Dionysus", which by the mid-nineteen-fifties had succeeded to the existentialist theatre in France, there is then a surrender to the "Absurd", in Camus's sense of the word. *La raison* has abdicated. Tension has disappeared, but anguish is left. The theatre of the Dionysiac has abandoned controlling devices and discursive thought; in defining the "Absurd", Camus was certainly attempting to contain it, whereas Ionesco is content to exemplify. The difference is one between estrangement and Dionysiac abandon. Sartre and Camus retain a sense of orientation and purpose; Genet and Ionesco do not.

A theatre which does not reflect but merely presents is inevitably far less literary than the existentialist theatre, or the theatre of myth which preceded it. Language has sunk to a subsidiary place; Beckett has written a play without words. For the language of dream is often wordless, and consists of objects, and components of our primary thinking; contemporary theatre is concerned with objects, and when externally seen, people are also treated as objects.

The search for the self, for a measure of identity has likewise been abandoned as a direct quest. In Duerrenmatt's *The Physicists* it is a subject of horrific farce. The lack of communication is of course no new theme for drama. It may be recalled that in Chekhov characters do not hear or answer each other, but talk like Piaget's infants (2); in Andreyev a drama takes place inside one man's head; in Pirandello there is no coherence in the selves that trade under a single name. Strindberg, who saw all relationships in terms of conflict, has been retranslated by Adamov, whose plays, from *The Parody* onwards, have been frequently built on his personal dreams. *Professeur Taranne* is a transcription of a dream, in which the professor's identity is stolen from him; when he has to meet an accusation, his friends deny him, the world presents a face of complete indifference, and he ends by committing the act of indecent exposure of which he has been accused.

Elements of Strindberg, Pirandello, the literary influence of James Joyce and surrealism combine in these plays to create total disorder. Small, fragmented objects float through the air, as in the paintings of Salvator Dali—a flower pot, a pair of boots, a whistle. No human relationships are possible, since the characters are too fragmentary to form them.

These plays depict man at the extreme limit of his being, where, as Pinter has said, he "is pretty much alone". The action lies only in tension, waiting, menace, without the release of a deed—the special Ordeal of our time. Waiting for an undisclosed and uncertain catastrophe, the blind, paralytic, deaf characters within these plays evoke dark satellite selves within the audience; they appeal to and play upon those responses that are below the threshold of conscious apprehension.

Large gaps in the dialogue, deliberate verbal insufficiency indicate the area of conflict, where words must be groped for. It has already been pointed out in Chapter Two that anything which is articulated or suggested in verbal form is raised to a level where it may be ordered with a much more precise set of tools, since it becomes at least vaguely associated with a rational system. The theatre of dream appears infantile and regressive in so far as its dark rôles of fantasy and violence are freed from the logic of ordinary perception. They can the more readily accommodate the primitive aspects of spectators' responses; yet in so far as they are related to common images (and the figures of this world provide a very restricted group) they effect some measure of adjustment.

In the preface to *L'Aveu* (1938) Adamov said, "All that I know of myself is that I suffer. And if I suffer it is because at the origin of myself there is separation, mutilation."

The chief image of man is that of the beggar, the tramp, or madman; the chief action is murder. The assumption of a fantasy world of aggressive horror is behind such plays as Ionesco's *The Lesson* and Genet's *The Maids*. Perhaps such fantasies have been played out in private often enough, but more recently, whole nations have been forced to live inside the fantasy world of someone else, a Hitler or a Stalin. For five years the whole of Western Europe lived in Hitler's fantasy world; this is why, in Ionesco's play, the mad professor at the end of the lesson puts on an armband with the swastika upon it. The consequences of living in fantasy worlds even in art have been put by Owen Barfield:

> they are appreciated by those who are themselves willing to make a move towards seeing the world that way, and ultimately therefore, seeing that kind of world. We should remember this, when we see pictures of a dog with six legs emerging from a vegetable marrow, or a woman with a motor bicycle for her left breast (3).

As Blake more epigrammatically put it, "We become what we behold".

The drama cannot, from the nature of things, become an abstract art; it must be representational and therefore employ distorted forms. Nonsense and violence have to be represented by human actors.

In the Theatre of the Dream there is nothing to drink but raw alcohol, for civilization is repudiated and the stimulus must grow ever stronger; the images, being comparatively primitive and therefore undifferentiated, allow little variety of response. Raw alcohol is stimulating but it does not train the palate. In the "estranged" theatre of the existentialists, a sparse and austere intellectual control was exerted by those who had known extreme violence, and had learnt discipline and responsibility in secret; the Theatre of the Dream is a reaction from this.

It is said that any great crisis may take a decade before its effects are registered in imaginative literature (4). After a stunning blow, time is needed to regain memory and a sense of identity. The Second World War, which Camus and Sartre recorded directly, in about a decade took imaginative form. What emerged was not, as in 1929, the horrors of battle, or war atrocities; it was the image of the Delinquent, the young criminal, the child from the wild gangs that roamed Italy and Germany; all that is represented in the career of Genet, "martyr" of the new theatre. The image of a prison, directly presented by Sartre in *No Exit, Men without Shadows*, and by Camus in *The Just*, becomes something else in Genet's *Death Watch*; in Beckett, Pinter, Gelber, it is an interior prison.

The clown Marcel Moreau, in one of his mimes depicts an invisible cage from which he slowly, persistently works his way out, gains human stature—only to find that outside is another invisible cage, of exactly the same kind.

Theatre of the Dream might be dated from 1953, when Beckett's *Waiting for Godot* appeared in French, and established an image and a theme. Adamov's *Theatre* was published the same year, Sartre's study of Genet had appeared a year before. None of the writers were young men; in 1953, Beckett was 47, Adamov 45, Genet 44 and Ionesco 39; all had been writing for some years without attracting attention.

Gradually, Beckett, Ionesco and Genet have established a lead over the other dramatists of the Left Bank.

Theatre of the Dream takes its form from the play-within-the-play. In *Waiting for Godot*, the chief characters are two stage clowns, playing some embryonic versions of the traditional clowns' scenes—the attempt to hang himself, losing his trousers. The limitless waste place with its single blasted tree is reminiscent of *Purgatory*. The invisible Godot may be a reminiscence of Balzac's omnicompetent M. Godeau; or the deity in an affectionate French diminutive (as in "Charlot") or a contemptuous Irish one (as in "boyo"). The clowns can only play at living and their games are trivial, but their brotherly love, though it is never looked at, remains assured. The double being, Pozzo-Lucky, opens up a deeper level ("Pozzo" means a well); their symbiosis is defined only by commands and babblings; the one is savagely dominating, the other abject. The angelic boy messenger—or messengers —is alien and his very identity uncertain; but his appearance belies the disquieting contradictions of his messages.

Beckett allows the audience a wide variety of interpretations; interpretations of Lucky and Pozzo have ranged from Id and Super Ego, Proletariat and Capitalist to Beckett and Joyce. The same freedom is not offered in any of his subsequent plays. The heroes become more and more derelict, more and more isolated, more and more derived from Joyce; if Gerty MacDowell and the Dublin sandhills are taken away from *Happy Days*, there is little left but Ionesco's conception of a world of encroaching objects (5).

In the plays of Ionesco, objects are more important than human beings, and all objects become hostile. The little horns that proclaim man is turning into a rhinoceros, Roberte's three noses and her extraordinary fecundity in laying eggs show matter encroaching upon life. In *The Bald Prima Donna* it is language which is the obstacle—in *The Lesson* this is complicated by the orgiastic frenzy of the killer. The objects that take possession of the stage—the growing corpse of *Amedée*, the furniture of *The New Tenant*—induce a panic which may become a joke; "When I want to write a tragedy, I make them laugh, when I write a comedy I make them cry," as Ionesco observed. Submission to a killer's knife by Berenger and the Pupil, submission to the family formula by Jacques is balanced by Berenger's later refusal to become a rhinoceros, even when all the rest of the human race has become transformed. He stands alone, bravely (like Bottom the Weaver) in a world of terrifying encroachments.

In two plays only does a certain respect for life inform the action. In *The Chairs*, the two old people, inhabiting a middle European past, share the tenderness of Beckett's clowns. Although the Orator who comes to proclaim their wonderful System to the imaginary audience turns out to be dumb, his appearance does not invalidate the rest of the play. In *Exit the King*, Ionesco is refashioning the deposition of Richard II, as the earlier playwrights refashioned Greek myth. This play of Shakespeare has long fascinated him, and from it he draws the ceremonious grandeur of deposition and death. Love and Necessity, the rival Queens, carry out the ritual of despoiling, which would be thoroughly in the vein of some late medieval writer. In this play Ionesco has reached a firm simplicity of outline, and a completely traditional theme. But whenever he sets out to convey a social message, as in *Rhinoceros*, he becomes heavy, banal, almost his own Orator. It is rather ironic to note that his attempts to *épater le bourgeois* have had their effect chiefly upon the emancipated sections of that same class. His inflation satisfies the craving for violence that lies in an affluent society, but his dream world does not stand up to confrontation with the world of events. It happened that I had been reading Ionesco when news came to me that a brilliant young friend had been murdered. His voice in such circumstances sounds absurdly pompous and self-assertive; I turned to Chaucer's *Book of the Duchess*, to modesty and balance.

The life of Genet has been that of an outcast; a child thief and the subject of a life sentence, he has developed a whole inverted religion of death. In *The Maids*, the servants play at killing their mistress, and in *Death Watch* the highest admiration is reserved for the gratuitous killer, the negro Snowball. This diabolism, however thin beside that of great French poets, in *The Blacks* achieved a peculiar naïve success. The savagery of its opposition of black and white masks does not disguise the fact that Genet's characters, unlike those of Beckett and Ionesco, inhabit a recognizable social world, even if it is a highly simplified one. Genet's characters play games of murder which turn out to be earnest; the game he plays with his audience is dependent on a mixture of conjuring and shocks.

The comic-horrific mood of modern French drama is claimed to be "beyond tragedy"—it belongs to a world too disorganized for the affirmations that make part of the tragic paradox. Yet it is strongly reminiscent of the grotesque forms of later medieval art, which eventually, as in *Dr Faustus*, became assimilated into tragedy.

2 THE ENGLISH REVIVAL

The English dramatic revival dates from the mid fifties; *Look Back in Anger* appeared in 1956, and gave to an image already established its dramatic form. In America, the same year saw the Manifesto of the "Beat" poets—Ginsberg's *Howl*—and for a year or two all young writers of protest or revolt were classed together; Amis, Wain, Osborne and the unfortunate Colin Wilson in England; Kerouac, John Clellan Holmes, Ginsberg and Burroughs in America.

Osborne never again quite equalled the force of his figure of raw youth and suffering in Jimmy Porter. His self-pity, his weak impulse to destroy and hurt, complementary to his wife's impulse to throw herself away, are designed to be provocative but they have no particular target. Jimmy Porter is a child casualty of the war before the last—the Spanish Civil War. "There aren't any good brave causes any more" he says, in the year of Suez. His torrents of invective are set off by Cliff, the decent Horatio to this Hamlet of the Butler Education Act, and by the Colonel, an honest man of good will, whose Army memories are of military bands in India. The heaviest invective is reserved for the Church.

It is only too easy to pounce on the absurdities of inverted snobbery, by which child-bearing can raise a girl to working class status; or the shrill self-righteousness that appears most absurdly in the dedication of a later play, *The World of Paul Slickey*:

> To the liars and self deceivers; those who daily deal out treachery; to those who handle their professions as instruments of debasement; to those who for a salary cheque or less, successfully betray my country; and to those who will do it for no inducement at all. In this bleak time, when such men have never had it so good, this entertainment is dedicated to their boredom, their incomprehension, their distaste.

The bloodthirsty antics that follow are close in spirit to those of St Trinian's; Osborne's protest represents that of the welfare state's beneficiaries, who, like children in an orphanage, have been issued with everything free except a sense of purpose. It registers the devaluation that this general issue implies; along with the free milk and the third class arts degree come all the risks of national and international catastrophes.

Osborne has great natural theatrical ability; he might be called a theatrical journalist, for he can quickly turn the mood of the day to the forms of the stage, and put it over. *Under*

187

Plain Cover is a suburban version of Genet, as *Luther* relies on Brecht's *Galileo*. Basically, Osborne is the entertainer he depicted in *Epitaph for George Dillon*; he is prepared to turn out film scripts, vehicles for actors—he himself began as actor—but his attempts to be shocking, the main device of engaging his audience, are really very conventional; the targets when provided turn out to be of an old-fashioned kind that, with a slight change of idiom, might have appealed to Shaw.

Harold Pinter, who like Osborne is an actor, but unlike Osborne has remained within the theatre as director, works at a far deeper imaginative level. The trap, the cage (which Beckett also used in *Endgame* and *Happy Days*) is the setting for *The Room*, *The Dumb Waiter* and *The Birthday Party*, which all end on a punitive climax. Unfocused feelings of menace, the emergence of irrational guilt, fear and rage, mark a society in which the individual is unable to feel much true responsibility, and therefore little genuine guilt; these fears are the fruits of impotence and frustration.

Like the characters of the French theatre, Pinter's are blind, or paralysed, or inarticulate; the murderers, tramps and demented in Beckett and Pinter live in an ominous timeless moment. It is Faustus' last hour, but the clock never strikes, Godot does not come, we never learn who Monty is, or the the nature of the nameless organizations to which Ben and Gus, Goldberg and McCann are bound. Responsibility is reduced to anxiety, conscience to fear, lit by the weak blaze of undirected rage. The old beggar is given many names— Estragon, Davies, Barnabas; he may be a nameless dwarf.

The end remains "nobody's funeral, for there is no body to bury"; nor is there any possibility of tragic action. The characters float, like space travellers, in a sort of weightless imbalance. A void or gap, which begins at the level of the speech, surrounds each character. In Pinter, this does not merely signify a lack of context beyond and a pile of rubbish within, but a sinister degree of mystification. In *The Birth-day Party*, the two killers who penetrate to Stan's squalid sea-side refuge break him down by a preposterous series of questions and insults, after getting him to obey the first simple command—to sit down. The bullying begins "What were you doing yesterday?" and rises to "Do you recognize an external force?" "Is the number 846 necessary or possible?", shot through with such insults as "Why do you pick your nose?" "You verminate the sheet of your birth" and finally:

> You're dead. You can't live, you can't think, you can't love. You're dead. You're a plague gone bad. There's no juice in you. You're nothing but an odour!

When the old deck-chair man, Stan's landlord, makes a last protest as the victim leaves, spruce and speechless, he is threatened in turn:

GOLDBERG: Why don't you come with us, Mr Boles?
MCCANN: Yes, why don't you come with us?
GOLDBERG: Come with us to Monty. There's plenty of room in the car.
PATSY (broken): Stan, don't let them tell you what to do! (They exit.)

The Caretaker, Pinter's most successful play, presents much clearer rôles; the blustering cringing Davies, the cool tech-nician Mick, with his dreams of interior furnishing out of glossy magazines, the touching beauty of his brother's stumbling mind. The poetry is in the pity. Unreal bargains and threats and demands are necessary to the Caretaker's mar-ginal hold on existence:

DAVIES: I told him, I told him he . . . I said to him, you ain't heard the last of this, man; I said, don't you forget your brother. I told him you'd be coming along to sort him out. He don't know what he's started, doing that. Doing that to me. I said to him, I said to him, he'll be along, your brother'll be along, he's got sense, not like you. . . .

The threat is Mick's natural accent, usually in the form of a question:

DAVIES: I tell you, he should go back where he come from!
MICK: Come from?
DAVIES: Yes.
MICK: Where did he come from?
DAVIES: Well . . . he . . . he. . . .
MICK: You get a bit out of your depth, sometimes, don't you?

In *The Dwarfs* a triangular group sustain much more precarious identities; in *The Lover*, a single pair go through a whole collection of rôles which they play with each other as a sexual game. The affinities of this play with Genet's are obvious.

In the centre of Pinter's early plays there is often a slatternly, maternal figure who stands for animal comfort and protection. In *A Slight Ache*, the wife is an all-powerful purveyor of security, and when she removes her attention from Edward, he takes the place of the beggar at their gate. Pinter's imaginative strength lies in the precision and control of the rhythms that guide the inarticulate speech of his characters; the effect is a poetic one, though it is not in the traditional sense poetry. Timing and pace are all important in his dialogue; it is oral literature that demands to be spoken aloud.

The audience at Pinter's plays are involved in a exciting but mysterious action, and are left with an unresolved or unconcluded puzzle. The effect of John Arden's best known play, *Serjeant Musgrove's Dance*, is also bewildering and contradictory. The protest of the soldier is a hackneyed theme on the modern stage, but the formality of this play, which is set in a northern town towards the end of last century, enforces the effect of its queer, surrealist story. The serjeant himself is a stupid, narrow fanatic, driven to rebellion by what he has seen, but without the vision to do more than repeat the methods of his superiors, to opposite ends. As with Brecht's Mother Courage, his vitality and his crude determination attract, but he is not fully sympathetic, and the audience is not allowed to take sides either one way or the other with the mutinous soldiers in their anti-recruiting campaign, still less with the forces that oppose. The final result, as in Brecht, is sardonic but exhilarating.

Private fantasies have become a popular subject for quite conventional plays, such as *Billy Liar*, as well as nonsense plays, like those of N. F. Simpson. His *One Way Pendulum* is set partly in subtopia and partly at the Old Bailey, a model of which court has been built in the suburban sitting room.

Besides this imaginative drama, more naturalistic forms continue to protest against society in general, in the manner which Osborne initiated. Wesker, Delaney, Kops and Behan all present dominating mothers, lonely soldiers, and acts of sporadic violence. The all-powerful mother is a natural image in an age of general insecurity; the huge vague menace of international catastrophe is felt to be like a maternal threat to the infant—perhaps the most imaginative version of this fear is Ann Jellicoe's *The Sport of My Mad Mother*, in which a gang of delinquent juveniles is presided over by a Kali-figure—an evil mother-goddess. Against this may be set the Lonely Soldier, trapped in outposts, bullied by N.C.Os, led on farcical exercises; these two figures represent power and helplessness, security and insecurity, comfort and discomfort. Such are the general relationships that modern drama is concerned to explore, and they are represented in scenic terms by mother's domain, the family's living room, and by the prisoner's cage. For the conscript Soldier, far from being a symbol of conquest, is the modern version of the Prisoner.

3 THE AMERICAN DREAM

The imaginative theatre was created in America in the nineteen-twenties by Eugène O'Neill, who, if his unpublished plays are included, wrote upwards of sixty dramas. O'Neill was the most Protean dramatist of his time; he began with "slices of life"—his own life as a merchant seaman—then flirted with Expressionism in *The Emperor Jones*; while in *The Great God Brown*, he resorted to masks.

Plays of love–hate relationship, like *Welded*, reflect his close study of Strindberg; *The Hairy Ape* and plays about negroes rely on a heavy emotional assault, in the cause of social justice. In his plays of New England, *Desire under the Elms* and *Mourning Becomes Electra*, O'Neill evoked the legendary severity and starkness of that country in the heroic age of the Civil War. In the last play he boldly reworks classical myth against the New England background.

The vigour of O'Neill's writing lacks much qualification or fine shading; his technical virtuosity, his readiness to explore new forms, his natural gusto and violence give value to his massive output. In spite of many technical experiments, some of which were very curious, his style is basically naturalistic and he conceives character almost in the terms of a novelist.

After a twelve-year gap, O'Neill returned to the theatre with a gigantic drama, *The Iceman Cometh* (1946), a study of derelicts based on Gorki's *Lower Depths*. The last refuge where his outcasts nurse their dreams is

the No Chance Saloon. It's Bedrock Bar. The End of the Line Café. The Bottom of the Sea Rathskeller. Don't you notice the beautiful calm in the atmosphere? That's because it's the last harbour.

No more dirty hope (it is Hope's Saloon); only the complete freedom to dream about hope, in complete irresponsibility.

The eager peddler of ideals who comes to clean up the place finally breaks down and admits that he murdered his wife because of the incessant strain of meeting her goodness and forgiveness. It is the general atmosphere of decay, the posthumous calm of the whole group that makes the statement of this drama.

The same season that saw the production of *The Iceman Cometh* saw also Arthur Miller's *All My Sons* (1947), and two years later appeared *Death of a Salesman* (1949). Here men are crushed by the demands of a society based on conformity and success; the inexorable pressure of family and public expectations are exposed, but the form of the plays seems actually to endorse it; they are very conventionally given to social protest. The fantasies of O'Neill's plays about Cornelius Melody, "hero of Talavera", and the theatrical family of *The Long Day's Journey into Night* are grosser and more broken up; the dramas of Tennessee Williams, who can enlarge the unsuccess story with powerful traditions of the Deep South, remain likewise within a regular pattern.

The difficulties of the dramatist in America are of a practical kind; and plays tend to be more conventional than other forms of literature. The *avant-garde* began their work in the lyric and the novel. The first literature of protest came from the "Beat" poets of the Pacific coast, the most affluent region of the Affluent Society. Grant Avenue, Venice West and Big Sur produced the prophets of total revolt. The destitute waif of Kerouac's novel, *The Subterraneans*, an Odyssey of San Francisco's "junkies", visits her analyst regularly. The disaffiliated, who substitute for success a cult of unsuccess, have taken over their critical position from the French (though sometimes the whole thing is more reminiscent of *La Bohême* than modern Paris), their peculiar vocabulary from the dope rings, their alternation of bland coolness and destructive fervour from delinquency. The gross inflation of self-esteem, the smashing of generally accepted idols provide an initiation to anarchy. A non-disciplinary form of Zen Buddhism opens up metaphysical deeps for those who require them (6).

Ginsberg's Bardic poems, in a style which is Dionysiac, diffuse and highly repetitive, invite the audience to join in by a strong opening exclamation—*America!* begins, "America, I've given you all and now I'm nothing." This verse is made for performance. It carries apostrophe to the point where it begins to recall the ancient minstrels with their "Lo", even "Hwaet!" The jazz beat of repetitive, ecstatic assertion implies tolerance of the extreme forms of living—tolerance of psychosis, cultivation of trance and dream. Only a very affluent society indeed could admit this cult of unsuccess—which makes the language of its claims rather unconvincing. In the introduction to *Howl* William Carlos Williams wrote:

> Literally he has, from all the evidence, been through hell. . . . It is the belief in the art of poetry that has gone hand in hand with this man into his Golgotha, from that charnel house, similar in every way, to that of the Jews in the last war. But this is in our own country, our own fondest purlieus. . . . Hold back the edges of your gowns, Ladies, we are going through hell.

Jack Gelber's play *The Connexion* (1959) presents a group of drug addicts who are waiting for Cowboy, their negro "connexion" who brings the heroin. He appears at last, escorting a Salvation Army sister; she thinks the ritual for which the addicts depart one by one is some kind of baptism; at the end she admits to being frightened of dying and rolls up her sleeve to show the needle prick she received in hospital—the stigmata that they share.

At intervals the play is broken into by a set of jazz musicians who are also waiting for a "fix", and by the author, theatre director and a couple of camera men, who get involved with Cowboy and his trade. Play-within-the-play provides some

194

action to relieve the motionless tension of the waiting group, who are stupified yet consumed with craving. They are victims of society, whose sufferings have been laid on them by the "absurdity" of events; exposed to the indifferent eye of the camera, they are more deprived even than the inhabitants of Harry Hope's saloon, since they have lost their peace.

Gelber depends on provoking and involving the audience in a manner that should by now be familiar. The play is otherwise almost a documentary, the record of the addicts. It neither comments nor judges openly.

The unmasking of society by Edward Albee uses techniques which are close to those of Pinter. In *The Zoo Story* (1958), the bourgeois is induced to knife the outcast; in *The American Dream* (1960), all the clichés of cosy success are paraded—the lovely apartment, the desire for successful children; the theme of this play is repeated with much greater mastery in *Who's Afraid of Virginia Woolf?* (1962), where successive acts expose the depths of what at first seems a familiar story. A second-rate history professor, who has married the daughter of the college president, is humiliated by her in front of a couple of young newcomers to the campus. But the end of the all-night party shows the husband in command of his hysterical alcoholic wife; she has been rejected by her father and they have reassured each other with a secret game in which they invent a supremely successful young son. Martha, however, mentions this imaginary child to the others, and in revenge George announces that he has been killed in a motor smash. Anything which can be corroborated by an outsider must be true, according to the rules of the game, and the younger woman confirms that a telegram has arrived. The continuous exploration of hatred between husband and wife—it begins with a mock murder—recalls the furious games of the brothel in Genet's *The Balcony* rather than the fantasies of Pinter's *Lovers*; but Albee's scene remains

195

cosily domestic throughout. Circling round, probing each other's defences, changing the rules of the game, the two fighters take up one pretence after another, assume successively the rôles of bully, mentor, servant, lecher, indifferent scholar. George sits down to a book while his wife and her guest retire for an amorous session; Martha is coaxed into a naïvely idyllic account of herself as a mother so that George may smash the image. The relationship that finally emerges as basic in this strange marriage is one of complete inner destitution and yet of mutual trust—a symbiosis based on failure.

The usual setting for any American drama seems to remain that of the single family. Only a very fluid society would provide so many roles to discard; yet behind them all there remains a certain solid acceptance of the basic family group— parents and children, husbands and wives. Here is no "metaphysical questioning" of the selves that trade under a single name; nor is there any doubt that in spite of their many disguises, George and Martha can communicate with the very finest precision. The dream is one they can share. Yet the pattern is formal, with ironic echoes of older myths. George and Martha—these names evoke the memory of America's primal parents, George and Martha Washington; but as the ritual drinking proceeds, the rôles expand to those of Sky Father and Earth Mother. The Sky Father of the Greeks devoured his children; by claiming that he ate the telegram announcing his son's death, George meets Martha's challenge to produce evidence for his story; at the same time, the manner of this death is taken from the climax of George's first novel, which he had been forced to suppress (or devour) by his father-in-law. The murder of the dream child avenges the death of the brain child.

CONCLUSION

In spite of its present success and its undoubted power, I doubt if the Theatre of the dream is likely to persist. This is because it has put what was formerly the latent content of a play in the position of being its overt subject, which leaves as latent content a good deal that can not be transferred. Antitheatre could not exist if there were no theatre to protest against; in this way, it is parasitic. Ionesco's dependence on Shakespeare in *Exit the King* is a case in point. Theatre of the Dream has a profound although unacknowledged relation to the society from which the dream material of which it composed arises. Pinter and Arden are recognizably caricaturing British suburbia, Genet the French bourgeoisie, Albee the American dream. Their drama is loaded with fantasy and therefore unconsciously dependent on all the social considerations that are overtly excluded, at least by the first two. Except to an audience familiar with the society which is assumed as the background to these plays of nonsense and violence, they would be not only incomprehensible but devoid of emotional charge, words spoken without power to communicate. As the poets of the "Beat" generation are imaginable only in an affluent society (a society of poor whites or beggars would be quite unable to understand the cult of beggary), so this chaotic disorder is possible only in an environment which is, even if temporarily, secure.

If read or seen in the context of real violence, it seems improbable that the plays would work. On the one hand, these writers challenge reality too closely by their violence and on the other they are too sharply dissociated from it by the devices of "antitheatre". In so far as these plays are valid art, therefore, I would expect them to be ephemeral, perishable, like the Jacobean masque, African mud sculpture or Japanese flower arrangements. What is overtly presented in these plays is the waking dream, the unconscious aspects of daily

197

living, and therefore what is implicit will be increasingly inaccessible, that is, the ordinary habits and assumptions of society. This will reduce the emotional force of the plays.

While the attempt to portray man "at the extreme edge of his living" is a triumph of recovery and recall, it is also unlikely that any playwright would be able to sustain this type of creation for very long. Adamov and Ionesco have already abandoned the extremes of irrationality for a more rational framework. One man's capacity for invention in this area, being dependent on his own fantasy, is likely to be limited. There is a great deal more variety in the outer society than the inner society, and nonsense tends to become repetitive.

If the "games" of our new society themselves become the subject of this sort of play, it may, however, develop conventions of its own. The sexual games of *The Balcony*, *The Lover* and *Who's Afraid of Virginia Woolf?* belong to a recognizable if bizarre area of general experience.

The "Happenings" of the Parisian studios are an old form of game; the middle ages called them "Marvels" and expected them to precede a feast. The chief characteristic of a Marvel is that its appearance is unexpected, its form unceremonious, and that it erupts into some formal occasion with a pleasurable shock, not unmixed with the horrific. This revival of a "game" in the theatre confirms that the writer's rôle is declining in favour of the mime, and the more primitive languages which are put forward by the advocates of "total theatre". If so, the return to non-verbal forms of communication can only be regarded as part of the general concern for the inarticulate, the partially expressed, which the language of the modern theatre, based so largely on what is *not* said, might also be held to display.

There has been great theatre in the past where the poet's imaginative art played little or no part. It would be unwarrantable to confine great theatre to great poetic drama. However, it seems to me that poetic drama is not only permanent, it is also more deeply permeative of the audience's minds; and it is the tradition of this kind of drama that I have attempted to recall.

And if at the present moment imaginative drama seems largely concerned with the inarticulate, the irrational, the borderlands of consciousness, this indicates, I think, a process of reclamation. The functions of language are being extended and the inner self is becoming accessible, not in the limited vocabulary of scientific description, but in common words and for ordinary recognition. As in any living structure, the point of weakness and incompleteness is often the growing point, so it may be that the very limitations of dramatic speech at this time are an index not of failure but of achievement.

NOTES TO CHAPTER TEN

(1) Denis Donoghue, in *The Listener*, 12 July 1962.

(2) Jean Piaget, *Language and Thought of the Child* and *Judgment and Reasoning in the Child*, records the conversations of small children to prove that their "conversations" are largely not intended to communicate, but are a series of running comments, boasts, imaginary events.

(3) Owen Barfield, *Saving the Appearances*, 1957, p. 146. This account of the development of self-consciousness is pertinent to the whole question of dramatic response.

(4) Gertude Stein made this observation about the effects of the First World War, in a paper she once gave at Oxford.

(5) The connexions between Ionesco and Beckett are interesting; *Embers* (1959) seems to contain an indirect reflexion of *The Lesson*. The encroaching objects of Ionesco are at their most powerful in *The New Tenant*, and for Beckett in *Happy Days*, which carried further the imprisonment of Nagg and Nell in *Endgame*.

(6) So quickly does the American system digest revolt that a college teacher's book of extracts from Beat poetry appeared in 1961, complete with bibliography and a list of questions for classwork; these included:

An essay on Zen Buddhism, using an encyclopedia article and one book.

A definition of 'Bohemian' and a list of five books relevant to the problem of defining the term.

A comparison of the first part of Ginsberg's *Howl* with Whitman's *Respondez! respondez!*

INDEX

INDEX

Works are listed under authors' names. The most important entry is in bold type, and within this, individual works are not cited separately.

INDEX

*Printed in Great Britain
by Richard Clay (The Chaucer Press), Ltd.,
Bungay, Suffolk*

(7

CHRISTMAS AT THE CUPCAKE CAFÉ

CHRISTMAS AT THE CUPCAKE CAFÉ

Jenny Colgan

WINDSOR
PARAGON

First published 2012
by Sphere
This Large Print edition published 2013
by AudioGO Ltd
by arrangement with
Little, Brown Book Group

Hardcover   ISBN: 978 1 4713 4499 2
Softcover   ISBN: 978 1 4713 4500 5

Copyright © Jenny Colgan 2012
'Baking your first cupcake' piece, copyright ©
The Caked Crusader 2011

British Library Cataloguing in Publication Data available

Printed and bound in Great Britain by
TJ International Ltd

To anyone who still leaves a mince pie out for Santa (and a carrot for the reindeer).

A Word From Jenny

Hello! Even though *Meet Me at the Cupcake Café* was my thirteenth novel, I found it was a harder one to leave behind than some of the others. Maybe because it was the longest book I'd ever written, I really felt that I'd grown fond of the characters. I found myself going into Christmas mode after it came out—I love Christmas—and starting to make my Christmas cake and some mince pies and thinking—I know this makes me sound totally ridiculous, by the way—I wonder how Issy would do them? So I figured I'd better just write them down. Plus, if you enjoy the recipes, it's nice to have a few together just for this time of year. We've also reprinted (so when you see it, don't think SWIZZ!), the Caked Crusader's brilliant introductory guide to baking cupcakes from the last book, in case you're just starting out.

It's weird, because although I like reading sequels, I've never written one before. There are a couple of things I sometimes don't like about them, though, so I have tried to avoid paragraphs like: 'Jane walked into the room. "Hello, Jane!" said Peter. "How are you ever since you were abandoned in that shipwreck and had to take part in human cannibalism then a dolphin picked you up and gave you a ride home where you married your true love who turned out not to be your brother after all?" "Fine," said Jane.'

I have also tried to avoid the opposite, where you have to remember everything yourself (come on, we're all busy), like: '"This is worse than Bermuda," spat Jane, hurling her prosthetic leg across the room.'

So. Instead of having to shoehorn everyone in, here's a quick rundown (and also, welcome if you're new!).

Issy Randall lost her job in an estate agency, and threw her redundancy money into opening the Cupcake Café in Stoke Newington, which is a mixed, villagey area of London (her grandad, **Joe**, had been a baker in Manchester and she had always loved to bake and decided to turn it into a career).

She employed **Pearl McGregor**, who is bringing up **Louis** mostly single-handedly, although his dad, **Benjamin Kmbota**, swings by from time to time; and **Caroline**, who is in the process of divorcing her rich husband. And Issy broke up from her estate agent boyfriend Graeme, who was horrible, and has started dating **Austin Tyler**, the local bank manager, who is raising his brother, **Darny**, after their parents died. Austin was offered a new job overseas, but that got delayed—it's now over a year since the last book, if that makes sense. Well, anyway, Louis is four now, and in reception, Darny is eleven and in his first year of secondary school, and Issy's best friend **Helena**, a nurse, has had a baby with her doctor boyfriend **Ashok**.

So hopefully we're all up to speed!

With grateful thanks to BBC Books and Delia

Smith for allowing me to use her recipe. And another thanks to The Little Loaf for the recipe in Chapter fifteen. For more recipes go to http://thelittleloaf.wordpress.com

Let us know at www.facebook.com/jennycolganbooks or @jennycolgan on twitter if you try any of the recipes, and may I wish you the merriest of Christmases.

Very warmest wishes,

Jenny

Author's Note

All these recipes have been successfully tested by
me, many repeatedly and greedily. If you have time
to do the Christmas cake a good four weeks in
advance, it really helps!

NB: altitude cookies are very, very sweet indeed at
ground level.

Sitting under the mistletoe
(Pale-green, fairy mistletoe),
One last candle burning low,
All the sleepy dancers gone,
Just one candle burning on,
Shadows lurking everywhere:
Some one came, and kissed me there,

Walter de la Mare, 'Mistletoe'

Chapter One

Gingerbread

This is not for gingerbread men, which is more of a cookie recipe as it has to stay hard and crunchy. And it is not for gingerbread houses, unless you have endless time on your hands and (let's say it quietly) are a bit of a show-off who would rather their cakes were admired than devoured. No, this is old-fashioned soft, sticky gingerbread. It doesn't take long to make, but you'll be glad you did.

   NB Oil the container before you fill it with treacle. Otherwise you and your dishwasher are going to fall out really badly.

50g white sugar
50g brown sugar
120g butter
1 egg
180ml treacle
300g self-raising flour

1

1 tsp baking powder
1 tbsp powdered cinnamon
1 tbsp powdered ginger (or a little
  more if you like)
$\frac{1}{2}$ tsp ground cloves (I just threw in a
  'lucky' clove)
$\frac{1}{2}$ tsp salt
60ml hot water

Preheat oven to 175°C/gas mark 3.
Grease a loaf tin or square baking tin.
   Cream sugar and butter together
(you can do this entire thing in the
mixer), then add the egg and the
treacle.
   Mix the spices, baking powder,
flour and salt. Fold in to wet mixture.
Add the water, then pour into baking
tin and bake for 45 minutes.
   You can sprinkle icing sugar on
the top, or make an icing glaze, or
just slice it like it is—proper yummy,
sticky Christmas gingerbread. Serve
liberally to people you like.

*   *   *

The scent of cinnamon, orange peel and ginger
perfumed the air, with a strong undercurrent of
coffee. Outside the rain was battering against the
large windows of the eau-de-nil-painted exterior
of the Cupcake Café, tucked into a little grey stone
close next to an ironmonger's and a fenced-in
tree that looked chilled and bare in the freezing
afternoon.

Issy, putting out fresh chestnut-purée cupcakes decorated with tiny green leaves, took a deep breath of happiness and wondered if it was too early to start playing her *Silver Bells* CD. The weather had been uncharacteristically mild for much of November, but now winter was truly kicking in.

Customers arrived looking beaten and battered by the gale, disgorging umbrellas into the basket by the front door (so many got left behind, Pearl had commented that if they ran into financial difficulties, they could always start a second-hand umbrella business), then would pause halfway through wrestling with their jackets as the warm scent reached their nostrils. And Issy could see it come over them: their shoulders, hunched against the rain, would slowly start to unfurl in the cosy atmosphere of the café; their tense, anxious London faces would relax, and a smile would play around their lips as they approached the old-fashioned glass-fronted cabinet which hosted the daily array of goodies: cupcakes piled high with the best butter icing, changing every week depending on Issy's whim, or whether she'd just received a tip-off about the best vanilla pods, or a special on rose hips, or had the urge to go a bit mad with hazelnut meringue. The huge banging orange coffee machine (the colour clashed completely with the pale greens and greys and florals of the café itself, but they'd had to get it on the cheap, and it worked like an absolute charm) was fizzing in the background, the little fire was lit and cheery-looking (Issy would have preferred wood, but it was banned, so they had gas flames); there were newspapers on poles and books on the bookshelves; wifi, and cosy nooks and corners in which to hide oneself, as well as a long open table where mums could sit with their buggies and not block everybody else's way.

Smiling, people would take a while to make up their minds. Issy liked to go through the various things they had on offer, explain what went into each one: how she crushed the strawberries then left them in syrup for the little strawberry tarts they did in the summer; or the whole blueberries she liked to use in the middle of the summer fruits cupcake; or, as now, making customers smell her new batch of fresh cloves. Pearl simply let people choose. They had to make sure Caroline had had enough sleep or she tended to get slightly impatient and make remarks about the number of calories in each treat. This made Issy very cross.

'The "c" word is banned in this shop,' she'd said. 'People don't come in here looking to feel guilty. They're looking to relax, take a break, sit down with their friends. They don't need you snorting away about saturated fats.'

'I'm just trying to be helpful,' said Caroline. 'The economy is in trouble. I know how much tax avoidance my ex-husband does. There's not going to be the money to pay for cardiac units, that's all I'm saying.'

*   *   *

Pearl came up from the basement kitchen with a new tray of gingerbread men. The first had been snapped up in moments by the children coming in after school, delighted by their little bow ties and fearful expressions. She saw Issy standing

4

there looking a bit dreamy as she served up two cinnamon rolls with a steaming latte to a man with a large tummy, a red coat and a white beard.

'Don't even think it,' she said.

'Think what?' said Issy guiltily.

'About starting up the entire Christmas shebang. That isn't Santa.'

'I might be Santa,' protested the old man. 'How would you know?'

'Because this would be your busy season,' said Pearl, turning her focus back to her boss.

Issy's eyes strayed reluctantly to the glass jar of candy canes that had somehow found their way to being beside the cash till.

'It's *November*!' said Pearl. 'We've just finished selling our Guy Fawkes cupcakes, remember? And don't make me remind you how long it took me to get all that spiderwebbing down from Hallowe'en.'

'Maybe we should have left it up there for fake snow,' wondered Issy.

'No,' said Pearl. 'It's ridiculous. These holidays take up such a long time and everyone gets sick of them and they're totally over the top and inappropriate.'

'Bah humbug,' said Issy. But Pearl would not be jarred out of her bad mood.

'And it's a difficult year for everyone,' said Caroline. 'I've told Hermia the pony may have to go if her father doesn't buck up his ideas.'

'Go where?' said Pearl.

'To the happy hunting grounds,' said Caroline promptly. 'Meanwhile he's going to Antigua. Antigua! Did he ever take me to Antigua? No. You know what Antigua's like,' she said to Pearl.

'Why would I?' said Pearl.

5

Issy leapt into action. Caroline was a good, efficient worker, but she definitely lacked a sensitivity chip since her husband left her, and now he was trying to cut her maintenance. Caroline had never really known anything other than a very comfortable life. Working for a living and mixing with normal people she still tended to treat as something of a hilarious novelty.

'Well, it is nearly the last week of November,' said Issy. 'Everyone else is doing red cups and Santa hats and jingle bells. Frankly, London is not the place to be if you want to escape Christmas. It does the most wonderful Christmas in the world, and I want us to be a part of it.'

'Ho ho ho,' said the fat man with the white beard. They looked at him, then at each other.

'Stop it,' said Pearl.

'No, don't!' said Issy. She was so excited about Christmas this year; there was so much to celebrate. The Cupcake Café wasn't exactly going to make them rich, but they were keeping their heads above water. Her best friend Helena and her partner Ashok were going to join them with their bouncing (and she was very bouncing indeed) one-year-old Chadani Imelda, and Issy's mother might come too. The last time Issy had heard from Marian, in September, she'd been on a Greek island where she was currently making rather a good living teaching yoga to women who were pretending they were in *Mamma Mia*. Marian was a free spirit, which was supposed to make her romantic, but didn't always make her very reliable, mother-wise.

And then of course there was Austin, Issy's gorgeous, distracted boyfriend with the mismatched socks and the intense expression.

6

Austin was curly-haired and green-eyed, with horn-rimmed spectacles he tended to take on and off again a lot when he was thinking, and Issy's heart bounced in her chest every time she thought of him.

The door pinged again, unleashing another torrent of customers: young women in to have a sit-down after some early Christmas shopping. Their bags overflowed with tinsel and hand-made ornaments from the little independent shops on the pretty local high street, and their flushed cheeks and wet hair meant they brought the cold in with them in a riot of shaken anoraks and unwrapped scarves. Perhaps just a quick chain of fairy lights above the coffee machine, thought Issy. Christmas in London. Best in the world.

*   *   *

Christmas in New York, thought Austin, looking up and around him, dazzled. It really was something else; as dramatic as people said. Early snow was falling, and every shop window was lit up with over-the-top displays and luxury goods. Radio City Music Hall had a tree several storeys high and something called the Rockettes playing—he felt as though he had fallen through time and emerged in a movie from the fifties.

He adored it, he couldn't help it. New York made him feel like a child, even though he was supposed to be here very much as a grown-up. It was so exciting. His bank had sent him here on an 'ideas-sharing exercise' after the American office had apparently requested somebody calm and 'not a bullshit artist'. It appeared New York had tired of its crazed, risk-taking bankers and now desperately needed anyone with a reasonably level head to hold things together. Austin was disorganised and a little impatient with paperwork, but he rarely made loans that went bad, and was very good at spotting who was worth taking a risk on (Issy had most definitely been one of those) and who came in spouting pipe dreams and the latest management jargon. He was a safe pair of hands in a financial world that, increasingly, appeared to have gone completely crazy.

*   *   *

Issy had helped him pack, as otherwise he couldn't be trusted to keep hold of matching socks. She'd kissed him on the forehead.

'So you'll come back full of amazing New York know-how and everyone will have to bend and scrape before you and they'll make you king of the bank.'

'I don't think they have kings. Maybe they do. I haven't climbed up to those esteemed heights yet. I want a gigantic crown if they do.'

'And one of those pole things. For whacking.'

'Is that what those are for?'

'I don't know what the point is of being a king if you can't do whacking,' pointed out Issy.

'You're right about everything,' said Austin. 'I will also ask for fake ermine.'

She had gently pinged his nose.

'What a wise and gracious king you are. Look at me!' she said. 'I can't believe I'm balling socks for you. I feel like I'm sending you to boarding school.'

'Ooh, will you be my very firm matron?' said

Austin teasingly.

'Are you obsessed with whacking today, or what? Have I just had to wait all this time for your disgusting perv side to come out?'

'You started it, perv-o.'

*   *   *

She had driven him to the airport. 'And then you'll come back and it'll be nearly Christmas!'

Austin smiled. 'Do you really not mind doing it the same way as last year? Truly?'

'Truly?' said Issy. 'Truly, last year was the best Christmas I've ever had.'

*   *   *

And she had meant it. The first time Issy's mother had left—or the first time she remembered clearly, without it getting muddled in her head—she was seven, and writing out a letter to Santa, being very careful with the spelling.

Her mother had glanced over her shoulder. She was going through one of her rougher patches, which usually corresponded with a lot of complaining about the Manchester weather and the dark evenings and the sodding leaves. Joe, Issy's grampa, and Issy had exchanged looks as Marian paced up and down like a tiger in a cage, then stopped to look at Issy's list.

'My own piper? Why would you want a piper? We're not even Scottish.'

'No,' explained Issy patiently. Her mother had no interest in baking and relatively little in food, unless it was mung beans, or tofu—neither of which were readily available in 1980s Manchester—or some other fad she'd read about in one of the badly mimeographed pamphlets about alternative lifestyles she subscribed to.

'An icing piper. Gramps won't let me use his.'

'It's too big and you kept ripping it,' grumbled Grampa Joe, then winked at Issy to show that he wasn't really cross. 'That butterscotch icing you made was pretty good, though, my girl.'

Issy beamed with pride.

Marian glanced downwards. 'My Little Pony oven gloves ... My darling, I don't think they do those.'

'They should,' said Issy.

'Pink mixing bowl ... Girl's World ... what's that?'

'It's a doll's head. You put make-up on it.' Issy had heard the other girls in her class talking about it. That was what they were all getting. She hadn't heard anyone wanting a mixing bowl. So she'd decided she'd better join in with them.

'You put make-up on a plastic head?' said Marian, who had perfect skin and had never worn make-up in her life. 'For what, to make her look like a tramp?'

Issy shook her head, blushing a bit.

'Women don't need make-up,' said Marian. 'That's just to please men. You are perfectly fine as you are, do you understand? It's what's in here that counts.' She rapped Issy sharply on the temple. 'God, this bloody country. Imagine selling make-up to small children.'

'I don't see too much harm in it,' said Grampa Joe mildly. 'At least it's a toy. The others are all work tools.'

'Oh Lord, it's so much stuff,' said Marian. 'The commercialisation of Christmas is disgusting. It drives me mad. Everyone stuffing themselves and making themselves ill and trying to pretend they've got these perfect bloody nuclear families when everybody knows it's all a total lie and we're living under the Thatcher jackboot and the bomb could go off at any moment ...'

Grampa Joe shot her a warning look. Issy got very upset when Marian started talking about the bomb, or made noises about taking her to Greenham Common, or forced her to wear her CND badge to school. Then he went on calmly buttering the bread they were having with their turnip soup. (Marian insisted on very plain vegetables; Grampa Joe provided sugar and carbohydrates. It was a balanced diet, if you included both extremes.)

Issy didn't bother sending the letter after all, didn't even sign her name, which at that point had a big loveheart above the 'I' because all her friends did the same.

Two days later Marian had gone, leaving behind a letter.

Darling, I need some sun on my face or I can't breathe. I wanted to take you with me, but Joe says you need schooling more than you need sunshine. Given that I left school at fourteen I can't really see the point myself but best do what he says for now. Have a very lovely Christmas my darling and I will see you soon.

Next to the card was a brand-new, unwrapped, shiny-boxed Girl's World.

Issy became aware, later in life, that it must have

11

cost her mother something to buy it—something more than money—but it didn't feel like that at the time. Despite her grandad's efforts to interest her in it, she left the box unopened in the corner of her bedroom, unplayed with.

They both woke early on Christmas morning, Joe from long habit, Issy from excitement of a kind, although she was aware that other children she knew would be waking up with their mummies and probably their daddies too. It broke Joe's heart to see how she tried so hard not to mind, and as she unwrapped her new mixing bowl, and her lovely little whisk, all child-sized, and the tiniest patty pans he could find, and they made pancakes together before walking to church on Christmas morning, saying hello to their many friends and neighbours, it broke his heart all over again to see that some of her truly didn't mind; that even as a small child she was already used to being let down by the person who ought to be there for her the most.

She'd looked up at him, eyes shining as she flipped over a pancake.

'Merry Christmas, my darling,' he had said, kissing her gently on the head. 'Merry Christmas.'

*　　　*　　　*

Austin had his own reasons for hating Christmas. He'd never really bothered since that first one after their parents died, when a tiny Darny hadn't cried, hadn't yelled, hadn't moaned, had simply sat in silence, staring bewildered at the ridiculous number of presents from everyone he had ever met cluttering up the corner of the room. He hadn't wanted to open a single one. Austin hadn't blamed

12

him. In the end, they'd unplugged the phone from the wall (after Austin had turned down endless invites, everyone rang to coo pitying noises at them, and it was unbearable) and gone back to bed to watch *Transformers* on the computer whilst eating crisps. Somehow, watching ludicrous gigantic machine robots smashing lumps out of everything was as close to their mood as they could get, and they'd done something similar every year since.

But last year, he and Issy had been so new together, so wrapped up in one another, and it had been thrilling. He'd thought for ever about what presents to get her, and she had been utterly delighted: a going-out dress from her favourite little Stoke Newington vintage shop, and a fancy pair of shoes that she couldn't walk in. Oddly, it wasn't the fact that he'd bought them so much as what they represented: nights out, and fun, which could be hard to come by when you were working all hours.

'I thought you'd get me a pinny,' she'd said, trying on the blue dress, which made her eyes a vivid bluey-green and fitted her perfectly. 'Or a mixer or something. Everyone else always does! If I get one more cupcake jar, I'm going to start selling them on the side.'

And in the bottom of the bag, bought with his bonus—he had been the only person in the entire bank to get a bonus that year, he seemed to recall—a small, but immaculately cut, pair of diamond earrings. Her eyes had gone all big and wide and she had been completely unable to speak.

She had worn them every single day since.

And they had spoiled Darny horribly with games (Austin) and books (Issy), and watched telly in their

13

pyjamas and had smoked salmon and champagne at eleven, and the weather was too disgusting outside for anyone to mention a walk, and Issy had cooked an amazing lunch … Issy had … she had made it all right again. She had made it fun; made it their own Christmas. She hadn't tried to gussy it up, or push them into party games or silly hats or church or long walks, like the aunties would have done. She understood and respected entirely their right to watch *Transformers* all day in their pyjamas and had sweetly been there with them whilst they did so.

'I can't wait till Christmas,' said Austin at the airport. 'But I wish you were coming to New York.'

'One day,' said Issy, who longed to visit more than almost anything. 'Go and be clever and impressive and wow them all, and then come straight back home to us.'

*   *   *

And now here he was in the middle of Manhattan, Darny back in London with Issy. A year ago, the idea of leaving his headstrong, hyper-intelligent, super-cunning eleven-year-old brother with anyone other than an armed response team and a team of vets with tranquilliser guns would have seemed utter madness. Darny had bounced from school to school and run rings around his elder brother since their parents' death in an accident. Austin had immediately given up his college course and taken a banking job in order to keep a roof over their heads and prevent his brother being taken away by social services, or any number of well-meaning aunties. Darny had not repaid this by being particularly grateful.

14

Yet somehow, after being frankly abominable to all Austin's other girlfriends—girls who had cooed over Darny and gone all mushy-eyed at tall, handsome Austin, which made Darny want to vomit—he had really taken to Issy. Indeed, the fact that Darny had liked her so much had been one of the first things that had attracted Austin to her in the first place—along with her large eyes, generous mouth and easy laugh. Now when he thought of them together in the little house that had been, frankly, a bit of a midden when it was just the two boys together, but that under Issy's auspices had become cosy and welcoming, he got the sudden urge to ring her. He was on his way to a meeting and, not trusting himself to make his way around the subway system, had decided to walk. He checked his watch: 11 a.m. That meant 4 p.m. in London. Worth a shot.

'Hey.'

'Hey,' said Issy, struggling up the stairs with five kilo bags of finest milled Ethiopian blend. People were queuing for their afternoon pick-me-ups, or their post-school treats, but she was still delighted to hear from him. 'Wassup?'

'Are you stuffing plum pudding in your gob, by any chance?' teased Austin. 'You want to watch for wastage.'

'I am *not*,' said Issy, outraged, letting the coffee drop on the counter. 'Yes, hello, can I help you?'

'Do you have any Christmas cake?'

Issy arched her eyebrows at Pearl. 'Not yet,' she said. 'Apparently the little baby Jesus starts to cry if we start celebrating ten seconds before the official beginning of Advent.'

'That's a shame.'

15

'It *is*.'

'Don't disrespect my beliefs,' sniffed Pearl.

'So, anyway, here I am, hanging on the unbelievably expensive mobile phone from New York,' said Austin.

'Sorry, my love,' said Issy as the customer pointed, slightly disappointed, to a cherry-topped cupcake instead. They wouldn't be, Issy thought, when they got to the glacé cherries hidden inside. 'How is it?'

'Oh, it's amazing!' said Austin. 'I mean, just fantastic. The lights everywhere, and they're skating down at the Rockefeller Center ... that's this huge building with an ice rink outside it, and it's full of skaters and they're really good, and there's music playing around the street corners, and Central Park is all lit up with these amazing lights, and you can take a horse and cart ride through it with a blanket and mistletoe and ... well, it's just fantastic and amazing and wow.'

'Ooh, really. Bugger. Argh, I wish I was there so much. Stop having such a good time without me!'

A thought struck her.

'Is it super-brilliant? Are they all being dead nice to you? They're not going to offer you a job, are they?'

She felt a sudden clutch of panic in her breast that he was going to up sticks and move away, an idea that would make her best friend Helena stop breastfeeding for ninety seconds and snort that that was ridiculous, which was all right for Helena, who was sitting there with Ashok dashing about trying to fulfil her every need, constantly glowing with the joy of winning such a magnificent prize as H, with her wild long red hair and triumphant bosom; her

16

way of sweeping through life felling lesser mortals as she went. Issy just wasn't that confident a personality.

'Nah,' said Austin. 'They're just showing me round, swapping ideas, blah blah.'

He thought it was best not to mention to Issy that someone in the back office had asked him if it was true they were shutting half the London branches. There was more spurious gossip in banking than there was in the Cupcake Café Stitch 'n' Bitch, and that was saying something.

Issy tried to stop her mind from racing overtime. What if they wanted him? What would she do about the café? She couldn't leave it. She couldn't just leave and dump everything she'd worked so hard for. But if Austin was in love with amazing, fantastic New York, and she was in love with Austin ... well. It was a pickle. No. She was being stupid.

She thought back to their parting at the airport. It had been rather a thrill—Heathrow had no compunction about when Christmas started, and had decorated its huge high-ceilinged terminal with long hangings of purple tinsel and gigantic silver trees.

'This is like that film,' she'd whispered to Austin, who was looking rather dashing in a smart green scarf she'd bought him.

'It isn't,' Austin had said. 'All the children in that film are cute.'

Darny was standing to one side and scowling. His hair stuck up in exactly the same place as his big brother's.

'Don't do that thing. It's disgusting.'

'What, this thing?' Austin had said, nuzzling

Issy's neck till she squealed.

'Yes, that thing,' said Darny. 'It's having a terrible effect on my development. I am basically scarred for life.'

Austin glanced at Issy. 'Worth it, though,' he said, and she had grinned with happiness. She'd watched his tall figure disappear into the crowds at passport control, turning at the last moment to give them a cheery wave before he disappeared. She wanted to shout it to the world: 'That's my man! Over there! That's him! He's mine! He loves me and everything!'

She'd turned to Darny. 'Just you and me for a week,' she said cheerily. It had been unorthodox, falling in love with a man who already had someone else in his life, but she and Darny rubbed along pretty well.

'I'm very sad,' said Darny, not sounding or looking in the least perturbed. 'Can you buy me a muffin?'

'I am *far*,' said Issy, 'too fond of you to let you eat airport muffins. Come on home, I'll make you something.'

'Can I use the mixer?'

'Yes,' said Issy. Then, after a pause, 'You mean to make cakes, right?'

Darny tutted.

*   *   *

Somehow, Issy supposed, she'd expected Austin to be desperate to get back home. Anyway, in New York they were all shouty and fast-paced and yelled 'buy buy sell sell' all day, didn't they? That wouldn't suit Austin at all, she was sure of it. He was so

18

laid-back. He would check a few things out, meet some people, then they'd all go along as before. They'd threatened to send him overseas a year ago, but with the economy being how it was, it hadn't transpired, and that was just fine by Issy. So she was a little put out to hear him so cheerful.

'That sounds great,' she said, a tad unenthusiastically. 'London looks amazing too. Everywhere is all dolled up with lights and decorations and windows. Well, everywhere except for here.'

Pearl coughed, unabashed.

'Oh yeah,' said Austin. 'Oh, but wow, you have to see it. The skyscrapers put special red lights in their windows, and there's snow on the streets ... it's just magical.'

Issy picked up a stack of chocolate-stained plates and cups that had just landed on the countertop next to her.

'Magical,' she said.

*   *   *

Austin frowned after hanging up the phone. Issy hadn't been quite her normal ebullient self. He supposed it was hard when there was a time difference. Everyone was at sixes and sevens with one another. He'd have to call again later anyway, to talk to Darny, even though Darny was entering adolescence and was thus quite likely either to answer every question with a grunt or, even worse, an invisible shrug, or to start castigating his brother for being in the finance industry and therefore, as far as Darny was concerned, responsible for bringing about the end of the world, massive

19

apocalyptic catastrophe and general evil. Austin deeply regretted letting him read *The Hunger Games*.

Explaining that Austin's job was necessary to put the enormous amount of food Darny got through on the table and buy him new trainers for his gigantic boat-like feet didn't seem to cut him any slack whatsoever. Darny only muttered about how come Issy managed to buy Fairtrade coffee, which somehow made her one of the nice capitalists. Issy would wink at Austin and try and explain to Darny that she couldn't have opened the shop without Austin's help, whereupon Darny would end the conversation by tutting loudly and slouching off, his thin shoulders hunched. It was going to be, Austin sometimes thought, a tricky next seven years.

*   *   *

The café bell rang and in rushed Louis, Pearl's four-year-old, with his best friend, Big Louis. Big Louis was substantially smaller than Louis but had been at the school first, and there was another Louis, smaller than both of them, so that was how it worked. Louis had explained this in painstaking detail to Pearl one night, and it had taken him almost the entire length of the number 73 bus trip to do so.

Pearl had tried to move from her south London estate up to north London to be nearer work and Louis' excellent, difficult-to-get-into school (they'd used the café address, which she'd told her vicar made her feel uneasy and he had patted her hand and told her that the Lord worked in mysterious ways and he'd heard William Patten was a wonderful school), but it was difficult: her mother, who lived with them, hated leaving the house, and Ben, Louis' dad, didn't live with them but popped in regularly, and she really didn't want that to stop. So it made for a long commute, but she couldn't think of a better plan right at the moment.

Big Louis' mum picked the boys up every day from reception, a massive favour she was repaid for in coffee and buns. Pearl left the counter and crouched down so Louis could launch himself into her arms. It was bad for her knees, but, she told herself sternly, there would come a day, who knew when, when he would no longer want to rush to her and give her a huge cuddle and a big wet kiss on the cheek and tell her all about his day and generally behave as if she was the best person in the world; which to him, of course, she was. She never grew tired of it.

'Hello, sweetheart,' she said. Although Big Louis' mum probably felt exactly the same way about her own little boy (there was, in fact, no probably about it), Pearl could never help but feel that the curve of Louis' smooth cheeks, his long black eyelashes, his soft tight curls, his round little tummy and ready smile were possibly the most beautiful things she had ever seen. And even to disinterested observers, he was an appealing-looking child.

'MUMMY!' Louis had a worried look on his face as he pulled a picture out of his *Cars* rucksack. It was a large butterfly, roughly painted in splurges with silver paper on its head and wired antennae. 'BUFLYS ARE BUGS! DID YOU KNOW THAT?'

'Well, yes, I suppose I did know that. Don't you remember the book about how hungry he is?'

21

'They are caterpillars. Caterpillars are bugs with legs but they are also butterflies. Like toast,' he added reflectively.

'What do you mean, like toast?' said Pearl.

'There is bread, and there is toast. But one is bread and then it is toast and is different. I hungry,' said Louis.

'I HUNGRY,' barked Big Louis, suddenly anxious in case he was missing out.

'Here you go, you two,' said Issy, appearing with some toasted fruit bread and two cups of milk. Being let loose in a cake shop every day wasn't very good for four-year-olds, so they all made sure they kept an eye on the boys, particularly Louis, whose body shape echoed his mother's, and who liked nothing better than settling down for a chat about diggers with a customer—anyone would do, although he particularly liked Doti, the postman—with a large wodge of icing in his chubby fingers.

'Mamma?' said Louis. 'Is it Christmas?'

'Not yet,' said Pearl. 'When it's Advent, and we start opening all the little doors up till Jesus comes. That's Christmas.'

'Everyone at school says it's Christmas. We have a big tree in our classroom and Miss Sangita says that it's a good time for everyone to slebate.'

'Slebate?'

'Yes.'

'Well, it *is* a good time to celebrate. In its own time. This is still November. Fireworks and Hallowe'en just finished, remember? Scary costumes and loud noises?'

Louis looked down at the floor and bit his lip. 'I'm not afraid of fireworks,' he said quietly. He had been, undeniably, very very scared of the fireworks.

22

And although he had enjoyed getting the sweeties at Hallowe'en, he had found running into ghosts and ghouls—particularly the big boys off the estate in their Scream masks, charging about shouting on their bicycles—rather off-putting too, if they were being honest about it. Miss Sangita had told Pearl that Louis was a little sensitive, and Pearl had sniffed and said that what she meant was not a total lout like the rest of the children, and Miss Sangita had smiled nicely and said she didn't think that attitude was really necessary, and Pearl had felt cowed again, and remembered that this was a nice school and she had to stop panicking about her boy.

She thought about it too as they rode the bus home together, Louis helpfully pointing out every Christmas tree and decoration in every house they passed—and there were many. When they reached the centre of town to change buses, his eyes grew huge and round as he looked at the window displays of the famous department stores: Hamleys, with its feast of magical moving animals in a woodland scene; the great cascade of lights down Regent Street; John Lewis, its windows seeming to brim with every form of bounty imaginable. The pavements were full of excited shoppers looking for bargains and soaking up the atmosphere, and already pubs and restaurants, festooned with gaudy garlands and turkey menus, were packed full of revellers. Pearl sighed. She couldn't deny it. Christmas was definitely coming.

*　　　*　　　*

It was just, it had been such a hard year. Not for her—the shop was doing well, and Issy had been

23

more than kind, making her a manager, paying her as much as she was able, as well as being flexible for Louis' sake. Pearl had even, for the first time in her life, been able to put a bit by; to begin, possibly, to think about a future; moving closer to the shop and Louis' school and away from the estate. Not that it was a bad estate, she thought loyally. Not the worst, by any means. But to move into a little place that wasn't exactly like everyone else's, where she could decorate how she wanted and have an extra room for her mum. That would be nice. That would be very nice indeed. And it had looked, briefly, like it might be possible.

That was before the economic downturn had taken its terrible toll on Benjamin.

If Pearl had had a Facebook page—which she didn't, as she didn't have an internet connection—her heart status with Benjamin would have been 'it's complicated'. Ben was absolutely gorgeous, and they'd dated and she'd got pregnant, and whilst obviously she wouldn't swap Louis for the world—he was the best thing that had ever happened to her—nonetheless, Ben had never lived with them and came and went in their lives far more than she would have liked. The problem was that Louis absolutely worshipped him; thought his tall, handsome, muscular dad was a superhero, swooping in on the family from time to time in between top-secret missions. And Pearl couldn't bear to burst his happy bubble; his cries of joy when Ben came round, and it felt, for a while, like they were a proper family. So she was stuck. She couldn't move on. It wasn't fair to Louis. Things had been starting to get better for Ben too, the work coming in more steadily ... until the last six

24

months.

The building site jobs had dried up, just like that. He'd got some work up at the Olympics park, but it felt like every contractor in the whole of Europe had bowled up there, and the competition was fierce. Elsewhere, there wasn't much either. People were putting off moving or building extensions or finishing renovations or expanding their premises till they found out how the cards would fall; whether they would lose their jobs, or have their hours cut or see their incomes fall; whether their pensions would flatline and their savings would become worthless against inflation. Pearl struggled with the one bedroom; sometimes, she thought, looking out at the rain, she had no idea how people managed to heat larger properties at all. Keeping her power key charged up was a job in itself.

It wasn't Benjamin's fault, it really wasn't. He was looking for work, trying everything, but there just wasn't anything for him, and he'd had a few problems with the benefit office in the past, so he got the absolute bare legal minimum.

She knew him so well. He was easily led, but he was a proud man. A hard worker when he had work, but if he didn't ... Well. He had a lot of friends who dabbled in things she didn't want Louis' daddy anywhere near.

So she'd been helping him out, here and there, and more and more, and she didn't know where it would end. Benjamin hated taking the money too, hated having to ask and beg like a dog from a woman. Which meant that their rare nights out, the odd meal, the odd staying over—it killed her to admit it, but he was still the best-looking man she had ever seen in her life—became less frequent. It

25

was no fun taking your woman out to dinner when she had to pick up the tab.

Pearl was really feeling the pinch. But oh, Benjamin was so good with their boy. He played with Louis for hours, was genuinely impressed by his daubings and scrawlings from school; would kick a ball round the waste ground or discuss diggers and cranes till the cows came home. Pearl would starve before she deprived her son of that.

It wasn't going to come to that. But Christmas was going to be tight, that was all, and she hated being reminded of that fact in every decorated window and expectant-looking face.

Chapter Two

Christmas Cherry Chocolate Biscuit Slice

This is a no-cook cake that is utterly delicious. You can add a slug of rum if you want to be extra seasonal, but bear in mind it won't burn off in the cooking. ☺

275g butter (I used about 200g
  unsalted)
150ml golden syrup (2 very generous
  tablespoons)
225g good-quality dark chocolate
200g digestive biscuits (roughly
  crushed)
200g Rich Tea biscuits (roughly
  crushed)
125g mixed nuts (walnuts, brazils,
  almonds) (optional)
125g glacé cherries
1 packet of Maltesers (plus if you
  have any other sweeties—Rolos,
  Munchies, etc.—lying around,

they can go in too)

Line a 15cm round cake tin or a
2lb loaf tin with a double layer of
greaseproof paper. (I used a silicone
loaf mould. There is no need to line
the silicone mould.)
   Melt the butter, syrup and chocolate
in a pan over a low heat. This took
some time as I used the lowest
setting on the hob. Make sure that
the pot is large enough to take all the
crushed biscuits, etc. Stir to mix the
ingredients thoroughly.
   Add the biscuits, Maltesers and fruit
and nuts (if used). Stir well. Make sure
to break the biscuits relatively small
as they will not fit in the mould/tin
otherwise.
   Transfer to prepared tin. Level it on
top and press down well to avoid air
gaps. Allow to get cold and hard. It
needs about two hours in the fridge
or about 45 minutes in the freezer.
The longer the better. It tasted much
better on Saturday. Wrap completely
in greaseproof paper and store in a
fridge.
   Decorate with holly. Do NOT count
calories. This is a time of joy.

                *   *   *

Helena picked up Chadani Imelda and gave a
grim smile of satisfaction that denoted the size

of her achievement. Even though Chadani had hollered unwaveringly, she was now dressed in frilly knickers, a frilled shirt, a ballet skirt and a pompom coat, plus lacy tights with small pompoms at the back, baby-pink Ugg boots with tiny stars and a pink pompom hat with long dangling ribbons. Her fierce red hair clashed outlandishly with all the pink, but Chadani was a girl, Helena thought determinedly, and therefore needed to be identified as such.

'Don't you look pretty?' she cooed.

Chadani gave her mother a ferocious look and tugged mutinously at the hat. To no avail; Helena had already tied it up for safe keeping. A one-year-old's hands were no match for the strapping power of a registered accident and emergency nurse. And she was still a nurse, she kept telling everyone. She was going back to it. Just as soon as she found the right person or nursery to take care of Chadani Imelda. So far, there had not been one to meet her standards.

Issy at first had thought Helena must be joking about being overprotective. Helena herself was so strong and confident and independent; how could it even be possible? And it might have taken Helena herself by surprise. Nonetheless, from the first squalling breath Chadani Imelda had taken, sunk deep into Helena's remarkable bosom, after a quick and utterly straightforward labour Issy felt would do nothing to help Helena's empathetic skills with the sick—she had marched into hospital under her own steam and popped the baby out in under ninety minutes without even an aspirin—Helena's entire life had become the Chadani Project.

Ashok's adoring family, once they'd got over

the shock of him fathering a child out of wedlock to a rather staggering and distinctly larger-than-life redhead, did nothing to deflect Helena from Operation C. Ashok was the youngest of six, four of them female, all of them noisy (one of the reasons why he had been totally unworried about taking on a strong woman), and all of them very keen to kick in with help, advice and gifts for the new baby, their own children grown up.

So Chadani never left the house without a couple of extra layers just in case, or an extra feeding bottle here and there so she didn't go hungry; every toy in the catalogue now subsumed Issy's old flat, which Helena and Ashok had bought. Once small and cosy, it was now small, cosy and completely hidden under vast amounts of plastic, drying babygros and a large sign on the wall that said 'Princess'.

Issy had narrowed her eyes at that.

'She'll have high self-esteem,' Helena had insisted. 'I don't want anyone pushing her around.'

'No one pushes you around,' pointed out Issy. 'I'm sure she'll inherit that from you anyway.'

'You can't be too sure,' said Helena, leaving Issy to clear a space on her own old red velvet sofa, now piled high with very small designer knitwear.

'Helena, this says "dry clean only",' said Issy sternly. 'Now, I may not be a parent, but ... '

Helena looked slightly shamefaced. 'I know, I know. But she does look so amazing in it. I'm surprised no one has stolen her, I really am.'

Issy made a nodding face, like she often did around Chadani Imelda. It wasn't that she wasn't a lovely baby—she was, of course; the daughter of her dearest friend. But she was very noisy and squally and demanding, and Issy did sometimes feel

30

that she would be more comfortable out of all those clothes; and perhaps if she didn't have Helena, Ashok and at least four other relatives jumping to attention every time she squeaked, she might do a little better.

'So,' said Helena, importantly. 'Let me know what you think. Here are the outfits I was planning for Christmas Day. Look at this little reindeer hat, isn't it *darling*? To die for.'

Chadani picked up the corner of the reindeer antlers and started biting it, angrily.

'Then I thought red velvet for church.'

'Since when do you go to church?'

'I think everyone at church might like to see a lovely baby at Christmas time. That's the whole point,' said Helena.

'Well, yes, the baby Jesus, symbol of light and hope for the world. Not just a random baby ...' Helena's face stiffened. 'Even though she's obviously a very, very special baby. And she's a year old now anyway. Does she still qualify as a baby?'

Chadani had cruised over to the television and was pulling Baby Einstein DVDs out of the rack and throwing them on the floor. Helena was completely ignoring it.

'Of course!'

'And Ashok's a Sikh,' Issy added, unnecessarily.

'We'll go to temple for Diwali as well,' said Helena. 'Now for that you need to *really* dress up.'

Issy smiled. She wanted to open a bottle of wine, but remembered that she couldn't because Helena wasn't drinking because she was still breastfeeding on demand, and at this rate looked likely to be doing so till about 2025.

'So anyway,' said Helena, 'Chadani is ...' and

she launched into a list of Chadani Imelda's latest accomplishments, which may or may not have included 'scatter all the Baby Einstein DVDs'.

Suddenly Issy had slightly lost the urge to confide in her friend. Normally they could chat about anything, but since Chadani had arrived, Issy had felt them drifting apart in a way she couldn't quite put her finger on. Helena had met a load of new, pushy mums through North London Mummy Connexshins, which she presided over by virtue of having the most natural birth and breastfeeding the longest, and their endless, stupefying discussions about baby-led weaning and sleeping through the night left Issy completely cold. Even when she tried to join in by bringing up Darny's latest misadventures (all the children had to be either perfect or awful, it seemed, there was no middle way; likewise, when you'd given birth you had to have either hardly noticed, or nearly died and required fifteen pints of emergency blood transfusions), Helena had looked at her patronisingly and said it would be different when she had her own. Starting a conversation about missing her boyfriend seemed a bit . . .

'I miss Austin,' said Issy, suddenly. She was going to at least give it a shot. 'In New York. I wish he was hating it.'

Helena looked at her. 'Ashok's on call,' she said. 'I've been getting up four times every single night, then he comes in and wants me to keep the baby quiet all day. In this tiny, crappy apartment! I ask you.'

Issy loved the flat, and still felt very proprietorial about it.

'Oh dear,' she said tentatively, then ventured,

32

feeling cut off from her own feeble complaint, 'Should Chadani still be waking up at night?'

'Yes,' snapped Helena. 'She's very sensitive.'

As if in answer to this, Chadani toddled over to the large pile of freshly washed clothes on the sofa and upturned her beaker of supplementary milk all over them.

'No!' howled Helena. 'NO! Don't! I just ... Chadani! That is behaviour of which I am critical! Not that I am criticising you as a person and as a goddess. It is because this behaviour at this time ...'

Chadani stared at Helena, continuing to hold the beaker upside down, as if conducting an experiment.

Issy decided not to press the boyfriend matter any further.

'I'll just head out ...' she said.

As she went, she could hear Helena saying, 'Now, I would be very happy if you would give me that cup now, Chadani Imelda. Very happy. Make Mummy happy now and give me the cup. Give me the cup now, Chadani. Give Mummy the cup.'

Chapter Three

Whatever Pearl thought, Issy decided when she got home, it was time to start the Christmas cakes. She gathered together the huge bags of sultanas, raisins and currants—wondering, as she passingly did once a year, and once a year only, what the difference between them was again—along with the glacé cherries and candied peel. If she didn't start them now, she wouldn't have enough time to feed them and they wouldn't be good and strong and delicious in time.

Darny thumped through to the kitchen as soon as he got in from homework club. As he marched through the door, Issy jumped; he sounded like a grown man already, even though he was only eleven. And of course he'd had his own set of keys since he was six years old.

'Hey,' he shouted. Normally he swung straight past her up the stairs to his bedroom to play on his Xbox—unless, of course, she was making something good to eat.

The house Austin and Darny had inherited from their parents was a rather pretty red-brick terrace, with a large knocked-through downstairs sitting room and a back kitchen, and upstairs three little bedrooms. There was a patch of garden out the back which was in no way large enough to play football, rugby, handball, volleyball or Robin Hood, not that it had stopped the boys trying over the years. Five years of just two chaps there, one small and one overworked and dreamy, had left the place in a very unpleasant state, even though they had a despondent cleaner. Issy was, gradually, trying to do up bits of it: a coat of paint here; a new flagstone floor there. The bones of the house were reasserting themselves, though Issy had kept intact a little square of the skirting board that had a long procession of racing cars drawn on in indelible ink in the hand of a five-year-old.

'Why didn't you stop him?' she'd asked Austin.

'Well, I rather liked it,' he'd said mildly. 'He's good at drawing; look, he's got all the wheels in the right positions and everything.'

Issy looked and decided it was sweet. She cleaned up the rest of the paintwork and kept the cars. The rest she was trying to make over.

She couldn't help it. She never felt she needed to see a therapist to confirm that it was because of her insecure childhood—her mother a restless spirit; her father a traveller she'd never known. The only constant in her life had been her beloved Grampa Joe, whose bakery had always been a warm and cosy haven for her. Ever since then, she'd tried to reproduce that cosy, comfortable feeling wherever she went.

Pre-Austin, Helena had said once that she was a people-pleaser. Issy had asked what was wrong with that exactly, and Helena had pointed out that all her boyfriends had been really horrible users. But Issy could never march through life like Helena

35

did, doing what she felt like doing and damning the consequences. Meeting Austin, who liked the fact that she liked to please him ... well, the boys had complained at first about the house—who really needed curtains anyway, Darny had said; they were just bourgeois (a word he clearly had no concept of the meaning of), about shame and a fake privacy the state didn't even let you have—but Issy had persisted, and gradually, as the windows were cleaned, and a new kitchen table brought in (they let Darny keep the old one, covered in ink spills and old glue and that part where they'd played the knife-throwing game that time, as a desk upstairs) with a comfortable wall bench covered in cushions, and all Issy's kitchen appliances, which she bought like other women bought shoes; lamps in the corner of the room rather than bare bulbs (Austin had complained he couldn't see a thing until Issy had told him it was romantic and would make romantic things happen, which changed his outlook somewhat), and even cushions (which were constantly being secreted upstairs for Darny to use as target practice), the house was beginning to look really rather cosy. More like a home, Issy had pointed out, like normal people had, and not a holding pen for delinquent zebras.

Austin might have grumbled cheerfully—because, on the whole, it was expected of him, and also because it was exactly what all his interfering aunts had been saying for years, that the place needed a woman's touch. In the past there had been plenty of women who'd promised to supply that and tried to inveigle their way in. Austin and Darny had even had a name for them: the Awws, because of the concerned expression they got on

36

their faces and the way they said 'awww' when they looked at Darny like he was an abandoned puppy. Austin hated it when someone said 'awww'. It meant that Darny was about to do or say something unspeakable.

But somehow with Issy it was different. Issy didn't say 'awww'. She listened. And she made them both feel that coming home to somewhere cosy and warm every evening might actually be rather pleasant, even if it did require them to start making their own beds and remembering to put the rubbish out and eating with cutlery and having fruit and stuff. Yes, there were more soft furnishings and bits and bobs about, but that was just the price you paid, Austin reckoned, for all the lovely stuff too; for something that felt not a million miles away from happiness.

*   *   *

Darny took off his winter jacket and rucksack, scattering school books, hats, scarves, Moshi Monster cards and random small pieces of plastic everywhere.

'Hello Darny,' said Issy. He padded through into the kitchen.

'What are you doing?' he said. 'I'm starving.'

'You're always starving,' said Issy. 'You can't eat this, though.'

He gazed into the huge pans. 'What are you doing?'

'Oh, this is the easy bit. Just marinating the fruit.'

Darny took a sniff of the bottle she was applying liberally to the mix. 'Phew. What's that?'

'It's brandy.'

'Can I—'

37

'Nope,' said Issy without hesitating.

'Come on, just a taste. In France they let the kids drink wine with their meals.'

'And they eat horses and have mistresses. When we decide to be French, Darny, I'll be sure to let you know.'

Darny scowled. 'What is there to eat, then?'

'Have a couple of bananas, and I made you some fruit toast,' said Issy. 'And there's a lasagne in the oven.'

'Fruit toast? I can't believe you run a cake shop and all I get is fruit toast.'

'Well, learn to bake your own cakes then.'

'Yeah, not likely,' said Darny. 'That's for girls.'

'Scared?' said Issy.

'No!'

'My grandfather baked hundreds of cream horns a day till he was seventy years old.'

Darny snorted.

'What's funny?'

'Cream horns. It's rude.'

Issy thought about it for a while. 'It is a bit rude,' she allowed eventually. 'Men make wonderful bakers, though. Or they can do.'

Darny had already scarfed the fruit toast and was peeling a banana. He glanced at the phone.

'I'm expecting him,' said Issy. 'Any minute.'

'I don't care,' said Darny instantly. 'He's probably in stupid meetings anyway.'

He looked out of the back French windows that led on to the dark patio. He could see their reflections in the glass. The house looked cosy and warm. He wouldn't admit it, but he did like having Issy there. It was nice. Not that she was ... she wasn't his mum or anything like that. That would totally NEVER happen. But compared with the drippy women Austin had brought home over the years, she was probably all right he supposed. And now she was here, well, it was almost like they had a nice house like his friends did, and everything was kind of all right when it really hadn't been all right for a really long time. So why was his stupid brother in stupid America?

'You know the schools in America, right?' he asked, faux-casually, trying to steal some raisins from the mixing bowl. Issy smacked his hand lightly with the wooden spoon.

'Yes,' she said. Issy had, in fact, never been to America, which made it a bit difficult to calm Darny's fears.

'Do they have ... do they have a LOT of guns at school and things?' he asked, finally.

'No,' said Issy, wishing she could be more sure. 'I'm sure they don't. Absolutely not.'

Darny's mouth curled in contempt. 'And do they sing all the time?'

'I don't know,' said Issy. 'I just don't know.'

The phone rang.

*   *   *

'Sorry,' said Austin. 'The meeting ran on. They wanted me to meet a few more people and pop into their board meeting ...'

'Wow,' said Issy. 'They're obviously impressed by you.'

'I don't know about that,' said Austin. 'I think they just like hearing me talk.'

'Don't be modest,' said Issy, cheerful, but with a slight wobble in her voice. 'Of course they love you.

39

Why wouldn't they love you? You're amazing.'

Austin heard the emotional tone in her voice and cursed internally. He hadn't wanted to think, hadn't wanted to even consider, what it meant if he was offered a job here—and it seemed to be shaping up to be more than that. Not just a job; a real career; an amazing opportunity. Given the state of banking at the moment, he was lucky to have a job at all, never mind a career that was going places. And the idea of making some real money for once, instead of just bobbing along ... Issy had the café, of course, but it was hardly a big earner, and it would be nice for the two of them to do some lovely things ... take a nice holiday ... maybe even ... well. He didn't want to think about the next step. That was a bit too far in the future. But still. It would make sense, he told himself firmly. For whatever lay ahead. It would make sense to have a nest egg, to have a cushion beneath them. To be secure. Together.

'Well, they have been very nice ...' he conceded. 'How's Darny doing at school?'

Issy didn't want to say that she'd seen him in the playground in the company of a teacher being marched quickly to the gate. She tried not to get too involved in the school, even though she worried about Darny, the smallest kid in the year, and the only one without even one parent, almost as much as Austin did.

'Hmm,' she said.

'What are you doing?'

'Making Christmas cake. It smells amazing!'

'It smells foul,' said Darny down the speaker phone. 'And she won't let me taste it.'

'Because you said it smells foul,' said Issy,

40

unarguably. 'And it's about twenty per cent proof, so you can't have it anyway.'

'Austin would let me have it.'

'No I wouldn't,' came the voice down the phone.

'When we have proportional representation,' said Darny, 'I'll have more of a say around here.'

'If you get on to teen voting rights, I'm hanging up,' warned Austin.

'No, don't . . .' said Issy.

There was a silence as Darny gave the phone a rude gesture, then, muttering darkly about how things would change around here when teens got the vote, he grabbed a bunch of bananas and disappeared upstairs.

'Has he gone?' said Austin eventually.

'Yup,' said Issy. 'He seems in a pretty good mood tonight, actually. Maybe school wasn't as bad as all that.'

'Oh good,' said Austin. 'Thanks, Issy. I didn't really think puberty was going to kick in till a bit later.'

'Oh, it's not too bad yet,' said Issy. 'He's still talking to us. I think that goes altogether soon. Although his trainers . . .'

'I know,' said Austin, wrinkling his nose. 'I'd kind of stopped noticing the smell before you came along.'

'Hmm,' said Issy. There was another pause. This wasn't like them at all. Normally there was no end to the conversation. He would tell her what was up at the bank; she would mention funny clients or whatever it was Pearl and Caroline had had their latest fight about.

But what she was doing was the same as always. For him, life seemed to be becoming very different.

41

Issy racked her brains to try and think of something to talk to him about, but came up short—compared to New York, her day had been the usual: talking to sugar suppliers and trying to convince Pearl to let her hang some tinsel. And the rest of the time ... well, she couldn't say this, because it felt like it would be unfair on him, that she was blaming him for being away, or turning into one of those awful clingy women she didn't want to be, always moaning at their other halves. So she couldn't tell him that pretty much all she'd been thinking of, all that was filling her head, was how much she missed him and wanted him home and how much she was dreading him uprooting their lives just as, for the first time in years, she felt she was coming into safe harbour.

So she didn't say anything at all.

'So what's up?' said Austin, confused. Getting Issy to talk was rarely a problem. Getting her to not talk when the cricket was on was usually far trickier.

'Oh, nothing really. Same old.'

Issy felt her face grow hot as the silence drew out between them. Austin, however, was waiting to cross a four-lane highway without being entirely sure of which way the traffic was coming, and was blind to minor emotional nuance. He thought she was cross with him for leaving Darny with her.

'Look, Aunt Jessica said she'd be happy to take Darny ...'

'What?' said Issy, exasperated. 'There's nothing wrong with me and Darny. He's fine. Don't worry about us.'

'I'm not worried,' said Austin, as a yellow taxi cab honked loudly at him for having the temerity to pause before crossing the road. 'I was just saying.

42

You know. It's an option.'

'I'm coming home every night after a full day's work and managing to check his homework and make his supper. I think it's fine. I don't think I need options, do you?'

'No, no, you're doing brilliantly.'

Austin wondered just when this conversation had started to drift out of his grasp so badly.

'Sorry,' he said. 'I didn't mean to ...'

His phone was beeping. Another call was coming in.

'Listen, I have to go,' he said. 'I'll call you later.'

'I'll be in bed,' said Issy, sounding more huffy than she meant to. 'We can speak tomorrow.'

'OK ... all right.'

*   *   *

Issy felt alarmingly frustrated when she hung up the phone. They hadn't managed to talk at all, not about anything proper, and she'd no idea what he was up to or how it was going, apart from the definite sense she'd got from talking to him that he was having a really good time.

She told herself she was being stupid; this was a big fuss about nothing. She was getting all wound up for no reason. Her last boyfriend had been very emotionally distant, and had treated her like dirt, so she was finding her new relationship sometimes very difficult to manage. With Graeme, she couldn't say anything at all or he would coldly close up; she knew Austin was very very different, but wasn't sure exactly how far she could go. Men—no, not just men, everybody—shied away from neediness. She didn't want to look needy.

43

She wanted to be warm, casual, breezy, reminding him that they were building a loving home, not defensive and shrewlike.

Issy sighed and looked back down at the fruit she was mixing.

'No,' she said, feeling a bit self-conscious and daft. 'You can't have negative thoughts when you're making the Christmas cake. It's unlucky. DARNY!' she hollered up the stairs. 'Do you want to come and drop twenty pees in the cake mix?'

'Can it be two-pound coins?'

'NO!'

*   *   *

Austin sighed. He didn't want to worry Issy, but sometimes it was easy to do. He'd been called in just before he left. Kirsty Dubose, the primary headmistress, had always been very soft on Darny in the past, knowing his background. Plus, unbeknown to Austin, she had had the most enormous crush on him. Mrs Baedeker, Darny's new head at secondary, had absolutely no such qualms. And Darny's behaviour really was appalling.

'We're looking at what you might call a last-chance situation,' Mrs Baedeker had barked at Austin, who sometimes found it difficult in school situations to remember he was meant to be a grown-up.

'For answering back?' protested Austin.

'For persistent class-disrupting insubordination,' Mrs Baedeker said.

Austin's lips had twitched.

'It's not funny,' she added. 'It's stopping others from learning. And let me tell you this. Darny Tyler

44

might be clever and sharp and well-read and all the rest of it, and he may well turn out noisy and fine and all right.' She hit the desk with her palm to make her point. 'But there are a lot of kids at this school who don't have what Darny's got, and do need good teaching and organised lessons and proper discipline, and he's stopping that process from happening and it's not right and not welcome in my school.'

That had shut Austin up very quickly indeed. He'd put Mrs Baedeker's argument forcibly to Darny that evening, and Darny had argued back, equally forcibly, that formal examinations were a total waste of everybody's time so it hardly mattered either way, that those kids kept trying to set him on fire at playtime so it was righteous vengeance, and surely critical thinking was an important part of education. Issy had hidden in the kitchen and made a smoked haddock quiche. But Austin found it hard to worry about Issy and Darny at the same time, and his thoughts at that moment were with his brother, even as Issy was thinking endlessly of him.

Chapter Four

Perfect Christmas Cake

I make no apologies for this, wrote Issy in her recipe book for the extra staff she liked to think she would employ one day. It was a tradition her grampa had started, and she was determined to continue with it; she had kept all his hand-written recipes and her friends had bound them for her into a book. She never, ever let herself think about perhaps one day having a daughter to pass it on to. That would never do. And anyway, she thought, if she did have a daughter, she'd probably be just like Marian and only eat mung beans and run off travelling and send mysterious postcards and interrupt crackly Skype conversations with long, involved stories about people Issy didn't know. Regardless.

Most recipes I tend to tweak and move around to suit what I like, in the hope that my customers will like them too. I'm not fond of anything too fiddly, or overly fancy, and if I'm looking at American recipes I know they'll probably be too sweet for

British people, while French recipes probably won't be sweet enough. So all of that is fine, but this is different. This is one of those occasions where a recipe has been written that can't be bettered. Some people may do fancy things with whole oranges or surprises or various bits of malarkey, but this, as it stands, is one of the best, most reliable recipes ever written. It doesn't matter if you've never baked before in your life. You can make a wonderful, wonderful Christmas cake, and it's by St Delia Smith.

Although Delia isn't officially a saint quite yet, and fortunately for everyone still alive and well, it will, one day, be a mere formality down at the Vatican. No one has made cooking so clear, and no one is quite as successful. Whilst we all know— naming no names—famous chefs who say their dinner takes half an hour when it takes all afternoon and some crying, or who leave ingredients out altogether because they are too busy tossing their hair, Delia can always be relied upon, and rarely more so than here. Do what she says—exactly what she says, neither more nor less—and a lovely Christmas cake will be yours. Not to mention the smell of your kitchen as you make it. You should do it ideally by the end of November to give it a few weeks to ripen, and if I were to make one change it would be to add a little more brandy, but that is completely up to you.

The Classic Christmas Cake
By Delia Smith

This, with no apologies, is a Christmas cake that has been in print since 1978, has been made and loved by thousands and is, along with the Traditional Christmas Pudding, one of the most popular recipes I've produced. It is rich, dark and quite moist, so will not suit those who like a crumblier texture. Recently we took some of these cakes along to book-signing sessions up and down the country and were quite amazed to see so many people take a mouthful and then buy a book!

1lb (450g) currants
6oz (175g) sultanas
6oz (175g) raisins
2oz (50g) glacé cherries, rinsed, dried and finely chopped
2oz (50g) mixed candied peel, finely chopped
3 tablespoons brandy, plus extra for 'feeding'
8oz (225g) plain flour
$\frac{1}{2}$ level teaspoon salt

$\frac{1}{4}$ level teaspoon freshly grated
  nutmeg
$\frac{1}{2}$ level teaspoon ground mixed spice
8oz (225g) unsalted butter
8oz (225g) soft brown sugar
4 large eggs
2oz (50g) almonds, chopped (the
  skins can be left on)
1 level dessertspoon black treacle
grated zest 1 lemon
grated zest 1 orange
4oz (110g) whole blanched almonds
  (only if you don't intend to ice the
  cake

You will also need an 8 inch (20cm)
round cake tin or a 7 inch (18cm)
square tin, greased and lined with
silicone paper (baking parchment).
Tie a band of brown paper round the
outside of the tin for extra protection.
  You need to begin this cake the
night before you want to bake it. All
you do is weigh out the dried fruit
and mixed peel, place it in a mixing
bowl and mix in the brandy as evenly
and thoroughly as possible. Cover the
bowl with a clean tea cloth and leave
the fruit aside to absorb the brandy
for 12 hours.
  Next day pre-heat the oven to gas
mark 1, 275°F (140°C). Then measure
out all the rest of the ingredients,
ticking them off to make quite sure
they're all there. The treacle will be

easier to measure if you remove the lid and place the tin in a small pan of barely simmering water. Now begin the cake by sifting the flour, salt and spices into a large mixing bowl, lifting the sieve up high to give the flour a good airing. Next, in a separate large mixing bowl, whisk the butter and sugar together until it's light, pale and fluffy. Now beat the eggs in a separate bowl and add them to the creamed mixture a tablespoonful at a time; keep the whisk running until all the egg is incorporated. If you add the eggs slowly by degrees like this the mixture won't curdle. If it does, don't worry, any cake full of such beautiful things can't fail to taste good!

When all the egg has been added, fold in the flour and spices, using gentle, folding movements and not beating at all (this is to keep all that precious air in). Now fold in the fruit, peel, chopped nuts and treacle and finally the grated lemon and orange zests. Next, using a large kitchen spoon, transfer the cake mixture into the prepared tin, spread it out evenly with the back of a spoon and, if you don't intend to ice the cake, lightly drop the whole blanched almonds in circles or squares all over the surface. Finally cover the top of the cake with a double square of silicone paper with a 50p-size hole in the centre (this gives extra protection during the long slow cooking).

Bake the cake on the lowest shelf of the oven for $4^{1}/_{2}$–$4^{3}/_{4}$ hours. Sometimes it can take up to $^{1}/_{2}$–$^{3}/_{4}$ hour longer than this, but in any case don't look till at least 4 hours have passed. Cool the cake for 30 minutes in the tin, then remove it to a wire rack to finish cooling. When it's cold, 'feed' it—make small holes in the top and base of the cake with a cocktail stick or small skewer, then spoon over a few teaspoons of brandy, wrap it in double silicone paper secured with an elastic band and either wrap again in foil or store in an airtight container. You can now feed it at odd intervals until you need to ice or eat it.

*   *   *

Pearl looked at Issy. 'You're doing this on purpose,' she said.

'I am not,' said Issy. 'It needs time to sit.'

Everyone who had walked through the door had raised their noses and sniffed appreciatively and smiled.

'You know, you can buy this smell in a scented candle,' said Caroline. 'It's only fifty pounds.'

The others looked at her.

'Fifty pounds for a candle?' said Pearl. 'My church sells them for thirty pence.'

'Well, they're for gifts.'

'People give candles as gifts?'

51

'Smart people do,' said Caroline.

'Smart people give gifts that say, here, take this, I think your house smells really terrible and you need this stinky candle to make it better?'

'Hush, you two,' said Issy, putting on the noisy coffee machine to stop them bickering. She glanced over at the fireplace, where she had hung a small red stocking for Louis. Pearl followed her gaze.

'Are you *smuggling in* Christmas decorations?'

'No,' said Issy hastily. 'It's just leftover laundry.'

'That is the most Christmassy smell I've ever come across,' said the young customer Caroline was serving. The child next to her shot her a wide-eyed, beaming glance.

'SANTY IS COMING,' she said.

'Ssh,' said Issy. 'I know, but don't tell everyone.'

The child smiled with her mouth closed, as if they shared a secret. Pearl rolled her eyes.

'Fine. Fine. Drape the place in tinsel that will gather dust and make a total mess for me to clean up and start those stupid Christmas songs until if I have to listen to "Stop the Cavalry" one more time I'll want to punch something. Do you want me to wear a Santa hat for five weeks? Maybe I'll tie some bells round my waist and I can jingle solidly for a month and a half. Will that suit you?'

'Pearl!' said Issy. 'It's just a bit of fun.'

'I'm having all-white decorations this year,' mused Caroline. 'Hand-made by the Inuit. They don't sparkle or light up, but they're sustainable. The children complain, but I explain to them how a stylish Christmas is a better Christmas.'

Issy was watching Pearl closely. She didn't normally take offence.

'Seriously, are you all right?' said Issy. She was

52

worried she'd been too wrapped up in her worries about Austin to notice that Pearl was feeling the pressure of her own.

'I'll be fine,' said Pearl, looking shamefaced. 'Sorry. It's just, it happens so fast and there's so much to do ...'

Issy nodded. 'But it will be lovely, won't it? Louis is at just the right age for it.'

'But it's expensive,' said Pearl. 'Getting him all those toys.'

'Louis is the least demanding child I've ever met,' said Issy. 'He isn't going to demand toys.'

'Benjamin keeps going on about him getting a new garage and everything he sees on TV and football kit and stuff,' said Pearl. 'But I don't even ...'

Issy looked at her. 'Pearl McGregor, you are the most sensible woman I've ever met in my life. I can't believe you're talking like this. Craig the builder asked Louis who his favourite football team was last week and he said Rainbow United.'

Pearl let out a smile.

'He means Brazil.'

'He doesn't know what he means! He's four! Don't worry about it! *And*,' added Issy as an inspired incentive, 'the more Christmassy and lovely we do things, the more we're going to sell so the bigger bonus you can have. Hmm?'

Pearl shrugged.

'I still think people forget why we celebrate this time of year.'

'Would you like me to make a gingerbread nativity?' asked Issy, assuming that Pearl would laugh off the suggestion. It was a fiddly job and would take absolutely ages.

Instead Pearl said, 'I think that would be lovely. Could we put it in the window?'

*　　　*　　　*

Caroline wasn't looking forward to Christmas either. It was Richard, her ex-husband's turn to have the children. Well, she had told everyone, that was just fine by her. She was going to spend the day pampering, using her day spa bathroom and detoxing early, avoiding all that awful bloat everyone got at Christmas time.

She knew she was being miserable—and so snappy and sarcastic—and she was aware that Pearl and Issy were about the only two people on earth who could put up with her at the moment, but she didn't seem to be able to help it. Richard had originally left her for a woman at work, but now he'd apparently moved on, and she couldn't for the life of her find out where he was staying or who he was with. He was only contacting her through lawyers. Had he met someone else? Was he going to fall in love and have thousands of babies with another woman and spend Hermia and Achilles' inheritance? And the house cost a lot to run, *and* City bonuses were way down, everybody knew that. It was getting impossible to live in London.

Deep down the fear gnawed away at her, and she took it out on almost anyone. Pearl and Issy understood and tried their hardest to be good about it. Pearl had said out loud several times that putting up with Caroline was going to guarantee her place in heaven. Issy liked to think in her dreamier moments that if she and Austin had daughters, this was what the teenage years would be like.

54

'How's that hot boyfriend of yours doing in New York?' Caroline asked her as they handled the lunchtime rush together—Pearl had let Issy change the sandwich order to include turkey, stuffing and cranberry sauce, and they were flying off the shelves as fast as they could load them.

'He's fine,' said Issy, in a tone of voice that Pearl and Caroline realised immediately meant anything but.

'Oh well, you know New York,' said Caroline in a superior tone.

'No, I don't,' said Issy. 'Not at all really. I've never been.'

'You've never been?'

'Neither have I,' said Pearl. 'And I haven't injected poison in my face either. Isn't it amazing what people haven't done?'

Caroline ignored her. 'Oh well, it is full of the most incredible-looking women, really beautiful, and all totally desperate for a man. What they'll do for a tall, handsome banker with an English accent ... they'll be all over him like vultures.'

Issy looked shocked.

'Is this something you know for a fact?' asked Pearl heavily. 'Or is it just something you've made up from watching television programmes?'

'Oh no, darlings, I've been there. The women there make *me* feel ugly.' Caroline let out a tinkly laugh that was presumably meant to sound self-deprecating and charming but failed utterly.

'He's coming home soon,' said Issy.

'I wouldn't count on that,' said Caroline. 'They'll snap him up in no time.'

This didn't improve Issy's mood in the slightest, even when the latest batch of Christmas cake

55

in the big industrial oven started to perfume the entire street and brought over a crowd of scaffolders from across the road. They were from Ukraine, and could normally only ever spare the money to share a cake. Somehow, every single member of staff, without telling the others, always managed to slip them an extra bit of something.

*　　　*　　　*

Austin couldn't deny that this was proving an eye-opener.

Merv Ferani, vice president of Kingall Lowestein, one of the largest Wall Street banks still standing, was manoeuvring him through the tables of the oak-panelled dining room, following the shapely form of the most beautiful waitress Austin had ever seen. Well, maybe she wasn't a waitress. She had been standing at the front desk, checking names off on a list and being very rude to the people in front of her, but when Merv had marched in—he was very short, very fat and wore flamboyant bow ties—she had come over all smiles and gushing and eyed Austin up in a very forward way he found completely unnerving. He wasn't used to very beautiful people being nice to him. He was used to quite normal-looking people asking him to please take his son off the bus.

They threaded their way through the tables, all of which were filled with affluent-looking people: men in expensive suits with pointed shoes; beautiful women, sometimes with much older, much less beautiful men. Merv stopped often to shake hands, exchange witticisms Austin didn't understand and clasp people on the shoulder. To one or two he introduced Austin—'he's just come over from London'—and they would nod and ask if he knew so-and-so at Goldman Sachs or someone at Barclays and he'd have to shake his head and try not to blurt out that he was in charge of small business loans at a very small branch on Stoke Newington High Street.

Finally they reached their table. Two more waiters came dashing up to pull out their seats and pour them some water. Merv glanced in passing at the heavy embossed menu, then tossed it to one side.

'Ah, what the hell. It's getting towards that time of year. I love Christmas food. Let's see if they do anything Christmassy. And a bottle of claret, the 2007 if they have it. Same for you?'

He cocked an eyebrow at Austin, whose stomach still thought it was night-time and was therefore more than happy to oblige. He did wonder, though, what would have happened if he'd asked for a green salad. He'd certainly have failed a test in some way.

The dinner plates were the size of heads. Austin wondered how much he was going to have to eat.

'So, Austin,' said Merv, starting in on the bread basket. Austin supposed that when you hit a certain level of wealth and success, you were just allowed to eat however you wanted. Manners were for little people.

*   *   *

It had happened very suddenly the previous afternoon. Austin had been in the offices of KL, feeling rather anxious about everything. The place was full of sharp-looking young men who must have been about his age but looked rather more groomed, worked out, somehow smooth; perfectly shaved with weirdly shiny skin and buffed fingernails, in expensive suits and shined shoes. (The only time Austin had ever been in a gym had been to pick Darny up from Scouts, and that had only lasted till Darny insisted that it was against his human rights to be sent to a quasi-paramilitary organisation.) And that was before you even got to the women. The women in New York were the most terrifying specimens Austin had ever seen. They didn't even seem vaguely on the same planet as everyone else. They had incredibly muscular legs that ended in really sharp stiletto heels, and pointy elbows and pointy faces and they moved fast, like giant insects. They were beautiful, of course, Austin couldn't deny that. They just seemed somehow other-worldly. Still, they had all looked over at him when he came in and had been very friendly. Austin wasn't used to being scrutinised by women who looked like they could be models when they were finished with their banking careers. It was unnerving.

Another Brit, Kelvin, had walked him round. Austin knew Kelvin a little from before, from various courses they'd taken together when the bank was still stubbornly trying to promote Austin and Austin was still stubbornly trying to resist it. Back when he thought working in the bank was some kind of temporary manoeuvre.

Austin was impressed to see that Kelvin had lost weight, smartened up and generally seemed different. He'd even adopted a strange kind of transatlantic accent. Austin thought this made him sound a bit like Lulu, but didn't want to mention it.

'So you're liking it here, then?'

Kelvin smiled broadly. 'Well, the hours are a bit of a killer. But the lifestyle ... amazing. The women, the bars, the parties ... it's like Christmas all year, man.'

Austin really didn't want to say 'man' at the end of his sentences.

'Okay. Um. Kelvin.'

Kelvin lowered his voice. 'They're short on men here, you know. As soon as they hear the accent and you lay it on a bit thick and pretend you know Prince William, they're all over you.'

Austin frowned. 'Kelvin, you were born in Hackney Marshes.'

'Still London, isn't it?'

They rounded the corner into the main trading floor. Austin looked around carefully.

'Where the magic happens, bro.'

Austin only had one bro, who was almost as annoying as Kelvin.

'Hmm,' he said.

Kelvin winked broadly at one of the girls on the floor, who was tapping ferociously on her computer whilst on the telephone, but still managed to find the time to shake back her beautiful long black hair that looked like something out of a shampoo advert. The huge open-plan room was a hive of frenzied, scurrying activity: men standing up and shouting into phones, a ticker running overhead on an LCD display, people dashing about with files and looking busy.

'Yup, here's where the magic happens.'

'Hmm,' said Austin again.

'What's the matter? You're not impressed?'

'Not really,' said Austin, a bit glumly. This was

only a finding-out visit, and it was already obvious to him that he wouldn't fit in here in a hundred years, so he might as well say what he thought. 'I can't believe you're still pulling all this bullshit like it's 2007.'

He pointed at a flashily-dressed trader bellowing into a telephone. 'Come on! We've tried all this shouting bollocks before and it didn't work then. This is a total waste of time. I bet no one in here really understands what a derivative is or why it's such a terrible idea, except three quants in a back office taking five minutes off playing World of Warcraft. Banks have spent years pulling the wool over their own eyes. It's not sustainable, and we know it now. Why isn't the money flowing properly? To help real businesses, real people grow and build and make things? Because that castle-in-the-air stuff fell right down. Still, nice suit, Kelvin.'

Austin turned round and got ready to go. That was when he saw the little man with the large bow tie who had been standing in the middle of the trading floor with an unlit cigar, watching them intensely.

'You,' he said, stabbing a stubby finger at Austin. 'You're having lunch with me.'

*   *   *

And now here he was, sitting in front of six different types of bread that were being explained to him by a ludicrously handsome young man. Austin wondered vaguely where all those fat Americans you heard about were. Maybe Manhattan's skinny buildings and tiny living spaces simply discouraged it.

'Two olive, one rye, but not if it's warm,' ordered Merv, and settled himself down to look at Austin. His eyes were small and curious.

'London tells us you're a bit of a curveball. Young, on the up, incorruptible … might be ready to jump from clearing while you still can.'

'Um,' said Austin. 'That was very nice of them.'

'They also said you were the only person in the entire company whose loans had never lost money.'

Austin smiled at this. It was a nice compliment to get. He loaned on his gut instincts for people; how hard he thought they could work, how much they wanted it. When Issy had walked into his office nearly two years ago, Austin could see beyond the nerves and anxiety and the frankly total lack of preparation to the person beneath; she had more steel in her than you would think by looking at her. Well, an unusual upbringing could do that to you, as he knew only too well.

'Do you know how much my bond traders lost me last year? Those klutzes in the trading room?'

Austin shook his head politely.

'About seventeen billion dollars.'

Austin wasn't entirely sure whether this was, in context, a lot of money or not.

'We have to get back to basics, Austin.' Merv refilled their glasses with claret. 'We need decent, honest brokers with no blotted copybooks. We need transparency. We need to do something before the public decide we should all be in jail, capisce?'

Austin nodded.

'Guys like you … making smaller loans, more cautious investments. Not behaving like drunk fucking beavers at the wheel of a 747, you know what I'm saying? Not acting like coked-up weasels who exist simply to spunk cash down the panties of cocktail waitresses and buy themselves fucking indoor fucking trampolines.'

Austin was slightly lost, but he smiled gamely nonetheless.

'Sustainable banking?' he tried. This was a phrase that had gone down well at head office.

'Yeah,' said Merv. 'Exactly. You married?'

'No ...' Austin was confused by the curveball question.

'Kids?'

'Uh, I look after my brother.'

'Why, what's up with him?'

'He's eleven.'

Merv nodded. 'Oh yeah, one of my kids is eleven. From Mrs Ferani number two. Doesn't know if he's coming or going. Half of him wants to play *Star Wars*, half of him wants to race in the Indy 500 ...'

'Is that like Formula 1?'

' ... so I said to him, "Well, fine, you can have the damn car, but don't drive it off the ranch."'

The waiter came over and started to explain the enormously complicated list of daily specials, in such a friendly way that Austin wondered for a few moments if they'd been at school together, but Merv waved him away.

'It's Christmas, isn't it? Bring us something with turkey. And cranberry sauce and the rest of that bullshit. And some more claret.'

*   *   *

Austin, his body clock slightly messed up, and having drunk some very good but rather rich claret

62

at lunch, lurched out of the restaurant at 4 p.m. A black town car appeared silently out of seemingly nowhere to pick up Merv, who seemed to be suffering no ill effects at all and offered Austin a lift. He declined. The New York city air was absolutely freezing in his throat, but he wanted to clear his head a little and think things over.

'Sure thing,' Merv said. 'But you're one of my men now, OK?'

They shook hands and Merv pulled him into a large bear hug. It was extremely unsettling.

Austin found himself just by the Plaza Hotel at the south-east end of Central Park. Long rows of horses and carriages lined up opposite, with jingling bells and icy breath. The horses wore blankets, and Austin went to take a picture of them on his phone before remembering that Darny would probably think this was infringing the rights of horses or something, so decided against it. Opposite the park was FAO Schwarz, the massive toy shop. Even Darny, Austin suspected, would have liked a peek in there. He headed on to Fifth Avenue, among the crowds of excited shoppers hopping in and out of Barneys and Saks and the other great department stores that lined the sidewalk. The lights and window displays were almost overwhelming, and snow was starting to fall. Wrapped up in warmth and the excitement of new people and new places ... it was enervating.

A whole new world? Really?

He hadn't told Issy because he didn't want to worry her, but there was every chance the Stoke Newington branch wouldn't make it through the next round of cuts. And to make the dizzying leap from local to global banking ... it was almost unheard of. The bank had only ever been meant as a stopgap. He'd known he was capable of more, but life was so complicated, and providing stability for a terrified and confused four-year-old had been paramount at the time.

Now, though … maybe it was time for him to reclaim some ambition for himself?

He thought of Issy. She'd often said how much she'd love to go to New York. She could come … she'd love it, wouldn't she? Would she? He thought with a sinking heart of how happy she was in the Cupcake Café; how she'd worked so hard to build it into a lovely cosy place for people to come and sit for a while; how she'd got to know the locals and the regulars and how the café had taken its place in Stoke Newington like it had always been there. It gave him an ominous feeling.

But she could do it again! Maybe get her green card, start up something wonderful. Americans had invented the cupcake, surely? Two very tall women pushed past him to get into the Chanel store, talking loudly about their dates. Austin buried the thought that Issy wouldn't feel at all at home here. That she possibly wasn't tough enough and sharp enough for New York. He decided to buy her a present. Something lovely to show her how magical the city would be.

In his slightly fuddled state, he couldn't believe it. The smell. He'd just been thinking about Issy, and suddenly, out of nowhere, he'd smelled her. He followed his nose off down a side street. And sure enough, right there on the corner was the most adorable, charming, perfect little cupcake café he'd ever seen in his life.

Outside, the little corner building was painted

pink. It was completely covered top to toe in little white fairy lights, with more lights strung inside visible through the windows. Mismatched dark-coloured sofas—greens and burgundies—were dotted around, covered in tartan rugs, and the walls and the floor were dark mahogany. The smell of coffee and baking cakes made Austin nearly tearful with homesickness. He pushed open the door, and it clanged just like Issy's did.

'Well, hello there,' said a friendly voice from behind the counter. The back wall was entirely lined with red and green twisted candy canes. 'What can I get you today?'

Chapter Five

Polar Bear Cupcakes

These little cakes are irresistible. Cut
the liquorice into tiny eyes and a little
nose, and use white buttons for the
ears. Or if, like me, you hate liquorice,
use chocolate chips. Try not to feel
too sad when you bite into them; let's
face it, anyone who can eat a jelly
baby can eat a coconut baby polar
bear.

125g unsalted butter, at room
   temperature
125g caster sugar
2 large eggs, at room temperature
125g sifted self-raising flour
2 tsp vanilla extract
2 tsp milk

For this recipe you need two different
sizes of cupcake tin, one smaller than
the other.
   Preheat oven to 190°C/gas mark 5,

and put paper cases in the tins.

Beat butter and sugar together, then add eggs, flour, vanilla and milk and beat until the mix drops slowly off the spoon (add more milk if it won't).

Spoon into paper cases, put in oven. Check with a toothpick after 12 minutes—if it comes out clean, we're ready.

For the topping

125g unsalted butter
250g icing sugar, sifted
1tsp coconut extract (you can also use
 Malibu, if you're feeling frisky!)
splash of milk
desiccated coconut
chocolate chips, large and small
white chocolate buttons

Beat the butter and add the icing sugar, then add the coconut extract and the milk until you have a light frosting.

Spread the frosting all over one small and one large cupcake, then stick them together so the little cake makes the polar bear's head. Carefully roll the bear in the desiccated coconut.

Add chocolate chips to make the eyes and the nose, and the white chocolate buttons to make the ears— and voilà! Polar bear cupcakes!!!!

Merry Christmas!

*　　　*　　　*

'So we're going full Christmas,' said Pearl in a resigned tone of voice.

'They're polar bears,' said Issy. 'Polar bears are for life, Pearl, not just Christmas. Anyway,' she added, 'it's the first of December today! It's Advent! It's all official! Ta-dah!'

She unveiled her *pièce de résistance* from her shoulder bag: a huge Advent calendar. It was in the shape of a traditional snow-coloured village, and the brightly coloured windows of the houses formed the numbers of the calendar.

'First child every morning gets to open a door. Except for Louis.'

Louis looked up from where he was sitting engrossed in a book about frogs.

'Do you have your own calendar?' she asked.

Louis nodded gravely.

'Grammy did give me one. It has sweeties. I get chocolate every day! And Daddy gave me one too.'

Issy looked at Pearl.

'Don't look at me,' said Pearl, who had some trouble watching Louis' weight. 'I told them both,' she said. 'I took one of them away.'

'For the poor children,' said Louis gravely. 'Poor, poor children. I kept Grammy's because I ate that first.'

'OK, good,' said Issy. 'Don't open this one, if you don't mind. You can open the big doors on Christmas Eve.'

Louis studied it carefully. 'Issy!' he said urgently. 'It has no chocolate left, Issy!'

'Not all Advent calendars have chocolate, Louis.'

'Yes! They do!' said Louis. 'I think a robber came.'

'Well, I'm glad I'm not going to have too much trouble keeping you away from it,' said Issy.

She unfolded the calendar on top of the fireplace. It looked lovely, but wouldn't stay up.

'Hmm, I wonder what would keep that up?' she said. 'Oh, I know. Perhaps this long rope of holly I just happen to have in my bag.'

Pearl snorted. 'Yeah, all right,' she said. 'You've made your point.'

'Did you know who started with the holly and the ivy?' said Issy cheerfully.

'Baby Jesus!' hollered Louis.

'Well, yes,' said Issy. 'But also the Romans. And mistletoe is from even further back, from the Druids, their midwinter festival.'

Pearl sold another six polar bear cakes and didn't say anything. Caroline turned up to let Issy get back downstairs to the baking. Her face fell when she saw the holly on the fireplace.

'Oh,' she said. 'You've decided to go with red and green, have you?'

'At Christmas?' said Issy. 'Well. Yes, funnily enough.'

'But there's so many more chic ways to do it!' said Caroline. 'I was thinking maybe an all-silver motif, or those clear plastic trees they do in the Conran shop? So stylish.'

'If I wanted to be stylish, I wouldn't wear clothes from a catalogue,' said Issy. 'I want it to be nice and cosy and comfortable, not scary like those posh places where they make you sit on jaggedy chairs and everyone is blonde and skinny and wears leather trousers . . .'

Realising she was exactly describing Caroline, Issy fell silent. Fortunately Caroline, despite having zero body fat, managed to be very thick-skinned.

'We'll never make it into the *Super Secret London Guide*,' she said. 'They choose the most select hidden shops of the year and run a special issue. There's a prize for the most stylishly decorated.'

'We will not,' said Issy. 'I will try and get through it as stoically as I can.'

Caroline pouted. 'Don't you want to at least make the effort? They run a special supplement in January.'

'The problem is,' said Pearl, 'if we were in it, we'd fill the shop with other people who looked like you. And people that look like you are bad for turnover. Don't eat enough cakes.'

'Yes, but we take up less room,' pleaded Caroline. 'So you can fit more of us in. And let's face it, we'll pay almost anything for a smoothie, especially if it's green.'

Issy smiled. 'Well, even so. We wouldn't win and I don't want to spend a lot of time doing stupid stuff.'

'You might,' said Caroline. 'And it might bump you up the ladder a bit. It's time you were expanding anyway. That's how the Bastard grew his business. Well, I think. He used to talk about it, but I didn't really listen, obviously—very boring.'

'I will never understand why you two split up,' murmured Pearl.

'At least I was a married mother,' sniffed Caroline.

Thankfully, the bell tinged, and Helena entered, carrying Chadani. She had a gigantic buggy that had cost about as much as a small car, with personally commissioned muff, hood, foot cosy and car seat in pink and purple tiger stripes, so that from a distance it looked, as Austin had pointed out (quietly), like a small monster that had just eaten a baby, then exploded. It didn't fit up the stairwell of their apartment, through the doorway of most shops or in the boot of their Fiat, so Helena regularly left it in the middle of the pavement, which managed to make it look even more like a monster, and meant it got in absolutely everybody's way. This didn't stop her from recommending it as the very best in buggies to everyone she met. Issy was rather grateful it didn't fit inside, but she'd had to insist that Helena chain it to the little tree that grew in their courtyard, after she kept leaving it outside the door and it tripped up four people in one morning (it had an extra, malevolent wheel that jutted out the front, and was used mostly to jar people's heels at pelican crossings).

'Hello!' said Issy cheerily, glad she wouldn't have to break up Pearl and Caroline. 'Hello, Chadani!'

Chadani yelled and contorted her face.

Issy looked at Helena.

'Tell me that isn't real fur.' Chadani was practically buried in a huge fur coat with a matching bonnet and her pale pink Uggs.

'No!' said Helena. 'But doesn't she look so CUUUUTE? Ashok's great-aunt wants to pierce her ears.'

Issy didn't say anything to this, but kissed Chadani on her little button nose. Once you got past all the fluff and nonsense, she was a very endearing baby.

Chadani smiled cheerfully and pointed at the largest cake on the stand, winter raspberry with pink icing confection that Issy, in whimsical mood, had covered in sparkly stars. They were very pretty and shiny, she conceded.

'WAAAH!' shouted Chadani.

'Will I get one for you to share?' said Issy, firing up a cappuccino for Helena.

'Oh, Chadani doesn't really like to share,' said Helena. 'She's a bit young to be forced into that, don't you think?'

'It's a very big cake,' said Issy.

'Yes,' said Helena. 'You really shouldn't have made them so large. You have to think about children too.'

Issy decided not to roll her eyes, and put another batch of bear cakes into the oven. Then she decided to take a quick break—Pearl and Caroline weren't talking to one another, which made them both work really quickly and efficiently in a gigantic huff—and sat down next to Helena, who was looking at toys in the Argos catalogue whilst Chadani made shorter work of a gigantic cupcake than Issy would have believed a one-year-old capable of.

'Hey,' said Issy.

'Do you know,' said Helena, flicking through the catalogue, 'Chadani has every single one of these, just about. They really need to invent some new toys.'

'You love having a daughter, don't you?' said Issy, suddenly.

Helena beamed. 'Well,' she said, 'yes. Yes, I do. I mean, obviously we got a very special child, not everyone gets that. But yes. In general. I mean, obviously, it can be ...' She stopped herself. 'Yes. It's wonderful. So when are you and Austin going to get to it, then?'

72

Issy bit her lip. Ever since they'd got together ... well, everyone had just seemed to think that it was the end to a fairy tale, a happy ever after; there was Austin and Issy, and wasn't it funny, she fell in love with her bank manager, ha ha, bet she'll never be short of a few bob, ha, well, you can guess where he's putting his deposits ... oh, she'd heard all the jokes. And now it was more than a year ago, and everyone was expecting some kind of announcement, or at least for something to happen. But Austin's work had gone on and on and she'd got caught up in the shop and moving, and, well ...

Something in her expression penetrated Helena's baby haze.

'You two are all right, aren't you? There's nothing wrong? I refuse to believe there's anything wrong. After all the goat's arseholes you've dated, I won't let anything bad happen to you. Don't you dare. I mean it. I'll march Austin round at gunpoint. I will put him in a wrestling hold. I will remove his horn-rimmed glasses and stuff them up his—'

'I'm sure it's nothing,' said Issy hastily. 'I'm sure he's just ... you know, a bit caught up in New York and a bit excited. That's all. Nothing bad.'

The doorbell rang. Issy looked up. It was a delivery service. She wasn't expecting anything.

'Issy Randall?' the man in the uniform said.

Issy signed for the box, noticing with excitement that it was from Austin.

'AHA!' she said. 'Look! I shouldn't have mentioned anything! Look! He's sent me a present from New York!'

Helena beamed as Issy cut through the brown tape. 'Hurrah! Now never think badly of him again!

73

You need a relationship like Ashok and me.'

'What, where you tell him what to do and he lies down and kisses the ground you walk on? Hmmm,' said Issy, but she was smiling with happiness.

Inside was a bright green box, wrapped with a paler, pistachio-coloured ribbon.

*   *   *

The girl in the New York cupcake shop was called Kelly-Lee. She was very pretty, with a snub nose and wide grey eyes and a few light freckles that looked as though they were dusted on like icing sugar. Her hair was thick and auburn, in a high ponytail, and she wore the pink polo shirt uniform of the shop in a way that was pert but not too sexy.

She'd been so excited to move to New York— Queens, to be precise—to finish her masters, but she was finding it hard to make ends meet. Everything was so expensive, and she'd hoped to find a good job—like Ugly Betty— on a cool magazine, or in an art gallery or with a photographer. She'd been a bit shocked to find out that those jobs didn't actually pay any money; you were expected to work for free—how you paid for food didn't seem to come into it—which clearly meant that any of the cooler jobs were only open to really rich people, which seemed unbelievably wrong and had opened up a distinct glow of unfairness in a life that up to now had been nicely skewed in her favour, as she was pretty and clever and had grown up in a happy Wisconsin family.

So she had taken this stopgap job to make ends meet, but now it had dragged on for three years and none of the other cool stuff seemed to be happening, and frankly she was getting tired of it. That was before she even got to the New York men. She'd been asked out, of course, and had been wined and dined by handsome guys, sexy guys, crazy guys, nice guys, and every single one of them had asked her at the end of the evening if she wouldn't mind remaining non-exclusive, and every single time Kelly-Lee had said no. She was worth more than that. She was sure of it. But it was getting a bit tiring waiting around. Her roommate Alesha thought she was a buttoned-up idiot, but then Kelly-Lee had noticed Alesha get home several times early in the morning with her silver dress still on from the night before, so she was trying not to pay too much attention to what Alesha thought. Then, after two years she'd changed her mind on that one too. Sure enough, the guys that said they were going to call called her about the same as before—i.e., not at all. But at least she occasionally woke up with someone in her bed. Alesha had smiled unpleasantly and made remarks about Little Miss Snooty being brought down a peg or two, and how you had to kiss a lot of frogs. Then Alesha had moved out with someone that she'd met, and Kelly-Lee felt more alone than ever.

You didn't meet many men in the cupcake shop, though. Well, you did, but not very useful ones. Some fat, some gay, some buying for their wives or girlfriends. (That was the worst, if they were nice. Imagine having a husband who also bought you cakes. Kelly-Lee sometimes had trouble finding a guy who would buy her a drink, even if they'd only just met.) And some obviously feeling sorry for something they'd done and hoping the cupcakes would make up for it, which, in the case

75

of a woman, very much depended on whether they were on a diet or not. Kelly-Lee was always on a diet. She had to try the new cupcake recipes at the beginning of every month, but she always made sure she restricted each one to a mouthful, and spent an extra ten minutes at Aquabike Extreme.

Her mother wanted her to go back to Wisconsin for Christmas. It would be about ten degrees below zero, snowed up to the windows, and her relatives would spend the entire time banging on and on about her amazing life in the Big Apple and was it really like what they saw on TV, and then they'd all fall out about gay marriage and her mom would say something that was meant to be conciliatory, like how she knew Kelly-Lee wasn't quite married yet, but if she wanted to bring a boy home, they could probably overlook the sleeping arrangements, and Kelly-Lee would look at her prom queen picture (truly, her proudest moment at the time) and want to scream. She sighed. Then the doorbell had rung and she'd hopped up to her perky best.

'What can I get you today?'

Foreigner, she thought. Cute, but a bit rumpled-looking.

'Uhm, hello,' said Austin, blinking and taking off his glasses.

Ah, thought Kelly-Lee. English. So probably drunk. Still cute, though. She checked his finger automatically. No ring.

'Are you looking for something sweet?' she asked, cheekily. She liked Englishmen, you could have a laugh with them. Not like American men; they always took you seriously, then carried on talking about themselves anyway.

Austin smiled. 'I just liked the smell.'

'Have you been in New York long?'

'About two days,' said Austin. 'It's been a long two days though.'

'It's confusing at first, isn't it?' said Kelly-Lee. 'When I first got here, I just stared upwards all the time. I nearly fell down a manhole.'

'Oh no,' said Austin. 'Well, it could have been worse. A giant anvil could have fallen from the sky.'

'Are you looking for some cakes?'

'Yes,' he said. 'My girlfriend runs a cake shop.'

Kelly-Lee liked the word girlfriend. It could mean anything. It could mean girl I just met, someone I know in passing, near ex. It didn't mean fiancée or wife.

'Which one?' she asked happily.

'Oh no, you wouldn't know it. It's in London. London, England,' he clarified needlessly. She smiled.

Better and better, thought Kelly-Lee.

'Oh no,' she said. 'So you're all the way over here and she's over there? Are you going to be separated for long?'

'Hmm,' said Austin. 'I'm not sure. I hope not. You know how things go.'

Kelly-Lee did.

'Coffee?'

Austin did want a coffee, to clear his head a bit. 'Yes,' he said.

'So do you like running a cupcake café here?'

Kelly-Lee had learned long ago that moaning was not considered very attractive in a woman. Men liked perkiness and happy girls.

'I LOVE it,' she said. 'It's amazing! The smell of cinnamon in the morning! The first cup of coffee! Trying out all the new amazing flavours.'

'Do you bake them yourself?' Austin asked.

Kelly-Lee frowned. She had always considered it the hallmark of a sophisticated New Yorker to be unable to turn on her own oven.

'Well, kinda,' she said. 'The van drops them off, you know, half mixed? Then I just kinda heat them up. Like Mac and cheese.'

'But you like baking?'

'Love it,' smiled Kelly-Lee. 'Hey, you know, we deliver.'

'To London?'

'Sure! We've got a sister shop there. I can call them right away, they'll be there in half an hour.'

'Really?' This struck Austin as a fantastic idea. And it seemed there was absolutely nothing to stop Issy coming over here and baking if he took up a job. There were plenty of shops. It would be great!

He bit into a chocolate and vanilla that Kelly-Lee had put out for him. He hadn't protested, even though after the lunch he'd just had, he'd have put money on not eating again for about a week. It wasn't bad—a little sweet for his taste, and it didn't have the warm, fresh out-of-the-oven taste that Issy's cakes had. But that was fine; good in fact. Maybe she could come over here and make them even better! She would like that.

'Send a dozen,' he said boldly, thinking he was behaving like a New Yorker already. Kelly-Lee took down the address and promised to call it through.

'Well, I'm so glad you like us!' she said, smiling at him appealingly. But it was wasted on Austin. Sitting back after his second bite of the cupcake, in the cosy, familiar-seeming fug, he had fallen straight into a deep sleep.

78

Chapter Six

Recipe for a Bad Cupcake

2 cups bleached flour
2 cups corn syrup
1 cup partially hydrogenated soybean
  and cottonseed oil
1 cup sugar
1 tspn dextrose
water
$\frac{1}{2}$ cup high fructose corn syrup
$\frac{1}{2}$ cup whey powder
1 egg
1 tbsp soy lecithin (emulsifier)
1 tbsp corn starch
pinch salt
1 tsp sodium aluminium phosphate
  baking soda
3 drops white colouring
1 tsp citric acid
$\frac{1}{2}$ tsp sorbic acid
Send through machine. Bake for 20
minutes until partially cooked. Freeze
until needed fully cooked, then zap
for 10 minutes at high temperature.

Back in London, Issy unwrapped the box in disbelief.

'What the heck?'

Under the ribbon on the green box was emblazoned the large flower-embossed logo of a huge, internationally successful cupcake chain. And sure enough, inside was a selection of a dozen cupcakes in different flavours. They did look, it was fair to say, absolutely exquisite, all perfectly piped, and decorated with glitter, tiny stars and iridescent raspberry dust.

'Wow,' said Caroline. 'They are so chic. Look at the attention to detail.'

'That's because they're made in a factory,' said Issy darkly. 'You need a few wonky ones here and there to know they're home-made.'

'Why would he send you those?' said Helena. 'I don't understand. Are you sure they're from him?'

'Yes, look,' said Issy.

The card said, 'To Issy from Austin'. No kisses, nothing. It was very strange. It was less strange if you knew that Kelly-Lee had had only the barest of details to go on when she called in the order over the head of a profoundly fast asleep Austin. And possibly an ulterior motive when it came to not putting kisses on the card.

Issy shook her head. 'But why would he? I don't understand.'

'Maybe he's trying to show you they have better cupcakes,' said Caroline, helpfully.

'Maybe he's the least imaginative gift-giver ever and knows you like cupcakes,' said Helena. 'I mean, come on, he works in a bank. He's hardly going to be a super-romantic soul, is he?'

'He's perfectly romantic,' said Issy, going slightly pink. 'When he wants to be, and when he isn't running late or too busy or just generally a bit distracted because Darny's playing up.'

They all stared at the open box.

'Ooh, are those your new range?' said a customer. 'They look amazing.'

Chadani cruised over from the sofa, stuck a podgy little paw into the box and started smooshing the cakes all up together. For once, Issy didn't think Helena needed to say anything to her, which was just as well, as Helena was watching her daughter admiringly, as if feeling sorry for anyone whose baby wasn't as good at bashing up cakes as hers.

Pearl came past carrying a pile of empty dishes. She sniffed.

'What are you three all hanging around for?' she said.

'Austin has gone completely insane,' said Caroline. 'He's obviously trying to put Issy off him for some reason. Don't worry,' she said, touching Issy on the arm. 'I know break-ups can be messy. My divorce was just horrible. Awful. So I can help you through this.'

Normally Issy could laugh Caroline off, but this really was a bit odd. She bit her bottom lip. Pearl noticed immediately.

'Oh for goodness' sake stop being a big bunch of divs,' she said. 'He's thinking about you. Obviously.'

'But why send something so insulting?' said Issy.

'Because he's a man,' said Pearl. 'I said he was being thoughtful. I didn't say he wasn't being a total and utter idiot.'

'Hmm,' said Issy. 'I think I am going to go and

81

knead some panettone.'

Pearl and Caroline exchanged glances.

'You do that,' said Pearl.

Issy turned to go downstairs. Then she turned back. She sighed crossly.

'Well, I'd better try them, I suppose.'

She broke a bit off one of the big sparkly ones in the middle. It did look immaculate, there was no doubt about that; all the cupcakes perfectly even and exactly the same height. She took a bite and her nose wrinkled up.

'Oh, yuck,' she said.

'I think they say "gross" in America,' reproved Caroline.

'Too sugary,' Issy pronounced. 'And they're not using all butter. You can tell. There's a horrible oily aftertaste. That means industrial quantities, not hand-milled. This is raspberry extract, not real raspberry. And the crumb is too dense. Bleurgh.'

'There you go,' said Pearl. 'He obviously sent them to you to point out your clear superiority over them.'

'Or else he can't tell the difference,' said Issy, worried.

'Or perhaps he thinks these are better,' said Caroline, who always managed to go one worse than everybody else.

'Thanks, Caroline,' said Pearl pointedly. Issy turned away and stomped down the steps to the cellar bakery.

*   *   *

Doti the postman was finishing off his Christmas round outside the Cupcake Café. He liked to come to them last, especially on cold days. Partly because he had a sweet tooth, and partly because he had a soft spot for Pearl and liked to flirt with her. Pearl had Benjamin to contend with, but liked Doti very much.

Today, however, Doti was with someone else, a definite first. She was, Pearl noticed, rather pretty, in her thirties, long dark hair tied back in a ponytail, large hooped gold earrings and very white teeth. It was hard to tell what her figure was like in the unflattering postal uniform and fluorescent vest, but Pearl was putting money on pleasantly curvaceous. She sniffed. They were laughing together as they jangled through the door.

'Hello,' said Pearl, stiffly. Doti smiled.

'Ah, beautiful Pearl. This is beautiful Pearl,' he said to the woman.

'Hello, beautiful Pearl,' said the woman, nicely. That annoyed Pearl even more. Nice pretty people made her feel uneasy.

'This is Maya,' said Doti. 'She's my temporary Christmas postie.'

'Oh, hello,' said Pearl, trying not to sound narked. She shouldn't sound narked. It was just that Doti was the first person who'd shown the slightest bit of interest in her since Louis was born. Still, they couldn't be together, so she couldn't expect to be surprised if he liked somebody else. He was probably too old for Maya anyway. And they were only working together.

'Doti has been *soo* helpful,' said Maya, looking at him in a way that almost immediately put paid to their relationship being merely professional. Doti was pretty handsome, Pearl supposed. His hair was shaved, and he had a very finely shaped skull with small ears and a long neck and ...

'What can I get you?' she said.

'I promised Maya I'd let her try the finest coffee and cake emporium this side of N16,' said Doti. 'So here we are.'

'Oh, it's lovely,' said Maya. She glanced at the blackboard and her face fell a little. 'It looks expensive, though.' She lowered her voice and spoke directly to Pearl. 'I really needed this job,' she whispered. Pearl understood.

'Well, we're glad you got it,' said Doti heartily. 'Very glad. And coffee is on me.'

Louis ran in with his best friend Big Louis, scattering rucksacks, hats, scarves and gloves all over the place before the bell had stopped ringing.

'MUM!' he yelled, and Pearl put down the milk she was steaming and stepped over to give him a big kiss and cuddle.

'My special guy,' she said. 'My number one boy.'

Louis beamed. 'I was SOOO good today,' he said. 'Here is who was not good. Evan. Gianni. Carlo. Mohammed A and Felix ...'

'OK, OK,' said Pearl. 'That's enough.'

Louis looked grave. 'They have to sit on a rug. You would not like to sit on a rug.'

'Why not?' said Pearl. 'What happens?'

'You have to sit on a rug! And EVERYBODY knows you have done some naughty behaviour.'

'Hey, Louis,' said Doti.

Louis' face lit up. 'DOTI!' he yelled. They were great friends.

Doti crouched down. 'Hello, young man,' he said.

Louis looked suspiciously at Maya. 'WHO'S THAT?' he whispered very loudly.

84

'That's my friend who is also delivering post.'

'A lady postman?' said Louis dubiously.

'Of course! There are lots of lady postmen.'

'We're called post*women*,' said Maya. 'Hello. What's your name?'

Louis still looked at her suspiciously, and, unusually for him, didn't immediately start chatting.

'Doti has a friend already,' he announced loftily. 'He has me and also he has Mummy. Thank you very much.' Then he turned away.

'Louis!' said Pearl, genuinely surprised and secretly a bit pleased. 'Where are your manners! Say hello!'

Louis stared at the floor. 'H'lo,' he muttered.

'It's very nice to meet you,' said Maya. 'Oh, Doti, you weren't wrong about these mince pies.'

Pearl gave her a look.

'It's December,' said Doti. 'We can celebrate Christmas now.'

'Oh yes,' said Maya. 'Definitely. Yum.'

Louis tugged at Doti's trouser leg. 'Have you any letters for me?'

He asked this every day. Issy often reflected that it did slightly ameliorate the effect of getting endless and ever-higher electricity bills when they were delivered by a cheerful four-year-old wearing a hat shaped like a dinosaur.

'Well, as a matter of fact, I do,' said Doti. 'You know how normally you have to do a special delivery to Auntie Issy?'

Louis nodded.

'Well, today it isn't for Issy. Today it's just for you.'

Louis' eyes went wide.

'And you won't BELIEVE who it's from.'

85

Pearl was as surprised as Louis when Doti handed him an envelope covered in snowflakes and addressed Louis Kmbota McGregor, c/o the Cupcake Café.

Doti winked at her. 'The post office does it every year,' he whispered. 'I thought he might like one.'

Louis, who could recognise his own name printed in gold, was turning the envelope over and over like it was the most precious object he'd ever seen.

'Mummy!' he breathed.

'Are you going to open it?' said Pearl.

Louis shook his head. 'NO.'

'Who do you think it's from?' said Doti.

Louis held it away from him, still with a wondering look in his eye.

'Is it . . . is it from Santa?'

Doti took the envelope. 'See this,' he said, pointing. 'This is a postmark. Remember I showed you before? It tells you where the letter was posted and what date.'

Louis nodded.

'Well, this postmark says . . . the North Pole.'

'THE NORTH POLE?'

'Yup!'

'MUMMY! I've got a letter from Santa! At the NORTH POLE!'

'That's lovely,' said Pearl, mouthing a thank-you to Doti. 'Come on, darling, let's open it.'

Louis shook his head again and put the card behind his back.

'I can't,' he said. 'Too preshis.'

'Why is it too precious?' asked Maya.

Louis shrugged and kicked his foot against the counter, even though Pearl was always telling him not to.

'Monster garage,' he whispered. 'Santa might say I can't have a monster garage. Even though I did not do naughty behaviour and I did not have to sit on the rug. Like Evan and Gianni and Felix and Mohammed A but not me.'

Pearl bit her lip. That damn monster garage. Ever since he'd seen the advert, he'd been on about it. It was a garage that fixed monster trucks; big trucks, with big monsters inside. But every single monster cost a lot of money, and every single truck was sold separately and they cost money too, and the basic garage itself even before you bought a single monster or truck was well over a hundred pounds, and anyway they didn't have room to store it even if they got the damn thing, which she couldn't afford in a million years because she was going to have to buy Louis new trainers, as he'd grown out of the old ones and they were horribly shabby, and he needed a proper winter coat, and new pyjamas and loads and loads of basic stuff that probably other kids just got when they needed it and not at a special time of year, but that was just how it was.

And it hadn't helped that Benjamin had seen him looking longingly at the advert and said, without even thinking, of course you're going to have a monster garage; no son of mine is going without. They'd had a furious argument outside about it when he'd gone for a cigarette—which by the way also cost a fortune they couldn't afford— especially when he'd said, stubbornly, that he would get the fucking garage for his son and she could see by the glint in his eye not to argue, which just made her worry and panic even more because she hated to think what lengths he might go to to get it.

And every time Louis had mentioned hopefully about the monster garage and asked leading questions about whether Santa would bring him one on his sleigh or whether it would be too heavy and perhaps he would send some real monsters to carry it, or maybe a special dinosaur, she had hummed non-committally, and prayed for his little four-year-old head to latch on to something else.

So far, it hadn't. She hated Christmas.

'Well,' said Doti, 'when I went to empty Santa's letter box, he did say that he had heard that there was a particularly well-behaved boy in N17, so I think he'll probably try his hardest. And now we must be heading back to the depot.'

Doti and Maya departed together, chatting head to head like a couple of teenagers.

Pearl let Louis have a mince pie. Then she ate two more herself, crossly.

*   *   *

Kelly-Lee had let Austin sleep until closing time—he was sweet, it wasn't like he was a tramp or anything, although he did appear to be wearing odd socks, but perhaps that was some of that fabled charming English eccentricity she'd heard so much about. But finally it was seven o'clock, pitch dark outside, Hussein and Flavia had already gone and it was time to shut up shop.

'C'mon, Hugh Grant,' she said gently. He looked nice asleep; he didn't snore or dribble or fart, like that fat little TV producer she'd dated in the fall, who'd come round, eat all her food and then try and get in her pants—she wasn't that dumb, plus she'd felt his little dick prodding up against her thigh when they'd been making out, and frankly she'd lost interest pretty sharply after that. It didn't stop him talking almost constantly about how many beautiful actresses hit on him every time he stepped out of his condo, and dangling hints about her maybe working in the studio one day. She sighed. She bet this guy wouldn't do that. Kelly-Lee put on her perkiest smile.

'Hello, hello?'

Austin blinked. He felt awful. All he wanted to do was crawl under his duvet and sleep for a day and a half. For a second he couldn't figure out where he was. He pulled out his phone; the little red BlackBerry light was blinking at him ferociously. He had nine new emails and six new voicemails. The first was from the bank head in London.

'I don't know what you've done to the Yanks,' it started. 'Maybe they like staff with hair like an unmade bed. Anyway, they want to make you an offer. Get in touch.'

The next two were from his PA, Janet, insisting he call her as soon as possible. And there was one from Merv, saying how much they were looking forward to having him aboard . . .

Austin clutched the side of the sofa. This was going very fast. Much too fast. Half of him was excited by the rush of being in demand; half of him was petrified.

'Good news?' said Kelly-Lee, watching him stare at the BlackBerry screen in consternation and run his fingers through his lovely thick hair, all tufted up like a small boy's. Austin blinked several times.

'I . . . I've just been offered a job. I think.'

Kelly-Lee's eyebrows went even higher.

89

'Boy, that's great! Congratulations! That means we'll be seeing you again!'

'Yes, well . . . wow. I suppose.'

'That's brilliant.'

Kelly-Lee selected the largest of the day's leftover cupcakes—an enormous red velvet—and swiftly put it in a little box, which she tied up expertly with bright bows.

'Here you are,' she said. 'Congratulations. And welcome to New York.'

'I thought New Yorkers were supposed to be unfriendly,' said Austin.

'Well, you're about to discover that just ain't so,' said Kelly-Lee.

Austin shrugged on his heavy greatcoat and long scarf.

'Well, goodbye,' he said.

'See you again soon,' said Kelly-Lee, and flashed him her enormous smile.

*   *   *

Outside, the snow was horizontal and blowing into his face. He hurried along looking for a cab. New York in the snow was a lot more picturesque in the photos. In reality it was utterly bloody freezing, far colder than he'd ever felt in London. He found a yellow taxi and ordered it to take him to his hotel, then fumbled in his pocket for his phone again and made a resolution to buy a pair of gloves. That was odd, nothing from Darny and Iss. He checked his watch; what was the time difference again? Anyway, it didn't matter. This was news! Big news! A big job. Oh my goodness, a big job.

Austin had never meant to be a banker. He'd

never really thought of doing anything much. When his parents had died in a car crash, he had been ambling gently through a degree in marine biology, after enjoying many diving holidays with his mum and dad before the extremely late and surprising new baby had come along after a silver wedding anniversary party went a bit crazy.

In the hideous blur that followed the accident, his little brother was bombarded on all sides by well-meaning aunties, social services, distant cousins, friends of his parents he'd never met. Austin had had to grow up extremely quickly, cut his surfer hair (for the best, he thought now when he saw old photos), leave university and find a job that would allow him to take over his parents' unexpired mortgage on their little terraced house in Stoke Newington.

It hadn't been easy convincing everyone that they were fine the way they were, with or without the fifteen shepherd's pies that arrived every morning on their doorstep unsolicited. As long as Austin kept the front room and the hallway reasonably tidy, he'd found, and the upstairs windows open to circulate any boy smell, they got by all right. But it had been a struggle. A long road.

By the time he'd discovered he had an aptitude for his job, he was already caught up in getting Darny to school and running the house (badly) and getting to work on time, and before he knew it, he had become one of those working mothers at school who were always dashing in late with the wrong PE kit and never contributed to the Christmas fete. Except those mothers weren't particularly friendly towards him because all the stay-at-home mothers would cover for Austin and bake him Christmas cakes and have Darny round to sleepovers to give him some time to himself, whilst simultaneously sneering at or pitying the working mothers, which made the working mothers furious.

But Darny was older now, grown up enough to at least remember to brush his own hair once in a while, even though he'd rather not, and turn on the washing machine (turning it on was rarely the problem; removing the clothes when they were finished instead of leaving them there to stew was the main stumbling block at the moment), and now Issy was there too, and maybe it was, kind of, time for Austin to do something with his life, or rather something with his life that he himself had chosen.

He wouldn't have changed one thing about his life with Darny, not one thing, he told himself fiercely. That was the hand he had been dealt, and he'd played it. He loved his brother so much. But this was beyond his wildest dreams ... a big job in New York ... a cool apartment, maybe? Darny could go to school here. And Issy ...

He needed to talk to Issy.

'Hello?'

The voice was trying to be friendly, but struggling. By the time Issy had risen at six to start baking, worked a full day in the shop, cashed up and done the accounts, helped Darny with his homework and cooked supper, there wasn't much left of her. She went to bed very early.

'Iss?' said Austin. 'Iss, you won't believe this. It's amazing. This huge bank. They want me! They want me to work for them! They're offering ... well I don't know what they're offering but it seems like they really want me, and, I mean, well, obviously I haven't said anything, but, I mean, they have been talking about sending me overseas for a while, and well. Anyway.'

He was conscious Issy wasn't saying anything.

'Anyway. I just thought I should let you know what is going on. Kind of thing.'

*   *   *

Issy had been half asleep when she'd answered the phone. She was wide awake now. And she realised that on some level she had always expected something like this to happen. Who wouldn't want Austin? She did. Things were always too good to be true.

She suddenly wished Helena was here. Helena would tell her, ferociously, to buck up, that she was more than good enough for Austin, thank you, and that her stupid mind would talk her out of anything, which was how she had ended up with a loser like Graeme, and she didn't want that again, did she?

She did not.

But Helena wasn't here. She would be walking Chadani up and down the flat (Chadani was too sensitive to sleep well; it was a sign of hyper-intelligence), and there was only Darny, snoring loudly next door, a dark house with new, unhung curtains and, on the other end of the line, four thousand miles away, sounding happy and carefree and light, the only man she'd ever truly loved, telling her he was never coming home.

*   *   *

'Congratulations,' Issy had finally managed to stammer out. She had tried to cover up her

93

consternation by yawning ostentatiously for as long as she could; then it had turned into a real yawn that she couldn't stop until she could feel his impatience on the other end of the phone. 'I mean, well done. It's really happening. New York, New York! I mean. Wow. I'm so happy for you ...'

Austin winced. She didn't sound in the least bit happy. That fake yawn hadn't fooled him in the slightest.

'It's such a step up,' he said, feeling a note of pleading creeping into his voice. 'I mean, it just changes everything really. I don't even know how I could come back to London and say no to it.'

'No,' said Issy. 'Of course you can't. You've worked so hard. And you're good at what you do.'

'Thanks,' said Austin.

There was a windy, wobbling pause across the ocean. Then Issy remembered with a pang of annoyance the cupcakes he'd sent.

'I got your present.'

Austin couldn't remember at first, he'd been so sleepy and fuddled when he'd ordered them. Then he did.

'Oh, the cakes! Ha, yes, I thought you'd like those. So you see, they do cupcakes over here too.'

'Well of course they do,' said Issy. 'They invented them. Until the Americans, they were just known as fairy cakes.'

'Oh,' said Austin. 'I thought you'd think it was funny.'

'They weren't very good.' Issy hated sounding sulky. She had to stop this.

'Want to come out and make them better?' said Austin.

There was another pause.

94

'Austin,' said Issy. 'I miss you so much.'

'I miss you too,' said Austin. 'I really do. I only got the cakes because I was thinking of you. Was it a stupid thing to send?'

'No,' said Issy.

'Yes,' said Austin.

'Yes,' agreed Issy.

'Oh, bugger,' said Austin. 'It's hard, this long-distance stuff, isn't it?'

Issy felt an icy grip of fear in her stomach. What did that mean? Did it mean they were going to have to get used to it? Did he mean it was so hard, maybe they shouldn't bother carrying on? Did he mean they were just going to have a lot of trouble from now on?

'Hmm,' she said.

'I wish you could come out,' said Austin. 'Why don't you just come out? You'll LOVE it.'

'Well,' said Issy, 'I'll just kill Darny and leave his body in the garden for the foxes, set fire to the shop, then I'll be right there.'

Austin smiled. 'Look,' he said, 'I think I'm going to have to be here for a while longer. Whilst everything gets sorted out, you know. Contracts and stuff. And I have to meet a few people.'

'You are coming back?' said Issy, suddenly panicked. 'You're not asking me to parcel up your stuff and send it on, are you? Put Darny on a plane with a little ticket around his neck like Paddington Bear?'

'Of course,' said Austin. 'Of course I'm coming back.'

'But you don't know how long for,' said Issy. 'Or when.'

Austin didn't answer. He couldn't.

95

Chapter Seven

Mince Pies

If you don't make your own
mincemeat, you might as well just
buy mince pies from a shop. Using
pre-packed mincemeat, you're
basically just putting stuff in an
envelope. It isn't difficult to make,
and it is less expensive, and if you get
some of those nice-looking fancy jars,
you can give it away as Christmas
presents, although make sure you
give it to people who like stewed
fruit and know what to do with it,
otherwise they tend to look at you
as if you've just given them a jar
of fresh rabbit droppings, which is
rarely a welcome gift unless you have
a friend with a very very tiny garden
to compost.

The nice thing about mince pies is
that they can officially be made to
taste utterly delicious by the official
worst baker in the world. They are

as hard to mess up as peppermint creams. This is not one of those recipes where if you don't use precisely the exact measure of butter you might as well throw the entire thing in the bin. These are going to turn out absolutely perfect and fine. Trust me. Also, make them on a Sunday, as you can hang around and read the papers whilst the kitchen starts to smell absolutely and utterly delicious. The only weird ingredient is suet. Yeah. It's weird. Don't enquire as to what it actually is too closely.

Mincemeat

200g small cubes of apple
200g raisins
200g sultanas
1 tbsp nutmeg
1 tbsp mixed spice
Juice and zest of one lemon
Juice and zest of one orange
250g suet, cut into small pieces

The night before you need the mincemeat, put all the ingredients in a big bowl and mix well. Leave overnight covered in a clean dishcloth. In the morning add brandy (I'll leave it to your discretion how much) and then stick in the oven at 120°C/gas mark ½ for three hours.
   Let the mincemeat cool and then

pop into sterilised jars (to sterilise, dampen jar for one minute in the microwave). Cover with brown paper, then seal. It should keep for up to a year. If it keeps for up to a year, you're probably giving it to the wrong friends.

For the pastry, rub 200g flour and 200g cold, chopped-up butter together. Add 100g of golden sugar, a pinch of salt and a little water until it is ready to roll out and cut. Pop in baking tins, spoon in mincemeat and put pastry lids on pies. Brush top with beaten egg and sprinkle a little more golden sugar, then 20 minutes at 180°C/gas mark 4, and ... ta-dah!

*   *   *

Caroline stomped into the shop the next morning in high dudgeon. Issy looked at her with bleary eyes. She'd hardly slept a wink after speaking to Austin the night before and was on her third coffee. She felt so daft, but it was the unfairness of the whole thing that was getting to her. She'd finally got her life together; she finally felt like she was doing what she had always longed to do and had met a man she loved, and now it was all going horribly wrong.

On a deeper level too, she knew why she was so upset; why she was so bad at talking about all this to Austin. It being this time of year didn't help ... and now ... No, she was catastrophising. Taking the worst possible view of the situation. Surely London would give him another job and it would all be fine;

he couldn't possibly want to uproot what they had, how could he? Then she remembered something she hadn't thought about for a long time: she was at church on Christmas morning, wearing a too-tight red dress, with Startrite shoes that gave her blisters at the back, holding hands with Gramps, who knew everyone, of course, and would have been liked by them even without a bag in his pocket full of gingerbread. A woman she recognised from the shop, posh and loud. She didn't like her, although she didn't know why. The woman was wearing a blue hat with a large peacock feather in it, and she leant forward to Gramps and said, 'She couldn't POSSIBLY want to leave at this time of year,' and Grampa Joe hushed her, crossly, more cross than she'd ever seen him.

*   *   *

'So Richard is turning out to be even more of an UTTER ARSEHOLE than usual,' declared Caroline, banging the door and whisking her tiny arse—in white jeans, in December—into the shop. She was wearing a huge furry stole thing that made her legs look even more sticklike, and that Issy fervently hoped was fake. Issy blinked herself out of her reverie and tried to wake up as Caroline shook off the cold. It was freezing outside; everything was iced over, and the clouds in the sky were heavy and dense with snow.

'What's he done now?' she said. Caroline's divorce seemed to be taking rather longer than the marriage had lasted.

'He said no hampers. No hampers. Can you believe it? He stopped our hamper account.'

Issy looked puzzled. 'What do you mean? Those boxes with tins in?'

'They are not just boxes with tins in!' said Caroline in shock. 'They are traditional luxury items sent at Christmas as a token of esteem, and are therefore part of my totally normal family expenditure.'

'But don't they cost a total fortune for like a can of jam and some fancy nuts?' wondered Issy. 'And they're probably full of stuff you don't even like, like olives stuffed with beetroot. I always wondered who sent those.'

Caroline sniffed. 'Everyone does,' she said.

'So are the children looking forward to Christmas?' Issy tried to change the subject.

Caroline sighed dramatically. 'Oh well, you know what they're like.'

'Delightful,' responded Issy, promptly.

'Hermia is just looking forward to the opportunity to eat for the entire holiday. I will have to keep an eye on that girl. Can you believe it, she prefers eating a sandwich to practising her flute. A sandwich! I don't even keep bread in the house!'

Issy made Caroline her small decaf espresso, black, and handed it over. Caroline downed it quickly.

'Hit me again,' she said. 'And can I have it caffed?'

Issy raised her eyebrows. 'That bad?'

Caroline shrugged. 'Well,' she said. 'Well ...' She blinked heavily several times. 'It's just ... Richard said ... Richard said ...' And she dissolved into tears.

'What is it?' said Issy, rushing round the other side of the counter.

100

'He said . . .'

Issy suddenly felt terrified for her. He wouldn't fight for the children, would he? OK, Caroline left them with nannies and ignored them and denigrated them, but . . . no, surely not.

'He said that if he's going to keep paying for them, he wants them sent to BOARDING SCHOOL . . .'

Caroline collapsed into sobs. Issy put her arm round her.

'Oh no,' she said. 'But I thought you always said that boarding school was the answer to everything and would do all those rioters a lot of good?'

Caroline sniffed loudly and took out a cloth handkerchief. Issy was stunned that she carried a cloth handkerchief, but didn't say anything.

'Yes, but not for mmmyyyyyyy . . .' She couldn't finish the sentence.

It was odd, thought Issy. If you heard Caroline talk about them—although sometimes she seemed to forget she had children at all—you would think she wasn't really that interested; that having children was something she'd done simply because it was expected. She seemed to find them more of an annoyance than anything else.

'They would miss me,' said Caroline. 'I think they would miss their mother, wouldn't they? Achilles is only five.'

'They would,' said Issy, from bitter experience. 'Of course they would. It's ridiculous. He's being completely unreasonable.'

'I know!' said Caroline, bawling. 'What am I going to do?'

'Hang on,' said Issy, straightening up. 'I've got an idea.'

101

Caroline glanced up at her, her tear-stained face almost unrecognisable.

'What?'

'Why don't you just tell Richard to go screw himself? Say, sod off, Richard, they're not going to boarding school. You can send them to the local school! Louis goes there, it's great.'

Caroline paused for a second. Then she fell once more into massive gobbing sobs.

Pearl and Louis came in, tinging the bell.

'What's up with Princess Twinkle?' asked Pearl.

'Don't ask,' said Issy. 'I mean it. Really. Don't ask.'

'Don't be sad, Caroline,' said Louis, reaching up to stroke her fur wrap. 'I like your wolf.'

'Please don't touch, Louis,' Caroline managed between sobs. 'It was very expensive.'

Louis turned round to Issy. 'ISSY!' he yelled. 'I MOST FORGOT! IT'S SNOWING!'

Issy glanced up at the windows. Sure enough, in the early-morning gloom, the little lamppost next to the tree showed up the flakes that had silently begun to drift down into the little alleyway.

'Oh, so it is!' said Issy, almost forgetting her tiredness in her delight. 'Isn't that gorgeous!'

'Can you come out to play in it with me?' said Louis, grabbing her hand.

'I can't, my love,' said Issy. 'But I can make you a hot chocolate.'

Louis smiled. 'YAY!' He turned to Pearl.

'CHRISTMAS! It's snowing! It's snowing! It's Christmas! It's Christmas! YAY!'

Pearl half smiled. 'All right, all right,' she said. 'It's going to take us four hours to get home tonight, that's all I can say. Let's get that hot chocolate warmed up.'

As they bustled around, cleaning, scrubbing, baking and generally getting the shop ready for the first of their chilled, hungry customers, Louis stayed with his face pressed against the glass. It was barely light at all, with the blizzard and the clouds so close to the ground. People passing by on the main road had their scarves over their mouths and their hats pulled down over their eyes, and were leaning in to the wind at an angle, grimly set on their destinations. It was an extraordinarily cold storm out there.

'I might take some samples out to the bus stop,' said Issy, bringing up a huge tray of sticky gingerbread. 'More of a mission of mercy than anything else.'

'MAMMA!' shouted Louis suddenly, his chubby little finger pressed up against the glass, his breath forming a cloud of condensation on the window. 'MAMMA!'

Pearl rushed over and followed his finger.

'Jesus Lord Almighty,' she said, and without stopping to grab her coat, ran out of the shop.

Issy and Caroline were right behind her.

'What on earth . . .?'

When you opened the door, you realised how freezing and horrible it was outside; a true maelstrom, with flakes swirling every way, blinding you. The cold grabbed you with a metal grip; the wind bit at your throat.

Pearl's heavy figure was lumbering over to the other side of the alleyway. Issy was just behind her, and gasped when she realised what it was Louis had spotted.

Standing just behind the now bare tree was a

small boy, younger than Louis. He was in his bare feet, wearing nothing but slightly grubby cream pyjamas with fire engines on them. His hair was blond and standing straight upright, and he was crying his eyes out.

* * *

Pearl scooped the little thing up in her arms like he was nothing, and they all rushed back inside. Louis was excited at his discovery.

'I found the boy, Issy,' he said importantly.

Issy was horrified. She had dashed out on to the main road, expecting to see a terrified mother running up and down searching frantically for her little boy, but there was just the usual queue of frozen-looking early commuters. She said hello to her friend Linda and asked if she'd seen anyone looking for a child. Everyone had looked confused, but shaken their heads. Issy told them that if anyone did come looking for him, he was safe with them, then dashed back to the shop.

Old Mrs Hanowitz, one of their regular customers, was at the door already. She gasped when she saw the little boy, in his cream-coloured pyjamas, cradled in Pearl's arms.

'The Christkind,' she said, shaking her head. 'Look at him.'

She came closer and put her fingers through his golden curls.

'A child at Christmas,' she whispered.

'Don't be daft,' said Pearl. 'This child is lost. What's your name, sweetheart?'

By the time Issy got back, the child was wrapped up warmly in a tartan blanket that

104

normally sat on the back of one of the old leather sofas. The child, who looked to be barely eighteen months, seemed too shocked even to cry. He grabbed the label on the blanket and started to rub it gently between his thumb and forefinger, then stuck his other thumb in his mouth. He looked rather comfortable.

'He needs a cake,' said Louis. 'And an Advent chocolate. OH NO, THERE AREN'T ANY, AUNT ISSY.'

'Louis, hush about that stupid Advent calendar,' said Issy. 'It's not going to get chocolate in it.'

'It is a very sad Advent calendar,' observed Louis.

Pearl sat down on the sofa with the boy still wrapped up in the blanket. Issy tried to tempt him with a piece of gingerbread, but he wasn't terribly interested in it, preferring to stare around the room with wide eyes. His little feet were blue; he was wearing no socks or slippers.

'I'll call the police,' said Issy. 'Someone must be going frantic.' She glanced out of the window again into the blizzard. 'Where are they, though?' she said. 'Unless he's come from miles away.'

'What's your name?' Pearl asked again, but it elicited no response. Then Louis came forward.

'What is your name, baby boy?' he asked kindly. 'Can you talk, baby?'

The boy took his thumb out of his mouth.

'Dada,' he said.

'Well, that's a start,' said Pearl. 'What's your name, sweetie? We'll get you back to your daddy soon.'

'DADA,' said the little boy, louder.

'He's the Christkind,' said Mrs Hanowitz, who

had followed them back into the shop even though they weren't officially open and was looking openly at the boy's untouched gingerbread.

'I really don't think he is the Christkind,' said Issy. She took the phone from its cradle. 'Do you think this is a 999 situation? It's not, is it? Or is it? What's the one for things that aren't quite as important as 999? 888?'

'One oh one' reeled off Pearl at once. 'What?' she said, seeing Issy's surprised face. 'Oh, well done for you. You live somewhere where you're unlikely to be a frequent victim of crime.'

Just as Issy started to dial, she saw someone tentatively enter the alleyway and look around. It was a young, confused-looking woman, not dressed warmly enough for the weather. Issy put down the phone and went to the door and stuck her head out.

'Excuse me,' she said. 'Are you looking for a child?'

The young girl turned, looking relatively unconcerned.

'Oh, do you have him?'

Issy looked at her for a moment. She couldn't just have heard that.

'Are. You. Looking. For. A. Child?' she repeated in case the girl couldn't hear her.

The girl sauntered over. 'Have you got him?' She was chewing gum and her eyes looked tired and a little blank.

'Um, yes,' said Issy. She wondered for a tiny second if she was being a bit of a nosy old busybody—was it perfectly normal for small children to go wandering about in their pyjamas in snowstorms? Was it none of their business? Then she turned and saw the tiny thing sitting on Pearl's

106

lap and realised it wasn't.

The girl walked into the shop.

'Oh, there you are,' she said resignedly. 'Come on then.'

The boy made no move to go. Pearl looked at the girl.

'What are you talking about?' she said. 'Did you let this little boy walk out in the snow on his own?'

'Durr, nooo,' said the girl. 'He wandered off. Come on, Donald.'

'Dada no,' said the boy.

'Well, that explains that,' said Pearl. 'Is your name Donald?'

'Dada,' confirmed the boy, then stuck his thumb back in his mouth.

Pearl looked at the girl again. She didn't look old enough to be his mother. Plus, one would imagine his mother would probably be a bit more pleased to see him. Especially a mother who bought fire engine pyjamas.

'Right, I take him,' said the girl, looking bored.

'Have you got socks for him? A coat?'

The girl shrugged. 'It not far.'

'Hang on,' said Caroline suddenly. 'Is this Donald? Donald Gough-Williams?'

The boy's eyes lit up at the mention of his name.

'Yeah,' said the girl unwillingly.

'You *know* this child?' said Pearl. 'Why didn't you say?'

'Oh, they all look the same to me,' said Caroline. 'This is Kate's baby. Are you the new Gough-Williams nanny?'

The girl shrugged reluctantly.

'There are the twins too,' said Caroline. 'Where are Seraphina and Jane?'

The girl turned on her with exhausted eyes.

'Yes,' she said. 'The twins.'

'Who's looking after the twins now?' said Issy suddenly.

'CBeebies,' said the girl. 'Come on, Donald, let's go.'

Pearl stood up and handed over Donald, complete with the blanket.

'Bring this back later,' she said. 'Don't let him catch his death.'

'Yes, I say OK,' said the girl. Slinging Donald over her shoulder like a sack of potatoes, she turned and left the Cupcake Café.

Caroline stared after them. 'I wonder what's up with Kate?' she said.

'She hasn't been in here for ages,' said Issy. 'I think it was just after the baby.'

'No, she's gone completely off radar,' said Caroline. 'I just assumed she was in rehab.'

Caroline, Pearl and Issy looked at one another.

'Would you mind terribly . . .' said Mrs Hanowitz.

'Take it,' said Issy, without a glance. Mrs Hanowitz started to eat Donald's unwanted gingerbread. Issy knew it was difficult for the old lady to heat and eat on her state pension.

'Now, I don't have children . . .' started Issy.

'I'll have to have a word,' said Caroline, shaking her head. 'That nanny is just awful. There's obviously some very juicy gossip going on.'

'That girl looked about sixteen,' observed Pearl. 'What's she doing looking after three children? How old are the twins?'

'Six,' said Caroline. 'Little girls. One thinks she's a boy. Adorable, mostly.'

'They are,' said Issy, remembering. Kate was

108

always trying to separate them, but they insisted on doing everything together. 'I wonder what's happened?'

Caroline had already taken out her phone.

'Ooh, I wonder if it will ring in the Priory. Hello? Hello, Kate darling . . . Where? Oh, Switzerland?'

Caroline's voice dropped noticeably, but she pulled it back.

'How GORGEOUS! Got lots of the fluffy stuff? Oh DELIGHTS, darling. Say hello to Tonks for me . . . and Roofs . . . Oh, are Bert and Glan there too? Oh really, all of you . . . Sounds very jolly . . . No no, you know me, working girl these days, no room for that kind of stuff, just busy busy busy . . . Oh yes, Richard's coming down, is he?'

Her voice turned to steel.

'Well, that's great news. You and Richard and all our friends. I'm so glad to hear it. I do hope you all have a wonderful time. Oh, they're both . . . No, no, of course I don't mind. Why would I? He's nothing to me. He'd just better not be spending the children's fucking school fees, that's all I can say . . .'

There was a pause.

'Now, listen. We just had your Donald in the shop. He'd got out of the house. I think you need a new nanny . . . Yes, again. Well, you know, they don't know how to work, these girls. I agree, totally lazy. New Labour. Issy was on the point of calling the police.'

Issy was now very relieved she hadn't got to the point of dialling.

'Yes, well, no, he was totally fine. Yes, he was still sucking his thumb . . . seems like a bit of delayed development to me . . .'

They exchanged a few more words before Caroline hung up. Her face sagged, and Issy caught the hurt and pain there. Then she pulled herself together.

'That lazy girl. I think Kate's going to change agencies. She said they've sent her six totally useless characters now.'

'Maybe she should have all six at the same time,' said Pearl.

'Do you know, that's not a bad idea,' mused Caroline.

Issy rolled her eyes. 'The longer I spend in Stoke Newington, the less I understand it,' she said. 'Is everyone really rich now?'

'Hmmph,' said Mrs Hanowitz, across the counter. 'Although I am pleased the Christkind brought me this good luck. That was truly bitte good.'

*   *   *

Carmen Espito clicked her heels up the passageway in front of Austin. None of this, he reflected, felt quite real. But here he was, on the forty-ninth floor—forty-ninth! It even had a special express lift—of the Palatine Building at Forty-fourth and Fifth, right in the very heart of Manhattan. The office was on a corner, and consisted mostly of huge glass windows, one of which faced north and included the Empire State and all the way to Central Park; while to the east he could see the Hudson river with the Brooklyn Bridge spanning across into the warehouses and riverside cranes of Brooklyn.

All around the great tower snow whirled,

soundlessly turning the whole of Manhattan into an enormous snow dome. It was heartstoppingly beautiful, one of the loveliest things Austin had ever seen.

'Wow,' he said, standing so close to the floor-to-ceiling windows he felt as if he could step right out into the sky. 'My little brother would LOVE it in here. How does anyone get any work done?'

Carmen smiled. She was used to the bank staff being very sophisticated, and if they were impressed by anything, absolutely refusing to show it. Before she had lost sixty pounds, got her nose fixed and tattooed on her eyebrows, she had been just a normal girl from Oregon, and Manhattan had transfixed her too.

'It is nice, isn't it?' she said. Then her bright red lips closed again, and she sat down at the empty desk.

'Now,' she said. 'I'm a lawyer, specialising in immigration and employment rights. Mr Ferani wanted to get all of this red tape sorted out as soon as possible, and I'm sure you do too.'

Austin told himself this was just a bunch of paperwork; not at all irreversible, just some stuff to look at and think about later. Then he realised, looking at the obviously sexy but also obviously very serious Carmen Espito, that these were legal documents she had in front of her. This wasn't just a little American chit-chat. Obviously they liked things done and they liked them done quickly. And they doubtlessly expected him to jump at the chance.

As any sane person would, of course. The chance to grab a fabulous job, a whole new life, at his age, well. It was a dream come true. Anyone else, he was sure, would be biting her hand off.

'Can I . . .' he asked. 'Can I take the contracts and stuff back to take a look at, just before we're all done?'

Carmen raised an eyebrow.

'Of course, they're pretty much standard boilerplate,' she said. 'If you want to get your lawyer to call me . . .'

Austin's lawyer had been a seventy-five-year-old grandmother who'd advised him to ignore social services when they wanted to come and poke about and ask Darny if he was getting his five a day, to which Austin would always answer yes, having come to the conclusion some time ago that he was just going to have to include potato.

'Uhm, yes, maybe I will,' he said hastily, trying to sound businesslike. 'Great. These are great.'

Carmen handed him several heavy sheaves of documents.

'Just bring them back with your passport.'

'My passport?' said Austin, feeling slightly panicky. It felt a bit like they were trying to hold him against his will.

Behind him the door opened with a boom, and Merv Ferani marched in. Today his bow tie was covered in small leaping reindeer, and his waistcoat was red. He looked like a small Jewish Santa Claus.

'How are we going here, Carmen?' he said. 'Finishing up?'

'Mr Tyler wants to get his lawyer to look it over,' she said, swiftly. Merv's face registered surprise.

'There's something you're not happy with?' he said.

'Oh, no, I'm sure . . . It's just, you know, I'd . . . I mean. I kind of do have to talk it over with my little

112

brother.'

'He's your business analyst, is he?'

'No ... no, he lives with me. And my girlfriend,' he added hastily. 'I just ... I mean, it's a huge uprooting ...'

'To the greatest place on earth!' said Merv. He was genuinely confused—and he had a right to be, Austin conceded, given that Austin had agreed to come to New York in the first place.

'Well, yes,' said Austin. 'I realise that.'

Merv looked out of the ceiling-height windows.

'Hey,' he said. 'I've got a great idea. We'll fly 'em out for the weekend. What do you think about that, huh? Let them have a look, realise how great your life here is going to be. Take the kid to some museums and shit, catch a show, eat some real food. I'll get my PA to sort it out.'

Austin looked at him, stupefied. Then he remembered he was meant to be this super-cool hip banker from the UK who was completely blasé about this kind of thing happening all the time. He didn't think he could pull that off.

'Well ...' he said.

'That's my boy,' said Merv. 'I'll pass you on to Stephanie, you'll love her.'

*　　　*　　　*

Why did everything have to move so fast? thought Austin, feeling his throat tighten nervously. But then, Issy was going to love it. She *was* going to love it, wasn't she?

113

Chapter Eight

Peacekeeper Christmas Spice Cookies

225g butter, softened
200g sugar
235ml treacle
1 egg
2 tbsp sour cream
750g all-purpose flour
2 tbsp baking powder
5g baking soda
1 tsp ground cinnamon
1 tsp ground ginger
pinch salt
14g chopped walnuts
145g golden raisins
145g chopped dates

In a large mixing bowl, cream the
butter and sugar together. Add the
treacle, egg and sour cream; mix well.
Combine the flour, baking powder,
baking soda, cinnamon, ginger
and salt; gradually add to creamed

mixture. Stir in walnuts, raisins and dates. Chill for 2 hours or until easy to handle.

On a floured surface, roll out dough finely. Cut with a 2½ inch round cookie cutter. Place on greased baking sheets. Bake at 160°C/gas mark 3 for 12–15 minutes. Cool completely. Allow to be inhaled by hungry cross people.

*   *   *

Issy was at Darny's school, and, currently, feeling a complete and utter fraud. Actually, it was awful. She was surrounded by people who all knew each other and were chatting furiously amidst peals of laughter, under fluorescent lighting, the smell of cheap mulled wine failing completely to cover up the undercurrent that was still after all these years so familiar to Issy: sweat, horrific aftershave rendered by the bucketload, trainers, illicit cigarettes and a harder-to-place hormonal fug that made everyone a little louder and more excitable.

She shouldn't even be here; she had just been so horrified when Austin had remarked casually that he didn't normally go to Darny's end-of-term concerts any more because Darny hated him being there so much and played up and they both got embarrassed.

'I thought watching kids in nativity plays was the good bit about having them,' she'd said, outraged.

'After the year with the politically motivated capitalist innkeeper being portrayed as the leader of UKIP, and the dope-smoking shepherd? No. We all kept out of it after that,' Austin had said wearily. 'Anyway, now he's at secondary school they don't do a nativity any more, they do some contemporary stuff.'

'Shit,' said Darny helpfully. 'He means contemporary shit.'

'And have you got a part?'

Darny had shrugged his shoulders, which Issy took to mean yes, I do, and Issy had insisted they were going and both the boys had slumped in a way that made them look less like brothers and more like identical twins.

'You have to encourage young people,' said Issy, who felt strongly about this after a year of watching increasingly dejected teenagers turn up looking for work with barely literate CVs. None of these kids had a job or any experience and she wished she could do more for them; but the CVs were all full of grandiose claims about empowerment and being an envelope-pushing people person and horrible sub-*Apprentice* claims that, when she looked at the slouching, embarrassed adolescent in front of her, didn't seem to be helping anyone. Austin called her Jamie Oliver, but he agreed. Just not when it came to Darny.

'It'll make things worse,' he said. 'Darny doesn't need an excuse to open his mouth.'

'No, he needs to know when it's appropriate,' said Issy. 'That's why we need to be there for him.'

But then, of course, Austin had got called away to the land of women with pin-thin legs and spiky heels and amazing luxury and being cosseted all day long, and it was she who had to pull on as many layers of clothing as she could manage after

116

a long day at the café and try to catch out Darny as he insisted that they'd been instructed to be all in black as Miss Fleur had convinced them that that would make it more dramatically powerful. Issy had sighed and finally agreed.

It had been bracingly cold outside, and they'd passed other families rushing towards the main school building on Carnforth Road. Words of merry excitement filled the air, and Issy couldn't help but feel a momentary pang; everyone was excited about being with their families at Christmas time, and she hadn't even heard from her bloody mother, while Austin was miles away and Darny was already, before they'd even got to the school gates, disappearing into a vast sea of adolescents, most of whom were impossible to tell apart. Issy supposed it was a true sign of growing older when you couldn't really tell what young people looked like; individually they just looked young.

Oh, she missed her Gramps so much. He was good at young people. He liked them, encouraged them. He'd hired lots of apprentices in the bakery, some of them from awful backgrounds, and the vast majority had thrived and done well and gone on to other jobs and lives elsewhere, and for so long they'd received hundreds of Christmas cards every year from happy customers and family friends and ... Issy didn't even open email Christmas cards. She just couldn't see the point these days.

Of course everyone else knew where to go, so she played with her phone to make it look like she was very busy and engaged, and followed the general stream towards the gym auditorium. Someone had obviously tried to make it look festive—there were paper streamers hanging from the ceilings—but it

117

couldn't disguise the fact that this was an inner-city school trying its best, not a posh luxury private school with theatrical societies and fully equipped sound-mixing desks.

Issy paid a pound for a plastic cup of scorching, slightly bitter mulled wine to give herself something to do, and reminded herself to stay out of the line of sight of any of Darny's teachers; that was strictly Austin's department. One of the reasons, she figured, that she and Darny stayed on reasonably friendly terms was that she hadn't once interfered in his schooling or how he was getting on, even when her fingers itched to do so, and she knew it was the right thing. He had frequent letters home and detentions, and Austin would sigh and beg him to behave, and Darny would put forward very rational arguments as to why he shouldn't have to, and it would go back and forth until everyone was exhausted and frayed and Issy would retire to the kitchen and whip up some Peacekeeper cookies and hope that one or other of them would grow out of it.

She didn't know a soul at the school. She texted Austin quickly. He was just leaving another meeting and texted back, 'I told you not to go', which was of course not helpful and made Issy wonder what the emoticon was for mild frustration. She sipped her mulled wine—the second sip was slightly better than the first, on balance—and wondered who to text next. This was danger hour for Helena, who would be trying to settle Chadani into bed, a process that could take several hours. Then her other friends ... but it had been so long, and they all (she tried not to count, but they mostly did) had children now, and had moved away, or were travelling all the time, or didn't really know what to talk to her about once they'd got past cakes. She really needed someone to whom she could say, 'Isn't this just total hell?'

'OH MY LORD, isn't this just TOTAL hell?' came a strident voice. She glanced up. To her utter surprise, Caroline, in a bright red fitted dress that was almost totally inappropriate for a school concert, but which also still looked slightly amazing, was marching through the serried ranks of other parents, who parted to let her through.

'Darling, thank GOD there's someone I know here. Everyone else looks COMPLETELY feral.'

Issy winced and tried to make a 'she doesn't really mean it' face to the rest of the world.

'Sssh,' she said. 'What on earth are you doing here?'

'Oh GOD, well, if that bastard goes through with what he's threatening, I'm going to have to send Hermia to this hellhole one day and have her mugged for her watch and shoes before she's even made it through the metal detector.'

'Caroline, can you keep your voice down?'

Caroline looked mutinous. 'I was hoping they'd ban me, then the Bastard would have to keep them at their private school like any rational human being. I don't understand how he can be so evil.'

'I think it's rather a good school,' said Issy. 'It's integrated, progressive—'

'I don't want progressive,' hissed Caroline. 'I want them hit on the hand with a ruler three times a day and doing cold runs in their underpants. Build a bit of bloody backbone, that's what this country needs.'

'But doesn't that turn out bastards like your ex?'

119

said Issy. The mulled wine must be stronger than she'd thought.

'Well, quite,' said Caroline. 'He shafted me before I had the chance to shaft him. If it wasn't happening to me, I'd probably be quite impressed.'

A slightly fusty-looking older man was standing on the platform, speaking into a microphone that bent feedback in and out. 'Can everyone sit down, please?' he was saying, his tone of voice indicating that he fully expected to repeat that exact sentence several times before anyone actually listened to him. The sole spotlight reflected off his bald head as he bent over to look at his notes.

'Christ,' said Caroline. 'Is there anywhere we can get a drink round here?'

'I think he's asking us to sit down,' said Issy.

'Well, I can see what you were like at school,' said Caroline.

'Yeah, likewise,' said Issy, steering her gently up the aisle and passing over her mulled wine. Caroline tasted it and made a face. Everyone had started shuffling in and Issy couldn't see a seat anywhere. All eyes were on Caroline in her bright tight dress. Issy was burning up.

Finally they landed right at the front.

'Oh God,' said Caroline loudly. 'I think I've seen enough, actually.' She stared meaningfully at the teacher on stage.

'I will take you out,' said Issy warningly.

'What?' said Caroline. 'We're paying for this school, I think we deserve to see how it stacks up.'

'Actually it's a publicly funded school so everyone's paying for it,' said Issy. 'It can kind of do what it likes.'

Caroline snorted again. 'Ha, as if Richard pays

120

tax. Right, if he says "Winterval", I'm out of here.'

'I think Winterval is an urban myth,' said Issy.

'Like Kwanzaa?'

'No, I think Kwanzaa is a real holiday.'

'Welcome, ladies and gentlemen, to the Carnforth Road School Christmas celebration— happy Christmas, Hanukkah, Winterval or Kwanzaa, whichever you would like.'

Issy cringed as Caroline gave her a pointed look.

'We have, this year, with the help of our wonderful drama mistress Miss Fleur, put together something of an alternative event for you ... *The Tale of the Spaceman*.'

There was a flourish of excited applause, as the overhead speakers came on and started with an enormous burst of synth chords. The curtain went up to reveal a perfectly black stage with nothing visible on it except, hanging from the top of it, a torch.

'Hang on,' said Issy. 'Is that "A Spaceman Came Travelling"?' She glanced at Caroline. 'OK, it is. You win. Let's go.'

'I LOVE this song,' said Caroline, suddenly looking fascinated.

*   *   *

In fact, despite the inevitable silliness—some very painfully sincerely delivered homilies on being an alien sent to earth to discover the terrible fate that it had been left to; a long piece on polar bears dancing that was obviously meant to be very moving but in fact left most of the audience in uncontrollable fits of mirth; a line of girls dressed as sexy penguins which was obviously meant to be

121

funny but was in fact profoundly uncomfortable as row after row of fathers pretended they weren't secretly figuring out how old they were; and a truly horrible orchestral interlude that wasn't improved by being right next to the tuba player—on the whole there was a definite effort being made, which made Issy feel proud and Caroline fiddle with her telephone.

Then it was Darny's turn. One of the smallest in the lowest year in the school, he stepped forward boldly. Issy was used to thinking of him as a large presence in their lives, as denoted by his enormous smelly trainers and pots of cheap hair gel strewn across their only bathroom, but now he seemed tiny, a small boy amidst the hulking teens and young adults.

Issy, however, had finally relaxed. Something with a strong environmental message was surely well within Darny's remit for being on message. She quickly pulled out her phone and took an illegal photo for Austin. They were all supposed to buy the official, non-paedophile photo album afterwards, but she wasn't sure she could wait that long. And he would have been proud, despite himself, that Darny had such a large speaking role.

Darny walked confidently towards the podium with the microphone. Issy realised she was nervous for him. She couldn't bear speaking in public; even welcoming people into the café was hard enough some days. It didn't seem to bother Darny at all, though. Come on, she found herself thinking. A nice little speech about saving the planet for tomorrow and they'd be home free and ready for another glass of terrible mulled wine. Caroline might even take her for a real drink.

Darny lifted up his speech as he got to the podium.

'Written on recycled paper,' he quipped, which got an appreciative laugh from the audience. He paused, then began.

'I wrote a bunch of crap in this essay—which my teacher really liked by the way, so thanks, Miss Hamm—about how to save the rainforest and protect biodiversity for future generations ...'

Issy felt herself sit bolt upright all of a sudden.

'Well, you know it's crap and I know it's crap. Everyone in China wants a fridge, and everyone in India wants an air-conditioning unit, and to deny people that kind of thing when they're working incredibly hard under conditions we can't even imagine is frankly totally smashed up. So why do we waste our time sorting out our sodding milk cartons and tea leaves? It's not going to make one tiny blind bit of difference to the polar bears, you know that already. I guess we're just filling in time here at school and talking about stuff like this for OFSTED, but really we all know it's crap.'

Issy let out a low groan and her chin sank on to her chest.

'So instead of fannying about with recycling water bottles—which is a joke anyway; if they were serious about this, you wouldn't even be able to buy water in bottles because it's arse—we might as well—'

Darny's great ideas for a solution to all the problems of the world were cut off suddenly in their prime by a howling wail of feedback as Miss Hamm launched herself up on stage and grabbed the microphone out of his hands with a look on her face that indicated she regretted the passing of corporal punishment in schools to the very depths of her being.

'DARNELL TYLER, REMOVE YOURSELF FROM THE STAGE THIS INSTANT.'

She turned to face the crowd. Darny still stood there, looking totally unbowed.

'Ladies and gentlemen, I must apologise for the unprompted showing-off of one of our younger pupils ... Is the guardian of Darnell Tyler in tonight?'

With hindsight, there couldn't have been a better time for Austin to reply to the photo Issy had sent him with the words 'Want to leave the country?'

*   *   *

'Oh God, it was awful,' said Issy the next day. 'Awful awful awful. I was so embarrassed.'

'I don't see why,' Caroline was saying. They were making eggnog coffee in the shop. Issy had expected this to be disgusting—it certainly sounded disgusting—but had inadvertently become completely addicted to it and was mainlining it that morning. The night before had been tricky; she was in no position to tell Darny off, but neither could she let him think that he was the hero of the hour, as his classmates apparently had (it was unlikely they had listened to what he was saying, but they had adored the bravura and the disruption).

But every time she brought it up on the way home (it didn't help that Caroline had sighed and said, yes, she might have expected this kind of thing in a sink school, which as she'd just sat through over an hour of carefully put-together entertainment made Issy want to kick her), Darny

124

had just shrugged and said well if she'd only let him explain, and she'd had to say that wasn't the point, and Darny had said well that was hardly an argument was it, she must know he was right and everything was cyclical.

Issy tried to ignore Caroline's nihilistic take on the whole thing, but she was surprised when Pearl weighed in on Darny's side.

'I'm not taking his side,' Pearl explained patiently. 'I'm just saying, it was quite a brave thing to do.'

Issy tutted. 'Don't be daft. My mum was always trying to get me to do stuff like this. Talk about CND or refuse to wear a skirt or something. She wanted me to be some kind of school mouthpiece.'

'So what's wrong with Darny doing it?'

'I never did it!' said Issy, horrified. ''Cause everyone a bunch of trouble for nothing!'

Pearl and Caroline exchanged a rare smile.

'What were you like at school, then?' said Issy, stung.

'Mine was a great school and I loved it,' said Caroline, with a blank expression on her face. 'I made friends for life and I loved boarding.'

Now it was time for Issy and Pearl to glance at each other.

'What did you learn there, Caroline?'

Caroline ticked it off on her fingers. 'How to eat tissue paper if you get really really hungry. How to pretend to be ordering chips in a restaurant then change your mind at the last minute. How to never ever tell a girl you like her boyfriend or she'll call you a slut in front of the entire year. How to withstand prolonged and intense psychological warfare. And Latin.'

'Happiest days of your life?' said Issy.

Caroline shivered. 'Please. Please let that not be true.'

'What about you, Pearl?' said Issy in a gently mocking tone.

'I didn't see the point of school,' said Pearl. 'And my mum never made me go, not really. I liked sitting up at the back of the class and teasing the teachers and hanging out with my homegirls and just having a laugh really. We didn't care. We'd have eaten you two for breakfast.'

Issy agreed fervently with this.

'Yours sounds the most fun,' she said.

Pearl shook her head. 'I can't believe I wasted what I had,' she said, with only a trace of bitterness in her voice. 'They offered me a decent education and I chewed gum and smoked on buses. I envy Darny so much—he wants to learn, he wants to communicate and tell people stuff and engage. I couldn't be bothered doing anything like that.'

She shook her head. 'I tell you what, Issy, I hope Louis turns out like him.'

*   *   *

Issy sighed. And she hadn't even told them about Austin's job yet. She watched Louis patting the Advent calendar. 'I wish your chocolate comes back one day,' he was whispering to it. You were never supposed to want to swap worries with anyone, but for once she felt she could make an exception.

Chapter Nine

In fact, although she'd tried to make light of it, Issy
had been close to tears by the time they'd got home
the previous evening. She knew it was ridiculous—
Darny's outburst had nothing to do with her, and
he was completely unfazed anyway—but it hurt
that he didn't even mind that she was upset with
him. Everything she had ever told herself about not
interfering in Darny's life, not caring about him ...
well, she did care about him. Of course she did. So
it was galling to see that he didn't feel the same way
about her—why would he, some girlfriend of his
stupid big brother?

Deep down, too, she knew that if she had pulled
a stunt like that, no matter what the nuns at St
Clement's would have said, her mother would have
been delighted. Thrilled with her, so proud. Her
mother wasn't often very proud of her. It occurred
to her she ought to get Marian and Darny together.

'So you mean it?' Austin had said excitedly when
she picked up the phone, exhausted.

'What?' she said, dispiritedly. She'd thought he
was only sending her the message 'Want to leave
the country?' as a joke, and had texted back, 'YES
PLEASE.' 'Look, Darny did something ...'

'Did he bite anyone?'

'No.'

'Oh lord,' said Austin, thinking back to what Mrs Baedeker had said. She couldn't mean it, could she? She wouldn't seriously exclude Darny. No. He convinced himself she wouldn't. Darny hadn't hit anyone or stolen anything. It was freedom of speech. There'd be a row, but in that case it was an even better idea to get him out of the way for a few days. Yes. That would do it. And he'd make him apologise and everything would be fine.

'Listen, I've got good news: the bank has invited you guys out for a few days!'

'What do you mean, "out"?'

'To New York!'

'Why does the bank want me to go to New York?'

'To see if you like it, of course. And Darny.'

'Well, after Darny's little stunt, he'll probably be excluded,' said Issy.

'What did he do now?'

'He deviated from the script in his school play. A bit. A lot.'

'Oh yes,' said Austin. 'Yeah, I knew how he felt about that.'

'And you didn't tell him to stop it?'

'I think he's got a point.'

'But how is that the right way to make it?'

'I am imagining you as the goodiest goody two-shoes at school,' said Austin.

'Just because I behaved myself!'

'Well, as long as Darny didn't bite anyone, I'm sure he'll be all right to come. Don't you think it's amazing? Haven't you always longed to see New

128

York, Issy?'

This was a low blow. Of course she had. She paused.

'But … I mean, is this it? Are you staying there for ever?'

'Of course not!' said Austin. 'I can leave whenever I like,' he added, skirting round the truth. 'I mean, it's really just a taster, then I can take it or leave it.'

'If they're flying us out, it doesn't sound like they particularly want you to leave it,' said Issy.

'Well, tough luck for them, then.'

Austin didn't have, Issy reflected, that same desire to please everyone that she had. She admired that. Normally.

'But won't you owe them something?'

'Nope,' said Austin. 'I'm in demand, baby!'

Issy smiled. 'Anyway. I can't, it's a crazy, busy time of year for us.'

'That's why you've employed two excellent staff members,' said Austin. 'To cover for you. Cut down on the cake styles to the ones Pearl can do, or leave mix or whatever it is you do … It should be like leaving a dog in kennels, shouldn't it? Hey, you could take on a temp cook and—'

'A temporary cook three weeks before Christmas?' said Issy. 'Right.'

There was a silence.

'Well, I thought you would like it,' said Austin finally. 'It's only a few days.'

'I know, I know. It's just impossible,' said Issy. 'Come home.'

'I will. Soon,' said Austin, deflated. 'Can I speak to Darny?'

'Are you going to tell him off?'

129

'Um ... I'll do my best.'

*   *   *

Issy had sunk down on the bed, utterly deflated. Why was she doing this? Why was she lying? Of course she wanted to be in New York. Of course she wanted to get on a plane, leave everything behind her, fly to Austin, jump on his hotel bed ... of course she did.

But Austin, she had to be honest, wasn't the only thing she loved. She loved the Cupcake Café too. More than loved it; she had built it, nourished it, grown it. It supported her and her friends, and was the single best thing she had ever done in her life. And she knew Austin was pretending this didn't mean anything, that it was only a holiday, a bit of fun, that he could say no whenever he wanted to, but it didn't feel like that to her. It felt like soon, down the line, he was going to make her choose between the loves of her life. The thought was unbearable.

From the other room, she could hear Darny shouting. So Austin obviously had tried to give him a telling-off. She didn't know what he was going to do about Darny either. Moving him right now seemed to her a very bad idea. But she was only the girlfriend. What did she know?

*   *   *

'So you're going?' said Caroline and Pearl simultaneously when she told them about it.

'I can't,' said Issy. 'We're so busy, look at us, we're overrun. I need the cash this time of year.'

'A free trip to New York,' said Pearl. She shook her head. 'A free trip to New York. At Christmas. Can you even imagine how many people would dream of something like that?'

'Oh, I used to go with an empty suitcase,' said Caroline.

'Whatever for?' said Issy.

'To fill it up with stuff, of course! We'd just shop all weekend and then I'd take off all the tags to avoid paying tax at customs. Brilliant days.'

'Shopping and tax avoidance?' said Issy. 'Well, it does sound wonderful.'

'You're the one turning down the free trip to New York,' said Caroline. 'So I will decide not to listen to you.'

But she couldn't turn her head away for long.

'Where's he staying?' she said. 'Because 72 E45th is fine these days but the Royale is really going downhill and you won't believe what they've done to the Plaza ... all those awful condominiums.'

'What's a condominium?' asked Issy.

Caroline sniffed. 'You know. A condo.'

'I don't know,' said Issy. 'It's just something Americans say, like bangs, that I've never really understood.'

'Well,' said Caroline, bustling off to tidy up, 'I don't have time to explain it to you now. In fact, why don't you go to the States and find out?'

'And cilantro,' Pearl called to her retreating back. 'What's cilantro, Caroline?'

Pearl and Issy shared a smile, but it didn't help Issy's problem. The bell tinged as Doti came in, without Maya today.

'Where's your glamorous assistant?' said Pearl, far too quickly, in Issy's opinion, for someone who

131

was meant to be making a go of it with someone else and wasn't at all interested in the postman. Even Doti looked surprised.

'Oh, she's doing so well I've let her take some of the run on her own,' he said, unleashing a block of cards wrapped up in a small red elastic band, and a large box.

'Hurrah,' said Issy. She had been completely surprised when people had started sending Christmas cards to the shop—it would never have occurred to her to do so. But they'd had one from Tom and Carly; Tobes and Trinida; from the students, Lauren and Joaquim, who had looked longingly at each other across the smallest, cheapest cappuccinos for months on end before finally plucking up the courage to talk to one another and were now madly in love, which was fantastic for them, but a bit of a loss of income; from Mrs Hanowitz, even though she didn't celebrate Christmas, who thought Louis might like a picture of a polar bear wearing a hat (he did); and even from Des, the estate agent who'd rented them the property in the first place. And as Issy had strung the cards up around the shop (Pearl grumbling about dust), more and more people had joined in, and now they had a lot. So Issy had thought about it and decided as a marketing cost (she said this to placate Pearl and Austin) to get some printed up. She'd enlisted her printer friend Zac, and Louis' artistic talents, and now they'd come back and they looked lovely.

Caroline had sniffed and said why didn't they go for minimalist, and Issy had pointed out that when you sold cakes with three inches of pink glitter icing sitting on the top, nobody was going to mistake you

LOUIs

for a Scandinavian furniture shop, and didn't Caroline think Louis' drawing was nice, and Caroline had said you had to be careful not to over-praise children—it was bad for them and meant they'd never achieve—and Louis had overheard and asked Issy what ovah-pwaze meant, and Issy had come closer to sacking someone than she'd ever thought possible.

'Well, aren't they lovely?' said Doti.

Issy nodded, then sighed. 'Better add getting these out to my to-do list.'

Pearl rolled her eyes. 'She won't go to America to see her boyfriend on a free flight,' she said. 'Boo

133

hoo hoo.'

'Why not?' said Doti kindly.

'Because there's too much to do and I don't want to leave the shop,' said Issy, expertly making up three hot chocolates and handing them over to some backpackers while spraying whipped cream on a nut latte for a fourth.

Pearl slipped four cranberry and fig cupcakes decorated with holly on to a plate whilst pouring two orange juices, wiping the surface, taking money, giving change and rearranging the front of the glass cabinet.

'Why can't you leave the shop?' persisted Doti.

'Because we're too busy,' said Issy. 'Which is nice, but it means I can't really go.'

Doti looked confused, as Maya clanged open the door behind him.

'Oh, I love this place,' she said, beaming her lovely smile.

Pearl gave her a surly look. 'Hello, Maya,' she said. 'I like your outfit.'

Maya looked down at the standard-issue postman anorak she was wearing, which looked at least four sizes too big for her.

'Really?' she said, then anxiously, 'You're joking, right?'

'She *is* joking,' said Doti sternly. 'Pearl is actually very nice, aren't you, Pearl?'

'Do you want coffee?' said Pearl.

'I've finished my round!' said Maya. 'We're a good team.'

Doti looked at Issy. 'What's that, Maya? You've finished for the day? Wouldn't it be lovely to have an extra job at Christmas time?'

Maya glanced at Doti and then at Issy.

'You're not hiring, are you?' she said, a flare of excitement in her eyes.

Issy shot Doti a cross look.

'No, no.'

'It's quite hard,' said Pearl. 'You'd need training.'

'Ha,' said Caroline from down in the kitchen.

'I don't understand,' said Doti slowly. 'If Maya could work for a few days so you could go and see your beloved, wouldn't that be a good idea?'

'It's not that simple,' said Issy. She was very reluctant to say that she would worry about not being in charge.

'Can't Pearl be in charge?'

'Well . . .' said Issy.

'Don't you think I could do it?' said Pearl.

'Of course you could,' said Issy. 'Of course. I mean, yes, we could narrow our menu . . . I'll leave my book.'

'I'd be completely fine,' said Pearl. 'And also, when I cash up, mine comes out even.'

'Don't rub it in,' said Issy.

'I . . .' Maya's face looked excited, then fell a little. She looked extremely young. 'Sorry,' she said. 'It's just . . . I've been job-hunting for six months. The idea of getting two . . . well. It would be amazing.'

'It would only be for a few days,' warned Issy.

'It would be such a help,' said Maya.

'She's a fast learner,' said Doti.

'Issy, did you break the new bowl?' shouted up Caroline from the cellar.

Issy's phone buzzed with a text. It was from Austin and said simply, '17.35 Heathrow Terminal 5. YES!!!!!'

135

This should, she knew, fill her with joy and excitement. Instead, irrationally, it made her a bit cross. It seemed presumptuous and bossy, as if she was being railroaded into a decision that wasn't hers at all.

She noticed on her smartphone (a birthday present from Austin that Darny kept trying to show her how to use and she kept forgetting) that she also had an email. Most of her emails came direct to <u>cafe@thecupcakecafe.com</u>, so this was unusual. Trying to keep her cool as Pearl started firing questions at Maya as to whether she knew how to work a till and do more than one thing at once and Maya revealed that she had grown up working in her local Chinese at weekends which made her pretty undoubtedly qualified if the busy craziness of most Chinese takeaways Issy had ever been in had anything to do with it, she clicked it.

`Darling Isabel`, it began.

Only two people in her life had ever called her Isabel. Her beloved Grampa Joe, and . . .

`Well, here I am! Just to tell`
`you I won't be celebrating`
`Christmas this year as I have`
`met my soulmate. I now live with`
`a collective of Orthodox Jews`
`so we'll be passing it just as`
`any other normal day. However`
`Hanukkah is upon us as I'm sure`
`you know . . .`

Issy internally rolled her eyes. She did know it

was Hanukkah actually: Louis had shown her the menorah he'd made at school, and everyone had finally understood after a week of trying to work out what he meant by 'men over' with Caroline talking pointedly about speech therapy to Pearl and Issy having to stand between them at all times.

```
so I will be lighting a candle
for you in the window here in
Queens ...
```

'Caroline?' said Issy in a strangled voice. 'Where's Queens?'

'Oh, no one ever goes to Queens, darling,' came the voice from downstairs. 'Does that new girl know how to make royal icing?'

'Yes,' said Maya. Pearl shot her a look. 'I learn fast,' qualified Maya quickly.

Issy held up her hand to quieten everyone.

'Caroline,' she said, more slowly. 'Is Queens near New York?'

Caroline climbed up the narrow steps with a supercilious look on her face. She loved being in the know.

'Actually, it's part of New York,' she said. 'There's five boroughs ... Manhattan, Brooklyn—'

'Yeah, OK, all right,' said Issy. 'So it's close by?'

'It's part of it. You go through Queens on the way to the airport.'

Everyone stopped what they were doing to look at Issy, who threw up her hands.

'OK!' she said. 'OK, I give up. The universe is conspiring against me. Maya, get down there and learn to make royal icing. I'm ... I guess I'm going to New York!'

'Yay!' cheered some of the customers.

Doti smiled. 'This is all going to work out great.'

'Thank you! Thank you!' said Maya.

Pearl didn't say anything as she handed over a box of a dozen red velvet and mint icing cakes for an office party.

'Don't smoosh them in the photocopier when you're taking pictures of each other's bums,' she warned the giggly girls with reindeer antlers waiting to pick them up.

'No fear,' said one. 'We're going to hand-feed them to the best-looking men in the office.'

'Well, there's no way that can possibly backfire,' said Pearl as they disappeared, giggling their heads off.

Issy's mind meanwhile was in a whirl; half-excited, half-terrified, and trying to work out the practicalities. Pack ... tell Darny's teachers ... get organized ...

'I'll pick up Darny en route, he's at his friend's,' she mused. 'He'll be delighted ... No,' she corrected herself. 'He'll be the exact opposite to whatever emotion I expect him to have. Pearl, you're in charge.'

'It's a Christmas miracle!' said Caroline. 'This is wonderful.'

'Hmm,' said Issy, nervous and excited all at once.

'Hang on!' said Caroline and disappeared back down the stairs. 'I have something for you.'

Pearl looked up. Spontaneous acts of generosity weren't exactly Caroline's thing. Two seconds later she reappeared.

'It will be freezing in New York,' she said. 'Proper real American freezing, not a bit blowy and damp like it is here.'

138

She held out, at arm's length, her white fox-fur coat. It was cut very short, like a biker jacket, with great screeds of fur down the front and metal stud detail at the top, and a leather collar and cuffs, and was, beyond a shadow of doubt, the most hideous coat Issy had ever seen in her entire life.

'That's sooo kind of you,' said Issy in agony. 'But I couldn't possibly. How will you get home?'

Caroline shrugged. 'Can't I do something nice?'

'Yes, but you know, I don't really believe in fur ...'

'It's fake,' said Caroline. 'I know, it doesn't look it, it looks like the real thing. And it was practically as expensive as the real thing. But as I said to the Bastard, can't you share a little kindness in the world? I mean, he can't, obviously, he's a total bastard. So that's me rebalancing our chakras. My therapist says it's good karma.'

'Your therapist believes in karma?' said Pearl wonderingly, but Issy was just standing there, floored by the generous gesture.

'Send me lots of pictures of you wearing it,' said Caroline. 'I love New York so much and never get to go there any more. You can take the coat instead. It'll be almost as good as going myself.' Her eyes had gone a little misty.

'Uhm. Thank you,' said Issy. 'Thank you. That's very kind.'

'Try it on!'

'Yes!' said Pearl. 'Try it on!'

Caroline's narrow shoulders and thin frame meant that at least the ludicrous cut of the jacket made it look like it was done on purpose. On Issy's soft white shoulders and large, gentle bosom, it didn't have a hope in hell. Her arms stuck out at the sides like Buzz Lightyear's wings.

'I don't think it fits,' said Issy.

'Nonsense,' said Caroline, pulling and fussing with the creaking leather till it came to an approximation round her middle. The fur tickled Issy's nose and she could feel the studs through the shoulders. 'It's perfect.'

Issy risked a look at Pearl. Her face was utterly blank and she couldn't meet Issy's eyes, which told Issy all she needed to know. Even more when two seconds later she turned round to greet Louis coming in early from school.

'Issy!' he said, looking concerned. 'Is your coat sore, Issy?'

'Thank you, Louis,' said Issy. She glanced at her watch. 'Oh Lord, I'm going to have to go.'

She searched for the words that involved taking off the jacket without insulting anyone. They would not come. Pearl, still completely straight-faced, hung her handbag off her outstretched arm. Doti and Maya clapped and waved her a cheery goodbye, and she struggled her way out of the door, heart pounding, arms wide.

*   *   *

Just outside, in the chill of the courtyard, she turned back. Everyone except Caroline was, as she'd suspected, bent double with laughter at her new outfit. But that wasn't what she was looking at.

The little café was full to bursting with happy cheery people sharing their nut lattes and mince pies, showing each other their big bags of gifts, some with long rolls of red and green paper sticking out. Children were running around pointing at the Advent calendar, which Louis was guarding fiercely, doling out one window a day without fear or favour. The queue was almost out the door and steam was rising from the tea urn, and Issy felt, already, only a few metres away, a deep and abiding nostalgia for the place. She was on a journey now, heading somewhere else, far away, and she did not know if things would be the same when she returned.

Chapter Ten

Express Airlines Altitude Cookies

If you live up very high (or are flying) you have to bake differently, because things don't rise the same way or taste the same. In fact, hardly anything tastes of anything in the air, which is why you like to drink tomato juice even though at ground level it's a bit nasty. Here are some airline cookies you may want to bake in advance if you have to go on a plane. They make a lot, so you can hand them out on the plane and make a lot of new friends.

Altitude Cookies

125g salted butter
125g white sugar
125g brown sugar
1 large egg
1 tsp vanilla essence
350g sifted flour

75g hot chocolate powder
1 tsp salt
1 tsp baking powder
350g chocolate chips (whichever
  colour you like)
pinch cinnamon

Cream butter and sugar together,
then add egg and vanilla essence.
    In a separate bowl combine the
dry ingredients. Fold in the wet mix,
then mix the chocolate chips in (yes,
you can eat some; you don't have
to pretend they fell on the surfaces
or anything). Chill the whole mix in
the fridge for at least an hour, then
preheat oven to 180 degrees.
    Cut out with a glass to about $\frac{1}{2}$ cm
thickness and place on baking tray
covered in baking paper. Bake for
around 10 minutes, or until brown (9
minutes if you prefer a softer cookie).
    Attempt to avoid eating them till
you get on the plane—warning, they
are VERY rich for ground level!

*   *   *

Issy was dashing about the house in a panic.
Helena had agreed with frankly surprising alacrity
to take her to the airport, muttering something
about getting out of the house, but time was
running short. Issy had no idea what to take—
cocktail dress? Ballgown? Five hats?—and Darny
was point-blank refusing to pack anything apart

from his usual hoodie and fifteen DS games. He scoffed at every hat she held up as if it were for a five-year-old and couldn't seem to get his head around the fact that they were going to a different climate, which, since the only place he'd ever been to was Spain on a package trip, where it had rained every day, was possibly not that surprising but was infuriating Issy.

'Why are we even going?' he had grumbled. 'Doesn't Austin want to come back here? Why can't he come and see us?'

Issy had tried to come up with a good explanation. She wasn't doing very well.

*　　　*　　　*

'Hello!'

Kelly-Lee was delighted to see the rumpled-looking Englishman again. Now that he wasn't half asleep, she noticed how handsome he was, with a distracted look about him which implied his mind was on higher things. Austin was in fact wondering what exactly to say to Merv if Issy and Darny simply didn't arrive. He knew on one level that it was his fault for making everything so tricky; on another level, there was a bit of him, more childish, that said it was unfair that he didn't have anyone—truly anyone—around to say, wow, Austin, that's just so amazing! Even his PA, Janet, who was normally his biggest cheerleader, had got very sniffy about the whole thing and was making pointed remarks about how wonderful it was for people who got to go and work in America and how there wasn't much call these days for old washed-up PAs who got put out of work, and Austin had tried to laugh it off and

144

explain that he wasn't going, and she sniffed loudly and he remembered how many more things Janet seemed to know than he did and felt guilty.

So no, nobody was happy for him, not really. He did like to think that his mother would have been pleased. But would she? She hated bankers; both his parents had been totally unreconstructed old socialists. She had absolutely adored him going off to study marine biology, had loved the concept of him travelling the world and diving. And if she hadn't only gone and been hit by a bloody nineteen-year-old driver—well, then he might have been doing just that. At least he was doing the travelling the world bit.

He had a few photos of his parents, but not many; developing pictures was expensive in those days, and they were mostly of him and Darny, which as far as Austin was concerned was pointless and completely unnecessary. Sometimes they were with his dad—tall and with the same mop of unruly red-brown hair as Austin—but there were very few of his mother. He guessed it was always her behind the camera. He tried to conjure up her image, but he still found it hard to believe how young she had been. It became worse the older he got. Sometimes he would imagine her in the kitchen cooking up something nice, but this was a complete fallacy; his mother hated to cook and would dole up sad-looking vegetable stews or lentil hotpots under sufferance. The fact that Issy actively enjoyed being in the kitchen was something he could never quite understand; his mother used to mutter a lot about Germaine Greer and slavery. He saw so much of her in Darny. He missed her such a lot.

'You look like you've lost a dollar and found a

nickel,' said Kelly-Lee. Austin smiled weakly.

'Hello,' he said. 'Sorry, lost in thought.'

'Ooh, a thinker!'

'Well, I don't know about that,' said Austin, as she made him a cup of burnt-tasting coffee large enough to sail the QE2 in.

'So,' she said in a conspiratorial tone of voice. 'Did your girlfriend love the cupcakes?'

Austin frowned. 'Hmm,' he said. 'Not exactly.'

Better and better, thought Kelly-Lee.

'Oh no! That's too bad. Is she on a diet?'

'Issy? On a diet?' Austin grinned at the thought. 'Uhm, no.'

Kelly-Lee had been on a diet since she was thirteen years old, though she always claimed she wasn't and was just lucky she could eat what she liked.

'So what was the problem?'

'Well, she's a baker, so ...'

'They're all made to the highest of standards.' Kelly-Lee picked up a coconut cookie wrapped in cellophane. 'Here, try this.'

'Actually,' said Austin, 'I'm not that crazy about sweet things.'

He didn't even care for sweets. This was perfect, thought Kelly-Lee. They might as well have broken up already. He was moving here, she wasn't here, she didn't like his present, he didn't like her cakes ... No court would convict her.

She quickly glanced at herself in the reflecting side of the cake cabinet. She looked pretty good, her wide mouth painted a nice delicate pink and her teeth very straight and sparkly white. She blinked whilst looking at the floor—an old trick, but a good one, she'd found—then glanced up at

146

Austin through her lashes.

'Well, if you don't want anything sweet ...' she said tentatively, pretending to be nervous, 'maybe a drink later?'

'Uhm.' Austin furrowed his brow in confusion. 'I don't ...'

'I just thought a friendly thing when I finish my shift ... nothing more. Sorry. I'm just ... I'm new in town too. I'm sorry, I just ... I mean, I just get lonely sometimes.'

'You?' said Austin, genuinely surprised. 'But you're so pretty! How can you be lonely?'

'Do you really think so?'

Austin was starting to feel this conversation was getting out of his control.

'Anyway, I have to go to the airport tonight. My girlfriend is ... well, at least I *think* my girlfriend is arriving.'

'Oh, great,' said Kelly-Lee. 'You must come on by, show her the place!'

'I will,' said Austin, relieved.

'But you don't know if she's coming for sure?'

Austin winced a bit. 'Well, it's hard for her to get away, you know; she runs a business and everything ...' He checked his phone, instinctively, then put it away when it showed nothing.

Too busy to look after her man, thought Kelly-Lee without a qualm.

'Well,' she said. 'If she decides not to come, you come here and get me and I'll take you to this little Manhattan watering hole I know where they serve Jack Daniel's and play jazz. You'll like it.'

'I'm sure I will,' said Austin, gulping down as much coffee as he could handle—about an eighth of the gigantic cup—and heading for the door.

'Hang on,' said Kelly-Lee. She grabbed a notepad and pen and jotted down her number. 'Just in case,' she said, popping it in his top pocket.

*   *   *

There was a letter on the hall table that looked official. Even though Helena was honking furiously outside in the car and a pair of tights were trailing out of Issy's gigantic bag like they were attempting to escape, she stopped to pick it up. Darny was wearing shorts, mismatched socks, a hoodie and nothing else. Issy threw one of Austin's coats at him—very briefly she caught Austin's comforting smell of cologne and printer ink—and banged open the door with a clang. Helena was gesticulating wildly, Chadani Imelda howling her head off in the back seat. Behind them, a large white van was also honking, trying to get past on the narrow road that was lined both sides with parked cars.

'DARNY!' called Issy in frustration. Darny slouched out as slowly as he dared, pretending to read *The God Delusion* in one hand as he went.

Helena stopped honking when she saw what Issy was wearing.

'What ... ' Her mouth dropped open.

'Shut up. It's a favour to a friend,' said Issy. 'An acquaintance. Someone I don't like. Whatever.'

She tried to throw her bag in the boot of the car, but Chadani's gigantically oversized turbo buggy was already in there taking up all the room, so eventually, crosser and crosser, she laid it on the back seat and made Darny sit on it.

'We're going to miss this flight,' she grumbled.

'We won't,' said Helena, cheerily flicking a V at

the irate van caught behind her. 'And if you do, you can catch the next one, and if you don't want to, you can come home and have some wine with me and I'll show you all of Chadani's new photographs and finger paintings.'

Issy sighed. 'Hello, Chadani,' she said to the back seat. To her horror, Chadani was wearing a white fake fur coat not unlike Issy's own, except Chadani's was huge and had big pompom buttons. She looked red-faced, hot and cross.

'WAORGH!' she cried, then opened her mouth and started screaming again, and Issy began to think that paying a fortune to take the Heathrow express might not have been so bad after all.

'Hello, baby,' said Darny in a conversational tone.

Immediately Chadani stopped hollering and looked at Darny with huge chocolate-brown eyes.

'Stop crying,' he said, fastening his seat belt beside her. 'It's annoying and I have to sit next to you.'

Chadani held out her little finger. Darny took it, and she coiled her hand around his second finger, then held it tight. Issy and Helena looked at each other.

'How do you *do* that?' said Issy.

Darny shrugged. 'Because I don't judge everyone the second I meet them like you do.'

'Well, one, I do not do that,' said Issy. 'And two, Chadani is a baby.'

'She's a person,' said Darny.

Helena pulled out.

'I can't believe,' whispered Issy to Helena when Darny had put his earphones in, 'that I get all the annoyingness of a child and none of the cute and

149

cuddly bits.'

'Oh, you can keep your cute and cuddly bits,' said Helena. 'Chadani Imelda pooed on her own head this morning.'

'Maybe you could send that to *Britain's Got Talent*,' said Issy.

Helena snorted. 'She has many, many talents,' she said, her voice softening. 'But delicate, feminine pooing is not one of them. Although the other day—'

'It's all right!' said Issy quickly. Helena's ability to talk freely and enthusiastically about poo might, she supposed, be considered absolutely cool and normal in her parenting group, but Issy still found it a bit alarming.

Helena swerved round the corner and shook her head.

'I can't understand why you aren't excited,' she said. 'I can't imagine waking up one day normally then suddenly getting whisked off for free to New York. I mean, I have to look after Chadani every day ... FOR EVER.'

'But you love doing that,' said Issy.

'You love eating cupcakes, but you don't eat them every day ... Hmm, bad example,' said Helena.

Issy sighed. 'Actually,' she said, 'I hoped you'd understand. Everyone else thinks I should be over the moon to be going away, and I feel like the most ungrateful, selfish person on earth.'

Helena grinned, before fiercely flicking a V at a lorry driver. Issy didn't think he'd done anything wrong; it was just habit.

'What's the matter, it's not a posh enough hotel?'

Issy grinned back. 'No, it's not that. It's just ...

you know, the Cupcake Café is my baby.'

'Smells better than mine,' said Helena.

Issy looked at her curiously. It was very unlike Helena to talk in anything other than glowing terms about motherhood.

'What's up?' she said.

Helena let out a big sigh. 'Do you know how many hours junior doctors work?'

'Lots?' asked Issy.

'*All* of them!' said Helena. 'So it's just me and Chadani cooped up in that crappy little flat all day ...'

Issy bit her tongue.

'Then he comes home and he's knackered and has to study and we have to be quiet and all he wants to do is sleep and he thinks my life is very easy but all I get to do is change the baby and take her out for walks which is oh my God so boring, I just push a pram about all the time and no one will talk to me because apparently a pram makes you invisible and all the other mothers go on about their kids all the time and it's *so* boring and I miss my life.'

Helena stopped suddenly and took a deep breath as if she'd surprised herself by what she'd said.

'I love Ashok and I love Chadani Imelda,' she said fiercely. 'Don't get me wrong. I love them more than anything.'

Issy felt horribly guilty. She should have listened more, been around more for Helena. She hadn't thought motherhood made you lonely—how could it when there was someone new in your life?—but maybe it did.

'Why didn't you say?' she said. 'You always seemed so happy.'

'I *am* happy!' said Helena in anguish. 'I've got everything I've ever wanted. My stupid brain is just taking a bit of time to realise it. And whenever I try and see you, you're so busy and professional and successful and doing nine things at once and it's taken me three hours to leave the house and wipe banana off the walls, so I just think what could I possibly have to talk to you about, when you're jetting off on the spur of the moment to New York like a model or something.'

'You can talk to me about anything!' said Issy. 'Except Chadani's poo, I don't like that.'

There was a pause, then Helena burst out laughing.

'I've missed you,' she said. 'I really have. I just didn't know how to talk to you any more.'

'Well I've missed you too, so much,' said Issy. 'I have plenty of people I work with, and I have Austin, when he's not on the other side of the world, but I really really need my friend.'

'Me too,' said Helena.

'So aren't you going back to work?' ventured Issy. 'You love your job so much.'

Helena sighed. 'Well, Ashok and I felt it was so important for Chadani Imelda's first years . . . '

Issy shot her a look.

'Am I going on about "what's best for baby" again?'

Issy nodded vigorously.

'Sorry. I got into the habit at my mothers' group. So much for the sisterhood. It's like *The Apprentice* in there, but with breast pumps.'

She reflected.

'I mean, obviously I'm winning, but it takes a lot of effort. There's masses of puréeing and stuff.'

'So?'

'Oh fuck, yes, as soon as I possibly can. I am totally bored off my fucking tits. Also I need gin.'

Issy nodded. 'We do. We need to go out and get some gin.'

'We should,' said Helena. 'But you're leaving the country.'

'Yes,' said Issy. 'I shall return with duty-free gin.'

'Well, I am envious,' said Helena. 'But I do understand. And I would say, enjoy it as much as you can. December in New York—amazing! Forget all the other stuff. You and Austin will sort it. You're both reasonable people. Love will find a way.'

'Hmm,' said Issy. 'I will just have to try and remember the difference between compromise and giving up everything for a chap. My mother would be horrified.'

Helena smiled. 'And she spent a year in a nudist colony.'

'Please don't remind me about that again. Please please please please.'

'The photo Christmas card was my favourite.'

'Stop it! Stop it!'

*   *   *

When they arrived at Heathrow, Helena got out and even ignored—for five seconds—Chadani's cross mewling noises to give Issy a huge hug, which Issy returned with gusto.

'Now don't start buying too many presents for Chadani,' she said sternly.

'Sssh!' said Helena. 'She still believes in Santa Claus.'

153

Darny slouched out of the car.

'Have you got a hug goodbye for your auntie Helena?'

Darny regarded her. 'I wouldn't feel comfortable embracing you at this point,' he said.

Helena shot Issy a look. 'Good luck,' she said.

'Thank you!' trilled Issy. 'Come on, Darny, shall we go see Austin?'

Darny shrugged his shoulders. 'I'd have been all right in the house by myself.'

'Of course you would,' said Issy. 'Right up to the catastrophic fire at five past four. Come on!'

Helena held Chadani Imelda's arm up to wave as they disappeared into the futuristic glossiness of Terminal Five, lit up like a spaceship in shades of purple and blue. Then she cuddled her little girl close to her in her smart red coat.

'I love you so much,' she said. 'But Mummy has stuff to do too.'

'MUMMY!' said Chadani cheerfully, and bit her affectionately on the ear.

*   *   *

There was a queue of hundreds of people at check-in. It made Issy tired just looking at it; she'd been up since 5.30. Lots of screaming children, obviously travelling for Christmas, and loads of complicated-looking baggage being checked in. The queue wound round and round the metal poles with strips to pull out and fasten to mark the line; several children were pulling them back, hurting their hands and causing disagreements in the queue. One harassed woman at the check-in desk had a grim set to her jaw that said she was getting

154

through her day by sheer willpower alone, so not to try and cheek her.

Down in the main lobby of the terminal a brass band was playing 'Once in Royal David's City' so loudly Issy couldn't hear herself think. She felt a headache coming on. This was a stupid idea. They shouldn't have come. She had a very ominous-looking letter from Darny's form teacher in her pocket that she was taking to Austin that she recoiled from touching whenever her hand strayed in that direction and Darny was making the kind of loud sighs and eye rolls that generally precipitated an outburst against the world, and Issy felt ridiculously hot and stupid in her white coat; she knew her cheeks were red and her black curly hair had tangled itself in the humidity.

They heaved their stuff forward towards the front of the queue, where a man was checking boarding passes. Theirs had been lying on the hall floor when Issy had arrived home—she'd assumed Janet had dropped them in, but now she saw that they'd actually been couriered. She handed them over, feeling as she did so a mild panic that they were the wrong ones and the realisation in the pit of her stomach that she hated flying; it scared her stiff even though she'd never admit it in a million years.

The man studied the documents and glanced at her briefly. Issy felt herself go even redder. It would be entirely like Austin to get the date or the plane or the time wrong; once they'd been to Barcelona for a minibreak whilst Darny stayed with the dreaded aunties, and he'd booked the hotel for the wrong weekend. Typical. Issy chose to forget for the moment that instead they'd hired a scooter and

155

gone off and explored the countryside, ending up in this completely amazing finca with a waterfall in the grounds and the most amazing paella, and had had the best trip ever.

The man finally looked up, smiled brightly at them and said, 'This isn't the queue for you.'

Issy thought she might burst into tears. They were going to have to turn round and head all the way back into town with all their stuff, and Darny would be a nightmare and she'd have to explain to everyone what she was doing back in London and Austin would probably extend his trip and she'd have to spend Christmas by herself because her mum was Jewish now and ...

The man was pointing to the side. 'You go over there.'

She followed his hand. It was indicating a red carpet, leading off behind a purple-tinted wall with a sign overhead saying, 'Business and First-Class Passengers'.

Issy did an enormous double-take. She couldn't believe it. She looked at the tickets but still didn't really understand them, then smiled an enormous wobbly grin.

'Really?'

'Really,' said the man. 'Have a good flight.'

*   *   *

Suddenly, everything changed. It was, Issy told Helena later, like being whisked through the wardrobe to Narnia. There was an entire section for check-in just for them; no queues, no waiting to get through security. Even Darny was quietly impressed. They went up to the lounge, which had

156

every magazine and newspaper and snack and drink imaginable, then, on the plane itself, they went upstairs, which was beyond exciting.

If Austin thinks this will change my mind about everything ... thought Issy, sinking into the heavy pillows and pushing out the footrests as the plane banked over the twinkling lights of the city. For the first time ever (and with Darny in the window seat), she'd complctely forgotten to be nervous on take-off, quickly texting Austin to say they were on their way (which he'd received with some relief). If Austin thinks ...

But the weeks of late nights and constant early starts at the café, the worry and the work, coupled with the slow steady burr of the engines below, was too much for Issy, and she fell fast asleep, waking up six hours later to find, to her utter and total disgust, that they were commencing their descent.

'I missed dinner,' she said crossly.

'Yes,' said Darny. 'It was amazing. Delicious. You could have anything you wanted. Well, I wanted wine but they said no.'

'And I missed ...' Issy flicked quickly through the inflight magazine. 'Oh no! They had *all* the good movies I wanted to watch! I haven't been to the cinema in a million years. I can't believe I missed them all!'

She looked around. Businessmen were removing their slippers and putting their shoes back on; pushing back TVs and footrests.

'Nooo!' howled Issy. 'The only time in my life I will ever ever ever get to go business class on an aeroplane and I've wasted it all.'

'Your face looks crumpled,' observed Darny.

'Nooo!' Issy jumped up. The airline mirror

157

reflected the fact that she looked absolutely gruesome. She did her best with the make-up she'd managed to grab on the way out. Then she added a bit more. Then she put some lipstick on her cheeks to try and stop herself looking like the walking dead. Instead she looked like a clown. She told herself, sternly, that she had woken up to Austin every single day for over a year and he hadn't recoiled in horror yet, but deep down she realised how nervous she was. Not about him, but about what was going to happen. And maybe a little bit about him.

*   *   *

Austin was nervous too, standing in the airport arrivals. He was excited to see them, of course he was. It was just … he hoped … well, he just wanted everything to be good and happy and nice. But he also wanted—indeed, had pretty much promised—to come and live here now. To try things out. To travel, to experience life in the big city. He bit his lip. A brass band was playing 'Once in Royal David's City' in the terminal forecourt. It was dreadfully loud.

Issy and Darny came through passport control first. Darny looked excited and nervous; he burst into a huge grin when he saw his brother, then instantly tried to look cool and nonchalant, although his eyes were darting everywhere: at the security marshals with their guns and dogs; accents so familiar from the television but so strange at the same time; different signs and instructions coming over the tannoy.

Issy looked tired, and sweet, and had for some mad reason put red clown spots of make-up on her

158

cheeks, but he decided to ignore that for now. And she was wearing . . . what was she wearing?

'What are you wearing?'

Issy looked up at him. Had he changed? She couldn't tell. He looked the same—his thick browny-red hair flopping over his eyes as usual; his horn-rimmed glasses; his tall, slim figure with the surprisingly broad shoulders.

But he also looked—kind of at home here. Like he fitted in. He had a briefcase and a long overcoat and a rather nice red scarf and a suit, and suddenly Issy saw him as one of the men on her flight; casually bored of being in business class instead of finding it a big adventure; working every free moment they had. She had never thought of Austin as one of those people. But maybe he was.

'Hey,' she said. Then she let herself be enfolded in his strong arms; drinking in his scent and the familiar warmth of him.

'Hello,' he said. He kissed her firmly on the mouth. 'You haven't answered my question.'

'I liked the plane tickets,' she said.

Suddenly Austin stopped looking like a smooth, rich businessman and looked like himself again.

'I know, coool, huh? Did you play the games? Did you visit the bar? Did you get a massage?'

'No,' said Issy crossly. 'I fell asleep and missed all of it.'

'No way! Did you not even try the barbecue? What about the swimming pool?'

Issy giggled. 'OK, now you can shut up.'

Austin caught Darny in his other arm. 'Don't think you're getting away without a hug, you.'

Darny grimaced. 'Yuck, that's disgusting. Brothers aren't meant to hug anyway.'

159

'You'd do well in communist Russia,' said Austin. 'C'mere.'

Darny continued to grimace, but did not, Issy noticed, pull away.

'Shall we get going?' she said, eventually.

'No,' said Austin. 'Not until you tell me what you're wearing.'

'Ahaha,' said Issy. 'It's for the cold.'

'But it comes up past your bum. Is that real fur?'

'No.'

'Have you joined … a band?'

'Shut up.'

'Are you retitling it the Cupcake Café and Pole Dancing Club?'

'I'm warning you …'

'Am I being insensitive? Are you actually being eaten by a polar bear? Do I need to call an ambulance?'

'I'll just take a taxi by myself.'

'No, no, we'll accompany you. Pingu.'

The taxi queue was surprisingly short, which was a relief, as the cold hit them with the force of a wall when they left the heated building.

'Only a taxi?' said Issy. 'I was expecting a limo.'

'They did offer me a town car,' confessed Austin. 'But I didn't know what that was, so I said no.'

He didn't mention that they had offered to send a car to get Issy and Darny without him, so he could start picking up on things that were going on around the office, attending some meetings and getting up to speed. He didn't mention that at all.

* * *

Darny promptly fell asleep in the car, but Issy was

160

glad. At first she was a little odd with Austin—she didn't know why, she just felt slightly sad, which was ridiculous, as it was hardly his fault that he hadn't been around; it wasn't like he'd taken off on the holiday of a lifetime. But she couldn't resist his childish enthusiasm as they came over the crest of a hill in Queens and Austin nudged her going, 'Now! Now! Look! Look!' and grabbed her and pulled her on to his lap as she saw for the first time in real life the lights of Manhattan.

It was so strange and so familiar all at once that it took her breath away.

'Oh,' was all she could say. As if choreographed, the cab driver let out a string of expletives, and a light snow started to fall, wreathing the huge buildings in a cloud of smoky whiteness; softening the lights so that the entire island of Manhattan appeared to glow. 'Oh,' she said again.

'I know,' said Austin, their heads together out the right-hand window.

'What's that old song?' said Issy. 'The buildings of New York . . .'

' . . . look just like mountains in the snow,' finished Austin. 'Oh, except I don't know that song. I don't listen to girl singers. Mostly I like heavy metal and rap and boy songs.'

'You don't know any rap.'

'All Saints are rap,' said Austin.

'Yes, all right,' said Issy, squeezing his hand with hers. It was breathtaking. Whatever was going to happen, this was still them together, coming into New York.

'Put up that goddam window,' barked a voice from the front of the cab. They complied immediately.

161

'Well, it's not exactly the Plaza ...' said Austin, leading them into the lovely little old-fashioned boutique hotel on the west side of Central Park. It had stable doors beneath, and gabled windows, like an English country cottage thrown into the middle of the iron and steel of the city. A log fire burned in the corner of the lobby and the receptionist welcomed them like old friends, calling in a waitress, who brought them three foaming cups of hot chocolate with marshmallows in whilst she processed their check-in. It wasn't grand like big hotels she had seen before, Issy thought, looking at the cashmere throws over the sofas, but it was the most gorgeous, homey luxurious thing she could imagine.

Austin led them up a small creaking staircase into their bedroom, then he added, 'But look what it has ... ta-dah!' And he threw open the connecting door to reveal an extra bedroom for Darny, complete with flat-screen TV and its own bathroom and games console.

'Wow,' said Darny, whom they'd had to haul bodily out of the cab, suddenly wide awake. 'WOW!'

'I reckon these old beams are nice and soundproof,' said Austin, winking at Issy.

'It's beautiful,' she said, awestruck at their own room, which also had a fire burning in the grate. The room was small, but the bed was huge and gigantically soft and pouffy-looking, made up with soft white linen; there was a huge flat-screen television, a fridge and a bottle of wine. Outside the window, the snow was piling up on the sill; yellow cabs cruised the quiet back street, but further behind she could hear honking traffic and feel a buzz in the air with the looming skyscrapers above. She popped her head into the bathroom and noted the great claw-footed bath, lined up with luxurious full-sized products and towels that would need their own postcode.

'Oh yes,' she said. 'Oh yes oh yes oh yes. I want one of these very much. And room service, seeing as I didn't manage to eat a single thing on the plane as I am a total idiot. But even if I missed that, there is no *way* I am not enjoying every second of this.'

Her clothes felt stale and hot, and she sniffed the bubble bath with a smile, then winked at Austin.

'I am *so* glad I came,' she said suddenly, filling up with happiness. She went to embrace Austin, who was, however, frowning at his watch.

'Ahh,' he said. 'Well. Um, we're due at dinner in about twenty minutes. Sorry.'

'Dinner?' said Issy, who despite her nap was still feeling tired and distinctly grotty after the flight, and whose body clock thought it was about one o'clock in the morning. 'Can't we just stay in and have a lovely time?'

'I would love that,' said Austin firmly. 'But I'm afraid having dinner with you and ...' He nearly said 'my boss' but checked himself just in time, ' ... Merv is just part of the deal.' He grinned at her. 'Come on, we're going somewhere posh. It'll be fun.'

'I want to have fun here, in a bubble bath, with you, followed by my very first American cheeseburger, which I was hoping would be larger than my head,' said Issy a trifle sadly. 'Then falling asleep in about an hour.'

'I've booked the babysitter,' said Austin relentlessly.

'I don't need a babysitter,' came an adamant voice from next door. The rooms obviously weren't as soundproof as they looked.

'She's just going to pop up every half-hour,' said Austin. 'Make sure you aren't playing eighteen-rated games or touching your private area.'

'Shut up.'

Issy jumped in and out of the strong American shower, but it wasn't quite the same as a long soak followed by a long lie in bed with Austin.

'Smart?' she asked, remembering that she'd packed in about four seconds flat and couldn't actually remember what she'd brought.

'Oh yes, well, hmm, I don't know,' said Austin, who had enormous trouble noticing what women wore.

Issy suddenly remembered with horror that her best green dress that she'd bought for her birthday party was at the dry-cleaner's and she hadn't had time to pick it up. That was her only really lovely thing; everything else she wore was really to be comfortable to work and get around in, which meant lots of slightly faded floral dresses with elbow-length sleeves teamed with opaque tights and boots and a cardigan if it was cold; in other words, she dressed like the student she hadn't been for ten years.

She wasn't sure this was going to cut it.

She hauled through her suitcase—turning the perfect little hotel room into a midden in the process, she noted sadly—and came up with three near-identical grey floral dresses, two of which were far too light for the winter chill; two pairs of jeans (who needed two pairs of jeans on holiday? she wondered to herself); four formal shirts for Darny (what was she thinking?), and her old college ball gown, which was covered in netting and pinched under the arms and would be far too formal.

'Bugger,' she said. 'I think I will have to shop tomorrow.'

Austin, who never normally noticed time at all, was looking anxiously at his watch. 'Um, darling . . .' he was saying.

'OK, OK.'

With horror, Issy realised that the only thing she had that was mildly suitable was the black jumper and trousers she had travelled in—travelled in, and slept in for six hours. At least black could look a bit dressy, and she could stick a necklace on, and her boots could go under the trousers . . .

She sighed. Then, tentatively, pulled on her slightly stale clothes.

'I feel like Haggis McBaggis,' she said gloomily, gazing at herself in the tastefully soft-lit mirror. Austin glanced at her and just saw that the steam from the shower had made her cheeks go warm and pink, which he liked, and she was biting her lip like a nervous child, which was also cute.

'You look great,' he said. 'Let's go.'

Chapter Eleven

Bananas Foster

1 banana, peeled and cut in half
2 eggs, beaten
1 cup breadcrumbs
1 cup vegetable oil for frying

For the sauce
$\frac{1}{4}$ cup butter
1 cup brown sugar
$\frac{1}{2}$ tsp cinnamon
$\frac{1}{4}$ cup banana liqueur
$\frac{1}{4}$ cup dark rum

2 scoops vanilla ice cream

Heat the oil in a thick-bottomed pot. Roll the bananas in the egg then the crumbs to coat and set aside.
    When the oil begins to smoke, gently place the banana halves in pot and cook until golden brown. Less than 1 minute.
    Combine the butter, sugar and

cinnamon in a flambé pan or skillet. Place the pan over low heat on top of the stove, and cook, stirring, until the sugar dissolves. Stir in the banana liqueur. Remove from heat and add rum. Then continue to cook the sauce over high heat until the rum burns off—the sauce will foam.

Slice cooked banana into quarters and place in dish. Scoop vanilla ice cream on top. Generously spoon warm sauce over the top of the bananas and ice cream and serve immediately.

*   *   *

Pearl got home late and was bone tired. Louis had uncharacteristically whined the whole way. It had taken a lot longer to cash up and clear up without Issy there, and that was before they batched up for the next day. Because Pearl did so much of the cleaning, she often felt she worked very hard. Which she did, but as she filed the payroll reports, she realised she didn't quite appreciate how much Issy did to keep everything ticking over. No wonder she couldn't think about going to New York without falling into a panic. There were a million different things to remember.

Too tired to think about supper, she'd given in to Louis' proddings and as a special treat picked up some fried chicken on the way home. She knew she shouldn't; she knew eating it would only make her feel more tired in the long run. But right at that moment, resistance was low and the weather was freezing and wet and windy, and she wanted nothing more than to sit down in front of *In the Night Garden* and cuddle her (slightly greasy) son.

The doorbell rang. Pearl and her mother looked at each other and frowned. They didn't have many visitors. There wasn't the room, for starters. And Pearl usually met her friends after church, not at seven o'clock at night in the middle of a storm, unannounced.

She got up from the futon, her knees creaking as she did so. She cursed inwardly to herself; she was young, still. She shouldn't be creaking and huffing like an old lady. She shouldn't have eaten all that chicken.

Standing in the shadow of the alleyway, in the space that was meant to be lit by security lighting but that the council never got round to fixing, with his finger to his lips, possibly a little tipsy, was her ex, and Louis' father, Benjamin.

'Sssh,' he said.

*   *   *

In the cab, Issy suddenly sagged. The cold had cut through her like a knife as she'd stepped out of the cosy lobby of the hotel; her watch said 2 a.m. British time; and she envied Darny, who had gone straight to bed, very much. Never the less, she wanted to be as supportive as she could.

'So who's going to be there?' she said, trying to stifle a yawn.

'Well, Merv,' said Austin. 'He's the guy in charge. And his wife. I haven't met her. And some other director of the bank. I haven't met him. And *his* wife, I suppose.'

168

'We're walking into a massive group of people we haven't met?' said Issy, feeling suddenly terribly anxious. 'Who are basically interviewing you for a job?' She took out her make-up case nervously.

'Don't ... I mean, you've probably got enough stuff on your cheeks,' said Austin.

Issy's eyes were hugely round and fearful. 'What do you mean?' she said.

'Nothing,' said Austin quickly. 'Nothing. I mean, you look fine.'

'They're all going to be trendy New Yorkers, though,' said Issy. 'And I'll just be scuzz. Mind you,' she added, 'maybe that'll make them change their minds about the job and you'll have to come home on the next flight with me.'

She'd tried to sound light, but she was aware she'd touched on a sensitive issue. Austin looked at her, but in the passing street lights it was very difficult to see his face. As the cab bounced downtown on one of the large, open avenues, he pointed out the Chrysler Building, all lit up in Christmas colours. It was so familiar and so wonderful all at once that she couldn't help being impressed. Then she sniffed.

'They've done the BT Tower up in red and green,' she said casually. 'Oh, and the whole of the South Bank is a festival of light. And a Christmas market.'

The snow flurries were becoming thicker and thicker. The driver turned down a little old-fashioned-looking street lined with houses with brown steps up to their front doors, which reminded Issy of *Sex and the City* and the days when she and Helena used to watch it and wish they got their Chinese food delivered in little boxes, or that they too were asked out by suave gentlemen every five minutes (Helena did get asked out every five minutes, but only by drunks on a Saturday night when she was bandaging them up in Accident and Emergency).

The restaurant had large plate-glass windows that reminded her of the café, but this place was painted grey, not green. Inside, it seemed to glow; the lights were soft and warm and yellow and gave the place the most inviting, exciting atmosphere imaginable. Happy, stunningly beautiful men and women—all dressed, Issy noticed glumly, up to the nines—were chatting, laughing and generally having a wonderful time.

'Hello,' said Austin cheerily to the doorman. He never felt intimidated anywhere. Probably because he wasn't really noticing it, thought Issy. And that made him comfortable and that in its turn made him likeable and that made him confident and so things always went well. It must be nice. She smiled in an ingratiating way at the doorman and wondered whether to tip him as he opened the door.

Inside, a stunningly beautiful blonde woman gave Austin a smile that made her look as if she'd been waiting to see him all day.

'Good evening, sir!' she said, displaying gorgeous teeth. 'Do you have a reservation?'

But 'Austin! Hey, Austin!' was already booming across the room, and at the back of the restaurant—it was much larger than it appeared from the outside—a short, wide man was rising up from a comfortable-looking banquette.

The blonde whisked away their coats, then threaded them through the tables. Issy decided it

170

must be jet lag that had made her think she had just passed Michael Stipe having dinner with Brooke Shields. All she could say for sure was that every person in the room looked gorgeous, had obviously just had their hair done, was talking animatedly about interesting things and looked a hundred per cent absolutely like they were supposed to be there. Unless someone asked her about flour grading, Issy reflected sadly, she wasn't going to have anything to say. And, after all, she was only the girlfriend. If *Sex and the City* was accurate, there were millions of beautiful girls in New York just desperate to snap up some gorgeous hunk.

Issy tried to snap herself out of it and smile politely and the men stood up as they approached the table.

'Hello,' she said, as the women revealed themselves to be almost terrifyingly skinny. Merv's wife, Candy, was at least three inches taller and twenty years younger than him. The other couple's names she didn't even catch, and she muttered 'hi' whilst feeling nine years old, hopelessly intimidated, furious with herself and furious with Austin for some reason she couldn't quite articulate.

'Hi,' said the women, blankly and without interest. Presumably if you didn't have poison injected in your face every ten minutes and starve yourself to death 24/7, you didn't deserve even the faintest glimmer of attention round here.

Austin, on the other hand, was, she noticed, the object of ritual scrutiny. In her cornered state she couldn't help but be slightly mollified; yeah, she thought, you guys are all a lot thinner and richer than me, but at least I don't have to pretend I like having sex with Merv just because he's rich.

171

Mind you, that said, compared with everyone else there, Merv was a lot of fun.

'D'ya just get off the plane?' he said. 'There's only one answer to that. A martini! Fabio!' A stunningly handsome young barman appeared at Merv's elbow. 'Get this young lady a martini straight up. She needs a wake-up. Gin—she's a Brit. With a twist. Quick as you can, OK?'

Austin looked at Issy in a slight 'he's always like this' way, but Issy didn't actually mind. Anything that would make her feel more at home.

'Bottoms up,' she said when her drink arrived, and took a large gulp.

The only martini Issy had had before had been one her mother had made for her when she was fifteen and had come back miserable from a party because none of the boys had wanted to dance with her, which almost certainly had something to do with the fact that whilst all the other girls were in Lycra and legwarmers, she was in a macramé dress her mother had made for her in Peru and insisted on her wearing, and as it was one of her mother's periodic homecomings, she had given in. It had had martini bianco and lemonade and had been delicious, and she'd sat up late while Marian had told her that no man was to be trusted. As Marian herself was not to be trusted, and the closest man in Issy's life was Grampa Joe, who clearly was, Issy had gone slightly too far the other way and endeavoured to trust most of the men she ever met, far too much for far too long. Which had often turned out to be a mistake. Until Austin. She looked at him and took another gulp.

This martini, on the other hand, was pure alcohol and, frankly, rocket fuel. She put it down

172

spluttering, her eyes watering.

'Ooh, got ourselves a party girl,' said Merv approvingly, as the rest of the table looked on superciliously. Issy thought she heard the director's wife mutter something about 'British drinkers'.

'Actually, Isabel runs her own business,' said Austin.

'Oh, really? Doing what?' asked the other man.

'I make cupcakes,' said Issy.

'Oh, that's so *cute*,' said Candy. 'I wanna do that, Merv.'

'Course you can, darling,' said Merv.

'Oh, wow, it must be so much fun, you must just have such an awesome time!' said Candy.

'Every second,' said Issy. She glanced at Austin, glanced at the table, and determined to finish the entire drink, even if it did taste like very expensive petrol.

*   *   *

'What is it?' hissed Pearl. 'Ben, you've got to give me some warning when you come round! It's not right. I'm just about to put Louis to bed. He's got school tomorrow.'

'I know,' said Ben. 'Ssh. Come see this.'

He dragged her closer for a kiss, and she could smell hash on his breath. Her heart sank.

'You been eating chicken?' he said. 'Got any more? I'm hungry.'

'No,' she said. 'What is it, Ben? You haven't been by in weeks.'

'Yeah, but look.'

He beckoned her out in the freezing wind—she wished she'd grabbed her coat—to a beat-up old van

173

that wasn't his, as far as she knew, and flung open the back door.

'Ta-dah!'

Pearl peered inside, lit only by the street light. At first she couldn't quite figure out what it was. Then she realised. It was a huge box. The writing on it became clear.

'A monster garage,' she breathed.

'I told the little man I wouldn't let him down,' said Ben.

'But ... but ... I mean, have you been working?'

She knew what she meant by this. If he was working, he was meant to give her some money. That was the deal.

'Oh, just a bit, here and there ...' said Ben. He couldn't quite meet her eyes.

'Do you mean working properly, a proper job? Where? Was it cash in hand? With Bobby or who?' demanded Pearl.

'Oh, well, I thought you'd be pleased,' said Ben, cross now. 'I thought you'd be happy that we got the little man the one thing he wants more than anything ... thought we could wrap it up too, you know, with a big bow, the whole works. Maybe I'll just throw it away, huh? Just set it on fire because I haven't got my P60 and a receipt and everything else ...'

'Ben,' said Pearl, desperate not to start a fight. 'Ben, please. It's just it's so expensive ...'

'I know how much it is,' said Ben, his handsome face set like stone. Pearl swallowed. She wanted to believe he had a job, she did, but why couldn't she get a straight answer out of him?

She didn't say anything more. Ben cursed quickly under his breath then turned to go.

'Don't you want to come in and see Louis?' Pearl said, a little reluctantly.

Ben shrugged, then slouched past her in through the door of the little ground-floor flat.

'DADDY!' Louis' shout of joy, Pearl reflected, could be heard halfway down the street.

Pearl never swore. She thought it showed an uncontrolled mind. But she got extremely close to it right then. She looked around. Someone had built a snowman from the dirty leftover snow of a few days ago. Someone else had taken the carrot off its nose and put it where a penis would be. Pearl sighed, and went back indoors, out of the freezing cold, feeling very far away from wishing goodwill upon all men.

*   *   *

'So, Austin,' Merv was saying, sitting back in his banquette and grumbling, presumably not for the first time, about the fact that he couldn't smoke his cigar indoors. 'What would you say our prospects are vis-à-vis . . . '

Issy had realised that frankly there wasn't a single thing she could contribute to the conversation—Candy was playing with her phone, like Darny would have been doing, and the director's wife, who was called something like Vanya or Vania or something that sounded like it might be a name but wasn't really, was making a massive point of differentiating herself from Issy and Candy by insisting on joining in with the men's conversations in a highly technical and competitive way.

Candy yawned every so often quietly behind her hand, but then would lean in and stroke Merv's thigh in an affectionate manner. Issy realised that a charming waiter was refilling her glass every time she took so much as a sip of the ambrosial white wine, so she kept at it. Since neither Vanya nor Candy ate at all, Issy went at the bread basket in an almost passive-aggressive manner. Meanwhile Austin was talking about Europe and money and futures and micro-trading and other things Issy hadn't even heard of in a way that was completely beyond her and very impressive.

She wondered what Austin thought about her job—he saw her at work, she supposed, making coffee and baking cakes and handling the customers, but she didn't think he found it very impressive (she was quite wrong to think this; Austin thought what she did was amazing). Meanwhile, here he was, eating a very rare steak and explaining why the future of Europe was as luxury-goods merchants to roaring emerging economies, whilst everyone nodded sagely and listened to everything he said. Suddenly Issy wished Darny were there to wind Austin up and say something cheeky.

Cosy in the warm restaurant, drinking quite a lot of wine and eating her food without saying very much, Issy had felt herself start to slightly drift off when she heard her name.

'It's like Issy's business model,' Austin was saying. 'High-end products, immaculately made and presented, not mass-market. That's the future, because everywhere else we can't compete.'

The table turned towards Issy, who felt very fuzzy in the head.

'What?' she said.

'Is that true, Issybel?' asked Merv. 'Are you the

future of commerce? When you're awake?'

Everyone laughed as if he'd said something funny, and Issy blushed bright red and couldn't think of a single word to say.

'Well?' said Merv.

'Do you think your model is going to drive European-zone regeneration?' snapped Vanya, as if they were in court or something.

'Ha, well, hem,' said Issy. She was bursting with embarrassment and bright red. Austin hadn't told her this was a bloody job interview for her too. Even worse, because she hadn't been following the conversation, she didn't have a clue what to say. And even if she had, she didn't know what the right answer was anyway.

'Well, gee, it's nice to have a hobby,' said Vanya with a large fake smile, turning back to her salad and mineral water.

Austin took Issy's hand under the table and gave it a sympathetic squeeze. This made things worse as far as Issy was concerned; she didn't need his sympathy: she needed not to be put on the spot. The conversation moved on to real-estate prices, but Issy still sat there, burning up with crossness and feeling stupid and inferior.

Finally, when the pudding menu was coming round and Vanya and Candy were holding their hands up against it as if it were a list of poisons (which, Issy reflected, taking it, was probably exactly what they did think), Issy was ready. She launched in.

'The thing is,' she said, 'if you make stuff that's really good, people realise it's a superior product. Well, most of the time. They still sell lots of squirty cream in cans. Anyway, that's not important. The

177

important thing is that even if people have less money, they'll still buy themselves small lovely things as a treat. Sometimes even more because they're staying in a lot, trying not to buy too much, so they'll have a little reward . . . '

'Yeah, yeah,' said Vanya, sounding bored. 'But what does that mean on a macroeconomic level to you?'

Issy spluttered. 'It means . . . I'll tell you what it means,' she said, drunker than she'd realised, and suddenly sick of being patronised and talked down to and ignored and treated as the uninteresting dumpy girlfriend of the brilliant and fascinating man by these stupid, annoying glamorous Americans. 'It means I wake up every day and I do a real thing. I get my hands dirty. I create something from scratch, with my bare hands, that I hope people will love, and they do, they really do; and I turn out something perfect and beautiful, that is meant to be enjoyed, and people realise that, and they do enjoy it and they pay me money for it and that is the best job in the bloody world and we should all be lucky enough to do something like that and that's where we should be focusing our efforts. What did you create today, Vanya? Did anyone pick up one of your reports and smell it and give you a big smile and tell you it was absolutely bloody amazing?'

She paused to savour the open mouths round the table.

'No, I didn't think so.'

She turned to the waiter.

'Does the gateau de fôret noire come with fresh cherries or marinated? Tell the chef fresh if he can, it's far better; the acidity balances out the sweetness

178

instead of making it cloying and overbearing. Of course, I'm sure he already knows that. On a macro level. So I'll take it.' And she shut the menu with a triumphant snap.

*   *   *

The party headed out rather mutedly, except for Merv, who had suddenly found Issy a bit of a one and asked her lots of cake-based questions and whether she could make a decent kugel, which actually she'd never heard of, then described his grandmother making it in their little Long Island kitchen and complaining that she couldn't get kosher sugar and that the base wasn't right, and Issy tried to talk him through it to see if she could figure it out.

No one else spoke to her at all; even Austin seemed stiff, and Issy, through her slightly drunken haze, started to worry that in fact rather than putting her point in a cool and measured way, she had perhaps shouted at everybody else at the table completely unnecessarily. Oh well. She couldn't worry about that now.

As they got to the door, the beautiful waitress brought them their coats. Issy shrugged herself into Caroline's now even tighter ridiculous white jacket. Candy stopped short. Then she leaned closer.

'Oh. My. God,' she said, the first direct thing she'd said to Issy all night. 'Is that ... is that the new Farim Maikal?'

Issy didn't have the faintest clue who it was, but the name definitely rang a bell. And actually, now she thought about it, Caroline had gone on and on about the coat when it had arrived and been really

179

smug about it and how she'd got one over on her friends and this would show them and all sorts of other stuff that Issy hadn't really understood. But Farim she thought she remembered.

'Hmm,' she said non-committally.

'It IS!' breathed Candy. 'Can I touch it?' She held out her hand, reverently stroking the ridiculous white fur and collar studs. 'Wow, the wait list at Barneys for this was like . . . wow.'

Even Vanya was looking at it with a touch of jealousy.

'Shame they didn't have your size,' she said.

'Oh man, that doesn't matter, she looks amazing,' said Candy. 'Anybody would who got their hands on one. This is THE hot coat this winter.'

Issy bit her lip and suddenly felt a terrible wave of homesickness.

Chapter Twelve

Kugel

220g medium-wide egg noodles
65g butter
220g cream cheese
100g sugar
1 tsp vanilla
4 eggs
200ml milk
150g frosted flakes or corn flakes
  mixed with sugar
2 tbsp butter, melted
2 tsp sugar
2 tsp cinnamon
Cook noodles according to package
directions.

In a large bowl, mix butter, cream
cheese, sugar, vanilla, eggs and milk.
Stir until smooth. Drain noodles, and
add to mixture, then pour into a large
square pan, cover and refrigerate
overnight.

The next day, about two hours
before the meal, preheat the oven to
180°C/gas mark 4.

In a small bowl, crush the cereal and mix with melted butter, sugar and cinnamon. Sprinkle the cereal mix on top of the cold kugel, and then bake for $1\frac{1}{4}$ hours. Cool for 20 minutes before serving.

*　　　*　　　*

Issy fell asleep in the car, then sank into the beautiful bed, which made her feel like she was sleeping on a cloud, and even though she was woken incredibly early by both the jet lag and Darny banging hard on the connecting door, she already felt much better. She had been too tired even to give Austin a proper kiss, but as she turned over in the bed, she saw he was already up and in the shower.

'Hey,' she said as he came out with a towel wrapped round him and opened the door for his brother. Darny grunted at them, then headed into his own bathroom.

'Hey,' Austin said, without quite looking her in the eye.

Issy immediately panicked and sat up in the big soft bed. Last night was a bit of a blur.

'Was I . . .' Her voice sounded weird, a bit husky. 'Sorry, was I really bad last night?'

'No, of course not,' said Austin, but his tone was a little distant.

'Well, you put me on the spot,' said Issy, looking round for something to drink. She picked up a bottle of Evian, then saw a sign next to it indicating that it was $7.50, which even she with her poor arithmetic skills could tell was outrageous, so she put it down again.

182

'Just drink it,' said Austin crossly, when he realised what she was doing.

'What's the matter with you?' said Issy. 'What did I do?'

'You were just … you were just a bit aggressive, that was all.'

'*I* was aggressive? That Vanya girl wanted to bite me on the leg!'

Austin still looked unhappy.

'Austin,' said Issy, imploring him. 'Look, if you wanted me to behave in a certain way or dress like a tart and keep my mouth shut like that Candy girl … you should have said so.'

'I didn't,' said Austin. 'I just wanted you to be yourself.'

There was a terrible silence.

'Maybe that *was* me,' said Issy quietly.

Austin looked as if he wanted to say something, then bit his tongue and didn't. Instead he glanced at his watch.

'Look …'

'You have to go. I know. Me and Darny will go out and explore.'

'Good,' said Austin, looking relieved to be on safer ground. 'OK, cool. I'll text you. I should be able to get away this afternoon after five. I know this cool café we can meet at.'

'Well, we might need an afternoon nap,' said Issy. 'But definitely. OK.'

Austin came over and kissed her. 'We could do with some time, just the two of us,' he said. At exactly the same moment, Darny started up singing a loud and extremely tuneless version of a Bruno Mars song, whilst clattering loudly in the rainforest shower. Issy rolled her eyes.

183

'Mm,' she said. Then she smiled. 'Have a good day.'

Austin smiled back at her, but still, when he left the hotel room she felt a terrible anxiety in the pit of her stomach. Something wasn't right, and she didn't know if she could fix it. She didn't know the recipe for this.

*   *   *

'Well, *fix it*,' Pearl was saying, as patiently as she was able. Maya tried yet again, but her shaky hand meant that more of the latte slopped over the top of the glass.

It was Maya's first day, and Pearl had never had to be someone's boss before, especially not someone who was pretty, sweet, young, and appeared to have caught the eye of a person Pearl would never admit in a hundred years she had a bit of a soft spot for.

It was proving tricky for both of them. Maya was trying her best, but Pearl was so quick and efficient, she couldn't quite follow what she was doing; not only that, but she was nervous. Pearl seemed to have taken against her for some reason, and she couldn't work out why. And she'd been up since five on her post round and had been too anxious to eat any breakfast.

'Three lattes, a hot chocolate and four mince pies,' said Pearl, smiling nicely at the customer. 'Just ring it up like this.'

Her fingers flew deftly amongst the buttons and the till dinged open. Maya tried to remember what she'd done, but it didn't seem like it would be possible. She sighed, then went back to the

184

coffee machine. Grind, pressurise—the big orange Rancilio terrified the life out of her. Even Pearl admitted it was temperamental, and likely to give you a steam burn at any moment. Steam the milk but not too much (skin) and not too little (freezing). Then combine, spoon the foam on the top, and powder a little cupcake shape with chocolate and a template Issy had had made up. Repeat a hundred times an hour, serve up with a smile … Maya was getting panicked.

'Hurry up!' said Pearl, keeping a fixed grin on her face. Where the hell was Caroline? She'd been late the day before, too. When Pearl had called her on it, she'd shrugged and said, come on, the boss was away, and anyhow it was too cold to leave the house in the morning without her coat. Now she'd done it to her again. Pearl gritted her teeth. Sometimes it drove her beyond endurance to have to work with someone who only turned up as a sop to her ex-husband's divorce lawyer, and thought she was hard done by at that.

Maya turned round too fast and knocked the entire metal jug of milk on to the floor. Gasping apologies, she jumped to it, but Pearl was there before her.

'Please take these mince pies with our compliments,' she hissed, handing the customer back her money. 'I'll bring the coffees over when they're ready.'

Pearl got out the mop whilst Maya spluttered apologies that Pearl wasn't really in the mood to accept, particularly when they smelled burning and she realised she'd missed the oven beeper going off because she'd been crouched down cleaning up milk, and they'd lost an entire tray of Christmas

185

cake cupcakes and the beautiful warm-scented ambience of the shop had gone, giving it instead a charred edge that was going to do nothing for business.

'This place smells awful,' said Caroline, wafting in twenty minutes late. 'Good lord, look at that disgusting pile of dirty dishes all over the tables. Yuck, who'd want to eat here?'

'Can you keep your voice down?' said Pearl, wiping sweat off her forehead. 'And get cleaning up.'

'Can't the newbie do that?' sulked Caroline. 'I just got my nails done.'

'The newbie is trying to learn how to make a cup of coffee without exploding anything,' said Pearl.

'Oops,' said Maya.

'Maybe try again when we're a bit quieter,' said Pearl through gritted teeth, getting her to start on the dishwasher, which she figured even Maya couldn't mess up. Wrongly, she discovered, half an hour later, when Maya tried to refill the soap dish with dishwasher cleaner and managed to somehow scoop the overflowing foam over an entire tray of fresh lemon slices.

'Oops,' said Maya, again.

There was a queue out the door, but not a good queue—it was a grumbling bunch of freezing people who'd waited far too long for watery coffee and nothing-like-as-good-as-usual cakes, being served up by three grumpy, stressed-out people instead of being soothed by the normal gentle smile and greeting from Issy. If one more person said 'Boss on holiday, then?' to Pearl, she was going to scream.

Just as one of their everyday regulars was

looming up to the counter bearing a cake with teethmarks in it and an ominous expression, the phone rang. Pearl ducked down the stairs with the handset, leaving Maya to put on an apologetic look and try to explain why the strawberry tart tasted a bit soapy.

'Hello.'

'PEARL!'

'Oh, well, you don't have to shout.'

'Sorry,' said Issy. 'I'm not used to phoning from abroad. Wow, it's good to hear your voice. How are things?'

Pearl paused. As she did so, she heard the tinkle of falling crockery.

'Uhm, fine,' she said quickly.

'Really? You're all doing great without me?'

Issy's voice sounded slightly disappointed. She had rather hoped they would find it difficult to struggle on without her being there. Mind you, Pearl was so capable and had reassured her so many times that she could manage on her own. It was hardly rocket science. She thought back to that snooty woman at dinner last night. Maybe she was right after all.

'Well,' said Pearl. 'It's certainly not the same.'

'PEARL!' came Caroline's imperious voice. 'Did you remember to reorder the milk? Only we appear to be running out and it's only one thirty. And the sandwich boy hasn't been, so we've missed an entire lunchtime.'

'Bollocks,' muttered Pearl under her breath.

'What's that?' said Issy. 'This is a terrible line.'

'Oh, nothing,' said Pearl. 'Just congratulations from cheerful punters.'

'Well, good,' said Issy. 'I'm glad it's all carrying

on fine.'

'Yup, don't worry about us,' said Pearl, catching with her foot an orange that appeared to be bouncing down the stairs. They didn't even sell oranges. 'Don't worry about us at all.'

*   *   *

Issy wrapped Darny up against his strongest protestations and took out her guidebook. 'Don't complain,' she said.

'I am complaining,' said Darny. 'I'm considering a citizen's arrest, in fact. I don't want to go out. I want to stay in and play computer games. They have *Modern Warfare 2.*'

'Well I'm afraid you can't,' said Issy. 'We're in the greatest city in the world and I'm not letting you miss it. Any other kid would be desperate to get out there and explore.'

Darny's brow furrowed. 'Do you think so?' he said.

'Yes!' said Issy. 'It's a huge world out there, full of all sorts of things. Let's go explore!'

Darny stuck out his bottom lip. 'I think this is kidnap.'

Issy, hung-over, stressed, tired, worried about the café—she had thought she would be worried if it was wobbling, but no, nobody even seemed to have noticed she was gone, so a fat lot of use she was back there; and here she was nothing but a liability—had finally lost her patience.

'Oh for CHRIST'S sake, Darny, just do what you're asked one FRICKING time and stop behaving like a spoilt baby. It's pathetic. Nobody's impressed.'

188

There was a sudden silence in the room. Issy had never spoken to Darny harshly before. It was the tightest of drawn lines. He was not her boy. He was not her son. She had always promised herself that she wouldn't cross that line.

And she just had. She had been harsh and hurtful and it was hardly Darny's fault; he hadn't asked to come here. And neither had she. Oh, what a mess.

In total silence, Darny stood with her as they waited for the elevator. As they descended into the lovely lobby, the charming receptionist smiled nicely at them and asked if everything was all right, and Issy lied through gritted teeth and said it was, then they both steeled themselves to go out into the freezing New York morning. The sky was a burstingly bright blue and Issy resolved that the first thing they needed was sunglasses; the sun bouncing off the glass panes of the skyscrapers and the snow was almost blinding.

'Wow,' she said. For a moment she forgot everything that was going on, just how impressed she was with the fact that she was actually here. In New York!

'Come on,' she said. 'Let's go shop! We can have Darny at Barneys! There's a shop called Barneys, you know, very famous.'

Darny didn't respond.

'Look,' said Issy, putting up her hand to hail a taxi. It really was impossible to be outside for more than a couple of minutes. 'I'm sorry, OK. I really didn't mean what I said. I was … I was frustrated about something else and I took it out on you.'

Darny shrugged his shoulders. 'Doesn't matter,' he said. But obviously it did.

Barneys turned out to be horrifically expensive, so they left after Issy had swooned a little over the staggeringly beautiful clothes draped on the mannequins, and marvelled at the young, beautiful American women who were storming through and picking things up right, left and centre, commenting on them all the while. She spied a Gap across the road and they hurried across. Everything was much cheaper there, and she bought Darny a few things she thought he needed (most notably new underpants) that neither Austin nor Darny ever seemed to notice. Then she thought about it again and bought Austin a whole bunch of new underpants too. Couldn't hurt. And some shirts and a couple of jumpers. She liked buying for him. She couldn't ever have bought clothes for her last boyfriend, Graeme; he was very anal and particular. Austin probably wouldn't even notice, or care, but it made her feel like she was looking after him, and at the moment she didn't feel that she was looking after anyone particularly well—and worse, no one, from her customers to her boyfriend to his brother, felt particularly like they wanted looking after either.

She sighed, especially when she came across a beautiful, soft checked lumberjack shirt. It was lined inside, which would have made it comfortable and warm for her grandfather, who had, in his last days, always been cold but found hard fabrics scratchy and uncomfortable against his skin. She held it briefly in her hands, wishing she could buy it for him. But she couldn't.

Laden with bags, they jumped into another cab— Issy knew she should probably take the subway, but was terrified of getting lost or hopelessly confused.

Anyway, she told herself, she hadn't had a holiday in over a year, she worked too hard ever to spend any money and the rest of the trip was free. She deserved a bit of time off and could afford to spend a little.

The Empire State Building didn't look like anything from the street; just another office block, except for the beautiful art nouveau signage outside. Issy hadn't considered that it was actually a working office block. Of course it was; what did she think, that it would just be empty, like the Eiffel Tower? She bought their tickets with excitement, glancing at the enormous, beautifully dressed Christmas trees in the lobby that seemed to stretch several storeys high, whilst Darny maintained his petulant silence. Issy tried to pretend he wasn't there. In the crush of the first lift, she watched the beautiful golden arrows on the floor indicator climb upwards and smiled to herself, feeling she was channelling Meg Ryan. But it wasn't the same, every time she caught Darny's tight-looking little face in the mirror.

Up on level 100, the cold and the wind and the sun were absolutely bracing. All Issy's jet lag and fuzziness was instantly blown away as she stepped out on to the smaller-than-she'd-expected platform. The jostling lift-load of tourists spread to all four sides of the building to gaze out over the far horizons: huge ships from China and the Middle East docking down in the Lower East Side; helicopters taking off south from Broad Street and circling round the island like giant wasps; Central Park, so ridiculously straight-edged and tidily cut, totally unlike the more organic outdoor spaces of London she was used to—then no other green

191

at all anywhere, just building after building, their jagged tops and mirrored glass walls making them look like an infinite reflection of a child's Lego set. The sun glinted off the river and the island—a shape as recognisable to Issy as London; possibly even more so than her home city of Manchester, she realised, with a lurch of shame. Her breath was visible in front of her face and she instinctively took out her camera, before realising that the vista laid out before her was probably better bought on a postcard rather than taken through netting.

'On top of the world,' she called out to Darny, who was huddling in a corner against the cold, looking anything but. 'Come on,' she said. 'Shall we go up and look at the mast? Do you know, it was built to tether Zeppelins to? Can you imagine what it was like, bringing one of those down? Only it was too windy, so they had to stop.'

Darny grunted again.

'Darny,' said Issy timidly. 'I know you're cross with me. But don't let it spoil your trip, OK. Or mine. I promise I won't think you're not cross with me if you have a tiny bit of a good time.'

Again, no reaction, and Issy bit her lip in frustration.

'Well, never mind about that,' she said, taking one last look around, lingering longest on the side with the little arrow that said it was 3,460 miles to London. 'Come on. It's time for lunch. There's someone we have to meet.'

Chapter Thirteen

Verity Deli Hot Chocolate Brownies

Calories: UK—a million, and can make you potentially nauseous all day; US—a light snack in between two gigantic meals, both of which have melted cheese on top. Can also be accompanied by caramel sauce, whipped cream, ginger ice cream, coronary surgery. Do make this, but please make very small brownies as a delicious melting snack. Death by chocolate is, truly, a horrible idea. The idea here is to feel delighted and pleased, not sticky and regretful.

185g unsalted butter
185g best dark chocolate
85g plain flour
40g cocoa powder
50g white chocolate
50g milk chocolate
3 large eggs
275g golden caster sugar

Melt butter and dark chocolate very slowly and carefully in the microwave. Allow to cool. Turn on oven to 160°C/gas mark 3 and line a baking tray with baking paper.

Sift flour and cocoa powder; chop the milk and white chocolate. Whisk together eggs and sugar till the mixture looks like a milkshake and doubles in size. Carefully and gently fold in melted chocolate mix until fudgy. Stir in chocolate chunks.

Bake for 25 minutes till shiny on top.

*   *   *

Issy followed the instructions she'd received in the email. Heartily frozen from exposure to the elements a hundred floors above ground, they were both relieved to escape back into the warmth of the building, then into a yellow cab. Issy was beginning to get the hang of cabs; Austin had explained that you didn't hail them and wait for them to come to you. You grabbed one and just opened the door and jumped in, otherwise someone else would take it. At first this had seemed rude and ill-mannered, till the first three times someone had managed to get there ahead of them and stolen their cab, which was of course even more ill-mannered, so now Issy was hopping in and out of them like a native, Darny at her heels.

They passed through the happy chaos of Times Square, full of pink-cheeked tourists looking around to see what all the fuss was.

A Santa was ringing a bell at every cross-walk. People were buying tickets to Christmas shows and staring at the fabulously lit-up buildings, with their holidays wishes from Coca-Cola and Panasonic. Everything was a riot of lights and trees and every street corner had carollers or bell-ringers or men selling knock-off handbags which Issy looked at slightly regretfully before coming to her senses and moving on. She couldn't imagine the look on Caroline's face if she turned up with a fake Kate Spade, not to mention her horror of getting caught at customs.

The place they'd been instructed to show up at—early, it had been insisted—was a large corner block with old-fashioned fifties-style lettering advertising a soda fountain. It was called the Verity Deli, and its walls were lined with pictures of its illustrious clientele—Woody Allen was there, as was Liza Minnelli; Steven Spielberg and Sylvester Stallone. There was already a small queue forming. An elderly waitress with dyed orange hair and an alarming bosom crammed into a green uniform took them straight away to a much patched and darned banquette. Issy asked for a cup of tea and let Darny, eyeing her closely, order a root beer float, even though neither of them had the faintest idea what it might be. When it arrived, it turned out to be a gigantic confection of ice cream and fizzy flavoured lemonade, in a glass the size of Darny's head. He glanced at her again, but she didn't comment and he plunged in without checking twice.

They were waiting a long time. The waitress returned repeatedly—the menu was absolutely gigantic, with all manner of things to order: roast beef side; knishes; pastrami on rye and lots of

195

other things that made no sense at all to Issy, who was already slightly shocked at the state of the banquettes and the slovenliness of the waitress. She wouldn't want to run her fingers across the top of the pictures.

After twenty minutes, as Issy fiddled with her phone and wished she'd brought a book, and Darny ate his way stoically through the root beer float until he looked like he was turning green, the door slammed open dramatically, bringing in with it a noisy gust of wind. A tall, imperious woman dressed in old-fashioned, very plain hand-made clothes and a large and rather elaborate hat swept in.

'Isabel!' she declaimed loudly, in an American accent.

'Mum,' said Issy.

Darny looked up for the first time that day.

*   *   *

Marian swanned across to their table. The elderly waitress was over in the blink of an eye, but Marian waved her away.

'Beverly!' she cried. 'Not until I've said hello to my precious daughter, whom I haven't seen in an age. Look at her, isn't she lovely?'

Marian wobbled Issy's cheeks up and down. Issy tried not to mind and hugged her mother back.

'And who's this? Have you had a child and not told me?'

'No,' said Issy and Darny simultaneously.

Marian sat down and waved away the laminated menu. 'We'll have pastrami on rye three times, no pickles. And three root beer floats.'

'No thank you,' said Darny, looking slightly

196

queasy.

'Two root beer floats. You have to try these,' said Marian.

'OK,' said Issy.

Their drinks appeared in record time, while Marian was still looking her up and down.

'I haven't seen you since ...'

'Gramps' funeral,' said Issy. She'd put a notice in the *Manchester Evening News*, and had been stunned by the response. Over two hundred people who had remembered her grandfather—worked with him or eaten his wares over the years—had contacted her, and his funeral was full to the rafters. It had been rather daunting. Her mother had wafted around gathering compliments and looking artistic and brave whilst Issy had attempted to cater for an endless parade of well-wishers and mourners, many of whom were kind enough to say that she had inherited his talent.

There had been so many stories. Credit given when the man of the house was out of work; an apprentice taken on out of prison; a thief rapped sharply on the knuckles and sent off with a stiff lecture, never to offend again. There were stories of wedding cakes; christening cakes; warm doughnuts for cold hands off to school; growing up with the scent of fresh bread always in the nostrils. He had touched a lot of lives, and people wanted her to know that, and she was grateful to hear it.

She was glad to be busy too, all through the funeral and the sorting things out; there was always something to do and she had her hands full. It was when everything was tidied away and she'd returned to London that she'd spent her nights crying into Austin's shirts. He had been very good about it.

He'd understood, perhaps better than anyone else could.

There had been a little money—not much. Issy was glad about that. Her grandfather had worked hard his entire life, and she had spent it all on the nicest home and the nicest people she could find to make sure he was as comfortable and happy as possible. She didn't grudge a penny of it. She had used her share to extend her lease and pay off some of her mortgage. Her mother had used hers to go to an ashram, whatever that was, and complain about all the inaccuracies in *Eat Pray Love*.

And here she was again, large as life, in a coffee shop in New York. It felt very strange.

'Hey,' said Issy.

'Well,' said her mother. 'Tell me everything.'

But before she could begin, Marian was looking over for the waitress.

'You know,' she confided, 'I shouldn't really be eating this. I went all raw food at the ashram. Apparently I have a very sensitive system and I can't process refined flour. But oy vey, as we say.'

'Mum,' said Issy. She looked at the sandwich in front of her. It was piled higher than her mouth could possibly open. She wasn't entirely sure what she was meant to do with it or how she should eat it. 'Are you Jewish now?'

Marian looked solemn. 'Well, I think on a very real level, every one of us is Jewish.'

Issy nodded. 'Except we're Church of England.'

'It's the Judaeo-Christian tradition, though,' said Marian. 'Anyway, I'm changing my name.'

'Not again!' groaned Issy. 'Come on. Remember the fuss you had with the bank when you tried to change back from "Feather"?'

198

'No,' said Marian. 'Anyway, it's not hard to remember. I'm going to be Miriam.'

'Why bother changing your name from Marian to Miriam? It's practically the same.'

'Except one honours the mother of Jesus, a great prophet to be sure, and one is the sister of Moses who led the Chosen People to the Promised Land.'

Issy had learned long ago not to take her mother up logically on any of her latest crazes. Instead she smiled resignedly.

'It's good to see you,' she said. 'Are you enjoying living here?'

'It's the most wonderful place on earth,' said Marian. 'You must come visit the kibbutz.'

'You're in a kibbutz?'

'Of course! We're trying to live as authentically as possible. Saturdays are difficult, but apart from that ...'

'Why are Saturdays difficult?' It was the first time Darny had spoken of his own accord all day.

Marian turned her attention towards him.

'And who are you?' she asked bluntly.

'I'm Darny Tyler,' he replied, his face heading back down towards his sandwich again.

'And how do you fit into all this? Is my daughter being nice to you?'

Darny shrugged.

'Yes, I am!' said Issy, cross. 'I'm nice to everyone.'

'You're too nice,' said Marian. 'Always trying to please people, that's your problem.'

Darny nodded his agreement. 'She always wants everyone to like her, all the teachers and stuff.'

'What's wrong with that?' said Issy. 'Of course I want people to like me. Everyone should like people to like them. The alternative is just wars and aggravation.'

'Or honesty,' said Darny.

'Quite right,' said Marian. They exchanged a glance.

'You two are ganging up on me,' said Issy, attempting at least the bottom half of her sandwich. It was absolutely delicious. As soon as she tasted it, all her doubts about the café and its standards completely disappeared. That was interesting, she realised, looking at the queue out of the door. People came here for one thing only: the amazing, fabulous food. The fact that the lino was a bit cracked or the windows smeary didn't matter in the slightest. She looked around at the other customers, rushing in, shouting out their orders, scattering salt sachets and coffee stirrers on the counter, jostling each other to get in. This was good. This was how people liked it. It might not suit her clientele, but it certainly suited its own.

'So tell me, how's school, Darny?' said Marian.

Darny shrugged. 'Awful.'

'It is not "awful",' said Issy. 'He gets top scores in maths and physics. And no scores in everything else, not because he's not bright but because he isn't interested.'

'I hated school,' said Marian. 'Got out as soon as I could.'

And got pregnant, Issy didn't say.

'Issy was such a little scholar, worked so hard, went to college, passed all her exams, proper little swot, and what does she do now? Makes cakes. Which is fine, I grant you, but it hardly needed her grandfather to pay for three years of higher education.'

'It's been very useful, actually,' said Issy, crossly.

'So you are who, exactly?' said Marian.

'I'm Austin's little brother. Austin's her boyfriend.' Darny made a face and Marian laughed.

'I didn't know you had a boyfriend,' she said.

'Austin,' said Issy patiently. 'The tall chap that was at the funeral? Whose house I live in? Whom I talk about on the phone?'

'Oh yes, ooh yes, of course I did,' said Marian. 'I must meet him one day.'

'You have met him,' said Issy. 'Four times.'

'Oh, of course I have. Good for you! Now, Darny, tell me some of the nonsense they've been teaching you in school.'

And to Issy's absolute surprise, Darny launched into a long story about their sex-education teacher who had got all wobbly and upset doing something unfortunate with a banana. It was a funny story and Marian listened carefully and asked pertinent questions, and then they both got stuck into a discussion of why they had to use rabbits for sex information and why couldn't they use those gay penguins, and Issy couldn't help but be struck by the fact that Marian was obviously enjoying the conversation—they both were—but also that she was talking to Darny as if they were both adults, or both teenagers, she couldn't quite tell which one. At any rate, in a way that they managed to understand one another. She watched them with some sadness. Darny was so sparky, so full of contrariness and argument. She found it wearing and problematic, but to her mother it was clearly a challenge. Yet she herself had spent so much time as a daughter trying to be good, and behave herself, and gain appreciation for that.

201

Well, Gramps had loved her for who she was. She knew that much. And Austin, too. No wonder he'd been so surprised by her outburst last night. She surreptitiously fingered her phone and wondered what he was up to. She glanced towards the restaurant kitchen, full of short-order cooks shouting, bantering, working the lunchtime rush. She wished she could bake something. It always calmed her down when she was agitated. But between the little hotel room and the big restaurant meals, that definitely wasn't possible. She was just going to have to grin and bear it. And be happy that Darny and her mother seemed to have made a connection. That was good, at least.

*   *   *

They added a hearty tip to the bill (Issy paid, and her mother let her), reluctant to leave the cosy banquette for the freezing street, but Marian mentioned that she had to go and pick up some knishes from Dean & Deluca, a sentence Issy didn't understand any of, so they headed out together into the cold.

'How long are you here for?' said Marian.

'A few days,' said Issy. 'Can we come and visit you?'

Marian frowned. 'Well, you know, it's very busy at the commune ... Of course,' she said. 'Of course. I'll send you directions.'

She kissed them both freely.

'Mazel tov!' she yelled happily, as she marched off in her funny home-made clothes, walking across a stop light as if she'd been born in America.

'Your mum's cool,' said Darny, as they took a

202

cab up to the Guggenheim Museum.

'People think that,' said Issy.

'Do you not see her very much?'

'No,' sighed Issy. 'But that's OK. I never did, really.'

A silence fell between them. But this time it felt a bit more companionable.

After an hour of trying to appreciate the art (and Darny running up and down the famous circular passageway), Issy was utterly exhausted. She was on the brink of suggesting they go back to the hotel and have a nap when her phone finally tinged. It was Austin, with one of the funny, short New York addresses made up of numbers. He was suggesting they meet up there, and Issy agreed.

*   *   *

Austin had sleepwalked through his meeting. He hadn't listened to a word anyone had said, just launched into an analysis of the business as he saw it. Amazingly, nobody seemed to have noticed that he hadn't listened. Maybe not listening was the way forward. Maybe it was how everything got done. But he couldn't help it. He was, he realised, unutterably miserable. Here they were, showering him with riches and offers and a whole new way of life; a way of life he'd never even dreamed of. Success, security for Darny and himself; a future.

But the person he wanted more than anyone to share it with didn't seem to want to share it with him.

Austin hadn't fallen in love with Issy straight away. He had found her quirky, then he had liked her, then it had gradually dawned on him that he never wanted to be without her. But it was more than that. He trusted her; he listened to what she had to say. They thought alike on so many things. And the fact that Issy clearly wasn't interested in being here with him ... it shook his confidence, it really did. He'd grown to rely on her so fully, even, he realised, to the point of taking her for granted.

He kicked his way through the dirty snow. Everyone he met thought he was crazy in this weather, but he liked walking in Manhattan; there was so much to look at, and he fitted in with his regular long stride because everyone walked fast, and he liked the pulse of the city in his veins and the hum and buzz of electricity. He did like it. Issy would like it too.

That made him groan internally. He knew ... he thought he knew ... that if he begged her, if he made a big point out of it and insisted and strong-armed the situation—which was not his style at all—she would come. She would. Wouldn't she? But even if she did, Austin knew she wouldn't be happy. Couldn't be. She'd worked so hard, and it was her ... her purpose, he supposed. Issy, in the Cupcake Café, her hands covered in flour, her cheeks pink from the heat of the oven; with a pat on the head for every child and a friendly word for every cold and weary London passer-by. It defined her. To stick her in some glass box high-rise apartment in Manhattan whilst he worked ridiculous hours every day ...

He would turn them down in a heartbeat.

That much had been running round and round his head. That much he'd decided. Unfortunately, there was something else. Something that made all his good intentions towards Issy hardly count at all.

The letter Issy had grabbed from the hall table as she had left for New York. The letter, with its impersonally typed address and frank. It was slightly crumpled and stained from its trip on the plane and being stuffed in and out of bags. Issy had left it on his side of the bed. She didn't know, of course, how far things had gone.

Dear Mr Tyler,
We at Carnforth Road School are afraid that the behaviour of your son/ward has become, despite repeated warnings, too much for our school to take on. We are recommending a permanent exclusion. We do not feel Darny's particular needs are being met by this school ...

There was more, much more. Mostly of a legal nature. Austin had skipped that.

There was only one other school in the district, King's Mount, and it had been terrible and dangerous in Austin's time and it was still terrible and dangerous now. Parents avoided it like the plague; people moved so their children wouldn't have to attend it. Fights were regular; it was the dumping ground for children who had nowhere else to go, or a halfway house to borstal, or for those whose parents just didn't give a toss. It had been on special measures for ever, but they couldn't shut it as it was absolutely huge, and nobody else wanted the children who went there.

Darny would never survive there. Austin couldn't possibly afford to send him to another school. Not in London. Even if they'd take him, which with his record was probably a bit tricky.

He gulped.

Merv had already handed him a brochure for the middle school his own children went to, assuring him he'd get a place for Darny. It had class sizes of twelve, its own pool, and weekly one-to-one seminars 'to develop social and creative potential' and encourage 'independence and clarity of thought'. Austin had had it half on his mind ever since. Part of Darny's intransigence was of course just down to his age; it was completely normal and would probably get thrashed out of him at King's Mount ... Austin couldn't bear it. Darny was small for his age. Small, not very brave, but with a big mouth. He remembered Issy saying in passing that she didn't like big gangs of schoolchildren in her shop (she let them in, but Pearl did bouncing if they got too rowdy), but felt like making an exception for the poor terrified mites she saw crawling out of King's Mount, with their pale, scared-looking faces.

Austin sighed. Would he drop everything, this job and everything else, for Issy? Of course. Yes, New York would be fun and an adventure, but he wouldn't jeopardise their relationship for that. Not if it was just him.

It wasn't just him. It was him and Darny; had been for a long time.

*   *   *

As soon as Issy saw the outside of the place where they were meeting, she knew, and couldn't help feeling a bit irritated. This was where Austin had got those other cupcakes. Those enemies ... She was curious, she couldn't help it. The New York

City Cupcake Store, read the old-fashioned writing on the window. This was where so many of the great cupcake makers had started in this city ... perhaps she'd just had a bad batch. It would be a good thing to try some others out, have a look around and see if she could get any new ideas. She wished she'd thought of this before, actually, rather than following the guidebook and having to try and explain stuff to Darny in the art gallery that she didn't really understand, then answer his follow-up questions, which she definitely didn't.

The smell of coffee wafting out into the street— although it had that odd, slightly burned smell that she'd learnt to associate with American coffee shops—calmed her down a little. It felt more like home somehow. She sniffed. Something was odd. She could smell baking for sure, a warm smell that encompassed half the street. And she could see the cakes in the window. But the cakes in the window didn't chime with the smell, which was much breadier. Something was up.

She peered through the steamed-up window. Austin, to her amazement, was already there. It wasn't like him to be on time, never mind early. He was inside chatting to someone. They were head to head. Issy blinked. He hadn't mentioned bringing a friend.

'Come ON,' Darny was saying, hopping up and down. 'It's FREEZING out here.'

'OK, OK,' said Issy, and pushed open the door. The doorbell made an electronic noise. Issy preferred her real bell.

Austin looked up, almost guiltily. The girl he was talking to was, Issy noticed, almost ridiculously pretty, with her perfect teeth and rosy mouth and

207

lovely scattering of freckles. Issy wondered if she was being paranoid, but the girl seemed to shoot an angry look in her direction. Issy was going too far in her harsh judgements of New York and its inhabitants. She needed to calm down and lighten up a little. Everything was going to be better now.

'Hello,' she said as cheerily and generously as possible.

Austin smiled. He still felt a bit awkward about this morning, and had a sense that things weren't turning out quite as amazingly as he had thought they should be in his head.

'Hello,' he said.

'New York sucks,' announced Darny cheerfully, as if it confirmed all his long-held suspicions. 'It's freezing and really boring. But the food is good,' he added, looking at the cupcakes.

'Hello,' said Kelly-Lee. She was slightly discomfited. Girlfriends she could handle, but she didn't know they had a child. That was annoying. And Austin didn't look anywhere near old enough. 'Have you come to visit your dad?'

'My dad's dead,' said Darny rudely, as he always did under the circumstances. 'That's my brother.'

'Awww,' said Kelly-Lee. Darny knew that 'awww'. He and Austin exchanged glances.

'Come here, tyke,' said Austin.

'Here, little man. Let me get you a cupcake. I don't know if you have them in your country. It's a special American treat, and here's a Christmas one just for you!'

Darny rolled his eyes, but he wasn't about to turn down a free cake.

Issy smiled tightly. Kelly-Lee glanced up at her. 'Oh yes,' she said. 'I forgot, you bake, don't you?'

208

'Yes,' said Issy. She had realised what was weird about the smell; they were pumping it in. It was chemical. They hardly baked here at all.

'For a real job or just for fun?'

'It's a real job,' said Issy.

'Oh,' said Kelly-Lee. 'I wanted to be an actress for a real job.'

'Well, it's nice to meet you,' said Issy, slightly confused.

'Me and Austin here have been hanging out, haven't we?' said Kelly-Lee, playfully putting her hand on his lapel. Then she came out from behind the counter to pick up some cups littering the tables, making sure she bent over at each one so Austin and Issy could both check out how amazingly tight and rounded her bottom was, after several hours of Pilates a week.

Issy raised her eyebrows at Austin.

'Um, she's been very friendly,' said Austin.

'And don't forget to call me!' said Kelly-Lee. 'Don't worry, I'll look after him for you when you're not here!' And she smiled her enormous wide American smile right in Issy's face and gave her a cheery wave with her dishcloth before disappearing into the kitchen.

Issy was fuming. 'Who the hell is that?' she said.

'I don't know, some girl,' said Austin, confused.

'Some girl? Some girl? You just happened to walk into a cupcake shop and start chatting with some girl?'

'It was just chatting,' said Austin.

'So you didn't take her number?'

Austin thought back. 'Well, she did give me her number ... but I didn't ask for it. I don't even know where it is. She only gave it to me in case you didn't

209

get on that plane.'

Issy blinked in disbelief. 'What, if one cupcake girl wasn't available, any one would do?'

'No! No!' said Austin. 'You're getting this all wrong. You're taking everything all wrong! You have done since the moment you got here.'

'I haven't seen you since the moment I got here,' said Issy, realising to her horror suddenly that she was on the brink of tears. They hardly ever fought. 'Which I suppose I'd better get used to, seeing as you're moving here with all the new people you know and all the cool New York stuff you do and I'll just go back home and get on with my dreary baking life, which, by the way, is REAL BAKING,' she shouted through the back so Kelly-Lee could hear. 'Not this plastic crap they're churning out here with fricking vegetable oils and sell-by dates. Do you know what the sell-by date of a cupcake is? It doesn't have one. About an hour. So this is crap and everything here is crap and you're coming here, for ever, and I realise I have to put up with that, but I don't see why you should bloody start flaunting your new girls and new interests in front of me before I've even left.'

Austin was stunned. He'd never heard an outburst like this from Issy before. He looked at her, upset. Also, he hadn't understood the bit in the middle about vegetable oil.

'Issy . . . Issy, please.'

'No!' said Issy. 'Don't turn this into me being all ungrateful and stupid. *You* make up your mind about what you want and don't tell yourself you don't know or that you're still weighing up options. I met the people you're going to be working with. They seem very confident that you're about to move away from everything we have. But don't worry about telling me, I'll just put it together all by myself.'

She turned round, grabbed her hat and stormed out of the shop.

'Is she all right?' said Kelly-Lee coming through from the back all wide-eyed and sympathetic. 'I'm sorry, I didn't realise she'd fly off the handle like that. Is she like that a lot? I hope I didn't say anything wrong. Some people are just very dramatic, aren't they?'

'Don't worry about it,' said Austin, not putting her straight, and leaving money for the coffee.

'This cupcake is awful,' said Darny. 'By any reasonable judgement, it's a terrible, terrible cake.'

'You're so cute,' said Kelly-Lee. 'I love your accent.'

Austin turned to Darny. 'Can you stay here for five minutes?' he said. 'I'd better go and get Issy.'

'With her? No chance,' said Darny. 'You can't leave me, it's illegal.'

'*Please*, Darny,' begged Austin.

Darny folded his arms and looked mutinous. By the time Austin had bundled him out on to the street, there was no sign whatsoever of where Issy had gone.

*   *   *

It was growing dark outside. It was icily, bitterly cold, as cold as Issy had ever known. People were dim outline shapes in enormous puffa jackets and huge hats and furs, like bouncy marshmallow men, hurrying and rushing to get inside. The sun was setting in bright pinks and reds and

211

golds, cutting through the skyscrapers and casting endless shadows across the busy pavements. Issy hardly noticed; she ran, blindly, up the street, tears pricking at her eyes. It was time to face the truth, she knew. Austin was going to move here. He was going to make his home, and Darny's home, over here, and that would be that. And all the girls would be all over him like a shot, and . . .

She could hardly think any more. She found herself back on Fifth Avenue, pushing blindly through the crush, the sheer weight of people slightly freaking her out when she was disorientated and just needed somewhere to have a really good cry, in private. There didn't seem to be a lot of privacy in this city.

Her phone rang. She fumbled for it in her pocket, her heart thudding. Was this it? What was she going to say? Sorry, Austin, this is it for us? I'm leaving you because you're about to leave me anyway and I don't want to go through four months of torture whilst you faff around between London and New York unable to make up your mind? Or, Please please please come back to London with me and give up all hopes of an exciting future to be stuck behind a desk in Stoke Newington for the rest of your life?

She was tempted not to answer—nobody's name would come up on her screen because she was abroad—because she didn't know what to say, and a snot- and tear-filled gabbling wouldn't really help anyone. But to not answer would be worse, passive-aggressive and horrible and scary, and if Austin was putting things off, it wouldn't help if she did too.

'Hello?' she whispered into the phone, her hand where she'd taken off her glove to press the green button already feeling cold and stiff. Automatically she kept walking north to where it seemed quieter; up through Columbus Circle and skirting the bottom of Central Park.

'Oh thank GOD,' said Pearl. 'There you are. Issy, I may have been … ahem … slightly exaggerating before. About how things are.'

'What?' Issy snuffled, wrenched back to reality.

'Um,' said Pearl.

*   *   *

Pearl was standing in the basement kitchen of the shop. It looked like a bomb had hit it. Strawberry cake mix that Issy had carefully made up in advance was dripping off the walls. Receipts and pieces of paper were piling up on surfaces all over the place. It was the middle of the night and Pearl hadn't slept properly in two days.

'I think,' she said, finally, 'I think I've broken the mixer.'

'Frick,' said Issy. The industrial mixer was a central part of the operation. 'But it's Saturday tomorrow! It's a huge Christmas shopping day. The entire world is going to be out.'

'I know,' said Pearl. 'And some cake mix landed on the calculator and I'm having, um, some trouble cashing up. And possibly there's a health inspection due.'

Issy made up her mind. 'Listen,' she said, with a heavy heart. 'It's all right. I've got this totally posh plane ticket.'

She paused and took a deep breath.

'I'll fly straight back. I'll see you in the morning.'

213

Chapter Fourteen

It didn't take Issy long to pack. Apart from Caroline's ridiculous coat, she'd worn almost none of the unsuitable clothes she'd packed so quickly, with such excitement. Flicking pointlessly through the television channels, she saw *Sleepless in Seattle* playing on TCM and nearly burst into tears.

Austin arrived back at the hotel shortly after her, a grumpy Darny in his wake.

'This really isn't good for me,' Darny was saying. 'Having to deal with conflict in an already difficult childhood.'

'Shut up, Darny,' Austin said. His face fell when he saw Issy with her suitcase out.

'It's not because of you,' she said. 'Honestly. Pearl can't cope without me. Things have gone really wrong.' She looked at him straight on. 'Sorry. I can't leave the café.'

Austin looked straight back at her. His heart was pounding in his chest. Darny was sitting in the corner, his face drawn and tense. Austin didn't want to mention the letter in his pocket. It wouldn't make anything better. It would make everything worse; Issy might think he was blaming her, because it had happened in his absence.

He never wanted her to think that she had done anything wrong; with Darny, with him. Not anything. He felt a terrible lurch. There was so much he wanted to say, but would any of it change that essential truth?

'I know,' he said, quietly.

There was a long silence after that.

Issy felt as if she'd been punched in the face. He was going to let her go, just like that. Without even vaguely trying to persuade her to stay. For some stupid job. For his career. Everything she had ever thought about her big, handsome, gentle Austin ... well, she hadn't imagined that this would happen. Not like this.

She put out her hand to steady herself. Austin saw her and wanted to burst into tears. She looked so vulnerable. But what could he do? If it wasn't now, it would be later. Should he just prolong the agony? He felt as if he were ripping apart inside; and yet here they were, words still coming out of their mouths, almost like normal human beings.

'I'm just going to phone the airline,' Issy said, feeling as if they were someone else's words, someone else's script. Surely she should be saying, let's take a ferry ride to see the Statue of Liberty; or go for a romantic evening in a cocktail bar where a pianist would be tinkling 'It Had To Be You' in the corner; or go and watch the adverts and the sailors down in Times Square and look at the great bows and Christmas lights that draped every corner of the city.

'I'll get someone to do that,' Austin was saying, like a robot.

'Someone at your office? In New York?' said Issy, then wished she hadn't. Everything was bad enough without being spiteful on top of it. 'Sorry. Sorry. I didn't mean that.'

'No,' said Austin. 'It's OK. *I'm* sorry. I mean ...'

He looked so thoroughly miserable, all Issy wanted to do was take him in her arms and hold him till he felt better. But what good would that do? she thought. He seemed to have made up his mind. Prolong everything? Pretend to carry on a financially ruinous and technically impossible career between two totally different continents?

'Ssh,' she said. 'Don't worry about it.' She indicated Darny. 'We can talk about it back in the UK.'

'Mm,' said Austin. He couldn't figure out where exactly this had all gone so terribly wrong. Issy hadn't even taken a second to look around or tried to see the positive side of New York. She'd been against the entire thing right from the start, almost as if she'd decided that it was going to be a disaster, and therefore it had turned into one. It made him incredibly cross.

They stood a little while longer with neither of them saying anything.

'Well, this is boring,' said Darny. 'I can feel my ADHD kicking in.'

'I'll make the call,' said Austin.

'OK,' said Issy.

After a tense ten minutes, it was arranged that Issy could go back on a flight leaving very early the next morning. Just one more night to go.

'Do you want to go out?' said Austin.

'I think I'm finally going to have that nice bath,' said Issy, trying to paste a smile on her face and stop her voice from wobbling, though she didn't quite succeed. 'Then an early night; I'm going to be

216

up to my eyeballs when I get back to the café.'

'Yeah,' said Austin. 'OK.'

But as they lay together in the huge, comfortable soft white bed, listening to the distant honks and whoops of the traffic, there was not the faintest possibility of sleep. Instead Issy cried; great silent tears, dripping down into her pillow. She tried not to make a sound or disturb Austin, until he turned over and realised her pillow was wet.

'Oh my darling,' he said, holding her tight and stroking her hair. 'My love. We'll work it out.'

'How?' said Issy, sobbing. 'How?'

But Austin didn't have an answer to that. Either way, it seemed, would leave one of them very unhappy. Which in the long run would leave them both unhappy; that much he understood. He sighed again. Why did life have to throw up speed bumps when they seemed to be running happily along? And this, he thought, stroking Issy's soft dark hair, this was a big one. Their tears mingled together on the expensive pillowcases.

*   *   *

Pearl had finally thrown up her hands and admitted defeat. She had phoned Caroline and asked her to come in early.

Caroline had turned up and tutted at the state of the place. Then she had made a call of her own.

'Perdita! Chop chop!' she had shouted at the pleasant-faced middle-aged woman who'd arrived, slightly frightened-looking, three quarters of an hour later. Perdita had instantly started scrubbing everything down from top to bottom, as Caroline briskly went through the figures.

'One thing divorce does is make it very easy to read a balance sheet, see where all the money's gone,' she growled.

Pearl was still gazing at Perdita. 'She's your cleaner? How can you have a cleaner and still come to work in a café?'

'Because Richard is an evil cunning bastard,' said Caroline. 'I've told you this before.'

Pearl eyed her shrewdly. 'But you must be getting close to a settlement now,' she observed. 'It's been dragging on for years.'

'Pearl, you're a terrific salesperson and a wonderful organiser in the café, but your paperwork is a dog's dinner and you bake like a wookie,' said Caroline tightly, ignoring her. 'Division of labour should have been sorted out properly before Issy flounced off.'

'She didn't exactly flounce off,' said Pearl. 'Caroline, I have a theory about you; do you want to hear it?'

'If it's about my astonishing self-control when it comes to food, I'll just tell you again, nothing tastes as good as skinny fee—'

'Nope,' said Pearl. 'That's bullshit. No, here is my theory: I think you work here because you like it.'

'*Like* it? Working? In a job a robot will probably be doing in two years' time? In a job that persistently refuses to recognise my creative interior design and organisational skills and insists on putting me in front of the general bloody public after I've already been a major player in the corporate world? Yeah, right. Perdita, you've missed a bit. And sort out the skirting while you're down there.'

'Yeah,' said Pearl. 'I reckon you really do like it.'

Caroline glanced at her out of the corner of her eye.

'Don't you ever dare tell a bloody soul. PERDITA! Did you bring those bags I asked you? Well, if it takes two runs at it, it takes two runs; just bring them in, would you?'

Perdita soon came in weighed down with two suitcases.

'What the hell is in there?' said Pearl.

'Aha!' said Caroline.

*   *   *

Maya arrived just afterwards, arm in arm with a girl with very short hair.

'Hi,' she said happily to everyone, beaming her lovely smile. 'This is Rachida. Rachida, this is Pearl and Caroline. They are being very patient with me.'

Pearl raised an eyebrow, feeling guilty because she had not been in the least bit patient.

'I've had her up all night practising,' said Rachida. 'Our friends have got a cappuccino machine. She's got it down to six seconds.'

'Thank you,' said Caroline. 'Do your friends do bookkeeping too?'

'Shut up,' said Pearl, looking at Maya and Rachida.

Rachida left, kissing Maya full on the lips as she did so. Maya took off her coat and hung it up behind the door, unconcerned. 'See you tonight!' she yelled cheerfully. Then she turned round.

'OK,' she said. 'I reckon I'm ready.'

Pearl smiled a huge wide smile at her, ridiculously cross at how pleased she was.

'OK,' she said. 'Go bring up that new tray of mince pies. Surely I got them right sixth time out.' And Pearl started to slightly relax, leaning behind the counter and turning on the stereo. 'Deck the Hall with Boughs of Holly' came thundering out of the sound system, and she found herself joining in on the falalas. She must need sleep, she thought.

*   *   *

Issy cried all the way to the airport in the cab. She cried as she sat in the posh lounge, where she completely wasn't in the mood to sample any of the luxury treats. She cried all six hours across the Atlantic, pausing only to watch *Sleepless in Seattle* so at least it seemed like she had an excuse. She cried all the way back on the Heathrow Express and all the way back up the Victoria Line and all the way across town on the number 73.

Then she pulled herself together and walked into the café.

*   *   *

She stopped, and gasped. She couldn't help it. She hadn't really noticed from the outside; there were a lot of people with their faces pressed up against the glass, but she hadn't really taken it in. But here, inside, the entire place was transformed.

Snow lined the fireplace, which was thickly wreathed with ivy. Ivy also hung down in garlands from the ceiling, linking up so the café appeared to have trees growing out of it. Every table had a display of silver ferns and holly, and there was a

220

huge wreath on the door, so the entire place felt like an enchanted forest. Most remarkable of all, however, was that some space had been cleared in the windows, taking out their display box. In its place was a snowy landscape, complete with white hills and a little wooden town, lit up with tiny lampposts. Figures were tobogganing down the hills; there was a school with children playing outside, a hotel with ladies in ballgowns descending the steps, and several cosily lit houses, and round it all ran a dinky steam train, with carriages with tiny people inside them. There was a station with a station master waving a flag and blowing a whistle, and vintage cars parked outside, and tucked behind the highest of the hills, against a backdrop painted with stars, was Santa Claus on his sleigh with all his reindeer. It was utterly enchanting.

'AUNTIE ISSY!' Louis hurtled out from behind the counter and leapt on Issy as if he hadn't seen her for months. 'AH DID MISS YOU!'

Issy let herself enjoy being bowled over and smothered in kisses.

'I missed you too, my love.'

Louis beamed. 'WE HAVE A TRAIN! DID YOU SEE OUR TRAIN? IT'S A REAL TRAIN! IT GOES ROUND AND ROUND AND THERE IS SANTA CLAUS BUT HE IS HIDING SO YOU DON'T SEE HIM!'

'I did see it,' said Issy. 'It's wonderful.'

'Well, my wretched children don't appreciate it,' sniffed Caroline. 'Why are you back so early? Did you get a stain on my jacket?'

Louis stroked Issy's hair. 'Did you bring me a present?' he whispered.

'I did,' whispered Issy, answering the easiest

question first. She reached into her hand luggage and brought out a snow dome she'd bought at the Empire State Building. It had all the lovely buildings of New York—the Empire State, the Chrysler, the Plaza—with little taxis on the ground, and when you shook it, a snowstorm commenced. Louis held it in absolute awe, shaking it again and again in amazement.

'I like my pwesent, Issy,' he said, quietly.

Pearl came round from behind the counter, looking at Issy carefully. She wasn't her normal ebullient self at all. Pearl thought it could just be jet lag. But no, it was more than that. It was as if a light had gone out somewhere behind Issy's eyes. Her face was drawn and pinched-looking, with none of its usual rosy glow.

'That's a beautiful present, Iss,' she said, using the gift as an excuse to give Issy a big hug.

Issy nearly lost it again, but felt she was pretty much all cried out. She turned to Caroline.

'Did you do this?'

Caroline nodded. 'Well. My interior decorator did. I think it's dusty and clutters the house up, so I brought it here. Achilles did look a bit sad at our minimalist look, but heyho. We should absolutely win that bloody *Super Secret London* prize for best shop.'

'It's beautiful,' said Issy. 'Thank you.'

She smiled at Maya, who was expertly balancing four coffee mugs on one arm whilst pouring off perfectly frothed milk with the other hand.

'Well, it didn't take you long to get the hang of things.'

'It did, actually,' said Maya. 'I've been up practising five hours a night.'

222

Pearl nodded to confirm the truth of this. Issy looked around. Everywhere were happy-looking people eating away. Many of her regulars waved. She wanted to cry again: it felt good to be home.

'I thought you were all having a total disaster,' she said.

'A temporary blip,' said Pearl. 'We're totally over it now.'

'I see that,' said Issy. 'Could I possibly get a cup of coffee?'

*   *   *

Austin cried all the way into the office, but hid it. Darny wasn't paying attention anyway. He washed his face in the men's room, installed Darny with his DS next to his secretary, marched into Carmen's office before he even had a chance to think, and signed the papers. Now he belonged to Kingall Lowestein.

'Hey!' said Merv, swinging by to shake his hand and have his photograph taken with Austin for the bank's newsletter. 'You won't regret it.'

Austin already did. 'Can your PA send over those school forms?' he said.

'Sure thing,' said Merv.

*   *   *

Issy started the batches for the next day's cakes so they could get a bit ahead of themselves. Maya was looking at her with wide frightened eyes, imagining her instant dismissal, but Issy smiled and said they were so busy with the window display bringing shoppers in that would she like to stay for a while,

223

and Maya grinned widely and gleefully acquiesced. Issy also thought privately that she wasn't sure she herself was up to being jolly in the shop all the time and might take some more time off. On the other hand, what else did she have?

* * *

'Can I come over?'

'Yes,' said Helena, with the fervour of someone who wasn't getting enough adult conversation. 'Whenever you like. Stay as long as you like. Bring wine. Chadani Imelda, stop putting that up your bottom.'

'Um,' said Issy. 'Um. Can I stay the night?'

There was a pause.

'Oh,' said Helena.

'Oh,' said Issy.

'Oh darling,' said Helena.

'Please don't start me off,' said Issy. 'At least wait till I get there.'

'Bring wine,' repeated Helena. 'I've suddenly decided to stop breastfeeding. Bring LOTS of wine.'

* * *

Helena had, Issy noticed blearily, actually tidied away some of the children's toys and clothes that normally littered the flat in anticipation of her arrival. This was almost more worrying really; that she would go to so much trouble.

'I also went out and got some gin,' said Helena. 'I think gin too. And tonic, obviously. Or perhaps martinis, what do you think?'

224

'When's the last time you had a drink?' asked Issy.

'Two years ago.'

'No martinis, please,' said Issy. 'Especially not for you; you'll fall out the window by five past seven.'

They sat down, whilst Chadani Imelda methodically emptied Issy's handbag of lipstick, change, tampons, and, heartbreakingly, a napkin from the New York City Cupcake Store. Issy picked it up and made to blow her nose on it.

'If I called this number,' she said, indicating the 212 dial code, 'he'd probably be there right now. It's only afternoon there.'

'Hush,' said Helena. 'Hush.'

She poured them both enormous glasses of Sauvignon Blanc.

'Now,' she said. 'You. Fantastic person. Him. Total delight. How the hell did you get yourselves into this mess, and how are you going to get out, you utter bloody blithering idiots?'

*   *   *

After Issy had explained—she could hardly bear to think about that last night, both of them lying there, totally alone in their hugely luxurious bed—Helena took a large slurp of her wine and let out a long sigh.

'Phew,' she said. Then, 'Well.'

'So I'm meant to give up my whole life and everything I've ever worked for for some guy?' said Issy, re-pouring.

'Well, it's not "some guy", is it?' said Helena. 'It's *Austin*.'

225

'AW-IN,' said Chadani Imelda, looking so like her mother even Issy couldn't help smiling.

'Why can't the two of you just talk it through?'

'We can't,' sighed Issy. 'This is a huge, huge deal they're offering him. Whereas the way things are in London, he might not even have a job for much longer. He doesn't feel he can turn it down for me. And I don't think I can destroy the Cupcake Café for him. Which makes me think ...' At this, Issy started to cry huge, racking, choking sobs, '... which means we can't love each other enough.'

Helena shook her head. 'You do. Of course you do. But you're human beings, and it's not a movie. You can't just dump everything and run off into the sunset. Life gets in the way. There's love and then there's things that are practical. You both have responsibilities. You have employees who rely on you, and he has Darny to look after.'

'Nobody ever looks after me,' said Issy.

'Well, that's just self-pitying bollocks,' said Helena. 'And completely unfair given how much time we all gave up to help you open that stupid café in the first place.'

'Oh yes,' said Issy. 'Sorry about that.'

She sighed and drank more wine.

'I was so happy, though, Leens. I thought I was tired and a bit stressed out and always super-busy and up at the crack of dawn and everything with the café, but ... actually, when I think about it, I had everything.'

'That's the ludicrous thing about happiness,' said Helena. 'You never know you're going through it at the time.'

Chadani Imelda hit her mother on the leg, rather hard.

'Apparently these are the happiest days of my life.'

'Oh yes, we're in our prime,' said Issy.

'I'll consider myself in my prime when I stop getting spots,' said Helena.

'And my heart broken,' said Issy.

'And eating fish fingers.'

'And learn self-control,' said Issy, pouring them both another glass.

'Bottoms up!' said Helena.

'You haven't even compared me to some kid that's getting its leg chopped off yet, like you used to when you worked in the hospital,' said Issy.

'Oh GOD, I am SO HAPPY WITHOUT A JOB AND NO SENSE OF PURPOSE OR DIRECTION IN MY LIFE!' shouted Helena, startling Chadani, who nonetheless burst out into giggles too.

'Ha, you girls sound happy,' said Ashok, opening the door to the sounds of hysterical laughter.

Issy and Helena looked at one another, then burst out laughing again. They only stopped when Issy accidentally burst into tears. Helena swallowed, then realised how drunk she was.

'Jet lag,' she tried to explain, but it didn't come out quite right.

Ashok came over and kissed her. He was slightly perturbed by all the empty bottles, but he hadn't heard Helena laugh like that in a long time, and Chadani seemed quiet for once, so perhaps on balance it was a pretty good thing.

'Hello, Issy,' he said. His face lit up. 'Did you ...'

'Bring you some cakes? I know, I know, that's all I'm good for ...'

'ASHOK!' Helena tried to whisper, but she

wasn't used to the booze and couldn't keep her voice down. 'Be sensitive! Issy's just split up with Austin!'

'Not officially,' said Issy.

Ashok picked up Chadani, who had cruised her way towards him, and gave her a huge cuddle and a kiss.

'This is not possible,' he said sternly. 'You have not split up. You cannot. It is unacceptable to me.'

'I should have tried saying that,' said Issy, gulping.

'So. What was it? Something ridiculous? And small? Did he tell another woman she looked nice? Did he not buy you a thoughtful present for your birthday? Men are not always perfect, you know.'

'Are you diagnosing our relationship?' said Issy.

'Sometimes it is useful to take a dispassionate view,' said Ashok.

'Oh, it is definitely dispassionate,' said Issy. 'It definitely definitely is that. He has a job in America. I have a job here. He has to move to America to do his amazing job there, otherwise he'll probably lose the one he has here. I have a quasi-successful business running on a long lease that employs three people but can't manage without me. What's the outlook, Doctor?'

'Well, one of you will have to move,' said Ashok stubbornly, nuzzling Chadani's neck. 'Look at this. This is happiness. You deserve happiness.'

Helena snorted loudly. 'Happiness and lots and lots of stinky laundry.'

Chadani giggled and squirmed in her father's arms, and Issy wanted to cry again.

'Well, I can't and he can't,' she said. 'This isn't north and south London. This is real life, with real choices and real consequences, and we both figured the sooner we faced up to that the better.'

'There is always a way,' frowned Ashok.

'Well, yes,' said Issy. 'If I wait five billion years, the tectonic plates will eventually fuse together and I'll be able to cycle over to his apartment ...'

She was off again. Ashok patted her on the shoulder and Helena rushed up with more wine and some tissues.

'I've got a great idea,' she said. 'Let's have a wonderful Christmas, all together. A big party, here.'

'Here?' sniffed Issy.

Helena looked innocent. 'I just thought it would be lovely to get everyone together at Christmas time. Chadani's aunties could all squeeze in, and you could see if Pearl and Louis want to come, and—'

'Not everyone would fit in here,' said Issy.

'But think how wonderful it would be, all together,' said Helena. 'So happy, such a great way to take your mind off everything.'

'But you don't have a big enough table!' said Issy.

'Oh, so we don't,' said Helena. 'If only we knew of somewhere nearby with great big ovens and loads of tables ...'

'I'm not cooking Christmas lunch for six thousand people,' said Issy.

'Just think of how wonderful it would be to be surrounded by the people who care for you and love you,' said Helena relentlessly.

'Care for me enough to banish me to the kitchen for the whole of Christmas Day?' said Issy.

'OK,' said Helena. 'Was just an idea. What were you planning on doing?'

'At the moment,' said Issy. 'I couldn't feel less in a goodwill-to-all-men state of mind.'

*   *   *

Pearl was on a half-day the next day, and she felt like she desperately needed it. She left early, rather guiltily ignoring Issy's red-rimmed eyes, a combination of jet lag, crying and an ill advised nightcap. She needed the time off and could make it back before Louis got out of school.

Doti caught up with her at the bus stop.

'Well, hello there,' he said, with his customary twinkle. 'How are things with you?'

'Not bad,' said Pearl. She was pleased, but still a bit cross with him for slavering all over Maya. It had felt insensitive.

'Christmas shopping?'

'I might be.'

'I was just heading into town myself. Maybe I'll wait for the bus with you.'

'If you like,' said Pearl.

'So, Maya's worked out well for you? I thought she might.'

'She is a hard worker,' agreed Pearl.

'Have you met Rachida? They're a lovely couple.'

'You knew she lived with a woman?'

'Of course I did; they're on my round. Don't get much past the postman, you know.'

'Why were you all over her, then?'

Doti looked confused. 'What do you mean? I really wanted her to get that job, she needed it desperately.'

'I thought you ... I thought you fancied her,'

230

mumbled Pearl, feeling her face grow hot. Where the hell was that bloody bus?

Doti burst out laughing. 'A skinny little thing like that? Not likely,' he said. He looked slyly up at Pearl under his thick black eyelashes. 'I like something a bit more ... womanly,' he said.

There was a silence.

'There,' he said, finally, kicking the heel of his black postman boot against the pavement. 'I said it.'

Pearl's heart was fluttering in her chest and she found it hard to get her breath. Her emotions fought with each other inside herself; she had an almost overwhelming desire—and it would be so, so terribly simple—to extend her right hand, just a few centimetres, to meet his left, just there, his large, strong, worker's hand, holding on fiercely to the uncomfortable bus shelter bench. She gazed at his hand, and then her own, and his eyes followed her gaze.

Then she remembered the sound of a little boy crying, triumphantly, 'DADDY!' Ben parading Louis round the sitting room on his shoulders like he was a football trophy or a crown; the two of them playing kung fu and breaking her mother's prized horse statuette; Louis laughing, laughing, laughing.

Her knuckles tightened involuntarily, and she froze.

'I can't,' she said, in a voice barely above a whisper. 'It's ... it's complicated.'

Doti nodded. 'Sure is,' he said.

Then he stood up, just as the 73 rounded the corner.

'I am actually going into town,' he said, in a much more conversational tone of voice. 'I wasn't

just looking for an excuse. So can I still come ...
just as a friend? As a normal person?'

Pearl smiled at him, touched. 'You will never be
a normal person to me.'

*   *   *

It was fun, in the end. Pearl hadn't realised it
would be; pottering around John Lewis, buying
a cheap little horse statuette for her mother to
replace the one the boys had broken; and walking
up to Primark to buy some underpants with
monsters on them so hopefully they would appear
to Louis more of a gift and less of a basic necessity.
All the way they looked at the beautifully dressed
windows of the posh shops, filled with expensive
goods, but Pearl, watching the sullen faces of the
thin blondes passing in and out of them, wasn't
sure they were having as good a time as she was,
and she could barely afford anything. Doti asked
her advice on buying make-up for his grown-up
daughter—he and his wife had separated years
before, when she had taken a job in a nightclub
almost comically unsuited to his hours and ended
up having an affair with a bouncer, for which
Doti did his very best not to blame her, which
Pearl appreciated, even if she thought his ex-wife
patently mad. Then he insisted on treating her
to coffee at Patisserie Valerie, down on Regent
Street, having once overheard her say how much
she liked it. Pearl was as touched by the fact that
he had remembered as she was by the treat itself.

They walked down past Hamleys, the huge toy
shop. As usual, there was an enormous crowd of
people, children and adults alike, gathered to see

the wonderful window display—this year it was a huge snowy fairground scene, with a real rotating wheel and carousel rides for the toys below. Outside a Santa Claus was ringing a bell, and several pirates and princesses were blowing bubbles to attract passers-by.

It was the first time Pearl had felt a pang all afternoon. Right by the main door, under a seasonal coating of white cotton wool, all lit up with fairy lights—there it was. The monster garage, with the monster mechanics and the monster trucks going up and down the special lift. She smiled at it and shook her head.

'Are you thinking about that for the little man?' asked Doti.

'Oh, no, no, he gets far too many treats,' said Pearl, fiercely and quickly. She was never, ever going to admit to anyone what she could and couldn't afford.

*   *   *

Doti stayed in town, and Pearl just made it back in time to hide all the little parcels before the door of the café flew open and Louis ran in.

'MAMMA! Oh, no.' He stopped himself. 'MUM!'

'You don't call me Mum,' said Pearl indignantly. 'I'm your mamma.'

'Noooo,' said Louis, shaking his head crossly. 'That's what babies say. I'm not a baby. You're my mum.'

Behind him Big Louis stood nodding gravely at this sad fact of the world.

'I don't want to be Mum. I want to be Mamma.

233

Or Mummy, at a pinch, if you want to sound like those namby-pamby kids you go to school with.'

'Whatever,' said Louis.

'Louis Kmbota McGregor, don't you ever say whatever to me ever again!' said Pearl, horrified. Issy looked up and laughed. It was the first thing that had made her smile all day.

Louis looked half terrified, half proud of himself for inducing such a reaction. He glanced at Issy, who beckoned him over.

'When you say "whatever",' she said, 'you have to make your fingers into a "W", like this . . .'

'Issy, you stop that right now,' said Pearl in a warning voice. 'Louis, that is not allowed, do you understand me?'

Issy and Louis made the 'W' sign at each other, then both chortled heartily.

'Dear Santa Claus,' said Pearl, writing out an imaginary letter, 'I am terribly sorry, but Louis Kmbota McGregor has been very badly behaved this year, and—'

'NOOOOO!' shrieked Louis in sudden terror, charging over and hurling himself into his mother's arms, and showering her with kisses. 'I'm sorry, Mamma. I'm sorry. Sorry, Santa. I'm sorry.'

'I think I'm coming round to Christmas,' observed Pearl.

'I'm not,' said Issy. 'I'm closing up early today.'

There was a massive groan from the customers in the café.

'Shouldn't you all be out getting stocious drunk for Christmas anyway?' she asked.

'The cake is soaking up the stocious drunkness from last night,' shouted someone from the back, and a few people vehemently agreed.

'Oh, all right,' said Issy. 'I may leave you all to help yourselves.'

'Yay!' said the crowd.

'Don't worry,' said Maya, yawning but appearing efficiently at Issy's elbow with a cup of coffee. 'I can handle it.'

Caroline ostentatiously tidied away the white jacket in a dry-cleaning bag. 'Hardly a thank you,' she sniffed out loud. Issy turned to her. She knew why Caroline was in such a filthy mood.

'So, Caroline, what are your plans for Christmas?'

'I am going to go through Richard's old address book and fuck all his friends in alphabetical order,' said Caroline brightly. 'Why?'

Caroline had been blinking very tightly all day and Issy had caught sight of a solicitor's letter in her pocket. She guessed it wasn't good news, as Caroline was being even more of a pain in the arse than usual.

'Only I thought,' said Issy, ploughing on. 'Well, I'm going to be here ...'

'Alone?' said Caroline sharply. Issy didn't answer. She didn't see why she shouldn't pull rank once in a while, in the case of major insubordination.

' ... and Helena and Ashok wanted to have some family around, so I was thinking I might hold a little Christmas dinner here, in the café.'

Caroline didn't say anything. Issy knew that if she hadn't wanted to be included, she would have said something very sarcastic.

'Would you like to join us?' Issy asked gently.

Caroline shrugged. 'Don't think I'll be doing the sodding clearing up,' she said, blinking rapidly.

235

'No clearing up, no coming,' said Issy. 'It'll have to be all hands on deck. But it'll be fun. Pearl?'

Pearl wrinkled her nose. Normally they just went to church and sat in front of the telly. But it might be more fun here for Louis, with Ashok's little cousins running about the place ...

'I'd have to bring my mum,' she said. 'I can't leave her on her own on Christmas Day.'

'Of course,' said Issy.

'And I don't know how we'd get here without buses or anything ...'

'Oh, I'll pick you up in the Range Rover,' said Caroline. 'I won't be doing much else in the morning.' She remembered herself. 'Of course it's great to be alone on Christmas morning. I'm going to have a bit of a spa day, some real "me" time.' Suddenly she burst into tears.

As Issy comforted Caroline, Pearl thought about Ben. She hadn't decided whether to ask him for Christmas. Well, that was what she told herself. She still didn't like thinking about where he'd got that bloody monster garage for Louis. But if she wanted to keep things civil—and she did, she did—she'd have to pretend that it was from a job, and that she hadn't noticed her maintenance had dried up. She'd tackle him again in the new year. She thought that he thought she made more money than he did, or that she somehow didn't mind paying for everything. She sighed. Everything did feel bloody unfair sometimes.

'Um, and maybe ...' Issy looked at her, raising her eyebrows. 'Louis' dad?' she whispered. Louis, however, was totally hypnotised by the Christmas train and didn't notice.

Pearl shrugged. 'Well, you know. He's hardly

236

Captain Reliable.'

'Hmm,' said Issy. She felt as if she had no idea who was reliable and who wasn't, not any more. Pointless trying to guess really.

'Fine,' she said. 'So we'll have a huge one. Right here. I'd better find the world's most gigantic turkey.'

'Can we come?' said a regular customer who'd been listening in.

'No,' said Issy. 'They don't do turkeys that big.'

There was a sigh from around the room.

'Be quiet and eat your cake,' said Issy, going over to phone her suppliers, see if anyone could recommend a really good last-minute gigantic turkey supplier.

'Merry merry merry merry Christmas!' Louis was singing to the train. It was a song they were doing at school. 'Merry merry merry merry Christmas. Ding dong! Ding dong! Ding dong!'

Chapter Fifteen

Chocolate Cola Cupcakes with Fizzy Cola Frosting

Makes approx. 12 large cupcakes

200g plain flour, sieved
250g golden caster sugar
$\frac{1}{2}$ tsp baking powder
pinch salt
1 large free-range egg
125ml buttermilk
1 tsp vanilla essence
125g unsalted butter
2 tbsp cocoa powder
175ml Coca-Cola

For the frosting
400g icing sugar
125g unsalted butter, softened
$1\frac{1}{2}$ tbsp cola syrup (I used Soda
   Stream)
40ml whole milk
popping candy, to taste
fizzy cola bottles, candied lemon
   slices, stripy straws or candy canes
   to decorate

Preheat the oven to 180°C/gas mark 4. Line two 6-hole muffin tins with papers.

In a large bowl, combine the flour, sugar, baking powder and salt. In a separate bowl, beat together the egg, buttermilk and vanilla.

Melt the butter, cocoa and Coca-Cola in a saucepan over a low heat. Pour this mixture into the dry ingredients, stir well with a wooden spoon, and then add the buttermilk mixture, beating until the batter is well blended.

Pour into your prepared liners and bake for 15 minutes, or until risen and a skewer comes out clean. Set aside to cool.

To make the frosting, beat together the butter and icing sugar until no lumps are left—I use a free-standing mixer with the paddle attachment, but you could use an electric whisk instead. Stir the cola syrup and milk together in a jug, then pour into the butter and sugar mixture while beating slowly. Once incorporated, increase the speed to high and whisk until light and fluffy. Carefully stir in your popping candy to taste. It does lose its pop after a while, so the icing is best done just a few hours before eating.

Spoon your icing into a piping bag and pipe over your cooled cupcakes. Decorate with fizzy cola bottles or a slice of candied lemon, a stripy straw or candy cane and an extra sprinkling of popping candy.

* * *

Austin's newly assigned PA, MacKenzie, was incredibly beautiful. She was tiny, with a gym-honed body that could only be arrived at by a lot of lettuce and early rising. Her face was tight, her nose probably not original, her hair extraordinarily bouncy and shiny. She had two degrees and a string of letters after her name, and Merv had called her a paragon of efficiency. She was also, Austin suspected, the most colossal pain in the arse. He already missed Janet terribly.

'So I've just typed up your sked-u-al?' she said, talking in a rat-a-tat voice with an upward inflection that sounded like everything was a question. It was not, Austin was learning, a question. It was an order. 'And if you could, like, be on time for all your appointments so I don't need to make so many calls to keep people waiting? And if you could, like, check out my colour-coded filing system so you always have the right files to take with you? And if you could, like, have your lunch order ready by ten thirty every day so I can get it right for you? And you need to look into contract apartment leases, like pronto? And we'll start work on the green card, like, before you go back to close down your London office?'

Austin bowed his head and did some quick nodding, hoping she'd leave him alone. She stood in front of him, arms folded. For such a tiny person, she made an awful lot of noise.

240

'And, you know, I realise you've just arrived,' she said, 'but I think it is, like, unprofessional to leave a child in my office? It's not really acceptable to me? You know I have a bachelor's from Vassar? And I'm not even sure that it's, like, legal?'

Austin sighed. He knew this was true. He couldn't keep dumping Darny around the place; it was driving both of them crazy. But he'd promised to stay a few more days and set everything up, then go home and work out a couple of weeks' notice—although Ed, his old boss, was so proud that his boy had gone to the big team, he wasn't really expected to do much more than go out for a few leaving pints. Ed had also confirmed what Austin had suspected: they wouldn't be filling his post. They did need to fillet; even though Austin had done well in the job, it was going to go to keep good on the bank's promise to shareholders. Which meant there hadn't really been a way back after all.

He didn't know what else to do with Darny. He wasn't enrolled in the school yet, and it wasn't like he could go to a nursery or a crèche, however much Austin wished he could.

'You would be prosecuted for doing this to a rabbit,' Darny had announced cheerfully as Austin had perched him on his sofa with a Spiderman comic and a packet of crisps the size of a pillow, which Darny crunched with a noise that drove Austin to distraction. 'I wouldn't mind seeing that old lady again. She was cool.'

'Which old lady?' said Austin, struggling to figure out who Darny was talking about. If she wasn't wearing a black pointed hat and living in a gingerbread house, he was willing to give it a shot at this point.

'Marian. No, Miriam. Something like that. Issy's mum.'

'Oh yes,' said Austin, warily. He'd forgotten she was here. They'd met a few times; he thought on the surface she seemed pleasant, a little batty, mostly harmless. Underneath, from stories Issy had told him late at night, he thought what she had done was much, much worse. But she could babysit, couldn't she? She owed Issy that much, at least.

Then he remembered, as he did afresh and anew dozens of times a day, the way things were with Issy, and wanted to howl with anguish.

He didn't. He couldn't. Darny shook out the gigantic packet of crisps so all the dust floated to the floor. Then he burped loudly.

'I'll call her,' said Austin.

*   *   *

Issy was up to her eyes in marzipan when the phone rang. Nonetheless, she knew, in the way that sometimes you just do. Some phone rings sound different to others. And it was just when she was thinking of Austin.

Although, if she was being honest, she had been thinking about Austin every waking moment and every sleepless-night moment and her few and far between early-morning dreaming moments too. So.

She wiped her hands down her striped pink apron and picked up her phone. Number unknown.

It wasn't unknown to her.

'Austin?'

'Issy?'

She swallowed hard. 'I mi . . .'

Then she stopped herself. It had nearly all come

242

tumbling out, all the heartache and the sadness and the terror she had that she was going to lose him. All her neediness and insecurities brought to the surface. But how would that help? What would it prove? That she could guilt him into giving up his amazing life? Did she think that would make them happy?

She tried again. 'I'm making marzipan. Acres of it.'

Austin bit his lip. He could just see her, pink with the exertion. Sometimes, when she was concentrating, she even let the very end of her tongue slip out of her mouth, like a character from *Peanuts*. There she was, doing what she loved best; happy and immersed in her kitchen. He couldn't take that away from her. He couldn't.

'I hate marzipan,' he said.

Issy gulped. 'Well, one, you are wrong. And two, you haven't tried mine.'

'But I don't like the flavour and I don't like the texture. I do think people should be allowed to have different tastes in food.'

'Not when they're wrong.'

'But you don't like beetroot.'

'That is because it is food for horses. Everyone knows that.'

'Well I think marzipan is food for … rabbits. Or squirrels. Nut-loving squirrels.'

'I think it's illegal to give marzipan to a squirrel,' said Issy.

'I wouldn't know, I missed squirrel marzipan week at school,' said Austin.

There was a silence. Issy thought she would burst with longing. Why was he calling? Had something changed? Had he changed his mind?

243

'So?' she said.

'Um,' said Austin. He didn't know how to get the next bit out without sounding like the most terrible heel. 'The thing is,' he said. 'I have to stay on here a bit longer . . . '

Issy's heart dropped out through her feet like a plummeting lift. She felt it crack and go, all the way down down down, and smash to bits, far, far below.

All she said was, 'Oh.'

'And, hem. Well. I wondered . . . '

'I can't come out again,' she said, quickly, fiercely. 'I can't. Don't do that to me, Austin.'

Oh Christ, thought Austin. This was going even worse than he'd thought. Although he realised that as he'd made the call, there'd been a bit of him wondering if she might possibly say, 'Darling. Let's forget the last week. Let me fly back over. Let's give it another shot.'

Of course she couldn't. She was up to her elbows in marzipan. He was mad.

'Um, no. No. Of course not,' he muttered. He wondered what Merv would say if he were here. Something straight and to the point, he imagined.

'I wondered if I could have your mother's number.'

Issy almost burst out laughing, but she knew that if she did, the tears would be right behind.

'For what, a date?' she said.

'No, no . . . for Darny. To help with Darny.'

'What, because I flounced off?' she said.

'No,' said Austin. 'You did what you had to do. For him really. He liked her.'

'She liked him.'

'So, maybe . . . I mean, just while I've got a few things to do . . . '

244

This would be Austin's life from now on, Issy realised. He would always have a few things to do. His phone would always be ringing; his work would always be his priority.

'Of course,' she said. 'I'll need to text it to you when I hang up.'

There was a pause. Neither of them quite knew whether this meant she was about to hang up; and if so, how final it was.

'Issy,' said Austin, eventually.

That was too much. She choked.

'Don't,' she said. 'Don't say it. Please. Just don't. I'll text you the number.'

*   *   *

'No Christmas?' said Darny, gazing at Marian in sheer amazement. 'How can that even be?'

'Don't you do religion at school?' grumbled Marian.

'Yeah,' said Darny. 'We do how all religions are super-great. It's rubbish. And I got kicked out of the class anyway for going on about the Inquisition.'

'They aren't allowed to teach the Inquisition?'

'I brought a book of pictures in,' shrugged Darny. 'Kelise Flaherty threw up all over the whiteboard. Well, she was the *first* one to throw up.'

Marian's lips twitched. 'You remind me of someone,' she said. 'Anyway, we have something much cooler. It's called Hanukkah.'

'Oh yeah. My mate Joel has that. He says it's rubbish.'

'But you get a present every night for eight nights! It's the festival of lights.'

'He says the presents get really rubbish by the

245

end, and him and his sister complained and drew Christmas trees all over the place, so his parents just gave up in the end and had Christmas too. So now he has Hanukkah *and* Christmas.' He glanced up at Marian. 'Maybe I'll do that.'

'Maybe,' said Marian. 'But it's very disrespectful.'

'Good,' said Darny, kicking his chair. His feet didn't quite reach the bottom of the bar stool he was sitting on so he could sip his root beer float.

'Do you like getting into trouble?' asked Marian gently.

Darny shrugged. 'S'all right. If I get into trouble with the teachers, I get into less trouble with the big kids. So, you know. On balance. Teachers hit less.'

Marian smiled. 'I know what you mean. I just used to bunk off all the time.'

'I do that too,' said Darny. 'Only problem is, where we live, everybody knows us. I get spotted by busybodies all the time and they tell Austin and he sighs and makes those big puppy-dog eyes at me. It's rubbish. I wish I lived where nobody knew me. Where did you go when you bunked off?'

'I used to go to the fairground,' said Marian. 'They gave me free goes on the rides.'

'Really?' said Darny. 'That sounds amazing.'

'Well, it had certain ... consequences,' said Marian. 'I would say I paid for it in the end.'

'Is that a metaphor?' said Darny. 'Or am I meant to understand it right away?'

'You are far too smart for your age,' said Marian. 'If there was a way of making young people understand any of it, and then actually act on it— ha. Well, I'm sure they'd have discovered it by now. But your mistakes are all yours to make.'

She handed him a small parcel wrapped in brown

246

paper.

'What's this?' said Darny. 'Can I open it now?'

'Have you not been listening to me at all?' said Marian, but with a smile in her croaky voice. 'Of course you can open it.'

Darny did. It was a small square wooden spinning top covered in letters. Marian had expected him to be dismissive of it, but had hoped to explain where it came from and what it meant. She liked this boy. He had something about him.

Instead of casting it aside as a child's toy, though, he picked it up and held it carefully and looked at it from all angles.

'I can't read the letters,' he said. 'They're weird, like something out of *Ben Ten: Alien Force*. Which blows.'

'It's a dreidel,' said Marian. 'You can play games with it.'

Darny spun it in his hands.

'That's right. A long time ago Jewish scholars had to pretend they weren't studying the Talmud—the holy book. So they pretended they were playing a game instead. And tomorrow you'll get another present, and that will be gelt.'

'What's that?'

'You'll see. You'll like it.'

'Can you eat it?'

'In fact, yes. Now, would you like to come for a walk with me?'

'It's freezing outside.'

'To the cinema. It's two blocks—they're showing *Miracle on 34th Street*. I think you'll like it.'

'That sounds like it's for girls,' said Darny dubiously.

'I won't tell a soul,' said Marian.

Chapter Sixteen

Caroline's Turnip Pie Surprise

Chop turnip, mushroom, radishes, Brussels sprouts and a red onion and put in a dish with a spray of flax oil. Add cumin (not too much).
  Cover with wholemeal pastry. Bake. Fumigate house. Call out for pizza.

*   *   *

Three days before Christmas, Caroline saw Donald again. Looking like a very small bear in his footsie pyjamas, he was creeping out of Kate's house. He saw her looking at him and blinked, his thumb in his mouth. Caroline gave him a stern look and mounted the imposing stone steps. The house had been remodelled beautifully by a builder she had had a fling with the year before. The affair had finished when he'd tried to buy her a bacon sandwich and they had both realised they had no future together. He was a good builder, though. Immaculate box trees stood either side of the forest-green-painted front door.

'Come on, you,' said Caroline, taking Donald's

hand. She rang the bell. No one answered, so she pushed the door open. The nanny was standing exhaustedly over a huge pile of ironing, while the twins charged up and down the stunning stairs, with their freshly painted balustrade and tasteful works of art, hitting each other with sticks.

'Um, missing anyone?' Caroline said. The nanny looked up, a defeated look on her face.

'Oh,' she said. 'Come here. Was he running away again?'

'He's a baby,' said Caroline. 'He's just looking for his mother. Where is she?'

The nanny shrugged. 'In bed. She say she needed lie-in after the jet lag. They just got back from Cyprus.'

'Cyprus?'

Caroline marched up the stairs.

'Kate! KATE!'

A door clicked open.

'Heinke? Could you keep those bloody children quiet for five seconds?'

'Kate?'

Kate was wearing an expensive-looking silk night shirt and yawning widely. Caroline glanced at her watch. It was after eleven; she'd been doing the early shift.

'Good holiday?'

Kate snapped awake. Her eyes went wide.

'Caroline? What on earth are you doing here?'

'Picking your children up off the street. What are *you* doing?'

Kate snorted. 'Oh, thanks for the lecture about children. And who's been doing all the complaining to Richard about school fees?'

Suddenly there was a male voice from behind her

in the bedroom. Both women froze.

'Darling, it's no one,' called back Kate, optimistically. But it was too late. Caroline had already recognised the unmistakable tones of her ex-husband. She felt like she'd been punched in the stomach. So this was where the bastard had been hiding! No wonder she and Kate hadn't been getting together so much.

Caroline may have been many things, but she wasn't a coward. She took a deep breath and stood up straight in the face of adversity, just as she'd learned at her hard-ass boarding school.

'Good lord, you do both get around,' she held on to herself long enough to say. 'I hope you used a condom, Richard; remember that time you gave everyone chlamydia?'

Kate went pale and gasped, as Caroline turned on her heel. Downstairs, the nanny was unplugging the iron.

'I quit!' she shouted. 'Is like being slave for crazy woman! I'm going to look for job for non-crazy woman. Bye! Stop losing child!'

The three children started wailing their heads off all over their smart Petit Bateau Breton shirts. Snot was going on the William Morris wallpaper. Donald dropped his juice carton on the pale landing carpet. Caroline carried on out of the house.

'And lock the bloody door behind me for once!' she shouted over her shoulder.

*   *   *

Later, she looked at her handiwork. She had made the children a pie. They were terrified of her cooking; normally she tried to get them to eat

raw food. Hermia especially, her daughter, tended, even at the age of nine, to shrink from her mother's highly critical gaze. She consoled herself at school, finishing up the thick stodgy puddings the other girls were already pushing away. It showed.

Caroline added turnip, cabbage, carrot and some pieces of apple for flavouring, and a spray of low-calorie oil. Then she put the pastry over the top. That would cover it up, then she'd suggest that Hermia didn't eat the pastry, just as she herself wouldn't be doing.

Perdita was bustling round the kitchen and looked dubiously at the pie, but a warning look from Caroline soon froze her off. Caroline also fired off an email to her lawyer, demanding additional damages for pain and distress caused by Richard flaunting his infidelity.

Then, at a loose end, with Maya taking the afternoon shift and Issy back, she found herself sitting down with her photo albums. Like many other things in her life, Caroline's photo albums were immaculate. She chose only the best pictures of them all in carefully staged perfect environments—round the fire in the ski chalet, wearing matching jumpers and toasting cups of hot chocolate (Achilles had screamed and refused to touch the snow or go outside; Hermia had been horribly bullied at ski school and woken up with nightmares for five months); on their island getaway (Richard had stayed on the phone to work pretty much the entire time; Caroline had gone mad without childcare and with all the mosquitoes); dressed up for a wedding (Richard had chatted up a bridesmaid, Caroline had burst into tears, the marriage had lasted six months before the bride ran away with the caterer). She smiled ruefully at the expensive albums and the stories they did not tell.

But there were other stories, too, real ones. Hermia putting her nursery angel on the Christmas tree, one branch totally weighed down by decorations (Caroline had immediately tidied the tree up once the children had gone to bed, so it looked nice). She glanced over at this year's tree. It was exquisitely tasteful in silver and white. But it didn't have Hermia's nursery angel on it. Caroline wondered where it had gone.

There was Achilles, in the same kind of footsie babygro Donald had been wearing. Her little snuggly boy, who now looked hostile and rebellious if she suggested he change his shirt or put down his DS. He was sitting in Richard's lap; Richard had just unwrapped an enormous, ridiculous puppet he'd brought back from a business trip somewhere. It was a huge gawky parrot with a purple and pink feathered crest and a manic grin. It had been hideous; Caroline had given it to Oxfam the second Christmas was over. In the picture, though, father and son were breathless with laughter and suddenly looked very like each other. It was a beautiful shot.

Caroline swore under her breath. Perdita had left, and the house—secondary glazed, of course, well set back from the road—suddenly seemed very quiet, only the ticking of the beautifully restored pale French grandfather clock in the hall disturbing the silence. Caroline didn't want to look at photo albums any more. She wanted to gather her children close to her, feed them pie, apologise on some level for the family she had put in the photo albums, and the family they had turned out to be.

On impulse, she went to pick them up from school—normally they stayed late for homework hour so she could have some me-time. The other mothers at the gate smiled at her nervously, but didn't engage her in conversation. Obviously they thought divorce was catching, like nits. Caroline ignored them. She also ignored the surprise—and, if she was being completely honest, worry—on the children's faces as they emerged in their smart hats and blazers, marshalled by a teacher who looked suspicious that they were skipping homework club.

'Is anything wrong?' said Achilles.

'Nothing at all, darling,' lied Caroline. 'I just wanted to see you, that's all.'

'Has something happened to Granny?' asked Hermia.

'No, but don't worry, when it does, you're getting a new pony. No, come on, let's all go home together.'

'I made a decoration!' said Achilles, holding up a misshapen Santa with a huge head.

Normally Caroline would have smiled politely. Today she picked it up. 'That's fantastic!' she said. 'Shall we put it on the tree?'

The children looked nervous.

'I thought we weren't allowed to touch the tree,' said Achilles.

'I would never say that,' said Caroline. 'Did I? Did I say that?'

The children swapped glances.

'OK, OK, never mind. Today it will be different. And I've made supper! Pie!' She caught Achilles' hand. Unusually, he let her hold it.

'What kind of pie?'

'Surprise pie.'

Their faces fell.

'Now, tell me all about your day.'

And to her surprise, they did. Normally she got Perdita to pick them up for karate or swimming or Kumon maths or whatever it was they were supposed to have scheduled that evening. But just walking along with them, she was amazed when Hermia launched into a long and detailed description of how she and Meghan and Martha and Maud had been best friends, but now they couldn't all be best friends and they had said to her that they would let her be best friends again when they'd got enough space and when she didn't have a tummy any more, and Caroline listened carefully to the saga, which Hermia told in a completely flat tone of voice, as if of course it was the way of things that a group of small girls would turn on you sometimes and explain that you couldn't be in their gang any more. She looked at Hermia's wilfully black, tufty hair, inherited directly from Richard, and mentally contrasted it, as she so often did, with the smooth blonde locks of her friends' daughters. Then she gave Hermia a big hug.

'Are you looking forward to Christmas?' she said.

Hermia shrugged. 'Don't know,' she said. 'I get scared at Grandma Hanford's.' Richard's mother was a terrifying old horsey bag who lived out in the middle of nowhere in a spooky old house that she refused to heat.

'Never mind,' said Caroline. 'We'll have a proper celebration the next day.'

When they arrived home, Achilles unpacked his school bag. There were mountains of books and homework.

254

'I know for a fact that Louis McGregor gets no homework till he's nine,' said Caroline. 'Do you get this much every night?'

Achilles winced, and suddenly his face, which often seemed discontented and mulish to Caroline, looked simply exhausted. He was such a little boy. Such a small thing to be sitting in rows at old-fashioned desks, competing with other children who were also overscheduled and anxious and doing their best to please everyone. Caroline stroked his face. She wondered if it would really be the worst thing in the world if Richard stopped paying the school fees. Maybe if they went to Louis' school, with their black history months and potato cut-outs and ... No. That would be ridiculous.

A horrible smell was coming from the kitchen.

'Shall we see if this pie is really terrible?' she said. 'And if it is, shall we call out for pizza?'

'Can we eat it in front of the TV?' said Achilles, pouncing on their mother's moment of weakness. Between the Aubusson carpet and the pristine reclaimed oak floors, this was absolutely verboten; no food, shoes, wine or animals were allowed in Caroline's front room. It was, she liked to tell the interviewer in the imaginary *Homes and Gardens* piece she occasionally did in her head, her oasis; a sanctuary from the hustle and bustle of London life. She would add that she often used the room to perform her meditations, even though she'd given up meditating when the divorce had started, because when she wasn't busy doing something, she started thinking about how much she wanted to kill Richard.

Caroline rolled her eyes. 'OK. Just this once.'

She scanned through the Sky TV guide.

'It's Christmas. They must be showing *The Wizard of Oz*.'

They were.

*   *   *

Issy's favourite Christmas song was Sufjan Stevens singing 'Only At Christmas Time'. It was so beautiful, and at the moment she seemed to be hearing it everywhere. It accompanied her as she did a huge food shop (Helena had come with her, then Chadani Imelda had kicked off like a maniac at the selection boxes, so Issy had sent them home), its refrain following her up and down the aisles: 'Only to bring you peace/ Only at Christmas time/ Only the King of Kings ... Only what once was mine'.

She felt as if she was regarding the world from behind a fuzzy mask, or through the wrong end of a telescope; all around her were families—she had none—and children—no—and happy couples giggling and pointing at mistletoe, and here she was piling loads of sprouts into the trolley because Ashok's relatives were vegetarian, and even though Ashok had assured her that they'd bring food, she was hardly going to greet guests with empty plates and a hopeful expression.

She threw in pâté and stuffing and mounds of potatoes and lots of nuts for the nut roast, and tutted loudly at the ingredients in the mince pies, and added an extra four boxes of crackers. Ashok had insisted on paying for the food, but as many of his relatives didn't drink either, she reckoned she'd have to do the booze, or perhaps everyone could contribute. She stood in front of the special seasonal shelves of spirits and liqueurs and lots of things she couldn't imagine people wanting to drink ordinarily, and sighed. She didn't know how she'd feel on the day; whether her awful black mood would bring everyone else down and she'd have to get a bit squiffy to perk herself up. Or the opposite; she'd be able to put a brave face on it until she'd had a couple of glasses, then she'd be a puddle on the floor.

A woman, younger than her, pushed a buggy into her and grimaced apologetically. 'Sorry,' she said. 'It's just so busy.'

'Not at all,' said Issy. 'Not at all. It's me who was ... just standing ...'

The woman smiled. 'Oh, you're so lucky. If I stop moving, he screams the place down.'

Issy smiled politely. She didn't feel lucky.

*   *   *

'So are we going home, or what?' said Darny. They were back in the New York City Cupcake Store. Kelly-Lee was absolutely triumphant when she saw that Issy had gone.

'Will she be back soon?' she asked pointedly. Austin tried to half-smile at her in a distracted way, then forgot about her completely.

'We can't go to Issy's mum's,' said Darny. 'They don't have Christmas.'

Austin bit his lip. He knew Issy wasn't staying at his house. He called the number deep into the night, letting it ring on and on, even though he knew it was stupid, and pointless. Although he guessed she must be at Helena's, he didn't call there. Just dialled his own number, letting it go,

257

letting himself imagine, just for a second, that she'd creep downstairs in that terrible old fleece he had left over from his diving days, complaining about the cold wooden floors, which creaked everywhere, and stand, bouncing up and down on the tips of her toes, telling him off for ringing her so late when she had to get up so early, then immediately forgiving him.

'No,' he said. 'Merv's invited us out with his family. If we want to. He said there'll be millions of them there, we'll fit right in.'

Darny stared glumly at his stale apple and cinnamon muffin.

'We won't,' he said. 'We'll be the weirdo foreigners with the funny accents that everyone wants to pinch.'

'I know,' said Austin. 'But here's the thing . . .'

He remembered last year. Giggling under the duvet. Refusing to get dressed, but wearing their 'formal pyjamas' that Issy packed away the next day and insisted they could only have on special occasions. Playing chicken with the Quality Streets until only the toffee ones were left. And later, when Darny had gone to bed, Issy had lit the candles and put in her new diamond earrings, and her pale skin had glowed in the light . . .

Austin blinked twice, hard. No. It was time to come back to reality. To do what he always did: make the best of it. Which meant it was time to break the news to Darny. He took the letter out of his pocket.

'Here's the thing, Darny. And I know I'm supposed to be cross with you, but I don't really know how, because I think, apart from the fact that you're really, really annoying, that you're doing brilliantly well.'

'Shut up,' said Darny, reading the letter upside down. The swagger left his face and he immediately seemed about two years younger. 'Expulsion? Really?'

Austin shrugged. 'Oh come on, Darny, you've been asking for it.'

'True,' said Darny.

'You really pushed it with them.'

'Hmm.'

'And you hated that school.'

'I hated that school.'

Darny swallowed. He was, Austin saw, genuinely upset.

'I thought ... I kind of hoped ...'

'What?'

Darny kicked the table leg. 'It's stupid ...'

'What?'

Darny grimaced. 'I thought they might kind of come round ... maybe think that kids should have a voice.'

Austin sat back. 'Tell me this isn't about your Children Should Vote campaign.'

'We *should*,' said Darny. 'Nobody listens to us.'

'That's all anybody does,' said Austin. 'Oh, bloody hell. They're going to bring this up when you're bloody prime minister.'

Darny suddenly looked very tiny.

'I didn't mean ... I didn't think it would be a big problem for you.'

Austin took perhaps the deepest breath of his life. 'No,' he said. 'No, you didn't. Because you are eleven, and you can't think like that yet. But oh, Darny. I really wish you had.'

'Am I going to have to go to King's Mount?' said

Darny, with a note of panic in his voice. 'They skin kids there, Austin. Especially wee kids. Remember that gang who branded all those year sevens?'

'I do remember,' said Austin sombrely. King's Mount was very rarely out of the local paper. 'And that's why,' he glanced round, 'that's why I think we're just going to stay here, Darny. They have amazing schools here, places you wouldn't believe, that like independent thinkers and do all sorts of amazing, cool things, and you'll get to meet kids from all over the world, and, well, I really think you'd like it . . .'

'We're staying? In New York?'

Darny looked at him. Austin was prepared for tears, shouting, defiance—anything but this.

'All right!' said Darny, punching the air. 'Can't be worse than that shit hole. Cool! I wish Stebson could see me now! Living in New York! Yeah! When's Issy coming back?'

'She . . . she might not be,' said Austin. 'It's hard for her to leave the shop.'

'Don't be stupid,' said Darny. 'Of course she can leave the shop, there's loads of people there.'

'It's not quite that simple,' said Austin. 'It's her business.'

Darny just stared at him. 'She's not coming?'

Kelly-Lee came over. 'Is everything OK over here? And I'm sorry, I couldn't help overhearing— is it true you're staying?'

'Looks like it,' said Austin.

'Oh, that's WUNNERFUL! I'll be your new friend.' She put her hand on his shoulder. 'Show you around. And you, sweetie. I'm sure we're going to be the best of friends.'

Darny looked at her without saying anything

and rudely kicked the table. After a while he said quietly, 'I think it was me. I think it was my fault.'

Austin squinted at him. 'What?'

'That Issy's not coming.'

'You think you drove Issy away?'

'I was bad at school, then I was mean to her.' Darny's face was terribly distressed. 'I didn't mean to, Austin. I didn't mean to. I'm sorry. I'm sorry.'

'Ssh, sssh,' said Austin, who suddenly found himself wanting to swear. 'No. Of course not. Of course it wasn't you. She loves you.'

Darny started to cry.

'It was me,' said Austin. 'Being a selfish idiot. And things moving and changing and me thinking, like an idiot, that it would be great and I should just go along with it, and well, here we are . . .'

Darny no longer looked like a truculent pre-teen. He looked like an upset, terrified little boy.

'Please make her come back,' he said. 'Please, Austin.'

Austin swallowed hard. He didn't answer.

Chapter Seventeen

Issy had unpacked all the food and drink down in the basement, along with as many small random gifts as she'd been able to grab charging through Boots in a tearing hurry. Upstairs, Maya was still on her rounds, and Pearl and Caroline were bickering happily about what age children should be told the truth about Santa Claus. Caroline felt that if the parents had worked hard for the money, children should appreciate that and learn the cost of things. Pearl did not agree. It was the Saturday before Christmas, and Louis was making a Santa beard for himself out of a huge roll of cotton wool and cardboard and sticky tape. He also had a Santa hat on that Big Louis had given him, and was smiling benignly at other children coming into the shop.

'I'm not the real Santa,' he said helpfully to one little girl. 'Would you like a beard?'

The little girl nodded, and before long Louis had turned his handiwork into a thriving cottage industry. Eventually a small woman who'd come in by herself and ordered only a green tea, then looked around for a long time and started writing furiously in a small notebook, leant over.

'Can I have one?' she said.

'Yes,' said Louis. 'But don't pretend to be Santa

262

Claus. You aren't him.'

'I don't think anyone would ever mistake me for Santa Claus.'

'Or a pleesman. You're not allowed to dress up as a pleesman.'

The woman looked puzzled and assured Louis she had no intention of masquerading as a policeman.

'Sorry,' said Pearl through her thick white beard. 'His dad let him watch *Terminator 2* and it scared him half to death.'

'I'm not surprised,' said the woman. 'It scared me half to death and I'm grown up.'

Louis fixed her with his warm brown eyes.

'It's not real, lady. It just in a film. Go back to sleep.'

The woman suddenly cracked open a huge grin and shut her notebook with a clunk. She turned towards Pearl.

'OK, OK,' she said. 'I give up. I've had enough. It's nearly Christmas and I'm really knackered.' She stepped up to the counter and held out her hand to shake. 'Abigail Lester. *Super Secret London Guide*. Style section.'

Pearl took her hand politely without having the faintest idea why.

'Um, hello.'

Caroline threw herself across the counter like a skinned cat.

'A-BIGAIL!' she screeched, as if they were dearest friends. The woman looked rather nonplussed.

'Um, is this your establishment?' she said.

'No, it belongs to the girl crying downstairs in the basement,' said Pearl. 'Hang on. ISSY!'

'Can I offer you a complimentary cake ... cup of hot chocolate? Glass of wine? We don't serve wine, but we keep some for Friday nights ...' Caroline was babbling, and Pearl still couldn't figure it out.

'No, no thanks. I can tell by the happy punters that everything's just lovely.'

Issy clumped up the stairs feeling red-eyed and dull. It was as if the jet lag she'd brought back from the States had never gone away, but thickened, and deepened, and settled into her skin, as if she wanted to wake up, rouse herself, but couldn't, because she knew that if she was wide awake, she would see the world as it was: a space where Austin was thousands of miles away and always would be.

'Congratulations,' someone was saying. Issy squinted and noticed the slender girl with the blonde hair. 'We'll officially announce it in the next issue, but you win our best-decorated independent shop award.'

Issy blinked.

'It's the little man that swung it,' Abigail said, looking at Louis, who knew he'd done something good and was waiting to find out exactly what. 'Giving free Santa beards away is a level of customer service that just goes above and beyond. Well done, young man.'

'Thank oo very much,' said Louis, without prompting.

'So, we'll send a photographer round ... And there'll be a cheque for five hundred pounds. Congratulations!'

Abigail obviously expected Issy to say something, but Issy couldn't do much more than mumble her thanks.

'Of course, the concept was all mine,' said

Caroline, moving in closer. 'I can take you through all my suppliers and my many inspirations in the world of interior design.'

'Well, I would like that,' said Abigail. 'Here's my card. We'll give you a call next week in the doldrums after Christmas—nice and quiet to take the pics.'

Caroline snatched the card before Issy could even raise her hand.

'Will do! Mwah! Mwah!'

As Abigail departed, to a kiss from Louis, wearing her beard, Caroline turned round in triumph.

'What just happened?' asked Issy wearily.

'Best-decorated shop! I KNEW we could win it. I think it was probably my clever *trompe l'oeil* tinsel.'

'I'm sure it was,' said Issy, trying to muster a smile. They'd done well without her after all. This gave her a bittersweet feeling. 'Five hundred pounds, eh? Well, I reckon you should split it as an extra Christmas bonus. I can advance it to you if you like.'

'Well, conceptually speaking it was really my . . .' began Caroline, but a quick look from Issy stopped her. Pearl's heart leapt, but she didn't want to be unfair.

'It *was* Caroline's concept,' she said. 'And she did enter us.'

Caroline looked at Pearl, amazed at her generosity.

'No chance,' said Issy. 'It was Louis' beards, she said so herself. If anything, it should be his. Plus, you've been cleaning and dusting all those new decorations every day.'

Caroline couldn't bear anyone being

magnanimous without her.

'Of course I wouldn't dream of taking more than my fair share,' she said. 'And, after all, it's not like I need the money.'

Pearl and Issy smiled at one another, and Issy, looking round at the beautiful shop, and the happy punters, felt that surely she ought to be able to squeeze a bit of Christmas spirit out, somewhere.

'I have made your beard for you here,' said Louis seriously, holding up stuck-together cotton wool and cardboard with sellotape loops for her ears.

'Thank you, Louis,' said Issy. And she put it on.

* * *

The traditional crate of wine—clearly her mother hadn't realised she'd moved house—arrived at the flat on Christmas Eve. It was kosher, she noticed. She called Marian, but no luck. Anyway, she supposed her mother didn't celebrate Christmas any more. Not that she ever had, not really.

Everything was ready for tomorrow, all the food prepped and covered in cling film, ready to pop into the big industrial ovens at the café. They could peel all the potatoes tomorrow, but there were many hands for the job. All the bits and bobs like cranberry sauce and buttered cabbage Issy had happily outsourced to Marks & Spencer. The kosher wine would join the bottles of champagne contributed by Caroline and the two bottles of whisky given to Ashok by a grateful patient.

She and Helena sat up late, chatting, as they wrapped presents for Chadani Imelda, who didn't know what was happening but knew something was, so was using it as an excuse to stay up late. Ashok was dealing with her. Every so often he would run past the sitting room door pursuing a tiny shrieking girl holding a dirty nappy above her head, and Helena and Issy would ignore it.

They were talking about the future.

'The flat above the café has come up,' Issy was saying. 'He's not sure whether to rent it or sell it. He reckons he'll get more for it because of where it is. So, basically, I've priced myself out of it just by making nice baking smells.'

'Well, see if he'll let you lease it. He already knows you're a good tenant. Then you can decide what you want to do later.'

'Hmm, maybe,' said Issy.

'And we won't be here for much longer,' pointed out Helena. 'As soon as I start working again, we'll get a bigger mortgage and move. We need a garden for Chadani Imelda anyway.'

Chadani Imelda was now riding Ashok like a horse and giggling uncontrollably.

'So you could have this place back.'

'I could,' said Issy, looking at the pink kitchen and the nice old faded floral armchairs, currently completely hidden under mountains and mountains of presents. 'I don't know. Maybe it's time to move on.'

'I've registered,' said Helena. 'With a nursing agency. Look.' She held up a sheaf of forms.

'Wow,' said Issy. 'What did you say when they asked why you wanted to come back?'

'I said, darlings, I can be fabulous simultaneously in many arenas.'

'Like that?'

'Yes, exactly like that. No, don't be stupid. I just reminded them how lucky they'd be to have me, and not to ask such impertinent questions.'

'Heh,' said Issy.

'Now, look away,' said Helena. 'I need to wrap your present.'

'Oh, don't be daft,' said Issy.

'I mean it! Look away, or you're not getting it.'

Grumbling, Issy went and stood in the doorway. Chadani Imelda now had pants on her head. Ashok was growling at her and pretending to be a bear. Issy watched them, smiling. It was a nice sight. Ashok realised she was watching and looked up at her. He stopped growling.

'You could have had this,' he said, seriously.

Issy felt herself stiffen.

'You two. You were very silly.'

'Ashok, STOP THAT THIS INSTANT!' came a voice from the sitting room that brooked no argument.

'I just want Isabel to be happy. Do you not want Isabel to be happy? You want her off renting new flats and opening new shops instead of saying well, Isabel, it was nice when you were happy because your friends were also happy so everyone was happy.'

'I'm warning you,' came the voice again.

Issy choked up. 'It wasn't my fault,' she said. 'I'm not the one who left.'

'Are you sure about that?'

'I'll be fine.'

Ashok gathered Chadani into his arms and nuzzled her soft olive cheek.

'I want you to be better than fine, Isabel.'

Helena stomped through.

'BED. Bed bed bed. For everyone.'

Chapter Eighteen

Figgy Pudding Cupcakes

100g unsalted butter
100g treacle
50g sugar
2 eggs
1 tsp cinnamon
1 tsp ground ginger
½ tsp cardamom
½ tsp ground cloves
250g all-purpose flour
25g unsweetened cocoa powder
½ tsp baking soda
2 tsp baking powder
1 tsp salt
100ml milk
1 tsp brandy
1 tsp vanilla

Preheat oven to 170°C/gas mark 3 and butter cupcake tin.
   Combine dry ingredients and sift; set aside.
   Cream butter, treacle and sugar on

medium-high speed until fluffy. Add eggs, one at a time, beating until each is incorporated, then add vanilla and brandy.

Mix in the dry ingredients in three batches, alternating with two additions of milk, and beating until combined after each.

Bake for about 20–22 minutes. Ice if you like with brandy butter icing.

*   *   *

'HAPPY CWISMAS! HAPPY CWISMAS EVERYBODY!'

Louis kissed his mother and grandmother hard.

'It's five thirty,' said Pearl. 'Go back to sleep.'

'SANNA CLAUS DID COME.'

Louis was pointing excitedly to the stocking under the little stubby tree they reused every year, and which was covered in his creations. Pearl had kept back his large gift till they got to the café; there was nowhere to hide it where they lived. But he had his little things, all wrapped.

'Can you go back to sleep?' she asked groggily. She felt bone-tired still, and the flat was freezing. She didn't keep the heating on overnight and there'd been a really cold snap.

'NOOO.' Louis shook his head vehemently to show how much he really couldn't. Pearl couldn't begin to imagine how you could get a four-year-old to go back to sleep on Christmas morning.

'All right then,' she said. 'Do you want to open your stocking really quietly . . .'

'I'm cold, Mamma.'

270

'. . . really quietly in the bed?'

Louis clambered in happily beside her, and proceeded to very noisily unwrap the cheaply sellotaped gifts Pearl had put together late the previous evening.

'MAMMA! A TOOFBRUSH!' he cried out in delight. 'AN I GOT AN ORANGE! AND SOME CHOCOLATES! AND SOCKS! Oh, socks,' he said in a slightly more normal tone.

'Yes, but they're monster garage socks,' said Pearl.

Louis' eyes darted round the room. There was not—could not be—a parcel big enough to be a monster garage. He tried to look nonchalant.

'I doan care about monster garage,' he said quietly.

Pearl was suddenly wide awake, pulsing with adrenalin. She'd sneaked the monster garage in after the shop was closed; rushing down to Argos with Issy's cheque only just deposited, heart in her mouth, clammy with excitement. She knew she had to put some of that money to one side, keep the power key charged and for the inevitable rises in her transport costs which were due in January. Really she ought, she realised as she fought her way through the freezing winds, to buy herself a new winter coat. This one was so thin . . . and she'd love some of those cosy-looking sheepskin boots girls seemed to wear these days. But no. She was going to make this one purchase. This one day.

'Do you have a monster garage?' she said, bursting into the shop, wild-eyed. She'd been panicked all day that there would be none left; the most successful toy of the year. There had been a piece in the paper about a fight breaking out in a

271

large toy shop over the last one; apparently they were changing hands on eBay for hundreds of pounds. But she had to try. She had to.

A silence had fallen over the shop, and Pearl registered that it had started to sleet outside and had soaked through her thin coat, then remembered that you didn't ask for what you wanted in Argos, you filled in a piece of paper. Everyone was looking at her. Then the nice girl had smiled. 'You are totally in luck,' she said. 'Our last delivery got delayed. It's only just arrived, far too late for most people. I've had people swearing at me for a week for one of these.'

She paused, dramatically.

'But yes, we have one.'

As Pearl filled in the order slip with shaking hands, she heard people all round her on their phones—'They've got them! They've got monster garages'—and starting to rush their orders in. People began to fill the store, drawn by the news.

'Whoops,' said the girl as Pearl took hold of the large, brightly coloured box. 'Looks like you've caused a stampede.'

Pearl had bought a sheet of terribly expensive, unutterably wasteful silver wrapping paper too, and made up the parcel reverently with a giant red bow, then hidden it under the oven until the next day.

She was nearly back home when her phone rang.

'Pearl,' Caroline was saying. 'I need some of that money back.'

*   *   *

'Well,' said Pearl, trying to keep the excitement out

272

of her voice. 'Remember, Santa knows you go to the Cupcake Café. I think he might have stopped there. Remember, they have a real chimney.'

'OH YES,' said Louis, brightening up immediately. He dived back into his stocking and came up with a packet of stickers.

'STICKERS!'

'Can you be a bit quieter?'

'Can you tell Santa I didn't really mean it when I said I din care bout monster garage?'

'I'm sure Santa knows that already.'

'Like Baby Jesus.'

'Exactly.'

'Thank you for the pwesents, Baby Jesus.'

Pearl decided to let that one roll. With a slight groaning noise, she pushed herself off the bed and went to light the Calor gas heater and make a cup of coffee. It was going to be a long day.

*   *   *

Caroline woke alone in the emperor-sized bed with its pristine Egyptian cotton sheets and numerous rolls, cushions, pillows and bits and bobs (less of a bed, more of a haven for the real me, she liked to think). At first she felt a stab of pain at waking up alone on Christmas morning.

Then she remembered the previous day. Outside, all had been sleet and freezing wind. Nonetheless, violin lessons and rugby were still on—many parents felt it wasn't ideal to give children holidays, as it made them slack. Hermia and Achilles had got up obediently enough and were just getting dressed when Caroline appeared in their bedrooms.

'Well,' she announced, still wearing her long

273

Japanese robe. 'I have decided.'

The children looked at her.

'It is disgusting weather outside. Who wants to stay in all day and not get changed out of their pyjamas?'

The children had roared their approval. So Caroline had turned the heating up (normally she felt a hot house was terribly common and bad for the skin) and they had watched *Mary Poppins*, then played snakes and ladders, then Achilles had had a nap (overscheduled and at a demanding school, he was almost constantly tired, which explained, Caroline realised, why he whined all the time and why Louis almost never did. Caroline had put it down to Louis getting everything he wanted. She was beginning to suspect this might not be the case), and she and Hermia went upstairs and Caroline let her try on all her make-up and clothes and looked at her in the mirror and realised how her beautiful little girl would, any minute now, be turning into a beautiful adolescent (if she could improve her posture, she couldn't help thinking), and that she would need to be armed for that.

Then she had ordered in noodles for supper and cracked open a box of chocolates afterwards, and they had sat round the tree and Caroline had had a glass of champagne and let them both taste it, then they had opened their gifts.

Unlike last year, Caroline wasn't trying to make a point this year. She wasn't trying to hurt Richard by throwing in his face how well she knew the children, or how they were her kids first, or how much of his money she could spend on them. She'd simply thought about them, and got them what she thought they would like, regardless of whether it

274

would clutter up her minimalist space, or whether she thought it would interfere with them getting into good universities.

So Hermia had a Nintendo with a fashion design program on it, and some fashion dolls, and Achilles had a Scalextric, which she even had the time and energy to sit down and piece together with him; and because the children were both getting so much of her attention, she noticed, they didn't bicker and snarl at one another.

This seems remarkably easy, thought Caroline. Perhaps I should write a book on the subject and become an international guru, like that woman in France. Then she looked around the sitting room, which was now an utterly disgusting mess, and burped those noodles she really oughtn't to have eaten, and wondered if Perdita would mind coming in on Christmas Day, and realised perhaps she couldn't be a parenting guru.

But she could do her best.

Richard arrived in the evening, expecting the usual litany of bitter complaints and sullen children and shining resentment, all fermented in the immaculate house whose mortgage he kept up and whose cleaning he paid for.

Instead, the house was a terrible tip, and the children were—were they laughing? Were they all laughing? Was Caroline wearing pyjamas? Pyjamas must have come back in fashion, then; they must be Stella McCartney and had probably cost him a fortune.

'Daddy!' the children had yelled. 'Come and see what we got! And what we've been doing.'

Richard half smiled nervously at Caroline. Kate, as it turned out, was being just as difficult as

275

Caroline—particularly about money, attention and general attitude. He cursed, yet again, his taste in aerobicised blondes. But Caroline seemed in a mellow mood.

'Well, I have a bottle of champagne open,' she said. 'If you want to come in for five minutes?'

He had. And they had managed to sit and talk, civilly, whilst the children played in the wreckage of the Christmas paper, about finishing off the divorce and finding a way to move forward, and Caroline might have mentioned that she had heard Kate wanted a huge second wedding party, incredibly luxurious, just for the pleasure of seeing him blanch a little, but on the whole she was on her best behaviour and they managed to toast the day like adults.

And for the first time, Caroline on Christmas morning, sitting up in bed looking at the gifts from the children, which she would open when she saw them that evening, didn't feel vengeful, or lonely, or angry. She felt, tentatively . . . OK.

Then she remembered the disgusting mess she was going to have to clean up in the kitchen, and sighed.

*   *   *

Issy woke with Chadani Imelda clambering on her face. Fair enough, she was in her room, although Chadani had insisted on sleeping with her mother since she was born (Ashok pretended he didn't mind; Helena told a bare-faced lie to anyone who asked her about it). It was rather nice, actually, the toddler sleigh bed with its brand-new mattress and pristine White Company sheets.

For a second, she almost forgot what was

276

happening.

'GAHAHABAGAGA!' said Chadani Imelda, her little face right up to Issy's, drool dripping from her mouth on to Issy's nose.

'Oh, yes,' said Issy out loud. 'My life is over and yours is just beginning, I remember. Good morning, Chadani Imelda! Merry Christmas!' And she kissed her.

Then she had to stand, clutching her coffee cup, for forty-five minutes whilst Helena and Ashok and Chadani, all dressed in matching red outfits, opened their gifts. They had presents for Issy too, of course, but mostly she took family photographs. Finally, the acres of wrapping paper were cleared away and Chadani Imelda had completely ignored her first computer, her first beauty bag, her miniature car and her new spotty Dalmatian fur coat in favour of trying to consume large quantities of bubble wrap. Then the door rang, and it was Ashok's family, all of them carrying vast tupperware boxes full of fragrant-smelling food and gigantic gifts for Chadani. Issy slipped off and got changed quietly, glancing outside at the grey sky. There was snow coming down; not much, but enough to powder the streets and chimney tops of Stoke Newington; the Victorian terraces and grand villas and occasional tower blocks and big mish-mash of lovely London all silent in the Christmas-morning hush. Issy leaned her head against the window pane.

'I miss you, Gramps,' she said softly. Then she put on the plain navy blue dress she'd bought that looked smart, though also, she realised, not really very festive. Well, that didn't matter, she'd be in a pinny all day. Which was the best way. She glanced out at the quiet city again and didn't voice who else she missed. Love was not a choice. But work was. She rolled up her sleeves.

'OK you lot,' she said to Ashok's family; Chadani's four aunties were cooing vigorously over her, whilst discussing competitively at the top of their lungs the most recent achievements of their own children. It was going to be a noisy day. She could do with a couple of hours to clear her head. 'I'll see you down at the café after you've had breakfast.'

*　　*　　*

Austin was dreaming. In his dream he was back there, back at the Cupcake Café. Then he woke up with a horrible start, his head throbbing. What had happened last night? Oh God, he remembered. Darny had been staying at Marian's, and Merv had taken Austin out for a couple of drinks, then he'd had a couple more on his own, which was stupid, because American drinks as far as he could tell were made from pure alcohol, then, unsteady on his feet, he'd tried to get back to his hotel and he'd run into that girl from the cupcake shop, almost as if she'd been hanging around waiting for him, and she'd helped him stagger on a little bit, then pushed him backwards in the snow and made what he supposed was meant to be a sexy face at him, then tried to snog him! And he had pushed her away and explained that he had a girlfriend and she'd just laughed and said, well, she didn't appear to be here, and had tried to snog him again. He'd got quite cross with her then, and she'd got really really annoyed and started yelling at him about how nobody understood her problems.

It got quite blurry after that, but he'd made it back to the hotel in one piece. It wasn't an evening he was particularly proud of. Great. Happy Christmas. And here he was, awake at an ungodly hour of the morning and all by himself. Brilliant. Well done, Austin, with your great new successful life and new successful career. It's all working out brilliantly. Well done.

He guessed he'd better go and get Darny. His PA hated him, it was clear; fortunately this was fine by him and he'd already put in for an urgent transfer for Janet, whose only son lived in Buffalo. Still, MacKenzie had asked him if he wanted any Christmas shopping done; apparently this was normal behaviour from support staff. So he'd asked her to get what she thought a fourteen-year-old boy would like (Darny wasn't even twelve yet, but Austin figured this would probably suit him) and she had come back with a pile of gift-wrapped shapes that she had thrown on his desk, so he didn't actually have the faintest clue what Darny was getting for Christmas. But the subways were running all day, so he was heading out to Queens to see Marian. It seemed on the one hand absolutely ludicrous that he was spending Christmas Day with his ex's mother. On the other, she'd assured him that they didn't do Christmas, that they would be eating Chinese food in a restaurant and they were quite welcome to sit on the sofa watching movies in their pyjamas all afternoon, which compared to Merv's exhausting schedule of party games and family in-jokes sounded just the tonic. He hauled himself out of bed and took a very, very long bath.

It was definitely droplets of steam on his face,

he told himself. He absolutely and positively wasn't crying.

*   *   *

'Only to bring you peace ...'

The song was playing again on the radio. Issy had peeled four thousand potatoes and was about to start on three thousand carrots. But she didn't mind really. There was something about the repetition of the work, and the forced bonhomie of the DJ, who was, presumably, at work on Christmas Day all by himself, and the sweet familiarity of the songs—ones you liked (Sufjan) and ones you didn't (Issy was done with travelling spacemen). Then she switched channels and listened to the boys singing carols from King's, even though listening to the boys made her think of Darny and even though Darny actually hated to sing anyway.

The turkey was glistening and turning golden in the oven, along with a beautiful glazed ham; the Brussels sprouts were ready to go, as was the red cabbage. She had tins of goose fat to make the best roast potatoes, and was planning on whipping up a fabulous pavlova for dessert; she liked to get the meringue just right. So everything was ticking over perfectly. Fine. Lovely.

At eleven, everyone started to file in; first Pearl, who had been up for a long time, and who immediately put on her pinny and wanted to clean. Issy tried to stop her. Louis was dancing along in her wake, full of chatter about church and the sweets the minister had given him and the singing and how Caroline had come to pick them up in her BIG CAR ('I like you more now I saw your car,' he had announced, to Pearl's utter horror, but Caroline had, amazingly, laughed it off and rumpled Louis' tight curls); then all Ashok's family had piled in, and Issy regretted immediately making all the vegetarian food, or indeed any food at all given the sheer heft that they had brought, and everything in the kitchen downstairs took on a spicier, more unusual tang and Caroline opened the first bottle of champagne.

Then, first things first, everyone scuffled around quickly under the tree so they could put out each other's gifts. Then everyone went very shy and said you first, no, you first, but actually it was totally obvious that it should be Louis first, so Issy went in and found his packages and hauled them out.

'Well, that's odd,' said Helena.

And it was. Because there were five large square packages, all exactly the same size and shape. Louis' eyes were like saucers.

'I said Santa would pass by here,' said Pearl, sending him forward. He ripped into the first one—Pearl's, with the beautiful silver wrapping and the huge red ribbon.

There was an enormously long pause. Then Louis turned round to his mother, his eyes huge, shining with unspilt tears, his mouth hanging open in shock and amazement.

'SANTA BWOUGHT ME A MONSTER GARAGE!'

Then everyone looked at the four other, identically shaped parcels, and realised immediately what had happened.

There was one from Issy, who had spent her lunch hour running down to Hamleys and paying a fortune for it. There was one from Ashok and

Helena, who had ordered theirs online months ago. One from Caroline, beautifully wrapped. Pearl's, of course. And the last one Pearl couldn't figure out at all. Then it dawned on her. It was from Doti. She shook her head in disbelief. She thought it was because everyone loved Louis so much. She didn't realise that it wasn't only Louis.

'Santa's made a mistake,' she said, cuddling him. 'I'm sure we can take the others back.' She waggled her eyebrows furiously at the others.

'I believe Santa trades things in for other toys,' said Issy loudly, digging in her wallet for the receipt. 'No wonder there was such a shortage.'

Louis didn't say anything at all. He was lying down right across the shop, oblivious to everyone else, making all the different monster noises and car noises and monster truck noises and talking to each monster in turn. He was completely in everybody's way. Nobody minded at all.

Pearl slipped off to text Doti. Then she added at the end, 'pop round if you're free xx'. Just as she was about to send it, a movement at the window caught her eye. She glanced up. It was Ben, whom she hadn't seen since that fight. He was looking apologetic, with his hands open.

She went to the door.

'Hey,' she said.

'Hey,' he said, looking at the ground.

'Look,' he said. 'You were right. I shouldn't have had that damn garage. I bought it off a bloke in the pub.'

'Ben,' said Pearl, bitterly disappointed.

'But I took it back, all right? I knew it was dodgy. I'm sorry. I've been working late shifts. It's only as a security guard, but it's work, right? Look, I'm still in

282

my uniform.'

She looked at him. He was.

'It suits you, that uniform.'

'Shut up,' he said, running his eyes up and down the curves of Pearl's soft old wool dress, the best thing she owned. It still suited her.

'Anyway,' he said, handing over a package. 'It's not the garage, right. It's what I could afford. Properly.'

'Come in,' said Pearl. She deleted, quickly, the message on her phone. 'Come on in.'

Everyone greeted him cheerily, and Caroline immediately handed him a glass. Louis jumped up, his grin so wide he looked like he could burst.

'SANTA BROUGHT ME A MONSTER GARAGE,' he said.

'And I brought you this,' said Ben.

Louis ripped the package open. Inside was a pair of pyjamas, covered in monster garage characters. They were fluffy and warm and the right size and exactly what Louis actually needed.

'MONSTER GARAGE JAMAS!' said Louis. He started pulling off his clothes. Pearl thought about stopping him—he was wearing a lovely smart shirt and a new pullover—but at the last minute decided against it.

'Merry Christmas,' she said to the room, raising her glass.

'Merry Christmas,' said everyone back.

*   *   *

After that, it was a present free-for-all. Caroline did her best not to wrinkle her nose at the tasteless candles and knick-knacks that headed her way.

Chadani Imelda managed to eat an entire rosette. Louis didn't look up from his garage. Issy, hanging back near the kitchen, noticed that she didn't get any presents, but didn't think much of it.

They had lined up all the tables in a row to make one long table with space for everyone, and Ashok's sisters jostled Issy for space in the kitchen, chatting and laughing and sharing jokes and handing out crackers, and Issy felt herself coasting along and letting the shared comfort of happiness and ease carry her with it. Chester from the ironmonger's shop was there, of course, and Mrs Hanowitz, whose children lived in Australia, and all in all they were a very long table by the time they sat down to eat, slightly drunk, carols playing loudly in the background.

The meal was magnificent. Bhajis and ginger beet curry nestled next to the perfectly cooked turkey, acres of chipolatas and the crunchiest roast potatoes, all delicious. Everyone ate and drank themselves to bursting, except Issy, who didn't feel like it, and Caroline, who couldn't, but did her best with the red cabbage.

At the end of the meal, Ashok stood up.

'Now, I just want to say a few words,' he said, swaying a little bit. 'First of all, thank you to Issy for throwing open her shop—her home—for all of us waifs and strays at Christmas time.'

At this there was much stamping of feet and cheering.

'That was a wonderful meal—thanks to everyone who contributed ...'

'Hear hear,' said Caroline.

'... and Caroline.'

There was a great deal of laughter and banging of

forks.

'OK, I have two orders of business. Firstly, Issy, you may have noticed that you didn't get any Christmas presents?'

Issy shrugged, to say it didn't matter.

'Well, aha! That is not the case!' said Ashok. He lifted up an envelope. 'Here is a small token of our esteem. Of all of our esteem. Oh, and we've hired Maya back.'

'Who's Maya?' Ben asked Pearl. His large hand was squeezing her thigh under the table.

'No one,' said Pearl quickly.

Issy, her hands shaking, opened the envelope. Inside was a return ticket to New York.

'Everyone put in,' said Ashok. 'Because . . .'

'Because you're an idiot!' hooted Caroline. 'And you can't borrow my coat again.'

Issy looked at Helena, eyes glistening.

'But I've been . . . I tried . . .'

'Well, you try again, you bloody idiot,' said Helena. 'Are you nuts? I bet he is totally bloody miserable. Your mum said he is.'

'I like the way everyone gets to chat with my mum except me,' said Issy. She glanced down at the date on the ticket.

'You have to be joking.'

'Nope,' said Caroline. 'Cheapest date to fly. And no time like the present; we've got Maya all of next week.'

'I can't even get to the airport.'

'Fortunately I treated a cabbie with renal failure,' said Ashok. 'He asked if there was anything he could do. I said could he drive my friend to Heathrow on Christmas Day. He sighed a lot and looked really grumpy, but he's on his way over.'

'And I packed for you!' said Helena. 'Proper clothes this time you'll be pleased to hear.'

Issy didn't know where to look. Her hand flickered to her mouth, shaking.

'Come on,' said Helena. 'Do you really have anything to lose?'

Issy bit her lip. Her pride? Her self-respect? Well, maybe they didn't mean so much. But she had to know. She had to know.

'Th … th … thanks,' she stammered. 'Thank you. Thank you so much.'

'I'll make you up a sandwich for the plane,' said Pearl. 'It's not business class this time.'

Caroline had managed to convince Pearl, when she realised how much Pearl needed the money, that the amount everyone was putting in the pot for the ticket was ten pounds. Pearl had only the fuzziest idea of how much flights cost and had chosen to believe her.

*   *   *

There came a honking outside.

'That's your cab,' said Ashok.

Helena handed her her bag and her passport. Issy had no words. They hugged, then Pearl joined in, then Caroline too, and they were all one big ball.

'Do it,' said Helena. 'Or sort it. Or whatever. OK?'

Issy swallowed. 'OK,' she said. 'OK.'

And the table watched her go out into the snow.

'Now,' said Ashok, swallowing very hard, and taking out a small jeweller's box from his pocket. 'Ahem. I have another order of business.'

But there was a cry from Caroline. Coming

out of the snow was the tiny figure of Donald, and directly behind him, chasing after him, were Hermia and Achilles. The baby headed straight for the Cupcake Café and everyone crowded round to welcome him.

'He ran away!' said Hermia.

'We ran away too,' said Achilles. 'It's really boring in there.'

Pearl winked at Caroline.

'Well, I'll put on some hot chocolate and then you're heading straight back,' Caroline said.

Caroline called Richard and he agreed that they could stay for afternoon games. Then there was a pause. 'Actually, could we all come over?' said Richard. 'It's dead boring here.'

Caroline thought.

'No,' she said, but not unkindly. 'It isn't my home to invite you. But we'll speak soon.'

*   *   *

Pearl, stacking the big dishwasher downstairs, wrote a text and deleted it, and wrote another and deleted it again. Then, finally, she texted the simple words, 'Thank you. Merry Christmas' and sent it to Doti. What else was there to say?

'What are you doing down there?' came Ben's deep voice.

'Nothing!' said Pearl.

'Good,' said Ben. 'Because I have an idea of a few things we could do.'

Pearl giggled and told him off, and felt the touch of his warm hand on her face and thought after that simply, Merry Christmas. Merry Christmas.

Chapter Nineteen

Galette de Rois, the Cake of the New Year

30g almond paste
30g white sugar
3 tbsp unsalted butter, softened
1 egg
¼ tsp vanilla extract
¼ tsp almond extract
2 tbsp all-purpose flour
1 pinch salt
1 packet of puff pastry
1 egg, beaten
one favour (traditionally a small
   china—not plastic!—figurine)
icing sugar for dusting
one gold party hat
Preheat oven to 220°C/gas mark 7;
line baking sheet with baking paper.
   Blend almond paste in the food
processor with half the sugar, then
add the butter and the rest of the
sugar, then the egg, vanilla and
almond extracts, then flour and salt.
   Roll out one sheet of the puff

pastry, about 20cm square. Keep the pastry cool; do not knead or stretch. Cut a large circle. Repeat and chill the circles.

Mound the almond filling on to the centre of one of the pastry circles on the baking sheet. Leave a large margin. Press the figurine down into the filling. Place the second sheet of pastry on top, and seal edges.

Egg-wash the top of the pastry and add slits (artistically if you like).

Bake for 15 minutes in the preheated oven. Do not open the oven until the time is up, as the pastry will not fully puff. Remove from the oven and dust with icing sugar. Return to the oven and cook for an additional 12–15 minutes, or until the top is a deep golden brown. Transfer to a wire rack to cool. Crown with gold party hat. Give gold party hat to whoever gets the favour (or Louis).

*   *   *

Austin turned up at Marian's with a bottle of kirsch, even though he wasn't quite sure why. He instantly felt a bit strange, being the only man there without a beard, but everyone seemed very nice— there were about four families, and dumplings were boiling on top of the stove. There were no decorations up, of course, no cards, no television; nothing to indicate that this wasn't just another day.

Which of course it was. To everyone else.

Darny was happily sitting chatting to one of the old men in the sitting room over a small, sticky-looking coffee.

'We're discussing the nature of evil,' said Darny. 'It's great.'

'Is that coffee?' said Austin. 'Great. That's all you need.'

He popped his head round the door. 'Hi, Maria . . . Miriam. Do you need a hand?'

'No, no,' said Marian, who was rolling out pastry, very badly.

'OK. Listen, is it all right if I give Darny his presents? I realise it's not really . . . '

'No, no, that's fine,' said Marian. 'Half of them get secret presents anyway, we're just not supposed to mention it.' She smiled naughtily.

'You seem really happy here, really settled,' said Austin.

Marian grinned and looked out through the kitchen door. In the sitting room, a man in his fifties, with a long beard and beautiful brown eyes, glanced up, caught the gaze and smiled at her.

'It's all right,' said Marian, colouring. 'Though of course everyone here is too smart for me.'

'Are you pretending to be stupid?' asked Austin, affectionately.

'No, that would be you,' said Marian, giving him a look that reminded him inexorably of her daughter. 'Now, give your brother his gifts. He thinks he isn't getting any.'

'Really?'

Austin went back into the room with the large bag of presents.

'Merry Christmas,' he said.

290

Darny's eyes widened. 'I thought I wasn't getting any presents.'

'What, because you're Jewish now?'

Darny shook his head. 'No,' he said. 'Because I've been so awful.'

Austin felt as though his heart would crack.

'Darny,' he said, kneeling down. 'Darny, whatever happens ... I never, ever think you're awful. I think you're amazing and brilliant and occasionally a bit tricky ...'

'And in the way.'

'Well, that's not your fault, is it?'

Darny hung his head.

'If ...' he said. 'If I hadn't got chucked out of school, would we still be living in England with Issy?'

'That doesn't matter,' said Austin. 'It's good that we're here. It's good. Isn't it?'

'So you can make lots of money and work all day and I'll never see you?' said Darny. 'Mmm.'

He sat down and started opening his gifts. Austin looked on, as did the other children, fascinated to see what MacKenzie had bought. There was something called an NFL game for the Wii (which Darny didn't have), and a long basketball shirt that came down to his knees and looked like a dress, and a baseball cap with a propeller on the top. Darny looked up at Austin. 'I don't know what any of this is for,' he said quietly. 'Is it to make me American?'

'Don't you like it?' said Austin.

Darny looked down, desperate not to appear ungrateful. He had been on his best behaviour. It was slightly freaking Austin out.

'Yes ... I mean, you need a computer and stuff

to work it ... but I suppose ...'

There was a pause.

'Thank you,' said Darny.

A much older boy with an incipient wispy moustache picked up the NFL game. 'I can show you how to work this if you like.'

'Thanks,' said Darny, brightening a bit. 'Cool.'

Marian came in from the kitchen and beckoned Austin over.

'I have a gift for you,' she said. Austin raised his eyebrows as she brought out an envelope. 'I want you to go see my daughter,' she said. 'No, I insist on it. Just for a day or two. See if you kids can't work something out without distractions around you. We'll keep Darny here; he has fun with the other kids. Just go and see her. She doesn't know it's finished. She doesn't know what's going on. I like you, Austin, but if you make her unhappy and leave her dangling, I will cut off all your fingers. Is that clear?'

Austin opened the envelope, shaking. He stared at it.

'Where did you get the money for this?' he said.

'Oh, a friend who made rather a lot of money in those computer things ... he died,' she said. 'Lovely man. Well, sometimes horrible. Very clever, though.'

Austin raised his eyebrows.

They both looked at the drifting snow in the little garden.

Austin looked at the ticket again.

'This flight leaves in two hours.'

'Lucky you're already in Queens, then, isn't it?'

*　　　*　　　*

This time, there was no sleeping on the flight. Full already from Christmas dinner, Issy couldn't face another one. The crew were very jolly and cheerful, but the flight was full of grumpy-looking people who hated Christmas, or plenty of people to whom it didn't mean anything, so their exuberance was slightly lost on them. She clutched her bag fiercely, biting her lip, trying not to think about anything except that for the first time in a fortnight she wasn't crying. And that, one way or another, they'd soon be in the same room again. Beyond that, she wouldn't let herself go, simply looking at the crackling ice over the oval window and staring into space.

Austin found himself on his plane so fast he didn't have time to think at all. He tried to order his thoughts, but he felt too full of gibberish. He drank an extremely large whisky and tried to sleep. He failed.

Their flights crossed over Newfoundland; Issy flying into a New York morning, Austin into a London afternoon, the pure white traces of vapour drawing a large X in the sky.

*   *   *

There was no traffic. Austin didn't stop to think; he knew exactly where she'd be. Where she'd always be. As the taxi driver—chatting animatedly about his recent miraculous recovery from renal failure, Austin barely listening—drew up just by the tiny little alleyway on Church Street, Austin's eye was distracted by the rows of fairy lights outside the Cupcake Café reflecting off the dirty white snow,

293

the steamed-up windows and, inside, the hint of shapes of happy people moving about.

As soon as he saw it, in an instant of clarity, he knew. He would come back. They could start again. He'd try something, anything. They'd figure it out. New York was harsh, a shiny dream. Not for him. He had given up everything once before in his life. He could do it again. Because at the end of the sacrifice was happiness. He knew that. And however much money he made, or however good Darny's school, they couldn't be happy—neither of them—without Issy. And that was that. He paused for a minute as the cab pulled away, the night coming on fast, his long overcoat flapping in the wind, his scarf likewise; paused and took a deep breath full of happiness before marching forward, cheerfully and with an open heart, towards his future. He pulled open the tinging door.

There was a long silence.

'What the *hell*?' said a slightly tipsy Pearl, as, just at the same moment, Louis launched himself at Austin's legs.

'AUSTIN! WEAH'S DARNY! I DID MISS YOU AUSTIN!'

One of Ashok's cousins blew a party hooter. It sounded a low note in the silence.

*   *   *

Snow was still falling. Issy could barely remember a minute of the trip, or the shorter-than-normal line at immigration. Sometimes it felt like the outskirts of London and the outskirts of New York could touch each other, that they were all part of the same metropolis of taxis and restaurants and businesses and people rushing with lots to do.

The cab dropped her at the hotel.

'I'm sorry, ma'am,' said the same lovely woman who'd been there before. 'I'm afraid Mr Tyler's been checked out.'

Issy swallowed. This had never occurred to her. She had no idea where he might be. Had he gone to his boss's house for Christmas? She didn't know how to contact him. And she'd kind of hoped ... she realised this was stupid, daft, but she'd kind of hoped just to meet him; to see him; to see his face—hopefully—break into that wide smile of his; to run into his arms. Not to have to call and have an awkward conversation and sound desperate—or worse, crazy. Much better just to appear and explain later, she thought.

'Do you have a room?' she asked.

'We have one room left,' said the woman, smiling nicely. 'It'll be seven hundred and eighty dollars.'

Issy snatched up her credit card like she'd been stung.

'Oh,' she said. 'Oh, I'll leave it for now.'

The woman looked worried. 'You know, it's quite difficult to find a hotel room in New York at Christmas time,' she said sympathetically.

Issy sighed. 'It's all right,' she said, shaking her head, stunned at how badly her mission was failing, with all the excitement and good intentions her friends had sent her off with. 'I can stay on my mum's couch.'

'Super!' said the friendly receptionist.

*　　*　　*

It would be best, thought Issy. Stay at her mum's

295

tonight, call Austin tomorrow wherever he was, meet up like civilised adults. That would be best. She could catch up on sleep and have a bath and all of that stuff. She sighed. Sit through her mum's lecture about not relying on men, or in fact anyone. All of that.

First, she wandered the streets. It was a beautiful day; sunny, with the ice crackling. As long as you stayed in the sun, it didn't even seem that cold. There were lots of people out and about, taking a stroll and saying good day to each other; tourists, not quite sure what to do on Christmas Day, hoicking rucksacks and taking photographs; lots of Jewish people noisily cramming into Chinese restaurants. It was ... it was nice.

She found herself, eventually, on a familiar back street. The big shops weren't open, of course, but it was amazing how many of the smaller ones were. Even at Christmas time, commerce was everything. She heard, suddenly, a snatch of her favourite Christmas song coming through an open door ... and caught a slightly off smell. She went through the door. She was, she noticed with a quick pang, the only customer. Well. He *might* have been there. The sole member of staff was standing red-eyed by the till, and didn't even look up.

'Hello,' said Issy.

Chapter Twenty

Vanilla Cupcake, Courtesy of the Caked Crusader

For the cupcakes
125g unsalted butter, at room
   temperature
125g caster sugar
2 large eggs, at room temperature
125g self-raising flour, sifted i.e.
   passed through a sieve
2 tsp vanilla extract (N.B. 'extract', not
   'essence'. Extract is natural whereas
   essence contains chemicals and is
   nasty)
2 tbsp milk (you can use whole milk
   or semi-skimmed but not skimmed,
   as it tastes horrible)

For the buttercream
125g unsalted butter, at room
   temperature
250g icing sugar, sifted i.e. passed
   through a sieve
1 tsp vanilla extract
Splash of milk—by which I mean,

start with a tablespoon, beat that in, see if the buttercream is the texture you want, if it isn't add a further tablespoon etc.

How to make
Preheat the oven to 190°C/fan oven 170°C/gas mark 5.

Line a cupcake pan with paper cases. This recipe will make 12 cupcakes.

Beat the butter and sugar together until they are smooth, fluffy and pale. This will take several minutes even with soft butter. Don't skimp on this stage, as this is where you get air into the mix. How you choose to beat the ingredients is up to you. When I started baking I used a wooden spoon, then I got handheld electric beaters and now I use a stand mixer. They will all yield the same result, however, if you use the wooden spoon, you will get a rather splendid upper arm workout . . . who said cake was unhealthy?

Add the eggs, flour, vanilla and milk and beat until smooth. Some recipes require you to add all these ingredients separately but, for this recipe, you don't have to worry about that. You are looking for what's called 'dropping consistency'; this means that when you take a spoonful of mixture and gently tap the spoon, the mixture will drop off. If the mixture doesn't drop off the spoon, mix it some more. If it still won't drop, add a further tablespoon of milk.

Spoon into the paper cases. There is no need to level the batter, as the heat of the oven will do this for you. Place the tray in the upper half of the oven. Do not open the oven door until the cakes have baked for twelve minutes, then check them by inserting a skewer (if you don't have one, use a wooden cocktail stick) into the centre of the sponges—if it comes out clean, the cakes are ready and you can remove them from the oven. If raw batter comes out on the skewer, pop them back in the oven and give them a couple more minutes. Cupcakes, being small, can switch from underdone to overdone quickly so don't get distracted! Don't worry if your cakes take longer than a recipe states—ovens vary.

As soon as the cupcakes come out of the oven, tip them out of the tin on to a wire rack. If you leave them in the tin they will carry on cooking (the tin is very hot) and the paper cases may start to pull away from the sponge, which looks ugly. Once on the wire rack they will cool quickly— about thirty minutes.

Now make the buttercream: beat the butter in a bowl, on its own, until very soft. It will start to look almost like whipped cream. It is this stage in the process that makes your buttercream light and delicious.

Add the icing sugar and beat until light and fluffy. Go gently at first otherwise the icing sugar will cloud up and coat you and your kitchen with white dust! Keep mixing until the butter and sugar are combined and smooth; the best test for this is to place a small amount of the icing on your tongue and press it up against the roof of your mouth. If it feels gritty, it needs more beating. If it's smooth, you can move on to the next step.

Beat in the vanilla and milk. If the buttercream isn't as soft as you would like, then add a tiny bit more milk but be careful—you don't want to make the buttercream sloppy.

Either spread or pipe over the cupcakes. Spreading is easier and requires no additional equipment. However, if you want your cupcakes to look fancy it might be worth buying an icing bag and star-shaped nozzle. You can get disposable icing bags, which cut down on washing-up.

Add any additional decoration you desire—this is where you can be creative. In the past I have used sugar flowers, hundreds and thousands, Maltesers, edible glitter, sprinkles, nuts, crumbled Flake . . . the options are endless.

Bask in glory at the wonderful thing you have made.

Eat.

*   *   *

It was amazing, the capacity for human sympathy, thought Issy. She would honestly not believe that she could sit here and listen to another human being pour out how unfair it was that Issy's boyfriend wouldn't get off with them.

'You'd met me,' she said finally. 'You knew I existed.'

Kelly-Lee kept weeping, big tears pouring off the end of her perfect retroussé nose. 'But you're foreign,' she said. 'So I figured it didn't really matter, know what I mean?'

'No,' said Issy.

'You're from Eurp! Everyone knows everyone has six girlfriends over there.'

'Does everyone know that?'

'Oh yeah,' said Kelly-Lee. 'And you have no idea how hard it is. Now I'm going to lose my job . . .'

'For trying to pull someone?' said Issy. 'Cor, your boss is miles tougher than me.'

'No . . . apparently my cupcakes are no good.'

'They are no good,' agreed Issy. 'They're terrible, in fact.'

'Well, they drop off half, then I'm meant to practise making them fresh, but I never really bothered.'

Issy rolled her eyes.

Kelly-Lee blinked at her. 'Does he really, really

301

love you?'

'I don't know,' said Issy, truthfully.

'Maybe when I'm as old as you I'll know what real love feels like,' said Kelly-Lee, starting to weep again.

'Yes, yes, maybe,' said Issy. 'Show me your kitchen?'

Kelly-Lee showed it to her. The oven wasn't even warm, but the place was amazingly well equipped.

'Look at all this space!' said Issy. 'I work in a bunker! You have windows and everything.'

Kelly-Lee looked around dully. 'Whatever.'

Issy looked in the enormous, state-of-the-art vacuum fridge. 'Wow. I would *love* one of these.'

'You don't have a fridge?'

Issy ignored her, and took out a dozen eggs and some butter. She sniffed at it. 'This butter is very average,' she said. 'It's a bad start. But it will do.' She added milk, then went to the large flour and sugar vats, and started pulling on an apron. Kelly-Lee regarded her in confusion.

'Come on,' said Issy. 'We haven't got all day. Well, we have, because it's Christmas Day and neither of us has anywhere better to go. But let's not think about that right now.'

Kelly-Lee listened, at first half-heartedly, then with closer attention, as Issy talked her patiently through the right temperature for creaming the butter and sugar, the importance of not overmixing, the right height for sieving the flour, which Kelly-Lee had never heard of.

Twenty minutes later, they put four batches into the oven, and Issy started to unravel the secrets of butter icing.

'Wait for this,' she said. 'You won't believe the

other muck you were churning out.'

She whipped the icing into a confection lighter than cream, and made Kelly-Lee taste it. 'If you don't taste, you don't know what you're doing,' she said. 'You have to taste all the time.'

'But I won't fit my jeans!'

'If you don't taste, you won't have a job and you won't be able to buy any jeans.'

The smell—for once, heavenly rather than overwhelmingly of baking soda—rose up in the kitchen, and instantly Issy felt calm and more relaxed. She was here. He was here, somewhere. It would all come good. She picked up the phone to call her mother.

'What the *hell*?' said Marian.

*　　　*　　　*

In Queens, the situation became clear. Issy turned up accompanied by two dozen of what her mother insisted on referring to as fairy cakes.

'Darny!' said Issy, as he flew into her arms. She wasn't expecting that.

'I'm sorry,' he muttered. 'I'm sorry. I was grumpy with you and you went away.'

'No,' she said. 'I was bossy and being like a mum and it was wrong and I hurt you. *I'm* sorry.'

Darny mumbled something. Issy crouched down so she could hear. 'I wish you were my mum,' he said.

Issy didn't say anything, just held him tight. Then she remembered.

'You know why my bag is so damn heavy?' she said. Darny shook his head. 'I brought you a present.'

It had been a last-minute idea; a silly one as she was toting it around. But she could get something else for Louis.

Darny's eyes widened when he saw it.

'WOW!' he said. All the other kids rushed towards it too.

'MONSTER GARAGE!'

Issy smiled at her mother. 'He's only little,' she murmured.

'He is,' said her mother. 'Well. Now. This is a mess.'

Issy sat down with a large glass of kosher red, which she was developing a real fondness for. She shook her head.

'I don't think it is,' she said wonderingly. 'I really don't. I can't believe ... he'd drop everything. Travel all that way. Oh, I wish I was there now. I wish I was.'

Then her phone rang.

'Don't say anything,' said a strong, humorous, familiar voice. 'And I'll text you.'

'OK ... I ... I ...'

But he'd already hung up.

Chapter Twenty-One

Issy had received a text message with a simple street address on it—cryptic, but to the point. When she got there, first thing on Boxing Day morning, it was quiet, but already people were starting to queue. He wasn't there. But if she'd learned anything, Issy thought, it was that she could no longer wait for Austin. Or anyone.

'One, please,' she said politely. She figured out her skate size in American and strapped on the black boots, then, wobbling slightly, walked out on to the ice. Gramps had used to love to skate; they'd built a municipal rink in Manchester in the fifties, and he liked to go round it with his hands insouciantly behind his back, a funny sight in his smart dark suit. Issy used to go with him sometimes, and he would take her by the hand and whirl her round. She loved it.

Slowly she rotated on the ice, the sun glinting off the surface crystals, 30 Rock towering overhead, people running in, rushing back to work the day after Christmas. She looked around at the pink light glancing off the high buildings. It was, she thought, spectacular. Wonderful. She and New York had had a rocky start, but now ... Lost in thought, she attempted a small spin, failed, then

305

stumbled. A hand reached out and grabbed her.

'Are you all right?'

She turned. For a moment, the sun was so bright she was dazzled and couldn't see. But she could still make out the shape of him, there, in that long coat, back in the green scarf she had bought him which matched the green dress she was wearing.

'Oh,' was all she could say. Now she could see again, she noticed he looked very tired. But apart from that, he looked so very, very happy. 'Oh.'

And then, balancing on their skates, they were completely and utterly wrapped up in one another, and Issy felt as if she was flying; rushing round and round like an ice dancer leaping through snow flurries, or racing down a snowy slope, or flying through the cold air faster than a jet plane.

'My love,' Austin was saying, kissing her again and again. 'I was such an idiot. *Such* an idiot.'

'I was stubborn too,' said Issy. 'Didn't give a thought to what you were up to. So unfair.'

'You weren't! You weren't at all.'

They looked at each other.

'Let's not talk any more,' said Issy, and they stood together in the centre of the rink, as bemused but indulgent skaters continued to weave around them, and the sun melted the ice, which dripped down from the high towers above them like crystal.

*　　　*　　　*

They checked back into the hotel and stayed there for a couple of days, then set about making it up to Darny with outings and exhibitions and treats until he begged for mercy. On the third day, Issy took a phone call and came to Austin with a very strange

306

look on her face.

'That was Kelly-Lee,' she said. The flash of guilt that crossed his face reminded her that she hadn't mentioned that she'd met her, and she decided not to tell him what Kelly-Lee had said.

'I ran into her and helped her make some cupcakes ... that's all,' she said firmly. 'Anyway, apparently her boss came in and was totally astounded, and wants to send her to California to open up a new store, and apparently Kelly-Lee feels she's much more suited to California.'

'I think she is too,' said Austin.

'Anyway, there's an opening to run the New York store if I want it, apparently ...'

Austin hadn't spoken to Merv. He looked at her carefully.

'Hmm,' he said. 'But we're going back to London.'

'It's raining in London, though, isn't it?' said Issy carefully. 'And we'd probably make a bit of money renting out your house. And mine, when Ashok and Helena move. Unless he gets her pregnant again, in which case she's going to kill him and *then* they'll split up.'

Austin kept his face completely neutral.

'It would be nice,' said Issy, 'to give Maya a full-time job. Her post office job has gone now, and she's such an asset. And with Pearl and Caroline getting on so well ...'

Austin coughed at that.

'Comparatively speaking ...'

Issy had been doing a lot of thinking over the last few days, now that she was finally rested. A lot.

Austin looked at her. She was lying on the white bed, looking luscious and pale and beautiful, and he didn't think he'd ever seen anything he liked quite as much.

'Mmm,' he said.

Issy looked at him steadily. 'Well, I suppose ... a couple of years in the world's greatest city, with Darny at the world's greatest school ... it might not be *too* bad ...'

Austin's eyes widened. 'We don't have to. I'm ready to go back. Well, I don't care. I just want to be where you are.'

Issy closed her eyes. She could see it in her head. The Cupcake Café. She could hear the jangle of the bell, and Pearl's throaty laugh as she grabbed the mop in the morning; she could see Caroline's taut face complaining about the price of ski holidays these days. She saw herself dancing to Capital Radio and feeling Louis' warm arms around her knees as he dashed in with a new picture for the back wall. She could remember the faces of so many of her customers; recall the day she'd first seen the menus back from the printers; how it had started out as a dream but had become real. Her Cupcake Café.

But it *was* real. It wasn't a dream. It wouldn't vanish if she stopped looking at it. It wouldn't suddenly disappear in a puff of smoke. Pearl was ready—more than ready—to step into her managerial shoes, and Maya's frantic practising and obsessive attention to detail boded well for her recipes. And Caroline would just be Caroline, she supposed. She couldn't do much about that. But she could leave now, confident that it could work, it could run without her. And maybe she could help the person she loved with his new life too. The café would, she fervently hoped, never change. But they

308

could.

'I want to be here,' she said. 'Where it's best for Darny. And close to Mum. But mostly … for us, Austin. You are us. It's great for us. And it will be great for me. I believe that. It's all decided. I'll go back once a month or so, check up on everything, make sure no one's killed anyone else, but for a couple of years … we'd be mad not to try the adventure. I've changed my life once already. I think I've got a taste for it now.'

Austin took her in his arms. 'I will devote my entire life to making it amazing for you,' he said.

'You don't have to,' said Issy, glancing towards the window, at the lights and the life and the buzzing, glittery, jittery streets. 'It already is.'

He stopped and thought. Then thought some more.

'You know,' he said. 'You won't be able to work here without a green card.'

Now it was Issy's turn to be surprised.

'Oh no? I thought, maybe in just a caf …'

'Nope,' he said. 'And normally they're quite hard to get.'

'Mmm?'

'Unless you're … with someone who has one.' He nuzzled her neck. 'You know, in all the madness, I never got you a Christmas present.'

'Oh no, you didn't!' said Issy. 'I forgot! I want one!'

'You know what they sell lots of in New York?'

'Dreams? Ice skates? Pretzels?'

He looked at her pensively. 'Aim higher.'

She looked back at him without saying anything, but her fingers unconsciously strayed to her little diamond earrings.

'That's it,' said Austin. 'You need something to go with those earrings. Definitely. But maybe ... on your finger?'

And they dressed warmly, and walked out hand in hand into the sharp, bright, exciting future of a honking, buzzing New York morning.

*   *   *

Back in London, Pearl looked at the post-lunch rush happily poking their fingers at the New Year range of apple and raisin cupcakes; rose blossom for the eventual spring; discounted gingerbread for the last few Christmas addicts, beautifully put together by Maya, and smiled.

'Cappuccino's up!' she yelled.

Acknowledgements

Firstly, thanks to everyone who read *Meet Me at the Cupcake Café* and was kind enough to let me know they enjoyed it, or even kinder to review it online and let other people know. I just can't thank you enough. I love hearing from people, especially if you've tried the recipes! And you can get me on Twitter @jennycolgan or my Facebook page is www.facebook.com/thatwriterjennycolgan. If you haven't read *Meet Me at the Cupcake Café*, don't worry; this book should stand alone.

Special thanks to Sufjan Stevens and Lowell Brams for doing their best to let us have a little Christmas miracle ... Everything lost will be found.

Also, many thanks to Kate Webster for letting me use her wonderful chocolate cola cupcake recipe (see page 238). For more of her delicious recipes check out her food blog: http://thelittleloaf. wordpress.com.

Huge thanks always to Ali Gunn, Rebecca Saunders, Jo Dickinson, Manpreet Grewal, David Shelley, Ursula Mackenzie, Emma Williams, Jo Wickham, Camilla Ferrier, Sarah McFadden, Emma Graves for the lovely cover, Wallace Beaton for the art work, everyone at Little, Brown, the Board, and all our friends and relations. Special hugs and Christmas kisses to Mr B and the three wee bees; I so hope your Christmas memories are magical. Even that time we couldn't get the Scalextric to work.

Baking your first cupcake
by The Caked Crusader

So, you've read this fab novel and, apart from thinking, gosh, I want to read all of Jenny Colgan's other novels, you're also thinking, I want to bake my own cupcakes. Congratulations! You are setting out on a journey that will result in pleasure and great cake!

Firstly, I'll let you into a little secret that no cupcake bakery would want me to share: making cupcakes is easy, quick and cheap. You will create cupcakes in your own home—even on your first attempt, I promise—that taste better and look better than commercially produced cakes.

The great thing about making cupcakes is how little equipment they require. Chances are you already have a cupcake tin (the tray with twelve cavities) knocking about in your kitchen cupboards. It's the same pan you use for making Yorkshire puds and, even if you don't have one, they can be picked up for under £5 in your supermarket's kitchenware aisle. The only other thing to buy before you can get started is a pack of paper cases, which, again, any supermarket sells in the home baking aisle.

Before making cupcakes, it's important to absorb what I think of as the four key principles of baking (this makes them sound rather grander than they are!):

- Bring the ingredients (particularly the butter) to room temperature before you start. Not only will this create the best cupcake but also it's so much easier for you to work with the ingredients . . . and why wouldn't you want to make it easy on yourself?
- Preheat your oven i.e. switch it on to the right temperature setting about 20–30 minutes before the cakes go into the oven. This means that the cake batter receives the correct temperature straight away and all the chemical processes will commence, thus producing a light sponge. Thankfully, in order to bake a great cupcake, you don't need to know what all those chemical processes are!
- Weigh your ingredients on a scale and make sure you don't miss anything out. Baking isn't like any other form of cooking—you can't guess the measurements or make substitutions and expect success. If you're making a casserole that requires two carrots and you decide to put in three, chances are it will be just as lovely (although perhaps a touch more carroty); if your cake recipe requires, for example, two eggs and you put in three, what would have been an airy fluffy sponge will come out like eggy dough. This may sound restrictive but actually, it's great—all the thinking is done for you in the recipe, yet you'll get all the credit for baking a delicious cupcake.

313

– Use good-quality ingredients. If you put butter on your bread, why would you put margarine in a cake? If you eat nice chocolate, why would you use cooking chocolate in a cake? A cake can only be as nice as the ingredients going into it.

Born on a Tasmanian sheep station, Timothy Bentinck is an English actor, writer, inventor and musician, Since 1982, he has played the part of David Archer in BBC Radio 4's *The Archers*. He is married to hat designer Judy Bentinck; they have two sons, Will and Jasper.

For more information about Tim, including photos and video clips of his work, please visit www.beingdavidarcher.net

BEING DAVID ARCHER

Tim Bentinck has played the part of David Archer in BBC Radio 4's *The Archers* since 1982. He is also the Earl of Portland — without an estate or riches — and the voice of 'Mind the Gap' on the Piccadilly Line. Timothy takes the reader behind the scenes of *The Archers*, the longest-running drama series in the world. With wry self-deprecating humour, he recounts his enormously varied life — a successful actor in TV, film and theatre; an HGV truck driver; a US tour guide; an inventor with UK patents; a farm worker; and a crossbencher in the House of Lords. *Being David Archer* is a dual memoir: of one of the country's most established farmers, and of a jobbing actor on the look-out for unusual ways to earn a living.

TIMOTHY BENTINCK

◆

BEING
DAVID ARCHER

(And Other Unusual Ways
of Earning a Living)

Complete and Unabridged

CHARNWOOD
Leicester

First published in Great Britain in 2017 by
Constable
An imprint of Little, Brown Book Group
London

First Ulverscroft Edition
published 2019
by arrangement with
Little, Brown Book Group
An Hachette UK Company
London

A catalogue record for this book is available
from the British Library.

ISBN 978–1–4448–3955–5

Published by
F. A. Thorpe (Publishing)
Anstey, Leicestershire

Set by Words & Graphics Ltd.
Anstey, Leicestershire
Printed and bound in Great Britain by
T. J. International Ltd., Padstow, Cornwall

This book is printed on acid-free paper

For my parents, Pauline and Henry

Contents

Introduction

'You're on,' said the stage manager.

'What do you mean?'

'Tim Curry's got food poisoning. You're playing the Pirate King.'

'I'm the second understudy, where's Chris?'

'He's off too.'

'This is a wind-up. It's because I'm five minutes late for the half, isn't it?'

'No.'

'Really?'

'Yes.'

'Seriously?'

'They're waiting for you in wardrobe. You've got twenty minutes.'

'Oh my God.'

'Cheer up, Tim, it's not often you get to play the lead in a West End musical.'

'But I've never even rehearsed it.'

'It's in your contract, love. Now get changed.'

This is what is known as the actor's nightmare, a curse we all endure; when you dream you're on stage either naked, or in an entirely unfamiliar play, or having absolutely no idea of your lines, or bonking your leading lady stark naked in a spotlight with your whole family watching from a box.

The nightmare was now actually happening.

1

It was 1982. An eventful year. While playing a pirate in *The Pirates of Penzance* at Drury Lane, we bought a house in north London, and I also landed the part of David Archer, son of the eponymous household in the world's longest-running radio series, *The Archers*. At the time of writing, I've now been channelling this guy for thirty-five years. It wasn't what I set out to do – I've always been happier with the sword fighting, really – but I bless the day I was lucky with that particular audition, and not just because it's given me a measure of financial security for over three decades.

I am now proud to be part of an Icon of Britain, a National Institution, and a source of excitement, enjoyment, anger and, sometimes, visceral emotional turmoil for some 5 million people every day.

So, I'd just come down on the train from Birmingham to do the matinee, having recorded an episode of *The Archers* at 9 a.m. The train was seriously overdue and, by the time I'd retrieved my bicycle at Euston, I was running very late for the first of two shows that day. The show was the West End transfer of the hit Broadway adaptation of Gilbert and Sullivan's classic, with Tim Curry, George Cole, Annie Ross, Chris Langham, Michael Praed, Bonnie Langford and Pamela Stephenson. If you ever saw that production of *The Pirates of Penzance*, I was the big bloke at the back – until that day, when I was suddenly the big bloke at the front.

I'd already done the movie. I was a pirate in that, too. At the audition for the film, this small, wired Argentinian ball of energy, choreographer Graciela Daniele, shouted, I want WAN HUNNERD TWENNY PO-SEN!! YANNER-STAN??!!' Luckily, I did understand, and because I was (and, indeed, still am) six foot three, and at twenty-eight was very fit and had boundless energy (cancel comparison), I gave her 130 per cent and got the part. Mainly because I didn't have to actually sing – we'd be miming to the original New York cast recordings in the film version.

I had performed in *Joseph and the Amazing Technicolor Dreamcoat* in Plymouth in 1979 but, I have to admit, I really wasn't a very good singer at the time. I got away with it, just, but always sang a wee bit flat. No one ever told me to sit on a note. Filming for months and earning pots of money (nearly all the pirates and policemen bought houses on that film) for just miming, dancing and faux fighting on a mock-up pirate ship in Shepperton Studios was about the best job a tall, energetic, not very good at singing, young-ish actor could possibly ask for.

Kevin Klein played the Pirate King. The inevitable and endless repetition of the scenes during filming meant that I at least knew the lines to the songs when it came to my turn to play the part on stage. The film's director was a man called Wilford Leach, and he wanted to do take after take from every conceivable angle, so the words were seared into my brain. When a fellow pirate, Mike Walling, asked him how many films he had directed before, he replied, 'Oh, this is my first one.' Mike came into the green room with a big thumbs up, 'We're in the money lads!' – and we were; what was scheduled as a three-week shoot took almost three months.

As Hollywood stars go, Kevin Kline is a diamond. When we once played a tedium-relieving silly game which ended with him getting slapped hard around the face, we all held our breath, waiting for a hissy fit. Instead, he smiled ruefully and said, 'I see, subtle British humour, eh?'

He came to dinner with me one evening, and when a friend of mine asked him if he was in 'this funny pirate film with Tim', he smiled his disarming Kevin-ish smile and said modestly, 'Yeah, I'm a pirate too.'

After filming had finished, Graciela told us that anyone who could actually sing had a part in the forthcoming West End show if they wanted it. I auditioned – and I was laughed at. However, the being tall and energetic bit got me in– 'Hey, we got back-op singas IN DA WINGS!!' Graciela said.

Three months later, we opened at the Theatre Royal Drury Lane to rave reviews and a sell-out nine-month season. As well as being a pirate at the back, I was asked to be second understudy for the Pirate King, which I accepted purely because it meant a slight pay rise. I never for one second thought that I would go on.

My preparation for playing the lead in a West End musical therefore was

1. I knew the words to the songs;

2. I had sung them at the piano precisely once

4

with the musical director; and

3. I had watched the show from out front on a Wednesday matinee.

That was it.

Tim Curry's costume for the show was about as sexy as you can get. This was 1982 and glam rock and New Romanticism were in their pomp. With bouffant hair and red headband, entire tubes of mascara, blousy, frilly white shirt, tight purple breeches and waistband and the coolest, tightest, longest black leather boots you can imagine, a fabulously flamboyant star like Tim Curry looked like a *sex god*. The problem was that none of his kit fitted me: it was far too small.

So, I didn't look like a sex god. More like an oversized kid in a school production of *Puss in Boots*.

I have very little memory of that afternoon, but a drug called adrenaline came to my rescue all by itself. While standing on the prow of the ship as it hove round from the backdrop and the curtain went up, I seem to remember laughing at the total absurdity of the situation. I pumped out my chest, lifted my chin, jumped off the ship and my hat fell off. I strode purposefully across the stage to begin the first number and was hauled unceremoniously back by Bonnie Langford to where I should have been. This continued all through the show. Bonnie pulled me one way, Annie Ross pulled me another and Pamela Stephenson ignored me completely, as she has done to this day.

All the swordfights that I did with Tim I now

had to do from the other side, so I kept missing the blade of the guy who was playing me. The jokey 'oh, the boss has missed catching the sword' shtick that the pirates all found embarrassing but usually got a big laugh just looked like the understudy had screwed up and was deeply eggy. It was only the power of the show and the professionalism of the rest of the cast that got us through.

Somehow, I survived. I asked the tech guys to record the audio as I thought it would be my one and only performance as the Pirate King, and I still have the tape. I'm not great. I just about survive but the cadenza at the end of 'I'm a Pirate King' is a train crash. I gabble my words and only through the comic genius and generosity of George Cole did any of my jokey sequence with the Major-General get any laughs. But one thing you can hear: I did have enormous energy and apparent confidence, and that, if anything, can disguise a multitude of sins.

That evening Tim was still ill but Chris Langham was back and so, as first understudy, he had to go through the whole thing himself while I went back to being a pirate. By his own admission, he had an even worse time than I did. After that a decision was made, probably by Chris himself, that I should take over as number-one understudy. The costume department started the job of making me a pair of the coolest, tightest, longest black leather boots you can imagine, but this time in a size twelve. By the time they'd done with me, I too had achieved sex-goddery.

Now, I was able to rehearse the part and I had

proper sessions with the musical director. I stopped singing so flat and learned how to time the jokes. However, in Tim's continued absence, the announcement 'Ladies and gentlemen, at this evening's performance of *The Pirates of Penzance* the part of the Pirate King will be played by Timothy Bentinck' was greeted with sustained groans of disappointment, which does little for your confidence as you stand shaking in the wings.

Kevin Kline helped my confidence, though. I was faced with having to do on the West End stage what this modest but big movie star had done on Broadway, so I wanted his advice and phoned him in New York.

'Are you paying for this call?'

'Yes?'

'Put down the phone. I'll call you back.'

We talked for nearly an hour about how to do it: timing of gags, thought processes, everything from how to kick a sword up from the floor and into another character's hand, to jock-itch, thigh boots and make-up – gold dust.

Eventually, Tim became very ill and had to give up the part, so I moved down from the fourth-floor dressing room that I shared with my pirate mates into the number-one dressing room on the ground floor, with my own dresser and my name slipped in the programme. It was the same dressing room that had sheltered the egos and insecurities of many of the great names of theatre and music for hundreds of years, including, thrillingly, my direct ancestor Mrs Dorothy Jordan. When I came out of the stage door every evening, hordes of young women were there, throwing knickers at me and wanting my autograph. This was it. I was a star!

It lasted about six weeks, which included Christmas and New Year. But one day in early January I came into the theatre on a Monday afternoon, cleared my stuff out of the number-one dressing room, trudged back up to the fourth floor, put away my sexy boots and shirt and watched from the back of the stage as Oliver Tobias swaggered his way through the part that I had made my own. After the show, I walked through the stage door as he was signing autographs and fending off knickers, and no one knew who the hell I was. My first lesson in the fleeting nature of fame.

Tasmania

'I was born on a sheep station in Tasmania.' I've always loved being able to say that.

My father had taken his wife and two daughters there in 1950, and I was born in 1953. We came back two years later so I have no memory of the place, but I have dual nationality, as do both my sons. When I finally returned to the land of my birth, to do a TV commercial there in 1998, I presented my virgin Australian passport to the guy at Sydney airport.

'How long have you been overseas, mate?'

'About forty-three years.'

'Christ, hell of a gap year.'

As a young man, my father Henry had absconded from Sandhurst, stowed away on a ship to America, ridden rough on the railroad to California and become a cowboy. Then, during the war, he had been wounded twice and made a prisoner of war in Italy. Faced with the beaten-up, grey, broke England that he came back to, he gave up his job as a talks producer at the BBC when he saw an advertisement in a paper saying, 'JACKAROO WANTED ON TASMANIAN SHEEP STATION'. A jackaroo is a farmhand and trainee. My father was a Count of the Holy Roman Empire (and I am too). It was a strange choice.

Bentinck is a Dutch name. We can trace it back

to a Helmich Bentinck, or Benting, who died in 1354. There are quite a few books about us but probably the most famous, or at least important, Bentinck is Hans Willem, later Earl of Portland, who came to England as the most trusted advisor of Prince William of Orange in the Glorious Revolution of 1688. There have been whisperings, handed down through history, that he was more than an advisor. This may have started because, when the young Prince was struck down with smallpox, Bentinck slept in his bed with him, as it was believed in those days that by catching a disease from someone, you took it away from them. Recent research suggests that while King William probably did 'swing both ways' – particularly with Hans Willem's great rival for William's affections, Arnold Joost van Keppel – my ancestor was a rather turgid statesman and, in the words of one historian, 'far too dull to be gay'. This didn't stop my distant cousin, Lady Anne Cavendish-Bentinck, when showing me the ancestral paintings at Welbeck, cheerily dismissing him, as we walked past his enormous portrait, with the words, '...and that's The Bugger'.

When the Prince was crowned King William III of England, there was a lot of tension between the English parliament and aristocracy and the new Dutch interlopers. To help assimilate his court into their new realm, he handed out titles left, right and centre. My father was never clear why Bentinck was given the title Earl of Portland, but family word-of-mouth had it that, as the Dutch fleet sailed towards their landing at Torbay, they passed close by Portland Bill in Dorset.

10

Turning to the ship's captain, the Prince asked the name of their first sighting of England.

'That's Portland Bill, my lord.'

'Vat iss a Bill?' asked the Dutch Prince.

There followed a lengthy explanation, which included the fact that Bill was also a diminutive of William, the name the Prince shared with my ancestor.

'Den I shall make you Earl off Portland, Bill!'

Cue helpless Dutch hilarity, probably the joke of the year, endlessly repeated to hose-wetting effect at parties throughout the Empire. This is the only known example of a joke in the entire 700-year history of my family, giving weight to the 'too dull to be gay' defence.

I have recently found out from the University of Nottingham that this is nonsense: the title was re-established through a connection with Hans Willem's first wife, Anne Villiers. Also, the Prince's first sight of land was Kent.

Hans Willem's son, William, was made Duke of Portland and his descendants married well, to the Harley, Scott and Cavendish families, and ended up with large estates in Scotland and Nottinghamshire, the seat of the family being Welbeck Abbey near Worksop. When the last duke died in 1990, there were no descendants of Hans Willem's son left, so the dukedom died out. However, the first Earl had married twice and we are the descendants of that second union, so at the age of seventy, Pa became the 11th Earl of Portland, a title I inherited. This came with a seat in the House of Lords, though without land or income. I'm often asked why not, and the answer seems quite clear –

11

the deceased duke was my father's sixth cousin twice removed. Would you expect to inherit anything from your sixth cousin twice removed? Do you even know who any of your sixth cousins twice removed are? Or what 'twice removed' actually means? It does, however, explain why I'm a jobbing actor and not managing an estate from a Subaru.

So, we are a family of counts. The Holy Roman Empire bit is complicated but doesn't mean Catholic. My Protestant great-grandfather was so formidably religious he gave up his Dutch castle and his entire inheritance for his belief. His son, my grandfather, was too dim to get the connection and continued being a slave to Jesus. My grandmother came from the Catholic Noel family, who disinherited her when she married a Protestant. When your father's the Earl of Gainsborough, being disinherited by him makes a difference. My father was therefore brought up by these impoverished warring Christian parents who had lost everything in the name of the Lord, and, understandably, the moment he became sentient he also became a staunch atheist. He married the daughter of a Yorkshire industrialist whose business had gone down the Swanee, which makes me a nicely mongreled half toff, half Sheffield steel.

My father's parents both died before he was out of his teens, and what bits of family stuff that were left, such as a house, some Gainsboroughs, a Titian and a Romney, were all sold by my sweet but totally naive great-uncle Arthur for practically nothing. He had become my father's guardian and he basically sold the entire inheritance in order to pay the death duties – Arthur's famous sayings have lived on, but his dismissal of these treasures with the words, 'not worth much, a few paintin's and a bit of rough shootin' for the boy' has lived on in infamy. It should be said that Arthur was also pretty much responsible for the Iraq wars, having been an important part of the British mandate that drew a straight line between Iraq, Kurdistan and Turkey. As we know, this led to more than just a 'bit of rough shootin''.

Arthur took his role as guardian very seriously. He once collected Pa from a party in Belgravia, from where they were due to drive to Scotland in his beautiful Lagonda. As they were walking towards the car, a pretty young French girl asked my father for directions. In the thirties, there were a lot of prostitutes in London, and a great many of them were French. Fearing 'the worst', Arthur grabbed Pa in the middle of his explanation to this perfectly innocent tourist, threw him into the car, reversed into a taxi and sped off into the night, engine roaring.

They drove in silence until they got to the A1, the romantically named Great North Road, when Arthur said, 'Now look here, Henry.' This usually presaged trouble. 'Were there girls at this party?'

'Yes, Uncle Arthur, of course there were girls.'

'Harrumph.'

They continued to travel in strained silence until they reached Scotch Corner, about eight hours later, when Arthur, who could contain himself no longer, suddenly shouted very loudly, 'Did they show their breasts?!!'

Arthur was a tragic relic of an aristocratic Edwardian childhood who, despite being a highly decorated major-general in the Coldstream Guards, badly wounded in the Boer and Great Wars, was quite simply out of his depth in the meritocratic twentieth century. One evening, Arthur had got tickets for a West End show. When they couldn't get a taxi, Pa suggested they take a bus. Arthur had never been on a bus in his life. When they got on, Arthur said to the conductor, 'Do you go to Piccadilly Circus?' The fact that the number 42 had 'Piccadilly Circus' written on the front of it hadn't registered with him. 'Yes, we do,' answered the conductor patiently. 'Will you take us?' asked Arthur, kindly. The fare was tuppence each, so Arthur gave the conductor sixpence and told him to keep the change.

I was brought up with these tales of odd relations. Arthur's sister Ursula drove around Europe in a VW Beetle, teaching the word of the Lord. She never discovered fourth gear so was a serious danger on speed-limit-free autobahns, going flat out in third in the fast lane – about forty. She picked up every hitchhiker she passed and one day a young man threatened her with a knife. She calmly pulled over to the hard shoulder, leant across him to the glovebox, got out a bible and gave it to the perplexed would-be mugger with the words, 'Now I don't believe you have read this. I want you to get out now, take this Bible with you, and when you have studied it thoroughly, come back to me and we will talk further. My address is on the flyleaf.' My great-aunts and -uncles were all devoted to God in such an all-embracing way that their own lives,

14

education, intellect and possessions were entirely secondary to their faith, which is why my father was so frustrated that he had no one in the family who he liked talking to, and the ones he did have anything to do with had managed to throw away his entire inheritance out of sheer ignorance.

So, when my parents left for Australia in 1950, they took just one crate of paintings and furniture to a modest settlement in the midlands of Tasmania. *One* crate. This was all this *nouveau pauvre* aristocrat had been left after a succession of forebears had managed to lose great castles full of the stuff.

So, I was born in a small hospital in Campbell Town, Tasmania, on 1 June 1953. As my family returned to England just two years later, the Australian adventure was like a part of my life that I'd completely missed out on. There were endless family stories of Hupmobiles and corrugated roads, of riding fast horses and climbing mountains, and two photograph albums of black-and-white pictures taken on my mum's Box Brownie camera, with me as a baby in this wonderful place that, to me, was so far away it might have been on Mars. My elder sisters, Sorrel and Anna, were full of memories, but I had none.

When I did finally get back there, some forty years later, I walked up the path to the hospital and approached the receptionist. She looked up at me and immediately said, 'Oh, are you Tim Bentinck?'

I was shocked. Had my birth made that much impression? It turned out that she was the wife of the old friend of the family with whom I'd

15

arranged to stay that night. When I asked her which room I'd been born in, she told me that the old maternity ward had been knocked down years before. She pointed out of the window at the car park. 'You'd have probably been born just underneath that little red Mazda over there.'

Wandering around Barton, the sheep station where we lived, about ten miles north of Campbell Town, I matched the locations of all the black-and-white photos of me as a baby to their present-day reality. The place was just the same, but in colour. When I dived into Broadwater, the wide, deep part of the river that ran through the estate, I saw in my mind the photo of me floating there aged one with my pa, and it completed a circle, restoring part of my childhood.

The owners kindly left me to my own thoughts, which were sad and jumbled and confused. I tried to picture my mum – naughty, funny, sexy, smoky Pauline Mellowes from Yorkshire, the aesthete, the jazz lover, singer, writer, the play-loving 'pretty one', as described by her older sister Pinkie. What on earth would she have made of sheep-shearing Aussie farmers, stuck in the heat in the middle of nowhere with no one to talk to, two young children and a baby on the way? How had my father persuaded her? He was always thinking ahead and in the post-war years with the fear of MAD – Mutually Assured Destruction – he had read somewhere that the only place in the world that would be almost free from the resultant radiation was Tasmania. That's why he went. In doing so, he made what became known as Pa's Great Mistake.

As far as I can make out, when Pa (broke

aristocrat) married Mum (daughter of once wealthy Yorkshire industrialist), said industrialist gave his daughter a sum of money to be used to buy a house. This money was in a form of trust called a Marriage Settlement, administered by a law firm called Bird and Bird (names which I heard my parents utter in the same way a Jewish family might refer to Himmler). Ever a one for the greater picture and often impatient with the petty details like contracts, Pa's Great Mistake was not to read the small print.

He was going off to Tassie to be a farm labourer, but that was just while he pursued his real goal: he was out there to buy a farm with thousands of acres, ride the range and start a dynasty. The small print, however, decreed that any property purchased with said Settlement was to be 'within the borders of the United Kingdom'. The pragmatic Grandpa Mellowes didn't trust this intellectual, flighty, handsome southern fop and wasn't about to see his daughter whisked off to the colonies. That's why Pa stayed a jackaroo for four years. Twit.

So, in 1955, he made an enormous crate out of Tasmanian oak, painted 'HB London' on the side of it, filled it with all the family furniture and paintings, and came home. I know this because there's a photo of him up a ladder painting the words on the crate. After he died, of cancer in 1997, I inherited his huge book collection, the bookshelves of which were made from this packing case. As I was dismantling them and stacking them together, I found the shelves with the writing on them, which was impossibly moving.

Berkhamsted

Back in England, my parents rented a house in Finchley while they went house-hunting. In fact, 'house-hunting' was one of the first phrases I remember, because that's all the grown-ups seemed to do all day. I used to wonder what sort of House they would eventually catch, and whether or not it might be a dangerous sort of House once they'd found it. It turned out to be quite benign, a four-bedroom detached house called 'Thorn Bank' in a quarter-acre of garden, just outside a village called Potten End, near Berkhamsted.

The garden was my playground, my fantasy world, with a sandpit and Wendy house, where I built camps and treehouses and later a stage with a curtain for putting on plays that I had written. The kitchen, where we ate, was the scene of great philosophical debates with my parents' friends, and sisters' boyfriends, with diagrams written in pencil on the blue Formica top of the dining table. It was also the place where, in January 1967, waiting to be taken back for my second term at boarding school, my father came downstairs and told me that my mother was dead. She had taken an overdose. I still don't know why they never gave her a funeral.

Until that day, my childhood had been pretty happy. After a rocky first day at a kindergarten called Rothesay in Berkhamsted, when I refused to let go of my father's hand and had to be dragged, screaming, into morning prayers, I settled down to a life of conkers, marbles, swimming, fighting and football. I do have some vague memories of sitting in classrooms while formidable women called Miss and dotty old gents with military titles droned on about things that scared me stiff because I didn't understand them, like Maths, which is odd given my later utter delight in computer programming. There are certain smells that take me straight back to my school-days. Rothesay is wet leaves on new tarmac (they had just relaid the playground when I arrived), Berkhamsted Prep School is wet white woollen polo-neck jerseys after games, and Harrow is an incriminating mixture of cigarettes and burning electrical motors from the overworked Vent-Axia extractor fan in the first-floor bogs.

The countryside around our house was beautiful, and for an adventurous child it was a bucolic idyll, of which I was the king and my bicycle was a thoroughbred charger. I biked everywhere. My best friend Johnse (his name was Johnson Merrix, a moniker with which his mother used to assault him in full when angry – he's been a relieved John for a while now) and I used to build camps. Our playground was a mixture of the paths, bracken and woods of common land, and the bicycling heaven of the fairways and bunkers of the local golf course. The area had been used to train the troops before they set off for the front in the Great War, so it was dotted with zigzag trenches, foxholes, slit trenches and bomb

19

craters. Our camps were made by covering these holes with branches and leaves – a technique learned from Pooh when making Heffalump traps. I can't really remember what we did when inside them; we were too young to smoke; maybe it was a desire to return to the womb or an early manifestation of nest-building, a trait which has been an important part of my life – building a home, making things, repairing, being practical. Basically, it was nine-year-old DIY.

I loved my bike for the total freedom it gave me. Some of the shell craters made amazing bike courses, like modern-day skateboard parks, and we would spend hours finessing our techniques and timing our runs. I used to bicycle to school, which in the morning meant crossing the common, then a death-defyingly fast downhill run of about a mile, past the Norman Berkhamsted Castle and into the town. Going back was a grinding slog, but my God I was fit. My first bike was a second-hand boneshaker, but putting black-and-white check tape down the side made it go like a rocket. When I was finally given a new one – a Raleigh three-speed – the twist-grip gears were about the most futuristic, coolest things I had ever seen. It felt like being on a motorbike. I learned to do wheelies and I saved up my pocket money to get special off-road tyres, which slowed the bike down a lot but looked great when covered with mud. Instant smell-memory: 3-in-One oil. I never knew what three things it did, but the fact that you were getting three things for the price of one made it important, grown-up and highly technical. A must for boys who wanted to be spaceship-pilots like Dan Dare, racing drivers like Stirling Moss, pilots like Biggles or land-speed record holders like Malcolm Campbell. A world of fantasy and invention, the joy of Wednesdays when the *Eagle* comic would arrive, and the sadness of Thursdays knowing you had another whole week to wait for the next one.

We would watch *Doctor Who*, *Robin Hood* and Westerns – classic black-and-white cowboy shows on a small screen. I'd lie on the floor about a foot from the tiny TV and live every minute of *Bronco Lane*, *Rawhide*, *The Lone Ranger* and *Bonanza* and, as you only saw it the once – no replay, no catch-up – you had to literally replay it yourself. So I'd strap on ma six-gun, pull on ma chaps, slip on ma weskit and flip on ma Stetson. With my trusty steed 'Raleigh Roadster', I was ready. First, I had to check for Injuns. Keeping low, I gained the cover of the hedge. From there, I made my way slowly and quietly to the top of the garden and the overhanging bough that I could climb up to reach the extensive, camouflaged treehouse I had built. I could reconnoitre the whole garden, judging whether it would be safe to continue the mission on to the Wendy house. To keep ready for any trouble, I would practise my quick draw. Johnse and I would have shoot-outs, and of course who-ever went, 'Peeeew, peeeew' first, won. I became lethally quick: I was like the gunfighter Johnny Ringo. This skill was to bear fruit some forty years later when I was in a Western myself. The problem was I couldn't stop going 'Peeeew, peeeew!' even in tight close-up. Some things are ingrained.

We had a beagle called Jasper and a black cat

called Oospoo. Jasper was great: he could roam free and would be called back for food in the evening with a bugle. That's why I can play the bugle – again, nothing wasted. One day, he came back in the van of a farmer who said the next time he chased his bloody sheep he'd 'shoot the bastard hound!' As a result, I have a vague recollection of taking Jasper for a walk through a field, showing him a sheep, and saying, 'NO! UNDERSTAND? NO!'

My first paid job was working on a farm in Nettleden. This gave me the farming experience I still use in my imagination for *The Archers*, and in my mind the farm remains the location of the yard at Brookfield. Later, when my father and stepmother created an organic smallholding in Devon, I did more farm work, but the traditional family farm at Nettleden, with its cows, sheep and pigs, is also a great source of inspiration. There was a big bloke with massive sideburns and a strong old Hertfordshire accent called Jess, and a weaselly, naughty kid called Nobby who used to take me out poaching. All my scenes with Jethro and later Bert Fry have resonances with those two, and that's where I learned to drive a tractor, muck out a pig sty, build a barbed-wire fence (I have the scars to prove it), toss a bale to the top of a haystack and roll a crafty fag.

I've always been able to imagine a mile in my head because, just down the road from our house, was 'The Mad Mile' – a stretch of almost straight country road on which my father, and later I, used to test the speed of our Beetle. The answer was always the same, about 68 mph, top whack.

His other trick was to see how late he could leave it before braking for the T-junction. He'd worked out that if he hit the anchors at the second he passed the T-junction sign, he'd stop just in time. One night he was returning from work, over the limit (the norm in those days), missed the sign due to thick fog and went straight through the fence at the end and into a field. The barbed wire on the top of the fence ripped the sunshine roof clean off and the rest of the car was battered and bruised. In the morning, when I got up to find the pitiable remains of my favourite thing in the world, I stormed into my parents' bedroom, purple with rage and streaming tears, and shouted, 'What have you done to Folksie?!' A few days later, no doubt to make up for his idiocy, Pa bought me a toy Beetle. Not a Corgi, Dinky or Matchbox, but a large, blue, beautiful model with a pull-back engine and opening doors. Within a week I had taken a hammer to it and bashed it to make it look like our own. I have it still.

It was typical of my father that, having gone through a war where the Germans had nearly killed him, taken him prisoner and amused themselves by subjecting him to a mock execution, the first car he had bought when we got back from Tassie was Hitler's iconic People's Car, the VW Beetle. Compared to everything else on the road in the late fifties, it looked like a spaceship. Pa was fascinated by modern things and the future, so to him it made perfect sense. Crowds would gather when we stopped at traffic lights, asking what on earth it was. It was metallic bronze and I was brought up to the sound of its air-cooled flat-four

23

engine, as my place was the 'back-back' – the luggage space behind the back seat which was like a cot, and I would sleep there on long journeys. And boy did we have some long journeys.

Every Christmas we would drive up to visit our cousins in Forfar, Scotland. It's only an eight-hour drive these days, but in the 1960s it meant a marathon journey on the Great North Road with a family of five and all their clothes, plus Christmas presents, jammed into a tiny Beetle with an underpowered 1200cc engine and a six-volt battery. The headlights were only slightly brighter than candles but we would drive through the whole night, often in freezing hail, fog or snow. One time, it was so cold that the windscreen wipers froze up and my father, damned if he was going to stop because he'd managed to overtake a lorry four miles back after an hour of trying, got my mum to stick her head up through the sunshine roof to free the wipers.

The reason we had all managed to fit in the car was because my mother had won the packing prize at school. Every spare space in the car was used, even around the engine. Wine bottles and Christmas crackers were fitted round the fuel tank, which made Christmas lunch at Fotheringham a spectacular affair when the petrol-soaked crackers were pulled.

Scotland was magical. Flinging curling stones down bumpy frozen lochs, driving wildly around the estate in a Jag that smelled of oil and leather, playing in the massive loft full of generations of memories, and togging up for fancy-dress dinners in the clothes we found there.

24

The other great thing about our car was that I was allowed to drive it from a very young age. Can you imagine the pride, aged about ten, on hearing your father say, 'Timmy, can you get the car out please?' I would rush out, open the garage doors, start the car, back it out ten yards, turn the wheel, put it in first, drive forward another ten yards and stop it outside the front door. I passed my test about a week after my seventeenth birthday and got my HGV Class 2 licence when I was twenty-three. One of my great regrets is not being a Formula One driver. It all started with that Beetle.

After Rothesay, I went to Berkhamsted Prep and then Junior School. I had a pretty good time, at least until the last year, but my standout memories are of being punished. One teacher was very partial to grabbing chunks of our hair and twisting it until it nearly came out. His other hobby was rapping us hard on the back of the hand with a ruler. The headmaster's beatings had an especially perverse cruelty about them. You would wait on a bench in the table-tennis room, which smelled of lino and polish, and be summoned into the headmaster's study, which smelled of pipe smoke and leather. You would then take down your trousers and underpants and bend over the back of a leather armchair and be hit six times, hard, with a cane. I remember him actually saying, 'This hurts me more than it does you,' and I had to shake his hand at the end and say 'Thank you, sir.'

The decision to send me to Harrow had a disastrous effect on my last year at Berkhamsted.

The norm for the boys was to go from the Junior School straight into the Senior School, but my parents had other things in mind. I never asked my father about it and now it's too late. It's not as though he could afford the fees – his salary as an adman at J. Walter Thompson was ridiculously small as he never asked for a raise and remained stupidly loyal to them. I believe he got help from richer relations, one of whom admonished me once for not thanking her – I would have done if I'd known.

Once my friends found out I was going to a posh school, and was having to take private Latin lessons to get me through Common Entrance, they ceased to be my friends. I was sent to Coventry, teased, baited and mentally bullied. The most hurtful thing of all was that my closest friend, a boy called Jeremy, became the ringleader of my tormentors. I used to hide during break so they couldn't gang up on me, and no one came to my birthday party that last year.

Jeremy and I had acted in lots of school plays together. I distinctly remember the first one, *The Dear Departed* by Stanley Houghton, in which we were both playing women. He got a huge laugh when he shot out of the wings and leapt into my arms in fear of being caught by the baddy. It took trust and friendship. After the first night, I went outside to look for my parents, forgetting to take off my make-up, and found myself being noticed by the departing audience. I came back inside and remarked on the attention I was getting. 'Oh, I'm not interested in that sort of thing,' Jeremy replied superciliously, putting me in my place and making me wonder if that was the 'sort of thing' that I wanted. Fifty years later and still an actor, I suppose the answer must be yes, a bit.

The change from best friend to chief tormentor was harsh and cruel, and I never forgave him. His treachery stuck with me for a long time, but when I discovered, well into my forties, that he had been killed in a car accident, I didn't know how to feel. I was shocked and saddened at his death, but, selfishly, I also felt cheated of confronting him with his betrayal of our friendship. I'm sure that as an adult he would have apologised, and I could have laid that period of my life to rest, but he wasn't able to, so it still hurts. It explains why I was so oversensitive to bullying when my two boys were at school, and why I have such a dislike for the cowardice of trolls and cyber-bullies today.

Another lesson learned at that school was that parents should be very careful about complaining, as it's usually the child who suffers. I once got full marks on a test in maths, which was highly un- usual but I'd done some work for a change. I was accused of cheating and given 0/10 and a punish- ment. Upset, I told my mother, who complained bitterly to the teacher. The result was that at the next test, where I got my usual middling marks, the teacher said, 'Bentinck, 5/10. However, we'd better give you full marks. We don't want your *mother* complaining again, do we?' Bastard.

Harrow School

When my father dropped me off on day one at Harrow in 1966 he remarked, 'Hasn't changed much since my time' – his time being 1932–7, which meant it hadn't changed much since the nineteenth century. The main difference, which he never stopped going on about, was that we had central heating, whereas they froze in Harry Potter-like dormitories with open fires and an allowance of about one lump of coal per week.

The school is divided up into houses of about sixty boys each. I was in Moretons, which is right smack in the middle, making getting to class-rooms a lot easier than for the boys at the end of Harrow Hill. When I arrived I was put in a room with two other wide-eyed innocents. The houses are like rabbit warrens with bits added on over the centuries, so that finding my way around took months to learn. This made responding to 'boy calls' even harder. The fagging system at Harrow was complex but more or less phased out by the time I left. This was annoying because I willingly submitted to being treated like a virtual slave for my first year only because I knew that when I got to be a sixth former, I too would have someone to clean my shoes, make my tea, go shopping, run errands, clean my room and generally do as they're told. I had to do all that shit, and never got to dole it out later.

Those were 'private' fags. A boy call was made by a sixth-former whose private fag was out or unavailable and it went like this. Said sixth-former stands outside his room and shouts, 'BOY, BOY, BOY, BOY, BOY!' upon which anyone in their first year has to drop what they are doing or, if they're on the bog, stop mid-effort, and run at full speed through the warren of corridors to where the shouting is coming from. Last boy there gets the job. This explains why I and my contemporaries were highly skilled at leaping down an entire flight of stairs in one go, and tended to win at rugby.

I can't say that I hated Harrow. I made some very good friends, some of whom remain dear to me to this day. My mum took her own life just after my first term at boarding school – maybe she wasn't too keen on the last of her children leaving home, and was alone and sad. It was tough, but those friends helped me through, especially Noël Diacono, who was my new room-mate that term. He was essentially brutal and didn't allow me time to wallow in sadness, but he knew what he was doing. Now in our sixties, he's the brother I never had.

I once read a psychiatrist saying that five years at a boys' boarding school does untold psychological damage, ruins sex lives, screws up a man's ability to have relationships and triggers a budding psychopath into full-on barking lunacy. Well, no one who decides to be an actor can be described as completely normal, but I seem to have survived, if not unscathed, then just about able to cope. Part of the reason for that has been the love of my older sisters, Sorrel and Anna, whom I adore, an easy and happy life with my mother in the short time I had with her, a close relationship with my father, then, later, the incredible luck of meeting my beloved Judy when I was twenty-one, and the joy of bringing up our amazing boys, Will'm and Jasper.

I perfectly understand why some people think of boys who went to places like Harrow and Eton as out-of-touch, privileged toffs, without a care in the world. Funnily enough, that's exactly what we thought of Etonians. Most of my friends' parents weren't rich but had scrimped and saved from fairly modest middle-class incomes to send their sons there, and had nothing left over for any luxuries. That's not to say that some kids weren't minted, but as a rule the brash rich tended to be disliked and it was considered bad form to boast of wealth. Of course, everything is relative and we had no understanding of real poverty or suffering; the only ethnic minorities we ever met were African or Arab princes and kings; and a lot of boys were picked up at the end of term in Bentleys and Jags, although my pa brilliantly used to turn up in winter in his rusty convertible Beetle with the hood down, long white hair and beard flowing, wearing a black eyepatch and his grandfather's Canadian racoon-skin coat, with massive furry collar turned up.

Sports were an important part of life at Harrow. I was quite good at most sports, but not outstanding. The one thing at which I excelled was swimming. I learned how to swim fast from Pa, who had the most graceful freestyle stroke, and it is written of my Great-Uncle Henry, who died at the Somme, that to witness 'Bentinck off the high board was worth travelling miles to see' according to the school magazine, the *Harrovian*. The Harrow pool was called Ducker, as it used to be a duck pond. Before it was abandoned in the seventies, it was the longest outdoor private pool in Europe, some 250 yards long, incorporating a 50-yard racing section, and was unheated. It was here that my father found himself in the thirties swimming naked against the Hitler Youth (swimming trunks were only made compulsory in the late 1950s when they built the nearby hospital that overlooks the pool). During the war, my father was comforted by the knowledge that 'extremely cold water has the same shrivelling effect on a Nazi as it does on a Harrovian'. It was inspiring to find in the changing rooms one's own father's name carved on the wooden boards for cups and prizes won, and I set out to emulate him.

I was used to cold water as our local pool, the Deer Leap in Little Gaddesden, was an unheated outdoor lido   blissful on summer days but so cold it made your head ache if you swam too fast. The Berkhamsted School pool, by contrast, was indoor, heated and only 25 yards long. I'd been swimming captain there and also had the school underwater distance record, so I arrived at Harrow thinking I was the bee's knees. I had a rude awakening. One fifty-yard length of the pool in near freezing water was a massive shock to the system, but probably explained why the school won everything – we just wanted to get out of the bloody water as soon as we could.

I was the fastest boy ever to swim in that pool, as I still held the individual medley and freestyle records when they shut it down and built an indoor replacement. I also swam the last ever length there when, many years later, my dear friend Noël and I, on a nostalgic, alcohol-fuelled ramble about the old place, scrambled through undergrowth to find the pool ruinous, abandoned, but so full of memories. There was about three feet of rainwater, so I stripped off to the buff and swam the last length. My great-uncle had spent his final week's leave from the Front at the pool, so there was a palpable sense of sadness and closure in that act.

Having a cool dad but having lost my mum; being a swimmer and a smoker (the two went inextricably together); being not great at footie but a demonic tackler; playing the guitar; having a tuck box full of Mr Kipling's Almond Slices (probably the most delicious thing ever made) left over from one of Pa's advertising shoots; doing Modern Languages – these things made me accepted in such relieving contrast to the tormented, excluded year I'd come from.

Of course, I look back now with rose-tinted glasses, but there were satisfying moments, including getting into a bath full of hot muddy water after freezing games of rugby or Harrow Football, then having tea and toast before setting off in the dark for more lessons, bruised and bleeding but wrapped up in the traditional long Harrow scarf. In a perverse way, the feeling of having survived without having any limbs ripped off was a good one.

And Ducker was magical, beautiful, serene. When we weren't racing or diving, there were 'log mills', a mill is a fight, and a log is a log. There were logs floating in the water and teams of about twenty boys would fight each other to get a log to their side of the pool. The log had splinters, the pool was rough concrete, and like so many things which 'wouldn't be allowed today', it was great.

As the sun set, we'd walk back to the Hill, avoiding the cow pats on the football fields that were grazed by Friesians, munching our Ducker Biscuits – huge rich-tea wheels that cost a penny each – and a Coke that was sixpence, bought from the small hatch in the door of the pool-keeper's cottage, run by Mr Campkin, who had been there in my father's day and remembered his swimming. Mr Campkin had treasures of chocolate inside, which you could just see through the hatch but could only afford on special occasions. Glowing and exhausted, we walked across fields and up to our rooms in the huge houses on top of the Hill.

All of that was pretty blissful.

On the other hand, I was pretty much constantly homesick. I just counted down the days until I could go home. There was a thing called 'Exeat Weekends', when our parents would come and collect us on Friday night, and we had to be back on Sunday evening. Even the word 'evening' felt like a very grown-up luxury, to be allowed back so late. I would feel the joy of release on the Friday night when I'd hear from way up the road the sound of the familiar VW engine of my childhood come gurgling round the corner, and I'd rush down with my bag and leap in the car before Pa had hardly stopped, and we'd be away from what was essentially a prison term, locked up in a building, with no choice but to stay, beaten if we misbehaved, made to attend classes, chapel and cadet force, required to wear starched collar and tails, compulsory exercise, no drinking, no girls, no smoking (!) – no wonder we wanted to go home.

In the first summer holiday after Mum died, my father borrowed a Commer camper van and we set off together to tour round Eastern Europe. I never asked him why, but I imagine it was a desire for a father/son bonding exercise and guilt about my parents' deteriorating relationship, which had contributed to my mum's depression and suicide. That summer I wrote a poem that began:

> *I went round Eastern Europe in a Commer with my Dad.*
> *It was nineteen sixty-seven, my mum had gone to heaven,*
> *We saw the sights in black and white and both of us were feeling*
> *Understandably*
> *Quite sad.*

It was an odd trip to take in the years of the cold war: East Germany, Poland, Czechoslovakia, Austria, Switzerland and back through France. We had an amazing 1960s Philips Mignon portable record player that purported to play 45s on the move. It was very futuristic as you slid the record in like a modern car CD player, and it had dampers to stop it jumping. My dad used to like to play Scott McKenzie's 'San Francisco (Be Sure To Wear Flowers In Your Hair)' because it filled him with hope for a better post-war future, run by peace-loving hippies. I got into trouble for leaving the discs on the dashboard in the sun, and they all warped except Nancy Sinatra's 'You Only Live Twice'. I wrote in the poem:

> Of all the songs that melted in the dormobile that
> day
> The one song that survived it was the one that made
> him cry.
> The one I'd brought, when he'd asked not, the Bond
> theme about living twice.
> Because my
> Mother hadn't.

Memories of that trip include his outrage at having a massive military bayonet confiscated at the East German border, doing black-market cash deals with a Polish woman in a petrol station toilet, me being pulled off the roof of the camper as I took photographs of Soviet troops parachuting into the Danube, and pouring water from the sink into the radiator (the engine was between the front seats) as we puffed and steamed our way over the Alps.

Happier times with my father were spent at home and abroad on the film sets for the TV commercials he produced for J. Walter Thompson. These included ads for Mother's Pride, with Dusty Springfield, Joe Brown and Andy Stewart, and Mr Kipling (it was Pa who wrote the lines 'Mr Kipling makes exceedingly good cakes' and cast the inimitable voice of James Hayter).

These days TV commercials don't generate the iconic status that they used to, but back then some ads became part of the national consciousness. If you say to anyone of my generation, 'Do you remember the Nimble balloon adverts?' they will nearly all say yes. The strapline was 'Real bread, but lighter'. 'Bingo,' thought Pa, 'strap it to a balloon.'

Expanding on this idea, he imagined a girl eating a Nimble sandwich in a balloon basket with a beautiful Spanish castle in the background. Why a Spanish castle? Probably because Pa fancied a trip to Spain. In those pre-green screen days and with massive budgets, films were made in exotic locations simply for the jolly! Which is how he found himself in Segovia with a hydrogen balloon, a film crew and me. It was an amazing adventure for a fourteen-year-old, and it's probably why I feel so at home on a film set to this day.

On the first day, they inflated the balloon with hydrogen bottles but discovered the first major problem: the 'Nimble Bread' banner was so small you couldn't read the lettering. Cue Bentinck improvisation skills. He got the art director to go around the town buying as many large white cotton sheets as he could find. He then co-opted the hotel ballroom and laid them out on the floor where the art director pencilled out the new lettering. Next, he found a willing local with a sewing machine to stitch them all together, then overnight got everyone, including me, to work with buckets of paint filling in the lettering. By the morning it was dry and ready.

In the ad, you can see a flock of rooks flying past as the balloon takes off with Segovia Castle in the background. That was me in a wood, armed with a walkie-talkie. On 'action', I had to set off fire-crackers so that the rooks flew past, in the right direction, at the exact right time. I was terrified I'd get it wrong but it worked. Just imagine today letting the producer's fourteen-year-old be in charge of something like that. Today, the entire thing would be done on a computer anyway, which is why it's not so much fun doing adverts any more!

Once the balloon was airborne, the second problem became apparent. Where exactly was it going to end up? It was the balloon crew department's job to retrieve it. An incredibly cool babe-magnet and ex-soldier called John Spear followed it across all terrain with the aid of a four-wheel-drive Land Rover and binoculars, but he was amazed to find that, having bounced and skidded across impenetrable Spanish desert for hours, he'd been beaten to the balloon's final resting spot by a film producer with a black eyepatch and his young son. Our only resources had been a beaten-up convertible Beetle and the question, 'Ha visto un globo?' The phrase has gone down in family history.

The Nimble girl was an incredibly brave model from London called Emily Gumming. She wasn't a stunt girl or a balloon expert, and for the long shots of the balloon in flight, she was replaced by Christine Turnbull, the daughter of the balloon manufacturer, Gerry. However, the following year they used a hot-air balloon in Switzerland, and that was when Emily earned everyone's admiration for her extraordinary bravery. This time, instead of a castle as a backdrop, Pa wanted the Eiger. So, they built a steel-frame mock-up of the bottom of the balloon, which was then suspended from a helicopter. Emily was slung beneath the steel frame, and the whole contraption was then lifted to a photogenic spot, about fourteen thousand feet high, in front of the mountain. These days she'd be wearing a parachute harness and every safety device known to man would be employed; and no way on earth a totally inexperienced but immensely brave model would be handcued, from another helicopter filming her a few yards away, to reach into a small hidden backpack, take out a slimming sandwich and eat it as though she were taking tea on the lawn. In fact her harness was just a few straps sewn together, designed by my father. Terrifying.

The location for the very first Nimble ad was less glamorous, and involved a very young Joanna Lumley diving into a freezing and muddy river in Gloucestershire. I was there too, and Joanna held my hand. I've been in love with her ever since.

So at least I was having some fun in the holidays, which took my mind off missing Mum.

I was finally released from Harrow in 1971. I was amazed to find that fellow pupils whom I thought I knew were setting off to become accountants or to work in banking. I thought they were bonkers, but of course most of them are now multi-millionaires who retired at forty. The friends from Harrow that I've kept in touch

38

with are more like me: teachers, charity workers, psychologists, alcoholic writers, hippie drop-outs, that kind of thing. Mind you, there's a smattering of eccentric lawyers, lords and land-owners who are good chums too!

The subject of my schooling came up when I worked with a communist-voting actress called Marjorie Yates in a production of *Hedda Gabler* at the King's Head Theatre in London. Hedda was played by Elizabeth Quinn, the profoundly deaf actress famous for *Children of a Lesser God*. I played her loving husband, Tesman, which was terrifying as she couldn't hear a word any of the cast were saying, so if anything went wrong, as can happen, a line missed or misspoken, where a hearing actor adjusts accordingly – she couldn't adjust accordingly. Still that's acting: a lot of the time it's just balls-out terror. One night in the dressing room, Marjorie asked me where I'd been to school. When I said Harrow, she said, 'Oh, so that's why you're so fucking confident.' That got me thinking. Was I able, insanely and without the talent to justify it, to walk out on stage just be-cause of a confidence I'd gained at school? The younger me would have said, no, I did it all my-self, but perhaps I might not otherwise have had the chutzpah to have made the bloody stupid decision to be a freelance, hand-to-mouth, job-bing actor, trading on a fleeting artistry that will fade with age while still hoping to be finally discovered by Spielberg.

Mind you, it's been fun.

Mind the Gap year

I got lousy grades in my A levels so if I was to have any chance of going to university, I'd have to resit them. I found this out in a phone box on a beach in Sardinia during a serious bout of food poisoning. I was hungry, broke, living in a tent, feeling like I was dying, and I had to decide whether to come home and do the exams again instead of continuing my journey to India.

I was eighteen, and after hitchhiking and working around Europe for a few months I'd bought my first car, a VW 1500N step-back, the saloon version of the Variant, and I had set off down the Indian hippie trail, stopping every now and then to earn enough money for food and petrol to get me to my next stop. I'd spent a fortnight in Florence where I'd worked handing out leaflets for a discotheque. The deal was that if I could get British and American girls to go for free, the local men would pay in droves to get in. I'd write my name on the leaflet and get paid for everyone that took me up on it. So essentially I was being paid to chat up all the girls in Florence! I found a cheap café that did spaghetti bolognese and a glass of wine for a few lire, which has given me a life-long love of the combination. I stayed in a campsite just outside town, and when I tried to leave without paying, the poor bloke on the gate accepted as surety for my return my much-loved but essentially valueless

Man from U.N.C.L.E. identification card. I still feel guilty about that.

I took the ferry to Sardinia where my sister Sorrel had got me a job as a child-minder and cleaner for an Italian family. She came to visit me but had no idea where I was, so in typically forthright fashion she simply walked through the town yelling my name. When the job ended and Sorrel had left, I finished up in my tent on a beach, where I now had to make a big decision about my future. After a lot of soul-searching I decided to come home. I drove back up Italy, over the Alps, and was halfway through Germany when the front-right wheel bearing seized solid on the autobahn. By amazing chance, I had stopped within sight of a major VW dealership. I stood in wonder as the chief mechanic sat by my jacked-up car like a surgeon with his patient, as fawning underlings slapped spanners into his hand like nurses with scalpels. Finally, he resorted to a blow torch and burned the entire wheel assembly clean off and replaced the whole thing. The entire procedure took about an hour and I remember wondering how on earth they had lost the war.

I was aiming to get back in time for my old friend Jamie Borthwick's birthday party the following night, so I kept driving, napping in the car when my eyelids started to droop. In Holland at 4 a.m. I ran out of fuel by a dyke and had to hitchhike to the nearest petrol station, sleeping by a pump until it opened. I reached Calais mid-morning, only to be told that all the ferries were full until the next day. I'd been through enough; I wasn't going to miss the party. I drove to Dunkirk,

41

figuring it to be a historically good place to get to England from. Amazingly I found a merchant ship that was loading goods onto its deck and blagged a lift. I drove the car onto a large net, and they hoisted us both aboard. I lunched with the captain in some style and was dumped on the Dover docks a few hours later.

In those days, Dover to Brancaster in north Norfolk was a good six hours, but setting off at two I reckoned I'd be just in time. I nearly didn't make it. On the north Norfolk coast road about a mile from my destination there's a rather hairy chicane, and, pumped up with a massive sense of achievement at having made it from Sardinia in one go, I approached it at about sixty and went straight into the ditch. Still my luck held; a passing tractor hauled me out and I drove the last mile to the party, only to find it was a black-tie event. Resplendent in oily T-shirt, jeans, greasy hair and thick stubble, I was fit, tanned and safe so I couldn't have cared less.

I had managed a 'B' in English and my French just needed some more work, but I'd failed my German, so my father arranged for me to stay with cousins in Hamburg for two months. Wilhelm and Ise von Ilsemann, together with their children Andrea and Godard, had been briefed by Pa not to speak English with me at all. I didn't know this and thought, right until my last day, that he had stupidly managed to find the ONLY well-educated family in Germany that didn't have a word of English. Wilhelm was a director of Shell and he got me a job in market research.

It wasn't all work though. I was taken out for

weekend adventures by a wonderfully eccentric cousin called Baron Joska Pintschovius and his barking-mad friend, the artist, satirist and radio comedian Heino Jaeger. They were older than me and had grown up to believe that the death and destruction that fell from the skies as they played in the ruins of Hamburg was normality. When the Allied bombardment was over they both experienced a kind of post-traumatic stress disorder in reverse, in that they found they missed it. Heino's art is predominantly to do with the iconography of bombs, destruction, war and Nazis, and when we went off in Joska's smoke-filled Mercedes for the day, we were on the hunt for bunkers, steel helmets and swastikas. When they came to visit me at university the following year, it was as if the concrete campus just outside Norwich had been built specifically for them.

'Da! Da ist noch ein bunker!'

East Anglia

The University of East Anglia (UEA) looks something like a spaceship that has landed on a golf course. Designed by Denys Lasdun, it shares its architectural style with the National Theatre on the South Bank, which he built some ten years later. Rough concrete, steel and carpet – the perfect 'bunker' for my war-damaged German friends.

I arrived in 1972 and read History of Art, not

43

because I initially had any special interest in art, but because I knew I wasn't going to be a scientist and I was done with studying languages.

I often wonder if the whole 'confident' thing wasn't just my enormous relief at being free. After all, not many Harrovians went to UEA – I'd been attracted to the university because there'd been a student sit-in the previous year and that sounded so radical and anti-establishment. If I had been more industrious, I might just have scraped into Oxbridge, but at the time it seemed to me to be an extension of Harrow, with possibly a few girls thrown in. Tales of having to avoid college porters and sneaking out at night didn't appeal to me. At UEA, I had a car and could come and go as I pleased. Academic demands aside, my days were my own and I filled them as I wished; I played Frisbee, went water-skiing in the local gravel pits, played guitar, went to concerts, rehearsed and performed plays. Even the lectures and seminars were given and led by people who loved their subjects and discussed them with you on equal terms; it was very different from the teacher/pupil relationship that I had endured at school – I was learning how to learn. Perhaps I wasn't so much confident as full of the joy of life – I was happy for a change.

Unfortunately, the self-assuredness didn't extend to dating. Maybe that shrink's assessment of public schoolboys is right about one thing: I was always hopeless at getting girls into bed. I once popped the question to a girl I fancied wildly at about two in the morning after we'd spent the whole evening talking and listening to music.

'Christ,' she said, 'I thought you'd never ask.' I look at pictures of me in those days and I suppose I was a fairly handsome chap, but I didn't think so at the time, and never dreamed that anyone fancied me back. That's not to say I was awkward with girls, quite the opposite: I just didn't want to offend them!

In my first year, I shared a room in the iconic ziggurat residence of Norfolk Terrace with Dave Robinson. I don't know if the authorities did this on purpose but Dave Robinson and I had completely different backgrounds and interests. He was from a state school, he had long black hair and a moustache, and was reading physics and chemistry. The only things we had in common were getting wrecked and watching Monty Python. Which was enough really. He'd never met anyone like me before and vice versa, but he was a lovely bright lad and we learned a lot from each other. I was astonished and relieved to find myself surrounded by northerners, communists, women, cockneys, Glaswegians, Asians and black people who weren't royal; I discovered a whole new world and I loved it.

It's quite odd doing a degree in something you know absolutely nothing about, and I had a huge amount of catching up to do on the history of art, but the great joy was that I was doing it because I wanted to, not because I was being forced; it was my idea and mine alone. I discovered that I loved architecture. Maybe this is because I like to make things; I want to see the physical skill in something and wonder 'How did you do that?' I like the idea of 'finding the figure' within a stone carving, as though it was always there and just needs the artist to reveal it. I love the strange importance of proportion, and the mystery of why the Golden Ratio just feels 'right'. I have a sneaking regard for Rachel Whiteread's *House* – filling a terraced house with concrete and then knocking the walls and roof away to display a concrete version of the space inside. And I love buildings because they are like the sea and the sky, they are seen by everyone who passes by; they are the same now as when they were first built and somehow embody the zeitgeist of the period. Buildings are like time travel, especially ruins which, in their decay, seem to express the past so much better than the roped-off furniture and paintings of a National Trust stately home. I've also always wanted to build my own house, from scratch. Now that would be my kind of art!

I found that I wasn't that turned on by paintings. To this day, I'm not a fan of non-figurative and more abstract art. It was pretty clear to me very early on that whatever I was going to end up doing for the rest of my life, it wasn't going to involve dealing with other peoples' art, I wanted to be the one who created stuff. There aren't many jobs for which a degree in History of Art qualifies you anyway – academia was not my world and otherwise working for Christie's, Sotheby's or an art gallery was not a seductive prospect either. Nonetheless, I enjoyed the detective part of finding a painting's provenance and the research required to find how an artist was influenced in his life, and I enjoyed the discussions and gaining a deeper understanding of art. Just being able to bandy about the word 'painterly' made me feel like I was a real undergraduate, able to verbally spar with academics on Radio 4 discussion programmes who can't get through a sentence without saying 'in a sense'. Such are the linguistic shibboleths of learning, worn like badges or secret handshakes of identification, and I enjoyed being accepted into this new club.

However, the theatre at UEA was where I was happiest. On the first day, at the Freshers' Fair, I joined the Drama Society, and that was where all my focus lay for the next three years. We did a play every term and it was really what I lived for. At Harrow, I used to devise and produce end-of-term sketch shows with music, but I only ever did one school play. I'd always been good at accents, voices and mimicry and just wanted to make people laugh. Shakespeare had seemed impenetrable and was performed only by a small coterie of classicists and scholars, and if you weren't part of their circle, you didn't get invited. The UEA Drama Society was more like a rep company, a mongrel assemblage of oddballs who were having loads of fun. This was where I cut my teeth and discovered my strengths and weaknesses.

I discovered drying. I now know that you can walk on stage for the umpteenth performance of a play, get to a line that you have delivered perfectly every night for months and suddenly find yourself enveloped in a dark blanket of memory loss. You experience not just the loss of the line, but everything – who you are, where you are, what the play is, what you had for lunch – nothing remains. The first time it happened to me was on the first night of Joe Orton's *The Ruffian on the Stair* – I just stopped. It instantly shattered my blithe confidence, and to this day drying is one of my worst fears. It can have you shaking in the wings, and, unfortunately, it gets worse with age: Laurence Olivier, as a younger man, once said to Anthony Hopkins, 'Remember, nerves are vanity – you're wondering what people think of you; to hell with them, just jump off the edge.' But in old age he could barely go on, and directed the other actors on stage not to look at him, so terrified was he of drying. Much later, I discovered how to stop this. If your head is in the right place, the lines are only a guide to what the character is thinking, and since you are *being* that character, not just pretending to be him, then it's much harder to forget a line as this would mean also forgetting who you actually *are* and what you believe. That's the theory anyway.

I discovered corpsing. In James Saunders's *A Scent of Flowers* there's a scene where a coffin is lowered into a grave. Just prior to this, the 'corpse' walks, trance-like, past the mourners and into her final resting place – all very symbolic. In our production, as we solemnly lowered the heavy oak coffin, borrowed from a local undertaker, my fellow pallbearer's foot slipped and he dropped his end of the coffin straight on top of the unfortunate corpse. The audience then heard the deceased, played by Belinda Oliver, scream, 'FUCK!' I looked for help to the guilty party, a Scottish bloke with an impish face, which was now streaming with tears. I turned upstage to find that the mourners were no longer gazing sorrowfully, but instead had turned their backs on the audience in a forlorn attempt at concealing their convulsions. When they began to emit a strange, strangulated mewling, the vicar broke down and began to weep openly with laughter. Just when we thought it couldn't get any worse, the injured corpse suddenly arose from her grave and, with the words 'Sorry, but I'm actually bleeding', staggered off the stage. I really don't think I've ever heard an audience laugh so long or so loud.

I also discovered 'The Pint After the Show', which is without doubt the most sublime drink in the world. There's an old actor's tale of a seasoned thespian who offers a young actor a drink before they go on. When the youngster politely refuses, the old boy asks in horror, 'You mean you're going on *alone?*' Drinking before the show is not to be recommended; I've tried it and it doesn't help, but drinking afterwards is pretty much the entire point. Relief, achievement, pride, release, basically not being shit scared any more – all these things go so well with a pint or three. I'm sure there must be actors who don't touch a drop, but personally I've only ever met the ones who have been told to stop by their doctors.

Where did this love of performing come from? Thankfully I have one recording of my mother's voice. On it, I'm aged about twelve and I'm showing her how our new Grundig reel-to-reel tape recorder worked. The banter between us is lovely, we do Pete & Dud voices, and she reels off great swathes of Shakespeare, rueing the fact that at that very minute she is missing seeing Richard Burton playing Dr Faustus in Oxford. My mum adored the theatre and could easily have been an actress, and when my sister Anna went into the business, I was hooked. Strange how it took me three years of not enjoying History of Art to come to the conclusion.

In my second year, I shared a houseboat with another Robinson, Michael. My friendship with Mike began during my very first night at the student bar when I dropped the 10p I was going to feed into the jukebox. Mike picked up the coin and told me I could have it back as long as I played something decent which, of course, was David Bowie. I was a Bowie freak – the first Ziggy Stardust concert that I went to was at the Friars Club in Aylesbury in 1972 and had a profound effect on me: I got both my ears pierced and dyed my hair – my father actually fell over when he first saw me, which, considering what a rebel he'd been, was quite a result. (One of the ear piercings went septic and I ended up wearing a single big gold earring in my right ear for years afterwards. What everyone failed to tell me was it signified that you were gay, which I wasn't, but it explained the friendly looks I used to get on Old Compton Street.) Luckily Mike approved of my choice of song and we've remained friends ever since. The houseboat, which was once owned by George Formby, was moored on the river Bure near Horning. It looked like a railway carriage, with a large room at one end and three bedrooms off a corridor that ran the length of the boat. It had gas heaters and the electricity came from a small Honda generator. The owner was a drummer who worked on cruise ships, and after a thorough briefing in September, he left us to it and went off to the Caribbean for nine months, with no way of getting in touch with him. Within a week, the generator packed up, leaving us to survive on a dangerous system of car batteries and a 12 to 240 volt converter. Dangerous because the boat leaked permanently and was only kept afloat by an electrical bilge pump, so if the batteries ran down, we would sink.

Our days therefore went like this. Wake up in freezing damp room and turn on gas fire. When room warm enough to get out of bed, put on two layers of clothes and make tea on gas hob. Put two batteries in dinghy and row 200 yards upstream to where VW Beetle was parked. Drive to Roy's Garage in Wroxham (everything in Wroxham was owned by Roy) and put the batteries on trickle charge. Drive into uni and go to shower block. Stand under hot shower until thawed out, clean teeth and head off to lectures/seminars/rehearsals/somewhere warm. Head back to Wroxham before garage shuts at five. Collect charged batteries and put in dinghy. Row back to boat and add batteries to four others wired in series connected to said transformer. Get half an hour of telly or four hours of music from 240-volt output, leaving just enough for dim lights and bilge pump to work.

Sometimes I'd persuade a girl who had been attracted by my wellies, thick jumper and tales of my glamorous houseboat life to accept an invitation to share a takeaway on said boat. She'd end up staying the night only because she couldn't really row back and hitchhike in the dark. It's a pity there was a spare room.

I spent hours fixing that boat: re-felting half of the roof, painting it and keeping it afloat. One day, though, I wired the batteries up wrong and the converter exploded. No more telly or music, and when the owner finally returned, bronzed from his cruising, all I got from him was a bollocking for 'screwing up the electrics'.

We soon moved back onto the university campus, but that had its own perils. One term, a whole lot of us went down with hepatitis A from infected food in the refectory. It used to be called 'infectious hepatitis', and while nothing like as serious as hep C, it means that you have to be isolated from everyone, so I wasn't allowed to remain in residence and went to stay with my friend Maggie Wheeler in a cottage at Caistor St Edmund. I had my own plates and cutlery and had to live in solitary confinement. I was treated by a naturopath called Shyam Singha, who put me on a diet of boiled onions, Vichy water and live goat's yoghurt for a week, followed by raw food only for another week. As for alcohol, I was limited to one unit of vodka a day for six months. I recovered quickly – unlike some of my *Archers* colleagues who contracted the same virus when they went to collect their Sony Award for Broadcasting in the late eighties. They pooh-poohed my suggested cure and some have sadly remained weak-livered ever since. Singha was a controversial character, and some said he was a fraud, but the simplicity of the diet, I think, helped to purge out the toxins.

University life was filled with great days and great friends. I devised and performed sketch shows along with Maggie, my close friend and fellow Bowie nut Philip Bird, Arthur Smith, later of BBC comedy fame, the force of nature that is Adam Wide, and other friends. I hung out as a threesome with two girls called Alexandra and Clare, until Clare and I went non-platonic and I moved into her flat above a fish shop.

Work occasionally interrupted my university life. I did my thesis on 'Berlin Cinema Architecture', which meant the university paid for me to spend two weeks in West and East Berlin, researching cinemas, many of which had either been destroyed or heavily damaged during the wartime bombing. Some had been converted to other uses: I wanted to get a photo of an auditorium that was now a porn cinema, but they wouldn't let me, so I paid for a ticket to watch the matinee. I'd never seen porn before – it wasn't exactly hardcore, just bad acting and jiggly breasts – and after a while I walked down to the front, turned around and took a flash photo of the interesting thirties décor. Unfortunately, the small, dirty mac-wearing audience were not best pleased at being caught on film and I was chased out through the fire exit. Great photo though!

I got a 2:2, but I have never used my degree since. I regret that I don't even have a graduation picture, as the university had decided that, instead of wearing flowing black gowns and mortar boards, we should be modern and cool and be attired in ghastly blue and green polyester cloaks and tricorns. I didn't bother to show up.

Foreign Study League

While at UEA, I saw an advert on the 'Jobs Offered' notice board for a company called Foreign Study League (FSL), an offshoot of *Readers' Digest*, that organised European trips for American school kids as part of their study curriculum. They needed people to work in the office and in the field as tour reps. I thought it looked like fun and made a mental note to go along the next day at 5 p.m. when the interviews would take place. I'm not sure how that mental note got deleted, but, at 6.30, I remembered and kicked myself for having forgotten. Then a tiny little thought completely changed my whole life: 'Hmm, maybe I'll just pop down there anyway because, you never know, they might still be interviewing.' So I did, and they were, and I got the job working in tourism for the next three summers. I was based in London and New York, and got to drive minibuses around the States and Canada. As a result, I also met my future wife, bought the house that we still live in, and had two children. And this was all down to one little thought.

When I was at Harrow, we had fold-down beds, which had a tendency to collapse when sat on hard. One day, Noël sat down hard on mine and it landed on my big toe. The doctor told me he would have to remove the nail. He broke the needle of the syringe injecting it with local anaesthetic, so it was fully sensitive when he yanked the nail clean out. I believe it's a fairly well-known form of torture – I still remember the pain. So from that time on I've always had a damaged big toenail that doesn't grow properly and is not a pretty sight. I'm also a great one for not wearing shoes, so when Judy Emerson walked into the FSL office on her first day, she didn't immediately think that she'd one day marry the bloke with the wonky toenail sticking out from under his desk, gold earring and stripy hair.

I, however, instantly fell for the girl with the frizzy perm, kooky smile and come-to-bed eyes. She remained oblivious until I rescued her by bringing the sixty packed lunches she'd forgotten down to her group of students at the port in Dover. We saw them off onto the hovercraft, and laughed at how grateful the poor kids were to have finally got their pretty woeful pre-packed meals, and she started to see beyond my calamitous exterior. Two weeks later we shared my tiny bed in University of London's Goldsmid House on Oxford Street, accompanied by the roar of traffic and the cries of an ice-cream seller from the street below. We were twenty-one. We've been together, through a lot, ever since.

FSL was a great job. It taught me professional organisation – making and checking bookings, finding people and passports, and going to the US Embassy when we couldn't find one or the other. After a while, I was promoted to 'Airport Rep' and I had a security pass at Gatwick Airport. This meant that when a student arrived from the States on a jumbo jet, the first English voice he or she heard was me, standing on a luggage trolley, welcoming them to these shores. On one occasion, a kid who looked like something out of the Waltons, dressed in dungarees with long blond hair and an imaginary straw stuck between his teeth, came up to me after such a speech and said, with a thick Tennessee accent, 'Goddam, y'all speak good English. They teach it to you in the schools over here?'

The following summer, 1976, I worked for the same company, but this time organising European tourists in New York. My boss was the utterly delightful and eccentric Fran Lazar, who very soon came to be a kind of mother figure to me, indeed to everyone who worked there. Small, feisty and funny, she could get anything from anyone, and she taught me a lot about chutzpah. On the flight from London, I remember saying to the person sitting next to me that my idea of New York was that if you left your hotel after dark, you'd be shot, and I did actually see someone get shot within hours of my arrival. Nonetheless, I was incredibly naive. Once, after watching the Independence Day fireworks from Battery Park, I managed to walk my party of tourists deep into the Lower East Side, at that time a dangerous ghetto. A friendly local stopped us and said, 'Man, where you heading?' 'That way,' I replied, pointing ahead. 'No man, y'all turnin' around an' headin' back the way you came. Lord, it's a miracle you got this far.'

Fran's husband Stan Feig used to organise the Schaefer Music Festival in Central Park, and I got to see Cheech and Chong, Kingfish, Donovan and B. B. King, all for free. At the B. B. King concert, I was taking my seat and a big black dude sitting behind me, dripping with gold, in a white suit and fedora hat, said to one of his minions, quite audibly, 'I hate whites at my concerts.' Without hesitating I turned and said, 'No, it's all right man, I'm not white, I'm English.' There was a pause, a long pause, during which my knees slowly turned to jelly, but then he just burst out laughing. By the end of the concert, having partaken of some of his extremely fine weed, we were, as Ving Rhames says in Pulp Fiction, 'cool'. Confidence and naivety can either get you far, or dead.

Death also threatened on a weekend office adventure on a houseboat on Lake Ticonderoga. This was where I learned how to navigate an unseaworthy, square, underpowered small bungalow through a force-seven gale and huge waves. I had to fight my English co-worker for the steering wheel as his belief that you should present the boat sideways on to the waves was putting us in very serious danger of capsizing, and everything not tied down on deck got swept away. Good team bonding exercise, though, and I got very good at boat parking.

The following summer I got one of the best jobs I've ever had, driving for Trek America. I flew from London to Los Angeles and joined a mixed party of English, American, Australian and Japanese tourists for a three-week trip to New York through the southern states, learning the job from the English driver. We were in a thirteen-seater

Dodge minibus loaded with camping gear on the roof, and we went from one campsite to another, driving around 300 miles per day. When I picked up my own group from a hotel in downtown NYC, the mainly Antipodean party were less than impressed at having a Pom drive them, and the fact that we were now driving the northern route meant I'd never been to any of the places we were visiting on the way. The convention that they took it in turns to put my tent up at the end of the day wasn't accepted as cheerily as it had been on my training run, and the fact that I'd forgotten to bring my driving licence from the UK meant that I had to be extremely careful not to get stopped by anyone in uniform.

I managed to convince the party that a 150-mile detour to Wounded Knee was a good idea, solely on the basis that I'd heard of the book *Bury My Heart at Wounded Knee* and thought it sounded impossibly romantic. Great name, crap place. In 1977, there was absolutely nothing there. One shack. Closed. On the other hand, driving through the night to witness sunrise at the Painted Desert was worth every minute. It is the most extraordinary place, with a sort of pre-historic beauty. I was the only one awake. I parked the van. 'Hey guys, wake up and check this out!' A few disgruntled raised heads. Roo slurred, 'Oh yeah?' Then silence. Then more sleep.

As we crossed over the Golden Gate Bridge, what should come on the radio? Scott McKenzie singing 'San Francisco', reminding me of my pa and the melted 45 in the portable record player. Saying goodbye to the group before picking up my next lot for the return journey, I finally admitted that I'd never done the trip before. 'Strewth,' said Roo, 'I'd never have known. You ought to be an actor.'

Meanwhile, for the second time in his life, my father had decided to again up sticks and drastically change his life. The first time – taking the family to Tasmania – had been for fear of a nuclear war. This time, he foresaw a world famine, which only the self-sufficient would survive. So he sold the house in Potten End, my stepmother Jenny sold her flat in London, and they bought a ten-acre smallholding in Devon and headed off west to live 'The Good Life'. This time, I was involved with the house-hunting, and an extraordinary set of requirements needed to be fulfilled. Firstly, it had to have a fast-flowing stream so that he could use the water to generate electricity. It needed enough land to be able to produce food and to farm sheep, turkeys, pigs, a house cow, chickens and ducks. Finally, and most disturbingly, it needed a 'killing ground' to defend the place from the marauding gangs that would be coming for us once the Great Famine had begun. I'll never forget the look on the estate agent's face when he overheard my father approving the view from an upstairs bedroom as 'a perfect spot for the Bren gun'.

It was to be an organic farm, this in the days before organic became fashionable and farming without pesticides was a forgotten art. We went to the Centre for Alternative Technology in Wales to find out about wind turbines, solar panels and the rest, and Pa read countless books on sustainable lifestyles and joined the Soil Association. Finding a hilltop fortress with running water proved impossible so they settled on a beautiful Devon cob and thatch long-house called Wigham that nestled on the side of a hill just outside the village of Morchard Bishop. It had been run as a dog kennels and in the year after university and in our holidays from drama school Judy and I stayed there to help them turn it into an organic smallholding. We tilled the fields with a two-furrow plough and harrow pulled by a lovely old grey petrol Ferguson tractor. We hand-milked 'Easy', the beautiful Jersey cow, and made butter and clotted cream. Pa harvested the wheat with a scythe and piled up stooks, which we threshed by hand. We built pigsties and bought in Tamworths that had piglets the same colour as the Labrador, 'Chumleigh', who as a result got confused and thought that he was a pig too. We raised, sheared, weighed, dagged and ate lambs; kept hens for their eggs; and I learned how to wring a chicken's neck (it's much harder than it looks). Judy too learned skills she still uses today.

In order to make some money, Pa and Jenny ran the place as a guesthouse. It became enormously popular because all the food was home-produced and my stepmother was a wonderful cook. However, they never turned it into a successful business because they didn't charge enough, and my father slowly turned into a Fawlty-esque host, hating having to play the part of fawning waiter after spending the day where he was happiest – out in the fields, working.

Happy memories, driving the short-wheelbase Land Rover to the abattoir with a pig in the trailer, and coming back with supper; trudging through drifts with our cat in a basket strapped to my back when the house had been completely cut off by snow, getting to the small station just in time for the only train that day, clambering aboard feeling like Scott of the Antarctic, observed with disdain by commuters in their shirt-sleeves; nailing down lethal corrugated iron sheets in a gale that was threatening to blow the whole roof off; plucking ducks until our thumbs were raw; coming down to breakfast wearing a crash helmet to stop getting brain damage from constantly hitting my head on the low beams and doorways; building a bedroom above the workshop with a trapdoor entrance; table tennis in the barn; then down to the pub in the evening with local tales, roaring fires and strong Devon ale. Proper job.

So much of that experience is still in my imagination today in *The Archers* recording studio, where the straw is tape, the cow is a sound effect, and the physical work is done for me by someone else. It helps if you can see the reality. It's like mime on stage – if you can see the brick wall in front of you, then so can the audience, but if you just pretend you can see it, they can't.

In the summer of 1976, Judy and I went on holiday to Morocco. We took the coach to northern Spain, then hitchhiked down to Algeciras, took the ferry to Ceuta, then a local bus into Tétouan. Stepping out of the bus was like travelling back in time and gave an arresting meaning to the term 'culture shock'. It was the first time either of us

61

had been outside a Christian country and the noise, clothes, smells and people were like nothing we had ever known. We were immediately royally ripped off and got serious food poisoning, which made the continuing bus journey to the Rif mountains a formidable exercise in the control of bodily functions. It was hardly surprising that western tourists were seen as easy game, but as we headed south we experienced nothing but friendliness and generosity, the poorest people sharing their bread and soup with us to break Ramadan, and in the mountains, cool air, water fountains and delicious food in hotels that felt like private homes being shared with honoured guests.

Back in Tétouan, our stomachs hardened to the local fare, we met an Australian guy (I'll call him Jeff) who had a plan to buy a Mercedes in Germany, drive it down to Persia and sell it for twice the price. Not having a licence, he needed a driver, and Muggins here, always on for an adventure, volunteered. I gave him my father's address and forgot all about him until a few weeks later when he turned up on the doorstep of the farm in Devon. Pa took an instant dislike to him and put him to work in the fields, which was not Jeff's thing at all. When I announced that I was going to drive this workshy ruby smuggler (as I found out later) from Frankfurt to Tehran, father and son had a flaming row. He accused me of being impetuous and reckless; I replied that I was simply following in his footsteps and a man who had absconded from Sandhurst, stowed away on a ship to America, ridden rough on the railroad to California and become a cowboy, then fought in a war, was not in a position to lecture me on putting myself in the way of danger. It wasn't until I became a father myself that I realised where he was coming from.

The trip didn't start well. We bought the Merc, rather the worse for wear, at night, from a very dodgy dealer for a suspiciously low price. In the cold light of day, we noticed the bad paint job covering up the rust. At the same time, the Iranian revolution was happening and even if we'd got to Tehran in once piece and sold the rust-bucket, we'd never have got the money out of the country, so Jeff announced we were going back to Morocco, which was *not* what I'd signed up for. I don't know where I get it from, but to this day I have a natural affinity for the underdog and a lack of ruthlessness. I would never have made a businessman and the family motto of fearing dishonour has given me an aversion for dishonesty and also for behaving like a dick. So I said yes, and off to North Africa we went.

Through Germany, France and Spain and once again on the ferry to Ceuta: two young men in a Mercedes with no baggage. At customs, they went through us with a fine-tooth comb. Jeff told me to give them a false address. This was getting worrying. In Tétouan we were flagged down by one man after another. 'You sell car?' Then tea, hashish, haggling and an offer of money just below what we had bought it for – because of the rust. This went on for two days until Jeff announced, 'Sod it, we're going to Iran.' I wasn't, I'd had enough and he was becoming a bit of a pain anyway. I said I'd drive him to the airport at Malaga where he would buy me the flight home and find some other willing dupe to take him on from there.

Coming back, the Spanish customs saw these two stoned idiots in their rusty Merc who had been in Morocco for forty-eight hours and quite literally took the car to pieces. We spent the best part of a day in a garage as they went through every square inch of panelling, upholstery, tyres, linings – they wrecked the car but finally, and very reluctantly, were forced to let us go. Sitting relieved on the terrace of a beachside café in Algeciras, Jeff casually reached into his nether regions and pulled out a small lump of hash. 'Christ, I need this,' he remarked casually as he skinned up. I nearly killed him.

Bristol Old Vic Theatre School

In the seventies there were things called 'grants'. Unheard of today, it meant that anyone could have free university tuition. The Tories stopped all that in 1989 so my two sons are now saddled with debt. Thanks, Maggie. There were still two hurdles for me to cross to get to a good drama school. One was the audition for the Bristol Old Vic Theatre School, the next was one for the London County Council, which meant that not only did I have to convince my future tutors that I was any good, but also a bewildered bank of civil servants, whose qualifications for judging budding thesps were iffy to say the least.

Having been accepted by Bristol I thought this would be a breeze. I boldly went into my Shakespeare piece, amazed them with my broad cockney modern piece, and fooled them into thinking I could sing with vast amounts of energy and sleight of throat. They were not impressed. Their leader then said, 'Hmm. And have you any other strings to your bow?' When I told them I had an HGV Class 2 lorry-driving licence, they all started nodding with approval and I got the grant.

This was another occasion on which to thank my father. I'd been signing on for a bit and was getting very bored from occasional jobs stacking shelves, door-to-door selling and farm labouring, so he lent me the money to do a truck-driving course. By registering with somewhere like Manpower you could get work daily, and drive different trucks to different places and never get into trouble if you had any kind of 'incident'. I've had three of these: turning a truck round in a petrol station in Wales and wiping out all the fluorescent lamps in the canopy; jettisoning an entire load of yeast on the M4; and destroying a parked car by misjudging the truck's width in Clifton. Despite these slight errors, I improved and paid my father back from my first month's earnings.

It was odd being a posh-boy trucker. One time I was sent as the agency driver to a scaffolding firm. I was taken into the yard and shown how to lay the back part of a flatbed truck laden with scaffolding onto the ground. A complex procedure featuring hydraulics and cables. My lesson lasted about ten minutes and I was then sent off on my first delivery. The address was a leafy suburb outside Clevedon and I had to lay the bed on a narrow road outside the house. In order to leave enough room for cars to get by, part of the bed landed on the verge, and some flowers got crushed. Jubilant that I'd actually managed to get the load off the truck, I was then assailed by the furious owner for having destroyed her flowerbed. It was revealing to find how a rude, arrogant, upper-middle-class harridan could be silenced by being out-poshed. She simply couldn't believe what she was hearing.

In my first year at Bristol, I shared a flat with Judy, a Welshman called Russell Roberts, a tall god-fearing Australian called Kim Wright, and a lanky, athletic, good-looking lad called Daniel Day-Lewis. Whatever happened to him?

The funny thing about drama school is that people who were just your mates – with their insecurities and weaknesses laid bare for you to see – can turn into international movie stars just a few years later. Dan's career has been exceptional, but quite a few of us have done all right – Greta Scacchi, Miranda Richardson, Amanda Redman, Nicholas Farrell, Jenny Seagrove and others. The *not* funny thing is the large majority who didn't. Some have continued to work without becoming well known but the majority have given acting up and done something sensible instead.

The training was wonderful. I remember thinking at the time that everyone should do this course, actor or not. Singing, dancing, voice production, acting, reading and understanding plays, losing the fear and the self-consciousness, all of these things leading to the tantalisingly exciting idea that, if we worked hard, but above all if we got really lucky, one day fools, idiots, suckers and mad people would actually pay us, sometimes a LOT of money, just to play Cowboys and Indians for the rest of our lives.

The scary thing is how much of it is down to luck. I'm not saying that the people who have become successful aren't hard-working and talented, it's just that at Bristol, for those two years, no one could have predicted which ones would make it. In the final shows, no one really stood out as different from the rest, even Daniel. His first professional role was as a walk-on in some little-known Restoration play at the Bristol Old Vic, where his only line was, 'The carriage awaits, m'lady.' Being Dan, he probably went over and over the role, working out who this messenger was, his back-story, his motivation for saying the line, what kind of carriage it was, the colour, how many horses, whether it was nearly ready, just coming round the corner, or if it had been waiting there for hours and the horses getting hungry, and the postilions impatient and bitching. So armed, on press night he strode on stage and, with all the bravura confidence of a future three-times Oscar winner, intoned, 'The lady awaits, m'carriage.'

In Bristol, hands roughened by hard farm work, I was loving learning how to be an actor. The theatre school has consistently produced good ones, and there's a reason for that: his name was Rudi Shelly. This tiny, ancient, bustling, waspish martinet, an Austrian Jew who had escaped the Nazis, with the body of a dancer, dressed in a

67

Norfolk jacket, used to drive us to tears of bore-dom, but every one of us has found that he was right about pretty much everything. Underneath the carapace of tetchiness, he had a heart of gold. He had little adages that summed up whole classes or even terms, including the most funda-mental one: 'Acting is the art of reacting.' Mean-ing you only do anything as a result of a reaction – to what someone says, to what they do, to what you think, to circumstances – and that requires you to *listen*.

Then there was the wonderful 'Watch out, actor about!' and 'Ducky, your technique is showing!' What every actor strives for is to make it appear that we're not acting at all. Very few achieve it. Dan Day-Lewis is one of them. Bastard!

In my final show at Bristol I played 'Master Hammon' in *The Shoemaker's Holiday* by Thomas Dekker. He opens the second half with a soliloquy and the school's principal, Nat Brenner, told me that this was the funniest scene in the play. I simply couldn't see it, but Nat took me through it line by line, using all the techniques that we'd been taught: where to pause, why, and finding out from the text alone what the playwright intended in terms of subtext, innuendo and double en-tendre. I still had little confidence that Nat was right, but sure enough, on opening night, I had the audience eating out of my hand, a laugh at every line, like doing stand-up comedy. It was so exciting. I was sharing a dressing room with dear friend David Heap, who had been listening on the tannoy. When I came back into the room he smiled and said, 'And just think, they're going to pay us to do this!'

After that, armed with numerous O levels, three A levels, a degree in the History of Art, two years at drama school and a radio competition prize, at the age of twenty-six I ventured forth for an actor's life. What the hell was I thinking?

BBC Radio Repertory Company

Being in the right place at the right time is horribly important. I've starred in sitcoms that sank without trace, dramas that no one watched and costume dramas that didn't quite catch the public's attention. The huge successes I've worked on, like *The Thick of It* and *Twenty Twelve*, have been in minor roles, so I've never built a starring reputation. I wanted to be a movie star, of course, but haven't quite stood out enough in the movies I've done so far. Maybe my 'Witness' in *Fantastic Beasts and Where to Find Them* will unlock the Hollywood door! I did get lucky twice, though, and that has been enough to keep me in work all this time.

The first bit of luck was winning the BBC Carleton Hobbs Bursary Award while I was at Bristol. This is a competition open to final-year drama-school students and one male and one female winner are offered a six-month contract with the BBC Radio Repertory Company, which in those days gave you an automatic Equity card – gold dust then, though not such a necessity today.

My sister Anna was the first of our family to take up the profession, and her advice to me about how to go about the audition was invaluable – she told me they were after versatility, so I tried to make my two pieces sound as though they came from two entirely different actors. I did a speech from Barrie Keefe's *Gotcha* about an angry young man sitting astride a motorbike with a lit cigarette held above the cap-less petrol tank. 'Wot about people 'oo don't do A levels? Wot about ME? EH?!' I then went straight into a very gentle, reflective RP Shakespeare soliloquy. I remember them sounding very different, so I thank/blame my darling sister for that advice, depending on however much/little work I'm getting at the time.

The bursary led to doing voiceovers and the whole world of voice acting, and thence to the second bit of luck, being asked to audition for *The Archers*. I have one man to thank for that luck and his name is Anthony Hyde.

He was the actual winner of the radio bursary competition and I came second, but he turned it down, presumably because he didn't want to sign up for six months with the BBC Radio Repertory Company, so they offered it to me. I've met him once since, when we were in an episode of *Sharpe* with Sean Bean, filming in the Crimea. I thanked him then – I'm not sure how he took it. He's since given up acting. He could have been David Archer.

The first radio play I did was *Westward Ho!* by Charles Kingsley in 1979. It was recorded in the wonderful Christchurch Studios in Bristol. I was playing a short fat boy with a squeaky voice –

about as different from me as you could get. That's just one of the many different things about radio acting: you don't have to look the part. Over the years, so many people have told me I don't look like David Archer and of course it's true: if there are five million listeners, then there are five million David Archers living in their imaginations – and none of them look like me.

It is said that on radio you have to be able to 'raise one eyebrow with your voice' – as there are no visual clues, you need to suggest movement, facial expression and feelings with voice and sound effects only. When I first started radio acting, I was all for doing it in a very naturalistic way, which is fine if the listener is wearing headphones or sitting in a quiet room and listening on DAB, but if someone is bowling down the motorway with the window open and listening on a tinny radio on medium wave, you won't be heard, so it has to be a cross between the two. Naturalistic, but not completely realistic.

Christchurch has wonderfully different acoustics. Because it used to be a church, the main studio room is vast and echoey. Then there are smaller rooms for intimate-sounding spaces, and a state-of-the-art 'dead room', where all outside scenes are recorded because it is acoustically 'dead' and there's no reverberation, no matter how loudly you shout.

There, I learned about the three-dimensionality of radio drama. In those days we still recorded in mono, but there was close to the microphone and far away, there was up and down too. I also learned to engage with props – one of the first things I ever had to do was chop logs while speaking, timing my grunt of effort with the spot-effects person whacking an axe into a wooden block. It's one of the most important things and so often done wrong. I hate it when I hear an actor saying his lines, with the sound of the activity he's involved in going on in a seemingly totally detached space – especially if that actor is me!

Performing at Broadcasting House in London was so exciting. My father took me around as though it were his alma mater – he'd been a talks producer there before going into advertising, and worked with Jack de Manio and others on the *Today* programme. I felt a tradition being passed on and still feel ridiculously attached to 'Auntie' all these years later. There were no security passes or gates in those days, just a doorman who either knew you or didn't, and if he didn't, you didn't get in. There was the famous canteen up on the top floor – dreadful food but cheap and filling and always full of famous names and faces, and Miriam Margolyes telling dirty jokes.

I did a vast array of work with the Radio Rep, ranging from *Vanity Fair* and *Moby Dick* to *Brighton Rock* and contemporary plays. I could be playing a lead in one play and then fourth policeman from the left in the next. I worked with many well-known actors and would watch and listen to their performances, learning all the while. As has been said, you can always tell a radio actor because he reads the newspaper silently. Different actors have varied ways of turning the pages of the script in silence. It's a terrible give-away if an actor is nervous because the pages will rattle uncontrollably and they might suffer the ignominy of being asked to put the script on a music stand and separate the pages. This should be done only as a last resort, because holding the script gives you the freedom to walk around, use your body and give a more dynamic performance. The trick is to try to keep the page taut as you turn it – loose paper is what makes the noise.

I once found myself in the actors' green room with Norman Shelley. Now there was a familiar name; a part of my childhood was being serenaded by his renditions of *The Hums of Pooh* on World Record Club 45 discs. When I asked him if he was indeed the same Norman Shelley, he replied, 'Oh dear me yes, in fact A.A. said that I was the *definitive* Pooh. Let me tell you about it...' at which point about eight actors suddenly got up as they all immediately had Sudden and Important Things To Do Elsewhere. Norman was known for going on, and on, and this young actor was fresh meat!

The recording studios were in the basement, and the tube trains on the Bakerloo line beneath shook the building. Quiet scenes had to be recorded between train departures and period pieces couldn't get away with too many distant rumblings of thunder, or earth tremors. The old iconic BBC ribbon microphones weren't as sensitive as modern stereo ones, though, so you could get away with a certain amount of outside noise, and they also gave a wonderfully rich, analogue feel to recordings, which is rather lost today. The other great advantage to recording in mono was that the actors could face each other across the mike, which gives greater eye contact. The downside, of course, was that you never got to kiss your leading lady, having to employ the old back-of-the-hand trick instead!

So much has changed. Firstly, the production team was almost exclusively male, from director to spot effects – the only women, apart from actresses, were secretaries. The directors also had a tendency to be hugely intolerant and often downright rude. Lateness was inexcusable, fluffing was a capital offence, and smoking almost compulsory. The older actors would be formally dressed in suit and tie, and the place was run with an almost military strictness. In the early days of radio, plays were recorded in one go straight onto disc, so that if you fluffed a line at the end of a half-hour recording, you all had to go back and record it again. This, combined with the poor quality of the broadcast, led to that familiar old style of 'Mr Cholmondeley-Warner' acting that now seems over-enunciated and artificial. By the time I started doing radio plays in the seventies, of course, recording was on tape, but it was still a palaver to edit – there aren't many engineers left now who remember the days of chalk pencil and razor blade. There was much more a feeling of doing it like a stage performance then, as though it were live, and to carry on through any slips or disasters regardless. Today, we just stop and go back to the beginning of the phrase, and the edit is usually done by the engineer there and then. Not nerve-wracking at all – unless you're doing just one day on *The Archers*.

Homebuilding

During this time, we stayed living in Bristol because Judy was the wardrobe mistress of the Theatre School. When she'd come down to live with me, she'd got a job as wardrobe assistant, but when the head of department left she was promoted, so at least one of us had a proper job. I was driving trucks and doing the occasional radio play and fringe theatre in Bath before I went up to London for the six months with the Radio Rep, staying at my sister Anna's house in Tufnell Park.

We once had a 'Terrorist Party' at our basement flat in Clifton. I realise how tasteless that sounds these days, but then the connotations weren't quite so bad as they are now. When Adam Wide, an old friend from UEA, arrived, he kicked down the door and sprayed the room with toy machine-gun fire, to the shock of the elderly couple next door whose flat he had mistaken for ours. Dan Day-Lewis knocked on the door, and when I opened it to find him dressed quite casually, he rubbed his knuckles up and down on the brickwork until they were bleeding. 'This all right?' he asked, and sauntered in.

My friend Peter Ackerman turned up driving his BMW motorbike sidecar, with Nick Farrell tied up and blindfolded in the passenger side. Pete added to the effect by being tied up and blindfolded himself. He was without doubt the funniest actor of our year at Bristol, but tragically died of a brain tumour not long after we all left – the comedy award at the Theatre School is named in memory of him.

I've always been one for a scheme. I'm not a businessman, and I don't have the interest or the killer instinct that seems to be required to be a successful one, but I've always tried to come up with ways of making money on the side. I'm sixty-three now and I haven't managed it yet. My brainwave at that time was buying Type 2 Jaguars and exporting them to California. Apart from anything else, it would involve driving Jags, which was almost enough in itself. Meanwhile, Judy had a better idea. She'd worked out that buying a house on the other side of Bristol would be a cheaper mortgage than the rent we were paying in Clifton, so she went to her parents to ask if they could lend her something towards the deposit. They were not wealthy people; Jack was an engineer who had lost three fingers in an industrial accident, and worked for Russell Hobbs where, among other things, he was involved with the design of their classic electric kettle. Did they think it was a good idea? she asked. They said yes, but are you going to get married? No, Judy replied. Consequently they agreed to give her the £1000 they had raised over many years to pay for her wedding.

Hence, the rather shoestring wedding we did subsequently have. But we were on the property ladder. The lovely three-bedroom terraced house in Stevens Crescent, Totterdown, cost a princely £8000.

I hate the term DIY as it sounds like something someone does in their spare time as a kind of hobby. My DIY has always been on fairly major works that I have undertaken myself, firstly, because I could never afford to get anyone else to do it, and secondly, because when I could, I'd find that they'd done a bad job and I'd have to redo it all myself. I've taken on rewiring whole houses from scratch, knocking down walls and fitting steel beams, plumbing, plastering, joinery, painting, hanging wallpaper, laying concrete floors and building kitchens out of brick and oak. I love it. One of the best feelings in the world is sitting at the end of the day with a beer in hand, bruised and aching from hard work, covered in dirt and rain, surveying what you've just created. I'd already been doing this for years for other people, and here was a house of our own – like a new toy!

That mistrust of others doing the work pretty much started there, with an Irish builder. Don't get me wrong, I've got nothing against Irish builders; in fact the best plasterer I've ever known was a fella from Cork called Billy Curtin, who was great company, good value and a real craftsman. This guy though was letting the side down. In Bristol, I was knocking through the two downstairs rooms so I jacked the ceilings up with Acro props, knocked down the brick wall and had everything ready for the builder to fit the steel joist, which essentially would take the weight of the whole house. He turned up with a wooden beam. Dismissing my worries with a cheery wave and a cloud of dope smoke, he explained knowingly that the wall above was tied into the side walls. 'Think of it like Lego,' he assured me. I very dubiously accepted and he put in the wooden joist. After the concrete under the supports had set, I gingerly let down the props, and the beam seemed to be holding. We went to sleep that night, our bed directly above the beam. In the morning, I saw to my horror that the floorboards in the bedroom now had a two-inch gap to the skirting board. I raced down the stairs and saw that the whole beam had a massive bow in it. I then did something that I really don't recommend: I jacked our whole house back up again. The Irish may pride themselves on their flowery use of the old Anglo-Saxon, but someone once described David Archer as 'having a good shout on him', and that comes from me. By the end of the day, we had a rolled steel joist in place, and the house is still standing today.

During the building, Judy saw that the Methodist church at the bottom of the road was being gutted prior to demolition. She asked if we could have any of the beautiful wood panelling that was lying on the pavement. 'The skip's coming in an hour,' said the builder. 'Whatever you can take before then is yours.' We helped ourselves to enough wood to panel both the downstairs rooms and build two alcove cupboards and shelves. Scrap yards and reclamation sites were, and really still are, some of my favourite places.

Meanwhile ... I was in a movie! *North Sea Hijack* with Roger Moore as 'Rufus Excalibur ffolkes', a maverick marine counterterrorism consultant who loves cats and hates women. I'd landed the part of Harris, ffolkes's right-hand man. Roger wasn't behaving like Bond. He had a thick beard to prove it and was quite wonderfully Roger Moore-ish, just as you'd hope he'd be, very funny, kind, easy-going, and totally in charge.

For the audition, I had been summoned to the Park Lane Hotel to meet Hollywood movie director Andrew V. McLaglen, son of the actor Victor McLaglen, and casting director Allan Foenander.

McLaglen was standing. He was six foot seven. I stood before him, six foot three. I felt like a child.

'Tell me something, kid, can you do a Scotch accent?'

I hadn't been told the character was Scottish.

'Mm, yes, I've spent a lot of Christmases in Scotland actually and … I mean … och right, aye, whellll, yeeees, I've Scoottish blud actually [which is true but a long way back], so that's no' a prooblem.' Blagging it here...

'Can you swim?'

Also not forewarned but, hey, result...

'Yes, I'm a good swimmer, I was captain of swimming at school...'

He walked towards me until his chin was an inch from my nose. Then he put his feet heavily on my shoes.

To this day I have no idea why he did that. A power thing? To see how I'd react? A fetish of some sort?

So I stared him out, what else could I do? Laugh? Nut him?

He stepped back, and then he said, 'Kid, I think

79

you just got yourself a part.'

Those were the very words; they are burned upon my soul.

We filmed in Galway. I'd never been to Ireland before. It was a bit of a dream; I'd just come out of drama school and I was in a Hollywood film, not only with bloody James Bond, but also Anthony Perkins and James Mason for heaven's sake! This was it, I was a movie actor. It could only go stratospheric from here. I was the trusty lieutenant, promotion awaited, Tinseltown watch out!

As it turned out, that was almost it, Hollywood-wise. But it was great fun while it lasted.

Every time the film is on telly in the afternoon, which is about once a month, I rue the fact that it was a buy-out. The fit young man in the film hasn't the faintest idea what he's doing, is by no stretch of the imagination a hard military man, has never commanded troops in his life, and is running around a ship and scuba diving in the open sea and Galway harbour, completely over-whelmed and totally bowled over at being surrounded by some of the hardest, most experi-enced stuntmen in the business. He is also having the most fantastic craic with the crew every even-ing in the bars of Galway, glugging water after a dive and finding it was potcheen, and being paid more money in cash per diems (as the daily allowances for expenses are known) than he had ever earned as wages before in his life. We spent one night at sea and I found myself in a mess room with Roger Moore, Anthony Perkins and James Mason, and we were all telling gags, and

these movie stars were laughing at my schoolboy
jokes! Roger was a wonderful raconteur, and
filthy with it. One joke he told ended with him
swatting a fly on the wall, but his hand was bandaged from a bad and painful cut. BANG!
'FUUUUUUUCKING SHIIIIIT!'

Said James Bond.

I was in heaven.

We had to climb on board the ship using ropes
from grappling irons that had been thrown up, so
we rehearsed in the woods with two ropes hanging from a wide branch, tied there by Roger's
personal stuntman, Martin Grace. Everyone else
had a go but no one could do it. 'Never mind',
said Greg Powell, son of the famous stuntman
Nosher, 'we'll climb up the fucking anchor chain.'
Then someone said, 'Oi, better let Tim have a go,
eh? Come all this way, Tim, wanna go?' with the
clear meaning of 'Yeah, come on then, posh boy,
show us what you can do.'

Well it's difficult in those situations when you
know you can do something, and one thing I
could do after about ten years of enforced school
gymnastics was shin up a couple of ropes; it was
like walking. So, should I do that, and show them
up in their eyes, or fail and be one of the gang? I
shinned straight up the ropes and sat astride the
bough. What the hell.

I got on a lot better with the stuntmen after
that, and then I pulled one of the guys back from
out in the bay one filming afternoon when he'd
got breathless and inflated his life jacket. I used
the old life-saving technique, and that was when
I drank the potcheen afterwards. I choked, but

81

from then on it was delicious.

There was a night scene where we scuba divers had to surface near a large ship in Galway harbour and begin to climb up the anchor chain. We were all kitted up. I was with a group of three other frogmen. Before take one, the word went out, 'Remember, fuck up the first two takes.'

Take one, someone comes up too early, 'Nooo!' from the loud hailer. 'On action, you descend, count to ten, then surface.'

The water was almost opaque with harbour pollution. I had encountered a very large turd on the surface and later developed a severe ear infection. 'Take two, and, action!'

Go down five feet. Wait. Come up looking menacing ... start to swim purposefully towards the ship...

'Cut!' Now what? 'One of you is swimming the wrong fucking way!'

Not me, thank God. Take three.

In the bag. Nailed it. Moving on.

It turned out that the stunt team were on £100 *per take!* And I found out later they'd made sure that I was paid, too. It was really nice to feel a little bit accepted by such a bunch of seriously hard nuts.

At the end of the shoot, I was invited to apply to be a stuntman and asked to the annual Stuntmen's Ball at Pinewood. After seeing that half of them there were bandaged and quite a few were in wheelchairs, I settled for the pansy-actor option. I was tempted, though.

Spliced

Judy and I were married on 8 September 1979 at Marylebone Register Office in London. It was a very low-key affair with parents only at the ceremony, which unintentionally upset my sisters. Also, the very informal invitation, 'Tim and Judy are getting married', was sneered at by some. The small party of family and close friends afterwards is recorded by a single photo, since our official photographer, old chum Bill Butt, was going out with Greta Scacchi at the time and he used up most of the film stock on her. It didn't matter, it was the best day of our lives.

Best man Jamie Borthwick provided his flat for the do, and then – a huge surprise – the bridal suite at the Ritz for the wedding night. When I came to return the compliment a few years later, I thought it would be funny to put up my Etonian pal and his beautiful bride Peng at the best hotel in Harrow – which sadly turned out to be a flea-infested dump and unsurprisingly closed down soon after.

We honeymooned in Spain, where the rain happened not to be staying mainly on the plain but directly overhead. Such was my frustration after four days of torrential downpour that I strode into the local police station and demanded to know when the bloody sun was going to appear. I think I had gone very slightly bonkers at that point.

I do worry sometimes when couples have weddings that cost the earth and take months to plan. Absolutely everything has to happen without a hitch, and the pressure for the relationship to succeed because of the amount invested in it can become intolerable. Our thinking at the time was that we'd publicly tell our nearest and dearest that we loved each other and were making it official, and then we'd see how it went. Two children and thirty-seven years later, it's just got better and better, so in our case at least that lack of pressure worked fine.

Tales of the Unexpected

For my first telly part, I got to drive a Rolls – *and* I had a bedroom scene.

For an episode of *Tales of the Unexpected*, I played 'Meech', Joss Ackland's chauffeur who is having an affair with the wife of 'Stinker Tinker', played by the incomparable Denholm Elliot. 'Stinker' was his character's nickname at school, where the Ackland character had bullied him remorselessly. The Rolls was a nightmare to drive as it was a chauffeur's vehicle with an almost solid bench seat; Joss, poor man, was beset by personal tragedies and hardly spoke; Denholm was just intent on getting almost anyone to sleep with him, including me; and I spent a lot of time in bed with Patricia Quinn. This led to a great moment many years later, when filming *By the Sword Divided*, when I asked the unshockable Robert Stephens who was the wife 'Pat' he kept referring to.

'Pat Quinn,' he replied.

'Oh,' I piped up. 'I've been to bed with her.' Cue look of brutal antagonism from the wild Sir Robert. 'On screen, old boy, on screen,' I hurriedly explained. Much relief all round. He once drew blood from me in a swordfight and I wouldn't have liked to have crossed him for real.

Being David Archer: The audition

My agent rang.

'Do you want to be in *The Archers?*'

'I've never heard it, what's it like?'

'It's about farming.'

'I know a bit about farming.'

'Not required, it's a radio soap. Wanna go for it or not?'

'Where's the casting?'

'Birmingham.'

'Why Birmingham?'

'That's where they record it.'

'Oh blimey. All right, then.'

We were what you might call a 'dum-di-dum-di-click' family – the moment my mother heard *The Archers* theme tune she turned off the radio, so I had never heard an episode of the pro- gramme before I auditioned for it.

At the BBC studios at Pebble Mill in Birming- ham. I met a charming man called Peter Windows, one of the producers, and a more enigmatic one, William Smethurst, the editor. The scene I was reading for the audition was a dialogue between David and Eddie Grundy. Trevor Harrison (Eddie) couldn't make it that day so I was asked to play both parts.

'Okay,' I said, 'what does Eddie Grundy sound like?'

A pause.

'Have you ever heard the programme?'

Gulp.

'Oh yeah, lots of times but I sometimes get confused which character's which ... you know...'

'Sure,' said Peter. 'Well, it's not an impersonation. For this just do all-purpose rural, you know, put a lot of arrs into it.'

Well, I honestly thought he said, 'Put a lot of *arse* into it', so I made Eddie rural and a bit bolshie, and by complete chance landed on a pretty close impression of Trevor's brilliant and inimitable Eddie. I hardly even thought about the voice for David, so I guess he must have sounded a lot like me, which in many ways he still does!

So, I got the part. I started recording almost immediately. By this time, I'd been a pirate for quite some time on screen and on stage, so my first appearance in *The Archers* green room was met by some raised eyebrows from the long-serving cast. I had long hair, my mouse-brown locks highlighted with great streaks of peroxide, I wore a thick gold earring in my right ear, and had a habit of wearing a bum bag and leg warmers with pale blue Levi's and a faux-leather jacket. Pretty normal for the 1980s but Ambridge wasn't used to it.

Paddy Greene, who has played my mother Jill

all these years, said I had the girls all aflutter, but all I remember is the terror of my first episode. Although I'd been doing radio for a while by then, a stray comment from a friend had got me into a bit of a state. She had told me that she – and all of her friends – listened to *The Archers* omnibus in the bath on Sundays (although presumably not the same bath). I combined this with another piece of information: that there were five million *Archers* listeners. So even if half the women were bone dry, that still made 1.25 million wet, naked women listening to my first words as David Archer, transmitted on 12 August 1982.

'Evening all.'

Shaking script? Thank God I didn't have to turn a page.

1982

Having met Judy and entered the world of radio drama, almost all the other major things that determined what my future was to hold occurred in 1982. I had been in *The Pirates of Penzance* movie, and was now ensconced in the Theatre Royal Drury Lane, giving my nightly pirate; I was still doing a lot of radio and voiceovers and I got the part in *The Archers* – and then we bought a house in London.

In *The Diary of a Nobody* by George and Weedon Grossmith, Mr Pooter's house is a semi-detached villa 'in a crescent in Holloway with the garden leading down to the railway line'. Well, that's our house. Nearly. The ones next to the railway are further round the crescent, but we have the iconic foot scraper, and I painted the bath red as an homage. When my sister Anna had got married and left home in the sixties, she'd settled in Islington, and so all my experiences of the capital had been in the north. South London is about as familiar and friendly a place as Beirut on a bad day, and I know the Southies feel the same about us. So, when we were house-hunting, we focused on the north, although Islington itself was too expensive, so it was Stoke Newington, Holloway, Hackney or Crouch End for us – basically anywhere with a prison near it.

Having sold the house in Bristol for nearly twice the amount we'd bought it for, the most we could afford was £28,000. We saw a photograph in the estate agent's window for a house in Holloway that looked lovely. It had a sitting tenant on a peppercorn rent, which meant it was cheaper, but £32,000 was too much. However, we toddled along to look, and just fell in love with it. Built in 1852, it had a large garden, two wonderful picture windows in the rear reception room, enough room for a family and half an hour by tube to the West End. It was divided into three flats. The basement contained the tenant, a Mr Crook, and his severely brain-damaged daughter. The other two flats hadn't been maintained or decorated for decades, so absolutely everything needed doing: new roof, new electrics, new plumbing, stripping out bathrooms and kitchens and building new ones, hardboard laid onto the floorboards and the whole house carpeted; every wall was lath and plaster, which would collapse when you tore off the woodchip wallpaper so would have to be plaster-boarded, skim plastered, painted, new skirting boards added and picture rails fitted. And the rest. For me, it was pure heaven.

We managed to get a mortgage for it through a dodgy dealer at the Woolwich.

'See all these questions? Just answer no to all of them.'

'Erm, but that's not strictly true.'

'Look, do you want this pile of bricks or not?'

We reckoned we needed another £5000 to get going so we started off in London with a £37,000 mortgage, Judy working part-time in costume, and me a jobbing actor. We were an optimistic couple, and we needed to be. Those figures sound absurd today, but it was a huge amount to find every month.

Mr Crook was a diabetic and was finding it impossible to look after his poor daughter, who was also incontinent, and then one day she was taken into care. His diabetes got worse and he finally had to have a leg amputated. One of the stipulations from the mortgage company was that we had to put in a damp-proof course, treat the timbers for dry rot and put in a concrete floor in the basement. Amazingly, we got all this done while he was in hospital. When he got back he moaned about the new carpet and the smell. It was a different smell; previously it had just stunk of damp, rot, toadstools and urine. We thought it was an improvement, but you can't please everyone.

Every now and then we'd hear 'Help!' from downstairs and have to get him out of the bath or clear up the Meals on Wheels dinner that he'd spilled on the floor. The poor man was in a terrible way and eventually an ambulance pulled up outside the house and took him away too. That was when I started turning three flats into a family home. I've spent thirty-five years working on it, and it's still not finished.

Along with a perfectly preserved dead rat that could have been a hundred years old, we found things under the floorboards that told tales of the previous inhabitants, rather like archaeology. They included a letter written in Swiss German, that when translated was found to be a legal document transferring ownership of a carpenter's studio in Berne. Two extraordinary coincidences convinced us we were destined to live there. Firstly, this letter had been wrapped in a copy of *The Times* in which there was a long article about a certain Army captain called John Emerson – Judy's brother's name. Strangest of all was that, when we got the deeds, we saw that the original document from 1852 had been witnessed by Lord Henry Bentinck, a distant cousin, whose signature, just *Henry Bentinck*, was almost identical to my father's writing (also Henry). That knocked me for six.

Being David Archer: Early days

My first day on *The Archers* was a shock. I imagine it is for most new cast members, but in those days it wasn't the easy bunch of modern actors it is today. On 30 June 1982, I entered a strange new world. These days the programme is recorded at the BBC studios in the Mailbox in the centre of Birmingham, but when I started we were out at Pebble Mill in Edgbaston, a building now sadly demolished, with a character all its own.

The drama studio was on the ground floor at the end of a long corridor. The cast didn't have a green room to wait in but lounged around in a large open area just outside the studio. The first thing that struck me was the clear separation between the assembled cast. They were divided into two factions: the actors, who sat on sofas on the right side and talked about agents and money; and the older characters, some of whom had come to the programme from a different route – genuine 'country folk' who had started in local radio and somehow made the jump to drama. They sat on hard chairs on the left and talked about agricultural shows and silage.

The older men wore suits, smoked pipes at the microphone and had fought in the war. Characters like Bob Arnold, a folk singer and teller of country tales, who was cast as Tom Forrest three months after *The Archers* began in 1951; he sat in a padded chair and would sing 'The Village Pump' at the drop of a hat – and, unless you were very careful, *all* the verses. There was George Hart, whose genuine accent was exactly the same as that of his radio character, Jethro Larkin – until the Worcestershire tones were sadly terminated by a swinging branch care of yours truly, David Archer; Mollie Harris (Martha Woodford) who proved her

Gloucester credentials by writing a fascinating and comprehensive guide to outside toilets called *Cotswold Privies;* and Chris Gittins, who, before Ruth's 'Ooooh Noooo', had the original and best catchphrase, Walter Gabriel's 'Me old pals me old beauties', uttered in an accent utterly unlike any other heard in these islands, all the stranger as the character's son Nelson sounded like a duke.

I thought I'd entered a madhouse when I started on the programme, as I was wholly unfamiliar with these voices that were the most famed in the country, and witnessed interchanges like:

'D'oh, dere yoo are Nell son me awd pal me awd bayooty!'

'Oh, for heaven's sake, do go away, Dyaad.'

The two factions never intermingled and woe betide a newcomer or guest actor who sat in one of the old hands' chairs. Almost the only time Bob Arnold ever spoke to me was after my character David had called off his engagement to the ditzy Sophie Barlow. He hobbled up to me with his walking stick and said, 'Now look here, David.' (He never knew my real name.) 'Nice girl an' everythin' but that Sophie would never 'ave made a Mrs Archer!'

The old country characters may not have been trained actors, but boy did they know what they were doing. Chris Gittins ended up in a wheel-chair for the last year or so of his career in *The Archers,* and I'll never forget watching him do an 'approach' to the microphone. The dead room used to create the impression of outdoors at Pebble Mill wasn't anything like as acoustically efficient as the new one at the Mailbox, and if you shouted too loudly, you would hear your voice bounce off the walls, which it doesn't do in the open air. I watched as Chris wheeled himself forward with one hand, the other holding the script, and turned away from the mike, directing his voice into one of the soundproof tiles. He executed the trick, which is difficult to master, of sounding like you're shouting while not actually projecting that much, the opposite of what you have to do in the theatre. Then, as he wheeled closer, he brought his head round, slowly, until he was facing the mike, all the time putting an effortful quaver in his voice to suggest movement. When I heard the broadcast, there quite clearly was a fit old man, walking towards us across a ploughed field, hailing us with a cheery. 'Well hello there, me old pals me old beauties!'

By the Sword Divided

When I was still strutting my Pirate Kingly stuff at Drury Lane, writer John Hawkesworth and director Henry Herbert came to see the show. They were casting a new twenty-part BBC series about the English Civil War, and one of the lead roles was the young Cavalier hero, Tom Lacey. As a result, I found myself sitting in a room on the first floor of the BBC offices on Shepherd's Bush Green, wondering if leg warmers were a bit over the top, sight-reading stuff about battles and horses. It all seemed like an impossible dream, but amazingly I got the part, and therewith two more years of earning my living with a sword around my waist and an earring in my ear. Obviously, I took the sword off to record *The Archers,* but only just.

We rehearsed at the 'Acton Hilton', the ten-storey BBC rehearsal rooms off the A40, now sadly demolished – Miriam Margolyes was there too, still telling dirty stories – and the interiors were recorded at BBC Television Centre. All the locations were filmed at Rockingham Castle in Northamptonshire over the two blissfully hot summers of 1983 and 1984. In those days, British drama was shot in two formats, multi-camera video interiors, shot in a purpose-built set in a studio, then with 16mm film outside. You got used to it but the jump from inside to outside was always deeply peculiar. Also, everything was shot out of order, so a character would exit the wooden set of the main hall of 'Arnescote Castle', shot in a studio in White City on video in freezing February, and continue their walk, now shot on low-grade film, into the blazing sunshine of the castle yard of Rockingham in July.

It's such a shame that the TV Centre studios are no more. So much classic drama was filmed there and everyone who worked in the place has tales of getting completely lost due to the circular nature of the building. The studios were divided into colour zones so if you mistook your Green for your Blue, you could find yourself, as I once did, dressed in full Cavalier rig (an amazing creation made by Judy, who was employed to make all my costumes), jangling in thigh boots with stack heels and spurs, and huge black hat which increased my six foot three by another seven inches, striding confidently into a live recording of *Only Fools and Horses*.

We were a happy company, led by Julian Glover as Sir Martin Lacey, royalist father of twins Tom (me) and Anne, played by the ethereal Sharon Maughan, and sweet, pretty younger sister Lucinda – Lucy Aston. When Anne marries a Cromwellian, the Laceys become divided, hence the title, which reflected the true stories of so many families at that time.

I became obsessed by the period, reading Antonia Fraser's *Cromwell, Our Chief of Men* and anything else I could on the subject. I was like a kid in a toyshop, riding horses, doing major sword-fights, defending the castle from sieges and working with some of the finest actors in Britain. My only issue was I was just a bit too keen, giving it the full 'My liege!' bravura period welly that we'd been taught at Bristol. The problem was nobody had told me that acting for the screen is completely different from acting on stage. The whole point about the theatre is you're a long way from the back of the auditorium, and you have to project your words, your thoughts and your emotions over a long distance. In *North Sea Hijack* and *Tales of the Unexpected*, I'd only had small parts in contemporary stories, so I got away with it, but here was my chance to shine, so Rudi's warning of 'watch out, actor about' was horribly appropriate for what I thought was youthful energy. The whole point about the camera is that it sees *everything*, so in total contrast to the stage, all you have to do is think, and the camera will see it. If only I'd thought about it more, and remembered that acting is about *being* and not about *pretending*.

In my defence, I wasn't entirely alone. The style at the time was much more mannered, but I was trying too hard. My enthusiastic gaucheness also led to a moment of acute embarrassment. One of the guest stars was the peerless Peter Jeffrey who was a magnificent Oliver Cromwell. Before I met him, I was reading the script of his first scene and the stage directions described a child being frightened by his 'warty face and bulbous nose'. Later that day, I saw him in full costume and went to introduce myself.

'My word,' I said, 'make-up have done a brilliant job on the warts haven't they?'

'No, no, old darling,' he replied with a tired smile, 'they come with the face, no make-up required.'

They were hot summers. Togged up to the hilt in a linen shirt, thick leather jacket and thigh boots, with a hairpiece that felt like a dead cat kirby-gripped on to the back of my head, topped off with the wide-brimmed black hat, I thought that I would cook, but after initially sweating profusely, the soaked linen shirt acted like a coolant while we rode into the castle on horses, had swordfights and ran meaningfully from place to place. Nevertheless, I smelled, the horses smelled, the straw and the sun and the hot stones smelled just as they did in the past. The Sealed Knot, members of the public dedicated to the re-enactments of battles, were our army and they smelled even worse – and drank all our beer.

One of the pitched battles featuring the Sealed Knot was a mounted attack on the castle, the defences of which had been reinforced with ditches and stakes. I'm pretty happy on a horse, having done gymkhanas when younger, so I'd been honest when they asked me up front if I could ride. Some actors, unwisely, lie about it, thinking, *How hard can it be?* The answer to that is that it's not hard to sit on a stationary nag, but galloping and jumping can be extremely danger-ous if you don't know what you're doing. This shot needed about twenty horses, the steeds provided by the horse master, Dave Goody, and the riders were volunteers from the Sealed Knot. They were led by Mark Burns, a real horseman who had left the King's Royal Hussars to become an actor, notably featuring as a cavalryman in *The Charge of the Light Brigade*.

Having gone off to check on the quality of the riders, Mark had a word with that episode's director, Brian Farnham.

'How many cameras have you got on this shot, Brian?'

'Four.'

'Right, well make sure they're all working be-cause there'll be no rehearsal and you'll only get one take.'

Sure enough, on action, a salvo of cannons erupted and the horses shot off, most of them bolting completely out of control, their panicking riders providing spectacular falls that no stunt-man would have even attempted. One was dragged along by his stirrups with shards of fibre-glass 'armour' sticking out of him, leaving a trail of blood. One of the cameras caught this in close-up. It looked like the most brilliantly dangerous stunt, which it was, because the silly idiot nearly died from it.

I got to do three major swordfights! Two rough and tumbles indoors and a formal duel in a field. The fight director on all of them was Malcolm Ranson and my three opponents were Malcolm Stoddard, Andrew Bicknell and Gareth Thomas. This was more like it. Having spent the best part of a year doing the same cod musical-type bish-bash stage fight, here was the real, choreographed, messy, brutal stuff of the movies. You can usually tell a Malcolm Ranson fight because he loves his signature 'moody' at the beginning, when the blades touch in close up, just a little 'ting' before the action begins. I'd watched *The Duellists* with Harvey Keitel, and so had Malcolm. We wanted the duel with Gareth Thomas to look like that, and in a lot of ways it does. It took all day to shoot, so if you watch carefully you'll see that it goes from a wonderfully misty, moody dawn shot at the beginning, to bright afternoon sunshine by the end. A few years later *The Princess Bride* came out, and Cary Elwes and Mandy Patinkin blew all previous screen duels out of the water, but still, it's for jobs like those that you put up with the insecurity, the ignominy and the rejection.

I recently worked with Gareth again after a gap of some thirty years. We were doing a *Doctor Who* audio play for Big Finish, and we talked about our epic duel. I was surprised when said he'd never seen it, so I got out the iPad and we sat together, two old geezers watching our younger selves. 'We weren't bad, were we?' he smiled. Tragically Gareth died about a year later, but I'm glad he saw himself in his gladiatorial pomp before the end.

The fight against Andrew Bicknell, though, led to one of my life's most mortifying moments, which has lived with me ever since.

Whereas I had done stage fighting at drama school and pretend stuff as a pirate, Andrew is a real fencer, and a good one. He was wickedly quick, and the swords were real. We trained for days, getting faster and faster, my skill at leaping down whole flights of stairs learned from my fagging days at school coming in handy. When we came to record it, the adrenaline levels went up and we got even quicker. On the first take, he cut me just above the eye, but we carried on, figuring it would look authentic.

A year or two later, when Kevin Kline the movie star flew to London for a red-carpet premiere, he came to our home. A massive limo pulled up outside Mr Pooter's house in Holloway, and re-mained, engine running and double-parked, while British Tea was taken.

Kevin's just lovely, bright, easy, not up himself – a mensch. So, he asks me what I've been doing since *The Pirates of Penzance,* and I tell him about *By the Sword Divided* and he's so happy for me that he asks if can he see any of it. Well, I've been recording it on videotape.

'Show me!'

'Okay, there's a fight scene you might like.' I wind it forward to the beginning of the fight, but he says, no, let's see the build-up.

Hmm. In the scene, I'm challenging Andrew's

character to a fight while, for convoluted reasons, pretending that I don't know that the woman who is sitting on his bed is my twin sister, so I'm doing awkward, trying-not-to-give-it-away acting on top of the already mentioned overdoing-it-somewhat style. The fight ensues, which is pretty impressive I think, and then I stop the tape. There's a silence. It's clear that to the eye of one of our greatest Hollywood screen actors, my acting looks like total amateur shit.

He left pretty soon after that. I haven't seen him since.

Being David Archer: History

I soon realised that I was involved in a series with iconic status, so I got to grips with some background research on the show. BBC Radio 4's *The Archers*, it turned out, was first broadcast nationally on the Home Service on 1 January 1951, and it isn't just a long-running radio series. It's the longest-running drama series in the world, ever.

It was conceived as a sort of 'farming *Dick Barton*' (*Dick Barton – Special Agent* was the adventure series that preceded it) and part of its remit was to educate farmers in the most efficient modern farming techniques for a post-war population that was struggling to feed itself. Rationing didn't finish until 1954, and so the content was part drama, part Ministry of Agriculture propaganda. Although today there is no government directive to that end, the sense of responsibility to the farming community endures, so one of the permanent jobs on the programme has always been that of agricultural advisor, whose task it is to keep up with the reality of farming and, as much as possible, to be ahead of the game.

I play farmer David Archer, and while I've had real farmers telling me I saved their harvest or helped rid their cows of warble-fly, it's not just about country matters. Over the years, the programme has covered so many difficult subjects: rape, arson, rural drug addiction, divorce, floods, dementia, cancer, family feuds, as well as addressing the changing values and attitudes of society. In recent times, as a result of the compelling story of Rob Titchener's controlling treatment of his wife, nearly £170,000 has been donated to Refuge's 'Helen Titchener Rescue Fund' for victims of domestic abuse. For a while, 'An Everyday Story of Country Folk' became 'A Disturbing Story of Emotional Abuse'.

One of the things that people complain about regarding *The Archers* is that there's not enough drama. The other thing that people complain about regarding *The Archers* is that there's too much drama. It is an unchanging certainty that pleasing every single listener is an impossibility. Listeners shout at the radio, they 'can't stand that man', they 'wish that woman would just stop moaning and get a grip', they engage, they argue with their friends, they care. I've heard people say that they want the programme to be 'nice', that their lives are full of conflict and nastiness and they want thirteen minutes of cotton wool every evening to soothe them and remind them that there is a calm, safe, friendly, bucolic world that they can dream about and, if not live, then live by proxy. *The Archers* tries to provide that. However, people wouldn't shout, get cross, argue at dinner parties and *care* about the programme if it were always so comfortable. Drama is about conflict, and story is about wanting to know what happens next. A balance has to be struck.

I can remember times in the past when three really serious, depressing storylines were going on at the same time, often in the same episode. That was a mistake, and acknowledged as such; it's better to temper heavy plots with levity – for every scene about marital strife you need a Grundy scheme about turkeys or Lynda finding Scruff after a year's absence. I'm told I once said that *The Archers* is 'life with the heat turned down' – maybe that's true as a general rule, but it would get awfully dull if it were always like that. You need to threaten that safe world occasionally in order to have the satisfying scene where it's all right again, when Elizabeth finally forgives David for inheriting the farm or causing Nigel's death, when Phil finally gets over his grief and marries again, when Ruth abandons Sam, or New Zealand, and comes back to the family – the two-timing hussy!

Musical auditions

One consequence of playing the Pirate King was that my agent then kept putting me up for musicals. I wasn't really cut out for musical theatre. I'd already auditioned for *Cats* in 1981 and gone through the equivalent of that scene in *A Chorus Line* where all the dancers are lined up on stage ready to strut their stuff, adjusting leotards and leg warmers and looking bitchily at the competition. I'd never done a *jeté* in my life. The choreographer's assistant, all pert bum and flounce, announced, 'Okay everyone, so we'll start off with a simple sequence, and *lunge* to the left, *pas de bourrée*, kick and step dig seven eight. Attitude round, three and four and step, ball, change, flick *jeté*, up and here and kick pa pa, finish with a double pirouette, shimmy and a tah.' I was still trying to work out what a lunge was when the rest of the company was on the other side of the stage halfway through the sequence, so I wasn't surprised that I was the among first to leave.

It had all started so well. I'd got through to this round because my agent had told me they weren't looking for dancers, but 'characters'.

'What does that mean?' I'd asked.

'No idea, darling, just do something original.'

So I wrote a song. I turned up at Drury Lane for my audition with my guitar, and there were Trevor Nunn, Andrew Lloyd Webber and the choreographer, Gillian Lynne. My song was a ballad about preparing for the audition and included the verse:

So I had Kit-e-Kat and cream for breakfast
I yowled on the wall all night
I purred when I heard the chirp of a bird
And I pissed in the pale moonlight
I got me some T. S. Elocution, I read about
Skimbleshanks and Bustopher Jones
I read all about Cats
Somethin' like that
In a feline baritone

I may not have got the part in the end, but at least I made an impact. Many years later, when I was in *Arcadia,* Trevor Nunn told me he remembered it. So did Gillian Lynne when she was directing her first television play, a strange piece about interracial love and racism called *Easy Money.* I got a call from her asking me if I'd write the music for it. I was amazed, but coincidentally had been working on a lovers' rock reggae riff that went perfectly with the story. I sang it with a light West Indian accent, something that would be anathema today. We recorded it in the same studio where, two months earlier, I had auditioned for *The Archers.*

After my brief stardom in *Pirates,* I was no longer going for parts in the chorus, but for leading roles. Sky Masterson in *Guys and Dolls* is a wonderful part. It was produced at the National in 1982 and I found myself on stage in front of Richard Eyre *et al.,* giving it plenty in 'Luck Be a

Lady Tonight'. They had been impressed with my Brooklyn accent and everything seemed to be going well right up until the very last line, where you have to hold the final 'To-niiiiiiiiiight' for about eight bars with gusto, vibrato and strength. As the agonising seconds passed and my increasingly obvious lack of technique became apparent, I saw the faces in the stalls go from smiling approval to regretful dismay. My musical career was officially over.

Being David Archer: Behind the lines

There are thousands of words written online every week arguing about *The Archers* plotlines, but those discussions are really for the listener. I have no control over or input to the story, I just do the acting! Over the years, though, I've grown to love the programme and I'm honoured to be a part of a team that takes its responsibility to the listener very seriously indeed. I care about David, his family, Brookfield, Ambridge and its residents, because I care about my own family, my home, my environment and the countryside, so I want the programme to have that same reality. Sometimes we'll finish recording a scene and say, 'That'll have them shouting at the radio' – it's not by accident that people get outraged or frustrated or weep for joy or laugh out loud: it was planned and produced that way on purpose.

I have been playing David Archer for thirty-five years. During that time he's gone from being the youngest child of a farming family, through marriage, children, inheriting the farm, marital crises, foot-and-mouth. TB, floods, nearly moving Oop North, being partly responsible for the deaths of Jethro, Nigel (only I know what really happened on that roof!) and the badger (okay, he shot the badger), and had countless other adventures amidst an endless backdrop of milking, drenching, dagging, fencing and fixing everything with baler twine, duct tape and WD-40. Now the tale has come full circle, with his own children having the same conversations about the future of the farm that David, Shula and Kenton had with Phil, and that Phil had with his own father, Dan. There is no other form of storytelling in the world that has this kind of longevity because even *War and Peace* doesn't happen in real time.

In all those years, David has never blasphemed or uttered an oath worse that the occasional 'damn' or 'for God's sake'. We *Archers* farmers are the only ones in the country who don't turn the air blue when they drop a hammer on their toe. I wrote a song once about Ambridge being a real village where once a day microphones descend from the sky and record fifteen minutes of random chat that the characters then have to repeat word for word the following day at lunchtime. The song had the line, 'watch out, they're listening in…' when everyone had to mind their p's and q's while the mikes were listening but could then carry on being rude, having sex and generally getting wasted once they had gone.

Equally, although the good denizens of Ambridge are exceptionally clean-minded, the actors behind them are certainly not. If the listeners ever hear a double-entendre concerning the size of someone's equipment or length of their prize marrow, they can be absolutely certain that the actors have had a field day with it in rehearsal. I hope it doesn't ruin the illusion to mention that at the read-through of the scene where David ejects Rob from the Bull, his parting words to the Controlling One were not as restrained as the ones in the script, but an earthy exhortation containing the words, 'Now', 'Just' and 'Off'.

Young Parents

William Jack Henry Bentinck was born on 19 May 1984. We wanted to call him Willem, after my ancestor Hans Willem and to keep up the Dutch connection, but when he went to kindergarten, they pronounced it Will-EMM, so at his primary school we changed the spelling to Willam. They then called him Will-AMM, so at prep school we gave him an apostrophe, Will'm, which has stuck to this day, although he's usually a good old English Will. The Jack was after Judy's father and the Henry after my father.

I was surprised to find that Pa was furious that we hadn't included 'Noel' in his grandson's name. He was Henry Noel Bentinck, I'm Timothy Charles Robert Noel Bentinck (thanks, Pa) and it was his mother's surname, from the Gainsboroughs, the side of his lineage with which he had most empathy. I thought that, three generations later, we could probably ditch it and imagined he'd be flattered to have his own name in there, but there's no pleasing some people. Will is Will and could now never be any other name, but in retrospect it was probably a confusing choice, as almost every Bentinck in history is either William, Henry, Robert or Charles. I'm the only Timothy Bentinck and it's better for Google having unique nomenclature, so I'm sorry Will, you are more unique than The Unique Person of Unique-town, but please don't go calling your son Ziggy or Moon-Breath by way of contrast!

So, the building site in which we lived was now a family home. The house still looked like a squat inside, but we didn't care, we'd had central heating installed, we had hot water and the roof didn't leak any more. We bought a second-hand cot, some nappies and went off to ante-natal courses at the National Childbirth Trust. I was well up for sitting on the floor holding Judy's tummy while she was taught how to breathe properly. I was astonished to learn that the agony of childbirth – a natural but dangerous function that, without modern medical intervention, has historically regularly killed both mother and child – could be obviated by small regular puffs of breath and the loving support of your partner. Nevertheless, I was proud to be one of the 'new men' who would play a full role in the whole process, and be there at the birth, unlike our forebears whose only role had been to smoke furiously while the screams of their loved ones were silenced by ferocious midwives behind locked hospital doors.

Some mothers supposedly give birth in a serene

and happy way, puffing fast to blow away those pesky contractions. That's not how it went with us. 'GAS AND AIR!' went the cry within a few minutes of the first serious contractions, and after two hours that included the full repertoire of Judy's gutter vocab list delivered at a volume that would have silenced Henry V at Agincourt, the epidural was administered.

Some memories are seared on the brain, and Will's eventual arrival is one of those, a moment of pure joy and love. I shot projectile tears across the bed onto the midwife as my child's head appeared, and more when I saw the size of his tackle. A worse memory was about twenty minutes before that, watching the junior doctor's hands shaking uncontrollably as he administered his first ever epidural – an injection into the spine, which, if done incorrectly, can paralyse permanently. The extreme contrast between my fear and Judy's agony one minute, and the delirious peace and joy the next, is extraordinary, and something that no one can ever prepare you for.

And it really was a life changer. One minute life was all about me, and us, then suddenly it was entirely about something else, that I loved beyond words and was the most beautiful thing in the world, and that I needed to protect and nurture – and I changed my attitude to poo, completely.

We didn't get much sleep. For the first six months, Will'm woke crying regularly throughout the night, and it's true that lack of sleep does send you a bit bonkers. It's extraordinary how fast you wake at the very first part of your baby's cry. I'm ashamed to admit I occasionally followed the cliché of male insensitivity and delayed my 'waking' by just a few milliseconds that ensured Judy was awake too before mumbling helpfully, 'Shall I go?'

She got wise to that pretty quickly, and then I'd go into his room at four in the morning and pick him up, rock him on my shoulder, and sing Helpful Sleeping Songs about Willo and Bilbo Baggins-oh, and after twenty minutes put him back in his cot fast asleep and tuck him up, and creep back to our bed...

'Waaaaah!'

We've carried on loving Will'm in the same house, until he was thirty, when we all agreed it was time to move on – to Hornsey. He got a first in Philosophy and was a professional croupier. He works in advanced computer training in Shoreditch, has a big beard and has sometimes been known to wear red trousers. He's also one of the cleverest people I know, so he's allowed to.

Walnut was the son we never had, he popped out two years later, but five months too early, though who's to say that if he'd lived, then Jasper would never have been born, and how could you have a world without Jasper?

I held Walnut in my hand. Above the kitchen sink. The doctor hadn't cleared up properly in our bedroom after attending Judy's miscarriage and, after he left, there was a bundle of towels on the bed. I found our son, about five inches long. I took him downstairs and washed him at the kitchen sink, I wrapped him gently in aluminium foil, then called the doctor. I don't know what I said to him. It probably wasn't very pleasant.

Two years later, when Judy went into labour six weeks early, I feared the worst. We had been talking about names, and we'd sort of decided on Jasper (a favourite name ever since I was a child and had a sheep-chasing beagle of that name) if it was a boy, and Lily for a girl (my suggestion of Tallulah was quashed). Judy was rushed in an ambulance to University College Hospital and I was to pack overnight clothes, change of underwear and washbag, then follow in the car. I was worrying about Judy and the baby, where was I going to park, and which knickers should I bring, all at the same time.

When I got there, parking badly on the pavement, I rushed into the hospital with the overnight bag, ready to endure together the agony of another lost child. I came into Judy's room to see her sitting up in bed, looking beautiful, but without a baby.

'It's a boy,' she said, 'it's Jasper.'

I actually said, 'What's a boy?'

'He's alive, he's Jasper, but they've taken him away for tests.'

Quite soon they brought him back and he was beautiful – small, a bit shrivelled, but perfect. The test results, though, were not so good.

Jasper was born with Listeria meningitis, was in intensive care for another six weeks, and developed septicaemia and hydrocephalus. Entirely due to the fantastic care of University College Hospital and in particular his doctor, Mark Rosenthal, he survived to become the indomitable man that he is today. I always reckoned that if you're born with the worst headache imaginable, then when it goes away everything else is just a bonus, and that's Jasp.

When he finished school, I asked him what he really wanted to do with his life. 'I want to be the lead singer in a rock band,' he replied, a quite reasonable aspiration, but one fraught with insecurity, as his jobbing actor father well knew. We finally agreed that he should get a degree first, and I couldn't really argue when he found a BA course at Cheltenham in 'Popular Music'. It sounded marvellous, but had little rigour (at the time at least) and, graduating three years later, he found himself lost and on the dole in Bristol. He had been doing temporary work teaching a Saturday singing class and really enjoyed it. When Judy discovered a week-long introductory course in TEFL (Teaching English as a Foreign Language), she booked it for him and he took to it like a duck to water, the teacher telling him that he was a natural. He then did a three-month Certificate in English Language Teaching to Adults course and got his teaching qualification. Days after getting his certificate, he applied for a teaching job in Tokyo and was offered it. Weeks later, we stood with our lovely boy at Heathrow as he set off for the other side of the world, to a totally different culture, where he spoke not a word of the language, to begin a job he had never done before. He's now been there nearly three years and is an enormously well-liked and respected *'Sensei'*. We simply couldn't be more impressed and proud, of both our wonderful boys.

TV commercials

Having been brought up on TV-commercial film sets, my first time on one as an actor was hugely exciting, and oddly familiar. In the very first commercial I did I wasn't yet an actor – I was still the producer's son. Michael Portillo made a fleeting appearance in a 1961 advert for Ribena, but I was the first 'Ribena Boy', in 1962, aged nine, when it was still promoted as a healthy drink: 'it does you so much good, we've known that since we read about all the Vitamin C in blackcurrants, that's what helps to keep you so sturdy and fit...'

I had to cycle through a water splash and we did take after take because I kept closing my eyes against the water. After about take five, my new corduroy trousers were so wet they split when I went to straddle the bike. I was scared my ripped crotch would show on camera, so I forgot about the eyes and instinctively closed them again.

'CUT! Eyes OPEN Timothy, please!' My first director's note, and one that I should have applied better to my whole life. They never did get me to keep my eyes open.

As an adult, I discovered that advertising castings are a cattle market where you abase yourself utterly for the possibility of a big pay packet. In the waiting area, there are usually six other blokes much better-looking than you, and then you are finally seen and have to give your all to the line you've learned, with a Welsh accent: 'Mm! Brain's Faggots! Crackin'!' More usually, there are no lines and you just have to stand there looking like a dick.

For some reason, I've done a lot of beer commercials. The main thing about these is that you have to be able to hold your drink, as industry rules decree that you have to use the real product when promoting it. One day, I found myself at Bray Studios to shoot a Guinness advert at some ungodly hour of the morning, feeling dreadful as I'd just gone down with flu. As our central heating hadn't yet been installed, I'd washed my hair under freezing cold water in the kitchen sink. This was when I really understood the best place to be on a film set – in make-up, as you can come in looking like death warmed up and emerge, after much pampering and mothering, like a screen idol – well, you feel like one anyway.

Then, around 8 a.m., I was required to drink copious amounts of Guinness for the closing scene, as the ad was being shot out of sequence. I was one of the 'Guinnless' and Angus Deayton was the doctor dispensing our 'cure'. My problem was that every time I savoured the delicious white Guinness head, I'd do what all Guinness drinkers do and suck the froth from my top lip, which apparently I wasn't supposed to. Like closing your eyes against water, it's an instinctive thing, and the more takes I did, the drunker I got and the less able I was to remember things like the director's note about not sucking my lip. By midday, I was tanked and feeling really ill.

After lunch, which didn't stay down long, we then had to film the first half of the ad, with me sitting nervously with my girlfriend in the 'waiting room' of the pub and then presenting my pint of lager to Angus for him to diagnose me as 'Guinnless' and hand me a prescription. I could hardly stand up. The first time I shoved my glass towards him, half of it went in his lap. After Angus's conclusion that I had 'Monotonous Pinticus', I was supposed to ask, 'Is that serious?' Which, after many takes, came out as, 'Issatsheeeriush?' Surprisingly, given that Guinness commercials have a great reputation in the industry, I wasn't edited out, so my slurring forms part of that iconic canon of films.

Terry's Logger Bar was a classic, too. The only photo I have of it looks like the set of a porn movie, with me as a lumberjack, holding an axe and lying on a log while surrounded by a bevy of adoring women – so eighties!

Will had been born the day before shooting and the producer turned up in the morning with an enormous box of Terry's chocolates for Judy as a thank you for her timing. There is a noticeable discrepancy in my hair. I still had long, high-lighted hair from filming *By the Sword Divided,* but immediately after filming the Terry's ad I had it cut for my next job – playing a colonial diplomat in India in 1890, so I'd had a short back and sides for the first time since schooldays. Then they changed the design of the chocolate bar and I had to come back to re-shoot the end of the ad.

'Sorry, I've had my hair cut,' was met with a grumpy, 'Oh, we'll have to make you a wig then.'

This would have been fine if the wig-maker hadn't taken for reference a photo of me heavily back-lit so that my hair appeared to be peroxide blonde – which is why, in the final cut, I look like a moustached lumberjack with a tranny wig. It was supposed to be a spoof of Python's Lumber-jack song, but the line, 'I put on women's cloth-ing and hang around in bars' was disturbingly apt.

One of the things you always hope for as an actor is the chance to go filming abroad. I was cast in *Man-eaters of India* with Freddie Treves, had all my jabs done and was about to fly off to the sub-continent when at the last minute it was decided that my scenes could be shot in Wales. I was enor-mously disappointed as I was due to have a week in a hill station in the foothills of the Himalayas. When I found that every single member of the cast and crew had gone down with serious dysentery on day one (waiters had refilled mineral-water bottles from the tap), I realised I'd had a lucky escape.

Since then I've done *Sharpe* in Crimea and other jobs in Europe but the two long-haul jobs were both commercials – one for the Australian Tourist Board and one for Wall's Feast ice-cream bar. The latter involved a week in the Maasai Mara National Reserve in Kenya and I was the Big White Hunter: 'You shouldn't be out here alone, Virginia, big cats are always ready for a feast!' It was an adventure.

Arriving in Nairobi, I went for a walk and was immediately taken in by a group of charming and incredibly persuasive Ugandan con artists, to whom I willingly gave all my recently acquired per diems for the whole shoot. I believed them when they said they would send me the money when they finally wrestled their savings from Idi Amin's clutches. It took me months to realise I'd been done.

Then we flew in an old silver DC3 Dakota into the middle of the Maasai Mara where an enormous camp had been built for us by Abercrombie & Kent. It was like experiencing the Raj. I had my own tent with separate bedroom, a manservant, and a hot shower – the water was carried from an enormous tank over a fire in the middle of the wooded encampment and poured into a canvas header tank over my shower. Unbelievable. We all ate together in a huge tent where the evening's entertainment consisted of massive liar-dice competitions. Armed guards patrolled the site, defending us from lion and elephant. It was impossibly exciting. However, that first night it rained, and the next day it was cloudy – too cloudy to film. Same the next day, and the next, and the liar-dice started to get boring, and I finished my book, and suddenly it wasn't exciting at all. All we did all day was listen to Paul Simon's *Graceland* and watch the skies.

When, four days later, the sun finally came out, we had to rush. The first shot was a close-up of me eating the Feast ice cream lasciviously next to my girl, played by the lovely Emma Harbour, with an acacia tree and the setting sun in the background. At the equator, the sun sets incredibly quickly, so we only had once chance at it that day. The Feast bars were kept in a cooler chest with bars of dry ice to keep them frozen, but it was so hot that only the bars right next to the ice were frozen. Having rehearsed with a soft one, on action, with the sun falling rapidly out of the sky behind me, I took a hunk out of the bar with erotic intent, expecting to bite through its soft deliciousness with one hearty crunch – and hit solid ice. So the take where I go, 'Ow! Christ, I think I've cracked a tooth!' didn't make it to the final cut and we had to do it again the next day.

The crew went on to shoot another commercial by the sea in Mombasa, so I got a couple of days R & R on the beach and took a photo of me on a sun lounger reading the *Daily Telegraph* with front-page headline 'Worst Winter for Thirty Years' above a photo of a snowbound London.

When I got home, full of sunshine and stories, I was greeted by three very dour and serious women: Judy, my sister Anna and my stepmother Jenny. Will had been in hospital for a week with suspected juvenile chronic arthritis, or Still's disease. While I was doling out presents, they were looking through catalogues for callipers and leg braces. I later wrote a radio play about it – it wasn't funny. Luckily, it turned out to have been an appalling piece of misdiagnosis – he'd put his neck out falling off a table, and got a temperature at the same time. Shyam Singha was again the one who got it right, but not before the doctors had given Will a massive dose of steroids, which did him no good whatsoever and took months to get out of his system.

Another weather-cursed TV advert adventure

followed a few months later, but this time in the Arctic. I'd been cast in a Carlsberg commercial to be a David Attenborough type walking across a mountain while talking to camera.

'I'm just over the rim now. To the west, Gustav Holm, but in front of me the spectacular Mount Forel Glacier. Since the Ice Age this mighty glacier has gouged its unstoppable path to the Straits of Denmark, where it breaks off into the sea to form massive Carlsbergs.'

'Cut!' says the director, and the caption comes up:

'Probably the easiest mistake in the world. Carlsberg. Brewed in the UK by Danes.'

Getting there was an adventure in itself. On the plane to Norway we were given some cash by the production company to each buy two bottles of spirits, as the price of alcohol in the country was prohibitive. I was already enjoying this job. I also made a new friend in Michael Percival, playing the director, a delightful, clever and funny man who tragically died recently. We took a coach north on snow-packed roads for the best part of a day, then transferred to a military half-track troop carrier with no windows, and set off across frozen lakes and mountain foothills until we reached the most remote hotel imaginable. Utterly beautiful, with each one of us assigned our own log cabin. The first thing we did was pool our alcohol resources, which resulted in a large dining table groaning under the weight of dozens of bottles of hard liquor, thenceforth free to anyone in the company. We were then encouraged to use the huge communal sauna to warm up after our long, cold journey. Stark naked was a great way to meet the gorgeous Norwegian make-up and costume girls – oh and the Ski-doo riders in whose hopefully expert hands our lives were to be held the next day as they drove us to the top of the mountain. A hearty meal and far too much whisky later, we trudged off to our cabins for a blissful night of deep arctic sleep.

The costume call in the morning was the first one I'd ever had that was far more practical than cosmetic, as not getting frostbite was more important than looking good. First, a layer of silk long johns, then cotton fleece, then wool, then the outer waterproofs, then boots and gloves and Norwegian hat. Onto a Ski-doo and hang on tight to the driver as he takes 'route one' up the mountain – just vertical. Halfway up, we enter a fog bank. We keep driving through the fog. We stop at the summit – in thick fog. Optimistically the film crew unload all their kit, the camera is set up, we rehearse the scene, but can't shoot because of the fog. We wait, and wait, and wait. Someone has the bright idea of building an igloo. Well, there is little else to keep us occupied on the top of a fogbound Norwegian mountain, so that's what we do.

Suddenly the fog lifts and we realise why we had come all this way – the view is incredible, just magnificent, a vista of arctic beauty, mountain behind mountain behind glacier, and a bright blue sky. Panic. The camera is loaded, my radio mike pack is attached, I have to run the long way around to my start position so they can't see any footprints. I have a walkie-talkie with me. I stand ready. I wait ... then,

120

'Okay, ready Tim?'

'Yes, standing by.'

'Okay, turn over...'

'Sound speed.'

'Okay, Tim, and ... ACTION!'

I start walking towards camera.

'I'm just over the rim now. To my west, Gustav Holm, but in front of me...'

'CUT!'

I look up the mountain to find that the camera crew has completely disappeared again... The fog rolls down. I return to the igloo.

But now, instead of playing Eskimos with my new-found friends, I had to wait alone about fifty yards away in my start position, ready to go the moment the fog lifted again. Luckily, I had a book. So I sat on a rubber mat for the next five hours with three Mars bars while the fog didn't lift in the slightest.

At the end of the day, one of the Ski-doo drivers asked me if I'd ever done cross-country skiing, which I hadn't, only downhill, but he lent me a pair of langlauf skis anyway and I skied, fell, slid and bounced my way down the slope into the welcoming and warm embrace of steak, whisky and the sauna.

The next day we did it all over again, except this time there wasn't even a single break in the fog. And the next day too. If ever a production was going to turn me into a smooth-skinned alcoholic it would be this one. Finally, on day four, it broke and we got the shot. One-take wonders the pair of us, wide shot, mid-shot and close-ups. But in commercials you always do multiple takes, so

121

there was a lot of crunching through snow.

The director asked us to improvise some dialogue at the end for them to fade out on, which we did. When I came to see it on TV a while later, they hadn't faded our dialogue at all, but kept it all in, so the thirty-second commercial ends with this:

ME ...to form massive Carlsbergs.
PERCIVAL Cut!
ME Sorry. Are the footprints a problem?
PERCIVAL Just wait at the bottom, there's a good chap.
ME I feel a complete amateur.
PERCIVAL No, honestly you mustn't...

Which did make it a lot funnier.

Years later, I was waiting in reception at the advertising agency who had produced it and saw that it had won some copywriting award. Did Percival or I get a mention? Nah, mate, you're just the actors! And the real irony of it all was that once the fog had lifted, the bright sunshine and blue sky looked far too pleasant for the story, so in post-production they had to add wind noise and fake snow, which ultimately made it look as though it was shot in a studio.

I have danced with the Bolshoi Ballet. Yes, in another exercise in 'unusual ways of earning a living', that particular bucket-list entry got ticked in the late eighties when I landed a part as a travelling businessman for Austrian Airlines. In a dream sequence, he finds himself in a line-up with the Bolshoi doing Cossack dancing. It was a night shoot in a cold barn just outside Vienna, the dancers had just flown in from Moscow, and, never having done any such dancing before, they had to bring me up to speed in about half an hour. They promised they would send me a tape of the finished advert but never did, and despite recently writing to Austrian Airlines to try and find it, this classic still eludes me. There is, however, a lasting legacy from this job – one evening when I was in my mid-fifties, Judy and I were out to dinner with friends and I related this story.

'Go on then, Tim, show us your Cossack dancing!' said the ever-daring actor Rupert Farley.

Three glasses of wine told me I was up to this challenge, despite my age and weight being quite significantly different to the fitter, younger Tim who had no trouble with it twenty years earlier. So, down on my haunches, stuck my leg out … and snapped an anterior cruciate ligament. I was on crutches for six months and will never ski again. Quit while you're ahead.

My favourite ad though is the commercial for Herte Frankfurters that I did with my son Jasper. My character is a Dad teaching his son to ride a bike and making them both a meal of frankfurters. At the casting they said they were looking for a young child who could just ride a bike, and I mentioned that I had the perfect candidate, so the next day I brought Jasper in, and he got the part. I've got the tape of the casting, and as posh put-downs go it doesn't get any better than when the director asked Jasper if he'd seen the film 'The Aristocats', which he pronounced Aristocats'. With just one word, Jasp nearly lost himself the gig, but it would have been worth it. '_A_risto-cats,' he corrected, completely dead-pan, aged four. We shot it on a lovely summer's day in a wood and a pretty English cottage, and all day people were telling Jasper he was a star. At the end he was given the bicycle. When he got back to school and was asked about it by his teacher, he said, 'I'm a star, and I got a bike,' neatly summing up the entire acting profession.

Being David Archer: Contractual obligation

When I started following my sister Anna's path into the acting world, she gave me a great piece of advice, 'Keep your mouth shut and never be late.' With the former I try, honestly I do, but I'm not very good at it. With the latter I'm better, because I'm aware of what's at stake – after all, if you're late for the theatre, a show with no understudies can't go on; if you're late for filming, it can cost millions; and if you don't turn up for an interview, you won't get the job.

When, fairly early on in my _Archers_ career, I answered the phone at 9.05 a.m. on a Monday morning, in bed at home in London, and Jane, the _Archers'_ P.A. in Birmingham said, 'Tim?' and I said, 'Yes?' and she said, 'Oh God,' and I realised I wasn't there for the nine o'clock episode, it did not go down at all well.

When I joined the programme, echoes of the last war still permeated an old-school-tie BBC, and the male-dominated hierarchy ran it like the

Army, either because they'd been in the services themselves or, probably more often, because they hadn't and were trying to make up for it. So, something as horrendous as not just being late but actually not getting there at all was Bateman-cartoonish in its horror. As a result of my one lapse, I developed a reputation for being late that was entirely unjustified but lasted until Ian Pepperell (Roy Tucker) did something similar in the late 1990s and had to take a taxi to the studio from London. Consequently, he took over as the protagonist in the 'Worst Late Story Ever'. He has just been usurped by James Cartwright (Harrison Burns) who was in Leeds at the time of his episode. The thing is, these more recent diary failures are treated with banter, jokes and teasing. When I did it, it was akin to murder. I nearly lost my job.

Another hairy moment was when I was offered a very high-paying TV commercial for the Australian Tourist Board – four weeks in Oz being filmed in all the most exotic locations in the country. Not only was it a dream job but I was spectacularly broke at the time, so much so that we were thinking that we would have to sell the house – this job would rescue us. The problem was I had one *Archers* episode to record slap bang in the middle of the shoot dates. When I asked if I could get out of it, I was told no 'because someone has to be at Brookfield for Christmas'.

'Where's everyone else?' I asked.

'They're all doing panto.'

So, after a lot of thought, I did something I'd never done before and have never done since – I broke my contract. I was off to the land of my birth. If I lost my part in *The Archers*, then so be it. In hindsight, it was an incredibly risky call.

When we arrived in Sydney they let us lie by the pool for five days to recover from jet-lag and get a bit of a tan – not a bad way of earning money. It was around Christmas time and I remember lying in the sun, listening to 'Jingle Bells', watching kids the same age as my boys play in the pool and missing them like mad, wondering whether I'd have a job when I got back. For the next three weeks, myself and the actress pretending to be the love of my life were flown everywhere, diving on the Great Barrier Reef, flying a seaplane, driving a four-wheel drive across the Northern Territory, canyoning, joining in an aboriginal corroboree, kissing on the sand as the sun set behind us, and bedroom scenes in five-star hotels – basically everything I dreamed of when I joined up.

While I was there, I received the *Archers* bookings for the following month – eight episodes! Well, I thought, either they're killing David off, they're recasting or they've forgiven me. When I got back, along with Paddy and Arnold Peters (Jack Woolley) I was interviewed on the *Wogan* chat show, and in the hospitality room afterwards I was handed a letter. I feared the worst, but luckily it was an official rap over the knuckles, full of phrases like, 'we reserve our position', which I didn't understand. When I asked what that meant, I was told, 'Do that again and you're out.' Thought so. I still owe our then temporary editor, Neil Fraser, a bottle of vodka – apparently that was what it took to persuade the powers that be not to sack me.

The coda to that tale is that when I arrived for said recordings, Peter Windows, who was directing that month, asked me to come into the studio to listen to something that had just been recorded. This had never happened before. Again, I was worried. I stood in the studio with Felicity (Ruth) and Graeme Kirk (Kenton) as they played the following scene over the speakers:

KENTON Hi Ruth, how's the honeymoon going? I bet Spain is a lot warmer than it is here!
RUTH (ON PHONE, DISTRESSED) Oh Kenton, something terrible's happened, we were on the coach travelling to the hotel and it crashed, and ... and David...
KENTON What? What's happened? Is Dave okay?

As the scene was playing I was getting progressively more concerned. Felicity and Graeme were looking at their feet, while behind the glass Peter and the crew had their backs turned; I knew I was done for.

RUTH Well he's alive, but when it crashed he was drinking a can of Coke, and the can has sort of got stuck in his throat, and the Spanish doctors say that even if he gets his voice back, he may never sound the same again!
KENTON Oh shit, Ruth, that's terrible!

Only when Kenton said 'shit' – a word which

127

has never been used in *The Archers* – did it finally dawn on me that it was a wind-up. This was confirmed by my colleagues and, up until this time, my friends, collapsing on the floor with laughter. When he'd recovered, Peter finally came on the talkback and said, 'Just remember, Tim, it's that easy.'

Point well made.

Sitcoms

After *By the Sword Divided*, I continued to work in TV and theatre, playing Archer (ha ha) in *The Beaux' Stratagem* at Southampton, which involved more sword fighting and my first male-to-male full-on kiss, and an episode of *Boon* with Michael Elphick and Anthony Head – playing an arrogant toff property developer with a shotgun. Was I becoming typecast? When I got my next part, the answer appeared to be 'yes'.

In a new sitcom series for LWT called *Square Deal*, filmed in 1988–9, Nigel Barrington was a young, posh, heartless estate agent married to the Sloaney Emma (gorgeous, Irish, Lise-Ann McLaughlin) and next-door neighbour to oiky but annoyingly good-looking Sean (naughty, funny, Brett Fancy). Brilliantly written by the ever-youthful Richard Ommanney, and directed by similarly young at heart and follicularly challenged genius Nic Phillips, once more I thought that fame and fortune beckoned. Quite what it is that determines whether a new comedy series becomes a hit or languishes on a 'Forgotten Sitcoms' website is a mystery. Rich had a great track record, having written four series of *Three Up, Two Down* with Elphick and Angela Thorne, and Nic is a wonderful and experienced director. It did all right at the time and ran to a second series, but hasn't gone down as one of the icons of British comedy.

It was my first sitcom and the format takes some getting used to. The problem is the studio audience. It's like doing theatre, but not, and like recording telly, but not either: it's halfway between the two. In the theatre, you wait in the wings and when you emerge on stage you are in character, which provides a kind of carapace of security because whatever you do isn't really you, so if anything goes wrong you can cover it up as the person you are playing. As long as you don't corpse, you'll usually get away with it. In a sitcom, you're waiting in the wings as the warm-up man goes through his shtick, then get introduced to the audience, one by one, as yourself.

'Ladies and gentlemen, playing Nigel Barrington, TIMOTHEEEE BENTINCK'

Big round of applause but, of course, we were all unknowns so unlike David Jason in *Only Fools* … where the audience knows that everything Del Boy says is going to be funny, we had to earn their laughter from scratch. The public buy into the fact that they are a part of the production and kindly laugh at anything that sounds vaguely like it's meant to be a gag, but problems arise when you have to do another take. If it's an actor's fault, like they get a line wrong, or corpse, or dry

129

up completely, the audience love it, as they become complicit with the unseen workings of the show and know that it will probably appear in an out-takes programme. But if the problem is technical, like a wrong camera angle or a sound boom in shot, their patience starts to wear thin and they stop laughing dutifully at the same weak gag. By the time they've heard it eight times, you can hear the tumbleweed.

The other problem is that the technicalities of acting on stage and acting for camera are two very different things. One is big and the other is tiny. When filming, there is always 'quiet on set' and you're utterly immersed in your own reality. On stage, the audience becomes another performer, particularly in a comedy where you have to ride the laughter (or deathly quiet) and time your performance to something that will vary every night. When doing a sitcom, you're acting small for the camera, but timing it like you would on stage. All of us were new to it, so we had to find out the hard way, and made plenty of mistakes in doing so. After a while, just by the sheer volume of scenes and episodes, we got used to it and not so frightened, but later in my career when I had the odd guest part in a long-running series, I realised why successful, experienced actors who came into our show for the odd scene or few lines were in a blue funk of terror and would very often totally dry, speak in tongues or spend most of the recording on the loo.

Nigel's partner at 'Barrington and Grout' was the kind face of estate agencies, Max, played by the late, great, Jeremy Sinden. In one scene,

Nigel is flipping through *The Times* obituary column, looking up the widows of the recently deceased in the phone book, then ringing them and offering to sell their houses. In 2013, we nearly sold our house in London, with a mind to do what my pa had done and start a new life in the country. It didn't work out but on the way we had to deal with the extraordinary world of enormously plausible and entertaining estate agents, who all turned out to treat the truth with cavalier abandon. I mentioned to one of them what Nigel had tried and showed him the clip. Far from laughing at the immorality of it, he was hugely impressed and assured me he would try it out.

The series climaxed with Nigel challenging Sean to a boxing match, which given that he had been fisticuffs champ at Marlborough and Sean very much hadn't, he was cockily sure of winning. Neither Brett nor I had ever been in a ring in our lives, so LWT sent us down to the Henry Cooper Gym on the Old Kent Road to learn. Our teacher was a former British cruiserweight champ called Billy who didn't really get the idea that this was for telly, and who's teaching technique was to shout, 'Go on, 'it 'im … just fuckin' 'it 'im in the face, will ya?'

Stage fighting, and fighting on screen, is all about making it look like you're beating the living daylights out of someone, without ever touching – unless of course you're Mickey Rourke or Robert De Niro or Sly Stallone in which case you train for a year and get your nose busted and become good enough to win real boxing matches. That wasn't us, and when Billy asked me if I'd like to spar with him, and I said, 'What, actually hit each other?', you should have seen his look of utter disdain.

Not wanting to come across as a complete wuss, I agreed and got togged up with head guard, groin guard and mouth shield. I was pretty fit at the time, I worked out, did weights and bicycled to work, so I thought I was ready. The first thing I did was incredibly stupid. I let my jaw drop in what I thought was a boxer-ish look of casual aggression – so he hit it. I honestly thought he'd broken it, first punch. So I hit him back. I realised I'd never actually hit anyone in the face before in my life, so when his head snapped back (apparently I've got a very fast jab!) we were both pleasantly surprised, me because I'd made contact, and Billy because clearly his sophisticated teaching methods had paid off.

In the story, Sean is being totally trounced by Nigel right up to the end, when he distracts him by shouting 'Don't shoot, Emma!' Nigel turns in panic and Sean knocks him out. So, we were rehearsing doing very bad boxing, not actually hitting each other, and we were watched by a group of young boxers who were waiting impatiently to use the ring. Sitting in the sauna afterwards, one of these bad boys came in and sat next to us with a towel over his head and a look of glowering contempt on his face.

'You two looked terrible up there, man, you know? Really amateur.'

Well, I wasn't having it.

'Yeah, well that was the point, mate, we're

132

actors and it was meant to look crap. I mean if I asked you to stand up on stage and play *Hamlet* you'd look a bit of a twat wouldn't you?'

I turned for confirmation to Brett, who was staring at me with a look of 'What. Have You. Done?'

After a long and extremely scary pause, I was relieved when instead of driving my nose into my brain, the boxer replied, 'Yeah, fair enough, good point.'

Phew.

Actors are an easy target. The common perception is that our only conversations revolve around agents, money, and jealousy. While that's often perfectly true, I've also had the most interesting political, artistic and philosophical debates with my fellow thesps, and laughed long and loud with some of the funniest people in the world. If I had to describe my class – rather than upper, middle or working – I'd say I have most in common with other actors, in that your class is really the kind of people you feel most comfortable with, and with whom you have a common life experience, a common language – an understanding without having to explain. My father called it 'ping' – when a few words are enough. We come from all walks of life – education, accent, family or income all count for nothing when everything about you is exposed on stage and you are utterly dependent on your fellow actor saying the right words at the right time. That trust and shared terror is the unspoken link that binds us all together, and, along with a shallowness that enables us quickly to forget the brotherly love for the person with whom we've just shared months of 'shouting in the evenings', is why we all call each other 'love' and 'darling' – it *is* genuine affection, but it's usually because we can't remember their ruddy name!

I may feel a sense of kinship with my fellow actors, but I can't stand divas. There are a few famous people in the business who have a reputation for being up themselves, rude, arrogant and generally unpleasant. One of the things I've always loved about coming into long-running series like *EastEnders, Casualty, The Bill* or *Born and Bred* is how welcoming, respectful and polite the major characters usually are, and in *The Archers* we always go out of our way to make guest actors welcome, as we all know what it's like guesting on something where you don't know anyone. Of course, if someone turns up being a bit grand they'll soon get the silent treatment, especially if they're crap, and the two do tend to go hand in hand.

There's a silly game that is sometimes played in bored moments in the green room called 'Arse or Angel' (or words to that effect). Someone says the name of an actor and everyone else has to reply immediately with either 'Arse' or 'Angel'. The fun is hearing five actors instantly saying 'Arse' in unison when [redacted] is suggested. There's also something very special when you find yourself working with people who are huge stars and who you admire enormously, and find that they're charming, generous, selfless and interested in others. I was so sad when John Hurt died – I'd worked with him on a *Doctor Who* audio drama only a few months before. I told him he'd once been to a party at our house in the sixties. 'Oh no, did I misbehave?' he asked wretchedly. I hadn't the heart to tell him the dampers on the piano he spilled a bottle of wine into still produce what became known as 'the Hurt octave'. Now there was a man who would always get a 'Lovely' from everyone.

Sometimes, in the heat of the moment, we can all let ourselves down and have a 'Christian Bale meltdown', even on a happy set like *Square Deal*. In one scene, Nigel is seen belting a punch bag in an uncontrolled fury in preparation for the boxing match. Takes one to three didn't work for technical reasons and I was getting a bit tired. On take four, I got a note from Nic up in the control room, delivered by the floor manager, to lift my head. Take four, he asked me to hit the bag harder. Take five, he told me to keep my guard up. Take six, I'd had enough. Pouring with sweat, with bruised hands and in a fury of antagonism, I yelled out, 'All right! You come here and show me how you bloody want it done!' Deathly silence from the audience. The floor manager came up and whispered, 'Nic's coming down.' Long embarrassed pause as the director came down the spiral stairs from the control room and took me round the back of the set. Ego massaged, profuse apologies from me for having lost it. Thirty years later, while having a lovely dinner with Nic and the series writer Richard Ommanney, I asked if they remembered the episode. 'Remember?' Nic spluttered. 'I thought you were going to kill me!'

To publicise the first series of *Square Deal,* we were taken on a jolly to the Montreux Film Festival and paraded before the press for photos and interviews. Lying in my bed in the five-star hotel, looking out onto Lake Geneva, I really thought my time had come. I was getting used to this press interview lark I thought, so when I got home and was asked to do a centre spread for the *Daily Mirror,* I jumped at the chance. So then came the reason why you should never believe what you read in the papers, in the form of an article by a seasoned *Mirror* hack by the name of Sharon Feinstein.

'BABY ANGUISH SENT ME MAD SAYS SQUARE DEAL STAR'

Well, as I'd been at pains to point out, it hadn't. Jasper's birth had been a very worrying time, but the brunt of it was borne by Judy as I was down in Southampton doing *The Beaux' Stratagem,* but Sharon was having none of it. We sat in the garden, she was as nice as pie, and I spoke to her in an entirely unguarded way, as you would to a friend. I happened to mention Jasper and how he'd nearly died, and from then on that subject monopolised the conversation.

'Surely you must have been worried sick. Weren't you angry or frustrated? Did your relationship suffer?'

'Not really, by the time I was doing the play he was out of immediate danger, but Judy had to cope with it all as I could only get home at week-ends.'

'Did you take it out on inanimate objects at all?'

'I don't think so. Well, there was one funny moment when I was coming downstairs with a full tray of coffee cups and the cat nearly tripped me up, almost had me crashing all the way down the stairs!'

The *Mirror's* translation: 'KICKED his cat around in wild temper fits.'

'And I guess I got a bit forgetful. I once locked the keys in the car and went a bit Basil Fawlty on it...'

The *Mirror's* translation: 'SMASHED in the roof of his car...'

It went on like that. I really should have learned the lesson but I'm a trusting soul and journalists are generally extremely good at finding an 'angle' if you don't provide them with one. Since then people have advised me that you should always come ready with your own 'angle', as it's a lot easier for the writer than them having to invent one, but I'm still pretty bad at it, I'm far too truthful. And saying things like, 'this is off the record' doesn't work at all – nothing is, ever.

Just recently Felicity Finch (Ruth Archer) and I were interviewed about *The Archers* for the *Observer* and right at the end, after the journalist had packed away her recording device, she asked me, 'Why is David always out of breath?' This is a rather sore point. Ninety per cent of the time he's not, but when engaging in hard work, in order to let the listener know there is physical activity going on, then effort in the voice is required! I can't stand hearing actors who are meant to be

137

belting seven kinds of crap out of a ploughshare sounding like they're having tea with the vicar, so with an exasperated smile I said, 'Well, he's out of breath when he needs to be. I mean, you try digging a four-foot hole for a fence post without breathing, fucking hell!' So, of course, that got printed verbatim.

I rang Sean, our editor, to apologise for saying 'fucking' to the *Observer* but he was entirely supportive– 'It was you swearing, Tim, wasn't it? Not David.' Exactly.

After *Square Deal,* I was in three episodes of *Three Up, Two Down,* my first casting against type as the heavily moustachioed and cockney George the barman, but my next regular part in a sitcom wasn't until ten years later, with Chris Barrie in *A Prince Among Men.*

Written by old chums from the *Pirates* film, the 'Sitcom Boot Boys' Tony Millan and Mike Walling, this was the tale of retired footballer Gary Prince, a Scouser with more money than business sense and a childish love of expensive gadgets. I played his posh accountant, Mark Fitzherbert. Coming on the back of the hugely successful *The Brittas Empire,* this was clearly going to be massive and we would all become huge telly stars. How many times have I thought that over the years?

It's hard playing a comedy character who is completely obnoxious. Having been a posh, selfish, opinionated, ruthless landlord and estate agent with no real redeeming features in *Square Deal,* I tried to make Mark – a posh, selfish, opinionated, ruthless accountant – a bit more likeable, but it wasn't easy. Twelve episodes later, Mark had spent most of the time sneering at the working class and doing barely legal business deals that relied for humour on his utter lack of morality. I was talking to Martin Clunes recently about how his Doc Martin, despite being completely ghastly to everyone, nevertheless manages to remain such a sympathetic character. Part of it is down to Clunes's subtlety as a performer, but also because the character has a vulnerability that comes from being cruelly abused as a child. When you're trying to get laughs from ringing up old chum Tubby McKinnon to arrange a Vicars and Tarts party, any vulnerability from being abused at Marlborough is hard to reveal.

Chris Barrie was my second encounter with a *Red Dwarf* actor, but my meeting with Craig Charles was not as an actor, and the blows exchanged were not stage fighting or choreographed. The blood was real. I'd been travelling down by train from recording *The Archers* in Birmingham and was sitting with Charles Collingwood, June Spencer and Moir Leslie who was in her first *Archers* incarnation as David's fiancée, Sophie. We were in a non-smoking carriage, and when the loud, drunk pair at the far end lit up their third fags, Muggins here decided it was time to ask them to cease and desist. This was a couple of years before *Red Dwarf* and I had no idea who Craig Charles was. It turned out later that he too had just been at Pebble Mill, doing a TV appearance as a 'Punk Poet', but faced with his aggression – 'Oh, here comes the rugby club!' – I was lined up for my first ever fight.

Remembering that Lord Byron was renowned at Harrow for fighting dirty, and figuring that this coiled spring of Liverpudlian aggression probably had more pugilistic experience than me, I decided to get my defence in early and kicked him in the balls and under the chin. The problem was my stage-fight training: I pulled both the blows and delivered a soft kick to his inner thigh and a light tap to his chin (although that did crack a tooth). My intention was that he should now be incapacitated, but his immediate response was to nut me twice on the nose, causing blood to gush over us both and it was only Charles Collingwood's timely intervention that stopped it developing into a brawl. Luckily, the visual anonymity of being a radio actor and Craig only being on the cusp of stardom meant that few people realised that David Archer and David Lister were having a scrap.

We then stopped at Coventry where, bizarrely, we were joined by another actor friend, Daniel Hill, who also knew Craig, and politely introduced us. I spent the rest of the journey trying to apologise to him, with that strange sense of fellowship one gets with people you've had a fight with. As we got off at Euston, far from leaving me with a sneering Parthian shot, Craig's last words were, 'Blessed is the peacemaker.'

One of the strangest aspects of recording sitcoms is that as well as doing the indoor stuff in front of a live audience, you also have to shoot all the exterior and location shots beforehand, and these get played in the studio during the recording so the audience can understand the story, and to record their laughs. This means that you must anticipate the response and leave a suitable pause so your next line doesn't get drowned out by the gales of hilarity. This is fine when the script is funny but deeply eggy if you leave a long pause and there's stony silence in the studio.

A first for me on *A Prince Among Men* was acting while driving. I'd done a parking sequence in *Square Deal* but that was just talking to myself. This was a long, involved scene with Susie Blake, made harder because they rigged the camera on the driver's side door, started the camera, clapper board, 'Action!' and we drove off, with only the sound guy on board lying on the back seat and no director monitoring it. I then had to drive around a council estate with a car that had thousands of pounds' worth of camera equipment sticking out about four feet from the right side of the car. The dialogue ensued, leaving appropriate pauses for laughs, and when we got back to the crew, the director rewound the tape and decided if it was any good. Looking at it now, all I can see is my eyes frantically checking whether I was about to wipe out the camera on a passing car.

Sometimes we *Archers* actors get to work with each other outside of Ambridge – I do a lot of additional dialogue replacement (ADR) with Alison Dowling (Elizabeth Pargetter), Becky Wright (Nic Grundy) and Roger May (James Bellamy), and I keep getting brutally murdered by Andrew Wincott (Adam Macy) in a strange German audio drama series in which I'm a vampire. We record on separate days so disappointingly I never get to bite him. I once sang and played my

141

banjo on a gig featuring a couple of my songs with John Telfer's band, the Bushido Brothers, at the Tobacco Factory in Bristol – when John sings he is a rock god, and totally unrecognisable as the Ambridge vicar, Alan Franks.

The Archers cast sometimes find ourselves doing other voice work together, including ELT (English Language Teaching) recordings with the afore-mentioned plus Carole Boyd (Lynda Snell). I once did a hysterical re-enactment of *Dick Barton* onstage, in costume, with original BBC micro-phones and sound effects, with me as Dick and Terry Molloy (Mike Tucker) as 'Snowy'. Ironic really, as that programme was axed to make way for *The Archers* in 1951.

However, *A Prince Among Men* was the first time I'd ever done a long scene in vision with any of *The Archers* cast. My character Mark Fitz-herbert had been sent to a factory that Gary Prince had just bought, with information for the long-time owner that we were closing it down. The factory owner was played by Arnold Peters, Ambridge's own Jack Woolley. You get very used to radio actors gurning, contorting themselves, doing anything that will make their voice sound right with no attention whatsoever to how they look. It was so strange to see Arnold without a script, proving why his final scenes as Jack with Alzheimer's, when he too was suffering the early symptoms of the disease, were so rightly praised and won the programme the Mental Health Media Award in 2007. In vision, he was a lovely, subtle actor, the master of baffled incompre-hension, and when I told him I was closing his factory, he nearly had me in tears.

Being David Archer: Phil and Jill

On the actors' side of the room at *The Archers* there were my 'parents', Norman Painting as Phil and Paddy Greene as Jill. By an extraordinary coincidence, Norman, who was also a writer on *The Archers* from 1966 to 1982, had used 'Bentinck' as a nom de plume. He wrote hundreds of episodes as 'Bruno Milna' but for some reason he also used 'Norman Bentinck'.

Painting and Bentinck are slightly homophonic – but it was a pretty amazing chance that the actor playing your son would turn up with that very name.

Although Norman was nothing like my real father physically, or in almost any other way, the one thing they did have in common was a love of pontificating, authoritatively, on almost any given subject. Norman had been a postgraduate research student at Oxford and was extremely well read, and liked to show it. I was brought up to challenge or at least query everything, which he might easily have taken agin in one so callow, but it was only because I was genuinely interested. We used to have wonderful long talks on so many subjects, notably the Civil War – because I was filming *By the Sword Divided* and he lived about a mile from the site of the Battle of Edge Hill.

Thank goodness the eating-averse Twitterati weren't around when he was at his on-mike eating prime; these days they give us a hard time

143

if we so much as crunch a piece of toast, so they'd have got their knickers well and truly twisted to hear him talking while eating a full English – an imaginary one, mind you, as he was always proud of his munching technique with nary a BBC biccy in sight. I also learned two other radio techniques from him: the art of slowing a scene if the episode is running too short, which he used to do by stroking his chin a lot, and the end-of-episode, pre-music rallentando. I used to call him the *rallentando-meister:*

PHIL I don't like the look of that marrow
    Jethro, I don't … like it … at all.
(MUSIC)

One of Norman's claims to fame was that, as the longest-running character in a drama series, he had once been invited to the *Guinness Book of Records* annual dinner. He had been seated between a Russian air stewardess who had survived the longest fall from an aircraft without a parachute, and who spoke no English, and the fattest woman in Britain, who needed two chairs and preferred eating to speaking. Loquaciousness being Norman's best thing, he suffered the whole dinner in tortured silence.

Once Paddy had got over my streaked hair and earring, she soon started being more to me than just a radio mum. She called me 'Timlet' and took me under her wing. You can hear her beautiful dry wit in her impeccable acting. When the script calls for this:

JILL Yes.

Or this:

JILL I see.

– in Paddy's hands those words can have limit-less meanings. She describes the role of Jill as essentially cooking and agreeing with the men, which she endured with the patience of a saint until Norman's death, when Jill was finally allowed to blossom and reveal gravitas and wisdom – though never abandoning the ability to imbue the words 'fruit cake' with innuendo, sexual or otherwise. Paddy gave a wonderful speech on the day we all left Pebble Mill, talking about Margot Boyd (who played 'the dog woman' – Marjorie Antrobus) giving her dress size on the phone – 'Forty-two, forty-two, forty-two!' She also told us that when Jack May (the inimitable Nelson Gabriel) came back to the programme after a few years' absence, and was told by the producer Tony Shryane that 'We now do the read-through in the narrator's room,' he replied, 'My God, you've made enormous progress in the last ten years.'

Her comic timing is impeccable. After Norman died, she was in many episodes to record the passing of Phil, her radio husband of over forty years. I asked her what it was like doing her scenes without Norman. When she replied, 'It's strange, very strange...' I thought I understood. When she added, '...nice though,' I was in bits.

The dangers of mucking around...

Most of my contemporaries started their careers doing rep theatre and tours. Apart from *Joseph and the Amazing Technicolor Dreamcoat* in Plymouth, *Henry IV* and panto at Coventry, *Charley's Aunt* in Watford and *The Beaux' Stratagem* at Southampton, my theatre experience has been a lot of fringe in Bristol, Bath and London, or in the London West End. Having been in the RAF TV drama *Winter Flight* in 1984, I continued the military theme, playing a young National Service conscript called Tone in the play *Reluctant Heroes* by Colin Morris at the Churchill Theatre, Bromley, directed by John Alderton.

We were all hugely impressed to have such a big telly star directing us, but although he's a wonderful comedy actor and all-round nice bloke, he had never directed anything before and had the unnerving habit of showing you how to do it. Since he was extremely good at pratfalls, double-takes and baffled innocence, it just showed up the fact that I wasn't.

The play had been a huge hit for Brian Rix in 1950, when the entire audience had been through the war and the younger ones were still doing National Service. The French's Acting Edition of the play had stars in the script that marked where the laughs would come. They didn't. By 1985, the topicality had worn off somewhat. The play also

146

starred the lovely Jeff Rawle, who recently reminded me that once it had opened, John and his wife Pauline Collins sloped off on holiday to Portugal, leaving us to cope alone for the three-week run which he, mistakenly, believed would be transferring to the West End. So we started misbehaving.

In one scene, as the gruff sergeant, played perfectly by ex-Grenadier sergeant Shaun Curry, is leaving our barracks, he says, 'Any questions? No? Lights out in five minutes,' and exits. One empty matinee, I decided it would be a good idea, when he said, 'Any questions?' to say, 'Yes Sarn't.'

A wicked smile playing around his moustachioed lips, Shaun said, 'What is it, Tone?'

'I need to report a terrible case of piles, Sarn't.'

'Piles?' He was now about to corpse. 'Piles of what, Tone?'

'Piles of haemorrhoids, Sarn't.'

He had now lost it but managed to utter, 'Report to the medical orderly in the morning. Lights out!' And off he went.

I thought that was the end of it. No such luck. The next scene was set in the morning with us recruits in vest and underpants lined up for inspection. In marched Shaun.

'Tone, touch your toes!'

Five years of school cadet force and three weeks playing an obedient recruit meant that I immediately did as ordered.

'Medical orderly, got that syringe? Man here with a bad case of piles.'

I shot upright. 'It's all right, Sarn't. All cured now, Sarn't, thank you. I'm fine.'

Appallingly childish and unprofessional I know, but you can get bored doing long runs, and the house was half empty – or so I thought...

Ten or fifteen years later, I was auditioning for a TV part and the casting director mentioned that she saw me in 'some play in Bromley about the Army.'

'Oh yes, *Reluctant Heroes*. Did you enjoy it?'

'Not much, there was a long sequence about piles that I simply didn't understand.'

Whoops. Lesson to us all – you never know who's in!

Being David Archer: Bristol Court Hotel

I retain happy, and some not so happy, memories of Pebble Mill. The thing that's changed most from those days is the sense of togetherness that *The Archers* actors had as a company. For one thing, everyone ate lunch in the staff canteen on the top floor, and this was where the gossip, stories and intrigue would be traded, until the producer came to join us, when, depending on who it was, mouths would be zipped and careers protected.

Another thing we miss about Pebble Mill is that in the evening we would all troop round to the BBC club, which was in a separate building, and for staff and performers only. You could eat there too, which was preferable to the hotel, where the term 'food' was stretching the definition of the word.

These days the cast stay in many different hotels and eat at a huge choice of bistros and restaurants in central Birmingham, but back then there was really only the famed Bristol Court Hotel, or 'Fawlty Towers' as we called it. Jack May loved it because the bar served Bell's whisky, and since it seemed that was all he ever consumed, he had no truck with his fellow cast members moaning about cold rooms that stank of stale smoke, the damp, the nylon sheets, the single beds with a thirty-degree slope from decades of overweight travelling salesmen trying in vain to reach their socks, the tiny televisions with lousy reception, or the blue or pink plastic shower cubicles with tepid water dribbling through limescale-encrusted shower heads. The heating was turned off during the day, and one winter afternoon between recordings stands out in my memory – watching daytime TV in black and white, lying in bed fully clothed under the polyester duvet (TOG rating minus twelve), running a hair dryer to raise the ambient temperature above freezing, wondering seriously if I'd made the right choice of career.

The owner was a friendly chap called Don, far more affable than Fawlty, but otherwise the place was almost identical to the eponymous 'Towers', right down to the actual 'Major' in the form of Ballard Berkeley (Colonel Danby), joining Jack and Margot Boyd for a post-prandial Bell's or three in the bar. So much has changed in just one generation; Margot was never seen without her 'face' on, her hair perfectly coiffured, an impeccable wool skirt suit and sensible shoes, and in the evening a cigarette in one hand, a whisky in the other, telling filthy stories – she was one of the funniest women I've ever met.

At her funeral, Charles Collingwood told the story of how, in her later years, she decided to change agent. The new agent's office was on the fifth floor of a building in Soho. Her large frame and weakened knees and hips made the climb excruciating. Entering the room and gasping for breath, she announced imperiously, 'I have two things to say … [wheeze]… firstly, you will never see me again, …. [gasp] … and secondly, [massive inhale] I don't want to work.'

Swordless

Aside from commercials and sitcoms, I was offered a healthy range of roles on stage and television following *By the Sword Divided*. After the excitement of playing the lead in a twelve-part costume drama, and effectively earning my living with sword and earring for the past four years, by contrast my next TV job was about as unglamorous as you could imagine.

Winter Flight was the story of a young RAF serviceman (Reece Dinsdale) and his waitress girlfriend, with the Falklands War in the background. I, my flowing locks shorn to a short back and sides, was a flight controller who makes the mistake of going to bed with Sean Bean's girlfriend, played by Shelagh Stephenson. In revenge, he picks my sports car up with a JCB and smashes it into my barracks bedroom as I and said girlfriend are on the job. Simulating sex with a total stranger while an MGB GT comes through the window isn't something you get taught in drama school. With no read-through it was literally, 'Tim, this is Shelagh, Shelagh, this is Tim. Okay, here's the bed. On action have sex.'

We filmed it in a deserted barracks that was about to be knocked down, so the room was ruinous, freezing and damp. It had been dressed to look lived-in but the single bed had starched sheets and just one regulation RAF blanket. We were alone in the room because the first shot was a POV, or point-of-view shot, from outside, as Sean peeps through the window and sees us making love. On take one, we didn't hear the director shout 'action' so a runner was sent to put a walkie-talkie in the room. We waited, frozen and silent, lying side by side in a single bed in an empty room, for the thing to be delivered. Then, absurdly, there was a knock on the door. 'Come in?' In crept the runner, averting his eyes from the bed, saying, 'Sorry, sorry,' put the walkie-talkie on the floor and shot out again. I've often wondered what on earth he thought we were doing. Well, at least it broke the ice, not the real ice that was forming on the bed, but at least we laughed, which made what happened next slightly easier.

Naked from the waist up but with underwear just hidden by the blanket, trying not to actually touch each other at all, a wonderfully British scene evolved. The walkie-talkie crackled into life.

'Okay, turn over.' 'Sound speed.' 'Aaaand, ACTION!'

Snog snog, writhe writhe, move on top, bump bump, grind grind, moan moan, quiver quiver, please God can we stop...

'CUT!'

Instantly roll off, maintain distance. 'Sorry, you okay?' 'Yes, fine, no, sorry, you all right?' 'Yes, well at least we're a bit warmer now!' Silence. Oh shit, too much information.

Crackle crackle.

'Okay, we're going again. Guys, can you try and make it look like you're enjoying it? In fact, I think it would be good if you were actually both climaxing, it'll give Sean more motivation. Okay, so on action you're both about to come. Thank you. Okay turn over.' 'Sound speed.' 'Aaaaand, ACTION!'

'Aaaah, aaaah, ohmygod, mmm, mmm, aaaah, aaaah, AAAAAAAHHHHHHHHH!'

'CUT! Great. Okay, moving on. Let's get the JCB in...'

We then had to do it again, many times, but now with the whole crew in the room, while dust and rubble were thrown on us to simulate the car smashing through the window. When all the reaction shots were finished, we then came to the bit we'd all been waiting to see. With a remote camera in the room in case the entire building collapsed, and another two outside, there was only going to be one take of this. The stunt driver fired up the JCB, picked up the MG in its bucket, drove towards the building, where the brickwork around the window had been weakened, and smashed it … and smashed it again … and made no impression on the wall whatsoever. RAF barracks are built with bombs in mind, and even the mighty Sean Bean couldn't get through that.

Being David Archer: Ruth

For a moment, Shelagh Stephenson, having barely survived simulated sex with me in *Winter Flight*, was in danger of becoming my wife.

David Archer is six years younger than I am, so when I joined he was only twenty-three, single, handsome and deeply eligible. Older actors kept telling me, 'Don't let them marry you off, darling, you won't get any episodes.' David went through a succession of girlfriends: before I took over the part from Nigel Carrivick, he'd lost his cherry to a Kiwi sheep-shearer called Michele Brown; in my time he fell first for Jackie Woodstock, then Virginia Derwent the ice-maiden, had a brief fling with a divorcee called Frances, then there was Sophie Barlow the fashion designer to whom he got engaged, and a Ford Escort XR3 (seriously, he loved that car).

One day in 1987 I was asked to come up to the studio to help audition for David's new squeeze. I suspected at the time that this might mean wedding bells, so I was in the difficult position of choosing a wife from a list that I hadn't made – like an arranged marriage. Very odd. It came down to a choice between two great actresses who both, for me, had the same disadvantage – they were tiny. I'm six-foot-three and, to address the microphone at the same level as anyone around the five-foot mark, I have to adopt a less than dignified splayed-leg posture, which I have now been doing with the girl who got the part, Felicity Finch, ever since. Who knows if the other applicant – the equally tiny Shelagh Stephenson – would have still gone on to be a hugely successful playwright had she got the part.

Ruth Pritchard was from the north-east and was on a year's work experience before going to Harper Adams Agricultural College. When she arrived at Brookfield it was as a farmhand, and her modern farming views and feisty attitude instantly got up David's nose. He was completely sexist, reckoning that no woman could possibly do his job. However, in the familiar path trodden by buddy movies and love stories since time immemorial, sure enough opposites attracted and within a few months they were rolling in the hay, or at least our spot-effects person was rolling in discarded recording tape while we were snogging the backs of our own hands. 'Ooooh nooo' didn't happen till later; then it was 'Ooooh yes please' – as often as possible.

Since Ruth's arrival, Felicity – Flick – and I have been through some amazing stories, have become enormously fond of each other, and can sometimes be heard bickering like a real husband-and-wife team. For instance, she insists that the meal you eat in the evening at Brookfield is called 'tea', whereas for me that's a mug of builder's and biccies around four-ish. She can't travel anywhere without at least three suitcases, assorted carrier bags and the last three days' newspapers, but, once she's taken about a week to discuss the menu with the waiter, we've had some great evenings together, happily disagreeing about almost everything. In all this time, apart from the occasional very small toy being tossed out of the pram, we have never fallen out.

She's a great actor and an extraordinary person. Wearing her journalist hat she's travelled, usually alone, to make radio features in Rwanda, Albania, Pakistan, Cambodia and, most recently, Afghanistan, for which she had to undergo a 'hostile environment training course'. And they say Ruth is plucky.

Made in Heaven

In 1985, stardom beckoned yet again. On paper, it sounded superb: a pilot episode of a new long-running series that was billed as the 'British *Dallas*', which was the biggest thing on TV at the time. This UK pilot was called *Griffins* and revolved around a high-class health resort set in a country-house estate and catering to the rich and famous. I was the sports instructor and was there to get everyone fit, including all the beautiful female inmates who I would get to exercise in bed. I wondered how to play him, and asked Judy what I should do to come across as smoulderingly sexy.

'Play him Irish,' she suggested.

The opening credits are hysterical. Over throbbing music, the major characters are shown in a montage, doing their thing, then turning to camera with a cheesy grin. I was rowing a boat in a shell suit. It went downhill from there.

My first 'conquest' was the delightful and beautiful Debbie Arnold. The opening scene was me teaching her how to shoot a bow and arrow (the producer was an *Archers* fan and this was his little joke); we then graduated to the indoor pool where I was teaching her to swim (we both got ear infections). Next was the bedroom scene. Debbie is splendidly endowed but, not wanting the entire crew to cop a look, she stuck circular Band Aids on her nipples to stay decent (albeit with eyelashes painted on!). There is really only one memory I have of that show: Debbie and me in helpless fits of laughter.

When it came to the cast and crew showing we knew it was doomed. One of the main problems was the sound – filmed in the cavernously large rooms of the stately home, every footstep, movement and line was accompanied by a booming echo. You couldn't hear a word. At least you couldn't tell how unconvincing my Irish accent was. 'Sure, an' you'll need-need-need some extra-tra-tra tuition shun-shun in my room later-later-later so you will-will-will...'

It didn't go to series. Indeed, so much of a death did it die that you can't even find it on the internet. I probably own the only copy in existence.

How I landed my next leading TV role I've no idea. I was in the middle of doing *Hedda Gabler* at the King's Head in Islington and had quite a thick beard. I was up to play the role of Steve, a once famous Man United and England football player, who, having damaged his knees, was now running a wedding agency called 'Made in Heaven' – the title of the series. It consisted of four two-hour episodes with two weddings in each, and well-known names coming in as guest stars: Keith Barron, Kenneth Connor, Julie Covington, Colin Welland, Maggie O'Neill and the like.

I don't look like a footballer, I don't sound like a footballer, I had a thick beard (not a footballer look in 1990) and had last played soccer, badly, when I was twelve.

I got the part.

We filmed in Manchester. While the rest of the cast stayed in a hotel, I booked myself into what used to be the stables of a pub called the Rampant Lion. Set at the bottom of the pub's garden, it was like a tart's boudoir with a four-poster bed and lush chinoiserie. It was summer and the noise from the garden was intense until exactly eleven o'clock every night, after which it was wonderfully peaceful. I loved it. Meanwhile Louisa Rix, who played my wife, was fending off the attentions of one of said 'names' at the hotel, whose bravura chat-up line was, 'Would you like to come upstairs and see the size of my room?'

It was all going swimmingly until the read-through of the third episode when the guest writer, a well-known grittily northern playwright who cannot be named, clearly saw through this southern wuss and decided to cut nearly half my lines, which when you're playing the lead is a bit off. She then took her name off the end credits – did she really hate me that much just from a reading? I think maybe she couldn't tune in to the appropriately estuarine footballer accent I was using, and just saw me as posh boy.

157

Louisa's character and mine were married but separated and I was having an affair with the equally gorgeous Maggie O'Neill. The day came when we had a bedroom scene, although unlike the freezing RAF fiasco, this involved leaping out of bed mid-howsyerfather stark naked to check my diary. My first 'closed set' – where only necessary crew were allowed. We rehearsed the scene. I leapt out of bed, grabbed my diary and stood there starkers madly checking appointments. I looked down to find the continuity girl sitting on the floor making notes. The only continuity she could possibly have been recording was the tumescence, or otherwise, of John Thomas, but thankfully he had remained well behaved under all that scrutiny.

After we'd finished filming and were back in London, Judy and I asked Louisa round for dinner. She was going through a rather difficult divorce at the time, and, needing another singleton, we also asked old chum Richard Ommanney, the writer of *Square Deal,* as he too was in the aftermath of a separation. At first, we thought the evening was a disaster as they hardly spoke to each other, Rich and I talked computers all night, while Louisa and Judy became firm chums. Around midnight, Rich mumbled something about him possibly driving back in Louisa's direction and would she maybe like a lift, sort of thing, or not. She grudgingly sort of accepted, a bit. It turned out they'd fallen madly in love with each other at first sight and had both been struck dumb. They're still blissfully happily married. A wonderful coda to a television series called *Made in Heaven.*

Being David Archer: Sound effects

'Rolling in discarded recording tape while we were snogging the backs of our own hands'? I should explain. Kissing the back of your hand started in the days of mono recording when you were physically separated by the microphone. It's also slightly easier to control as the real thing runs the risk of scripts clashing, and you've also got lines to read. The fake often sounds better than the real in radio.

An ironing board, old quarter-inch tape and a pot of yoghurt are all handy for sound effects. In thirty-five years of being in *The Archers*, it's always been the same ironing board – old and rattly, and it's used for all the metal gates and cattle crushes. The yoghurt is used for all the squelchy farming sounds, like calves and lambs being born, and the recording tape sounds much more like straw than real straw – also it doesn't smell or rot, so is perfect for a recording studio.

Lambing is a good example of the teamwork required to make the 'picture' of a radio scene. On one side of the soundproofed glass is the recording team – the director who runs the show and makes the final decisions, getting good performances out of the actors and, eyes closed, listening to the mix and balance of the various ingredients, which are all recorded in real time. Next to the director is the production coordinator who times the scenes and writes down everything about the process. Then there's the sound recordist at the panel, who 'drives' the whole thing, sat at a huge desk of faders, twiddling and tweaking to get the sounds just right. Behind them all are 'grams' – what used to be turntables with vinyl records of sound effects, then CDs, are now MP3s which play at the touch of a button.

On the other side of the glass are the actors and the 'spot-effects' person – in effect an actor who never speaks but makes all the live sounds, like teacups, opening Aga doors and digging fence posts, and who sometimes rolls around on the recording tape, simulating cows in distress. So, for instance, a lambing needs the distressed baaing of the ewe (grams track 1), other ewes in the background (track 2) and the atmosphere of the barn (track 3). Then you need the actor cajoling the beast,

DAVID Come on girl, you can do it, (squelch) that's it, (squelch) just a bit more, nearly there (big squelch … and … there we are…

while the spot person is squelching yoghurt with rubber-gloved hands. At the moment of birth a large towel soaked in water is dropped from high onto a pile of recording tape, at the same time as which the grams play the lamb's bleating entry to the world (track 4). *Voilà* – one new addition to the farm!

Regular listeners to the programme will have heard David and others getting down from the tractor. You may be surprised to hear that this is done with a bucket. It's an old, metal bucket filled with a manky pillow to deaden the sound and I can remember my first encounter with it. I hadn't been in the programme long when I walked into the dead room at Pebble Mill to find a very wobbly Chris Gittins standing on top of it.

'Hello, Chris, why are you standing on a bucket?' I asked naively.

'D'oh, this ain't a bucket, David,' he scoffed, 'this m's me tractor!'

The explanation is that you need something to sound like the steps down from the cab. Obsessive listeners will have noticed that the single step of a petrol Ferguson in the 1950s and the enormous flight of stairs required to get out of a modern Fordson behemoth have exactly the same sound.

Year of the Comet

So many false dawns.

Another Hollywood movie! Not only that but written by probably the most successful screen-writer ever, William Goldman, he of *Adventures in the Screen Trade,* the bible of movie wisdom, containing the famous line, 'Nobody knows anything.' Coming on the back of his *Butch Cassidy and the Sundance Kid, All the President's Men, Marathon Man, Magic* and *The Princess Bride, Year of the Comet* was bound to launch me into the stratosphere, we'd have to move to LA and the boys would grow up as Americans and say 'was like' instead of 'said'.

I wore a three-piece pinstripe suit for the

audition with famed English director Peter Yates to play the spoiled, arrogant, upper-class, stuffy Brit half-brother of American star Penelope Ann Miller in a film about a Europe-wide chase for the most expensive bottle of wine in history – they told me later it was the suit that clinched it. At the read-through I was one of the first to arrive. There was a friendly American there called Bill. I asked him how he was involved with the movie. 'Oh, I'm the writer,' he answered shyly.

I only had a few scenes, but they were all indoors, while most of the filming was on location, so I spent weeks in Skye and the south of France on 'weather cover'. This means that if it's pouring with rain, they've always got a set built for other scenes and actors on standby to shoot inside if necessary. My father was played by Robert Hardy – the most wonderful company for a young actor, he taught me so much and was hugely generous. We used to go for dinner in Nice and he'd order lobster, always picking up the tab. I once offered to pay– 'Dear boy, don't be ridiculous, I earn *far* more than you do.' Sadly, his availability ran out before we ever got to our scenes and the part was taken by the equally fascinating, but more serious, Ian Richardson.

It was the French actor Louis Jourdan's last film role before retiring – what style that man had. While in Scotland, we actors were put up in a three-star hotel in Fort William. As we gathered in the bar after checking in, M. Jourdan's chauffeur-driven Rolls pulled up outside, the driver got out and opened the rear door. Louis, coat draped French style over his shoulders, Gitane dangling from his lips, sauntered into the lobby, ignored us completely, looked around for a moment, turned to the driver, sighed, said quietly, 'Non,' and sashayed out to the Rolls again. He ended up in a massive suite in a nearby castle.

A week later we were introduced to the best restaurant in Skye by fine actor and gourmand Ian McNeice. Louis was sitting alone in the bay window overlooking the loch. He acknowledged acquaintanceship but didn't ask us to join him. When we looked at the handwritten menu, we noticed a recent addition in different ink – 'Haricots Verts à la Jourdan' – he had obviously had a word with the chef.

After weeks of touring Europe in wonderful locations but never even turning over, we eventually filmed my scenes in the Electricity Board's offices in Islington – about two miles from home. I was enormously flattered when Peter Yates asked me to be sure to let him know next time I was appearing on stage. It wasn't until many years later that I had a light bulb moment and realised it was a very English, polite way of suggesting to me that I was overdoing it – again!

Tim Daly, who played the dashing male lead, and Penelope were pretty good and quite friendly but, still, American actors need to be careful working with British film crews. Tim was a bit short with one of the crew once, which resulted in a classic wind-up routine one morning.

Tim arrived on set. A passing grip said, 'Oh 'ello, Tim. Are you still...?'

'What?'

'No, sorry, we thought you'd been...'

'What?'

'No, no, never mind...'

Tim walked on. The gaffer walked by. 'Tim! Oh. Are you...?'

'What?'

'No nothing, we just heard that...'

'WHAT?'

'No, it's fine, just surprised to see you that's all...'

How to get an actor completely paranoid.

The film, which was released in 1992, was William Goldman's only ever flop. He wrote: 'There was nothing we could do because no matter how we fussed this was a movie about red wine and the movie-going audience today has zero interest in red wine.'

Tim Daly summed up my experience too, in an interview with the A.V. Club in 2014: 'What a bummer, man. I loved that movie, I loved doing it. It was just a great part for me! And that was my shot, right? That was my shot to be a movie star. I mean, on paper, it was a William Goldman script, Peter Yates directing, it was a Castle Rock production, it had a good budget – and the movie just did not work.'

Year of the Comet proved to be one of the biggest flops in Castle Rock's history. It was released in the United States on the weekend of the Rodney King riots and no one was going to the cinema, so Tim didn't blame himself for its failure.

I wasn't in it enough to think it was my fault either!

Sharpe's Rifles

One of the great attractions for becoming an actor, beyond the cerebral art of it all, is the idea that you'll travel the world and be paid huge sums of money to be filmed entwined with beautiful women in exotic locations, shoot guns, drive fast cars and scream 'Land ahoy!' from the crow's nest of a pirate ship. Maybe that's just us men, or just me – well, anyway, they were on my bucket list. I'd ticked the box on the exotic entwining front with the Australia ad, but flying out to Russia shortly after the fall of the Berlin Wall to face a massed cavalry charge of Cossacks and, with my dying speech, bequeathing my sword to Sean Bean, was altogether another kind of adventure.

I actually died twice, once in a manger with Paul McGann and once with Sean. I'd read all the Sharpe books, and when I got the part of Captain Murray in the first of the new Sharpe series, filming in the Crimea, I couldn't have been more thrilled. The British Airways flight to Moscow was fairly uneventful, then we changed to a different airport – and a Russian charter plane.

The Ilyushin, parked on the far side of the Moscow air base of the Russian Air Force, smelled strongly of damp. The hold wasn't big enough to fit all the camera equipment so they simply piled it up in the aisle and across the seats at the back.

This created a kind of private cabinette that contained assorted newly met chosen men and other ne'er-do-wells. The Pathfinders of episode one were on their way.

When I say 'on their way', it took about an hour to get the engines started, and when they finally caught, huge clouds of smoke belched from the jets under the wings and the whole plane shook violently. Vodka seemed the only sensible option and the cabinette turned into the bar.

Three hours later, we started our descent into Simferopol. Within thirty seconds, we had landed. Apparently the captain was a military jet pilot whose technique for landing a plane was almost identical to that for vertical dive-bombing. Jason Salkey (Trooper Harris) used the plummeting plane to demonstrate his skateboarding skills. The rest of us curled up and prayed – even the atheists.

We were transported by minibus to Simferopol town centre, immediately dubbed 'Simply Awful'. A faceless hotel looking out onto washing lines. Welcome to Crimea.

The adventures that followed made up for it. I was soon facing a cavalry charge of twenty Cossacks dressed up as French Hussars, swords drawn, coming at me at full gallop, led by the guy who was supposed to slash me across the chest – he was a Scot on horseback, and I imagined therefore spurred on by acts of woad-painted, Sassenach-hating frenzy. The camera crew were safely tucked behind strongly built wooden barriers, and I was in front of them, alone, with a sword. No acting required here then. Having been sliced (he actually missed me by about six inches), I had to stagger midst the onrushing cavalry and collapse on the hill, whence to be carried off to die by Jason, who has very muscular but bony shoulders.

I remember sitting with Jason in the back of a Lada in a forest, with two Russian mafiosi in the front seat trying to sell us tank helmets with attached infra-red night sights. In order to prove it worked, one of the Russians got out and hid in a bush. I then put the helmet on and they plugged me into the cigarette lighter. Wow, green binocular night-vision, lit by an eerie glow, which turned out to be the cigarette the guy in the bush was smoking. I bought four and Jason equipped the entire cast and crew.

The reason for this was that our daily per diems were more than anyone there earned in a year, and it took us a while for that to sink in and to respect it. But we did buy a lot of caviar and fur hats. I think Jason just bought weapons.

We took a day trip to Balaclava and Sebastopol and saw the 'Valley of Death' of Light Brigade fame. An ancestor of mine, General Sir Henry Bentinck, had led the Coldstream across the Alma, and here was I with a video camera in a Russian Army encampment in the Crimea pretending to be a soldier, about five miles from where that battle had taken place.

I was filming the pack of nuclear submarines in the harbour at Balaclava from the steep hill that guards its entrance, when my view was blocked by a Russian sailor with a Kalashnikov pointing idly at me. This was an area that had only just come out of fifty or more years of military control. I explained that I was an English tourist, pointed at the submarines, said 'Glasnost' a lot and gave him ten dollars. Everything was smiles and joy.

Julian Fellowes, who was playing my commanding officer, entertained us with lectures on the relative architectural merits of Soviet bus shelters, and we lunched on the ridge where Raglan saw the Russian dispersion of guns and troops that he so tragically failed to convey to Lucan and Cardigan. To see the view is to understand everything about what happened. Earlier, we had driven to the head of the valley where the Light Brigade were formed up, and the misunderstanding is so clear.

Meanwhile, everything with the filming was going wrong. There was no stunt coordinator, so people started to get injured. The food really was appalling and those uninjured became ill. There was no way to phone home so everyone got frustrated and homesick. Then in an episode of almost suicidal bad judgement, one of the producers, playing football on the beach, tackled Paul McGann (the original Sharpe) hard and buggered his knee. The following day, Paul had to lead an attack up a steep hill under fire from the 'French', who were in fact all Russian conscripts who delighted in shooting us capitalist running dogs and fired their blank cartridges straight in our faces if they possibly could. Paul soldiered bravely on but it soon became apparent that his leg was too bad to continue, and eventually the production was pulled under an insurance contingency called 'force majeure' and, after a month of really quite dangerous work, we all came home.

Julian and I are cousins by marriage, but we had never met before. We had a wonderful dinner on the return journey in a brand-new hotel just outside Moscow airport. This was 1992 and Russia was like the Wild West in the days of the gold rush. Driving past puttering Ladas and ancient ZiL limousines on roads that hadn't changed since the war, we saw an enormous petrol tanker billowing smoke and flames in a field with no one paying the least attention, then turned a corner to find this brand new, state-of-the-art European hotel. In the lobby, prostitutes in mink coats flashed their nakedness at you as you checked in; then caviar and champagne in the bar with businessmen from all over the world, there to rape a country that was on its knees and utterly ignorant of the scheming ways of the West. How quickly did they pick it up? Well, who owns Kensington and Chelsea now?

Paul was replaced by Sean Bean, and after a few weeks of sitting at home on full salary, we flew back out to do it all over again. This time we were on the coast in Yalta, in an enormous sanatorium complex usually occupied by the KGB. One night we were playing the Risk board game and the table in my room wasn't big enough, so we borrowed the enormous desk that was manned by the two soldiers in the lobby.

'Hope you don't mind, Boris, we need this to play a capitalist game of world domination – a game it seems you have recently lost.'

The contrasts were so great, and really sobering. I had never seen such poverty. I went out one day to buy toothpaste, *zubnaya pasta* but there

169

was none to be had; no shops stocked it. I eventually bought a half-used tube that was sitting next to a single AA battery and a comb on a table of other paltry offerings in the flea market. Roubles were worthless, our US dollars were far too much, so we paid with coupons: 100 coupons represented about one US cent. The toothpaste was five coupons.

Jason Salkey is a professional Frisbee player and we made friends with inquisitive students and others as we played in the park. What struck me most, when talking life and politics with these fellow humans who had been raised and educated in such a radically different system, was how, looking westwards at my privileged life, it seemed so shallow, so preoccupied with earning money, a raison d'être built entirely around the need to get work in order to survive. I'm no communist, but what was so apparent was that these young students had absolutely no idea what we were talking about when we tried to explain. Their lives were financially poor but they had no opportunity to change anything, so for them life was about learning, about art, philosophy, theatre and literature, with an engagement that was different to ours. For us, those things are, in a sense, luxuries to be studied at leisure and for pleasure. For them, it *was* their life. For all our money, they pitied us. It was an eye-opener.

The contrast really hit me one night in the hotel bar when, fuelled with local vodka, the Russians started singing – beautiful, achingly sad, three-part-harmony folk songs, every note an expression of suffering and oppression, and they wept as they sang. We were invited to sing in response. The only thing we could think of was 'The Hokey Cokey'.

Being David Archer: High drama

There are two episodes that Felicity and I agree were unforgettable.

We usually receive our scripts about four days before recording, but sometimes, if we're away when they arrive or there's a delay, it has happened that we only see the lines just before we record, but there's always a read-through beforehand so we get to know what it's about. In one case, though, I'd been off filming, hadn't got the script and we had to hurriedly record a scene that I hadn't even looked at. We went straight for a take without a rehearsal, so I was sight-reading.

The green light came on and an actress whom we had barely met sat across a table from me and Flick, and nervously told us that Ruth had breast cancer. I hadn't seen it coming and nor had my character David, so in the words of Robert Mitchum, there was 'No acting required' – we were both really struggling to hold back tears. And it saved someone's life. Felicity received a letter from a woman who, but for the storyline about Ruth's breast cancer, would not have noticed a lump that then got treated just in the nick of time.

I prepare the scripts with a pencil, underlining DAVID and then a vertical line by the side of each speech. We all do it differently, some use highlighters, some biros, some scribble all over the page, others leave it almost pristine – whatever works. I usually do it at home, but sometimes on the train or in a hotel. Having done that, I read the scene and think about what David's train of thought is, whether he means what he says, what is the time of day, whether it's outside and raining and he's digging a ditch, or inside curled up with the missus. They all sound different, and you need to be in the right place in your head. When I read the scene in which Ruth tells David she's in love with Sam the dairyman, I was in a hotel room in Birmingham, and I remember it making me nervous for the first time since I'd started in the programme. Written by the longest-running of our team of wonderful writers, Mary Cutler, it twisted David's mind like nothing had ever done before. This was a turning point, a *Wendepunkt*, and it had to be done well.

Now here I need to give you David's side of the story. There have been suggestions that his attentions to Sophie blew Ruth into Sam's arms. This is palpable nonsense. The whole point about David Archer is his integrity. In the years I've been playing him, I've portrayed that integrity being tested, over and over. Usually he wins, but when he falters, it's like a morality play – he stumbles, is tempted by the Devil, nearly succumbs to temptation, then pulls back from the brink at the last minute.

In this case, he didn't even come close. His own wife was behaving extremely oddly and he became convinced that her cancer had returned and she wasn't telling him. His ex-fiancée Sophie turns up and is friendly and funny and listens to

172

his worries. The idea of having an affair with her *doesn't even cross his mind!* His wife meanwhile, without his knowledge, has become hopelessly sexually attracted to a farmworker and, having lied to David for months and treated him like an irrelevant idiot, has planned to go to a nearby hotel to have sex with a hunky stranger while her husband is cooking spaghetti bolognese at home for their children. Get real people, there is no comparison. And give it up for spag bol – it saved their marriage!

So, there we were recording this scene. Ruth is in floods of tears in the bedroom, David is comforting her: what is it love, tell me, what is it? Oh David... What, please tell me, I've been so worried (it's the cancer come back isn't it?). Oh David... Yes?... I... I... Aaaaaaaaaah! (tears of desperation) What Ruth, darling, please tell me... I... Yes, say it... I'm ... I'm in love with Sam and I nearly had sex with him in a hotel last night (or words to that effect) – (MASSIVELY LONG PAUSE) You. Did. What? Cue David losing it big time and Flick generating extraordinarily committed amounts of mucus to the reality of the situation. Finally, it ends. It's been a long, very emotional scene. We're drained. One take. Nailed it. A seminal radio moment.

Our director Kate Oates comes onto the talkback,

'That was great, guys. I'd like to do it again. Tim, page 12 line 4, can you pull back on "lied" – I think it'd be stronger quieter. And Flick, a bit less snot, darling. Okay, green light coming...' So we did it all over again.

Back to school

Back home from Russia and back in the theatre. I was cast as Torvald Helmer in a fringe production of Ibsen's *A Doll's House* at the Bridge Lane Theatre, Battersea, directed by Polly Irvin, produced by Adjoa Andoh and with Sophie Thursfield as Nora. This was a fascinating example of how a lack of preconceptions can help to create something original and new. We were in our thirties, traditionally too young to play the main parts, where the controlling Torvald demeans and patronises his 'doll' of a wife, using diminutives and pet phrases that belittle and dehumanise her. One of the things we were taught at drama school was 'text study' – the only thing you have as source material is the text, not how the play has been done before, or what has been written about it by critics, academics or even the writer himself. Acting is an interpretative art, and as long as you're true to the words, plays can be done in so many different ways. In our case, we started with the idea that Torvald and Nora had a very active sex life, and fancied each other madly. If you start like that, the rest of the play changes quite radically, and the diminutives become endearments, his protestations of love and loyalty, which later sound like empty half-truths, we played as male weakness rather than chauvinist manipulation. Probably not what Ibsen intended, but it had a

174

validity and was an original interpretation. We contrived to make Torvald a sympathetic character, and by the end the audience was torn as to who to feel sorry for when she left him. Judy brought Will, then aged eight, to see it one night and he felt sorry for his pa, and cried. The audience didn't know he was my son and were amazed to hear a child so moved.

We received a lovely review in the *Observer,* as a result of which we were invited to the annual Ibsen Stage Festival in Oslo, to put it on in the Nationaltheatret for a week's run. We were terrified that the Norwegians would think we were taking the mickey, and on the first night we took our bows to a slow handclap, facing serried ranks of dour academics with moustache-less beards, frowning intensely. We didn't know that this was the ultimate Norwegian accolade, and the reviews the next day were unanimously glowing. With wonderful performances from Sophie, Thane Bettany, Julia Barrie, Yvette Rees and Chris Mc-Hallem, this was the most rewarding play I'd ever been in.

A few years later, Yvette died and we went to her funeral. At the reception afterwards, I found myself talking to the amazing Ken Campbell, one of her oldest friends. I was telling him I'd once been in his first play, a fringe production in Bath of *You See the Thing Is This* and was being complimentary about his brilliant writing. After a pause, he looked me directly in the eye and said, 'Yeees. Actually, I think I'm going to go and find somebody more interesting to talk to,' and wandered off. It remains the most staggeringly rude thing anyone has ever said to me.

In the mid-1990s, I had a proper chance to work out how to do this screen-acting malarkey. I was cast as a running character in *Grange Hill* – Lucy Mitchell's father, Greg, whose wife had recently died. In shock and mourning, he then discovers the cause of death – AIDS. He goes mental, assuming she had been having an affair. It turns out they'd had a car crash in California, she'd had a blood transfusion and the blood was infected. A great storyline about father/daughter relationship, grief, guilt, blame and anger. After a while, he starts seeing someone new, so from Lucy's perspective the story was about step-parents too. I've always been a better actor when the part is very different from me, and after seventeen episodes of sounding like a proper geezer from Billericay, I finally learned the most fundamental lesson of all, that the camera doesn't lie, it sees the truth: you just have to immerse yourself in someone else's reality.

At the same time, I was playing a very different character, in Tom Stoppard's *Arcadia* at the Theatre Royal Haymarket, directed by Trevor Nunn. The contrastingly posh Captain Bryce has some funny lines in the first half and doesn't appear in the second, but I had made a bit of a mistake – I was understudying Roger Allam. That's Roger 'Never Off' Allam, as I discovered far too late. After *Pirates*, when understudying had changed my life, I thought I might get the chance to do it again, but hadn't reckoned on Roger.

'Roger's been shot!' came the cry down the

narrow corridors of the Theatre Royal dressing rooms. My heart leapt in terror and anticipation. How had I allowed myself to get into this situation again? And this time in one of the most complex and difficult parts in Stoppard's oeuvre, but a triumph if you can pull it off.

'Shot?' I squealed.

'Someone's shot him in the head with an air rifle.'

'My God. Is he dead?'

'No, he's in his dressing room, putting on a plaster.'

'He's going on?'

'Of course he's going on. Roger's never off.'

Another day he twisted his ankle running for a bus – went on with a limp. Bastard.

At the end of the nine-month run, we understudies auditioned in front of Trevor to take over the main roles. I didn't get it. Win some lose some, but that really would have made a difference.

As a result of doing these two jobs at the same time, plus a load of *Archers* bookings, I was unable to go on a big family holiday, which is one of my life's greatest regrets. This was the whole family: my father, my stepmother, my sisters and their children, and Judy, Will and Jasper. They had rented a huge villa with a pool in Italy for two weeks, and it happened without me. Pa died three years later, and it was my last chance to spend some real quality time with him, and when I hear the stories about the adventures and fun they had, I feel a real pang. These are the perils of being an actor, though: you have to take the work when it comes along.

That work in the mid-1990s included the lead in *Strike Force*. I was very nearly a pilot. When I was at school, I imagined my future either doing what my pa did, advertising, or flying planes. I flew light aircraft with the Combined Cadet Force and got *Flight* magazine monthly. My favourite reading was about Spitfires and Hurricanes, and I seriously considered joining the RAF for a while. The appeal of flying never left, though, and when I landed this part, it was as though it had been written by my guardian angel.

Wing Commander Jonathan Raikes was 'awesome in the air', as one of my pilots put it. Bliss. I so nearly blew it. Having got the job, two weeks before filming I was meeting Judy in a pub in London for my birthday when someone smashed a pint glass full in my face.

I was millimetres away from being blinded in one eye and my face was cut to bits. I had to go up to Manchester to show the producers the damage. I remember standing in a hotel car park as the two executives peered at my lacerations.

'No, I don't think we'll have to recast.'

Phew, but it meant that I spent hours in make-up every morning and was the palest fast-jet pilot you've ever seen.

The 'Strike Force' was an elite group of Tornado pilots based in Cyprus and trained to instantly answer the call to scramble anywhere in Europe. This pilot episode (yes, we did that joke to death) was about the selection for the team. I was the boss. If the pilot episode was successful it would go to series – like *Soldier Soldier* in the air – so we were all very keen to make it work. We filmed it on location at RAF Leeming in York-shire, and we pilots met up on a train at King's Cross. We'd clearly all had the same idea – look butch. Leather jackets, shades, stubble and monosyllabic grunts failed to cover the fact that we were all like excited schoolchildren, let loose with millions of pounds' worth of toys.

We were '555 Squadron' and, amazingly, as we wandered around the base in uniform, the real RAF would fire off salutes and call us 'sir'. One day we were lounging in the mess room and one of our number, a delicate soul, came in flapping and saying, 'Oh my God, I've just been saluted!'

We, butch as hell and Ray-banned to the nines, said, 'Yes, and what did you do?'

'I went "Aaaaaaaaahhahaahahhaaaa!"'

'Nooooooo!'

We were filming in a stationary Tornado just off the main runway with me fully togged up in the pilot's seat, when the Queen's flight took off in formation for a fly-past over Buckingham Palace. The leading plane was hit by complete engine failure and, in order to miss him, the plane behind pulled up and to the left, heading straight for us. Someone was filming it on a camcorder and when we looked back at the footage, its wing can't have missed us by more than a foot. 'Not ideal,' as they say in the forces.

I was invited to follow the real Wing Com-mander around on his duties, to get the style of the man and see how it was really done. We went into the 'hard' bomb-proof shelter for a briefing and instead of introducing me as 'the actor prat who's pretending to be me', he said, 'This is Wing Commander Raikes, O.C. 555 Squadron.' I left the briefing walking on air. He offered to take me up for a flight but the insurance wouldn't cover it. I'd practised for hours at home on a Tornado computer game, but when it came to the simple matter of shooting down a Russian MiG with cannon on the training sim – a computer in an office – I was dead meat within seconds. However, I did get to land in the full-size simulator – real cockpit, full G-kit and helmet, communicating with the ops room as they talked me down – and I didn't crash, which made it easier to play the part.

The pilot didn't go to series. The problem with pilot episodes like these is they try to cram too much in. The RAF wanted it to be a recruiting film, and kept changing the lines to make it accurate but dull, and the writer wanted to fit everyone's back-story into an hour, so there were about four storylines going on at the same time. The result was laudable but messy. The flying shots were great and it would have got better – good actors and great potential. We heard that the caterers had been booked for Cyprus, but that was it, it was broadcast but never picked up.

Is there a pattern here? Am I jinxed?

Being David Archer: 'Shocking Ambridge to the Core'

They say that every cloud has a silver lining but I know that real farmers who went through the horror of foot-and-mouth disease in 2001 won't be in the slightest bit mollified to hear that the extra *Archers* episodes I was in when Brookfield was affected by the disease paid my tax that year.

From the production point of view, it's always a difficult decision to know what to reflect in the real world, and what to ignore. We sometimes have to rush up to Birmingham to record what are known as 'topical inserts' where a piece of important breaking news needs to be recorded on the day of broadcast – taking the place of a scene that had been laid down weeks before. In the case of foot-and-mouth, it was impossible to ignore as it was a terrifying crisis for all farmers. Far from the odd mention, the story took centre stage as our family, along with Bert Fry, were barricaded inside the farm for the duration. Over 2,000 cases of the disease were recorded across the country, leading to the slaughter and burning of more than ten million cows and sheep. The story was handled with accuracy and sensitivity, and received praise from reviewers and farmers alike for doing what *The Archers* does best, combining drama with much-needed information.

To mark our fiftieth year at around the same time, we were all invited to St James's Palace where we were feted by Prince Charles and an enormous number of celebrity fans (who would have thought that Phill Jupitus was a closet listener?). I was photographed with the heir to the throne beneath a massive painting of our common ancestor, William IV – although my lineage is not as respectable as his, as I'm descended from the King's illicit liaison with Dorothy Jordan, the actress who trod the Drury Lane boards 200 years before I did.

The famous guests kept staring at us. It's different from being recognised from the telly: when *Archers* listeners finally put a face to the voice they've been listening to for so many years, they stare and stare. I've always wanted to do a play at the National Theatre, so when Richard Eyre locked onto my eyes with a probing gaze of fascination, I thought I'd be in his next five productions at least, if not a lifetime regular. Sadly, he's obviously typecast me as a farmer – I've never had the call.

So, when the sixtieth anniversary came around, we were all awaiting a party that would outdo that one. Instead, Nigel Pargetter fell to his death from the roof of Lower Loxley (I didn't push him, honest!) – a difficult and controversial decision that was taken hard by many listeners. The distinctive voice of Nigel lives on in the form of actor Graham Seed, so mourning *Archers* addicts can still get a dose of his tones in the theatre and on TV, along with appearances on *Saturday Live* and *Broadcasting House* on Radio 4. His one-off performance as the very un-Nigel-ish abattoir owner in the hour-long jury special at the end of Helen's trial showed what a good actor he is.

We had been told that one of our characters was going to die to mark the sixtieth with an event that would 'Shock Ambridge to the Core', but for weeks none of us knew which one. None of us that is except Graham, who had been told in advance but asked to keep it quiet, so the poor bloke had to sit with all his mates discussing who might be going, all the time knowing it was him. *The Killing of Sister George* for real. I think the intention was to balance the death with the birth of Henry Archer, and the subsequent reconciliation of Tony and Helen, and the celebrations continued into the year with the appearance on the programme of the Duchess of Cornwall, but the focus of course remained on Nigel.

We recorded his demise in the dead room, a horribly apt description. On the speakers we heard the wind whistling around the chimney pots. We edged carefully along the floor while John, the spot-effects artist, chinked bits of tile and brick together – it sounded pretty hairy (John had provided tiles from his own house, and they are now framed in his living room). When I listened to the broadcast, it was in the early days of Twitter and I was following this new thing called a Tweetalong. The moment David shamed Nigel into coming up with him to get the banner down– 'Are you a man or a mouse?' – someone tweeted, 'DON'T GO UP ON THE FUCKING ROOF!!' and I think from that moment there was an inevitability about what was going to happen. Graham and I discussed the length of the scream, imagining the height of Lower Loxley and figuring that the scream would be quite short. He slipped, yelled as he backed away from the mike (he didn't need the script for his last ever line), I screamed, 'NIGELLLLLLLL!' – and that was that.

I asked John to take a photo of us. I posed with what I thought was a face of sympathy, but in the picture I just look insufferably smug. They lengthened the scream in post-production to make it more dramatic, but the office was then flooded with letters and emails from people who had worked out that given the feet per second rate of acceleration of a human body at sea level, Lower Loxley must be the height of Salisbury Cathedral.

Night Must Fall

When an actor says, 'When I was doing *Charley's Aunt* at Watford...' you know they're the real deal. So, when I was offered *Charley's Aunt* at Watford, despite hating the play, not loving Watford and having a nasty chest infection, I felt I had to do it or I'd never be taken seriously by my peers.

Everything comes in handy. Five years of wearing a detached stiff collar at Harrow meant that I was in white tie and tails before the others in the dressing room had got their trousers on. That and getting my car broken into in the Watford multi-storey car park – after twenty-odd years of vandal-free parking in Holloway, for heaven's sake – are about my only memories of that box-ticking exercise.

Soon afterwards, in 1996, I had a nice part in Emlyn Williams's *Night Must Fall*. Jason Donovan is a lovely bloke but his Welsh accent is not as good as his singing. As he has admitted, he was also going through his cocaine period, which didn't help with the accuracy of his lines in *Night Must Fall*. I'm so glad he's cleaned up his act now, as I was genuinely fond of him and he was on the path to nowhere.

We opened in Leatherhead where the weaknesses of the production were forgiven by a ready audience of teen fans who were in thrall to the Antipodean blond one. When it came to the West End, though, the critics were unsparing. And I didn't escape either. David Benedict wrote in the *Independent,* '"This is all getting pretty terrible, isn't it?" That observation by the walking blue blazer masquerading as a character is both an understatement and the nearest you'll get to dramatic truth all night in this preposterous revival.' I was that blue blazer, with a stick-on moustache and a pipe. The moustache tended to flap off mid-speech and I hate pipes.

When it transferred to the West End, at the Theatre Royal Haymarket again, we were set for a long run, but about two weeks in, after the dreadful reviews that slayed everyone involved, our notice to quit was given. Sadly, it was on the night that Jason's dad Terence, himself an actor, had flown over from Oz to see his son. I was in Jason's dressing room, meeting his dad, when the company manager brought the bad news. Father and son greeted it with cheerful Aussie disdain – they do stiff upper lip even better than we do. I felt very sorry for him, he's a good actor and a lovely bloke, but sometimes you just get completely miscast.

He wasn't put off the stage – he has been in several successful musicals since – but it would be a long time until I trod the boards again.

I sought solace back in the television studio,

and in the world of Robin Hood that had brought me so much joy as a child, but the unlucky streak continued. It's almost impossible to be good in something that's dreadful, especially when it's produced by American control freaks whose only criterion for success is the bottom line. *The New Adventures of Robin Hood* was one such production. It was like panto on telly – enormous fun to do, but quite mind-bogglingly execrable. It made Mel Brooks's *Men in Tights* look like a historical documentary. I was dreadful, and therefore fitted into it perfectly.

We filmed in the Lithuanian National Film Studios just outside Vilnius, so it was a bit of an adventure. I'd lost my glasses on day one so could be found sitting three inches away from my hotel TV watching the football – the European Championship – with prescription sunglasses on. In my episode, I was the evil Count Frederick who looked like Ming the Merciless with a hangover. Pouring sweat in wig, beard and heavy velvet in a boiling studio with massive brute lamps and no air conditioning, Frederick had to battle with an enchanted sword while it destroyed four banqueting tables laden with food. So, the brief was to swipe specific parts of the table settings but not others, all the time making it look like the sword was doing it, and I was trying to hold it back. Not easy.

It's at times like these, when you're draped on your throne, confronted by a Ninja warrior (in Sherwood?), and delivering lines like, 'Who do you think you are?' and worrying whether you should hit the 'who' or the 'do' that the will to live is to be glimpsed scuttling out the side door, never to return.

'I'm a grown man. What on earth am I doing?' I often think this.

Being David Archer: Deaths and recasting

Although Richard Derrington had been told that his character Mark Hebden was going to die, he still found it a shock when he came to read his final script. He told me, 'I was just marking up the script as usual, I'm driving along in wet weather, I hit a bend, the car skids, I go off the road and hit a tree, I turn the page and there it is, I'm dead. Bit of a shock, I can tell you.'

At least David wasn't involved with that death, unlike Jethro, who David did for with a falling branch, or indeed the badger that he shot and then threw in the road pretending it was roadkill – and he was chairman of the Parish Council at the time! I play a lot of evil characters for computer games and the like, but as harbingers of doom go, David takes some beating.

Mary Wimbush (Julia Pargetter) died as most actors would like to go, at work. An old friend of my parents, we used to visit her idyllic cottage in Aldbury, Hertfordshire, that she shared with the poet Louis MacNeice, and in which, age twelve, I smoked my first cigarette in an upstairs bedroom with her son Charles, while the grown-ups partied below. Mary lived life to the full, and believed that taking the safe path was supremely dull and to be avoided at all costs. She finished recording an episode at the BBC recording studios at the Mailbox in Birmingham and, aged eighty-one, died on the stairs in the arms of her radio daughter-in-law, Alison Dowling (Elizabeth Pargetter).

When an older actor passes away their character usually dies with them – out of respect if nothing else. If the actor decides to retire, or is forced to by ill health, or, as can happen, is simply given the boot, then they might be recast, which can be quite a thing. It's asking a lot of the listener to believe that someone whose voice, mannerisms and style they have come to know intimately over a period of years can overnight turn into a completely different person. In a way, it's even more difficult than when it happens in vision, where you can at least see that it's palpably a different actor, but when it's just the voice, you're imagining the same body that you've always known, but the voice is suddenly someone else's.

Often, the new actor will do an impression of the previous one, and then gradually change it to something that they're more comfortable with. When Eric Allan took over the part of Bert Fry on the death of Roger Hume in 1996, his impression was uncannily accurate, and he has kept it up ever since. Heather Bell created the character of Clarrie Grundy, followed by Fiona Mathieson, who tragically took her own life after a very short time in the part. She in turn was replaced by Rosalind Adams who made the character her own over fifteen years. When Ros sadly decided to retire to spend more time with her family, we were thrilled to find Heather back again after all that time, but some new listeners of course complained that she sounded nothing like 'their' Clarrie – hugely ironic.

I'm a replacement myself. Baby David was actually Judy Bennett (who plays Shula), then as an adult he was first played by Nigel Carrivick, but David was sent to an agricultural college in Holland for a year, so by the time I turned up, I hoped that people had forgotten what he sounded like. I was never played a clip of the previous actor, and indeed I have never heard a recording, but when I met Peter Windows recently at William Smethurst's funeral, he told me that I was a shoo-in for the part, so I must have sounded pretty like him – unlike recent changes such as Pip, or Tom, or Tony, or Kate, or any number of characters over the years who have undergone a pretty radical vocal transplant.

When Tony Archer had a heart attack, listeners were not aware that the actor Colin Skipp also had one at about the same time. Life imitating art, like Jack Woolley getting Alzheimer's as Arnold Peters took the same sad journey, and continued portraying him with such poignancy until his own condition made it impossible. Colin was replaced by the distinguished Shakespearean actor David Troughton, who did sound very different. When Tom Graham was then replaced as his son Tom Archer, listeners complained that the new actor sounded nothing like 'Tony's son', which was odd because he actually is – William Troughton.

These cast changes are nothing new. Dan Archer was played by four different actors, as was John Tregorran. Until Annette Badland made the part her gloriously nasty own, Hazel Woolley tended to be played by whoever was available from the radio rep on the day. Nigel Pargetter was played by Graham Seed, then Nigel Carrington, then Graham again. When Sam Barriscale decided to leave the programme, he found out pretty soon that there was no coming back when his character, John Archer, was crushed beneath a Ferguson tractor – Colin Skipp's finest acting moment, but a closed door for Sam. I recently took a slightly surreal photograph of Ysanne Churchman and Paddy Greene – the long-dead Grace Archer with Phil's second wife, Jill.

In the past producers would cast radio actors with their eyes closed – after all, it was only the voice that was important. In these days of social media and the occasional big press story, it's helpful that Timothy Watson looks suitably handsome and dangerous as Rob, and Louiza Patikas as beautiful and vulnerable as the emotionally damaged Helen. Of course, from the actors' perspective we all look exactly the same as our radio characters, but in every case five million people would disagree.

Henry Noel Bentinck

In 1997, my father died. The cancer slowly wore him down. He had a morphine drip that would take him off to his 'other world' as he described it. One of the last things he said as he woke from a reverie was, 'You know, they used to walk more slowly in the nineteenth century.' I'm so happy his final thoughts were about gentle things like that. He died too young and I miss him still.

There wasn't much to inherit, just the proceeds of the house in Devon, split three ways with my sisters. After tax, there was just enough to buy a cottage somewhere. For years we'd been loading up the car and taking the family down to Devon for Christmas and summer holidays, and we wanted to buy somewhere near there to continue the tradition. Then it occurred to us that Devon would only have sad memories, and it was a five-hour drive, so why not look nearer to London?

When my mother had died in 1967, I used to get farmed out to stay with friends in Norfolk, and those chums, and my best man Jamie Borthwick, were still there. We started looking for somewhere in north Norfolk, and very soon we found the perfect place. We brought the boys up to see what they thought, and Will said, 'You must be mad!' It was a cold, unloved holiday cottage with lino, poky rooms, a minute kitchen, and it didn't do itself any favours by having a spectacularly ugly name – 'Preshute'. We ceremoniously burned the name and got to work. One thing Judy and I have always been good at is seeing potential in houses, and we knew what could be done.

In a quiet village by a large duck pond, the honking geese and quacky mallards kept us awake at first, but soon became a kind of lullaby to a rural idyll in what is now a lovely home. I knocked two rooms into one, built a new kitchen and enlarged it, and we stuck a conservatory on the back. I built a gazebo in the garden that

191

looked odd for a bit but is now almost entirely grown over, and is where I sometimes write. Whether writing words or music, some places are like a muse; the ideas float in through the windows and the blank sheet of computer screen fills up as though the ideas were someone else's.

Norfolk locals have an unwarranted reputation for being rude to 'foreigners' – meaning people from London. I've never found that myself. They just have a perfectly justifiable dislike of people who are up themselves. Anyway, not only was my pa brought up in Heacham on the north Norfolk coast, but lots of things in King's Lynn, including roads, pubs and farms, are called 'Bentinck' because, without the efforts of one of my Dutch ancestors who knew a thing or two about drainage, large parts of East Anglia would still be under water. Consequently, it's one of the few places in the world where they spell my name right.

I lost one source of inspiration but gained another. My father's portrait looks down at me as I sit and write or play the guitar or piano, and his smile is an encouragement to be brave and original, like he was.

Armando Iannucci

Improvisation. The very word fills some actors with dread; to others it is what they thrive on. It's about quick thinking, having an imagination and going with the flow. If someone says, 'I love your hat,' the answer is not, 'I'm not wearing a hat,' but 'Thank you, it was my father's.' 'Deer-stalker?' 'No, pig-stalker, he used to stalk pigs. He got three years for porcine harassment.' Or some such. Rule number one is 'don't block' – always accept a situation that's being presented.

I was quite good at it at drama school but when I attended a workshop at the Donmar Warehouse for a thing called Theatre Sports, it got a lot harder because you had to be funny. This is stand-up comedy territory – one of the few things I've never tried because you have to know your limits. If you listen to Paul Merton on *Just a Minute*, riffing for a full sixty seconds on washing lines, you have to take your hat off and wonder at an imagination that can think that fast. You can improve with practice, and I have done, but when the *Theatre Sports* people asked me to be in their first performance, I was well outside my comfort zone.

In the first sketch, audience members were asked to pose us into a frozen tableau. I was positioned with clenched fists held up either side of my neck. I started with 'Javelin thrower's off target again,' and got a big laugh, and I have a memory that an improvised opera about a barber wasn't bad – 'I'm all alone, with my comb!' Although I got away with it, I knew it wasn't a strength, it takes practice. I've got that practice over the years and these days I'm pretty good, but watching the likes of *QI* and listening to radio panel shows, I know that there's a way that certain people's brains are wired to be on hand with the witty line all the time. I can be amusing, quick-witted and can always hold my own, but a laugh is not absolutely guaranteed. Merton once said that sometimes he puts his foot on the accelerator and there's nothing there. I know that feeling too.

So, when I went to meet Armando Iannucci for his series, *The Armando Iannucci Shows,* I didn't think I'd get the part as I probably wasn't funny enough. As it turned out, though, the brief was to be real in a funny situation, and I was asked to join a wonderful cast of talented oddballs, all of whom were as astonished as I was that they'd been picked, but who had in common an ease with being inventive in front of a camera, and being real.

The Armando Iannucci Shows were a series of absurd sketches that took the audience to the edge of their taste and comfort limits. Although scripted, we were encouraged to 'loosen it up' by Armando, which stopped us being script-bound and allowed for invention. On the day of filming, where I would be a Catholic priest whose congregation falls in love with him, Armando asked if I played guitar. I said yes. He said would you play a song from the pulpit? Okay, what song? Well, nothing that's copyrighted or we'll have to pay. Okay, shall I sing one of mine? Sure. Which is how 'Quangos in the Shelter', a song about how civil servants will be the only ones to survive a nuclear holocaust, came to have its one and only public performance.

That sketch has since become a bit of a classic. The congregation persuade the priest to take them back to the rectory for coffee and they all end up in bed together. Poking my head round the bedroom door in the morning to find a queue for the bathroom snaking down the stairs was extremely bizarre. The priest goes into a toy shop and comes out with twenty-five teddy bears. Kicking leaves, all holding hands, they romp through a park, full of the joys of new-found love, before going out to dinner with the parents, all fifty of them! Sitting in the restaurant with seventy-five cast and extras, I asked the producer, Adam Tandy, how they got the BBC to cough up for such an expensive production. His answer was revealing– 'Nobody said no.'

Armando is such an original talent, so off the wall while representing the new wave of alternative comedy, that the uncomprehending bosses at the BBC gave him an office and free rein to do whatever he wanted. Some of it wasn't funny in the laugh-out-loud sense, but all of it was wildly imaginative, absurd and totally original. I was an inmate in the 'Home for Men aged between 42 and 55' in which we were told that our life was basically over bar the certainty of incontinence and dancing to Abba tribute bands – 'You will never be astronauts.' And I was the Yorkshire mayor introducing a 'Knife Attack Reunion' party where attackers and heavily scarred middle-class victims chatted sociably about the violent events that had brought them together.

I thought that would be the end of working with Armando, but years later he asked me back to star in the opening fifteen minutes of *The Thick of It*.

Hailed as one of the best TV comedy series ever,

The Thick of It showed the inner workings of government, allowing us to view the august corridors of power as teeming with power-hungry, foul-mouthed cynics. The political advisor was Martin Sixsmith, and when I once asked him how much of it was accurate, he replied, 'Oh, it's actually much worse.' The character of Malcolm Tucker, played with scary Glaswegian venom by Peter Capaldi, was based closely on Alastair Campbell. While Peter is the most charming and generous of actors, being sacked by Tucker from my post as Minister of Social Affairs was a terrifying experience.

Armando had a unique way of working. The cast met for the first time at the BBC rehearsal rooms in Acton, were presented with a script and did a read-through of the episode. Then Armando asked us to put the scripts down, move over to the other side of the room and go through what we remembered of the essence of the scene. The scriptwriter, Jesse Armstrong, sat in, and he and Armando took notes on our improvisation. We then went home. A while later, a new script arrived, which was a mixture of the original script and our improvised gems.

On the day, in order to get the fly-on-the-wall, faux-documentary feeling, the rooms had no film lighting, we did no rehearsal and didn't even block out our movements, and there were two hand-held cameras that just followed us around. Having filmed a scene a few times until Armando was happy with it, he then sprinkled the whole thing with his special stardust.

'Okay, so let's loosen it up a little,' he said as he

handed me a sheet of A4. 'Here's some lines you might like to throw in, and I've given Peter some of his own, so it'll be a little different.'

And this is why the whole series was so unique: the actors really are reacting to something they have heard for the very first time. I have to say I did feel a bit awkward about saying, 'stuffing a cat up my arse and having a wank', but it was worth it for the flicker of a smile on Peter's face, particularly as he had just given me what one commentator describes as 'the first manifestation of the Malcolm Tucker Death Stare'.

In a later summer-special episode, 'Spinners and Losers', I'm in the back of a black cab driving round and round Parliament Square with another scary Glaswegian character, Jamie Mc-Donald, played by Paul Higgins. The scene has developed a reputation, with its own internet meme. So much so that once, when I was performing my Earl of Portland duties on board HMS *Portland*, a Chief Petty Officer came up, introduced himself and said he had a message from the crew.

'Oh really,' I said, intrigued, 'what's that?'

'The message, my lord, is, "Are you a horse?"'

Working with Armando proved Rudi Shelly's adage at Bristol that 'acting is the art of reacting'. When Paul threw in a line about my horsey wife, which was a last-minute 'loosening' line from Armando, my reaction to hearing my wife insulted included a flash of anger in my eyes which is almost unactable. I was so shocked that all I could come up with was, 'Okay, leaving the wife aside for a second...', which I felt at the time wasn't witty or clever, but in fact was completely perfect for the character. That's Armando's genius, getting genuine reactions from his cast, along with writing biting political satire couched in glorious filth.

Being David Archer: Freelance

The listener might imagine that the *Archers* cast is up in Birmingham the whole time, and that we don't do anything else. This couldn't be further from the truth. The programme is recorded over eight days per month, each episode takes two and a quarter hours and we do four episodes per day. How much we're up there depends on how many episodes we're in, and we only get paid per episode – there is no retainer fee. We are also not paid per line – we could be in every scene or only one. Ted Kelsey holds the record for 'Fewest Lines Spoken' – he got a full fee for Joe Grundy's only line of an episode – the final one – which was:

JOE Uuuugh!

So, one month I might get eight days' work, and get paid accordingly; the next month nothing at all, and not make a penny. When people say, 'I saw you moonlighting on *EastEnders* last week', I'm not taking time off from the farm: I'm just being a jobbing actor like the rest of my profession. Tamsin Greig continues to be a stage, film and TV star while Debbie Aldridge is in Hungary. Michael Cochrane is a regular telly performer while Oliver

Sterling is in Italy. Josh Archer wasn't heard during the 'Are They Moving to Northumberland' marathon because Angus Imrie was in three plays at Shakespeare's Globe. Some actors' other work takes over to the exclusion of *The Archers*. Felicity Jones stopped playing Emma because she was getting too much work and ended up with Best Actress nominations across the board for *The Theory of Everything*. Lucy Davis was Hayley but after her bravura turn in *The Office* left in 2005 to work in Hollywood. Our previous Pip, Helen Monks, went on to be utterly brilliant in *Raised by Wolves*.

Some of us do loads of voice work, including voiceovers, computer games, narration and audiobooks, and still more are theatre and TV/film regulars. In a disturbing crossover, I was the voice of the helicopter pilot that wiped out most of *Emmerdale!*

After watching J. K. Rowling's *Fantastic Beasts and Where to Find Them*, in which I pretty much open the movie as 'Witness', who describes the magic force in a Bronx accent, someone tweeted, 'David Archer doesn't look like that!' It's hard to know where to begin with that one.

It's always great when actors and celebrities 'moonlight' in the other direction and appear as guest stars in the programme, for they are often as excited about being in *The Archers* as we are about meeting them. You would have thought that Sir Bradley Wiggins, having already won the Tour de France, four (now five) Olympic gold medals and been knighted, would think nothing of standing in front of a microphone and playing himself, but, great bloke that he is, he told us he was bricking it. Guest stars that I have met include Zandra Rhodes, Chris Moyles, Colin Dexter, Anita Dobson, the Duchess of Cornwall, Judi Dench, Terry Wogan and Victoria Wood. One guest was the Duke of Westminster, who I was at school with – 'Hi Tim'; 'Oh, hello Gerald.' I turned up in jeans and T-shirt when everyone else had togged up. I fondly recall the wonderful Richard Griffiths, who made the only ever appearance of Ruth's father, toilet-roll manufacturer Solly Pritchard.

Now we have the fun of working with new regulars Eleanor Bron and Simon Williams, but there were raised eyebrows among the cast when Bristol Old Vic School chum Alex Jennings, who had come in for an episode, was introduced as 'a proper actor' – dammit I've done *Charley's Aunt* at Watford, that's as 'proper' as it gets!

Going Deutsch

My father survived the war because, when lying wounded in a shell hole near the river Po in northern Italy, he understood the German for, 'What's in that shell hole, Gunther?' 'I don't know, Hans, but shoot away,' and stood up and yelled, *'Freund!'* very loudly.

I've always loved languages and accents, so when I went to Harrow, beyond the simple attraction of doing Modern Languages, there was the thought that without Pa's smattering of Deutsch, I would never have been born. I took it up with his encouragement and it has served me well.

I've been employed a number of times to speak the language, but also to speak English with a German accent, which is harder than it seems. It's not the cliché 'Ve haff vays…' of *'Allo 'Allo* fame – the vowels are subtler and the rhythm is different. It really makes a difference if you can speak the language, and the point is that the speaker is trying to speak English as well as they can, so they're not putting on an accent, but trying hard to speak without one.

In 2000, I was cast to play the U-boat captain in the film *Enigma*. After the read-through, we were invited to go on a trip to Bletchley Park to see the huts where the real code-breakers had worked – it wasn't open to the public then, so, with my software programmer hat on, and always intrigued by codes and cyphers, I was fascinated to see it. The cast had already started to get into their roles so, although Jeremy Northam used to be our lodger and Kate Winslet lived opposite us in Holloway, everyone was slightly reserved with the bloke who was commanding the U-boat – they treated me as though I were a spy!

In the script my lines were written in English, and I was surprised to find that they trusted me to do the translation, which involved German naval commands and compass bearings – not something you can just busk. It took days of research to get right. We filmed it in the enormous outdoor tank at Pinewood, with the mock-up of the sub's conning tower in front of a vast green screen. The director, Michael Apted, handed me an enormous pair of completely opaque goggles with the words, 'Your agent's not going to like this.' It was a night shoot, and in the story the U-boat captain, looking through binoculars, sees a sentry on a British destroyer lighting a cigarette, at a distance of about a mile. I said, 'But Michael, these are for wearing down below to get your eyes accustomed to the dark. When we come up here, they're taken off, otherwise we can't see a thing.'

'Sorry, Tim, it's the military advisor. Have to do what he says.'

I didn't argue, mainly because it was Michael Apted, but I did think it was his movie and he was the boss, and it was quite obviously non-sense.

While we were chatting, he asked me what I'd been up to recently.

'You mean my U-boat captain is David Archer?' he asked, horrified.

My next German part was in 2003 in *Born and Bred* as a war veteran who comes to England, dying of his wounds, to make peace with the parents of the English soldier that he had shot, and who had shot him, and who died before the medics got to them. They were holed up together in a barn and had become friends at the last. It was a sweet story and a friendly and welcoming cast of regulars made it a joy to work on. One of my scenes was with John Henshaw, who played Wilf, the railway station master. John is a Mancunian and only started acting at forty having been a binman for ten years. This is what I love about being an actor, an ex-binman and an old Harrovian working together as equals.

I hated learning German, but the next gig was worth the whole five years of hell at school – mastering the grammar, three genders, umlauts – when I found myself teaching Claudia Schiffer how to perform her German lines for a movie.

'Claudia's overslept. She'll be with you in a minute,' her PA apologised as I arrived at her flat in Bayswater. She appeared a few minutes later, hair tousled, in pyjamas and robe, and curled up on the sofa for her 'lesson'. She was intelligent, funny, modest and quite jaw-droppingly beautiful. The part she was playing was in a film called *666: In Bed with the Devil*, and she had a cameo role when Mephisto turns first into Boris Becker, then into Claudia Schiffer. She has to whisper sweet nothings into Faust's ear, then kiss him passionately. So, I'm with a supermodel in her jimjams, she's looking at me adoringly and whispering *'Ich liebe dich, ich liebe dich so* ... and then we go mwah mwah mwah...' and I'm trying to resist the temptation of saying that I'm a method actor and we really ought to do the kissing thing properly, and all the time thinking, *IT WAS ALL WORTH IT, EVERY BLOODY MINUTE!*

The sixth of June 2004 was the sixtieth anniversary of D-Day and a drama/documentary was made about it. At the audition for *D-Day 6.6.1944,* I read in English with a German accent. They then asked if I could speak German. I said yes. They passed me a photograph of a 1940s poster written in German *Schrift,* which is the old-fashioned, really difficult to read stuff. At school, half the books we'd studied had been written in

Schrift and I'd always thought it was completely pointless – now it was getting me a part playing a Nazi general.

I was Rommel's second-in-command, General-leutnant Hans Speidel. Rommel was played by another Englishman, Albert Welling. We met on the Eurostar and have remained close friends ever since. It was filmed at Château de la Roche-Guyon, the very same castle north of Paris that housed the real German High Command during the invasion, and on the walls were photos of our characters and of how the castle had looked at the time. One morning, I came out of costume in full Wehrmacht rig and frightened the life out of an elderly resident, who thought the Boche had returned. When I assured him in French that, 'non, non, n'ayez pas peur, je suis Anglais!' he was even more confused. 'Anglais? Mais non, c'est pas possible – les Anglais ont gagné!'

The other actors playing Germans were all real Deutschers and were mighty fed up that the two leads were being played by Englishmen, but having lost the war they felt they really couldn't complain too much and resorted to teasing and banter. I threatened to have anyone who complained shot at dawn, thus repeating the gag that the real German officers had played on my father.

I'd rung my cousin, Wilhelm von Ilsemann in Hamburg, to ask his advice on pronunciation, and when I asked if he'd ever heard of Speidel, he answered, 'Heard of him? I knew him!' – which was odd.

Albert's mother was German and between us we made a pretty good fist of it, and to an English ear it sounds fine. We were re-voiced for the German broadcast, though, because we're quite obviously English. It would have been like watching a German film in which Churchill says, 'Ve vill fight zem on ze bitches...'

The great spin-off to this job was that during the shoot, Albert and I came up with the idea for a book.

In the sixties there were two very popular books called *N'Heures Souris Rhames* and *Mots d'Heurres Gousses Rhames,* which, when read out loud, sound like *Nursery Rhymes* and *Mother Goose Rhymes*. They contained spoof French poetry which followed this conceit. 'Un petit d'un petit' was Humpty Dumpty. Albert had an idea to update this idea with modern pop and folk songs. I was amazed because I'd had a similar idea, called *Crises, Masques, Rôles* – Christmas Carols. We had just the best time inventing new poems after dinner in the hotel. We asked the friendly French waiter to audition them for us.

'But zis is nonsense!'

'Yes we know, but please read it out and see if these Brits understand.'

'Okay... *Et joue deux. Dans mais quitte bas de. Thé que ça de sang, animé quitte bête heure. Rime même beurre, toilette heur y ne tu Euro arte. Seine y ou Cannes ce tarte, tout mais quitte bête heure.*'

The crew were falling about because what they'd heard was *'Hey Jude, don't make it bad...'* etc. We knew then it was going to work. Over the next couple of years we wrote a lot of poems, because you can actually use this technique to write anything you want in English, using French words. When you translate them they are of course complete nonsense, but are not unlike the Dada poetry of the early 1900s. So we invented a 'lost' Dada poet called Paul Déaveroin (pull the other one) and an Icelandic professor of Phonetics called Isskott Belsohn (it's got bells on) and called it *Avant Garde à Clue* – published it on Kindle and then went round touting it to literary agents and publishers. The idea was to make it like a real academic work and fool the experts, but the problems with copyright were insurmountable. 'Are you writing Beatles lyrics?' asked the lawyers. 'No, they are French words, but they sound like Beatles lyrics.' They couldn't give us the go-ahead because there was no precedent. So it sat idle for four years until the copyright law changed in 2015 allowing quotes of copyright lyrics if they are 'Caricature, Parody, or Pastiche' – which they are! So we're having another try – meanwhile you can read it on Kindle, or to put it another way, *Y où quand ris dit-ons qui ne d'Arles!*

Being David Archer: Editors

The recent cast changes in *The Archers* were all the doing of the man who took over as editor in 2013, Sean O'Connor. Because he had once edited *EastEnders,* he was accused by fans of bringing the ethics of Walford to the village – before he had even started the job. And now that he has gone back there, you can of course hear the cows mooing in Albert Square and everyone's comparing the size of their melons – although the latter is probably par for the course. The 'EastEnderisation' of Ambridge is nothing new; when John Yorke took over briefly in 2012, having once been the executive producer of *EastEnders* (besides being the Controller of all drama series – *Holby, Casualty,* etc.), knickers were manically twisted that he would bring Walford to Ambridge. No doubt because the latest boss, Huw Kennair-Jones, was also once tainted by 'Enderness, the same mud will be slung at him.

Along with the cast changes, Sean's arrival brought a new perspective. His stated intention was to re-establish the values that had been the genesis of the programme – community, family and the land, more Thomas Hardy than Albert Square. While these had all been there to a greater or lesser extent under previous editors, he wanted to re-emphasise the core qualities. He gave more focus to Jill and the Brookfield Archers, looked at the long-term effects of soil erosion due to intensive farming with the flood story, the threat to the community with the long tale of the Route B bypass, and gave David and Ruth a tortuous choice between self-interest and land custodianship in the 'Moving North' story.

Hearing his father's voice during his near nervous breakdown brought home to David the responsibility he bore to carry on what previous generations of Archers had created through hard work and sacrifice. When we recorded that scene, so subtly written by Joanna Toye, I was alone in the studio with a pair of headphones and Norman's voice in my ears. It wasn't hard to get emotional, for I can hear my own father's voice giving words of advice in times of crisis. It was a blurring of fiction and reality, and an actor should always use their genuine emotion, experience and thoughts to create a believable performance. It's not pretending.

Every new editor comes with their ideas about the direction of the show, and consciously or not will always bring subtle, and sometimes noticeable, changes. The really challenging brief is to attract a new generation of listeners without losing the old one, a difficult and very fine line. When William Smethurst left in 1986 he was replaced by our first female editor, Liz Rigbey. Among other adjustments to the cast, it was she who decided that Sophie wasn't farmer's wife material, and brought in the Geordie Ruth, after successive Scottish characters, named variously Anne, Heather or Thistle (to suggest spikiness) were rejected.

Most of my *Archers* career, however, has been under the guiding hand of the longest-running editor, Vanessa Whitburn, who despite 'previous' on *Brookside,* for twenty-two years steered the ship through the hazardous waters of social and political change with enormous skill and professionalism. She modernised Ambridge in a way that often attracted traditionalist ire, but without which the show would slowly have started to lose any contemporary reality. Her performances on *Feedback,* dealing with the brickbats thrown by the presenter Roger Bolton and irate listeners, whether you agreed with her decisions or not, were masterclasses in diplomacy, worthy of the most experienced politician. She could have been a diplomat.

She lost her temper with me once, though, with very good reason. For a good many years, the actors used to receive all the scripts for the month, no matter whether they were in them or not. This meant I had huge piles of scripts that, when the boys were young, were perfect for drawing and painting on. As they got older, we used them less and the pile got bigger and bigger. One day when I was about to chuck them all out, I had a thought that for many people these scripts were gold dust, so I put it about that for a donation of £5 to the NSPCC I would send them an old script, signed by me if required. This went very well and I was soon spending hours each week filling the stamped addressed envelopes and making decent money for the charity. The only thing I had to be careful of was that the scripts I sent out were of episodes that had already been broadcast. One day I got it wrong and sent one off that wasn't due to be broadcast for another three weeks.

This would have been bad enough but it was compounded by a sequence of incredibly bad luck. Firstly, the people I'd sent it to ran a pub, the Cock Inn at Gamlingay in Cambridgeshire. They were amateur dramatics enthusiasts as well as *Archers* fans, so they thought it would be a great idea to cast some of their regulars as the characters and do a public performance of the episode for charity. As chance would have it, there was a reporter from the local paper in the audience, who ran the story the next day. This still might not have got back to Vanessa but for the other major problem. The episode was not about the Flower and Produce show, or the panto, or any number of everyday stories of farming folk, but the top secret and *massive* story of the death of Mark Hebden in a car crash. So, far from hiding on the inside pages of the local paper, it was subsequently splashed across the front page of the *Daily Telegraph,* which I happened to be reading, in shock, when the telephone call came from a furious Ms Whitburn. Thankfully the papers didn't reveal the storyline but, knuckles duly rapped, my stupidity unfortunately put an end to that charitable fundraising exercise.

Terror

Conquering fear is one thing but living with abject, self-imposed terror is quite another. When, in 2004, I was asked to play Frank, the Michael Caine part, in *Educating Rita* at the Watermill Theatre in Newbury; I hadn't been on stage for almost a decade. It was a daunting task. I hadn't had a lead in a play since drama school, it was a two-hander, I would never be off the stage for the full two hours, and it was scheduled for a six-week run with matinees on Wednesdays and Saturdays.

The Watermill is a lovely theatre, misleadingly intimate in that you feel the audience is close but the wooden construction absorbs the sound so you have to belt it out to reach the back. My Rita was the supremely talented Claire Lams and the director was Jamie Glover, the son of my *By the Sword Divided* father, Julian. It was like being on a small university campus and we lived in a little cottage on the site, which was bucolic but ultimately boring and lonely. Claire soon mastered both the Scouse and the lines, while I, very much out of practice, struggled to get fully on top of the learning – it's like a muscle, use it or lose it.

The night before the first producer's run, when you're off the book for the first time and watched by the heads of department, I didn't manage to sleep a wink. I couldn't remember that ever happening to me before and it worried me a lot. During the producer's run, I was in a state – not only was I still not word perfect, but the lack of sleep meant I was barely at the races at all. It was pretty disastrous, I kept calling for a prompt, mistimed the gags, forgot props, generally gave them hundreds of reasons to recast or cancel the show.

That evening I Skyped my close friend, actor Tony Armatrading in LA and gave vent to my fears. I really wondered if I hadn't bitten off more than I could chew. It was the first time in my life that I'd ever thought I actually couldn't do something. Tony got really angry with me and told me I was being a complete wimp and coward and of course I could do it, standing on my head if necessary. That's what friends are for and, even if I didn't necessarily believe him, the fact that a man who is only ever quite brutally honest about everything was certain I could do it made me gird my loins and plough on. I must add that, of course,

Judy was saying the same thing, but sometimes you need the cold, hard appraisal of a fellow actor, which is more professionally bolstering than that welcome but unconditional loving support.

The day when you see the stage set for the first time and move out of the rehearsal room is always hugely exciting. Frank's office was surrounded on three sides by bookshelves. The books were real, gleaned from charity shops in the area – there must have been hundreds of them. As part of the action, I had to climb the library steps to reach a book on the top shelf, so, getting used to the space, I climbed them and reached out at random for the first book that came to hand. What was the book I was now holding in my hand? *Night Must Fall* by Emlyn Williams, the last play I had done. Spooky or what!

The relief at the end of the first night was like a kind of ecstasy – I'd done it, it had gone down well, there was a great reaction from the audience and thunderous applause. It was only when I was wandering back to the cottage in a beer- and adrenaline-induced cloud of smug satisfaction that it occurred to me that I now had to do it another forty times, starting tomorrow. And so the fear returned.

I must have got used to the adrenaline, and perhaps I'd started to go cold turkey, because finding myself broke from having been away from the voice circuit for two months, I needed to drum up some work fast. Charles Collingwood had made a great success of a one-man show that he'd been doing on and off for years, so I reckoned I'd give it a go in 2010. I thought I'd combine the funny or interesting things that I'd done in my life with my inner geek, so I devised a PowerPoint presentation that allowed me to combine stories, live and pre-recorded music and the odd bit of stand-up.

I needed a title, and the ever-generous Collingwood came to the rescue. I'd once told him a story about meeting the vicar who was to conduct my father's funeral. As an atheist, Pa had never met the man, but he was enough of a sucker for tradition that he'd wanted a church service at the end, probably hedging his bets. I was worried that the vicar might pronounce Pa's name wrong on the day, so as we were having tea in the house in Devon, I checked with him that he was going to be able to get 'Bentinck' out okay, as most people get it wrong.

'Oh yes, absolutely,' he assured me, 'a well-known and familiar name.'

As he was leaving, he turned in the porch, looked me in the eye and said, 'Oh, and before I go, can I just say...' Usually when people start off with 'Can I just say...' they continue with, 'I've been listening to *The Archers* since it started and I've never missed an episode?' or words to that effect. Which is fine because I'm always more than happy to talk about the programme, I'm a great believer in *noblesse oblige* which, translated into the acting profession means that whatever success you've had in the public eye is only there *because* of the public eye – acting without an audience is spectacularly pointless, so being gracious to people who like what you do is a very pleasant and rewarding part of the job. I did think that in this case the timing was a bit off, what with my father being dead and all, but I smiled and waited for him to complete the sentence. 'Can I just say,' he repeated, 'that my wife and I *love* your chocolates? Bendicks Bittermints – our annual Christmas treat!'

'That's your title!' cried Charles.

And that's why I toured a show called *Love Your Chocolates* for the next three years.

'Bendick' is not the only misspelling or mis-pronunciation of our name. If it were spelled 'Bentink' people would pronounce it correctly, after all it's just 'Bent' and 'Ink'. It's the 'c' that throws them, and I've long since ceased correct-ing people who call me Mr Bentinick, but for a time I used to collect misspelled envelopes and stick them on the downstairs loo wall. Here are some:

Monsieur Beatnick I now always use this in
  France
Tim Fenting This is good for N. Ireland, where
  Bentinck is associated with King Billy and the
  Orangemen
Mester Tom Bentyick Russia and Poland
Mr P. Bening Annette's ex
Tim Bentwick I wouldn't have survived this at
  school
M. S. J. Bertinck A Jamaican ring to this one
Mr. T. C. Bestnick Just plain ugly
Mr Bentlack Starting to take the piss really
Mrs Cenpink And this was a letter to me!
Time Bentinck Yeah, man, hippy dude parents
Tom Benstink Yes, I chose this name when I
  became an actor

214

Signore Timoteo Benedictine I adore this, thinking of a deed poll job

The Right Honourable, The Earl of Bent Just so wrong in every possible way!

Mr Bentdick Again, what parent would have allowed their child to bear this name at school?

The County Inspector This was actually addressed to my mother – the writer had misheard Countess Bentinck!

In creating my one-man show, I wrote down everything on yellow Post-it notes and stuck them on the bedroom door, whittling down the material to a satisfactory running order. In retrospect, I should have got a director, or at least an editor, to curb my excesses and *folie de grandeur*. The first time I rehearsed it, in the cottage in Norfolk in front of an open fire, it took just over three hours. Cut, cut, cut. Did it again, two hours forty. Cut, cut, cut. Two and a half. The problem was I wasn't sticking to the script, so I was waffling away ad lib and taking for ever. The fireplace was getting bored. Cut, cut, cut and just read what you've written – better, just over two hours.

My first performance was at the Westacre Theatre in Norfolk and, as the days got closer, my terror increased. I'd never known anything like it. I'd wake up and immediately be hit by a shock of almost debilitating anxiety that would last all day. I knew that such nerves came from the fear of the unknown, and that rehearsal and preparation would cure it, but no matter how many times I went through it to the fireplace, and practised the songs on the guitar until my fingers were raw, I couldn't dispel it. Looking back, I think it must have been the lack of any support system – no director, no writer, no other actors, just me. I'd created the most enormous rod for my back and the decision to do ten songs was completely barking mad.

The Day of Reckoning dawned at last and, loading the car up with props, including yoghurt, audio tape and wet towel for the lambing sound effects, an old ironing board for the gates and cattle crush, I drove with increasing trepidation to the theatre. The only things I had no control over were the microphones, the projector and the RGB cable connecting it to my computer. I started setting up. Immediately there was a disaster. The RGB cable was displaying the Green and the Blue perfectly, but there was no Red, thus rendering all the carefully chosen photos and videos unviewable. A helpful techie leapt into his van and shot off to Fakenham to get a new one but the seeds of doubt had now taken root and were growing into triffids of uncertainty.

Then the calm and unflappable theatre director, Clive Hadfield, came to the rescue. It was still early afternoon and he suggested I run through the whole show, on my own, to an empty auditorium. The cable arrived and the pictures looked fine. He closed the doors and I started from the beginning. Two hours later I knew it would be all right, I knew the songs, I had PowerPoint to prompt me, the theatre was intimate and the audience close to the stage, and one thing I'm perfectly happy with is nattering away to people, so that's what I did.

By the time I walked onto the stage at seven that evening, I was calm, happy and really looking forward to it. It went well. It was too long and I immediately set about cutting another half-hour from it, but the sense of achievement was massive. Alone in the cottage again that evening I swore I would never ever get that scared about anything again. Of course, I was wrong, and over the next three years every time I did the show I'd get the same build-up of tension and uncertainty, wondering why I'd volunteered to do it, until the end of the show when I'd feel on top of the world. What a ridiculous way to earn a living.

I was booked all over the country, in village halls, churches and theatres. I'd load the car up, 'Have Ironing Board Will Travel', and head off to a far-flung destination, sometimes for two or three consecutive nights. Generally, the more intimate venues were better and being able to see the audience meant more engagement. Sometimes, when you're downstage during a play and looking out, you can see the first few rows, all eyes on you and your own eyes on someone's groin or chair arm, anything but catching their eye. By contrast, the requirements for doing a show like mine meant that eye contact was beneficial. I found it strange that the moment I walked on stage I effectively became someone else, the nerves disappeared, I was ready to engage and the only thing I had to worry about was just droning on too long!

As with all theatrical tours, I had my good nights and my bad. Towards the end of the run, I had three nights in a row in Norfolk. The first two went really well, and then ... well, I realised afterwards that up until then I'd been lucky. I had a huge advantage in that most of the people who'd come to see me were *Archers* fans who loved the programme, if not necessarily David, and I started on a wave of goodwill. On a cold evening in a desolate village hall in the fens my luck finally ran out.

It started the moment I arrived.

'Why are you here so early? You're not on till seven.'

'Oh, I just like to make sure everything's working, I've had problems in the past.'

'Are you suggesting we don't know what we're doing?'

'No, no, just need to check my own equipment.'

'Well, I have to tell you I don't listen to *The Archers* and nor does anyone else in the village.' Ah, *that* sort of village. A bit like Ambridge where, surprisingly, no one listens to *The Archers!*

'Right, well never mind, there's plenty of other stuff.'

'When was your publicity photo taken?'

'Oh, a couple of years ago, I think,'

'It's longer than that, you're much older.'

Right. Didn't realise there was an age limit.

His stage introduction continued the theme.

'You probably won't recognise him from the photo on the flyer, it must have been taken about ten years ago, but anyway please welcome Timothy Bent ... Bentin ... Benny ... well, here he is.'

Ironic really considering that the very title of the show was about how no one could pronounce my name.

When the audience consists of about twenty farmers, their wives, their children and their dogs

218

– all with their arms folded and that look of 'Come on then, entertain me', and the first few *Archers*-related gags are greeted with stony silence, you know it's going to be a long night.

At the interval I popped outside for a breath of fresh air – a Joe Grundy clone was there having a fag.

'Are you enjoying it?' I asked.

'Not really.'

The show started by explaining the title with the story of the vicar and 'love your chocolates', and it ended with David Frost saying the same thing when I was on *Through the Keyhole*. I'd got my son Will to do a clever bit of Photoshopping on the 'Bendicks' logo, so I was able to top and tail the whole thing with the line, 'Well, if you can't beat 'em, join 'em! Introducing *Bentinck's* Chocolate Mint Crisp!'

Desultory round of applause and everyone got stuck into the beer, which was obviously the only reason they were there. No questions, no queues for signed scripts, nothing.

As I was clearing away and loading the kit back into the car, Joe Grundy came up to me. *Ah,* I thought, *I've won him round!'*

'Scuse me.'

'Yes, hello!'

'So, where is your chocolate factory then?'

All that effort.

Being David Archer: Fame

I do get recognised every now and then. 'Video

Killed the Radio Star', of course, but occasionally the papers do a feature on *The Archers* and our photos crop up. Even though most people don't know my name, they have a nagging suspicion that they either know me from somewhere, and I've appeared on screen in their living rooms enough times that the face is vaguely recognisable.

I went to a Michael Jackson concert at Wembley once with my old chum Rena. Although wheelchair-bound, she still drives like a racing driver and I was pleased to have got there in one piece. We couldn't find the disabled entrance that had a lift so I ended up carrying her on my back up about ten flights of stairs. As we appeared in the Royal Box (Rena knew the tour manager), the whole of Wembley rose as one with a mighty cheer. For a brief moment I thought there was an extraordinary crossover between Michael Jackson fans and *Archers* addicts, until I looked to my left and saw that Charles and Diana had appeared at the other entrance at exactly the same time.

I sometimes find myself baffled at a party when a complete stranger admonishes me for the way I treat my son, until I realise they're talking about my *Archers* son, Josh.

'You'll drive him away, Tim, if you keep behaving like that.'

It's the 'Tim' bit that's the most confusing.

If I ever state an opinion on Twitter, or even a wry observation, some wag will ask me why I'm not milking. This blurring of reality and fiction goes with the territory and I completely accept it now. After all, it's only being teased and nothing like the real abuse and sometimes violence actors can endure if they play rapists or paedophiles. Now that's scary.

When I was younger and on TV a lot, particularly with my *By the Sword Divided* long hair and earring, I was recognised much more. At first, I was flattered and quite enjoyed the attention. After a while, though, I began to find it a bit intrusive, and realised that anonymity was something to be cherished and that privacy is a privilege. Radio celebrity is more enjoyable, and can sometimes surprise the hell out of people. Doing 'celebrity' quiz shows are enormous fun and I wouldn't have got all the wonderful travel articles without my *Archers* association.

But these are just perks. The real joy is when someone thanks me for all the pleasure I've given them over the years, reveals that *The Archers* has helped them through their life or taught them something they didn't know, says that by adding my name to the fundraising gig will earn more money for a charity, or is over the moon because I have recorded a birthday greeting or donated a signed script. Fame comes with a price, and nowadays it's a price that I'm all too happy to pay.

Shorts

I love doing short films, mainly because I get the leading role and often play characters very different to myself. When you start off in this business, you're required to be listed in *Spotlight,* a directory of every professional actor in the UK, containing photograph and contact details. It's divided into two categories, Leading and Character Actors. It's a misleading distinction really, but, aiming high when I left drama school, I chose Leading. In retrospect, this seems to imply that you can only play types like yourself, whereas I've always felt far more comfortable playing characters very different to me. I wonder if Dan Day-Lewis put himself in Character; after all, it is his astonishing ability to utterly transform himself that has resulted in three Oscars.

I never believed that I would ever star in a Western. My incessant childhood practice with a six-gun and a reverence for cowboy programmes meant that, if the time ever came, I would be ready, but the idea of getting the call was a distant dream. So, when I met Séan Brannigan for the title role in *The Pride of Wade Ellison* – his half-hour graduation movie for the National Film and Television School – I couldn't believe that my dream might come true. It's often said that acting is just 'playing Cowboys and Indians' but Ambridge is, let's face it, very far from Wyoming.

To prepare for the role, my great buddy Kevin Howarth, a master of the broody close-up, brought round four DVDs, *Shane, Unforgiven, A Fistful of Dollars* and *The Gunfighter,* to give me a proper reminder of the genre. It's an oft-told story – retired gunslinger comes out of pig-rearing retirement for one last (fatal) shoot-out. I practised my Clint voice, real deep and real slow, sashayed around the house with bandy legs for a week, spent an afternoon at a riding stables to get my inner thigh muscles working again, and remembered just how quick I was with a six-gun. We filmed in Black Park, near Pinewood, and at a genuine Western town called Laredo in Kent. Built by enthusiasts, they gather there at weekends for hoe-downs, shoot-outs and sing-songs with the honky-tonk piano. When I asked a fully kitted-up gunslinger if they did the accent too, his pure London reply was, 'Oh no, mate, we don't pretend!'

It was a good script, and the film looked fantastic; me and ma boy (Elliot James Langridge) escaping our burning cabin at night, wading into a lake to bathe the wounds from a horse-whipping, flying out of the livery stable on my prancing grey, challenging the villain to a duel, galloping through the woods and facing four ornery-looking villains for the final bloodbath. I was wired up with six explosive squibs under my shirt for the Tarantino-style climax where I get blown to bits. The squibs were the pride of the film school special-effects department but due to budget constraints we only had two goes at this, and I had to react to the gunshots at the right moment and in the right place – it was no use if my right shoulder exploded while I doubled up from a groin shot. So I was to be seen wandering around the set twitching peculiarly from imagined gunshots until I got the sequence right. I die saving my boy, and the final shot is him riding away from my freshly dug grave, on my horse, wearing my hat. I got buried in *Sharpe's Rifles* in the Crimea too. It's an odd thing, looking at your own grave.

Equally unlikely is me being cast as a bank robber, but in *Locked Up* (winner of Best Foreign Short, Lanzarote Film Festival) that's precisely who I was. Directed by the wonderfully monikered Bugsy Riverbank Steel, we rehearsed and improvised it for many evenings before the two-day shoot, which Bugsy then edited down to a crisp and funny six minutes. A bank-robbing dad and his two sons lock themselves inside their getaway car because number one son dropped the keys when he went to buy himself a haloumi wrap.

I do love playing villains; in another short, *The Club*, I get to give my London hard man, but I have a recurring dream that I'm in a gangster film with Ray Winstone, both of us East End villains, when he suddenly says, 'You're a what, a fucking Earl? Fuck off!' and smacks me in the face. Jung would say this is fear of being found out generally but I don't care, I'd take the beating, just for the enormous satisfaction of being allowed to call Ray a dozy twat!

Although my father's side of the family is 100 per cent toff, my mother's roots were pure Sheffield steel. My mum was sent to a school in the south so she lost her northern vowels, but my two aunts, Pinkie and Bell-Bell, were like female versions of Alan Bennett. Hearing a strong Yorkshire accent always reminds me of family. In *The Turn*, a short directed by Christian Krohn, I was Stanley Kovack, drunken northern has-been stand-up being usurped by a younger, funnier generation, so I just channelled my Yorkshire blood. None of the comedy routines were scripted, so I found myself onstage in a seedy club, having to make up a sequence of lame, tired, sexist jokes that only get boos and heckles from the restless, unsympathetic audience. I loved it!

My co-star was James Phelps, one of the tall, long-haired Weasley twins from the Harry Potter films. A lovely lad, he told me an interesting fact about his fellow child actors on the early Potter films. He said the atmosphere on set was like being at school: in the same way that swots get teased in class for trying too hard, anyone who did too much 'acting' was sent up. Hence, the 'just say the lines' acting technique that became almost a trademark style of the movies.

Doing improvisation with other actors is one thing, but doing it when the other people are real, and you're effectively fooling them, is quite another. I've done role-play a couple of times, spending entire days convincing groups of bright law students that I was in fact a Ukrainian oligarch, trying to wrest billions of dollars from my business rival. It's an entirely different exercise, much more like being a spy or a criminal – hugely exciting. The first time I found myself doing it, though, was purely by chance: 'My name's Don, I'm fifty-four years old, I'm single, and I'm into plastic.'

So began a rather charming student film directed by Wyndham Richardson. Don was a Dorset-accented plastic toy manufacturer with ideas above his station, but at the end of the film he goes out of business and we find him selling his old stock from the layby of a dual carriage-way. The camera was using a long lens from the other side of the road, so with a big sign announcing, 'FREE TOYS!' cars kept stopping to see what was on offer, and I strung them along, figuring the director could use this guerrilla footage in the film, which indeed he did.

The quality of these short films varies, but professional productions, like *Locked Up* and *The Club*, have very high production standards and often do very well on the film festival circuit. They're fun too – spending a night in a pub with Nicholas Hoult and Imogen Poots in *Rule Number Three* or being a nasty Glaswegian police interrogator in *Esau Jacobs*. Also, I'm now at an age where I can be useful to young film-makers if they want advice. If not, I'm perfectly happy to follow my sister's advice and just keep my ruddy mouth shut.

Being David Archer: On stage

We once did an *Archers* 'event' at a holiday camp on the south coast. It was fun, we did 'turns' on stage like a talent competition, and performed a couple of scenes from the programme. We all stayed the night so we were able to meet the fans properly and, at dinner that evening, we were encouraged to go around all the tables and chat to people. One woman was quite vociferous in her insistence that I looked nothing like David and that I had completely spoiled her entire listening experience. I told her that I'd heard this before and that I was sure it was just a temporary blip. 'Don't worry,' I said cheerily, 'I'm sure that in a couple of weeks your David will come back to you.' To my horror, she instantly burst into floods of tears. It turned out that her husband's name was David, and that he had died two weeks before. Oh dear.

Events such as the holiday-camp convention, as well as theatre and cruise-ship shows, were organised by 'Archers Addicts', a fan club set up by Hedli Niklaus (Kathy Perks), Terry Molloy (Mike Tucker), Trevor Harrison (Eddie Grundy) and Arnold Peters (Jack Woolley). The club ran from 1990 to 2013 and provided its 10,000 members with books, annuals, diaries, calendars and loads of other merchandise along with a quarterly newsletter, which I used to narrate for the RNIB. When I started, I used to read it first, then record it and edit it properly in Pro Tools, cutting out fluffs and coughs and any outside noise, much like narrating an audiobook. One day though, when a goose honked particularly loudly from the pond outside the cottage, I commented on it, saying it sounded like I was in Ambridge. From then on, I used to sight-read it as though I were simply sitting next to a blind friend, and laugh and make appropriate comments. Much more fun and it was well received.

It's such a shame the company had to close: the membership started to dwindle as the internet provided more and more of what listeners wanted. Celebrity members included George Michael, Norma Major, Judi Dench, Jane Asher and Maggie Smith, and even Jeremy Paxman admitted to listening.

We used to have stalls at agricultural shows, and sometimes recorded scenes there too. The first

Addicts' convention was held at Malvern, opened by huge fan and *EastEnder* Wendy Richard. I sang my song, 'Ambridge Time', and the cast threw themselves into the fun of the show – it was a huge success. At the end, one poor woman couldn't find her car. The stewards and police were assembled to help but just as all seemed lost, she suddenly realised she hadn't brought the car, her husband had driven her there. She'd been so carried away by the event she'd gone a bit doolally.

To celebrate the fiftieth anniversary, Archers Addicts organised an enormous day-long event at the National Indoor Arena in Birmingham. There were all kinds of stalls manned by the cast, cookery, skittles, quizzes, the Milk Marketing Board, sound-effects demonstrations, welly-wanging... It was like a small village – called Ambridge! Some 3,000 people attended, coming from all over the world. Hedli remembers a bemused sheikh who had been dragged along by his two burka-dressed and *Archers*-mad wives. One person arrived in a hospital bed, complete with drip and attendant nurses. I was amazed by the long queues for autographs and the contented hum of wonder from this vast throng. In the evening, we did a show on stage, MC'd by the late Nick Clarke, such a lovely man, taken by cancer far too young. When Norman and Paddy came on stage, 3,000 people stood and cheered. Just wonderful.

Some people, though, hate seeing us in the flesh. Like the poor widow at the holiday-camp event, for many it ruins the illusion and they even get cross if they see pictures of us in the newspaper. *The Ambridge Pageant* (1991) and *Murder at Ambridge Hall* (1993) were the only full-blown realisations of an *Archers* story on stage – I wasn't involved but when I went to see them, they both fitted perfectly into my imagination because, of course, to me all the actors look like their characters. However, for some of the audience it was a slightly surreal experience – right voice, wrong body. It's such a shame we don't get to do these appearances any more, but apparently the Beeb can't afford it. I know it's a radio show, but the joy on people's faces when they meet their favourite characters, even if they don't look like them, is palpable, and bringing a bit of joy into the world can never be a bad thing, can it?

The Royal Bodyguard and Twenty Twelve

So there I was in 2011, making a decent living out of being a jobbing actor, but still with the permanent sense of insecurity that afflicts most people in the profession. I was much luckier than most having *The Archers* as a constant, but even that was, and still is, subject to the vagaries of the storyline, and if I'm not in it, I'm not being paid. I'd pretty much resigned myself to the idea that the heady days of fame that I'd enjoyed in my youth were over, and that I should be content to muddle along with *The Archers*, voiceovers, computer games voices, travel writing, ADR, dubbing and the occasional lead in short films, or supporting roles in TV and films.

Then I got two auditions in one day. *The Royal Bodyguard* was a six-part comedy series featuring 'Sir David Jason's return to comedy after ten years!' as the publicity had it. It was a leading role, starring in all six episodes. Excited, I learned the lines for the audition and headed up to Hat Trick Productions in Camden to meet the directors Mark Bussell and Justin Sbresni, fresh from the success of *The Worst Week of My Life*. The casting director was Sarah Crowe, who had got me *The Armando Iannucci Shows* and *The Thick of It*, so I was quite hopeful. The audition went okay, but I was in and out like a shot, which usually means I am totally wrong for the part and that I'd ironed my shirt and polished my shoes for nothing.

I went straight from there to the BBC to meet John Morton and casting director Rachel Freck for a really nice part in the second series of *Twenty Twelve*, the comedy about the forthcoming Olympics with Hugh Bonneville. I really wanted the part. This was much more difficult to learn, as the lines are very bitty; full of 'yes, no, yes…' and ums and ahs that are all completely scripted and rigidly stuck to by writer/director Morton.

I got them both! A lead in a series with David Jason, name above the title, good money, options on two more series with a 20 per cent increase each time and worldwide DVD sales. I was going to be the next 'Trigger'! Fame beckoned again, and with it the security of becoming a bit of a household name, part of the 'rep' of British actors that work regularly in TV. No more scrabbling about for work, I could put my feet up, secure in the knowledge that all the persistence and work had paid off. Debts could be settled, new car, holiday, the lot. If only I'd known...

I started to have my doubts when I received the scripts. I thought that it probably wasn't my kind of thing, but given Jason's popularity, it was bound to be a success. The idea behind it was that it would be a return to a more old-fashioned, safe, non-edgy comedy for the whole family. It relied on a lot of slapstick and silliness. I imagined Norman Wisdom in the role of Guy Hubble, an ageing and hopeless retired Army officer, now in charge of Her Majesty's car park, who, having saved the Queen's life when her carriage horses bolted from the noise of a crisp packet that he had popped, is promoted to the role of royal body-guard. Wisdom might have saved it, Jason, despite the genius of the falling-through-the-bar gag on *Only Fools...*, sadly couldn't. I played Sir Edward Hastings, a Whitehall mandarin, alongside the wonderful Geoffrey Whitehead as my Hubble-hating colleague, Colonel Dennis Whittington, and Tim Downie as the hapless fall guy, Yates.

I'd heard that David Jason could be tricky to work with but he was utterly delightful on set, generous and complimentary to all.

Our Whitehall office scenes were filmed at Gaddesden Place, coincidentally just down the road from where I was brought up, and in the stables of which I had learned to ride as a child. It was a happy shoot, all of us admiring of seventy-three-year-old David's willingness to throw himself into stunts that actors half his age would have thought twice about, but it felt slow. Good comedy has to

231

take its audience by surprise, and I kept getting the feeling that they would be ahead of us.

This was confirmed at the cast and crew showing of the first two episodes where the laughter was either forced or totally lacking. Sir David did not attend, citing a cold, but it wasn't a good sign. Then there was the scheduling. It might have worked on children's TV, and indeed it went down well with the younger audience, but inexplicably the first episode went out at 9 p.m. on Boxing Day probably the most pissed, jaded and cynical audience you get all year. I, along with eight million others, settled down with my family to watch it, and within ten minutes the Twitter feed gave depressing forebodings of the disaster to come.

'About as funny as a bad case of the Trotters.'

'This has to be the worst programme on TV this Christmas.'

'The Royal Bodyguard may return next Monday but I doubt any viewers will.'

And indeed a million turned off during the show and the next episode played to half the original figures. The next three attracted a mere two million and the series was axed.

So, no fame, no security, no joining the comedy rep, only the occasional, 'Weren't you in that dreadful thing with David Jason?'

By contrast, *Twenty Twelve* was a huge success, winning awards and flattering praise all round. Proving that success is not judged by viewing figures alone, the first series aired on BBC4 to 400,000 (nonetheless a huge figure for that channel), and when the second series was broadcast on BBC2 it rose to 1.2 million. And there lies the difference between a popular and an artistic success.

Some actors hate them but I generally love read-throughs. It's the chance to meet the cast and crew and to find out the style and tone of the piece, so you're not acting in limbo. Some friends say they get terribly nervous and I've witnessed plenty of well-known names getting deeply uncomfortable, but what with *The Archers* and the amount of narrations and audiobooks I've done, I'm very used to sight-reading, so for me it's like a first performance. With *Twenty Twelve* it was different. I was a huge fan of the first series and had never worked with any of the actors before, so when we all met for the first episode of series two, I came into the room convinced that these were all actually real people, and that I'd be the only one acting and therefore stand out a mile. Thankfully my first line, with Hugh Bonneville, got a big laugh, I relaxed, and it went fine from then on.

When we came to the filming day, slotted in between *Bodyguard* location scenes, it was technically fiendish. We were sat in front of three TV screens, the idea being that in trying to organise a conference call with Sebastian Coe and the Algerian foreign minister, it all goes horribly wrong and Islam is irredeemably insulted. In these situations, you never actually see what's on a screen – it gets added in later, so all of our eyelines had to be on the correct screen at the same time, which combined with the quick-fire banter for which the show was famous, surrounded by a cast who'd been practising it for an entire series, was tricky to say the least. We did multiple takes, sometimes just recording a line on its own, so at the end of the day I had no idea if it had gone well or was a disaster. I therefore arrived at the cast and crew showing a few months later with some trepidation, to be greeted by director John Morton, whose first words to me were, 'Don't worry, you're funny.'

Phew.

Casting

My very first agent was a man called Nick Legh Hepple, who had no experience in the business but was from a PR background. His attitude was that you had to go out of your way to attract the attention of important people, and that would get you work. I took his advice, sometimes to my own detriment. When I heard about a new mini-series being cast, featuring modern-day aristocratic families – I thought I'd be perfect. I went to the boating lake at Alexandra Palace and asked if they had any broken oars. So, the next day I walked boldly into the offices of the production company with a six-foot oar, tied to which was my CV and photo, accompanied by the words, 'I just thought I'd get my oar in first.' I didn't get the part.

They say you usually succeed or fail the

moment you walk through the door. My dear friend Jon Dixon had travelled down from Derby one evening and stayed with us in London for a nine o'clock casting the following day. It was a TV commercial for VW and he found himself sitting with about twelve other hopefuls just outside an office with a glass wall, so they could all see what the previous actor was doing. One by one they were called in and Jon saw each of them shake the director's hand, have a little chat, then do the lines, each time two or three times. Then thank yous, smiles, another handshake, and goodbyes. When it was Jon's turn, he walked in, big smile, hand outstretched to the director who had his head down writing something. He looked up, saw Jon, said, 'No,' and put his head back down. After a sympathetic look from the casting assistant, Jon turned on his heel, exited, and went back to Derby. Cruel.

It is always best to do some research before you go up for a part. I was once told by my agent that I had a casting for a comedy series that was 'kind of like the Comic Strip' (the comedy group featuring Ade Edmondson, Rik Mayall, Dawn French, Jennifer Saunders, Alexi Sayle and others). I was up to play a 'student terrorist'. I thought this meant someone at university who was trying to blow the place up. When I got to the casting, they told me it was a school for terrorists, so totally different. Then Peter Richardson, who was directing, said the show was, 'you know, standard Comic Strip sort of stuff'.

Figuring that this must be their direct competition I offered, 'Yeah, I liked their early stuff but I think they've gone a bit off the boil recently.'

Silence and puzzled looks.

'Right...' said Peter.

'Um ... sorry, but my agent never told me who you are. What's actually the name of your show?'

'We're the Comic Strip.'

I just fell about laughing, 'Oh bugger. I'm not getting this part, am I?'

Amazingly, I did, but I couldn't do it because I had an *Archers* episode that day. Damn!

Others that have got away? Boromir in *Lord of the Rings* – I had two recalls, the last one with Peter Jackson – *Downton Abbey* and *Game of Thrones*. It's not so bad when you find the actor who got the part is physically different: Roger Ashton-Griffiths, who got the part as Mace Tyrell in *GoT*, and I are poles apart.

One of my best audition moments was for the part of Major Heyward in *The Last of the Mohicans* with Daniel Day-Lewis. I remember the casting, in an office on Frith Street. The director Michael Mann greeted me with the words, 'Hey, Tim, Dan says hi but he's working out.' So my old mucker had put in a word! I hadn't seen the script so just sight-read some lines. I could feel the director staring intently at me and when I'd finished, he turned to the casting director and said, 'Honey, give Tim a script. Tim, I want you to go to a pub, have a beer and read the movie. Can you be back here in an hour?' Are bears Catholic? Minutes later I was nursing a Guinness in the Dog and Duck, reading the script. 'Oh my God I'm rescuing my betrothed from the Indians ... oh wow I'm shooting the rapids ... Christ I go over a waterfall

... oh oh oh I'm being tortured, bones inserted through my breasts and hoisted over a fire on ropes ... a mercy shot from Dan puts me out of my pain ... bliss, a real movie part!'

Steven Waddington got it.

Being David Archer: Writers

Without the writers, there would be no *Archers*. While the overall storyline comes primarily from the editor in discussion with the writers, turning the generality of a months'-long plot line into believable dramatic scenes takes enormous talent and hard work. When faced with tales of great moment and emotion, I hear the actors rise to the occasion and give sometimes sensational per-formances, but they couldn't do any of that with-out great writing. However, it's more difficult when absolutely nothing in the slightest is hap-pening and we have to make turnips sexy, and hardest of all is being able to weave Ministry of Agriculture (now DEFRA) advice or propaganda into believable dialogue. Here's how they *don't* do it:

RUTH David? Where are you off to in the new
    four-wheel-drive tractor that will plough eight
    furrows instead of six, thus increasing our
    profit margins by 2 per cent over the course of
    the year?

DAVID Oh I'm just going to spray this new
    systemic insecticide that provides you with

control of pollen beetles in oilseed rape and
mustard, aphids in Calabrese broccoli,
Brussels sprouts, cabbage, cauliflower, carrots,
parsnips, peas, oilseed rape and potatoes and
a reduction of damage by orange wheat
blossom midge in wheat. I'll be back in time
for tea.

It's hard enough trying to make it sound natural
even when it's done well.

Our agricultural editor and writer Graham
Harvey takes the top prize for negotiating these
minefields, and I'm sure the other writers curse
him for introducing the plots in the first place.

There have been many scriptwriters over my
time, and while impossible to mention them all,
those who've been around the longest – Mary
Cutler, Joanna Toye, Caroline Harrington, Simon
Frith, Tim Stimpson, Paul Brodrick, Adrian Flynn
and Keri Davies have moulded and shaped the
character of David more than I ever could. I've
oftentimes found myself impossibly moved when
reading through a script, and once texted Keri to
say, 'You made me cry you bastard!' They really
are the unsung heroes – I can make you angry,
sad, sympathetic or shout at David in frustration,
but without the right words to say, you wouldn't
feel a thing.

Sometimes the script gets chopped to pieces.
The read-through is timed and has to come in at
around twelve and a half minutes. Any shorter
and we have to stretch time, but if it's too long,
great swathes of dialogue have to be cut. Unfortunately, it's usually the gags that go, as the

plot is paramount, and I often feel for the writer when their carefully constructed shtick is deleted at the stroke of a pencil.

Name checks are a bit of a minefield. There's a limit to how many times I can call Ruth 'Ruth' and she can call me 'David' in a single scene, and regular listeners obviously recognise our voices immediately in any case. However, we constantly have to cater for the new listener who needs all the help they can get. Joe Grundy is enormously useful in this respect: his habit of calling us by our full names makes it abundantly clear for the rookie listener exactly who is who.

The Year of the Roth

Despite what happened to Jon Dixon and his wasted trip from Derby to London, theatre, film and TV auditions are usually a lot better than the cattle-market hell of commercial castings – you're generally treated with more respect. They've changed a bit over the years. In the early days, the first question was often, 'So what have you been up to recently?' – which was a tricky one if the truth was watching daytime TV, collecting the kids from school and trying not to kill yourself. Also, you had a fair time to prepare – the scripts would come through the post a few days before and the whole process took longer. Mostly, though, you would just turn up and sight-read and if you did okay you'd get a recall to do it 'off the book'. These days, you can get an email at 6 p.m. for a casting the next day and be expected to produce a memorised and polished performance in one take. However, 'self-tapes' are also more and more common, where you have to film yourself at home and send it in. Often, fifteen minutes after a casting you suddenly realise how you should have done it, so self-taping at least has the benefit of giving you a few more cracks of the whip.

In 2015 Judy and I were on our first Mediterranean holiday in ages. We'd rented a villa with a pool on a Greek island for two weeks and were seven days into unwinding the stress of the last three years when I got an email from my agent asking me to do a self-tape to play the writer Frederick Forsyth in a Jimmy McGovern TV play called *Reg* – the true story of Reg Keys, who had taken on Tony Blair for the seat at Sedgefield in the General Election of 2005. His son had been killed in the Iraq War and Forsyth was helping him on the campaign trail.

The audition comprised the entire part of three monologues. I had two days to do it, so I spent the first one learning the lines while sunbathing next to the pool, the second day we set up to shoot it indoors. I was tanned and swimming-toned, the light inside the villa was gentle and flattering, Judy didn't have to do any off lines, and we did each scene in one take on an iPhone. Two days later I had the part, which was a result considering the wildly expensive holiday was all paid for with a credit card and optimism, and the job exactly paid it off in one go!

I was also delighted because Reg would be played by Tim Roth, and I had just finished filming with his son. Early that year, I'd had a delightful interview with casting director Shakyra Dowling, director Joe Martin and producer Danielle Clark. I was there for the best part of an hour, chatting about the part and life in general. The film was a low-budget British movie called *Us and Them*. Written by Joe, it was a thriller about a home invasion, in which I was auditioning to play a rich banker whose house gets taken over by Jack Roth and his gang, who tie up him and his family and broadcast their torture on YouTube. Nasty stuff, but with a contemporary and poignant message about the haves and have-nots.

I was offered the part but at first I was in two minds. In the plot, Jack's character half drowns me in my private pool and there's a lot of violence with his sidekick, played by Andy Tiernan. I looked them both up and they seemed to be seriously hard. I was worried in case they were method actors and would be just as nasty off screen as their characters were on. Still, it was a lead in a movie and things had been quiet for a bit so I accepted.

Jack, it turned out, is a total softie and we had the best time. He's a livewire and a seriously good screen actor, bouncing off the walls with energy and generous to a fault to make a scene look good, while Andy is a cuddly, loveable rogue, even when stabbing me viciously in my walk-in wardrobe. Joe is a hugely talented young director who will go far, and the whole cast, from my stoical wife, Carolyn Backhouse, and drop-dead gorgeous daughter, Sophie Colquhoun, to the very funny Danny Kendrick and Paul Westwood (it's impossible not to laugh when a man spends the entire day with 'Wanker' written on his forehead) were a delight to work with. For the first time in my life, I was the oldest, most experienced person on the set, and was often deferred to and consulted for advice. That's a real rarity, and felt good. The film went on to have great success at the SXSW Film Festival in America.

So, I was chuffed to monkeys to find myself in three nice scenes with Jack's dad Tim. The main scene for me in *Reg* was when Frederick Forsyth stands in front of a war memorial, with Reg beside him, giving an impassioned speech to a large crowd about how Tony Blair was a war criminal. When you're in front of a large crowd, and you've got a major Hollywood star next to you, and you've got a long speech written by Jimmy McGovern, and the light's fading ... that's kind of what you join up for.

When I came to watch it I was alone in a hotel room, and I was terrified. It was so good, Anna Maxwell Martin was amazing, Roth was quietly mesmeric, the story was tragic and compelling, and I was awaiting my first appearance. *'I'll be crap, I'll let the whole thing down, oh God, oh God...'* When it came to it, I was okay, thank goodness. The quality of the production, filming and writing lifted me and I rose to the occasion. This is what it's like, up one minute, petrified the next, and always only ever as good as your last job.

When the next job starred Tim Roth as well, it

started to get spooky. *Rillngton Place* is a three-part series about the serial murderer John Christie, an update of the 1971 movie starring Richard Attenborough – I played his doctor, Dr Odess. The last time I'd seen Tim he was a spiky-haired Brummie, but six months later, a bald, whispering Yorkshireman of intense creepiness shuffled into a cold, disused office in Glasgow.

'Are you stalking me?' he smiled.

'No, Tim, I'm your new good luck charm. Forget Tarantino, get me in all your productions from now on and I can guarantee your success.'

Being David Archer: Feedback

These days *The Archers* receives a lot of feedback on Twitter and Facebook. There used to be the BBC bulletin boards, known as 'Mustardland' because of the colour of the website. When that started, people used to write reams of often highly articulate critique, worthy of university dissertations, suggesting aspects of the story that I hadn't even thought of. Over the years, these got fewer and fewer and I went off it rather when it all started to get a bit abusive. It started off quite gently – 'David and Ruth Archer, the moral and intellectual vacuum at the heart of *The Archers*' – but after a while some bitter trolls made it unpleasant for everyone and the service was withdrawn, although if you do a search for 'Mustardland' there are independent sites that carry it on. Twitter hashtags and Facebook sites provide more outlets, and it's wonderful that people talk and analyse and argue and feel so strongly about the programme. How dull it would be if they didn't. These days, I have to admit to occasionally basking in the loving endorsements of the David Archer Appreciation Group.

It is said that imitation is the sincerest form of flattery and I was thrilled one day to hear myself being lampooned on *Dead Ringers,* despite the fact that Jon Culshaw didn't seem to sound like me. Have I got any noticeable ticks as David? I honestly don't know.

The Archers spoofs started in 1961 with Tony Hancock's 'The Bowmans' when he forces the producers to use a script in which the whole village falls down a disused mineshaft. These day there are some wonderful spoofs. The *Shambridge* podcast is a bravura turn by Harriet Carmichael, taking on and absolutely nailing all the women of the village. John Finnemore's sketches of 'How *The Archers* sounds to people who don't listen to *The Archers'* is wicked, but very well observed. My favourite, though, because it's so weird, is a series of tableaux done with Duplo figures, called 'The Plarchers' – on Twitter as 'Ambridge Synthetics'. Rob Titchener as Dracula is just perfection!

Before the internet, we used to get letters, and one such has gone down as a classic. There was a fair amount of controversy about the fact that when Pip was born, the whole process was, as it were, recorded live. David was present, and the actual birth was simulated for the scene. Flick doesn't have children but spoke to friends who had been through childbirth, did a lot of research and, because I had attended my son Will's birth, she asked about my experience. 'It was loud,' I said. 'There was a lot of pain.'

When it came to the recording, she really went for it. For my own part I can remember distinctly shedding projectile tears when my first-born appeared, so I used that experience to enhance David's emotion at witnessing his daughter's arrival. A week after this was broadcast two letters were published in the *Radio Times*, one very complimentary and another from a retired major:

I have attended the births of all five of my children, and I can assure you that my wife didn't sound as if she was being murdered, and that I didn't turn into a snivelling wreck like David, and neither did any of my friends.

It was the phrasing of the letter that made us laugh – how many of the major's friends were at the five births? I imagined them all standing around with their G & Ts, 'Come on Marjory, get on with it, the rugger's about to start!'

Dear old David, he may not be a searing intellectual but he's not thick. He's just more interested in the farm and his family than he is with discussing art, or politics, or philosophy – so he and I are a bit different really. The only things we share are the voice and the love of physical work and making things. I once went to a book launch in Norfolk. The book was a Marxist view of the Roman Empire.

'You're brave,' a posh local ventured to the author.

'Oh, why's that?' he asked, clearly flattered.

'There aren't any Marxists in Burnham Market,' came the entirely accurate reply.

When it came to Q & As, I asked a couple of questions because the Romans have always fascinated me. Over wine and canapés afterwards, a woman who had been sitting in front of me said, 'It was extraordinary, that voice! I mean it was David, but you sounded *so intelligent!*'

Voice work

I have a recording of me doing a Mother's Pride voiceover for my father when I was about twelve: 'But misery, Mum cannot abide, so in she trots with Mother's Pride.' You then hear my father on talkback saying tersely, 'Again.' I repeat the line. He says 'Again' over and over. I sound terrified.

Little did I know that this was the preparation for how I would be earning the majority of my income for my adult life. Over the last thirty-odd years, I've done thousands of television commercials, radio commercials, corporate voiceovers, stadium announcements, narrations, audiobooks, voice-unders (vocal subtitles), museum audio guides, dubbing, re-voicing, ADRs (additional dialogue replacements), loop groups (most movie-screen deaths you hear are me and my friends), language tapes, teaching tapes, training courses, computer games voices, cartoon and animation voices, in-store announcements, documentary narrations, medical instructions, film trailers, celebrity voices – and 'Mind the Gap' on the Piccadilly Line.

There's a recording studio called Side on Great Portland Street where I do a lot of computer games voices. The irony is not lost on me, as the Earl of Portland walks down the street, not owning it, but having spent the last two hours screaming fearful incantations as an undead vampire necromancer.

Winning the Carleton Hobbs award led to my radio career, but also opened me up to this whole other world of voice-related work. My sister Anna, the queen of audiobooks, paved the way and introduced me to a producer called Tony Hertz at Radio Operators, who remains the most original and inventive creator of radio commercials I've ever known. His thirty-second ads were mini dramas, well written, funny, poignant and required acting rather than mere voice technique. For some reason, he rated me and taught me the secrets of the soft sell. When I went off to Plymouth to do *Joseph* in 1979, I managed to get some work for the local radio station, which taught me the techniques of precisely the opposite – the hard sell. Hard sell involves cramming as much information into thirty seconds as you can possibly manage at town-crier volume, in the manner of a crazed salesman who has just discovered that frozen peas at £2.99 a packet are better than sex, and that if you don't RUSH OUT immediately to buy them from your local Co-op you'd be MAD, MAD, MAAAAD!

In the radio studio in Plymouth, there was a home-made, Devonian block of wood beneath the microphone with a series of LED lights stuck on it that counted down from thirty to nought, and I had to get the script across in exactly that time. I have an extremely accurate ability to judge thirty seconds as a result. I also mastered three things.

1. The Clarkson: 'Probably the best frozen peas … [one second pause] … *in the world!*'

2. The end of advert Terms and Conditions nightmare:'Peasmayvaryinsizenotallhandpickedp easwerepickedbyhandsomepeasmaynotbesuitabl eforchildrentermsandconditionsapply, and

3. The Voice: that particular and peculiar commercial advert voice that is classless and inoffensive to as many listeners as possible – an everyman voice. I've used it ever since.

The hard sell has gone out of fashion in the UK, but to be a successful voiceover you need to learn all the techniques and be able to do them convincingly and fluently on take one. I've now had a lot of practice, and, despite an inbred reluctance to boast, I have to admit that these days I generally get it right straight away. This can sometimes confuse the room full of people who are there for the one-hour recording session, each of whom feels that they have to contribute. The producer, the writer, the client, the client's mum, the client's twelve-year-old and their dog all have to justify their presence. I'm booked for the hour and I'm happy to take anyone's notes, but we do sometimes go around in a circle: 'Okay, can we get the first line of take six, which I thought was good, then the middle bit from take four, and put the last three words from take nine, because we loved that, at the end?' They play back the result. They look dubious. Then some kind soul says, 'Actually, could we listen to take one again?'

At its best, voice work is a genuine art form. At its worst, it is akin to slavery. Let's start with the hardest.

Corporates

Early days. Brighton in winter. A freezing basement studio. No table, just a wobbly music stand. A three-day job in the cold, sight-reading for eight hours a day – the instruction manual of how to operate a rolled steel mill in Lancashire. Terms whose meanings are like a foreign language, detailed and complex instructions that are, to my mind, gobbledegook, but I know about tools, and I like machines, so I get into a sort of zen-like state where I'm channelling the semi-literate writer of the piece, thinking about things at home, where I'd left the car keys, Charlotte Rampling, all the while sounding hugely authoritative about rolled steel mills. That's the job, that's what you're paid to do, sight-read as though you'd thought of it.

Then there are the medical ones. You're meant to be the doctor, so Latin-heavy, didactic tomes of medical philosophy are presented to you on arrival in the form of a weighty, bulldog-clipped

A4 script. You're ushered politely into someone's garage and asked to sound like you're the expert. That's when school comes in handy – those hated Latin lessons, those slightly better Italian tutorials with the rather fit housemaster's wife, the years of French and German that seemed at the time to have no point at all, but now mean I can read, on the fly, lines like 'such conditions as Choledocholithiasis, Menometrorrhagia and Bradykinesia...' with ease and without hesitation.

Well, that's what it sounds like in the final edit – the original recording is often entirely different: 'Choledodolith ... Choledotholid ... Cholethodoly ... oh bollocks!' It is not just medical terms that can trip you up. With an audiobook, I'll get through three pages without fluffing difficult stuff with long names and multiple character voices, and I'll be feeling just a bit chuffed with myself and bang! I'm suddenly completely unable to say 'the'. Then I'll get into fluff mode. Eventually I get through it and I'm off again. But it's feeling a bit pleased with yourself that's always your undoing.

Documentary narration
This isn't so bad because the pictures do a lot of the work for you. Usually there isn't so much to say, and sometimes the content can be fascinating. I was hugely honoured to find myself narrating a documentary about my father's old friend James Lovelock, the environmentalist; he was equally amazed and happy at the coincidence. My favourite doc narrator is Samuel West: I think

he gets it just right. The speaker should not sound as though they're reading it and shouldn't suggest an opinion on the content either; they don't use a special voice and don't perform, but at the same time they command the viewer's interest because of their engagement with the subject.

Audiobooks

Audiobooks can be tough, depending on the material and the studio. Sometimes, you're stuck in a tiny box with no window and an iPad in front of you, so no chance of a quick rest as you turn the page like you used to, blathering on about some mind-numbingly boring subject that will probably never be listened to anyway.

I once did a series of books called *How to Do Business the* _____ *Way:* the Richard Branson way, the Philip Green way, the Bill Gates way, etc. I was reading about how someone had an idea, wrote it on the back of a matchbox and a week later was a billionaire at the age of twelve. Meanwhile, I was freezing my arse off in a box in Notting Hill earning around 50p a page. Not fun.

On the other hand, you can be in a light airy studio where you can see the producer, reading a wonderful novel, and it's like doing a radio play where you're not only the narrator, but you're playing all the parts too. There's an app on the iPad called iAnnotate, which allows you to high-light all the dialogue with different colours. This makes it slightly easier when there's a Yorkshireman talking to a Geordie, a Scouser and a Scot, and the narrator is from New York. Sometimes it can get really complicated. In *Corroboree* by Graham Masterton, about the early days of Australia, not only are there scores of Aussies and English, but then they go out into the bush where there's about eight Aborigines, male and female, and everyone should be given a different voice. The main character then learns their language, so they're all speaking together, in Aborigine, but it's written in English. It didn't help that I had a bad chest infection at the time, so there's a lot of very butch Aussie women in the audiobook.

I've heard tales of actors who didn't even look at the book before the recording and, having spent three days voicing a story where they'd given their main character a standard southern RP accent, reach the last page only to find, 'said Albert, his Irish brogue softening the cruel impact of his harsh words'.

I've been guilty of this too. One of the first books I recorded was *Dracula* by Bram Stoker. I thought I knew the story so didn't prepare it. I invented characters' accents and voices on the fly. When it got to Mina, I gave her a high-pitched, very girly voice. My heart sank when I discovered halfway through that large extracts are taken from 'Mina's Journal' so suddenly the narrator is a shrill girl's voice, but the dialogue is still full of van Helsing's deep Dutch tones and Dracula's creepy Transylvanian.

Voice-unders

The 'vocal subtitle' is used when you've got a documentary with interviewees speaking a foreign language. Sometimes this is subtitled, but often the dialogue is subdued and an English voice comes in, providing the translation. Producers vary as to how they want this done. Sometimes they want you to match the colour and emotion of the speaker, and 'act' the lines, but more often the brief is to just provide the words, with no expression at all. There's a skill to this, as sometimes reading it totally flat can be a performance in itself and detract from the mood of the interview.

TEFL and ELT

Teaching English as a Foreign Language and English Language Teaching are recorded as learning aids for foreign students. Usually they consist of simple words and phrases, depending on the level that is being taught, from beginner to expert. At higher levels, you're doing Dickens and Shakespeare. Probably the most demanding job in this discipline is reading the rubrics: 'Chapter three, page nineteen, exercise five. One.'

The king and queen of Rubrics are Ken Shanley and Nicolette McKenzie, who both seem to adore doing it, and are peerless.

I was once booked to go to a studio in Milton Keynes to do some pickups of a session I'd recorded the previous month. The weather was appalling – huge snowdrifts and abandoned cars, treacherous icy roads, and driving, horizontal sleet. It took me nearly three hours. I staggered into the studio to be told, 'Ah, Tim, thanks so much for making it through in this weather. Very simple really, we just need you to record the alphabet.'

'The alphabet?'

'Yes, just A, B, C etc. Can't think how we failed to do it last time.'

'Right.'

I sat in the booth and when the green light went on I read the alphabet.

It took five minutes. I then got back in the car and drove home through the arctic waste, another three hours. An actor's life for me...

Mind the Gap

'Tim, job for you tomorrow at two, studio in Horsham. Station announcements,' says the lovely Tania from Hobson's International voice-over agency.

I got there early.

'So, station announcements. Which station is it?'

'It's the Piccadilly Line.'

'What, Mind the Gap?'

'Yup, and the rest.'

So for something like fifteen years I and fellow Hobsonian Julie Berry were the voices of the Piccadilly Line between King's Cross and Earl's Court. I achieved English icon status with this: 'Please mind the gap. This is Holborn. The next station is Covent Garden. Please stand clear of the closing doors.'

My boys grew up to the sound of their father watching out for them on the tube, which they both found strangely comforting. I use the Piccadilly Line almost every day, and when brash foreigners used to take the mickey out of my warnings, 'Ho ho ho, Mind ze Gepp!' I'd fantasise about seeing them fall down the gap, and I would lean down and whisper, 'I warned you!'

One day I was listening to *I'm Sorry I Haven't a Clue* on the car radio – they were on my favourite round, 'Mornington Crescent', when Graeme Garden introduced this piece of incidental information, 'On the Piccadilly Line, commuters hearing a recording of the phrase, Mind the Gap, are listening to the voice of Tim Bentinck, who plays David Archer in *The Archers*.' Now that is what I call fame!

People often ask me if I got paid every time it was played. Oh, I wish. Sadly, it was a £200 buyout. You win some...

TV voiceovers

Some people have made a great deal of money from voiceovers and I've done all right, but mostly from the less glamorous types of job. My first one wasn't a voice but a whistle.

'Tim, can you whistle?'

'Yes?'

'Okay, Soho Studios tomorrow at nine.'

I walked in.

'Oh hi, Tim, can you whistle?'

'Yes, I think that's why I'm here.'

'Great, it's just we employed an actor to play a

255

milkman, but it turns out he's the only member of your profession who has a complete inability to whistle, so we need to re-voice him whistling cheerfully as he delivers the morning pinta.'

'Okay.'

'Right, so we'll just show you the film; if you want to whistle along we'll take some level.'

'Fine.'

I watched a milkman get out of his milk float, go around the back, pick up two bottles and put them on a doorstep. I whistled along cheerfully.

'That's perfect, Tim, we actually put a tape on that and it sounds great. You're done, mate.'

I've been in the studio for five minutes max. I've earned £2000. It doesn't usually work like that.

I once did a TV voiceover for L'Oréal. So, I did take one. And it was fine.

There were seven women in the control room all looking baffled, desperately searching for something to criticise. We did another take because we could, they looked happier, then a third one which was pretty slick and everyone was smiling. Then the client, the representative of L'Oréal in the UK, early twenties, earnest, serious, justifying her presence, says, 'Sorry, but you're not saying L'Oréal correctly.'

'Okay, fine how do you want it?

'L'Oréal.'

'L'Oréal.'

'No, L'Oréal.'

'L'Oréal.'

'No, like this. L'Oréal.'

'Okay, so do you want it more French-sounding?

More in the area of L'Auréalle with a sort of vocal Gallic shrug? Or would you rather it was inclining more towards the cheerful Anglicised timbre of a 'Lorry-al' sort of sound?'

'It's L'Oréal.'

'Right. Okay, Steve, let's go again.'

I think we did twenty-six takes. The nature of the deal was that I would get paid a studio fee to record it, but if my voice was accepted I would get a buy-out, which was a whole lot more, so I was concerned to say L'Oréal in every conceivable way known to man. As we left, I felt a lack of enthusiasm and thought I'd blown it. I went on holiday. On my return, I got a call to come back and do it again. Only one person there this time, the agency producer.

'Is it the way I said L'Oréal?'

'No Tim, not at all, they *loved* the way you said L'Oréal, they adore the whole film. It's such a powerful commercial. Natalie Imbruglia's wonderful, you're wonderful. No, it's the way you said mascara.'

'How did I say it?'

'Mass-cara.'

'How do you want me to say it?'

'Ms-cara.'

'Mscara?'

'That's it.'

'Okay Steve, let's go. "The first two-step mscara from L'Oréal..."'

Cut to a month later and Judy and I are watching TV and the L'Oréal ad comes on. I haven't told her about recording it and I say, 'Oh this is me...'

As it comes to an end, there's a pause, and I say, 'There you are – because I'm worth it!'

And Judy says, 'Yes, very good darling. But...'

'What?'

'Why did you pronounce it *mscara?*'

Dubbing and re-voicing

This is one of my favourite types of voice work. There are two types of re-voicing, each demanding different skills. Dubbing usually refers to replacing foreign dialogue with English, and re-voicing when it's English to English, for instance, when the director has decided that he hates the actor's voice so replaces it entirely. This happened to Oliver Tobias in the 1983 film *The Wicked Lady* when director Michael Winner, without telling him, got my old *By the Sword Divided* chum Mark Burns to completely re-voice him in a starring role. Oliver didn't find out until the premiere.

The effectiveness of a foreign to English dub is almost entirely down to the translation. You have the raw translation in front of you, but that will rarely sit with the mouth movements of the actor, so you watch the footage without sound, and try to imagine what English words will convincingly replace the original. The reason I love it so much is that you're doing two things at once, being completely technical about getting the lip synch right while giving a performance that's as good (or in some cases better) than the original. My most high-profile dubbing work was voicing Chow Yung Fat from Mandarin to English in

Crouching Tiger, Hidden Dragon. Mandarin is quite easy as the speakers don't move their mouths too much, unlike Japanese, which is completely impossible.

I cut my teeth on hundreds of episodes of dreadful German TV series such as *Derrick* and *Black Forest Clinic.* These were done using the 'band' technique, where you would just sight-read scrolling words at the bottom of the screen as they passed a vertical line, and they would be in synch. I could get through mountains of work in a day, and it was great training for what was to come.

I've now re-voiced three French actors speaking English – it seems Americans are bad at under-standing a strong French accent, and I've had to tone it down for them, while still remaining 'vay Frenche' – Gérard Depardieu in *Battle of the Brave,* Xavier Duluc in *A Tale of Two Cities,* and most recently, and I'm proud of this, working with Paul Conway for a week in the Soundsquare Studios in Prague revoicing Marc Lavoine in ten episodes of the Eurocop drama, *Crossing Lines.* I've re-voiced Depardieu in a number of productions, and apparently he asks for me as our voices do have a similar timbre. Oddly, we have the same shaped face, apart from the nose, which in his case is becoming more cauliflower-like as the years go by. I once had a dream where I was on a film set, Gérard was in front of the camera, miming, and I was squatting on the floor, just out of shot, pro-viding his voice. And that is kind of what it's like.

ADR

'Additional dialogue replacement' is a catch-all term that encompasses any vocal sounds that were not actually recorded during the filming. There's another art called Foley, which is recreating all the sounds, like car doors, chopped-off heads, footsteps, creaking doors etc. On a big movie, you can be sure that practically nothing recorded at the time gets into the final mix: everything is done in post-production.

Loop groups are also a part of that. I've had regular employment in this most invisible, and usually unheard, area of voice work for over twenty years. My first encounter with this world was working on Mel Gibson's *Braveheart* where I was amazed to find that the screams and battle cries of the massed armies of the English and the Scots were created in full by multi-tracking twelve big-lunged actors in a Soho studio.

There are two requirements for this job: a willingness to sacrifice your throat for the cause because dying horribly, screaming military commands and being a tribe of Orcs all day long needs strong vocal chords; and an ability to improvise period dialogue, modern dialogue, do all English-speaking accents and preferably have another two languages as well. It can be great fun. I've often heard directors say that the improvised scenes we invent on the spot for the characters in the background are far more interesting than the principal dialogue. Our regular company is made up of leading West End actors, film and TV stalwarts and improv specialists. Despite the fact that practically none of it will ever be heard above a mumble, it keeps our improvisation skills up to scratch, makes us laugh a lot, and sometimes produces little gems – everything from fiendish East End burglary plans that are utterly plausible while Tom Hardy is being both the Krays to mechanics' detailed comparisons of different types of early twentieth-century motor cars while his lordship is arseing around in the Downton foreground.

Unfortunately, for many years the Internet Movie Database (IMDb) had me as 'Best Known For ... Conjoined Gnome Left' in the animated film *Gnomeo and Juliet,* not David Archer or any of the lead parts I've had in TV and film. This is because one day we were providing all-purpose background Gnome chatter and the sound editor said, 'Oh and we need two voices to replace the temp dub that the director did for these Conjoined Gnomes.' I volunteered, as did the resultant Conjoined Gnome Right, Neil McCaul, and we got a credit in the film. The IMDb's algorithms put at the top of your credits the highest grossing film you've ever been in, not the biggest part you've ever had, so if I'd died my major acting legacy, for the rest of internet time, would have appeared to have been Conjoined Gnome Left. Fortunately, IMDb have now allowed me to alter this, saving me from further ignominy, but it's one of the things that drove me to write this book – to put the record straight.

Computer games

I used to play a lot of computer games. Judy didn't. She hasn't the slightest interest in shooting things, whereas my *Desert Island Discs* luxury would probably be a Mongolian war bow. This led to a period in our lives where we would hardly see each other in the evenings, which I regret. So when *Myst* came out, I was delighted that we would play the game together. *Myst* was a completely different kind of game. Set on a beautifully drawn, photorealistic island, it involved a series of fiendish logic puzzles that unlocked doors, rooms and chambers to allow you to progress to the next level. What spoiled it totally was the dreadful acting. The game designers thought that it would be fun to provide their own jokey little dramas between levels, the appalling amateurishness of which meant that all involvement in this brilliantly created other world was entirely lost. Thankfully this has all changed now.

As the industry grew, and games creators started to make serious money, it finally dawned on them that their creations were being let down by the low standard of dialogue. Put it this way, if you're confronted by a ten-foot Vampire Necromancer wielding a blood-steeped battle axe, the effect is totally ruined if it sounds like an insurance salesman from Basildon. So they introduced writers, actors and directors, who brought with them all the hard-learned rigours of our profession. These days, the major games writers produce dramas that can be as good as a movie.

Every actor's bucket-list job is probably Bond. When Timothy Dalton got the gig, I knew I would never get the call, not least because they were never going to cast another Timothy with a two-syllable surname. However, I have got that credit on my CV as I am the voice of James Bond in *The World is Not Enough*. Of course, in the movie it's Pierce Brosnan, but he didn't want the computer game gig, so they cast around for a voice match and I got it. Brosnan's got a great voice, and it's hard to match as it's sort of Irish, sort of English and sort of American – very hard to pin down, so before each line of the game they would play me his voice in my headphones so I could tune in to it. So yes, professionally, I have uttered the line, 'The name's Bond, James Bond.' Die happy.

In 1988, I played a Finnish race announcer in the TV movie *The Four Minute Mile*. The character had to deliver the very first example of a mile time starting with 'Three minutes...' and I had to learn some Finnish. Once you've learned the Finnish for 'Three minutes, fifty-seven point nine seconds' you never forget it. Recently I was doing some dwarfish computer voices at Mark Estdale's Outlook Media with the producer on a video link down the line in Helsinki, and I told him this story.

'Oh, yes please, let's hear it,' he enthused.

'Kolme minuuttia, ja viisikymmentäseitsemän pilku yhdeksän sekuntia,' I announced with pride.

'Aha! Yes, yes, yes! And with a Swedish accent!'

While listening to *The Archers*, you can always play the game of telling how many Orcs I've been recently by the raspiness or otherwise of David's voice.

Animation

This is a different skill. It's more like radio drama but the fun is that your character is brought to visual life with the skills of the animator. I did an American children's series about Robin Hood in which I was the Sheriff of Nottingham and Richard the Lionheart. The Sheriff was my well-used snarly, imperious, evil posh voice, à la Severus Snape, but when it came to Richard, for whom I was being deep, warm and kindly, the note I received from the director, who was listening in 'down the line' at four in the morning somewhere in California, was, 'Can the King have less accent?'

'Sorry, what accent?'

'Less British accent?'

'But he's the King of England!'

'Yeah, but he sounds kinda evil.'

This is the problem with my fellow thesps getting good work in Hollywood playing bad guys. In American movies, practically all the villains are now English. With the exception of Harry Potter, if you're a toff, you're the bad guy, which probably harks back to the American Revolution. She said 'British', but she meant English, and not Scouse or Bristol or Geordie, but posh, sneery, superior – basically Alan Rickman at his best. It seems the rule about class war is that it's fine to take the piss out of people who used to oppress you, and since the English oppressed just about everyone, including the Welsh, Scots and Irish, and the toffs oppressed the workers, the posh English are fair game for anyone, any time. So that's why the King of England sounds like he's from Pasadena.

I've trodden the movie premiere red carpet only once. I auditioned for the part of Roger Radcliffe, the owner of Patch and a hundred other Dalmatians for Disney's *101 Dalmatians II: Patch's London Adventure* and was quite astonished to get the part. Astonished because the bulk of the role was singing a close-harmony duet, and in that department I'm a journeyman at best.

Technically it was fiendish. We recorded it at the famed Air Studios in Hampstead, often used for orchestral movie scores, and we did it live with my 'wife', the American actress Jodi Benson, a 'Disney Legend' who was at the end of an ISDN line in a studio in Los Angeles. The problem with this was latency, or delay. No matter how fast the signal comes down the wire, there is always a slight delay, so we were singing either ahead or behind each other. The studio engineer had to get it, by trial and error, so we were both singing at exactly the same time. I was also at the absolute upper limit of my vocal range and the song was musically tricky, and it was for Disney, so everyone else involved was the very best in the business. Intimidating.

The film won an award for Best Musical Score, so I guess take 103 must have been okay. When it came out I was invited to the premiere at Grauman's Chinese Theatre, downtown LA. My dear friend Tony Armatrading had moved to California some years before so this was an opportunity to visit him, too. The slightly deflating thing about being 'the voice of...' in a Disney film is that on the red carpet no bugger knows who the hell you are, so all the rent-a-celeb mums had brought their kids and were being snapped by the paps, and Tony and I just sauntered in unnoticed. We settled down in our tortuously uncomfortable seats to hear myself in my only Disney movie ever. So excited. The curtains drew, the titles rolled, on comes Roger, he opens his mouth ... and it isn't me. I've been replaced! This guy's got a high-pitched voice that isn't anything ... oh ... oh, wait a minute ... oh, it *is* me! Christ! Nearly had a thrombie. It had been months since I'd done it and I'd forgotten that I'd pitched it like a fourteen-year-old.

The party afterwards was interesting. The theme was 'London' inasmuch as there was a guy on stilts outside dressed as a guardsman and two 'Bobbies' in Keystone Cops outfits giving it plenty of Dick van Dyke. Inside it was just an American party, which is much the same as any other party only louder – those open plains. I was keen to meet Jodi after singing a duet with her and recording scenes of marital love and happiness when we'd been a thousand miles apart. I felt there was a bond. And she was like, 'Yeah, like it was such a pleasure working with you,' with that long emphasis on the 'you' that Americans do when they don't mean it.

The Equity voiceover strike
In 1997, we were told by Equity not to work for anyone who wasn't adhering to the long-estab-lished Equity agreements on voice work. The person who was seen to be responsible for this was Enn Reitel. He had been probably the most suc-cessful voiceover artist for many years and the

story goes that after an article about him appeared in the press, in which he said he sometimes couldn't get in the front door because of all the cheques piled up behind it, some admen got the hump and started asking why they were paying actors all this money.

The arguments are pretty simple. On the one hand, if a TV commercial has persuaded someone to buy your product, then part of the reason for that is the performance, in that one showing, of the voice behind it, who should therefore get paid for that one performance. So, if the ad is shown a hundred times, the voice artist should be paid x times 100. On the other hand, the advertising industry was saying that paying someone thousands of pounds for saying 'Blooper Soap is Best' is ridiculous, and they could get the tea boy to do it, it doesn't require any skill and the product is sold by the filming and the writing.

So Equity went on strike, and the admen got the tea boy to do it. And very effective he was.

Up until then, I had been regularly employed, not so much on TV ads but on radio certainly, selling products with a kind of classless but nevertheless educated southern English accent, the idea being that a voice of enthused authority was what people wanted to hear. The success of the new, post-strike amateurs proved the opposite, particularly among the young, for whom posh and enthusiastic were the opposite of cool. A perfect example was a telly ad for Vodaphone. The end line was, 'Use it, don't use it, it's your call.' Great line, and delivered with the kind of laid-back attitude of a rude boy sitting at the back of the classroom with his feet on the desk. It was saying, 'Look mate, there's this thing, right? Just saying. Up to you if agree with me. If not, cool.' That voice wouldn't be right for selling Bentleys or Ferrero Rocher, but it's perfect for mobile phones.

My income plummeted and, although things have got better since, no one's having problems with their front doors any more. Enn bought a stud farm and retired. You can still hear the difference in today's voiceovers, for which the preferred performance is not to sound as though you mean it, which wouldn't be cool, but as though you've been told to read it, which is acceptable.

Even with reduced rates, it was a lucky day when Anthony Hyde turned down the Radio Rep job and I got it instead, and with a bit of luck, as long as the old dulcets hold out, I may continue to be employed making odd noises in front of a microphone.

Radio drama

Since I've been in *The Archers*, the huge output from my days on the Radio Rep has dwindled and now BBC radio drama has almost disappeared. I do the odd play but the powers that be frown on *Archers* regulars turning up in other work: they think David will be heard no matter what I do. That's fair, I suppose. I can hardly complain I'm not on the radio enough, and these days I get to flex my radio-acting chops in a huge variety of roles for Big Finish, who have the licence to make *Doctor Who, Torchwood, Survivors, The Prisoner, Sherlock Holmes, The Avengers* and much more. I love working for them, I die almost every production I'm in, often more than once, I get to do all the accents and characters in my repertoire, the lunch is superb and it means that I have now worked with every living Doctor bar Matt Smith – and if I'd got a part I was up for in *The Crown* I'd have the full set.

Being David Archer: Technique

The older generation on *The Archers* had the experience of recording onto acetate disc, which meant it couldn't be edited – if the actor fluffed they either soldiered on embarrassed or, disaster, they had to start again from the beginning. The first hour and a half was spent in rehearsal, with the last thirty minutes or so devoted to the recording itself. It was effectively a live performance, which, together with the lo-fi quality of the broadcast, is part of the difference between the acting style of those early years and the more naturalistic style of today.

Also, in the last sixty-odd years, our language has changed so much. In usage and accent, early *Archers* recordings sound like a forgotten world. However, certain things remain the same. Telling a story within the time constraints means the structure has hardly changed, and the subjects are much the same – farming, intrigue, gossip, love, feuds, natural disasters, etc. These are the eternal archetypes and the scenes are about the same length as they have always been. The difference is the freedom we have in recording, which allows us the opportunity of invention – occasionally what we say isn't necessarily what is written on the page. As long as the cue for the other actor is the same, it can be liberating sometimes to be a bit free with the lines. Also, adding grace notes like pauses, deliberate stumbles, ums, errs, 'sort ofs', 'you knows', 'but…' or 'so…' can loosen up the script.

We can only do that because of digital recording – nowadays if you make a hash of it, the results are so easy to edit. I do a lot of technical work with music and voice recording, and I know how quick editing is compared to the razor blades and sticky tape of years gone by. Make a mistake? Pause a second, go back to the beginning of the sentence, say it again. Today, a fluff is just a deleted region of a digital waveform. The taped mistakes of the past are now only heard as the crunching of straw underfoot.

At Pebble Mill, in the days of tape, there was an 'edit room' where actors would wait, coats on, suitcases in hand, taxi waiting, to hear if the edit was clear and they could race for their train. If it wasn't, they'd have to go back into the studio to re-record, never a popular demand.

If you listen to a playback of a natural conversation in which the speakers don't know they're being recorded, natural speech patterns have a rhythm and a song that is almost impossible to replicate. I say 'almost' because sometimes an actor's job is to get as close to that as possible, and occasionally you can achieve it. Being in a drama for a very long time means you can just immerse yourself in the reality, and say it the way you think it. The lines in the script aren't just words to say: they're clues as to how you're thinking, what people are saying to you, why you might want to reply. The words on the page are simply the things that come out of your mouth as a result. You just have to react.

The cast are all very good at sight-reading. This helps with audiobooks and narration of any kind, especially when you turn up to a studio for a three-hour booking and you haven't been given the script in advance. The trick is to read ahead to see where the sentence is going, your heart sinking if it's a medical one, and that sentence is heading inexorably towards

Patients were treated with lymphodepleting conditioning chemotherapy (intravenous cyclophosphamide [60 mg/kg] daily for 2 days followed by fludarabine [25 mg/m²] daily for 5 days, followed by a single intravenous infusion of autologous TILs and high-dose interleukin-2 [720 000 IU/kg] every 8 h). *(Lancet)*

Of course, it's nothing like as bad as that in *The Archers*, but Bovine Spongiform Encephalopathy still springs effortlessly off my tongue!

Quiz shows

I learned two lessons from quiz shows. One, you can't win 'em all and, two, quit while you're ahead.

Call My Bluff (1996)

I'd been brought up on *Call My Bluff,* which started in 1965. I have great memories of Robert Robinson chairing the panel game, with team captains Frank Muir and Arthur Marshall, but that era came to a close in 1988. I really enjoyed the format, in which two teams of three were given a word that no one had ever heard of, and asked to give definitions. Two definitions would be false and the opposing team had to guess the correct version.

The show was resurrected in 1996 with Bob Holness as chairman and Sandi Toksvig and Alan Coren at team captains, and I was asked to do one episode in this new incarnation, on Sandi's team.

I wasn't very good. I'd always loved Frank Muir's technique, which would start, 'You're on a desert island...' or 'You're a daffodil...' and I thought I would copy him. I also thought I should throw in as many accents as possible to prove what a versatile and varied performer I was. All I remember is Alan Coren saying, 'God, is this an

272

audition?' In the break, he tried to convince me that there were such things as 'Bentinck's Chocolates'. I said no it's Bendick's, as usual, but he was adamant. Exhaustive Google searching has come up with one tantalising reference, but nothing more. Have you ever heard of them? After all I based my one-man show around the misconception!

Hidden Treasures (1998)

This was such fun – working with the Toby jug of loveliness that is Henry Sandon. Chaired by Lars Tharp, *Hidden Treasures* was a radio antiques quiz that each week came from a different stately home. We were in Harewood House, but the problem really was the format. Antiques are visual, and describing them doesn't have the same impact. We were asked to bring along an interesting *objet,* and that went down well as I brought along a fascinating naval journal written by an ancestor, Captain William Bentinck, which contains this tantalising entry, which I read out: 'Breakfasted with Sir Jos. Banks, where I met Capt. Bligh, late of the ['Discovery' crossed out] Bounty, taken by Pirates going round the world.'

This led to historians contacting me and the eventual loan of the two volumes to the University of Nottingham for transcription. I love the idea that Bligh told his fellow officers that he'd been 'taken by pirates' rather than cast adrift by a mutinous crew.

University Challenge (2004)

'How would you like to do *University Challenge: The Professionals?*' asked the impossibly glamorous and brilliant Kate Oates, producer of *Emmerdale* and then *Coronation Street*, but at that time working as producer at *The Archers*.

'Oh definitely! Are we "The Archers"?'

'No, you're "Actors". You're representing the entire profession.'

'Strewth, that's quite a responsibility'

'Yes, and you're the captain.'

So, a few weeks later I was sitting at our kitchen table at home with Charles Collingwood (Brian), Louiza Patikas (Helen) and Felicity Finch (Ruth) with four battery-operated doorbells in front of us, being quizzed by the late, very much lamented, Nick Clarke, who was armed with the *University Challenge* quiz book, and being filmed by Will and Jasper to add to the mood. My worry was that we would be embarrassingly bad and have to live with, 'Oh yes, you're the thick one on *University Challenge*,' and have thespians across the country telling us that they knew all the answers. So I learned the periodic table, the kings and queens of England, British prime ministers, US presidents, the romantic poets and all the major artists and composers, and doled out subjects for revision to the others. A professional and competitive approach.

A luxury minibus was sent to drive us all together up to Manchester, and we continued our preparation on the journey. During this trip, Charles suddenly got rather serious.

'Now look, chaps, I've done a few of these

things, and I'll just say that in my experience it's not a good idea to have anything to drink before you go on, it takes the edge off the speed of thought.'

We all agreed that this was sound advice.

When we got there we found we were up against a team of 'Soroptimists', a term we had never heard of but it turned out they were from a global women's charitable organisation. They were pretty nervous and they were also huge *Archers* fans, so they were doubly intimidated when Charles sauntered charmingly up, glass of red in his hand and said, 'Hello ladies, how delightful to meet you. Of course, this is all a bit of fun, but if I can offer a bit of advice? I've done a few of these things and in my experience it never hurts to have one or two glasses of the old vino before the show – takes the edge off the nerves, you know.'

Charles was almost a professional cricketer, and what he doesn't know about gamesmanship isn't worth diddly squat.

Well, we stormed it. I was on fire. Not one thing that I had prepared came up, but I was so in the zone that, supported by Collingwood on sport, what I didn't know anyway I guessed and got lucky. We agreed that we were all bad at classical music, so if any such question came up we'd say Beethoven. 'And the first starter for ten...': immediate result.

Oh, how I wish I'd left it at that.

A Good Read (2006)
This was not a quiz show, but it was another

275

opportunity to sound like a dunce. It didn't help that my fellow guest on the Radio 4 programme was Andrew Graham-Dixon, a man who knows how well qualified he is. His introduction took up a fair amount of the programme: his degrees, awards and achievements were a good read in themselves. Then Sue McGregor got to me– 'The voice of David Archer and Mind the Gap.' That was it. No mention of degrees or awards or education, and my choice of book didn't help. I'd gone for levity and chosen *Bryson's Dictionary of Troublesome Words* because I'm a bit of a grammar Nazi, an apostrophe abuse spotter and a spelling fiend. The problem was it sounded like I needed an American to help me speak my own language. Then I had to wax lyrical on Graham-Dixon's choice, the monumentally clever poem *War Music* by Christopher Logue, based on Homer's *The Iliad*. I love poetry and can write sonnets in the style of Shakespeare, French Dada-ist poems that are really English pop songs, and translate French erotic novels into English, but in-joke translations of Homer are for the classics scholars, not me.

Sue's choice was not much better: *The Turn of the Screw* by Henry James. There had recently been a film based loosely on the premise called *The Others,* which is wonderful and spooky and scary – all the things that the book is not. I left nineteenth-century fiction behind a long time ago, for a very good reason – life is too short, and outside Hardy, Conan Doyle and Dickens I haven't got the patience, so I wasn't much help there either. I suppose I was vaguely amusing, but the invitations to literary symposia didn't flood in after the broadcast.

Through the Keyhole (2008)
Humiliation.

So, there I am on the computer about five in the evening when the doorbell rings. Will shouts up that there's a cab for me. Wrong street, I say. 'It's for Tim,' he says. Still wrong street, different Tim. 'It's for Tim Bentinck,' he says.

I come downstairs. It's a large Mercedes waiting to take me to Riverside Studios for the *Through the Keyhole* interview. It's just that nobody bothered to tell me. The car satnavs me to the studios and drops me round the back so I have to walk round.

'Hi, I'm here for the recording.'

They put me in with the audience.

'No, I'm in the show?'

'Who are you?'

'Tim Bentinck, I'm one of the stars?'

'Oh, you're late.'

Um, yeees!

I'm shown into a tacky green room with some curling sandwiches and fizzy drinks. The only high point of the evening is that two of the other celebs are England rugby internationals, so now I've got a free pass to watch Wasps any time I want. I go into make-up and, since I've just got back from Australia and am fairly tanned, ask the make-up artist not to put too much slap on. She is clearly miffed.

A woman comes in. 'Darling, darling, you're so gorgeous, here let me massage you, isn't this fun?'

277

I feel I ought to know her so I give plenty of 'Darling, darling, yes indeedy' in return.

Then she says. 'Years ago, I went out with Eric Clapton and for the first four hours I had no idea who he was. Do you know who I am?'

'No darling, no idea, sorry.'

'I'm Paula Hamilton, the model who was in the VW ad where I put the keys in the dustbin. Now I'm a recovering alcoholic. Who are you?'

'I'm Tim Bentinck. I play David in *The Archers.*'

'Oh God, I love your voice I love that programme' etc., etc., gush, gush, until she finds herself next to Sir David Frost's PR man, after which I don't exist.

So now I'm on. I'm hidden in the wings while a film of my house is shown, and the 'celebrity' panel has to guess who I am. I'm in a chair looking into the TV camera and watching my own face on screen. It is deathly pale, the make-up woman's revenge. The studio audience clap if the panel is getting warm and stay silent if they're not. For some reason, the film shows a lot of military stuff in the house, swords, they think I'm a soldier. They have to be told I'm an actor.

'Is he a TV actor?'

Silence.

'Is he a film actor?'

Silence.

'Is he a theatre actor?'

Silence.

Having done thirty years of telly, film and theatre and forgetting that I'm on camera, I start to say, 'Oh for fuck's sake.' I see myself in shot halfway through and turn it into 'Oh for fahahaha...' smiley, smiley.

'Well, what other kinds of acting are there?' says Gloria Hunniford, who I've met at least twice and claims to be an *Archers* fan.

'Radio.'

'Oh, radio!' they sneer.

Eventually, they get around to the longest-running series in the world, a national icon and the most successful show on Radio 4, broadcasting to five million people daily.

'Is it Nigel Archer?' (There is no such character.)

Eventually they have to be told.

In the edit pause, David Frost comes backstage and says he used to live next to my father in Carlisle Square. 'No, David, that's the DUKE of Portland, my father was the Earl, as am I.' This is not going well.

So I come on. I want to say to the panel, 'Don't worry, I've never heard of you lot either,' but my natural politeness prohibits me. I do say, 'So, thirty years of telly out the window then.'

'Oh, have you been on television? What have you been in?'

This is the dread curse of the nearly famous actor. If you start to reel off the names, they always go, 'didn't see that' or 'never heard of it' or 'oh, who were you in that?' – you're on a loser to nothing. Actually, the usual phrase is, 'What might I have seen you in?' To which my answer now is, 'I don't know, what have you watched?'

So then Frost asks me about the banjo and guitars and recording equipment in my room, ending up with, 'Have you ever had a hit?' I have to admit that I haven't.

'So, Tim, you're an inventor.'

I tell them about how I spent a fortune on patents when I was younger.

'So, Tim, you're the voice of Mind the Gap on the Piccadilly Line?'

I tell them the story of getting only £200 for twenty years of being the station announcer on the whole Piccadilly Line.

'Can you do it for us?'

Oh God. Okay. 'Please Mind the Gap. This is Holborn. The next station is Russell Square. Please stand clear of the dosing doors.' Big round of applause.

'Well, Tim, it's been great having you on the show.'

So, I'm the guy that no one's ever heard of, who is a failed songwriter, a failed inventor and whose only claim to fame is that he says 'Mind the Gap' on the tube. Thanks a bunch.

The mixed blessings of being a radio star.

Celebrity Eggheads (2012)

I'd always wanted to meet Judith Keppel. When she was the first person to win the jackpot on *Who Wants to be a Millionaire?* I fell for this gorgeous, posh, coolest of women. We also had a history in common. The first Earl of Portland had been ousted from the affections of King William III by Judith's direct ancestor, Arnold, and poor Hans Willem retired hurt to the country where he died only a few years later.

So, there we were, Charles Collingwood again

(captain this time), Andrew Wincott (Adam), Charlotte Martin (Susan), Rachel Atkins (Vicky) and me, lined up against Judith Keppel and the other members of 'arguably the most formidable quiz team in the country'. The host, Dermot Murnaghan, announced that the first subject was 'Science'.

'Ambridge Academicals, who wants to start off?'

'I'll do Science,' I piped. I didn't care what the subject was, I wanted to go face to face with Judith and didn't want anyone getting in before me.

'Okay, Tim, and who would you like to take on?'

I have the recording, and what I said was this: 'Well, I'm going to choose Judith simply because our families have history. It goes back to 1689. Keppel took on Bentinck then – a certain Arnold Joost van Keppel got rid of my ancestor Hans Willem Bentinck from the favours of William III, so I think it's revenge time, Judith!'

She was delighted. As we walked together round to the booth that's separated from the main area, she said it was the best challenge she had ever faced, and we've since become good friends. And I beat her, so Bentinck/Keppel honours are now even.

We didn't win the competition, though, the blame for which I lay squarely on Collingwood's shoulders, but never mind, we had fun in Glasgow.

On the plane home, I found myself sitting next to Sandra Dickinson, who'd been doing a different episode. We were getting along fine; her squeaky American voice was very cute. There was a pause and then she said, 'Have you ever thought about having your moles removed?'

Well, of course, I've thought of nothing else since, Sandra.

Celebrity Mastermind (2012)

Only a month later, it was time for the big one. I would get to sit in The Chair! When they'd asked me for my chosen specialist subject, I'd said 'Winnie the Pooh' for the sole reason that I wanted to be the only person who had ever sat in The Chair and said 'Heffalump'. They said the subject was too small, so it had to be A. A. Milne and Winnie the Pooh', but at least it wasn't 'The Extended History of World War One' or 'Everything that Tolstoy Ever Wrote' – after all, there are only two Pooh books. So I learned them. I went through them both, imagining what possible question could be asked after each paragraph, writing it down and giving the answer. Then I learned what I'd written, like a script. For Milne, I figured they would only ask two or three questions, and they were likely to be about his upbringing, where he lived, his schools and teachers, so I learned that too.

In the week before the recording I started to get the serious wobbles. By a horrible coincidence, there were two *Mastermind*-related things on telly, which didn't help at all. Harry Enfield and Paul Whitehouse did a sketch where Harry passed on every question, and Paul couldn't even remember his chosen subject, and an actual episode where a woman did this for real: a total brain fade, rabbit in the headlights, panicked freeze.

There's nothing you can do to prepare yourself for the General Knowledge round, but I really swotted the Pooh questions and figured I'd do all right. I was up against actor Guy Henry, Bucks Fizz's Cheryl Baker and astronomer Mark Thompson. Cheryl and Mark were very relaxed and we agreed that all we wanted was to not make total prats of ourselves, but Guy was clearly in it to win it, pacing up and down outside in the Manchester rain, smoking furiously.

It's an odd thing, but with these TV game shows, no matter how apprehensive I may be feeling beforehand, by the time we walk out onto the set I'm usually completely calm and really looking forward to it. I suppose it's because TV and film sets are my favourite places, and I'm very familiar and comfortable there.

We had to wait for Cheryl to have a hairpiece fitted and she was first on. She did okay on James Taylor and got 10. Then it was me. The Walk To The Chair. I remembered my name, and my subject. The questions came fast. Milne's early life – I knew his house, where he went to school and his English teacher. Now Pooh. Correct, correct, correct. 'Heffalump' – I smiled! And then came the one to separate the men from the boys. There's a poem in the first book in the chapter on finding Eeyore's tail that goes,

Who found the tail?
'I,' said Pooh,

'At a quarter to two
(Only it was quarter to eleven really)
I found the tail.'

I'd noticed that this could be a trick question, and John Humphreys nearly got me.

'At what time did Pooh find Eeyore's tail?

'A quarter to t ... eleven!'

'Correct.'

Phew. All correct and no passes!

Mark was next, on the history of coffee, and did okay. Finally, it was Guy's turn, 'The Life of Peter O'Toole'. He did better but got a few wrong and I was in the lead.

General Knowledge. Going well, sailing along, then an impossible question about an obscure Turkish town. No idea. Pass. And this is when the brain starts to let you down: your concentration dims because you're thinking about the previous question.

"Who is the current presenter of *A Question of Sport?*'

Oh. Tennis player, blonde, you know ... thingy ... damn, pass. I knew it was Sue Barker.

'Hero of Troy and sailed on voyages of adventure?'

I heard 'Troy' and said 'Paris'. Odysseus. I KNEW that!

'Who famously interviewed Richard Nixon on TV after Watergate?' I heard 'TV interviewer' and got an image of Princess Diana and Martin Bashir.

'Martin Bashir?' David Frost. OF COURSE I KNEW THAT!

I was pretty sure I was now losing to Guy.

'What oil is used to stop cricket bats from drying and cracking?'

Aaaah. I could smell it. Things from your past that at the time seem completely pointless, like German, chapel, and in this case compulsory house cricket when I'd much rather have been swimming, last in to bat, lying in the grass playing with worms, and rubbing the bat with...

'Linseed oil.'

Correct.

I won by one point. Standing next to Humphreys, holding the trophy as the *Mastermind* music played out, was as close as I'll ever get to winning Olympic gold.

Guy was livid.

Pointless Celebrities (2013)

Kellie Bright played Kate Aldridge in *The Archers* from 1995, and I was delighted to find myself on *Pointless Celebrities* with her, as she hadn't been cast in the programme for a while and was now an award-winning star of *EastEnders* – she has since turned superstar as the runner-up in *Strictly Come Dancing*.

It was a 'Record Breakers' episode, so we were up against Linford Christie (100m British record holder), Sally Gunnell (400m hurdles British record holder), the tallest man and woman in Britain (seven foot seven and six foot ten), Janet Ellis and Ayo Akinwolere from *Blue Peter* (longest-running TV series), and me and Kellie (world's longest-running drama series).

What a clever game show it is, a great leveller, not relying so much on education as a wide-ranging life experience, helped occasionally by getting lucky with a subject you know about.

Linford and Sally went out first – we had beaten the fastest man and woman in the country. Then we beat the tallest, then *Blue Peter*, and now Kellie and I were going for the money. We had to name obscure counties in New York State. Now I'd worked there, and led my Trailways bus tours all around it, and I couldn't even think of a well-known one. For some reason, the name Hoboken came into my head, mainly because Jasper was writing a song once and asked me what rhymed with 'broken'. I knew it was a district of New York City, but we couldn't think of anything and it sounded good, so we said it anyway.

Clang! Big red cross.

We didn't win the money for our charities, but we got the *Pointless* Trophy, which stands proud next to the *Mastermind* pyramid – a lifetime of trivial achievements in clear plastic.

So, when they asked me again, exactly a year later, of course I came back for more – my first indication of the advisability of quitting while you're ahead.

Pointless Celebrities (2014)

The great thing about going out in the first round in *Pointless* is that you're paid the same and you get to go home for supper. Dame Jenni Murray and I were teamed together as part of a whole Radio episode, and were joined by Ken Bruce, David

'Kid' Jensen, Liz Kershaw and two modern DJs of whom I hadn't heard. Just because you're a bit well known doesn't stop you being slightly smacked-of-gob when meeting the superstars of your youth. Kid Jensen! Ken Bruce I knew from before and is every inch the gentleman he sounds on Radio 2, although balder.

Our first task was to name a country whose first vowel is an 'A'. I toyed with Kyrgyzstan, but wasn't totally sure of the two Y's and plumped for Zambia. Jenni unfortunately said Wales, which is a Principality, so out we went. Poor Jenni was distraught, and my limo driver had barely had time for a fag.

University Challenge (2015)
So, quit while you're ahead.

One day I got an email from *University Challenge* asking if I'd like to be on a Christmas Special team of former students from the University of East Anglia. I accepted like a shot.

I'd been waiting for this. I'd done the Professionals game but that's not the same as being on the uni team; this was the real deal, and my whole life of watching the programme, shouting the answers and learning from each one had been my preparation for this. I'd nailed it the last time so this would clearly be my intellectual zenith.

We were up against a formidable team from Manchester, with comic Lucy Porter and Jesse Armstrong, who wrote the first episode of *The Thick of It* that I was in. My captain was Labour MP Caroline Flint.

I had no idea of the first three starter questions, and nor did any of our team. Manchester, and Lucy Porter in particular, were very quick. I finally knew an answer, pressed the buzzer ... too late. I thought, *Gamble, just go for it early, and get the answer in the time it takes Roger Tilling to say your name*. Bzzzzz. 'UEA, Bentinck.' Answer. 'No, you lose five points.' So, we're now on *minus five!* They're on fifty-something.

'What Woody Allen film has a name derived from an instruction manual?'

Everything You Wanted to Know About Sex but Were Afraid to Ask – I press the buzzer!

'Manchester, Armstrong.'

'Er ... Everything You Ever...'

Bugger!

I got us back to a massive plus five points by knowing the board game 'Go' and also redeemed some credibility as a university graduate by casually tossing out 'Machiavelli' for another ten. We ended on 35 points. They got more. Sort of 150 more. In the broadcast, they didn't cut me quipping, in a stiff upper lip sort of way, hoping for a laugh, 'It was close,' and Paxman's waspish retort, 'No it *wasn't*.'

Being David Archer: Perks of the job

There are perks to being in *The Archers* – you do get invited to some rather special things. We once did a live performance onstage for a show called *The Great Event – Forty Years of Broadcasting for Her Majesty*. The green room was packed with stars – and us! Stirling Moss, Frank Bruno, some of the 1966 World Cup football team, Seb Coe and Steve Cram, Cliff Richard, Wogan, you name it. It's weird being a radio star – nobody knew who we were – until we went on stage and then all the people we'd previously been asking for autographs were suddenly our best mates.

After the show, we were lined up to shake hands with Her Majesty and her family. Now the thing is that the Queen's grandmother is a Bentinck, so I was prepared for her to say something along the lines of 'Are we related?' the answer to which would have been, 'Yes, ma'am, we're seventh cousins', but she said nothing. Then came Philip, irascible as ever. I was introduced, 'Timothy Bentinck, sir.'

'Hmm, that's a familiar name?'

My cue! 'Yes, sir, that's possibly because...' Then I couldn't think how to refer to the Queen when you're talking to Prince Philip. I mean he obviously knew she was the Queen, and I couldn't really call her Elizabeth, seventh cousin or no, so instead I said, '...your wife's grandmother was a Bentinck.'

'YOUR WIFE'? What was I thinking?

Anyway, he didn't bat an eyelid at that but just said grumpily, 'Oh, Bentinck. I thought you said Bentine.'

He meant Michael Bentine, who among many other things was on *The Goon Show* – the Duke of Edinburgh, Goon fan.

Then came Diana, and I suddenly realised what the whole obsession with her was all about. The way she looked at me, I saw that she was immediately madly in love. I was the only one. Her marriage with Charles was a sham and she and I were destined to elope in secret to a desert island and damn the consequences. I was weak at the knees – and then she spoke. The conversation went like this:

'Gosh, a radio star, how exciting.'

'Yes, it means you don't get recognised in the street.'

'Oh God, I could do with some of that.'

'Well, your royal highness, perhaps you'd like to move to Ambridge and be our radio princess, and never be seen again.'

She smiled, leant towards me slightly, and whispered, 'Sounds divine.'

I was besotted.

Charles was next.

'I love the way you use a bicycle pump and cork for the champagne-popping sound effect. I was allowed to do that for the Goons once you know.'

I couldn't believe it, Goon references from both father and son, but I also suddenly felt so sorry for him, the 'I was allowed to…' summing up an entire life of never being 'allowed' to do anything he really wanted to at all. I got cheeky, seeing as how he was now clearly the cuckold in this three-way relationship.

'Well, your royal highness, perhaps you'd like to come up to Ambridge and do our special effects for us?'

He gave me a rather old-fashioned look then came up with this cracker.

'Sounds intriguing, but I think I'll stick with this. I get to travel more, do you see?'

Brilliant.

Other benefits include, I suspect, getting off a driving ban because of being in *The Archers*. I'm a good driver – you don't pass your HGV test unless you are – and what with driving tourists round America and VW Beetles round Europe, I've had a lot of experience, but sometimes you get caught out by those pesky cameras. These days cruise control and a more adult perspective has cut down the problem but in my more impetuous thirties, I once got up to twelve points and was facing a ban. In these cases, you can plead 'Exceptional Hardship' and in the dock of the civil court at Market Harborough, having explained that I was in a 'long-running drama series on Radio 4', I felt the decision might be going my way when one of the magistrates leant across and whispered to her colleague, 'I think it's David!'

I wasn't banned, but driving for the next three years knowing that just one flash of a camera would mean the certain loss of my licence radically changed my driving behaviour.

As 'David' I've opened fetes, done after-dinner speaking, reviewed the papers on *Broadcasting House* and done a load of 'celebrity' TV game shows. It's also helped hugely when publicising my children's book, *Colin the Campervan*. This fame only goes so far though, and I'm never going to be asked to eat dead lizards in the jungle or go stir-crazy in *Big Brother*, to both of which I'd say 'Thank God' were it not for the huge piles of cash involved.

To be honest, I'm very happy with not being

recognised in the street, although I do secretly relish occasional delicious moments like once when at a dinner party, having spent most of the evening chatting about anything but acting with a charming but rather tiddly countess who, over coffee, joined in someone's conversation about *The Archers* and announced loudly to the whole table, 'Oh my God, can you imagine actually meeting someone from *The Archers?* I mean, really, if I did I think I'd probably DIE!'

Travel journalism

After our *University Challenge* triumph – the Actors one in 2004, not the UEA debacle, I received an email from Frank Barrett, editor of the travel section of the *Mail on Sunday*. He was inviting me to join him for the annual Irish Tourist Board Pub Quiz, held between representatives of the press. *The Mail* had won the previous year, and were determined to do so again. I figured I'd just got lucky with *University Challenge* but Frank was insistent, and an *Archers* fan, so I felt I couldn't let him down.

We got to the final round. Sports. We were neck and neck with *The Times*, so every point counted. The final question was, 'What is the animal on the top of the Calcutta Cup?' This is the annual rugby match between England and Scotland for the oldest rugby trophy ever, and the animal is an elephant.

'Lion,' said Frank firmly.

'No, it's an elephant.'

'No, it's a lion, I can visualise it.'

'How can it be? It's Calcutta. India. If it was going to be a large cat it would be a tiger, but anyway it's not, cos it's an elephant.'

He looked at me viciously.

'Are you sure?'

'I'm absolutely sure.'

'An elephant?'

'An elephant.'

'Look, this is pretty crucial, you know, because we're neck and neck with...'

'Frank, it's an elephant.'

Grudgingly he wrote it down. It was an elephant. We won by one point.

'Can you write?' Frank asked.

'Yes.'

'Where in the world would you like to write about?'

'Wow. Well, I've always wanted to go back to the land of my birth. Tasmania.'

'Okay.'

When Frank says, 'Okay,' he means it.

A few months later, Judy and I flew business class to Tassie. Courtesy of the Tasmanian Tourist Board, we stayed in all the very best hotels, had amphibious plane trips that landed on narrow rivers, had zip-wire adventures, walked Maria Island, had two weeks' free car hire, and were shown the very spot where I was born – under a red Mazda in the Campbell Town hospital car park. Oh, and the food and wine were out of this world, and I was commissioned to write further travel articles. Not a bad result for an elephant!

Writing about that trip was easy, but the deal was to write about Sydney too, where we had a two-day itinerary, arranged by the NSW Tourist Board – a crammed seventy-two hours. Everything was painstakingly planned down to the last tiny detail. As it turned out, all went well but these tight itineraries can be a recipe for disaster: if everything goes well, all you ever feel is relief, but if the car breaks down, the hotel's half-built or a child suddenly goes cold turkey for wifi, you experience that dreadful frustration of having catered for every eventuality except what usually happens – Murphy's Law. I'm thinking of starting a company called 'Bentinck's Serendipity Tours': no expectations, so no disappointments.

We had an itinerary-free trip to Ireland when the boys were young, driving round the Ring of Kerry and just finding somewhere to stay each night. One night we saw a battered sign pointing towards the 'Portland Hotel'. Obviously, we had to stay there. They'd had a massive party the night before, so at dinner, when I asked for the wine list, the waiter pointed at a side table with two bottles sitting on it.

'What would you be wanting, the Blue Nun, or the French?'

When Will locked himself out of his room, the cheery and untroubled solution was to completely remove the French windows, retrieve the key, put the window back, then walk round to the door and unlock it.

Judy and I did a similar thing in Croatia once; Ryanair were offering flights to Trieste for 4p, so we just up and went, hired a car and simply drove south. When it got dark we looked for a hotel. Luckily the Serbo-Croat for hotel is *hotel* so asking directions was fine. One evening we clearly crashed a meeting of the local paramilitaries doing gun drill, which was exciting, but the wine choice was similar to Ireland: under the heading of 'Red Wine' was the single word, 'Merlot'.

This sort of adventure makes for fun copy in the paper, as does becoming a PADI qualified scuba diver in the Cayman Islands on your sixtieth birthday, but being sent off on a journalists' jolly to New Zealand in 2010 was an eye-opener. Travel journalists get treated like royalty, way ahead of an earl or an actor. The *Mail on Sunday* has the highest circulation of any paper in Britain, so a complimentary article about your hotel or restaurant is priceless advertising, and learning the tricks of the trade from my new seasoned professional friends was an education. Airline upgrades? Damn right, from Business to First on Etihad, which allows you to have a stand-up shower, starkers at 30,000 feet, an extraordinary experience, although getting back into T-shirt and jeans instead of flowing white robes is the equivalent of wearing a shell suit to a polo match.

I was in New Zealand with the bunch of real journos to tour the country's rugby stadia before the following year's Rugby World Cup. On the first day, we were given a choice: tour the vineyards on the islands north of Auckland, or fling yourself off the highest building in the southern hemisphere. I have a phobia of heights, which is odd as one of my childhood pleasures was climbing trees. In fact, the instant and categorical reply from all of us was: 'Vineyards.'

Two of the things that journalists and actors seem to have in common is getting full value out of a freebie and a taste for fine wine. Having spent the whole morning not spitting out any of the delicious samples, our defences were down when our young Kiwi guides suggested that not experiencing the Sky Tower's controlled wire SkyJump descent from 192 metres at 85 km/h was Pommie wimping-out on a grand scale. 'Mate, we had a ninety-year-old granny do it last week!' So, pathetically we all succumbed.

My Dutch courage lasted until I was on the platform where, dressed in a superhero costume with full harness, I ventured out onto the windy diving board, mortality staring up at me from below. I heard a click as a carabiner was attached to my harness and, with a cheery pat on my back, I heard, 'All right, mate, you're good to go.' I was clinging on to the safety rail with the grip of a crocodile's jaw. All I had as assurance that I wasn't going to simply plummet to my death was the word of a Kiwi teenager. Mentally saying goodbye to all my family and friends I leapt into the void, fell for twenty feet and stopped dead – for a photo opportunity! I was hanging in front of the café at the top of the tower, where safe people, sensible people, people who were drinking beer or coffee, could snap away at the rictus grins of terror on the faces of the mugs who thought this was a good idea. Then I fell again, 85 km/h straight down. And instead of splattering myself on the Antipodean pavement, I was brought gently to a halt, and landed delicately on my feet.

I have the film of it. I said one word, and it began with 'F'.

Inventions

When I announced to my father that I wanted to be an actor, he said, 'A freelance, eh? That's very brave.' I thought, brave? From a man who's been through a war, wounded twice and a POW? I just didn't get it. Now I do. He was talking about security – a proper job, a steady income and a decent pension at the end of it. These days the difference between freelance and employed is not so great, but it's meant that I've spent my whole adult life trying to come up with a business on the side, a lottery win – or an invention.

The best inventions are the simplest, as they are the most likely to find success – one-piece plastic moulds, like the book-holder-downer that fits on your thumb, the tennis-ball-thrower for walking the dog, or the cable tidy for phone chargers. If you can get the invention patented, it's even better as you're the only person allowed to make it. Hence 'The Hippo'.

As they grow, children get heavier. The 'terrible twos' can turn your delicate, angelic little baby into a lumpen refusenik who demands to be carried everywhere, especially when you're also toting five bags of shopping. When Will reached that age, I discovered that one of the things that men tend not to have is wide, child-bearing hips. I'm fairly strong but the dead weight of a child on your side is pretty heavy; I felt like I needed a sort of shelf – so I built one.

I made the first Hippo prototype out of wood, cardboard and coat-hanger wire, with a wide hessian strap to go over my shoulder. It worked, so then I made one out of wood, which was more comfortable but way too heavy. This was 1986 – long before the internet, and also pre-*Dragon's Den,* so finding out if there was anything like it on the market was much harder to do, but a couple of trips to Mothercare and John Lewis's baby department assured me there was a gap in the market, so I went to a patent agent.

The skill of drawing up a patent is to create an 'inventive step', that is, you have to cast your net as wide as possible so that no one can make a slightly different version of your idea, but at the same time not intruding on anything that has gone before. It's a real skill, and you pay for it. You also pay for the patents themselves. At the time, I was earning quite well, with *The Archers,* telly shows and commercials, and the money I could have put into savings accounts or pensions went into the patents.

Eventually, with the help of my brother-in-law John Emerson, I teamed up with one of the greatest industrial designers in the world, Sir Kenneth Grange, who had designed the InterCity 125, the first UK parking meters, Kenwood food mixers, Parker pens, London taxis and a host of other design classics. He took the concept and created a plastic mould, a beautiful lightweight design that worked perfectly.

By the time we'd finally got a product ready to pitch to manufacturers, the patents were about to need renewing, at a cost of £10,000, and I was no longer so flush. I was offered a one-off payment of that amount by a company and there was a chance that I could have earned a percentage of every item sold in perpetuity; but I lost my nerve. This is why I'm not a businessman.

Kenneth included the Hippo many years later in an exhibition of designs that never got off the ground called *Those That Got Away*. With the patents lapsed, another company came in with a similar, and I have to say better, product, the Hippiechick, that you can still get today. Damn. It was fun while it lasted, though, and now I have a wall full of Hippos.

I had caught the inventing bug, though, and I carried on coming up with ideas. The next one was an orrery – well, sort of. An orrery is a mechanical representation of the solar system, with planets going around the sun on their unique orbits. Mine was a desktop object to show what part of the world was in sunlight.

My desire to invent has long been entwined with my passion for electrics and technology. From a very early age I used to wire things up, often with dangerous results. At boarding school, I took the power from the central light fitting and ran multiple lights around the room, twisting the wires together using Sellotape as insulation. When it fused the whole house, I was in serious trouble.

When computers came along, it was clear I was going to have to get involved. I wrote my first program within minutes of opening the box of my first computer, and I wrote my first website in 1996 – I couldn't understand why people were paying thousands or millions of pounds to people to write their 'Start-up Sites'. It was just HTML and I could write a site in a day, but as usual, I failed to monetise my talent and just made pin money from doing websites for friends. I bought a Psion 3a for its electronic diary and address book, but it came with a programming manual for its inbuilt language called OPL, which is a doddle. I typed in a sample program which converted miles to kilometres and started to expand it. Six months later I'd written an immensely complex program, called Conversion Calculator Pro, that converted absolutely everything to absolutely everything else. On Compuserve there was a thing called a Bulletin Board, and in the Psion section, people were posting their programs. I put up my Conversion Calculator, with a nag screen to encourage people to register for £10. Within a year it had become one of the most downloaded programs ever.

I also wrote an *Archers* adventure game in a weird language called Professional Adventure Writer, and missed another opportunity when I wrote a comprehensive relational database program called Agent that could be used to run a voiceover agency, but I only sold it to two companies. I wrote it for my then voiceover agent, Sheila Britten at Castaway and she continued to use it until she retired in 2012 – not bad for an Amstrad programme! I sold the PC version to another agency, Speakeasy, but maintaining the systems took up a lot of time, and as I was pretty busy acting at the time, I never got serious about selling it to anyone else.

I also came up with an early virtual reality concept that would be a strap-in fighter simulator that hurled you all around and upside down as you played. I worked out how this could be done, but it wouldn't fit in a bedroom. I have had other virtual reality ideas that lay dormant, and are now on the market courtesy of someone else.

I still think my 'Your Satnav' website concept is a good idea – it used to be possible to replace the generic voice of a satnav with one of your own, so you would use our app to record your daughter saying, 'Turn left, Daddy, etc. and we would then send you the code for TomTom, or Garmin, and you would have a personalised satnav. I don't know if it's still possible these days but, if so, go for it. As far as I know, no one's done that one yet.

I did create a little bit of a stir with Faceliftbook – a social networking site for the over-fifties that, following a chance joke at a dinner party just after I'd turned fifty, I created with a service called Ning. I put a link to it on Twitter, it got picked up by Christine Hamilton who had zillions of followers, and it suddenly took off. People really bought into the idea that this computer thing that our generation had created was now being completely taken over by our children, and we wanted a different place to play. However, the site was nothing like as sophisticated as Facebook and, of course, I didn't monetise the idea, so when Ning wanted to charge me an annual fee, I ditched it.

One of my ideas that I think could have a future is Minute Songs, an app for smartphones and a website where you can record or upload a song that is under a minute long. The idea is that this would appeal to the Twitter generation and be the musical equivalent of 140 characters: 'The Haiku of Music'. I'd often find, when I was writing a song, that once I'd done the first verse and chorus, that was enough. As ever, I got a job, put the idea on the back burner for a while and I ran out of steam. Interested? Let's do it!

Being David Archer: Rob and Helen

At the time of writing, the Rob and Helen story about domestic abuse has just reached its climax. Every now and then a real headline-grabber is needed to attract the next generation of listeners. There tends to be a perception that listening to *The Archers* is for old people, and indeed the demographic favours the over-thirties, so to stop it dying with a generation an injection of high drama is needed to up the profile.

When Sean O'Connor came in as the new editor in 2013, he followed through with his intention to make it more like Thomas Hardy, with a return to the traditional values of the programme and centring it on Brookfield, with Jill back at the heart of the story. However, Hardy didn't really do the kind of gentle, non-confrontational, happy tales of prize marrows and milking that are the familiar and beloved staple for most listeners: his books were in a way the *EastEnders* of their time, involving love, death, rivalry, deceit and shocking events. Sean is a great storyteller, so tales of the 'Great Flood', the will-they-won't they-move-north epic and the pressure on David and Ruth's marriage after Heather's death were like Marmite to the audience, loved by some, hated by others.

As Sean said in a *Feedback* interview, 'One thing that will always be true of *The Archers* – there is no consensus.' There really is no pleasing everyone, but the Rob and Helen plotline almost confounded that theory: it was the most intriguing story in the programme for years, brilliantly written and acted while bringing to the fore the little-discussed subject of emotional domestic abuse. While other stories dominated, in the background the listener was drip-fed the slow erosion of Helen's confidence and individuality, with Rob's charming but horrifically controlling dominance slowly undermining her entire personality. Then their story took centre stage, culminating in the stabbing, then her arrest, imprisonment and trial.

Of course, I am being hugely generous here because it meant that David and Ruth were almost unheard for months, and I was slowly going broke! But from the programme's point of view it was really remarkable, getting front-page headlines, dominating BBC Radio's output for months, and attracting so many donations for Refuge, the charity for domestic violence.

Relevant storylines in *The Archers* are nothing new and, after all, the raison d'être of the programme was to help farmers get the country fed after the war, dishing out propaganda and advice about modern farming techniques, which it continues to do. This, though, was different, and for me the most poignant reactions were from women who said that they had had no idea they were in such a relationship until the slow burn of the real-time story echoed the slowly dawning realisation that they were just like Helen – that's powerful storytelling.

Music

I suppose it must have all started because we had a piano in the house, and as a child I used to bash it. 'STOP BASHING,' my mother used to yell. Then I learned 'Chopsticks', so they arranged for me to have piano lessons. I still associate them with fear. When I'm standing in the wings waiting to go on stage, that terror conjures up sitting next to some fearsome gorgon of a music mistress waiting to pounce on my every mistake. All I remember of those lessons was scales, scales and more scales – and criticism. How that didn't put me off music for life I have no idea.

A teacher did manage to put me off being creative in another area. I still have a drawing of a robin that I did at Berkhamsted Junior School when I was about ten. It's a perfectly adequate drawing of a bird – with a beak, a red breast, wings and legs – instantly recognisable as a robin. Below this in red ink are the words: 'This is a very <u>BAD</u> drawing – 1/10.' I never drew again.

When I left Berkhamsted and went to Harrow,

I stopped piano and took up the guitar. I tried guitar lessons for one term but found I was being taught classical Spanish guitar, which involved scales again, when all I wanted to learn were heavy-metal riffs and James Taylor. From then on, I learned from books and by ear.

It's said that there is a correlation between music and being good at accents and languages. I play mostly by ear, in the same way that I can hear an accent in my head and reproduce it. It's a gift, in the sense that being 'gifted' is something you're born with. It's far more laudable to become proficient by grinding hard work.

The first exercise I worked at for my own pleasure was a twelve-bar blues called 'Trouble in Mind' – the absurdity of a thirteen-year-old public schoolboy singing what was effectively a slave song is not lost on me. Now, in my sixties, still living with the daily insecurity of being a jobbing actor, blues songs resonate with just a little more validity; while remaining resolutely optimistic, I have had my black-dog days, and the blues satisfies a fundamental need in me. Being lost in music is amazing. When your hands are doing things over which you have no conscious control, other than simply feeling the music in your head, it is lovely.

At school, I attempted to make an electric guitar out of oak, but it was far too heavy. My lovely pa, who was terribly pro youth, gave me an electric guitar for my birthday, which was probably even heavier than the oak one I had abandoned. It was something out of the fifties, massive, horrible, with the thickest set of strings possible. I was barely able to hold down a chord, let alone bend the screaming solo riffs of my dreams out of it. It wasn't until I bought a Fender Strat with ultra-light strings that I finally realised how bloody easy it is to be a rock god. If you can look good at Air Guitar, that's all that's required – feedback, distort and howl-around do the rest.

Thankfully the hell of scales, plus my love of computers, ultimately reaped their reward when I found out about Musical Instrument Digital Interface (MIDI) and digital recording. This meant I could play piano without being able to play the piano. Not only the piano, but the entire orchestra. It's like being a musical god: just using a small musical keyboard, I could record multiple tracks of any instrument – drums, violins, brass, woodwind – all playing along together and sounding very like the real thing, just by knowing my scales from fear of a harridan's bollocking.

I became obsessed, playing around with more and more equipment and programs. Judy didn't see me in the evenings as I spent every available minute writing and recording songs. Why? Because I was going to make a fortune out of my smash hit Novelty Song, wasn't I? My model for success was Joe Dolce's 'Shaddap You Face' or Men at Work's 'Down Under'. If it could be a Christmas hit, so much the better. I wanted to be like Hugh Grant's dad in *About a Boy*, who lived off the royalties of his Christmas song for life, as did all his offspring.

I once found myself in the office of a music producer who sat and dutifully listened to my latest effort, 'Russian Rap', full of internal rhymes and clever comedy, three-part harmony and multi-tracked with the full band, all played by me. There was a pause.

'Tim,' he sighed, 'your education is standing in your way.'

The songs were part of the constant theme of my life: the need to make some money outside of acting which will keep some dosh coming in when I'm too old to act any more. So far, my songs, inventions, computer programming, website creation, ideas for apps, playwriting, book-writing, translations, lorry-driving and the rest haven't cracked it.

If they made a film of my life, the guy playing me would get paid more than I did living it. Hey ho, mustn't grumble. Music, as well as acting, has opened doors to friendships and more, and let's face it, guitars are sexy as hell.

However, you don't expect David Archer to be able to sing and play guitar.

I discovered this when I did my one-man show, when in between anecdotes I would sling my guitar round my neck and belt out ballads with my incredibly complex pre-recorded backing tracks. It slowly dawned on me that the only thing people had really come for was to hear about *The Archers*, and every time this bloke called Tim Bentinck, who they'd never heard of, slung his axe and started to warble, they'd switch off.

These days, I have decided to spare the nation and I just play for fun.

Being David Archer: The Great Flood

Regular listeners tend to be disappointed that I often don't know as much about what's going on as they do. That's really because I'm not a regular listener. I listen if it's on in the car or if I'm doing work around the house, but only occasionally do I put a note in the diary to listen to something special. One such occasion was the 'Great Flood'.

Judy and I sat down in front of the fire to listen to the omnibus edition on iPlayer through the stereo on good speakers. There had been some criticism that listening to the individual episodes was confusing, but the omnibus was really an hour and a quarter radio play, and it had everything. Even Judy was in tears at the end. Creating epic soundscape audio drama is usually the preserve of the likes of Dirk Maggs but this was a technical masterpiece, and the production team of director Sean O'Connor, engineer Andy Partington and writer Tim Stimpson deserve enormous credit. When Charlie Thomas (Felix Scott) went underwater and was pulled out by Adam (Andrew Wincott), there was a genuine feeling that we were nearly drowning with him.

I remember the scene when Eddie was down the culvert – Trevor Harrison had a nasty backache and used the pain to add realism to the scene. He was on his knees with his head between two concrete breeze blocks, close to the microphone, hurting badly, while Liza, the spot-effects person, poured water over his head – now that's commitment. I was on a separate mike shouting encouragement. Listening to it we heard a very wet and pained Eddie down below and David clearly above him, which is an extraordinary effect to achieve in radio; far and near, left and right is easy but up and down is much harder.

Also, I wasn't used to hearing it in stereo, as for some unfathomable reason the DAB broadcast of the programme, which I get in the car, is in mono, which makes a nonsense of the amount of time and effort we put into the soundscape we try to create. Stereo, eyes closed, big speakers with the sound turned up – better than a movie any day!

It's often the case that Ambridge has its own microclimate, and while the village suffered terrible inundation, the rest of the country was puzzlingly flood-free. It was an interesting call by Sean to run this story, and had to do with something the programme tries hard to avoid – bandwagonning. The previous year the UK had suffered from severe flooding with loss of life and the ruination of homes and businesses, if Sean had run the story then, it would have seemed trite and insensitive when real tragedies were happening around the country. By telling the story the following year, they were able to do what *The Archers* does best: combine drama with information and suggest causes and lessons learned from the real thing, without being perceived to be exploiting genuine tragedy.

In order to make everything and everybody sound wet, there was a lot of water in the studio. Signs were put up saying 'Caution. You are now entering a Splash Zone!' I have pictures of us all dressed in hats, Barbours and wellies, standing in huge buckets of water – for once our workplace looked more like a damp farmyard than a recording studio.

When the studio at the Mailbox was built, they included a huge picture window to the corridor outside, the idea being that the public would be able to see us at work. They could have saved a lot of money by asking the actors first, as the curtain has remained resolutely closed since day one – there is no dignity involved when standing in front of a microphone, wearing a silly hat and standing in a bucket.

The title

So there you are, as Churchill said, 'buggering on' like everyone else, and then suddenly you're a lord. It's quite a peculiar experience.

If a title does not come directly from your father, you have to prove it. When the last Duke of Portland died in 1990, my pa was theoretically then the Earl of Portland, Viscount Woodstock and Baron Cirencester, but in order to convince the College of Heralds, he had to prove that all the other branches of the family, going back ten generations, had died out, and that some South American De Los Bentinck wasn't going to suddenly appear claiming his seat in the Upper House. Pa knew that there was no material benefit coming, but he was fed up with English toffs saying, 'Oh, he calls himself a count,' when in fact we were one of only two families entitled to do so. Most of all, he wanted a political platform to warn the world of the impending environmental catastrophe that was inevitable unless humankind, instead of putting its short-term best interests first, chose those of the planet.

Proving that people really had died when they were meant to have is more difficult than you might think. My father once found himself in a graveyard in Malta, where the headstones of the British had been torn out by angry Maltese and stored in a shed. He was looking for a certain Cavendish Cavendish-Bentinck, who was said to have drowned at sea, his washed-up body buried somewhere on the island. Pa never found him. He gave me various research tasks, and I remember sitting in the Reading Room of the British Library, feeling very Holmesian, flicking through a book, looking for a name that, if found, would mean I was a lord.

Eventually, after a long time and much expense, Pa took his seat in the House of Lords. He would come up from Devon on the train and stay at the Lansdowne Club. The job is unpaid and he was always broke, but he never claimed expenses. I get furious when I hear of lords' fraudulent claims as the whole point about being a lord used to be that it was beneath you to claim for things that you could perfectly well afford, so no one did. Or as Lady Anne Cavendish-Bentinck said when I asked her what it meant to be a lord, 'It means not being a shit.'

The whole family was there to support my father when he made his maiden, and only, speech in

1993, urging the noble lords to 'keep their green hats always on', and we were enormously proud of him – I gave him a lucky sixpence. He made a tremendous speech about the environment in Trafalgar Square in 1971 and his views were always ahead of and therefore out of kilter with everyone else. In his obituary, he was described as an 'intellectual eccentric', but everything he believed in and railed about has come true. As he predicted, his once alternative views on pollution, carbon emissions and climate change have become mainstream worldwide political policy. In that speech, he said: 'We know that if civilisation and population are allowed to continue unmodified on their present expansionist courses, they will cause an ecological catastrophe which will destroy that civilisation and most of our descendants. And yet we do nothing. Why is that?'

His novel *Isoworg* – the International Society for World Government – starred the Bond-like hero, Thorne. The book was written in the mid-sixties and within the first two chapters he foresees: the internet, *'Thorne was connected to a network of computers that housed the sum of the world's knowledge'*; the iPhone, *'he communicated with it via a radio device the size of a cigarette case'*; and Wikileaks, *'the job of Isoworg spies was to discover the secrets of all the world's governments and publish them in the newspapers.* He certainly didn't think he was eccentric, he just knew that he was right and everybody else was wrong. It turned out that he *was* right.

The great sadness was that he only had four years to live, pancreatic cancer getting him seventeen years after he'd quit cigarettes with the words, 'Giving up smoking is like giving up life.' I was devoted to him, not only because, from the age of thirteen, he was the only parent I had, but also because he was the most extraordinary person I have ever met. I've spent my life hoping he would be proud of me.

When he became the Earl of Portland, I was given the courtesy title of Viscount Woodstock, which for someone of my generation, brought up on the Woodstock festival, was about the coolest title you could possibly have, but for a jobbing actor in a left-wing meritocracy, it was also fraught with danger. When Pa died and I became the 12th Earl of Portland, it was even worse. I imagined the press getting hold of it: 'Lord David Archer takes his seat' ... 'Not another Archer in the Lords!' So, I kept my head down and never spoke in the House.

The preconceptions are completely understandable; if, on day one of a new stage job, someone had told me that one of the cast was a duke, or an earl, or a viscount, I wouldn't think that they were a proper actor at all. I'd imagine them tooling down from their estate in the chauffeur-driven Bentley and having a go at 'this acting lark' in a painfully amateur and condescending way, probably because they'd bribed the producer. That was my terror. You're only as good as your last job, and if anyone thought that of me, that last job would be exactly that, the last. So, I tried to keep as quiet about the title as I possibly could. Thank God for 'Mind the Gap' – you don't do that sort of job unless you need the work.

Let me dispel a few common myths. 'When you're a lord you can...'

1.'...get a table at a fancy restaurant.' False. Firstly, whenever I have rung a restaurant, no one has said, 'Are you a lord? If not, I can't help you.' I have to confess that right at the beginning it went to my head slightly. I had a credit card with 'The Earl of Portland' on it until someone said, 'Is that a pub?' And the first and last time I tried the restaurant trick, I was brought soundly down to earth. I tried to book a table at the Ivy and was told that the waiting list was three weeks. I rang back ten minutes later with a much posher voice and said, 'Oh, hello, it's Lord Woodstock here, I'd like to book a table for two for tomorrow night.' 'I'm very sorry, *my lord*, but at the moment the waiting list for the Ivy is six months.' Wrist duly slapped. Whoever still thinks that 'Everybody loves a Lord' is probably a hermit living on Sark. I was seriously regretting having booked a package holiday with the title, when the rep started calling out the names of the tour group at the airport. We would be with these people for the next ten days – and they'd hate us from the off. Luckily 'Viscount Woodstock' came out as 'Visco-nut and Wodstick', which is what Judy has called me ever since.

2.'...get a first-class upgrade on a plane.' You're far more likely to be asked to pay for an upgrade than anyone else because you're a flaming lord, and can *bloody well afford it*. Also flight bookings can't cope with titles. On my boarding card, my name is often given as 'MR THEEARLOF-PORT'.

Why people spend huge sums of money on bogus titles or 'Lordships of the Manor' I can't imagine. Mind you, Americans go weak at the knees for a lord. I once had a bizarre time in Miami Beach when I was doing a lecture tour on 'English Eccentrics' for the English Speaking Union – people came out in their millionaire face-lifted droves to see me. For them, it was like being in Downton for the evening. They were expecting someone in gaiters, preferably beheaded, so I was a confusingly modern anachronism. When I met them at the yacht club before the talk, they'd brought along a resident English 'lord' to check that I was the real deal. He said 'toilet' very early into the cross-examination and scuttled away when I gave him a knowing look – I thought it unfair to ruin his gig.

I don't think I've ever made a single penny out of being an earl, but there are some advantages. For a start, you get your own frigate.

Each Type 23 Duke Class frigate of the Royal Navy has an affiliation with the family of the ship's name, hence when the first HMS *Portland* for sixty years was commissioned in 2001, Judy and I were invited to begin our association with the ship. I was asked to design a flag based on the family coat of arms and colours, and I also told them of the family motto, 'Craignez Honte' (Fear Dishonour), under which she sails to this day. The strangeness of being both an earl and an actor is that in the morning, before heading down to the commissioning ceremony at Ports-mouth, I had been doing a radio commercial for

Finish dishwasher tablets. I arrived at the recording in a smart suit.

Someone asked, 'Off to a wedding?'

'No, actually I'm going to the commissioning of a Royal Navy frigate.'

'Blimey. Why?'

'Because it's mine.'

Being piped aboard is a privilege. I grew up on the Hornblower books and am a devotee of Patrick O'Brian's tales of Aubrey and Maturin, so being a part of the birth of a Royal Navy frigate was beyond my wildest dreams. We inspected the ship's company. Lined up on the helicopter deck, they were all at attention as the Admiral of the Fleet, Vice-Admiral, others with scrambled egg hats on, the ship's captain and me, the Earl, walked up and down, chatting to the sailors of the first company of HMS *Portland*. This was all new to me. The Admiral stopped and turned to one of the men. So did the Vice-Admiral, so did all the others, so I had to as well. It's at this point that you realise why Prince Charles always fiddles with his cuffs. I asked a sailor what his job on board was.

'Communications technician, sir!'

Desperate to say something vaguely intelligent, I imagined what might happen if all your sophisticated electronics had been disabled and you were back to basics.

'Do you still learn Morse code?' I thought this was pretty clever. He looked at me as though I was the most stupid, inbred, brainless twerp he'd ever encountered.

'No, sir,' he replied witheringly, 'we use semaphore.'

Judy and I, and the boys, have been welcomed aboard many times since for social events and for 'Thursday War', when simulated engagements are carried out. For the 'war', our arrival on board was very different. We were greeted at the quayside by two Pacific 24 rigid inflatable fast-attack boats and given all-in-one survival suits to don over our clothes. We then headed out to sea to rendezvous with the ship – at full speed. We came alongside doing a good twenty knots and they lowered a rope ladder down the side. I think it was a bit of a test to see what this posh actor chappie was made of. We were convinced we were going to end up in the briny, but despite looking a bit like Teletubbies, we made it!

We've spent the night on board at sea, and we could not be more impressed and humbled. The young, now 40 per cent female crew are hugely brave, bright, efficient and friendly, and I feel like a child playing Cowboys and Indians by comparison.

Being David Archer: Pip, Josh and Ben

As the father of two sons, the closest thing to daughters I've ever known in real life are my nieces: Anna's daughter Sophie, at the moment studying at LAMDA on the way to a promising acting career, and Sorrel's twins Melanie and Amelia, both the best working mums in the world. Gorgeous girls all three, but I've never known that very special father-daughter relationship. David's bond with Pip is the closest I'll get until I have a daughter-in-law, and it has been an education. Nothing I have learned as the father of boys is in any way relevant to bringing up a daughter. They don't do as they're told and their world is a closed book. I've always joked that I'm so glad I never had a daughter because I wouldn't have been able to cope with the boyfriends, and in the ghastly Jude, and now Toby Fairbrother, all my fears have been confirmed, but I also think it would have made me a more rounded parent, so for this gift of a fictitious and complex daughter, I am eternally grateful.

There have been three Pips. The first one was a loudspeaker, as were all our fictional children. Before they were allowed to come and work in the studio, the children would be prerecorded at home by recording assistant Sonja Cooper. She would sit with them and patiently get them to say the line in the way she wanted, and after multiple attempts finally come up with a selection of takes that would fit. The chosen take would then be played in to us on loudspeakers in the studio. This requires a special technique – instead of reacting, we had to, as it were, *pre*-act because you knew how the child was going to say the line, and it was the same each time. When they were tiny, it was just a gurgle coming out of the speaker and we would cuddle a pillow. I still have the manky old one I also used in my one-man show. Once, after a scene of mutual cooing over baby Pip with Paddy (Jill), I drop-kicked it across the studio. Paddy nearly had a fit.

After the pre-recorded Pips came Rosie Davies, then Helen Monks and now the wonderfully monikered Daisy Badger. Helen is a brilliant comic actor, as shown so well in a fat suit and Wolverhampton accent as Germaine in Caitlin Moran's *Raised by Wolves*. As usual, some listeners loved her, others thought her voice too high and her accent too West Midlands. When Daisy took over in 2014, the contrast couldn't have been greater, as Daisy's voice is very different – more mature and more RP. She's taller too which means I can stand up straight. My son changed as well when Josh also grew about a foot over-night from Cian Cheesbrough into lanky Angus Imrie. I have to admit that I had been a giant in my own family, as Felicity, Helen and Cian are all normal height, while I'm something of a cloud breather. Now it's Flick who feels she's in a family of giants – I think we should buy her some high-heeled wellies for Christmas.

At the moment, Ben is the unheard one. A loudspeaker for years, he then appeared for a while in the form of a bubbly lad called Thomas Lester but has yet to be cast in his adult form. Such is the nature of this ongoing saga, he may well be running the farm in another six months.

And now, sometimes almost word for word, David is having the same arguments with Pip and Josh as Phil used to have with David, and Dan with Phil – the same generational conflict, the arrogance of youth, new farming practices versus the tried and tested traditional techniques, and, charmingly, sometimes calls from younger voices to return to some of the old ways, putting the environment before profit, exactly as my own father had done for real in the 1970s.

One of Jill's lines in the clip we did in front of the Queen was, 'There's always been Archers at Brookfield.' What if Pip marries a Fairbrother – will it become *The Fairbrothers?* Over Jill's dead body, I think. John Peel wanted it to be renamed *The Grundys.* Or maybe Josh or Ben will want the farm and there'll he an inheritance struggle with Pip, just like we had with Kenton, Shula, David and Elizabeth. Whatever the future holds, one thing is for sure, for every listener who approves of the story, there'll be another who thinks it's rubbish, but I hope listeners keep shouting at the radio for many years to come.

An earl abroad

In the year 2000 we had a family adventure. To date, it was the most extreme example of the complete 'otherness' of possessing a title. August and September 2000 were two quite extraordinary months that culminated in an experience in Jamaica that almost no one outside the royal family will ever have. All as a result of inheriting a title from a distant cousin. It brought home quite how odd it is being a jobbing actor and a hereditary peer at the same time.

It had started in France. We'd hired an old mill house that slept nine – pool, pond, streams, etc. and had some close friends to stay. An *Archers* episode clashed with the flight so Judy and the boys flew out, while my friend Noël and I drove down the following day – twelve hours solid through the night. In ten days, we made a spoof Jackie Chan movie with the boys as Jasper Chan and his trusty sidekick Wilbur Force. Judy played harem queen Darling Jeeling. The other cast included Noël's wife and son, Sarah and Jack, old chum Jon and my sister Sorrel came in the second week and my other sister Anna, her partner Arnold and daughter Sophie came for a day. All were used in the film. We returned via Paris and Parc Astérix. I have been on the Goudurix. I know terror.

When we got back I had a week's *Archers* in Birmingham. I then flew to New York where I was collected in a limo and driven to the Holiday Inn, Yonkers. The next morning a talkative cabbie took me to Pearson Education in White Plains, where I was seated in a tiny office with a blue screen taped on the wall behind me and lights were shone at me for eight hours while I sight-read on autocue a grammar guide for an interactive educational CD-ROM. To this day, I have no idea why I couldn't have done that in a tiny office in the UK. At the end of the day I went back to the Holiday Inn with another talkative cabbie and ended up eating a hamburger in the bar with an even more talkative travelling jewellery salesman called Joe. We were then joined by a talkative tart who suggested a threesome. I honestly couldn't take the talking and went to bed alone.

While in New York, I visited old haunts from working there in the 1970s and found myself in the Manhattan Mall where I bought some soft loafers and a pair of Sta-Prest™ cream trousers – I had Jamaica in mind...

321

Two years earlier, I had received a letter from a man called Earl Levy (Earl is his first name, not his title), a Jamaican property developer, asking me to come to Jamaica as the Earl of Portland to endorse some building project that he was doing. The parish was called Portland, and it was named after Henry Bentinck, 1st Duke of Portland, a distant cousin, who had been the Governor of Jamaica for six years in the 1790s. I was suspicious, and when the *Daily Mail* rang up to ask me about it, I was flippant, which earned me a ghastly article sounding like I was broke and desperate for money. I heard nothing more and presumed that Earl Levy had read said article and thought *not a proper earl*.

A year later I got another letter, apologising profusely for the delay, with beautifully laid-out plans for the regeneration of the bay of Port Antonio in Portland, and an itinerary of things we were to do on our week-long trip, all expenses paid, to Jamaica.

So my Sta-Prest™ trousers, loafers and I caught the red-eye to London. I went to Amsterdam the next day for three days to celebrate a friend's fiftieth birthday, came back to London on Monday to re-voice St Peter in a TV movie called *Saul of Tarsus*, went with Kerry Shale that night to see Otis Lee Crenshaw at the Jazz Café in Camden, played a Catholic priest on *The Armando Iannucci Shows* on Tuesday, and flew to Jamaica with Judy, Jasper and Will on Wednesday.

That last section of the sentence sounds straightforward, but it wasn't. We had four free first-class return tickets to Kingston, courtesy of

Air Jamaica. However, as luck would have it, that week the Air Jamaica 747 was being serviced, so we were on a chartered Belgian 767 (two engines not four) with a Swiss crew and staff, and one Air Jamaica stewardess who sat the entire way in the front seat of first class and got the food before we did. The plane eventually took off seven hours late. Four of those hours were spent on the tarmac.

Problems encountered before the Belgian 'City Bird' took off:

1. Nose wheel needs changing. 3 hours.

2. PA system not working. 2 hours.

3. After boarding and taxi-ing to runway, warning light flashes briefly signifying possible starter motor fault. Regulations require return to departure gate.

4. Tow truck to get us back to departure gate attached to front wheel breaks down and bends connecting rod – can't detach from wheel so stuck. 2 hours.

5. Panicky passenger starts shouting: 'WHAT IS WRONG WITH THIS PLANE? THIS PLANE IS NOT SAFE. WE ARE ALL GOING TO DIE. MY WHOLE FAMILY IS ON THIS PLANE. I AM NOT GOING TO SACRIFICE MY FAMILY. WHY ARE YOU TRYING TO KILL MY FAMILY?'

6. Jasper has had enough and bursts into tears, needs comforting. I recognise David Baddiel. He and I help calm things down. Baddiel is baffled by my mumbling about being a Catholic priest one minute, then being...

We finally took off and were served alcohol for the first time. The Swiss crew would have been crap on a sixty-minute trip to Brussels but a nine-hour transatlantic flight was beyond them. Even in first class the seats were like rock and I don't remember the food. Belgian. Probably chips and mayonnaise. I didn't sleep as I was intent on swatting up on Jamaican history.

On the tarmac in Kingston, I was walking from the plane when an airline official asked me, 'Are you from London?' so after thirteen hours of Swiss service I answered rather tersely, 'Of course,' and walked on. She started talking to Judy, who called me back. It turned out she'd said, 'Are you Lord Portland?' Profuse apologies... Not a good start.

We were fast-tracked through passport control and customs, and with a cheery wave to Baddiel, who was in a long queue, we were met at the baggage carousel by Earl Levy and his wife Beverley. It was a further hour till all our bags, and Judy's hats, arrived.

Earl was short and wide, silver hair and glasses, a slightly sensuous mouth and Jamaican accent. He was of Spanish/Scottish descent and his family had been in Jamaica for 300 years. Beverley was charm itself. We felt welcome.

Finally, we walked out into the Jamaican night, the air filled with the smell of small fires, humidity and heat, and were met by a white stretch limo that only just fitted in the airport car park. This was more to do with the size of the car park than the size of the limo, but it was very long and the boys perked up. We drove with Earl and Beverley through the evening to our hotel for the night, before the journey over the mountains the next day to Port Antonio in the parish of Portland. We arranged to meet the following morning to go and visit the Governor of Jamaica. We, jetlagged and knackered, hit the hay immediately. I, however, having slept badly for a few nights and jetlagged from New York and now jetlagged back the other way, didn't sleep a single wink.

I had a long swim and lots of coffee in the morning and hoped that that would cure it, but it didn't really, I was feeling very spacy. I put on the Sta-Prest™ bought on Broadway, the handmade blue blazer that earned me such derision in *Night Must Fall,* suede shoes from *Casualty,* a $100 shirt from Palm Beach and an old Harrovian tie. Judy looked like an English rose with a brilliant hat. The boys were boiling so they were in white shirts and trousers. I realised this was not going to be the informal chat over coffee that I had imagined when the limo, having negotiated the long winding drive, pulled up in front of Government House, where a reception committee and the whole Jamaican press and camera crews were waiting to greet us. The driver got out, went around to the boot, got out a red carpet and unrolled it up the steps to where the governor was waiting. It was rather like doing something from the Armando show, but this time it was for real.

We were ushered into a large reception room with three huge sofas and large French windows, all open. Despite the breeze and the early hour, I started to sweat. Just as I found on *By the Sword Divided,* once my shirt had saturated it was better because the wetness was cooling, but my face was completely soaked. After initial pleasantries, I was introduced to Bev Cook who presented me with her book, *The Maroon Story,* a history of the Jamaican Maroons who escaped slave communities to live in the hills and resist the British. We stood in the centre of the room while she delivered a prepared speech that blamed the white man and the aristocracy in particular for all that was wrong with Jamaica. She told me in so many words that my wealth(!) came from the sweat, toil, torture and death of her slave forebears, and her book would give me a better idea of who I was, who she was, and what the hell I was doing there in the first place.

I had to answer, in front of two video cameras from Jamaican TV, reporters, Earl Levy, the Governor, Bev, my family, etc. Luckily I had looked up the Maroons on the internet, so I was relatively clued up. I did a lot of 'had no idea of the connection with my family', a great deal of 'How fascinating, I shall read it with enormous interest', a fair amount of 'my deep gratitude to Earl Levy and Air Jamaica for inviting me', and a smattering of 'I was Joan Armatrading's brother's best man so I'm not like the kind of earl who knows nothing of black culture...' This probably would have sounded patronising if they'd ever heard of Joan or Tony Armatrading, but they hadn't.

We were then shown around and given the history of the place, which was fascinating. At one point, the Governor said I sounded a bit like a Jamaican – the improv was slipping and I reverted to Prince Charles mode sharpish. I thought that was the end of the official functions. How wrong I was.

A limo arrived to drive us over the mountains. As we wound our twenty-foot absurdity through shanty towns and isolated shacks, the reaction veered between serious aggression and stoned welcome.

We arrived at Trident Castle, which we thought was a hotel but turned out to be Earl Levy's personal folly: an enormous, white-painted, twenties-built, eclectic beauty. Four guest rooms, each one different, and each with a theme. Our bedroom was the size of a large London flat with en-suite, squash-court-size bathroom. We couldn't stay long though. The Titchfield School Choir was waiting to sing for us, so we hurriedly got the boys into suits and got back into the limo.

As we rounded the corner to the school, we were greeted by a sign saying 'Titchfield School'. Underneath it was the Bentinck Cross, our heraldic cross. This was getting weird. We were greeted by the school's head and teachers, and again all the Jamaican press and two TV cameras. We were taken on a tour by two beautiful young girls who related the history of the school, which was in an old British fort, and we were shown the cannon and the dormitory buildings that now house the classrooms. It was a sobering sight to see such well-dressed, well-behaved teenagers with so few resources. It made me ashamed to think of the state of schools back home. Their school ties had Bentinck crosses on them too. I presented them with a framed print of the Marquis of Titchfield that I'd brought from home, and that had somehow survived the Belgian City Bird.

We stood in the sweltering sun for fifteen minutes while the choir sang, 'When the Going Gets Tough, the Tough Get Going' and I'd have happily stood there for an hour. It was beautiful. Four-part harmony and counterpoint. I want to record them. They'd be number one.

By this time, I was starting to feel extremely weird. I hadn't slept for seventy-two hours and my brain wasn't functioning properly. However, instead of heading gratefully for the castle, we were taken to the main civic building in the town centre to re-enact the signing of a peace treaty in 1846 between the Duke of Portland and the Maroons, who had been waging guerrilla warfare on the British for a century. I am the Duke's third cousin nine times removed, so not much of a link there, but despite my explanation to Earl Levy at the very beginning, I was seen as his direct descendant.

The Colonel of the Maroons, the MP for Portland East, the MP for Portland West, a few other guys in shades and gold watches and I re-enacted the signing and posed for the cameras. Then I was brought forward for the TV cameras and asked, 'So, Lord Portland, what are you doin' here?' This was accompanied by the *tooth suck*. Okay. What the hell *am* I doing here? I dried up at this point. The brain wasn't working, I was operating on my last vestige of mental capacity; and was being asked the *one thing I couldn't answer.*

He asked *me,* I thought, looking wildly at Earl, who brilliantly saved the day by giving me a three-point prompt: redevelopment of area, ancestral link, Bentinck cross on school ties. I compared them favourably to my own boys' ties, got a laugh, started to warm to it. Five minutes later, I was flying and it all sounded good, but I've seen the footage and careful editing could make me look either like a heart-warmingly human, concerned, knowledgeable, dignified aristocrat - or an inbred idiot.

That night I slept, and slept, and slept.

Halfway through the most glorious breakfast on the sunny terrace above the rocky seashore the next morning, Earl announced the arrival of the national TV crew who wanted to do an interview with me. Slightly better prepared, I had finally got to grips with what I really *was* doing there, and said that I'd do all I could to raise awareness of the regeneration projects in tourism in the area, specifically the dredging of the harbour to allow big cruise ships, and the building of hotels and tourist facilities. I also kind of intimated that the image of the Earl of Portland being supportive of the County of Portland would lend said county more credence with investors. This was all stuff I'd gleaned from Earl the previous night, shortly before passing clean out over brandies.

We swam that morning in the Blue Lagoon, except it wasn't blue. It was thick brown due to the recent rains. We couldn't see our hands in front of us it was so muddy, but that helped make the idyll a bit more real.

In the evening, there was a massive party in our honour. All of Jamaican society was there and I found myself flirting wildly with Errol Flynn's widow, Patrice, at seventy-three still formidably sexy and redolent of that old Hollywood excess. In this slightly Deco castle, we could have been in a black-and-white movie together and Bogart could easily have approached us with a whimsical line. Instead, a different Errol appeared: Errol Ennis, the MP for Portland West. He was an imposing figure, six foot four with a Stetson hat.

'So Lord Portland, your wife tells me you an actor.'

'That's right, I am.'

'Mm-hm. What sort an actor?'

'Well, everything really, I do theatre, TV, films, voiceovers, improv, radio, you name it.'

'Uh-huh.'

There was something about Errol that told me he didn't buy into this Earl of Portland thing. The only Earl he knew in Portland was his friend and my host Mr Earl Levy, and I could sense that Errol was here to suss me out.

'I've been in a radio series called *The Archers* for the last sixteen years...' I volunteered in a vain attempt to big myself up.

'You in *The Archers?*' His eyes opened.

'Yes.'

'Who you play in *The Archers?*'

'David.'

'You David Archer?'

'Yes.'

'Ha!' He turned around, bent down, slapped

himself three times on the thigh, then turned back to me.

'You know when I was in Wembley, '82 to '93, I never missed an episode!'

We got on like a house on fire after that. Great guy. I was glad that he liked me for what I did, rather than what I supposedly was, and I think he was glad that I didn't fit the cliché of what he'd expected.

On the next day, we found ourselves, along with an affable, humorous, Scottish attaché, being driven in a British Embassy Range Rover, with Union flags flapping on each side, to be shown the regeneration that had already begun in St Antonio. A large friendly crowd was gathered beneath the canopy of a petrol station because of the tumultuous rain, and I made a speech from a balcony on the other side of the road. By this time, I'd got it down pat and suddenly understood the whole thing of what it must be like to be a politician. Judy looked gorgeous in another wonderful hat, the boys had been stunned into an understanding that this was a bit serious and were on top form. We looked the business.

I was soon touring a house that had been newly reconstructed to the way it was in the eighteenth century, and was crowded with dignitaries. Emboldened by my new confidence in my role, when I was handed a guitar by someone who had seen from my website that I can play, I accepted the challenge.

'What you going to play?'

'Well, I think I should sing some reggae.'

'Bob Marley?'

'No, this is one of mine. It's called "Easy Money".'

And in that week's 'Hangin' Out' section of the *Sunday Gleaner*, there's a photo of me with axe slung low, in full voice, and with Portia Simpson Miller, the future first female Prime Minister of Jamaica, looking on in bemusement. The article begins, 'The Earl of Portland, an accomplished guitarist, sings reggae...'

Now that's a clipping to cherish.

As for the disadvantages of a title, people do have preconceptions, which I completely understand, but when you don't know that *they* know about the title, it can be tough.

For instance, the great adventure on the Australian Tourist Board ad had a downside. I like to think of myself as a 'Good Company Member' – someone who works hard, is generous and trustworthy, generally the kind of person who's fun to be on tour with. That's the image you want as an actor because the opposite is what is known in the trade as an arse.

On the Australian job there was something wrong from day one. There's an Aussie adage that goes, 'If we're not taking the piss out of you, it means we don't like you.' And they weren't taking the piss. We toured Australia for four weeks, being filmed in all the most exotic locations the country has to offer. People were perfectly polite, but I never felt included, wasn't asked out with the crew in the evening, never felt part of the team. I tried and tried but couldn't break through. On the last night, there was a wrap party and we all got pretty legless.

Late in the evening one of the sparks said to me, 'So, I hear you're a fucking lord?'

'How did you know that?'

'Everyone knows it. You're gonna have to make your mind up, mate, you can either be an actor or a fucking lord, you can't be both.'

Turned out the producer was a friend of my sister-in-law, who had inadvertently spilled the beans. If I'd have known I could have diffused the situation by explaining where the title had come from and who I really was.

So you might well ask, 'What did you do with your privileged position of power?

Well, when I took my seat in the House of Lords in 1997, I knew that the large majority of hereditary peers would be thrown out within the next few years. My dilemma was, do I become a politician and abandon acting, just to lose that position almost immediately? Or do I pretend it never happened and just take people to lunch in the Peers' Dining Room occasionally?

As a cross-bencher I was approached by the Liberal Democrats to join their party, and schmoozed by a number of peers who wanted my vote on various issues. I felt an onerous responsibility. I was torn between a sense of duty to continue what my father had started, and my own survival. I've always believed that if you're going to do something, you should do it properly, but I've never wanted to be a politician. The truth is that while I care passionately about a number of things, I believe that actors shouldn't use the accident of fame to presume they have a mandate to spout about political matters they've only read in the newspapers. We shouldn't pretend we know any more about a subject, or are anymore important, than someone banging on in the Horse and Crown. The only people from my profession who have the right to be taken seriously about politics are Glenda Jackson, who gave up the business for twenty-three years while she was an elected MP, and more recently my friend Tracy Brabin, who stepped in to become an MP after the tragedy of the murder of Jo Cox.

My views on hereditary power are divided. On the one hand, the idea that you should be able to decide government policy because of an accident of birth is utterly absurd. On the other hand, when they got rid of the old peers, they threw something out with the bathwater that I'm not sure has been replaced by the new system's babies: duty. In Thomas More's *Utopia*, the author floats the idea that anyone who seeks political power should automatically be disqualified from holding it. This simply doesn't hold up nowadays. I would hope that the vast majority of people who go into politics are there out of a genuine altruistic desire to make a difference, and deserve nothing but respect, but to quote Lord Acton, in 1887, 'Power tends to corrupt, and absolute power corrupts absolutely. Great men are almost always bad men.' I think I'd rather be told what to do by someone who didn't want to tell me, but thought it was right, than someone who made up policy in order to keep their seat.

The old hereditaries didn't come down to London and work long hours over tortuously dull documents of legislation for no reward because they wanted to, but because their fathers had told them that they *had* to; it was their duty. Present incumbents might tell me that this spirit survives, and if so then I stand corrected, but what we have now is still not a democratic alternative.

Power is sexy. I had no idea that was true until I entered the Upper House like a new boy on his first day at school only to be immediately treated like a house prefect, called 'M'Lord', respected, taken seriously and listened to. When it was taken away, I felt a palpable sense of loss. I was only there three years and I never gave a speech. Imagine what it must be like for a lifelong politician who is put out to grass. It must be like being sent to rehab after decades of intravenous drug use.

I've been invited to two royal garden parties at Buckingham Palace; one was as 'The Actor Who's in *The Archers*', the other as 'The Earl of Portland'. I'm prouder of my work than I am of my title. If the inheritance of an earldom from a distant cousin had carried with it the responsibilities of running an estate, or the duties of a position of power in the government, I hope I would have risen to the challenge and fulfilled the requirements that came with the job; but, as Stephen Fry once said when I did take him to lunch in the Peers' Dining Room, 'Your problem, Tim, is that you have a title, but you aren't entitled to anything.' And that's it in a nutshell.

The only time the title ever gets used is for charitable work and, even then, people are more impressed by me wailing about Ambridge than they are by the presence of a turfed-out peer.

Being David Archer: And finally...

There's a group of listeners called 'Archers Anarchists' whose conceit is that the programme is a documentary: there are no actors and everything that happens is real. In their book, there is a page devoted to each character. It takes the mickey out of each one of us, and their treatment of David is no exception. The last line of the entry, though, has always pleased me, '...still, at least he has a good shout on him'.

It isn't real, and we are all actors, but 'Being David Archer' is in some ways like having an alter ego. It gives me an idea of what it's like to be a farmer, and I'm humbled by that, as they lead a much tougher life than I do. By 'farmer', of course I mean the people who get up at five and get their hands dirty. They are at the mercy of nature and the weather, supply and demand, imports, radiation from Chernobyl, food fads, crop failure, disease – there aren't many who choose farming as a career if they weren't brought up with it, and so many stay in it with no profit, holidays or treats, just simply for the love of the land and the animals. They have my utmost respect.

To live and breathe this parallel, fictitious life in real time, to play the part of young upstart, then young parent, now older man, beginning to feel the next generation taking more and more control, is more like another life than an acting job, and I feel hugely privileged to have been allowed to do it for so long. Who knows what kind of man David will become in the future? If I'm lucky enough to continue to portray him on the wireless, one thing is for sure, he'll always be six years younger than I am, and for as long as I can manage it, he'll always have 'a good shout on him'.

The present

I have loved Being David Archer, but I have also enjoyed my simultaneous life Being Tim Bentinck, with its chequered history of ups, downs and everything in between: TV star, stage actor, voice artist, out of work, tiny parts, big parts, silly voices, singing, writing, inventing, computer programming, journalism, building houses, earl, son, husband and father.

Through it all I've managed to earn enough to keep the wolf from the door, and sometimes even feel a bit flush. I am at least proof to any budding actor that there is a living to be made from this mad profession without necessarily being famous. It's depressing hearing young people say that all they want to do in life is 'be famous'. I remember very well in our first year at Bristol, all of us felt that fame seekers were the ones who went to RADA, but we just wanted to perform great plays, entertain people, and play Cowboys and Indians, and if fame and fortune came our way it would be a bonus, a by-product, but not the thing itself.

My work continues to be eclectic. In 2015, Judy

and I both published our first books. *Designing and Making Hats and Headpieces* took Judy two years to write and is a comprehensive how-to book revealing the secrets of the traditional couture milliner, with step-by-step tuition and hundreds of photographs. It's already become something of a classic. You can see her beautiful creations at www.judybentinck.com. My book, *Colin the Campervan,* involved far less work. It's a story that I wrote for the boys when they were young, and which had sat on my computer for twenty years.

We had our own 'Colin' for many years, which I used to sleep in, parked in a field opposite Pebble Mill in Birmingham, to save on hotel bills when recording *The Archers* in the 1980s and 1990s. I modified it, putting in front seats taken from a scrapped Rover, cutting out the partition wall and, as the heating was almost non-existent, installing a gas central heating system, which was fine for the back but meant you still needed to wear moon boots in the winter and scrape the frost off the inside of the windscreen. The boys and I loved it. Judy absolutely didn't.

The book was a sort of wish-fulfilment for us all, turning an old rust-bucket into a state-of-the-art supervan with a personality. It's a sweet story and has been well received, so a sequel is on the way.

In 2015, I translated a French novel into English. The author, Laurence Casile, published as Laure Elisac, is an English teacher who lives in Lyon and improves her English by listening to audio-books. She wrote me a letter after enjoying one of the books I'd narrated, and after some fun correspondence asked me if I would like to translate her novel. It's called *Oh Lord!* and is the story of English aristocrats and their friends gathering at a country house in Kent for New Year celebrations and sex! Translating sex from French is a challenge, as they approach it in quite a different way: it's more of an art form. The gay sex was an eye-opener, but the most difficult thing was the food. They were all culinary maestros, in a way that the English upper classes simply are not. No spotted dick or custard, no gargantuan slabs of venison, no kedgeree, but lots of garlic, *fines herbes* and, for some reason, blinis galore. It took me the best part of a year to do, but I loved it, and it was like being paid to learn French all over again.

In recent years, I've flown to Budapest to be garrotted by a seven-foot Hungarian called Vlad in the TV series of *Dracula,* played a heart surgeon with a heart problem in *Doctors* (he was also having an affair with a nurse young enough to be my granddaughter, which was weird), 'moonlighted' as a lawyer in *EastEnders,* mastered the art of autocue as the newsreader in *Fast Girls,* worked with David Tennant in *The Politicians' Husband* and Brian Cox in *The Game,* been a police superintendent in *Gangsta Granny* and a Bristolian metal detectorist in *Gilt,* was made up to look like Ludovic Kennedy in *Lucan,* had a nervous breakdown in *Redistributors,* and spent three days in Gloucestershire, starring in a delightful film, *The Dead Dog,* as an eccentric gay duke and a week in Cape Town Brigadiering in *The Last Post.*

Then, after 'The Year of the Roth' and my first

movie lead role in *Us and Them*, I have now achieved legendary status in the eyes of Jasper's Japanese friends by being almost the first person you see in J. K. Rowling's *Fantastic Beasts and Where to Find Them*. In this business, some people who get to the top disappear up their own fundaments, while others remain modest and charming. When Eddie Redmayne came up to me in the make-up chair and said how much he loved my work in *The Archers*, he definitely got put in the latter category. This credit, together with being the voice of Victor Saltzpyre the Witch Hunter in the computer game *Vermintide*, Kor Phaeron in *Warhammmer*, and, my first TV *Doctor Who* credit, the voice of The Monk, now ensures my place in Comic Con conventions forever!

I narrated an audiobook for Marco Pierre White in which he talks about how writing was cathartic and, in visiting his past, he was better able to make sense of who he was today. I have found this too, so much so that I've been to a therapist for the first time. The thing that has become apparent was the traumatic effect that the years 1965 and 1966 had on me. First, being rejected by all my friends in my last year at Berkhamsted Junior School, when they learned that I was going to Harrow, then the overpowering strangeness of boarding school, and just after Christmas in my first year, my mother taking her own life. One minute I had a mother, and the next she was gone, and life was supposed to continue as normal. I've really been coping with that ever since. It may well have informed my choice of career.

To make up for a lack of funeral, we recently had a sort of memorial for my mother Pauline, celebrating her life. One of the main reasons for this was because her grandchildren knew so little about her. As my sisters and I told stories, read out her poems and played the audio clip we have of her, all of them (Sorrel's son Warwick and twins Amelia and Melanie, Anna's Gully, George and Sophie, and our own Will and Jasper) saw things in her that they recognised in themselves – looks, mannerisms, but most of all a palpable shared sense of humour.

When Pa was wounded and taken prisoner during the war, he was reported missing in action. She wrote this when she thought he wasn't coming back:

SONG OF A LONELY CARAVAN DWELLER

Why speak? For who will heed my voice?
The sea, the marshes, can they hear?
Why read? To dull a mind tormented,
There's still an ever listening ear.
Why sing? My songs are sad with seeking,
Longing for what can never be.
Why laugh? Such bitter empty laughter
That ne'er an echo answers me.
Why walk? Each path a fresh reminder,
Each tree, each cliff, a memory wakes.
Why eat? To live: They say life's precious.
Keep the heart beating while it breaks.
Why pray? Or seek to find an answer
Knowing my faith be all too small.
Why cry? My grief is never silenced,

There is no coming to my call.
Why write? The ink stares back, bleak, lifeless.
Words have no power to ease the pain.
Why sleep? When all my dreams are nightmares
In which I cry to you in vain

As I write, fifty years on from losing her, life goes on. On the good side, in the last year I've done three movies, four tellies, a load of voice work and some great family stuff in *The Archers*. On the bad side, we seem to be becoming a land without empathy and a world without truth. Beyond charitable work and donations, I feel guilty and frustrated that I am unable to do anything about it.

Meeting Judy was the best stroke of luck that ever happened to me. I loved her then and I love her more with every day that passes, and Will'm and Jasper are an endless source of joy and pride. I am surrounded by a loving and close extended family and good friends. So, whatever happens in the real world or in the little village of Ambridge, I count my blessings daily.

Acknowledgements

Writing this book has been hard because I've met and worked with hundreds of people through my life, and anyone who's bought it and searched in vain for themselves is going to think I'm a forgetful, ungrateful bastard. So, just so I can show my face in the green room when it comes out, dear *Archers* cast, I love you all, but here are those that must be mentioned in dispatches, or tearfully recited at the awards ceremony I will never attend:

My *Archers* family have been closest to me, and Richard Attlee (Kenton), Alison Dowling (Elizabeth), Judy Bennett (Shula) and Paddy Greene (Jill) feel much more than just colleagues; my new family Felicity Finch (Ruth), Daisy Badger (Pip) and Angus Imrie (Josh) grow and develop as characters alongside me, and my thirty-five years in Ambridge so far would not have been the same without the fun and friendship of Charles Collingwood (Brian), Angela Piper (Jennifer), Andrew Wincott (Adam), John Telfer (Alan), Michael Lumsden (Alastair), all the Grundys – Trevor Harrison (Eddie), Ted Kelsey (Joe), Heather Bell (Clarrie), Ros Adams (Clarrie), Barry Farrimond (Ed), Emerald O'Hanrahan (Emma), Philip Molloy (William) and Becky

Wright (Nic) – the Tuckers, now reduced to one, Ian Pepperill (Roy), the wonderful Snells, Carole Boyd (Lynda) and Graham Blockey (Robert), Sunny Ormonde (Lilian), Souad Faress (Usha), Stephen Kennedy (Ian), Eric Allan (Bert), John Rowe (Jim), Michael Cochrane (Oliver), William Gaminara (Richard), the now legendary Louiza Patikas (Helen) and Tim Watson (Rob), and new Archers family member, Buffy Davis (sex goddess Jolene). I have had the joy of listening to the sexual innuendo of chilli with Charlotte Martin and Brian Hewlett (Susan and Neil), the wonderful freshness of the younger members, Joanna van Kampen (Fallon), Ryan Kelly (Jazzer), Lucy Morris (Phoebe), Hollie Chapman (Alice) and the Yorkshire whirlwind James Cartwright (Harrison), and those Fairbrother boys Nick Barber (Rex) and Rhys Bevan (Toby) are top lads.

Recent replacements like Troughtons David (Tony) and Wiggsy (Tom), as well as Perdita Avery (Kate) and Will Howard (Dan) have become part of the team, as have those playing new characters, Eleanor Bron (Carol), Simon Williams (Justin) and Anneika Rose (Anisha). It's lovely having Annabelle Dowler back as Kirsty, but we still miss William Sanderson-Thwaite's Chris Carter and the Tuckers Lorraine Coady (Hayley), Rachel Atkins (Vicky), Amy Shindler (Brenda) and Terry Molloy (Mike), and hope they and Hedli Niklaus (Kathy) are not lost forever. The new Freddie and Lily Pargetter, (Toby Laurence and Katie Redford) are fresh new voices and although David had few scenes with them, Carolyn Jones (Ursula), Rina Mahoney (Jess), Isobel Middleton (Anna) and Michael Byrne (Bruce) were such an integral part of the brilliant Rob/Helen story.

And just so the long-time actors who crop up every so often don't hate me for not mentioning them, where would we be without Hazel Woolley (Annette Badland), James Bellamy (Roger May), Lewis Carmichael (Robert Lister), Snells Leonie (Jasmine Hyde) and Coriander (Alexandra Lilley), Amy Franks (Jennifer Daley), Charlie Thomas (Felix Scott), Annabelle Schrivener (Julia Hills), Alf Grundy (David Hargreaves), Horrobins Clive (Alex Jones), Bert (Martyn Read) and Tracy (Susie Riddell), Wayne Tucson (Clive Wood), Lucas Madikane (Connie M'gadzah), Mabel Thompson (Mona Hammond), Martyn Gibson (Jon Glover), Satya Khanna (Jamila Massey), the wonderfully annoying Graham Ryder (Malcolm McKee) and, of course, the star of the whole show, Sabrina Thwaite?

Without the tireless and patient work of the *Archers* staff, there would be no programme. To thank everyone I've worked with since 1982 would be a book in itself, but, though now retired, Jane Pritchard was our friend almost from the start. The present staff are editor Huw Kennair-Jones, business manager Ailsa Acklam-Drury, producers Kim Greengrass and Jenny Thompson, agricultural advisor Graham Harvey, assistant producer Hannah Ratcliffe, production coordinators Sally Lloyd and Andrew Smith, production management assistant Sandheep Johal and casual production coordinator Mel Ward. Directors Julie Beckett, Rosemary Watts, Peter Leslie Wild, Marina Caldarone and Gwenda Hughes are our present guiding hands and we hope Jenny Stephens and Sue Wilson will come by again, and, driving the ship, Andy Partington, Vanessa Nuttal, Liza Wallis and Kathryn Shuttleworth. The late and much lamented Mark Decker was studio manager at Pebble Mill and designed the new studio at the Mailbox, which was then run with the same dedication and efficiency by his successor, Michael Harrison. Thanks to you all, past and present.

There's one character I'd really love to return, as I want to know what happened to him: the drug addict Luke, cared for by vicar Alan Franks. Played brilliantly by Tom George, the bravest and sunniest of men, it would be lovely if Luke turned out to be as great a guy as the lad who plays him.

I'm so grateful for the guidance and support of all those who have gone before and are now no longer in the programme and the recent death of dear Sara Coward (Caroline) is particularly hard to bear. June Spencer (Peggy) is an inspiration to us all and I will never forget the kindness of unsung longest-serving continuous character Lesley Saweard (Christine), who together with Paddy and the eternally young Pat (Pat Gallimore), took me under their wings when I first arrived. Felicity Jones left and went to Hollywood (there's no coming back after *Star Wars*), Lucy Davis left and went to US TV, Sam Barriscale left and came a cropper with the tractor, poor old Heather (Margaret Jackman, previously Joyce Gibbs) passed away in a motorway services, Kim Durham (Matt Crawford) left but has recently returned, Tamsin Greig got famous but sensibly